A European Central Bank Standing Guard over a European Currency Union

International Banking and Finance Law Series

VOLUME 38

Series Editors

Professor Joseph Norton, Professor Ross Buckley and Professor Douglas Arner.

Subjects

Topical issues in international banking and financial services law, such as regulatory responses to the global financial crisis or regulation of alternative investment funds.

Objective & Readership

To provide authoritative analysis of trends and complex subjects for academics, regulators and practitioners involved in international banking and financial services law.

The titles published in this series are listed at the end of this volume.

A European Central Bank Standing Guard over a European Currency Union

Jan Meyers

Wolters Kluwer

Published by:
Kluwer Law International B.V.
PO Box 316
2400 AH Alphen aan den Rijn
The Netherlands
E-mail: lrs-sales@wolterskluwer.com
Website: www.wolterskluwer.com/en/solutions/kluwerlawinternational

Sold and distributed by:
Wolters Kluwer Legal & Regulatory U.S.
920 Links Avenue
Landisville, PA 17538
United States of America
E-mail: customer.service@wolterskluwer.com

ISBN 978-94-035-2148-0

e-Book: ISBN 978-94-035-2158-9
web-PDF: ISBN 978-94-035-2168-8

About the Author

Jan Meyers graduated from the Law Faculty of the Catholic University of Leuven (1974) and then, as a Harkness Fellow, pursued his legal studies at Harvard Law School (LL.M., 1975) and Stanford Law School (JSD, 1982). He practiced law at the international law firm Cleary Gottlieb Steen & Hamilton LLP where he became a partner in 1987 and Senior Counsel in 2016. He is a member of the Brussels Bar.

He wrote his doctoral dissertation at Stanford University about the possible architecture of a European Monetary System, at a time when a single currency still seemed a distant prospect. Now, so many years later, seemed a good time to take a fresh look at the subject.

Table of Contents

List of Abbreviations

ABSPP	Asset-Backed Securities Purchase Program
AMR	Alert mechanism report
APP	Asset Purchase Program
BICC	The proposed (but aborted) Budgetary Instrument for Convergence and Competitiveness
BPT	Buoni del Tesoro Poliennali
BVerfG	German Federal Constitutional Court (Bundesverfassungsgericht)
CAC	Collective action clause
CAP	Common Agricultural Policy
CBPP	Covered Bond Purchase Program
CDO	Collateralized debt obligation
CDS	Credit default swap
CET1	Common Equity Tier 1
CJEU	Court of Justice of the European Union (also referred to as the "Court")
CSPP	Corporate Sector Purchase Program
CSR	Country-specific recommendations
DSA	Debt Sustainability Analysis
ECB	European Central Bank
ECCL	Enhanced Conditions Credit Line
ECOFIN	Economic and Financial Affairs Council
ECU	European Currency Unit
EDP	Excessive deficit procedure
EFSF	European Financial Stability Facility
EFSM	European Financial Stabilisation Mechanism
EIB	European Investment Bank
EIP	Excessive imbalance procedure

ELA	Emergency liquidity assistance
ELB	Effective lower bound
EMS	European Monetary System
ERM	Exchange Rate Mechanism
ERPT	Exchange rate pass-through
ESCB	European System of Central Banks
ESM	European Stability Mechanism
ESM Treaty	Treaty Establishing the European Stability Mechanism of February 2, 2012
EU	European Union (also referred to as the "Union")
EUR	Euro
FOMC	Federal Open Market Committee
GC	General Court of the European Union
GDP	Gross domestic product
GNI	Gross national income
HICP	Eurostat's Harmonized Index of Consumer Prices
IDR	In-depth review
IMF	International Monetary Fund
LTROs	Longer-Term Refinancing Operations
MFF	EU Multiannual Financial Framework
MIP	Macroeconomic imbalance procedure
MRO	Main Refinancing Operations
MTO	Medium-term budgetary objective
NGEU	NextGenerationEU
OCA	Optimum currency area
OMT	Outright Monetary Transactions
PCCL	Precautionary Conditioned Credit Line
PCS	Preferred creditor status
PELTROs	Pandemic Emergency Longer-Term Refinancing Operations
PEPP	Pandemic Emergency Purchase Program
Protocol No 4	Protocol (No 4) on the Statute of the European System of Central Banks and of the European Central Bank
Protocol No 12	Protocol (No 12) on the excessive deficit procedure
PSI	Private sector involvement
PSPP	Public Sector Purchase Program
r^*	Natural (or neutral) rate of interest
RQMV	Reverse qualified majority voting
QE	Quantitative easing
QT	Quantitative tightening
REER	Real effective exchange rate
RRF	Recovery and Resilience Facility

SGP	Stability and Growth Pact
σ	Standard deviation
SMP	Securities Market Program
SRM	Single Resolution Mechanism
SSM	Single Supervisory Mechanism
TLTROs	Targeted Longer-Term Refinancing Operations
TPI	Transmission Protection Instrument
TEU	Treaty on the European Union
TFEU	Treaty on the Functioning of the European Union (also referred to as the "Treaty")
Treaties	The Treaty on the European Union and the Treaty on the Functioning of the European Union
TSCG	Treaty on Stability, Coordination and Governance in the Economic and Monetary Union of March 2, 2012

Acknowledgments

I owe a duty of gratitude to many. In the long run-up to this book, I am particularly indebted to Professor Victor Brudney (d. 2016) who, in his corporate finance classes at Harvard Law School, demonstrated brilliantly how to unlock financial issues using the Socratic method; to Professor John H. Barton (d. 2009), my patient and persevering thesis adviser at Stanford Law School; to Professor Ronald I. McKinnon (d. 2014), my teacher of monetary theory and international monetary relations at Stanford's Economics Department; and to Richard B. Webster (d. 2015), the partner at Cleary Gottlieb who actually taught me how to write when I joined this law firm at the age of 25. The one thing I hope most is that this book may in some small way honor their memory.

In writing this book, I have benefited greatly from the insights and counsel of several friends and contacts in banking, legal and academic circles. Any attempt at shortlisting them would do injustice either to those left out or to those mentioned, for associating them with the imperfections of this work. I have thanked each of them individually by sending them a complimentary copy so that they know.

I would also like to express my appreciation to Nadia Tielemans and Lieve Van Obbergen for their secretarial support, and to the staff of Wolters Kluwer for their editorial guidance and assistance.

The views expressed in this book are strictly my own and do not reflect those of my firm or indeed of anyone else.

Brussels, December 24, 2023

Introduction

1. This book tells the story of the euro and the European Central Bank ("ECB"). It is a truly fascinating story, with several plot twists and occasional drama. But it is also a subject of critical importance to the further course of the European project. Much is at stake, and it is important that the key policy issues and choices be broadly debated. There is an abundance of specialized literature about the subject—much more than anyone with a daytime job can hope to read and digest, even if one knew where to begin. My purpose is to condense the most relevant data and analysis (according to my inevitably subjective perception) into a single and reasonably short book, to raise questions about them, and to do so in a manner that is accessible and, dare I hope, moderately enjoyable to read for non-specialists.

2. Writing in such a manner is probably a special challenge for someone accustomed to legal writing and its penchant for opaque and occasionally suffocating prose. My legal upbringing may here and there get the better of me, and this may sometimes be more by indulgence than by inadvertence. To understand is to forgive. Much of the prolific literature on the subject is written by economists, and that does not always make for leisurely reading either.

In writing this book, I have pictured myself engaging in a dialogue with the reader over a summertime dinner in the garden, or more likely a series of dinners over a languid summer, and raising critical questions from simple logic and common sense. Technical complexities cannot always be avoided and, when that is the case, they must not be sacrificed on the altar of simplification. As Albert Einstein is believed to have said: *"Everything should be made as simple as it can be—but not simpler"*.[1]

When young Henry Kissinger published his 1954 Harvard PhD dissertation on the diplomatic exchanges between Metternich and Castlereagh in the early nineteenth

1. This quote is probably a shorthand version of a line from Einstein's Herbert Spencer Lecture of June 10, 1933 at Oxford University: *"It can scarcely be denied that the supreme goal of all theory is to make the irreducible basic elements as simple and as few as possible without having to surrender to adequate representation of a single datum of experience"*. It is reproduced in A. Einstein, "On the Method of Theoretical Physics", *Philosophy of Science*, Vol. 1, No 2 (April 1934), pp. 163-169, at p. 165, https://doi.org/10.1086/286316.

century,[2] a British reviewer wrote: *"I don't know if Mr. Kissinger is a great writer, but anyone who finishes this book is a great reader"*. Perhaps I should resign myself to the fact that my modest writing skills, applied to a sturdy subject, will indeed require a great reader.

3. At the outset, I owe a word of explanation to the reader about the reference to the "European currency union" in the title and elsewhere in this book and about what it implies for the scope of the book. The Maastricht Treaty of February 7, 1992 has set the European Union on the road to Economic and Monetary Union ("EMU") as a further step in European integration. EMU is a broader concept and a destination not yet reached. This book focuses on the architecture and functioning of the existing currency union within an incomplete EMU, *i.e.*, specifically, the single currency now adopted by 20 of the 27 EU Member States, the single monetary policy for this currency zone, its common fiscal rules and its financial support mechanisms. The book will not address the further initiatives toward the Banking Union and Capital Markets Union that have become attached to EMU, but that are of lesser immediate relevance to the central themes of this book and require separate treatment in their own right.

4. The monetary component of EMU is sometimes referred to as its monetary "pillar", as if standing side by side with its economic "pillar", *i.e.*, the coordination of the Member States' economic and fiscal policies. But "pillar" is not an apt term for EMU's monetary component. One would ordinarily expect to see this component rather as the finishing structure on the roof, put in place after a bottom-up process of progressive economic and fiscal convergence. The reader, my dinner companion, may, over pre-dinner cocktails already, find it counterintuitive that the construction team proceeded to place the roof on an unfinished construction—that 11 Member States, 12 as of 2001, later joined from time to time by others, "jumped the gun" to currency union while the vertical supports of economic and fiscal policy coordination were still under construction. It is a valid point. How this structure held up and evolved, with tensions and cracks, is a central theme of this book.

5. Europe's currency union is an incomplete, hybrid construction. It is a currency union under a single monetary policy conducted by a kind of federal central banking system consisting of a central institution, the ECB, and the national central banks of the euro area Member States.[3] But its 20 member countries retain substantial control over

---

2. H.A. Kissinger, *A World Restored: Metternich, Castlereagh and the Problems of Peace 1812-1822*, Houghton Miflin, Boston, 1957. This is an absolutely brilliant book and an intellectual joy.
3. This book generally refers to the monetary policy mandate of the ECB, which is somewhat of a shortcut. Formally, monetary policy is conducted by the ECB together with the national central banks of the Member States whose currency is the euro, which jointly constitute the Eurosystem, as a reduced format of the European System of Central Banks ("ESCB"). But monetary policy is effectively formulated and directed by the ECB, acting through its Governing Council (which consists of the six members of its Executive Board and the governors of the euro area central banks).

their economic and fiscal policies,[4] subject to a measure of peer review and coordination at the EU level, and with only limited centralized budgetary stabilization capacity. The co-existence of a shared currency and single monetary policy with relatively autonomous national economic and fiscal policies is an uneasy combination outside of a federal structure or without at least an adequate central budget to even out asymmetric shocks to or within the system. The European currency union was not an obvious proposition when it took off in 1999, and it still is not today. At the time, the euro was likened by some observers to a bumblebee: it was thought that, by all known laws of physics, it should not fly.[5] Yet it did, so far.

6. Under what conditions is such a currency union workable and sustainable over time? What minimum criteria do member countries need to fulfill, upon and after admission, for this to be and remain true? And what design or institutional features must a currency union have or develop for it to be sustainable?

These are the kind of questions addressed in the economic literature on "optimum currency areas" ("OCAs"). OCA theory was pioneered in the early 1960s by Robert Mundell and Ronald McKinnon[6] and has since gone through several developments, with ups and downs.[7] While the theory does not occupy center stage in today's (or even past) discussions on EMU, I will be forgiven for thinking that it still offers some useful intuitions and guidance on the issues that are discussed in this book.

7. In essence, OCA theory asks the question of when it makes economic sense for a multi-country geographic area to become (and remain) a currency union—under what conditions the current and future benefits of a shared currency exceed its costs. On the **benefits** side, a currency union (i) offers savings on currency conversion and hedging costs; (ii) facilitates intra-union trade, investment and resource allocation (*e.g.*, production chain optimization) by eliminating future exchange rate uncertainty; (iii) removes destabilizing exchange rate volatility and misalignment, including the temptation for countries to maintain their currencies at artificial levels or engage in competitive devaluations; and (iv) contributes to greater price transparency, thereby reducing market segmentation and fostering competition. The **costs** primarily derive from a country's loss of macroeconomic policy tools in that it gives up a currency of its own and relinquishes control over monetary policy.

4. In this book, the term "fiscal" is not used as (tax) lawyers may understand it but as it is used in economic and political literature to refer to the collection and spending of government revenue to influence macroeconomic variables affecting a country's economy.
5. The bumblebee metaphor was used by former ECB President Mario Draghi in his famous "whatever it takes" speech of July 26, 2012. He added that the bumblebee was now *"graduat[ing] to a real bee"*. The full text of this speech is reproduced on the ECB's website at https://www.ecb.europa.eu/press/key/date/2012/html/sp120726.en.html.
6. R.A. Mundell, "A Theory of Optimum Currency Areas", *American Economic Review*, Vol. 51, 1961, pp. 657-665, and R.I. McKinnon, "Optimum Currency Areas", *American Economic Review*, Vol. 52, 1963, pp. 717-725.
7. *Cf.* F.P. Mongelli, "'New' views on the optimum currency area theory: what is EMU telling us?", *ECB Working Paper Series No 138*, April 2002, especially pp. 7-17, and from the same author "European Economic and Monetary Union and the optimum currency area theory", *European Commission Economic Paper No 302*, February 2008, especially pp. 1-9.

OCA literature has identified various economic properties that should reduce these costs and make it more likely that they are outweighed by the benefits of currency union, including such characteristics as (i) price and wage flexibility; (ii) mobility of production factors and, in particular, labor; (iii) free flow of capital to ease financing of external imbalances; (iv) the degree of openness of an economy; (v) similarly low and stable inflation rates; and, as a kind of overarching property, (vi) synchronicity of business cycles and broadly symmetrical effects of supply and demand shocks. These and other characteristics do not constitute a clear-cut scorecard: authors occasionally disagree over their relative weight, and the strength of one characteristic may in some measure compensate for the weakness of another. By and large, the euro area does not score very highly on items (i) and (ii) and the evidence on items (v) and (vi) is mixed, as we will see.

8. OCA theory also proffers an "endogeneity" hypothesis to the effect that an initially imperfect currency union may itself generate virtuous dynamics that cause greater trade integration, higher correlation of income and employment, and more symmetry within the system and, hence, make the currency union "more optimal" over time. It is a hypothesis worth testing for the euro area, as we will do in Chapter 2.

9. The above considerations help to position important themes that will reappear throughout this book. For now, let me briefly introduce four of these interconnected themes in general terms.

10. ***First***, a country *X* that adheres to a currency union relinquishes a currency of its own. It gives up its ability to adjust its currency's exchange rate or let it float in order to correct external imbalances. Thus, when a country *X*'s exports diminish, it can no longer let its currency depreciate but will have to reduce its costs and particularly its wages to restore international competitiveness (what economists sometimes call an "internal devaluation"). This can be achieved by direct wage restraint (which may be painful politically), by structural reforms to raise productivity (which may take time and stretch beyond the electoral horizon of politics) and/or by deflationary fiscal policies and enduring recession for a while. Vigorous export performance of other member countries may contribute to country *X*'s trade deficit, and, conversely, these countries could ease country *X*'s adjustment pains by letting their wage and price levels increase and reduce their trade surpluses. But it may not be obvious how to make them do this.

11. Importantly, in order to finance its government deficit (or refinance pre-existing government debt), country *X* can no longer issue debt in a national currency under its control but must do so in the shared single currency over which it has no control. It is like issuing debt in a foreign currency. Nor can country *X* call on its central bank to provide liquidity (print money) in order to cover payments due on its sovereign debt. It will need to keep its house more or less in order and observe an appropriate measure of fiscal discipline in order to maintain its creditworthiness in the eyes of the financial markets and, hence, its ability to borrow at viable rates. If country *X*'s economic fundamentals are seen to deteriorate, markets may require a higher risk premium on its debt. And if it comes to the point where markets begin to worry about the sustainability of its sovereign debt, the risk of sovereign default (or debt restructuring) or even the prospect of the country's exit from the currency union, it may cause markets to overreact and set in motion the kind of destabilizing market dynamics that occurred in the euro area's 2010-2012 sovereign debt crisis. In this sense, speculative attacks on exchange rates may, in a currency union, eventually be replaced by speculative attacks on sovereign debt. One would not vastly exaggerate when saying that moving to a currency union shifts the locus of instability from foreign-exchange markets to government bond markets.

12. Currency union membership not only deprives a member country of the possibility to conduct an exchange rate policy of its own but also removes exchange rates as a direct external constraint on its domestic policies. Yet, it replaces this constraint with the need to maintain financial market credibility as to the overall soundness of its economic and fiscal policies and the sustainability of its debt. In a sense, this constraint tends to be more asymmetrical between currency union members than the exchange rate constraint. In a simplified model of reality, absent a currency union, exchange rate tensions tend to exercise adjustment pressure on countries with excessive external deficits or surpluses alike (albeit to different degrees). In contrast, in a currency union, the fiscal sustainability constraint will have a considerably greater bite for member countries with higher public deficit and debt—and the more so the higher and more lasting their deficit and debt. Generally speaking, currency union membership subjects deficit countries to a comparably greater constraint of fiscal discipline than surplus countries. It limits policy space precisely for the macroeconomic policy tools that are still left to currency union members, and it does so to a degree that increases notably with their levels of government deficit and debt.

13. This raises the question as to the need for common fiscal ground rules that do not one-dimensionally focus on greater fiscal restraint and structural reforms by deficit countries but also seek to bring pressure on surplus countries to assume some share of the burden for addressing imbalances across the currency zone. From the vantage point of the proper longer-term functioning of a currency union, there can be sin in excess of virtue—but this is never an easy message for the virtuous. Country *Y*'s structural trade surplus may aggravate country *X*'s trade deficit, particularly in a currency area with a high degree of trade integration. And Country *Y*'s fiscal conservatism may redirect capital flows away from country *X*. The currency union may in fact leave country *Y* with an undervalued real effective exchange rate ("RERR") allowing it to extract relatively more trade benefit from the union. The proper allocation of adjustment responsibilities among parties to an agreement that locks their currencies together is another recurring theme in this book. Europe has known variants of a "symmetry" issue of this kind in the (final) years of the Bretton Woods gold-dollar standard and under the joint floating arrangements that followed its disintegration and preceded today's European currency union. But it has not gone away. In a full currency union, it goes to the heart of the policy autonomy left to its members: it requires political arbitrage between (often engrained) domestic policy preferences that can be pursued with the fewer policy instruments left at the national level. Policy instruments are like the Sibyl's leaves: the more that are lost, the more precious those that are left—especially in times of economic adversity.

14. ***Second***, countries that become part of a currency union relinquish a monetary policy of their own for macroeconomic stabilization. They become subject instead to a single monetary policy that, in principle, is conducted in a one-size-fits-all manner. But one size will inevitably fit some less well than others, and one size may even fit none. A single monetary policy may be suboptimal on a country-by-country basis for several reasons:

(a) At a basic level, currency union members have different welfare functions, reflecting different *"contrats sociaux"* with their citizenry, and hence different levels of tolerance for inflation and unemployment. And, as economists may be inclined to put it, they have differently sloped Phillips Curves as to the (short-term) inverse relationship between inflation and unemployment. The single monetary policy in a currency union implies a choice of a single target level for inflation, and of a composite degree of tolerance for deviations from this level, for the union as a whole. Should the union-wide inflation target for monetary policy be set at 2% or at some higher or lower level? How vigorously must monetary policy pursue that target in the face of slowing growth and rising unemployment? What if there are significant country differences in growth and employment performance? How will these matters be decided and what measure of political control should be exercised over these choices?

(b) Countries may be in a different phase of the business cycle, experience higher peaks and lower troughs, have different levels of vulnerability to different external disruptions (or "shocks" as economists generally call them) or take more time to adjust. Some countries may be slower in recovering from COVID-19, and some are hit harder and longer by the economic fall-out of the war in Ukraine notably on energy and commodity prices. As a result, monetary policy rates at a given level may, to differing degrees, be too low for some countries and too high for others. At an elementary level, the degree of synchronicity and comparable amplitude of business cycles are key factors in facilitating the conduct of an effective single monetary policy.

(c) At a further level, even if business cycles are more or less synchronous, a given monetary policy stance may translate into monetary policy impulses of different intensity in different member countries due to various country idiosyncrasies. There is a wide variety of country-specific characteristics that may slow down, amplify or otherwise interfere with the pass-through of monetary policy through the various transmission channels and sub-channels and vary the strength of monetary impulses among countries. They are "bugs" in the monetary policy transmission mechanism. They include such variables as differences in inflation rates (which cause similar nominal interest rates to translate into different real rates), in elasticity of wages, in public and private debt levels, in income and wealth distribution (through their effects via the marginal propensity to consume) and in the mix of, and degree of dependency on, primary energy sources. In general, the more heterogeneity, the greater the potential for friction.

(d) And at a simple arithmetic level, smaller countries may be somewhat worse off since they have lower weights in area-wide inflation, output and other economic aggregates that determine the single monetary policy. They become subject to a monetary policy that, at least as a theoretical matter, has a greater probability of being less responsive to their particular needs. This may place greater weight on their fiscal policies, but smaller open economies tend to have less fiscal policy space to begin with. To test and illustrate this point, I have included Belgium and Portugal in several of the book's statistical tables, alongside the euro area's "Big Five" economies (Germany, France, Italy, Spain and The Netherlands).

15. ***Third***, it stands to reason that overall macroeconomic stabilization efficacy requires a measure of complementarity between monetary and fiscal policies or at least the avoidance of significant conflicts between them. This may be difficult enough in a single-country setting but the difficulties are obviously compounded in a multi-country currency union of now 20 member countries in which a single monetary policy co-exists and interacts with 20 relatively autonomous national fiscal policies that may differ to varying degrees. Tensions and conflicts may arise in different circumstances and different forms:

(a) Broadly speaking, in a low-inflation environment with subdued growth, monetary and fiscal policies tend to be more aligned, at least directionally, insofar as such a setting calls for monetary easing and fiscal stimulus. Yet, inadequate fiscal stimulus at national level, due to sovereign debt constraints or for other reasons, may play into deflationary risks and require the central bank to engage in more monetary easing for longer—thereby shifting a greater part of the burden of macroeconomic adjustment to monetary policy. This appears to have been the case in the euro area during a good part of the previous decade.

(b) In contrast, more direct tensions and conflicts are prone to arise in an environment of high inflation and low growth. The more restrictive monetary policy now required will raise interest rates which should depress investment and consumption and increase government borrowing costs and deficits, while fiscal stimulus will inject more liquidity into the system and, in this manner, work at cross purposes with inflation control. The central bank may come under pressure to moderate monetary tightening so as to maintain workable financing conditions and not to unduly compress the member countries' fiscal policy space.

(c) In an adverse scenario, subpar economic or fiscal policies by member countries with weaker macroeconomic fundamentals and/or higher levels of sovereign debt (possibly in combination with overly conservative fiscal policies by surplus countries with fiscal headroom) may cause a widening of sovereign bond spreads and eventually trigger destabilizing market dynamics. This may prompt central bank purchases of sovereign bonds which inject additional liquidity into the system[8] and, in a higher-inflation environment, work against inflation containment (unless such liquidity is somehow re-absorbed or "sterilized").

16. These and other potential conflicts in the macroeconomic policy mix suggest that the constitutional framework of a hybrid currency union like the euro area should have agreed ground rules for avoiding or mitigating such policy conflicts and some mechanism to arbitrate conflicts when they arise. As we will further discuss in this book, the European currency union presently has only fragmentary rules and procedures of that kind. In broad outline:

(a) Under the Treaty on the Functioning of the European Union ("TFEU" or the "Treaty"), the ECB must conduct a *"single"* monetary policy with the *"primary"* objective to maintain price stability. It must also *"support the general economic policies in the Union"* but *"[w]ithout prejudice to the objective of price stability"*. It should balance these considerations but, in case of conflict, should, at least in principle, give precedence to its inflation control mandate. In the exercise of its monetary policy mandate, the ECB may not take any policy instructions from EU or national authorities and is subject only to judicial control by the European Court of Justice. Yet, judicial review by the Court has to contend with the complexities and inherent uncertainties of monetary analysis and the ECB's need of a broad margin of policy judgment.

(b) The Treaty also summons Member States to regard their economic policies *"as a matter of common concern"* and to *"coordinate"* them within arrangements which the European Union has competence to define. But economic and fiscal policies substantially remain national competences, with the Union's competence being limited to their *"coordination"*. Common fiscal and macroeconomic surveillance frameworks have been put in place at the EU level that seek to prevent or remedy out-of-line national policies but, while these procedures have progressively become more elaborate and intrusive, their coercive power is limited, the record of Member State compliance has been mixed, and those frameworks have so far fallen short of genuinely aligning national policies into a coherent fiscal stance for the currency zone as a whole.

17. ***Fourth***, at a broader level, for a currency union between countries retaining economic and fiscal sovereignty to function properly over time, it needs rules of the

8. Central bank asset purchases in effect swap zero-risk liquidity for less liquid (but still marketable) government bonds or other securities with duration and credit risk. They extract duration and credit risk from the market and, in this manner, dampen the cost of financing.

game that achieve a workable balance between risk containment and risk sharing so as to unburden monetary policy and allow it to focus on price stability:

(a) Risk containment requires a credible common framework that incentivizes member countries to conduct responsible economic and fiscal policies that keep their government debt sustainable, implement structural reforms to address weaknesses in productivity and competitiveness and correct structural external imbalances. That framework must not merely focus on corrective action by deficit countries but must invite necessary adjustments by surplus countries as well. It should seek to avoid or mitigate conflicts with monetary policy.

(b) Risk sharing requires some centralized or pooled financial capacity offering temporary stabilization support to help countries overcome asymmetric external shocks or bridge imbalances pending structural reforms. Cross-country risk sharing also increases "skin in the game" for all member countries and diminishes the probability of some partial or total break-up of the currency union. Such stabilization support need not be (quasi-)automatic but may, in appropriate circumstances, be subject to policy conditionality aimed at avoiding, in particular, that beneficiary countries pursue unduly liberal fiscal policies or delay necessary structural reforms.

18. These two dimensions are largely complementary. If there is less risk sharing, more will be required in terms of risk containment. On both these dimensions, the European currency union's current architecture remains partially under construction. As we will see, the debate on risk containment and risk sharing comes up, sometimes cast in the stark terms of "discipline" versus "solidarity", in political discussions on the fiscal and macroeconomic surveillance frameworks, on stability support and related policy conditionality, and on (geographically selective) asset purchases by central banks to contain financial fragmentation.

19. At this juncture, euro area Member States face, to varying degrees, several longer-term challenges: a persistent decline in productivity growth in recent decades, considerable private and public debt, high levels of youth unemployment, an aging population, and climate change and the transition to a more carbon-neutral economy. These challenges are intimidating by their scale and simultaneity and, oftentimes, by inherent trade-offs and by the lack of historical data to guide current actions.

The governance of the European currency union will have to navigate these various challenges when defining the most suitable monetary policy stance and choosing and calibrating the monetary policy tools to be used, when setting effective common rules of fiscal discipline and administering them with the proper mix of rigor and flexibility, and when establishing adequate centralized stability support with appropriate conditionality to avoid moral hazard and political inaction bias. It is a question of finding the right dosage between complementary lines of action. But it is complicated. It is especially complicated in a treaty-based constellation of sovereign countries in which these countries retain significant economic and fiscal powers to deal with differing needs of their economies, and in which consensus is the rule when it comes to arbitrating conflicting interests. And there remains the virtually constant curse of the political horizon. Politics are locked into electoral cycles and the lack of synchronicity of these cycles in the euro area creates a state of affairs in which, at any point in time, there is a high probability that one or several Member State governments face the short-term prospect of national elections.

20. This all unfolds in a world of particularly elevated uncertainty. Things happen that cannot be foreseen, much less quantified *ex ante*. Crises occur episodically and seemingly randomly, and they do not come with labels identifying their scope, duration or consequences. The surge of divisiveness in the U.S. political system, the global spread of the SARS-CoV-2 virus, Russia's attempt at invading Ukraine and the tragic flare-up of the Israel-Palestine conflict are, in short succession, potentially major disruptive events that cast doubt on conventional assumptions and cloud the political and economic outlook. Climate change is another major source of "Knightian" uncertainty.[9] Today's economic and political environment is one of countless variables that interact in complex, ambiguous and occasionally non-linear ways. There can easily be competing but plausible narratives to explain the same observed trends and cycles, with different policy implications. And it is very difficult for policymakers to assign meaningful probabilities to various alternate outcomes. No theory or model can adequately capture everything of consequence in a reliable manner. Accordingly, it should not surprise that predictions of the best economists repeatedly turn out to be off the mark. Oftentimes, economists and policymakers will have to conclude, in the immortal words of a former mayor of New York City, that *"[w]e've got lots of theories, we just don't have the evidence"*.[10] Or perhaps the difficulty in the economic and monetary sphere is oftentimes the reverse, *i.e.*, that there is an abundance of data but no robust theories and models to reliably extract meaning and direction from them.

21. The most that can be expected from policymakers is that they engage in their best efforts at data-driven probabilistic analysis and think a few moves ahead. In the end, it may remain much of a gamble, like poker. But it is comforting that smart players experienced at poker tend on average to do much better than others. It is therefore entirely sensible to place confidence in a monetary authority that carefully explores that universe with the aid of sound monetary theory and the best possible but inevitably imperfect empirical data and models. In that sense, the ECB does not throw dice—which could be viewed as an alternative title for this book.[11]

9. So named after Chicago economist Frank Knight to distinguish quantifiable risk and unmeasurable uncertainty.
10. Statement attributed to Rudy Giuliani by Arizona House Speaker Rusty Bowers in his June 21, 2022 testimony before the January 6 Select Committee of the U.S. House of Representatives.
11. In a letter of August 15, 1942, to Fritz Reiche, Albert Einstein wrote that he still did not believe *"that the Lord throws dice"* to express his skepticism about the laws of quantum mechanics. Quoted in A. Fölsing, *Albert Einstein: A Biography* (translated from German), Viking Penguin, New York, 1997, p. 704. But in the present book, the ECB is put at the center of its universe, not the Lord.

22. Writing about events and developments while we are living them is, of course, a hazardous enterprise. Contemporary history does not pause. It does not follow a steady course. It is full of unexpected twists and bounds. European monetary history is no exception, and today is a time of great fluidity. I had to complete my research and writing at some point in time and I arbitrarily chose to put down my pen on Christmas Eve 2023. Books end, life goes on. I resisted the temptation to modify paragraphs, or even to add a post-script, to cover subsequent developments. But I hope that, at least for a short while, this book continues to offer some assistance to the reader in thinking about those developments.

CHAPTER 1

The First 25 Years: A Brief History

1 PRELUDE: THE CHANGING MORPHOLOGY OF A CURRENCY SNAKE

23. The European currency union saw the light of day on January 1, 1999, between a first group of 11 Member States, after a transition process that started in 1990. It did not rise from its shell as the Venus of Botticelli. It was preceded by much discussion and planning about the achievement of some form of economic and monetary union in what was then the European Economic Community.[12] Discussions intensified in the late 1960s and early 1970s against the backdrop of the unraveling of the Bretton Woods gold-dollar standard. They initially led to the establishment of a semi-fixed exchange rate system between European currencies, nicknamed the "snake", which, in its 1979 mutation, provided a runway toward the EMU project and today's currency union. It was very much a learning curve: the EMU project was assembled from the building materials and experience of arrangements tested in the 1970s and 1980s.

a The Unraveling of the Bretton Woods Gold-Dollar Standard

24. A flashback to the Bretton Woods gold-dollar standard and its disintegration in the early 1970s may seem to the reader like monetary archeology. It is necessary, but I will keep it as short as possible.

---

12. Part of this process, from the late 1960s to the early 1980s, is reviewed in my doctoral dissertation for Stanford University, *The Architecture of the European Monetary System*, January 1982, 279 pp. I was too busy at the time to pursue publication, and there were no digital platforms in those days to share the document. Students of those turbulent years of monetary history are welcome to contact me for a digital copy.

25. In very broad outline, under the gold-dollar standard based on the old Article IV of the Articles of Agreement of the International Monetary Fund, member countries other than the United States (the N – 1 countries) committed to contain the spot quotations of their national currencies within margins of maximum 1% above and below fixed (but adjustable) par values in terms of the U.S. dollar, while the United States (as the Nth country) guaranteed the convertibility of foreign dollar balances into gold at a fixed price of about USD 35 per ounce. During the 1960s, persistent U.S. balance-of-payments deficits (and systematic dollar-for-gold conversions of certain countries, notably France) led to a growing imbalance between the rising volume of foreign-held dollars and a narrowing gold base.

26. On August 15, 1971, then U.S. President Richard Nixon "temporarily" suspended the convertibility of dollars into gold (or other reserve assets), thereby closing the "gold window" (or, if you wish, the dollar-against-gold put option of the N – 1 countries). The Smithsonian agreement of December 18, 1971 attempted to rescue the system notably by establishing a new set of central rates relative to the dollar, now with wider margins of fluctuation of 2.25% on either side of these central rates. However, the agreement reached at the Rambouillet summit of November 15-17, 1975 and the further agreement on the substance of a revised Article IV of the IMF Articles at the meeting of the IMF Interim Committee in Kingston, Jamaica, on January 7-8, 1976, effectively legalized floating, without any commitment to return to a general system of fixed exchange rates.

27. Meanwhile in Europe, the original Treaty of Rome of March 25, 1957 had little to say on the subject of the Member States' currencies and their exchange rates. Under its Article 107, Member States had to treat their exchange rate policies *"as a matter of common concern"*, and, if a Member State changed its currency's exchange rate in a manner that *"seriously distorts conditions of competition"*, the European Commission could authorize other Member States to take defensive measures on a temporary basis. The Member States were then living under the umbrella of the gold-dollar standard which, absent changes to their currencies' par values, confined variability of their cross rates within a bandwidth of 2% (and thus an intertemporal spread of 4%). It appears to have been assumed at the time that this should not excessively inhibit or distort trade within the European "common market", at least so long as the currencies' par values remained correctly aligned in relation to underlying economic fundamentals. This last point is critical. While its Article 107 addressed the more obvious risk of competitive devaluations, the Treaty of Rome did not focus on the risk of par values becoming chronically misaligned due to one or more Member States' resistance to adjusting their currencies' par values in a timely manner, *i.e.*, the risk of one or more currencies being effectively maintained at overvalued or undervalued levels for any significant period of time. This would in fact produce as much a distortion in trade as would import tariffs or export subsidies.

28. A situation of this kind developed in the later 1960s when external imbalances made it increasingly clear that the French franc had become overvalued and the German mark undervalued. Both France and Germany tenaciously resisted adjusting their currencies' par values, each for their own domestic reasons, in a stand-off that lasted for many months and involved an elaborate play of tactical maneuvers, threats and reciprocal accusations of obstinacy. But the underlying dispute turned on the question of which country should bear what share of the burden of adjustment. It ended with an 11.11% devaluation of the French franc on August 8, 1969, and, following Bundestag elections and a brief period of floating of the German mark, a 9.29% revaluation of the mark on October 24, 1969.

b From the Werner Plan to the Snake

29. This Franco-German conflict and its eventual settlement and, in the background, mounting tensions in the Bretton Woods system (re)focused political attention on the need for an orderly monetary arrangement in Europe. The final communiqué of the summit meeting of the (then six) Member States held in The Hague on December 1-2, 1969 included a paragraph calling on the Council to work out *"a plan in stages [...] with a view to the creation of an economic and monetary union"*.[13] On October 8, 1970, a working group chaired by Pierre Werner, then Prime Minister and Minister of Finance of Luxembourg, submitted its (final) report on the subject.[14] This "Werner Plan" described the prerequisites of full economic and monetary union, to be achieved in a staged process. It did not set a precise time line but indicated that such a union should be *"realizable in the course of this decade"*.[15] It then focused on the steps to be taken during a first stage of three years. The Werner Plan proposed to progressively narrow fluctuation margins among participating European currencies until their cross rates could be irreversibly locked, at which point these *"national monetary symbols"* could be maintained or, preferably, replaced by a single currency so as to more clearly mark the irreversibility of the process.[16] By that time, the *"principal decisions"* of monetary policy should be centralized but, interestingly, the report considered that the utilization of monetary policy instruments could be differentiated from country to country *"within certain limits"*.[17] Monetary policy would then be conducted by a European system of central banks patterned on the U.S. Federal Reserve System.[18] In parallel, the Werner Plan placed considerable emphasis on reinforced coordination and harmonization of the Member States' economic and budgetary policies as of the first stage, in preparation for a centralization of key economic decisions in the final stage.

13. This final communiqué is reproduced in *Supplement to Bulletin 11-1970 of the European Communities*, pp. 31-34 and may be found at https://ec.europa.eu/economy_finance/publications/pages/publication6142_en.pdf. The relevant paragraph is §8.
14. *Ibid.*, pp. 1-29.
15. *Ibid.*, pp. 14 and 26.
16. *Ibid.*, pp. 10, 12, 22-23 and 26. The Werner Plan was written at a time when exchange rates were still embedded in the Bretton Woods gold-dollar standard. As a first step, it proposed that fluctuation margins between European currencies be reduced below those resulting from the cumulation of margins around their U.S. dollar parities, which was to be achieved by *"concerted action in relation to the dollar"*. *Ibid.*, p. 22.
17. *Ibid.*, p. 10.
18. *Ibid.*, p. 13.

30. By a resolution of March 22, 1971, the Council and the representatives of the Member States' governments *"expressed their political will to establish an economic and monetary union, during the coming decade"*, by a staged process substantially along the lines of the Werner Plan, and set out a series of measures to be taken during a first stage of three years.[19] This grand resolution was passed a few months before Richard Nixon's "bombshell" announcement of August 15, 1971, suspending the convertibility of U.S. dollars into gold. In the disarray surrounding the unraveling of the gold-dollar standard, the Werner Plan eventually fell by the wayside, leaving only fragments of the initial design, including some measures to improve economic policy coordination and, in the monetary space, a European exchange rate mechanism that became known as the "snake" (*see* paragraph 31 below). Separately, a shadow exchange rate scheme was developed for purposes of the Common Agricultural Policy ("CAP"), with "green rates" and "monetary compensatory amounts" (in fact, border levies and subsidies), to moderate the impact of changes in market exchange rates on the functioning of CAP, a policy area at the heart of the European construction.

31. The "snake" was essentially based on an agreement of April 10, 1972 between the central banks of the Member States (and those of prospective entrants) in which they agreed to keep their currencies within a 2.25% band around their bilateral central rates as well as, initially, within the 4.50% "Smithsonian" band about their central rates relative to the U.S. dollar.[20] It was a snake crawling in a widened dollar tunnel—the "snake in the tunnel". With another speculative wave against a weakened dollar reaching its crest, the dollar tunnel was abandoned hardly a year later, on March 12, 1973, and the snake became a (semi-)fixed exchange rate mechanism between participating European currencies, jointly floating vis-à-vis other currencies—*"le serpent dans l'espace"*. Thus, within a short time span, the morphology of the snake had evolved from the Wernerian conception of progressively narrowing margins around freezing parities in the perspective of economic and monetary union, to the temporary fix of a snake in a dollar tunnel and, in the event, to a "snake in space"[21]—and one that was in repeated trouble and shrinking.

32. Developments surrounding the 1973 oil crisis affected the Member States' economies asymmetrically and led to different policy responses depending on their different tolerance levels (indifference curves) for inflation and unemployment. Another source

19. Resolution of the Council and the Representatives of the Governments of the Member States of March 22, 1971 on the achievement by stages of economic and monetary union in the Community, *OJ* C28, March 27, 1971, p. 1.
20. For currencies other than the dollar, the widening of fluctuation margins to 2.25% either side of their respective dollar par values as a result of the Smithsonian Agreement of December 18, 1971 (*see* paragraph 26 above) implied that, at any given time, their cross rates could be as much as 4.50% apart and their intertemporal spread as much as 9%. This was thought excessive for Europe's common market, and the snake sought to limit the variability of cross rates to maximum 2.25% at any point in time.
21. I may note that there was yet another species crawling within the snake. Belgium and The Netherlands initially maintained the Belgian franc and the Dutch guilder within a narrower 1.50% band—an arrangement nicknamed the "worm". This creature was to survive until the French franc's second departure from the snake on March 15, 1976, when pressure on the Belgian franc prompted termination of these narrower margins.

of tension within the snake was that the German mark had increasingly become a refuge currency for the U.S. dollar in recurring episodes of dollar instability. As a result, the German mark often tended to drag along, "pull up", its partner currencies in the snake against the dollar and other third currencies. This could diminish the other Member States' competitiveness in international trade and repeatedly require them to intervene in the foreign exchange market in support of their currencies' central rates against the German mark, thus depleting their foreign currency reserves. The German mark's pull-up effect was initially constrained by the Smithsonian dollar band but, as said, this constraint fell away on March 12, 1973. The combination of these factors necessitated multiple realignments of bilateral central rates of snake currencies—all implying in effect an upward valuation of the German mark. More significantly, it also led to several defections from the snake,[22] with the consequence that snake membership eventually shrank to some smaller currencies (the Dutch guilder, the Belgian franc and the Danish krone) orbiting around the German mark.

c The European Monetary System

33. As was to become a recurring pattern in European monetary (and other) affairs, change came from a *rapprochement* of French and German positions:

(a) France, a traditional proponent of fixed exchange rates, had seen its efforts to preserve a fixed exchange rate system at international level founder at the 1975 Rambouillet summit and the 1976 meeting of the IMF Interim Committee in Kingston (Jamaica), which effectively legalized floating without any commitment to return to fixed exchange rates. France's own experience with floating, in between and after periods of snake membership, had been unsatisfactory, and it had grown suspicious that the United States and the United Kingdom sought to gain a competitive advantage by letting their currencies float downward. France had also become increasingly dissatisfied with the functioning of CAP's shadow exchange rate scheme which, by and large, turned out to be less advantageous for net exporters of agricultural products with a depreciating currency. Its major criticism of the snake's parity grid of bilateral central rates was that it required reciprocal interventions at the margins by both snake members irrespective of the cause of the disturbance. This, so the argument went, implied an asymmetrical allocation of the burden of adjustment that favored the snake members with the more conservative monetary and fiscal policies and the stronger currencies. This asymmetry was aggravated at times of dollar instability which caused the German

22. Thus, pound sterling and the Irish pound dropped out as early as June 23, 1972; the Danish krone withdrew on June 27, 1972 but rejoined on October 10, 1972; the Italian lira left on February 13, 1973; the French franc left on January 19, 1974, rejoined on July 10, 1975 and left again on March 15, 1976; the Swedish krona withdrew on August 29, 1977 and the Norwegian krone on December 12, 1978.

mark, as currency of refuge, to exert a pull-up effect on other snake currencies. Reciprocal intervention obligations then required other snake members to use their foreign currency reserves or borrow the harder currency, while the snake member with the harder currency could issue more of its own currency in defense of the central rates. Consequently, the snake effectively placed a greater burden on countries with weaker currencies than on those with stronger currencies (read: notably Germany). France therefore advocated a more "democratic" numéraire for the central rates, particularly some appropriate basket of currencies.

(b) Germany was (and is) traditionally strongly committed to price stability and inflation control but also wished to check excessive appreciation of the German mark to preserve export competitiveness, partly in deference to domestic industry and farmer interests. It regarded the snake as a means to contain upward pressure on the mark and to spread the burden of defense, particularly against dollar instability. Over time, however, the snake lost much of its efficacy in this respect as a succession of central rate alignments implied a revaluation of the mark and the snake's membership progressively shrank to a few smaller currencies around the mark. Germany became open to a new initiative to enlarge the European currency bloc.

(c) Back in France, the victory of the incumbent center-right majority in the March 1978 parliamentary elections and the ensuing malaise within the opposition on the left restored political maneuverability for the French Government. The stars had become aligned for a Franco-German entente.

34. After much discussion, including crucially a meeting between then French President Valéry Giscard d'Estaing and then German Chancellor Helmut Schmidt on September 14-15, 1978 in Aachen, the European Council on December 5, 1968 adopted a resolution on the establishment of the European Monetary System ("EMS").[23] The resolution focused on the initial phase of EMS, including notably its Exchange Rate Mechanism ("ERM"). Little was said about what should happen subsequently, except that the initial arrangements were to be "consolidated" into a final system no later than two years after the start of the scheme and that the final system would entail the creation of a European Monetary Fund as well as the full utilization of the European Currency Unit ("ECU") as a reserve asset and means of settlement. The two-year deadline was later extended and the final phase was postponed *sine die*.

35. The operating rules and procedures for ERM were worked out in an agreement of March 13, 1979 between the central banks,[24] again in the periphery of the European

23. Resolution of December 5, 1978 of the European Council on the establishment of the European Monetary System (EMS) and related matters, Annex 1 to the Conclusions of the Presidency, https://www.consilium.europa.eu/media/20762/bruxelles_december_1978_eng_.pdf.

24. Agreement of March 13, 1979 between the central banks of the Member States of the European Economic Community laying down the operating procedures for the European Monetary System, https://www.ecb.europa.eu/ecb/access_to_documents/document/cog_pubaccess/shared/data/ecb.dr.en.pdf?9eb78f0c5990c2385dbd3c690fb6ec59.

legal framework. ERM, at the heart of EMS, had a two-pronged structure reflecting a compromise between the French and German positions:

(a) The first prong, for purposes of the day-to-day exchange rate management, was a snake-like parity grid of bilateral central rates, now derived from each currency's base rate in terms of a weighted currency basket, the ECU. Both central banks concerned were required to intervene so as to maintain market exchange rates within 2.25% fluctuation margins from those bilateral central rates (with wider margins of up to 6% being temporarily allowed to previously floating currencies).[25]

(b) The second prong was a "divergence indicator", sometimes nicknamed the "rattlesnake", designed to prevent chronic strains from developing in the parity grid by serving as an early warning system to expose "deviant" national policies. Under this novel mechanism, whenever a participating currency crossed its "divergence threshold", *i.e.*, 75% of the maximum spread between the currency's market ECU equivalent and its ECU parity, this gave rise to a "presumption" that the relevant Member State should take appropriate corrective action by diversified (intra-marginal) interventions, monetary policy measures, changes in its currency's central rates or other measures of economic policy. A Member State's failure to do so would trigger consultations with other Member States, including, *"if necessary"*, at the European level.

36. ERM eventually extended to the currencies of most Member States, including the French franc and the Italian lira from the outset (the latter with the benefit of wider fluctuation margins of 6% until January 8, 1990). Pound sterling joined on October 8, 1990 (also with 6% margins) but, amid severe currency speculation in the summer of 1992, was forced to leave on September 16, 1992 ("Black Wednesday"), along with the Italian lira. In the following months, continued tensions in ERM led to occasionally massive interventions in the foreign exchange markets and four central rate realignments until, on August 2, 1993, the fluctuation margins were widened to 15% (except between the German mark and the Dutch guilder which were kept at 2.25%). Yet, while these developments did not bode well for the EMU project then approaching its

25. Intervention to support bilateral rates was obligatory at the margins, for both central banks concerned, with unlimited credit being available between central banks through a very short-term financing facility. Over the years, intra-marginal interventions, by way of preemptive action to contain incipient exchange rate pressures, became more frequent and, subject to certain limitations, were made eligible for financing via the then European Monetary Cooperation Fund under the so-called "Basle-Nyborg Accord" of November 1987. This agreement refers to a series of measures agreed by the central bank governors on September 8, 1987 and endorsed by the economics and finance ministers at a meeting of September 12, 1987 in Nyborg. *See Report by the Committee of Governors on the strengthening of the EMS*, September 8, 1987, https://www.ecb.europa.eu/ecb/access_to_documents/document/cog_pubaccess/shared/data/ecb/dr.parcg2009_0005_report_September1987.en.pdf?cc46f67b5676d33e6fd934cf09b515407.

Stage II, they did not derail it. The project had generated sufficient political traction by then.

37. Aside from those turbulent years, ERM had generally worked fairly satisfactorily, and more so after the early 1980s.[26] During this period, by and large, ERM helped to stabilize nominal and real exchange rates among ERM members (although not necessarily their effective exchange rates with the rest of the world). It led to closer interaction and dialogue between national central banks and governments on their exchange rate, monetary and economic policies and to a greater focus on inflation control. Before the currency crisis of 1992, there had been 12 realignments of bilateral central rates which generally had involved less delay and drama than in the Bretton Woods years, were broadly in line with underlying cost and price differentials (but without fully offsetting them) and, especially in the second half of the 1980s, were backed up by domestic stabilization measures. ERM even held up in the turbulence caused by the Wall Street stock market crash in October 1987 and the subsequent descent of the U.S. dollar, owing in significant measure to large-scale interventions and coordinated interest rate adjustments by the German and French central banks.

38. ERM may be credited for having contributed toward a certain convergence of the monetary policies of ERM members and a reduction of their inflation levels. There was less convergence in fiscal and external positions. While the ECU was nominally the *numéraire* of the system, the German mark remained its *de facto* anchor and hence the compass for monetary policy. Germany's low tolerance for inflation imparted a disinflationary direction to the system. In addition, given the German mark's status as a currency of refuge for the U.S. dollar in international portfolios, episodic dollar weakness would cause the German mark to further "pull up" the other ERM currencies and, in this manner, continued to be a potential source of destabilizing pressures within ERM. As a result, the symmetry debate did not go away. ERM members, especially those with weaker currencies, criticized ERM's *de facto* anchoring in the German mark for (i) imbuing the system with disinflationary, low-growth bias; (ii) determining the currency bloc's position in relation to third currencies, particularly the U.S. dollar, thereby potentially adversely affecting the other ERM members' international competitiveness; and (iii) placing a disproportionate share of the burden of adjustment on ERM members with weaker currencies, including in terms of the cost of intervention obligations.

d A Wall Came Down in Berlin

39. Academic debate on the proper form of a European monetary order never subsided but the subject moved back up the political agenda toward the mid-1980s in the context of the single market program and the Single European Act signed on February 17 and

26. An assessment of ERM's record requires cautious analysis, such as may be found in M.E.L. Griffiths & D.C. McDonald, "The ERM experience", in *Frameworks for Monetary Stability: Policy Issues and Country Experiences* (C. Cottarelli & T.J.T. Baliño eds.), IMF, 1994, pp. 139-161.

28, 1986. This Act set forth a number of significant institutional reforms designed in part to facilitate the roll-out of the single market program by the end of 1992. The belief that this ambitious plan of market integration needed a stable and more integrated monetary order gained momentum. The idea of moving toward some form of closer economic and monetary union was picked up again and, at its meeting of June 27-28, 1988 in Hannover on the implementation of the single market program, the European Council commissioned an *ad hoc* committee chaired by Jacques Delors, then President of the European Commission, to study and prepare *"concrete stages"* leading toward economic and monetary union.[27] The Delors Report, submitted in April 1989, outlined a step-by-step approach divided into three stages, without a precise calendar (advising even against explicit deadlines for moving from one stage to another).[28] It emphasized the need for sufficient convergence of economic policies and, hence, parallel advancement in economic and monetary integration and allowed for different speeds in the degree of participation by Member States.[29] This evolutionary process should lead, in its final stage, to irrevocably locked parities between participating currencies, which should then preferably (albeit not necessarily) be replaced by a single currency.[30] In this final stage, a single monetary policy and single exchange rate and reserve management would be conducted by a federal system of central banks *"in what might be called a European System of Central Banks (ESCB)"*, committed to the objective of price stability and being politically independent.[31]

40. Who could ever forget the images in the live broadcast of jubilant *Wessis* and *Ossis* climbing the Berlin Wall at its six checkpoints on the night of November 9, 1988? These events kick-started the process of German reunification. (Tactical?) reservations of then French President François Mitterand about German reunification eventually led then German Chancellor Helmut Kohl to commit to anchoring Germany more firmly in Europe, notably by agreeing to economic and monetary union under a new single currency, in order to overcome those reservations. To some degree, the euro could be seen as a *quid pro quo* for German reunification. Another Franco-German *rapprochement* was again of critical importance. It is a recurring theme in the history of European monetary integration: a Franco-German entente appears at all decisive moments—like the monolith in Stanley Kubrick's *2001: A Space Odyssey*.

41. In any event, the Treaty on European Union, signed on February 7, 1992 in Maastricht, *i.e.*, this time an actual act of EU primary law, called for the formation of an Economic and Monetary Union ("EMU") in a three-stage process which, in its final stage, would involve the replacement of participating national currencies by a single common currency, the euro, under a single monetary policy conducted by a European

27. Conclusions of the Presidency of the European Council of June 27-28, 1988, point 5, https://www.europarl.europa.eu/summits/hannover/ha_en.pdf.
28. Committee for the Study of Economic and Monetary Union, *Report on economic and monetary union in the European Community*, April 1989, §43, https://ec.europa.eu/economy_finance/publications/pages/publication6161_en.pdf.
29. *Ibid.*, §§42 and 44.
30. *Ibid.*, §§23, 26 and 58.
31. *Ibid.*, §§32 and 60.

System of Central Banks ("ESCB") centered around a European Central Bank ("ECB"). The third stage started on January 1, 1999—the default date set by the Maastricht Treaty: the euro was introduced for a first group of 11 eligible Member States, initially only in "paperless" form and circulating alongside the legacy national currencies (now as immutably fixed sub-units of the euro), and then, as of January 1, 2002, as exclusive legal tender, including in the form of banknotes and coins.[32] It was an unusually bold move in the history of European integration that is otherwise characterized mostly by small and hesitant steps. But the relative euphoria of renewed European integration dynamics and German reunification provided an inflection point and political traction.[33]

2 THE BUILDERS' PLAN: ARCHITECTURE OF THE EUROPEAN CURRENCY UNION

42. Summarized below are the key features of the new EMU plan, particularly its currency union, as conceived by its builders in the 1990s. The basic architecture still stands today, although certain elements have been strengthened and some added over the course of the past 25 years. The plan introduces a currency union well before completion of full EMU and does so at different speeds for different Member States, distinguishing, within the EU legal framework, between Member States admitted to the currency union and those not yet ready to join but, in principle, committed to work toward currency union membership at a later time.

a A Single Currency

43. The EMU project had a clear focus—and deadline set in the Maastricht Treaty itself—on moving from the preceding semi-fixed exchange rate arrangements to an

32. By and large, the particularities of the three-stage process and the technicalities of the two-phase replacement of national currencies by the euro in Stage III are of lesser relevance for present purposes. For an overview, *see, e.g.*, J. Meyers & D. Levie, "The Introduction of the Euro: Overview of the Legal Framework and Selected Legal Issues", *Columbia Journal of European Law*, Vol. 4, 1998, pp. 321-352.
33. This euphoria was not shared by all to the same degree. It was in those days that the Luxembourg Government in the greatest secrecy ordered the production of banknotes, bearing the image of the late Grand-Duchess Charlotte, in a total amount of 50 billion in a theretofore non-existing currency, the Luxembourgish franc. Apparently, Luxembourg, then in a monetary union with Belgium, harbored doubts about the prospects of the then Belgian franc to join any respectable European currency union. When the euro currency union fell into place on January 1, 1999 with Belgium as one of its members, the Luxembourg Government had the banknotes burned by the Luxembourg armed forces. Jean-Claude Juncker confessed all this in a speech of June 19, 2019 to a room full of central bankers at the ECB Forum on Central Banking in Sintra (Portugal), adding that this *"little story stayed a well-kept secret between the Grand Duke, the Prime Minister Jacques Santer and myself"*. Mr. Juncker's speech is otherwise worth reading for the perspective of a seasoned European politician on the currency union's first 20 years and is to be found at https://ec.europa.eu/commission/presscorner/detail/en/SPEECH_19_3320.

irreversible single currency. It was thought that this would avoid the episodic difficulties and possible asymmetries of managing and defending semi-fixed exchange rates, and also that it would more credibly convey immutability than maintaining national currencies with locked parities.

44. A Council regulation established the *"irrevocably fixed conversion rates"* at which the national currencies of Member States admitted to the currency union were replaced by the euro as of January 1, 1999 for the original 11 Member States, or the applicable later date for subsequent entrants.[34] Accordingly, as of the relevant entry date, euro area Member States traded in their national currencies for a single euro area currency, the euro, at a value relationship that is frozen in time, thereby eliminating any further nominal exchange rate variability between euro area Member States. Consequently:

(a) Within the **euro area**, there are no longer stronger and weaker currencies subject to upward or downward market pressures, nor bilateral exchange rates needing to be defended or adjusted. Terms of trade within the euro area are henceforth determined by cost and price competitiveness, undistorted by undervalued or overvalued exchange rates.

(b) Vis-à-vis **the rest of the world**, euro area Member States now share the costs and benefits of euro exchange rate variability against the U.S. dollar and other third currencies depending on the geographic profile of their foreign trade, regardless of which exchange rate level they might wish to target in order to suit their particular trading needs. Also, one would logically expect that the effects of occasional dollar instability, as previously occurred in the snake and ERM through upward pressure on the German mark as choice currency of refuge and its resulting pull-up effect on other European currencies, would be more subdued by an averaging-out effect now that the German mark is replaced by a supranational currency of a more diverse set of economies.

(c) At **both levels**, euro area Member States no longer have to worry about upward or downward pressures on their national currencies. By the same token, weaker economies are no longer able to adjust their currencies' exchange rates to restore international competitiveness and improve their trade balance.

45. All this is broadly fine, but financial markets cannot be sidetracked and stopped from making their own risk assessments and risk pricing. Currency union or not, they will at some point price in higher risk for deviant fiscal behavior or worsening economic fundamentals. At the time, it was only dimly apprehended in political decision-making that, while in a currency union markets can no longer speculate on exchange rate changes, they could shift their attention to government bond yields and require higher risk premiums for euro area Member States with out-of-line fiscal

34. Council Regulation (EC) No 2866/98 of December 31, 1998 on the conversion rates between the euro and the currencies of the Member States adopting the euro, *OJ* L359, December 31, 1998, p. 1, meanwhile amended nine times to add conversion rates for later entrants.

positions that could present a higher risk of default (or debt restructuring) or even compromise continued currency union membership. Speculation on exchange rates would then give way to speculation on sovereign bond yields. This was to occur episodically and became an immanent risk of the European currency union, particularly in times of high and strongly diverging government debt levels, as will further be discussed at various places later in this book and particularly in Chapter 5. The deflection of speculation from exchange rates to sovereign bond yields has a paradoxical side insofar as speculation previously targeting overvalued and undervalued currencies alike, including a refuge currency of a strong economy, is now redirected to government bond yields of weaker economies.

46. In any event, the introduction of the euro as of January 1, 1999 marked the end of ERM. It was replaced by ERM II, an exchange rate arrangement open to non-euro area Member States on a voluntary basis as an antechamber to currency union membership. ERM II involves fluctuation margins of 15% (or less if the relevant Member State so chooses) around (adjustable) central rates relative to the euro.[35] While ERM II membership is voluntary, smooth participation in ERM II for at least two years is one of the tests for admission to actual currency union membership (*see* paragraph 49(c) below). ERM II membership is currently down to the Danish krone (which joined from the outset with a fluctuation margin of ± 2.25%) and the Bulgarian lev (which joined on July 10, 2020).

b A Single Monetary Policy Primarily Focused on Price Stability

47. A single currency goes with a single monetary policy. In the later 1980s, a broad consensus emerged to the effect that monetary policy should focus first and foremost on pursuing (medium-term) price stability and should be conducted by a central bank or central banking system independent from government and not subject to its instructions. Germany in particular insisted that the single monetary policy should be hard-nosed about inflation and be ringfenced from political decision-making, much to the image of its trusted Bundesbank. The focus of the monetary policy mandate on maintaining price stability found support in monetarist theory which had become a dominant intellectual framework by the 1980s. In monetarist analysis, in essence, monetary authorities are incapable of structurally lowering unemployment and better concern themselves instead with what they can control, *i.e.*, the price level.[36] The architecture of EMU, laid down by the Maastricht Treaty, reflects the view that an

35. ERM II's main features are set out in the Resolution of the European Council of June 16, 1997 on the establishment of an exchange-rate mechanism in the third stage of economic and monetary union, *OJ* C236, August 2, 1997, p. 5. Its operating procedures are detailed in an agreement between the relevant central banks, *i.e.*, currently, the Agreement of March 16, 2006 between the European Central Bank and the central banks of the Member States outside the euro area laying down the operating procedures for an exchange rate mechanism in stage three of Economic and Monetary Union, *OJ* C73, March 25, 2006, p. 21, amended several times and last by an agreement of December 12, 2022, *OJ* C12, January 13, 2023, p. 3.
36. *Cf.* P. De Grauwe, *Economics of Monetary Union*, Oxford University Press, 13th ed., 2020, p. 166.

independent central bank can control inflation over the medium term (at least in significant measure), provided that it is not forced to finance fiscal deficits. This explains the explicit Treaty prohibition on monetary financing of the government sector (now Article 123 TFEU). By the same token, this prohibition was intended to encourage sound fiscal policies by keeping national governments subject to financial market discipline.

c Admission Criteria and Membership

48. With all of the experience acquired, progress made and setbacks suffered over the previous 20 years, it remained a daring move to introduce a common currency under a single monetary policy for an economically still relatively heterogeneous group of sovereign Member States retaining a high degree of autonomy in their economic and fiscal policies. Under the circumstances, is was a leap of faith to establish a currency union as an intermediate rather than as the final step on the path to complete EMU. It was recognized that, in order not to put the cart too squarely before the horse, admission to the currency union should be conditioned on an adequate degree of economic convergence particularly in price performance and fiscal positions.

Interestingly, while these convergence criteria serve as tests for a Member State's admission to the currency union at entry point, they are not conditions of continued membership. The fiscal criteria serve as benchmarks for the common rules on the members' proper fiscal conduct but, although a member's non-compliance with these rules may, at least in theory, give rise to other forms of sanction, it would not formally be a ground for suspension or termination of currency union membership. In fact, as we will discuss in Chapter 11, the Treaties do not contemplate a member's voluntary or forced withdrawal from, or suspension of, currency union membership. It is, on paper, a membership for life, in the full sense of legal fiction of this kind.

49. Thus, currency union membership is reserved at entry point to Member States that are found to meet certain minimum standards of low(er) inflation and sound public finances. These admission criteria deserve a closer look. They were initially set forth in the Maastricht Treaty and its protocol on convergence criteria and are now included substantially verbatim in Article 140(1) TFEU and Protocol No 13[37] for subsequent admissions. In substance, admission requires a finding of *"a high degree of sustainable convergence"* primarily (although not exclusively) by reference to four criteria:

(a) The Member State's price performance is sustainable and its average rate of inflation (as measured by the consumer price index), observed over a period of one year preceding the assessment, may not be more than 1.5 percentage points higher than that of, at most, the three best performing Member States in terms of price stability.

37. Protocol (No 13) on the convergence criteria. This protocol, like the other numbered protocols referred to in this book, is annexed to the Treaties and forms an integral part thereof (Article 51 TEU).

(b) At the time of the assessment, the Member State may not be subject to a determination by the Council under Article 126(6) TFEU that its government budgetary position is in excessive deficit, which, as a benchmark (subject to consideration of other relevant factors), will be the case if:
   (i) the Member State's actual or planned government deficit exceeds 3 % of GDP (at market prices), unless (1) this ratio has declined *"substantially and continuously"* to a level close to 3 %, or (2) the excess is *"exceptional and temporary"*, with the ratio remaining close to 3 %; or
   (ii) its government debt exceeds 60 % of GDP (at market prices), unless this ratio is *"sufficiently diminishing"* and *"approaching"* 60 % *"at a satisfactory pace"*.

(c) The Member State's currency has stayed within the normal fluctuation margins of the ERM or, for post-1999 entrants, ERM II, *"without severe tensions"* and without devaluation of its central rate against any other participating currency in the ERM, or against the euro in ERM II, for at least two years preceding the assessment.

(d) The Member State's average nominal long-term interest rate (on long-term government bonds or comparable securities) over the year preceding the assessment may not be more than 2 percentage points higher than that of, at most, the three best performing Member States in terms of price stability.

50. At first blush, these convergence criteria prompt several comments:

(a) The criteria show no particularly conspicuous imprint of OCA theory. While they generally seem sensible, some of their detail is not particularly scientific. In particular, there appears to be no compelling scientific basis for the specific numerical benchmarks of 3 % and 60 % for, respectively, the government deficit and debt ratios, especially since the sustainability of any given government deficit or debt level varies with interest rate levels and GDP growth. Predictably, economists have criticized those numerical values as arbitrary or even as a form of *"voodoo economics"*.[38] Yet, 25 years into the currency union and after several reforms of the common fiscal rules, these reference values still stand. Perhaps they are about something more than economics.

(b) There is a clear focus on a low level of inflation. This reflects Germany's concern that euro area inflation could be pulled up by a higher inflation tolerance of other Member States. A disinflationary effort to bring down their inflation rates close to best-in-class levels (read: including that in Germany) became part of the price for the entry ticket. The limits on government deficit and debt ratios—which have become continuing benchmarks under the common fiscal rules (*see* paragraph 54(c) below)—could be viewed from the same angle: these constraints should also serve to restrain inflationary public

38. *Cf.* P. De Grauwe, *supra*, p. 127.

spending and to avoid Member States ending up in a situation in which they might be tempted to tolerate higher inflation to "melt off" excessive government debt.

(c) Overall, the convergence criteria leave a significant margin for (political) judgment. This is especially the case for the fiscal convergence test (*see* paragraph 49(b) above) which refers to a Council determination on the basis of relatively elastic subtests. Moreover, the four criteria are not the sole criteria since the assessment must also take into account *"the results of the integration of markets, the situation and development of the balances of payments on current account and an examination of the development of unit labour costs and other price indices"* (Article 140(1), *in fine*, TFEU).

(d) The assessment horizon seems quite short: one year for inflation and long-term interest rates, two years for ERM or ERM II exchange rate performance, and no excessive deficit procedure pending at the time of assessment.

(e) The interest rate convergence test (*see* paragraph 49(d) above) may seem somewhat redundant. If a prospective member does well on the three other criteria, its government bond yields should ordinarily have converged to levels in the proximity of those of other Member States. The prospect of near-term admission to the currency union should provide further comfort to the financial markets and induce them to reduce the risk premium on the prospective member's government bonds. But, taking this reasoning one step further, one would almost think that, by the same token, the interest rate convergence test indirectly gives the financial markets a kind of no-confidence vote against admission by causing a widening of government bond spreads beyond 200 basis points if they lack confidence in the prospective member's eligibility for admission.

51. On the basis of those convergence criteria, 11 Member States, *i.e.*, Austria, Belgium, Finland, France, Germany, Ireland, Italy, Luxembourg, The Netherlands, Portugal and Spain, have been admitted to the currency union from the start, as of 1999. Greece has been admitted as of 2002, Slovenia as of 2007, Cyprus and Malta as of 2008, Slovakia as of 2009, Estonia as of 2011, Latvia as of 2014, Lithuania as of 2015, and Croatia as of 2023.

52. From the outset, the United Kingdom was exempted from the obligation to adopt the euro, unless it notified the Council of its intention to the contrary (which it never did).[39] The remaining seven Member States—Member States "with a derogation"—are, in principle, committed to achieving currency union membership, and their progress under the convergence criteria is assessed periodically. Denmark is treated as a Member State with a derogation but, in view of its constitutional requirement of a prior referendum, the procedure for its admission to the currency union may be initiated

39. *See* Protocol (No 15) on certain provisions relating to the United Kingdom of Great Britain and Northern Ireland.

only at its request.[40] The Treaty contains a loophole that cannot even be excused as unintended: while a currency's smooth participation in ERM II (which succeeded ERM in 1999) is a precondition to admission (*see* paragraph 49(c) above), participation in ERM II is voluntary, with the consequence that Member States can perpetuate their derogatory status simply by not joining ERM II. Currently, after the Croatian kuna graduated into the euro as of 2023, only two currencies remain in ERM II, *i.e.*, the Bulgarian lev and the Danish krone.

d A Common Fiscal Framework

53. The currency union took off in an incomplete EMU. In the euro area, a single currency backed by a single monetary policy is to co-exist with (mostly) national economic and fiscal policies of a relatively diverse set of sovereign Member States. Being deprived of exchange rate and monetary policy tools of their own, these Member States would need sufficient economic and fiscal elbow room to respond to business cycle fluctuations and external shocks. But, in a currency union, national economic and fiscal policies also need to remain consistent with overall price stability and longer-term sustainability of public finances. Fiscal sustainability remains a national responsibility, as underscored by the Maastricht Treaty's "no bail-out" clause (now Article 125 TFEU). Yet, it was recognized that political deficit bias and excessive public spending by Member States could create or fuel inflationary pressures, and that higher government deficits and debt could put pressure on the ECB to keep monetary policy rates lower than needed for inflation control—or might even tempt governments to "free ride" on the system in the expectation that the ECB would do so. Therefore, a common fiscal framework was established, in the Treaty and in the Stability and Growth Pact, that constrains the level of public deficit that governments can run and the amount of debt that they can incur. But, at least initially, that framework was largely limited to peer reviews, benchmarking and other soft forms of surveillance and coordination. Over the years, it has been expanded and sharpened in several respects and, on balance, has become more invasive, as we will discuss in Chapter 8.

54. Thus, in order to restrain public spending and deficit bias of national governments and guard against the "moral hazard" of political temptation to "free ride" on the system, rules and procedures have been put in place to ensure a measure of fiscal discipline of the Member States and avoid or mitigate conflict with the ECB's monetary policy and its price stability objective. This framework broadly applies to all Member States but is reinforced in several respects for euro area Member States. At the outset, it essentially included the following elements:

(a) Under the prohibition of monetary financing (now Article 123 TFEU), the ECB and national central banks may not extend credit to the European Union or any of its institutions or to any Member State's government sector, nor

40. *See* Protocol (No 16) on certain provisions related to Denmark.

directly subscribe to their debt securities. There is to be no monetization of government debt. While central banks may in times of crisis need to act as "lender of last resort" to the banking system in the interest of financial stability, they are barred from doing so for governments.

(b) Under the "no bail-out" clause (now Article 125 TFEU), neither the Union nor any Member State shall be liable for, or assume, any financial obligations of any other Member State's government sector—a rule which is not only a disclaimer but also a prohibition.

(c) Member States must continue to avoid excessive government deficits and debt, as measured on the basis of the same tests as under the convergence criteria (*see* paragraph 49(b) above). A Council determination that an "excessive deficit" exists triggers a procedure, referred to as the excessive deficit procedure ("EDP"), in which the Council may address recommendations for remedial action to the Member State concerned and, in the case of euro area Member States, eventually summon the Member State to take corrective measures by a specified deadline and even impose certain economic sanctions in case of non-compliance (now Article 126 TFEU and Protocol No 12 on the excessive deficit procedure).

(d) At its meeting of June 16-17, 1997 in Amsterdam, the European Council adopted a resolution on the so-called "Stability and Growth Pact" ("SGP").[41] SGP, which we will further discuss in Chapter 8, initially consisted of this resolution and two Council regulations of July 7, 1997:[42]

  (i) Under the original SGP, Member States committed to pursue budgetary positions *"close to balance or in surplus"* as a medium-term objective, which was believed at the time to allow Member States to deal with normal fluctuations in the economic cycle while observing the 3% deficit ratio.

  (ii) In broad outline, Council Regulation (EC) No 1466/97, concerning the so-called "preventive arm" of SGP,[43] set out rules and procedures for the content, review and monitoring of national programs (called "stability programs" in the case of euro area Member States and "convergence programs" for the other Member States), including an early-warning procedure in order to prevent the occurrence of an excessive deficit.

---

41. Resolution of June 17, 1997 of the European Council on the Stability and Growth Pact, *OJ* C236, August 2, 1997, p. 1.
42. The term became subsequently used to refer more generally to the body of EU rules on the surveillance and coordination of national fiscal policies at the EU level.
43. In EU primary law, the preventive arm of SGP is based on Article 121 TFEU. It is primarily implemented by Council Regulation (EC) No 1466/97 of July 7, 1997 on the strengthening of the surveillance of budgetary positions and the surveillance and coordination of economic policies, *OJ* L209, August 2, 1997, p. 1, amended by Council Regulation (EC) No 1055/2005 of June 27, 2005, *OJ* L174, July 7, 2005, p. 1, and Regulation (EU) No 1175/2011 of November 16, 2011, *OJ* L306, November 23, 2011, p. 12.

(iii) Council Regulation (EC) No 1467/97, on SGP's "corrective arm",[44] established a timetable for determining and remedying excessive deficits, clarified when a government deficit in excess of the 3 % ratio could be considered *"exceptional and temporary"*, and defined the sanctions that could be imposed on euro area Member States for failing to take appropriate corrective measures if so summoned by the Council as a final step in EDP.

3 1999-2007: THE EARLY YEARS

55. For a little short of 10 years, the new currency union sailed in seemingly clear blue water with favorable economic tailwinds. By and large, the first decade was marked by relatively calm macroeconomic conditions with limited volatility and steady economic growth. It was a time still of strong productivity increases (the low-hanging fruit of digitalization, increased globalization and outsourcing to lower-cost parts of the world), adequate labor supply (due in part to the Baby Boomers and their nocturnal activities) and the absence of disruptive external price shocks. Headline inflation (HICP) in the euro area evolved within a bandwidth of 2 % to 3 %, with an average of 2.35 %—although a steady increase in energy prices masked a softening of core inflation to an average of 1.7 % (*see* paragraph 114, Table 2.1, below). Sovereign bond spreads within the euro area stabilized within a narrow band of around 25 basis points most of the time. The financial markets tended to view government bonds of the euro area Member States substantially as close substitutes, without requiring significantly different risk premiums in relation to economic fundamentals.

56. Yet, pre-1999 budget consolidation stalled (consolidation fatigue?). The overall euro area government debt-to-GDP ratio eventually edged downward somewhat, albeit with significant country variations (*see* paragraph 116, Table 2.2, below). But few Member States achieved the medium-term objective of a budgetary position close to balance or in surplus, and several ended up in EDP. Early offenders even included Germany and France, which gave rise to the curious situation in which the Council held off on imposing corrective measures as the final EDP step, and the European Commission then (largely unsuccessfully) challenged the Council's inaction before the European Court of Justice.[45] Inadequate and uneven fiscal consolidation meant that

44. SGP's corrective arm is based on Article 126 TFEU, with the numerical reference values for the deficit and debt ratios being specified in Protocol No 12 on the excessive deficit procedure annexed to the Treaties. Implementing rules are set forth for the most part in Council Regulation (EC) No 1467/97 of July 7, 1997 on speeding up and clarifying the implementation of the excessive deficit procedure, *OJ* L209, August 2, 1997, p. 6, amended by Council Regulation (EC) No 1056/2005 of June 27, 2005, *OJ* L174, July 7, 2005, p. 5, and Council Regulation No 1177/2011 of November 8, 2011, *OJ* L306, November 23, 2011, p. 33.

45. CJEU, July 23, 2004, Case C-27/04, *Commission vs. Council*, ECLI:EU:C:2004:436. The Commission had proposed that, pursuant to Article 126(8) and (9) TFEU, the Council formally determine that Germany and France had failed to take effective action in response to earlier Council recommendations and summon each of them to take the necessary corrective measures by a specified deadline. At a meeting of November 25, 2003, the Council was unable to take these

insufficient buffers were built up.[46] Also, Ireland and several Southern euro area Member States (in particular Greece, Portugal and Spain), which experienced the strongest booms in economic activity, allowed wages to increase faster than productivity, with the consequence that their unit labor costs increased, and their competitiveness decreased, relative to other euro area Member States and trading partners[47] (*see* paragraph 132, Table 2.10, and paragraph 134, Table 2.11, below). It is also worth noting that the combination of a relatively high degree of convergence of **nominal** interest rates with greater variability of country inflation rates (*see* paragraph 114, Table 2.1, below) produced lower **real** interest rates in higher-inflation countries, in particular again certain Southern Member States, which likely fueled domestic demand and credit in these countries.[48]

57. As we will discuss in more detail in Chapter 8 (*see* paragraphs 583-585 below), SGP's less than stellar record prompted a first set of reforms in 2005 which were generally aimed at better accommodating country specifics in light of economic and fiscal heterogeneity within the European Union, encouraging structural reforms and offering a more flexible path for correcting excessive deficits:

(a) Thus, in SGP's preventive arm, Council Regulation (EC) No 1055/2005[49] (i) switched to country-specific medium-term budgetary objectives ("MTOs") which, for euro area and ERM II Member States, are to be specified in a range of –1% of GDP and balance or surplus in structural terms (*i.e.*, cyclically adjusted and net of one-off and temporary measures); (ii) for Member States falling short of their MTO, set an annual improvement of 0.5% of GDP as a benchmark; and (iii) allowed temporary deviations for structural reforms with direct long-term cost-saving effects (including, in particular, certain pension reforms).

---

decisions for lack of the requisite special voting majority and decided instead to hold EDP in abeyance in light of certain policy commitments offered by Germany and France. The Court held that the Commission's annulment action was inadmissible insofar as it concerned the Council's inability to adopt the proposed decisions under Article 126(8) and (9) TFEU, but suggested that the Commission could institute an action for failure to act under Article 265 TFEU. In contrast, the Court annulled the Council's decision to hold EDP in abeyance on the basis of policy commitments other than those initially recommended by the Council.

46. *See, e.g.*, X. Debrun, G. Ferrero *et al.*, "Monetary-fiscal policy interaction in the euro area", Report of the Eurosystem work stream on monetary-fiscal interactions, *ECB Occasional Paper Series No 273*, September 2021, pp. 38-40.

47. *See, e.g.*, P. De Grauwe, *supra*, pp. 33-34, Figure 2.5, and pp. 143-144, Figures 7.3 and 7.4. Later, over the 2008-2014 period, wage restraint and other austerity measures, oftentimes as part of the policy conditionality attached to EFSF/ESM loans, would put their unit labor costs back on a converging track. But, in the case of Greece, Portugal and Spain, some divergences seem to have re-appeared toward the end of the decade (*see* paragraph 132, Table 2.10, below).

48. *Cf.* J. Franks, B. Barkbu *et al.*, "Economic Convergence in the Euro Area: Coming Together or Drifting Apart?", *IMF Working Papers No 18/10*, January 2018, pp. 10-11.

49. Council Regulation (EC) No 1055/2005 of June 27, 2005 amending Regulation (EC) No 1466/97 on the strengthening of the surveillance of budgetary positions and the surveillance and coordination of economic policies, *OJ* L174, July 7, 2005, p. 1.

(b) In SGP's corrective arm, Council Regulation (EC) No 1056/2005[50] (i) provided for a broader set of factors to be considered in assessing Member States' fiscal positions (at least so long as the deficit ratio remains close to 3% and its excess is temporary); (ii) extended the deadlines for measures to correct an excessive deficit; and (iii) specified that Member States in excessive deficit will be required to achieve an annual budgetary improvement of at least 0.5% of GDP in structural terms as a benchmark.

58. Still, as we will discuss further in Chapter 4 (*see* paragraphs 198-199 below), in this relatively tranquil first decade, the ECB could conduct a textbook monetary policy. It was based on its policy interest rates and used conventional policy tools to steer money market rates (and indirectly the full spectrum of market interest rates) in the direction consistent with the monetary policy stance. These policy tools consisted primarily of (i) collateralized bank refinancing through open market operations, *i.e.*, mostly Main Refinancing Operations ("MROs") (regular weekly auctions of seven-day funds) and, to a lesser extent, Longer-Term Refinancing Operations ("LTROs") (monthly auctions of three-month funds), and (ii) standing lending and deposit facilities to provide additional liquidity to, or absorb excess liquidity from, the banking system. In the first two years, the ECB raised its main refinancing rate in several steps from 3% to 4.75% in October 2000, then gradually reduced it to 2% by June 2003, and from December 2005 onward progressively edged it up again to 4.25% by the summer of 2008. The marginal lending and deposit facility rates were consistently set at 100 basis points on each side of the main refinancing rate, thus producing a band of 200 basis points which effectively served as a corridor for interbank overnight lending rates.

4 2008-2012: THE GREAT FINANCIAL CRISIS

59. The 2008-2009 banking crisis, the problems with Greece's public finances that appeared in broad daylight toward the end of 2009, a widening sovereign debt crisis in the euro area in 2010-2012 and two successive recessions stretching into 2013[51] put the European currency union under severe stress and its governance in almost continuous crisis management mode. One can look at this crisis management through several lenses. In the narrative prevailing in official European circles, the crisis was successfully overcome in the time-honored European way: with patience and creativity, step by step, from one European summit to another. In his memoirs, Timothy Geithner, the then U.S. Secretary of the Treasury in the Obama administration, offers a different perspective: that of an outside observer perplexed by slow and hesitant decision-making, fiscal austerity bias and an inclination toward inflicting *"Old Testament*

50. Council Regulation (EC) No 1056/2005 of June 27, 2005 amending Regulation (EC) No 1467/97 on speeding up and clarifying the implementation of the excessive deficit procedure, *OJ* L174, July 7, 2005, p. 5.
51. The CEPR-EABCN Euro Area Business Cycle Dating Committee identified two recessions over the course of this period, *i.e.*, from 2008 Q1 to 2009 Q2 and from 2011 Q3 to 2013 Q1.

justice" upon "profligate" deficit countries, and poor execution and messaging to the financial markets.[52] As is often the case, the truth probably lies somewhere in the middle of the transatlantic narratives.

a The 2008-2009 Banking Crisis

60. The story of the 2008-2009 banking crisis has been told many times and in many variations. The *causa proxima* that sparked off the crisis was the bursting of the housing bubble in the United States—the wave of defaults in the subprime segment of mortgage loans as from 2007. In prior years, mortgage credit had been generously extended to low(er)-income households on the strength of continuously rising housing prices. Large amounts of subprime mortgage loans were repackaged (securitized), "sliced and diced", into collateralized debt obligations ("CDOs") and similar such synthetic instruments that received healthy credit ratings and obscured the underlying credit risks. These securities were dispersed widely across markets and geographies, in the portfolios of banks and non-bank financial intermediaries in search of higher yields. When housing prices started to decline and defaults on (subprime) mortgage loans to increase as of 2007, those securities became, in the words of Ben Bernanke, *"an agent of global contagion"* [53]—a kind of financial variant of a computer virus or SARS-CoV-2.

61. The contagious effects were transmitted and amplified by a complex dynamic of interactions that laid bare a series of pre-existing vulnerabilities in the financial system, including the high degree of leverage (stimulated, in the euro area, by relatively low real interest rates in the currency union's early phase), the excessive dependence of certain financial institutions (banks but also non-bank financial actors like money market funds and securitization vehicles) on unstable short-term funding, and forms of variable compensation in the financial services industry that incentivized undue risk taking. Tensions were exacerbated by the failure or near-failure of several financial institutions, including, most dramatically, Lehman Brothers' filing for bankruptcy on September 15, 2018. The crisis rapidly spread to European banks, especially, in the first instance, to banks in smaller economies (Iceland, Ireland and Belgium), and caused the interbank market to dry up.

62. As will be further discussed in Chapter 4 (*see* paragraphs 202-210 below), the banking crisis that followed the collapse of Lehman Brothers in September 2008 prompted forceful central bank action:

(a) National central banks provided Emergency Liquidity Assistance ("ELA") to banks, and the ECB (Eurosystem) stepped up to its role of lender of last resort

52. T.F. Geithner, *Stress Test. Reflections on Financial Crises*, London, Random House, 2014, pp. 441-450, 472-477 and 481-485.

53. B. Bernanke, *The Courage to Act: A Memoir of a Crisis and its Aftermath*, New York, Norton, 2015, p. 143.

to the banking system by engaging in large-scale liquidity operations to provide a backstop to dysfunctional interbank markets. On October 8, 2008, the ECB announced that, starting from the operation to be settled on October 15, the weekly MROs would be carried out through a fixed-rate tender procedure and with full allotment at the applicable main refinancing rate—meaning that the volume of liquidity supplied effectively became fully demand-driven.[54] In parallel, LTROs were also switched to full-allotment mode and, as the banking crisis unfolded and tensions began to build up in the sovereign debt markets, the regular three-month operations were supplemented by operations with longer maturities of six months, one year and even three years.[55] Also on October 8, 2008, the ECB facilitated access to central bank finance by expanding the list of assets eligible as collateral and by lowering the minimum credit rating for eligible collateral (other than asset-backed securities) from A– to BBB–.

(b) Between October 15, 2008 and May 13, 2009, the ECB lowered its main refinancing rate in seven swift steps from 4.25 % to 1 % and kept it at this level until April 13, 2011.[56] Interestingly, the spread (corridor) between the marginal lending rate and deposit facility rate around the main refinancing rate was temporarily narrowed from 200 basis points to 100 basis points between October 15, 2008 and January 21, 2009, moved back to 200 basis points between January 21, 2009 and May 13, 2009, and then reduced again to 100 basis points between May 13, 2009 and May 8, 2013 (and from then on kept within a range of 50 to 100 basis points).

(c) In the summer of 2009, the ECB also put in place a first—modest—asset purchase program, *i.e.*, the first covered bond purchase program ("CBPP1") which ran from July 2009 to June 2010 for a total nominal amount of EUR 60 billion. Subsequently, a sequel ("CBPP2") ran from November 2011 to October 2012 for a nominal amount of EUR 16.4 billion.

(d) Later, on December 8, 2011, the ECB lowered the minimum reserve requirement for banks from 2 % to 1 % (as of the reserve maintenance period starting on January 18, 2012).

54. The fixed-rate full-allotment approach had been "tested" in the summer of 2007, in the prelude to the financial crisis. When, on August 9, 2007, BNP Paribas Investment Partners froze redemptions from three of its investment funds invested in securities backed by U.S. subprime mortgages, serious liquidity tensions developed in the money markets in between regular weekly MROs. The ECB then promptly conducted discretionary fine-tuning operations, at a fixed rate with full allotment of all bids, for a total amount of EUR 94.8 billion. *See* M. Rostagno, C. Altavilla *et al.*, "A tale of two decades: the ECB's monetary policy at 20", *ECB Working Paper Series No 2346*, December 2019, pp. 144-145.
55. In fact, the first six-month LTROs were announced in March 2008. One-year LTROs were carried out in 2009 and 2011, and on December 8, 2011, the ECB decided to conduct two three-year LTROs (with prepayment option after one year).
56. Please note that these dates refer to the effective dates of the policy rate changes rather than to the dates of the relevant monetary policy decisions of the ECB Governing Council. This is generally the case throughout this book, unless it clearly appears from the context that the date of the monetary policy meeting is intended.

b The 2010-2012 Sovereign Debt Crisis

63. By then, the banking crisis had spilled over into a sovereign debt crisis in Europe. Between 2010 and 2012, several euro area Member States became subject to financial strain, and some even lost access to the financial markets and required financial assistance. It was partly the result (and, in the case of Greece and Portugal, probably more the cause) of an adverse feedback loop that became referred to as a "bank-sovereign doom loop". The banking crisis prompted several Member States to engage in significant public expenditures to recapitalize or resolve troubled financial institutions, which worsened their government deficit and debt ratios. This, in combination with increased market attention to sovereign credit risk, caused a widening of sovereign bond spreads to the detriment of higher-debt and/or smaller Member States and hence increased financial fragmentation in the euro area. Higher sovereign bond yields in these Member States depressed sovereign bond prices, which in turn adversely affected bank balance sheets.

64. On October 21, 2009, a surprise announcement by the new Greek government of George Papandreou had lighted the match: the Greek public deficit for 2008 was 7.7% of GDP, and not 5% as previously reported, and for 2009 was expected to be 12.5% rather than 3.7%.[57] These Greek confessions prompted or intensified risk repricing in euro area sovereign bond markets and caused credit rating agencies to reassess country risks within the currency union. Spreads between sovereign bond yields of euro area Member States started to widen significantly, to the detriment of Greece and other Southern Member States. Later, the Franco-German agreement on "private sector involvement" at the October 18-19, 2010 summit in Deauville and subsequent discussions in preparation for the Greek sovereign debt rescheduling of March 2012 (*see* paragraph 74 below) further fueled the dispersion of sovereign bond yields as these developments signaled to the markets, and the credit rating agencies, that they needed to differentiate credit risk among sovereign issuers of the same currency union in their pricing of sovereign bonds.

65. Table 1.1 below shows how the credit rating agencies (re)discovered country risk in the euro area sovereign bond markets, and how frequently they then adjusted their assessment of underlying sovereign risk, between the Greek confessions of October 21, 2009, and Mario Draghi's "whatever it takes" message of July 26, 2012 (*see* paragraph 75 below).

57. In the event, Greece's 2009 government deficit was revised upward to 13.6% in April 2010 and further to 15.4% in November 2010.

Table 1.1 Selected Sovereign Credit Ratings 2010 Q4–2012 Q2

	Greece	*Portugal*	*Spain*	*Italy*	*Ireland*
10/2009	A (S&P), A1 (M), A– (F)	A + (S&P), Aa2 (M), AA (F)	AAA (S&P), Aaa (M), AAA (F)	A + (S&P), Aa2 (M), AA– (F)	AA– (S&P), Aa2 (M), AA + (F)
11/2009					AA– (F)
12/2009	A– (S&P), A2 (M), BBB + (F)		AA + (S&P)		
3/2010	BBB + (S&P)	AA– (F)			
4/2010	BB + (S&P), A3 (M), BBB– (F)	A– (S&P)	AA (S&P)		
5/2010			AA + (F)		
6/2010	Ba1 (M)				
7/2010		A1 (M)			
9/2010			Aa1 (M)		
10/2010					A + (F)
11/2010					A (S&P)
12/2010		A + (F)			Baa1 (M)
1/2011	BB + (F)				
2/2011					A– (S&P)
3/2011	BB– (S&P), B1 (M)	BBB– (S&P), A3 (M), A– (F)	Aa2 (M)		
4/2011		Baa1 (M), BBB– (F)			BBB + (S&P), Baa3 (M), BBB + (F)
5/2011	B (S&P), B + (F)				
6/2011	CCC (S&P), Caa1 (M)				
7/2011	CC (S&P), Ca (M)	Ba2 (M)			Ba1 (M)
9/2011				A (S&P)	
10/2011		BBB– (F)	AA– (S&P), A1 (M), AA– (F)	A2 (M), A + (F)	
11/2011		BB + (F)			
1/2012		BB (S&P)	A (S&P)	BBB + (S&P), A– (F)	

	Greece	Portugal	Spain	Italy	Ireland
2/2012		Ba3 (M)	A3 (M), A (F)	A3 (M)	
3/2012	B– (F)				
4/2012			BBB + (S&P)		
5/2012	CCC (S&P)				

Note: "S&P" stands for Standard & Poor's, "M" for Moody's and "F" for Fitch.

66. Banks in the euro area held sizable and sometimes disproportionally large portfolios of (predominantly domestic) sovereign bonds. Increased yields on, and occasional downgrades of, sovereign bonds depressed bond prices and adversely affected the banks' balance sheets. Given the "home bias" in sovereign bond holdings, this tended to have a greater impact on banks in higher-debt and/or smaller Member States. As financial markets became increasingly concerned over the growing heterogeneity of government debt and financing conditions within the euro area and the sustainability of the currency union in its existing composition, differential pricing of sovereign credit risk began to include "redenomination risk"—an embellished expression for the risk of bonds of certain Member States being redenominated in some devalued substitute national currency upon partial or total break-up of the currency union. While in pre-crisis years markets had treated euro area sovereign bonds as close substitutes and had, by and large, been oblivious to underlying economic fundamentals that might differentiate sovereign risks, they now priced economic fundamentals with a vengeance and, in some cases, with a significant measure of overreaction.

67. At the same time, these developments reduced the effectiveness of both monetary and fiscal policies. The increase of sovereign bond yields and market interest rate levels in several euro area Member States translated into higher funding costs for financial intermediaries, businesses and households which countered the effects of the ECB's accommodative monetary policy in those days. And the public expenditures for financial support to banks and the higher government borrowing costs for Member States at the high end of the widening sovereign bond spreads reduced the fiscal policy space of several euro area Member States for counter-cyclical stabilization.

68. In a number of euro area Member States, the need to address government debt overhang and sustainability concerns and to preserve continued financial market access on acceptable terms prompted national governments to go into fiscal consolidation mode, then a pro-cyclical fiscal stance, during and in the aftermath of the sovereign debt crisis. Thus, when tensions spread to Italy's and Spain's sovereign bond markets and Moody's placed their sovereign bond ratings under negative watch in June and July 2011, respectively, the Italian and Spanish governments responded by announcing fiscal consolidation measures and structural reforms on August 5 and 7, 2011, respectively. Other Member States, particularly Greece, Ireland and Portugal, were forced into austerity measures as part of the economic policy conditionality attached to EFSF/ESM financial support. Fiscal restraint in a significant part of the euro area led to a rather unbalanced macroeconomic policy mix and, in a sense, shifted the burden of macroeconomic stabilization to monetary policy. In the sovereign debt crisis of those years, several euro area Member States required official financial assistance, including Ireland, Greece, Portugal, Spain and Cyprus. But by far the most acute and troublesome case was that of Greece, as we will discuss in the next section.

69. The ECB had initially increased its main refinancing rate from 1% to 1.25% on April 13, 2011, and then to 1.50% on July 13, 2011, in response to an uptick in inflation readings, but it soon reduced this rate again to 1.25% on November 9, 2011, and from there, in several steps, to 0% as of March 16, 2016, where it was to stay for over six years. Also, as mentioned above, during the build-up of the sovereign debt crisis in 2010-2012, the ECB engaged in longer-term liquidity provision to banks through several rounds of LTROs (*see* paragraph 62(a) above). Then, on May 10, 2010, over the opposition of then Bundesbank President Axel Weber, it launched its Securities Markets Program ("SMP") for the purchase of government and private debt securities in market segments subject to severe tensions.[58] SMP was to run until September 2012 (when it was effectively replaced by the Outright Monetary Transactions initiative discussed in paragraph 77 below) and led to the purchase of some EUR 218 billion in Greek, Portuguese, Spanish, Italian and Irish bonds. Interestingly, the SMP's liquidity effect was largely "sterilized" by weekly liquidity-absorbing operations until June 2014.[59]

c A Greek Tragedy in Three Acts

70. As shown in Table 1.2 below, in Greece's first seven years of currency union membership, from 2001 to 2007, its real GDP grew significantly more strongly than the euro area average (euro area statistics are indicated between parentheses and in italics). Its inflation rate was also consistently higher than the euro area average, by a margin of 0.9 to 1.6 percentage points. Its government deficit ratio substantially exceeded the 3% benchmark and the euro area average throughout this period, which suggests a measure of pro-cyclical public spending. Greece's government debt ratio remained in the low hundreds over the entire period, well above both the 60% benchmark and the euro area average. Importantly, Greece's relative unit labor costs also increased strongly over this period (*see* paragraph 132, Table 2.10, below),[60] causing a loss of international competitiveness and a sharp deterioration of its current account balance.

58. *See* the ECB's press release of May 10, 2010, https://www.ecb.europa.eu/press/pr/date/2010/html/pr100510.en.html.
59. These took the form of finetuning operations by way of quick tenders to collect one-week fixed-term deposits.
60. *See also* P. De Grauwe, *supra*, pp. 152-153, Figure 8.7.

Table 1.2 Greece: Key Economic Indicators 2001-2007

	2001	*2002*	*2003*	*2004*	*2005*	*2006*	*2007*
Real GDP *per capita* (% change over prior year)	3.6 *(1.8)*	3.5 *(0.4)*	5.5 *(0.1)*	4.8 *(1.7)*	0.3 *(1.1)*	5.3 *(2.8)*	3.0 *(2.4)*
HICP (annual average rate of change)	3.6 *(2.3)*	3.9 *(2.3)*	3.4 *(2.1)*	3.0 *(2.1)*	3.5 *(2.2)*	3.3 *(2.2)*	3.0 *(2.1)*
Government deficit-to-GDP ratio	–5.5 *(–2.0)*	–6.0 *(–2.7)*	–7.8 *(–3.1)*	–8.8 *(–2.9)*	–6.2 *(–2.6)*	–5.9 *(–1.5)*	–6.7 *(–0.6)*
Government debt-to-GDP ratio	107.1 *(68.1)*	104.9 *(68.0)*	101.5 *(69.4)*	102.9 *(69.7)*	107.4 *(70.4)*	103.6 *(68.4)*	103.0 *(66.0)*
Current account balance (% of GDP)	–	–6.8	–8.5	–7.7	–8.9	–11.5	–15.2

Source: Eurostat. Euro area = 12 (until 2006) and 13 (2007), except for real GDP *per capita* where euro area = 19. Government deficit and debt ratios as computed under ESA2010.

71. No longer able to devalue its currency, Greece eventually had to adjust by public spending cuts, tax increases and other austerity measures, largely negotiated with the "Troika" (the European Commission, the International Monetary Fund ("IMF") and the ECB) as policy conditionality of international financial assistance. These painful remedies led to serious political and social tensions that would bring Greece to the brink of currency union exit in July 2015.

72. Against the backdrop of a possible exit of Greece from the European currency union ("Grexit"), three successive financial assistance programs were laboriously pieced together in 2010, 2012 and 2015, at and between European summits, from a varying mix of bundled bilateral loans from euro area Member States, a stand-by loan from the IMF and long-term EFSF/ESM loans (*see* paragraph 719, Table 10.1, below). The programs were made subject to tough austerity measures and other economic policy conditions that led to street protests, left Greece with an unemployment rate of 25% by 2015 and, reportedly, even prompted then Greek Prime Minister Alexis Tsipras in April 2015 to seek assistance from one Vladimir Putin (who, uncharacteristically, appears to have missed this opportunity for sowing discord in Europe). Some of the political discussions surrounding this financial assistance, its policy conditionality and related fears of "moral hazard" had an unmistakable taste of Fontaine's fable of the ant and the grasshopper.

73. All in all, the Greek programs involved total financial assistance (on a disbursement basis) of approximately EUR 289 billion (including EUR 32.1 billion from the IMF). A sobering thought: Greece stands for roughly 1.5 % of aggregate euro area GDP. This begs the question of whether the currency union would have the means, tools and decision-making processes to effectively respond to a serious crisis of a significantly larger economy.

74. This was not all. Greece's first (2010-2011) financial assistance program failed to reassure the financial markets of the adequacy of the financial support and the sustainability of Greek sovereign debt. At a summit in Deauville on October 18 and 19, 2010, then French President Nicolas Sarkozy and German Chancellor Angela Merkel agreed on a German demand for "private sector involvement" ("PSI")—a euphemism for the proposition that private creditors should not be exempt from loss contribution when a euro area Member State's sovereign debt has become unsustainable.[61] This sent a clear signal to the financial markets to the effect that, even in the European currency union, they could not count on a member's sovereign debt necessarily being backstopped by the system. Credit rating agencies continued to downgrade Greek debt and, by the end of July 2011, Standard & Poor's had downgraded Greece to CC with outlook negative (a rating then below that of such countries as Ecuador, Paraguay, Pakistan and Vietnam). A Greek sovereign debt restructuring had become inevitable and the second (2012) financial assistance package effectively became conditional upon such a debt restructuring. This restructuring took place in February and March 2012 and involved about EUR 107 billion of debt relief (in nominal terms) on a total amount of participating debt of about EUR 199.2 billion.[62]

---

61. In the context of what was a summit meeting between France, Germany and Russia, the French and German delegations published a statement on October 18, 2010 saying that the future crisis management system (to be established by an amendment of the Treaties) should provide *"the necessary arrangements for an adequate participation of private creditors"*—suggesting that future financial assistance to euro area Member States should be made conditional on debt relief imposed on their private creditors. *See* https://www.eu.dk/~/media/files/en/franco_german_declaration.ashx?la=da. The ECB was opposed to any automaticity of PSI and its then President Jean-Claude Trichet made this clear in no uncertain terms at the ECB press briefings of March 3, 2011 (*"absolutely counterproductive"*) (*see* the transcript of the ECB's press conference of March 3, 2011, https://www.ecb.europa.eu/press/pressconf/2011/html/is110303.en.html, at p. 10) and July 7, 2011 (*see* the transcript of the ECB's press conference of July 7, 2011, https://www.ecb.europa.eu/press/pressconf/2011/html/is110707.en.html, at p. 2). *See also* European Stability Mechanism, *Safeguarding the euro in times of crisis. The inside story of the ESM*, Publications Office of the European Union, Luxembourg, 2019, pp. 95-96, 145 and 171.
62. For a more detailed discussion, *see, e.g.*, J. Zettelmeyer, C. Trebesh & M. Gulati "The Greek Debt Restructuring: An Autopsy", *Peterson Institute for International Economics Working Paper Series No 13-8*, August 2013, 65 pp. For an overview of the decision-making process leading up to the Greek sovereign debt restructuring, *see* GC, February 9, 2022, Case T-868/16, *QI et al. vs. European Commission & ECB*, ECLI:EU:T:2022:58, §§11-33. Legally, the restructuring was based on an idea of my former partner Lee Buchheit: given that a considerable part of outstanding Greek sovereign debt was governed by Greek law, the Greek legislature adopted a law that allowed a supermajority of bondholders to consent to changes in terms, including for outstanding bonds—in effect retrofitting a collective action clause in existing bond terms. For a fascinating account of how this controversial idea eventually prevailed, *see* P. Bolton, X. Fu, M. Gulati & U. Panizza, "The 2012 Greek Retrofit and Borrowing Costs in the European Periphery", University of Virginia School of Law, *Law and Economics Research Paper Series 2023-11*, August

d Calming the Seas

75. In the event, market tensions did not subside following the Greek sovereign debt restructuring. By the spring of 2012, differential pricing of country default risk led to increasing risk premiums on sovereign bonds of euro area Member States with high debt levels. The resulting widening of sovereign bond spreads fueled fears of a partial or total break-up of the currency union and consequent "redenomination risk" upon a more or less disorderly return to national legacy currencies. It was then that Mario Draghi, speaking at the Global Investment Conference in London on July 26, 2012, said that *"we think the euro is irreversible"* and proclaimed that *"[w]ithin our mandate, the ECB is ready to do whatever it takes to preserve the euro. And believe me, it will be enough"*.[63] At the end of his speech, he made the link with the ECB's monetary policy mandate in another short sentence: *"To the extent that the size of these sovereign premia hampers the functioning of the monetary policy transmission channel, they come within our mandate"*. Mr. Draghi had calmed the seas, although concerns over the euro lingered on in 2013 and 2014.

76. In his memoirs, Timothy Geithner suggests that Mr. Draghi had not planned to say this, could not be sure to have the support of the Bundesbank for it and did not have any specific plan to back it up, but that *"he was so alarmed by the darkness expressed by hedge funds and bankers at the conference that he ad-libbed an unequivocal commitment to defend Europe"*.[64] If Mr. Draghi's famous 23 words were indeed impromptu, they would be even more deserving of their place in history books. Yet, Mr. Draghi was not speaking in a void. In a brainstorming session at the ECB on June 17, 2012 and in the following days and weeks, a blueprint had been developed for sovereign bond purchases by the ECB linked to EFSF/ESM stability support.[65]

77. Thus, on August 2, 2012, the ECB announced that it may engage in outright open market operations to counter the excessive widening of sovereign bond spreads. Particulars of the new program, by the name of "Outright Monetary Transactions" ("OMT"), were published on September 6, 2012.[66] The program was reportedly adopted with near unanimity, with a single dissenting voice of the Bundesbank representative. Its stated purpose was *"to address severe distortions in government bond markets which originate from, in particular, unfounded fears on the part of*

2023, pp. 2-15. The retroactive application of the collective action clause was unsuccessfully challenged before multiple courts. *See ibid.*, pp. 19-20.

63. The full text of Mario Draghi's historic speech is to be found on the ECB's website at https://www.ecb.europa.eu/press/key/date/2012/html/sp120726.en.html.
64. *See* T.F. Geithner, *supra*, p. 482.
65. *See* M. Rostagno, C. Altavilla *et al.*, *supra*, p. 201. And in the press briefing following the Governing Council's August 2, 2012 meeting, Mr. Draghi claimed that *"there is not one word of these remarks that had not been discussed in the previous Governing Council meetings"* or that *"surprised my colleagues"*. *See* the transcript of the ECB's press conference of August 2, 2012, https://www.ecb.europa.eu/press/pressconf/2012/html/is120802.en.html, at p. 7.
66. *See* the ECB's press release of September 6, 2012, https://www.ecb.europa.eu/press/pr/date/2012/html/pr120906_1.en.html.

investors of the reversibility in the euro",[67] with a view to *"safeguarding an appropriate monetary policy transmission and the singleness of the monetary policy"*. Under this program, the ECB could, in the secondary markets, purchase bonds issued by euro area Member States receiving financial assistance with macroeconomic policy conditionality from the EFSF/ESM. The underlying idea was that OMT purchases would complement EFSF/ESM stability support by focusing on the shorter end of the yield curve. There would be no *ex ante* quantitative limits on the purchases but the liquidity created would be fully "sterilized". Ironically perhaps, the program has not so far been applied in practice. Its mere announcement sufficed at the time, at least for a while. We will revisit OMT in Chapter 5 (*see* paragraphs 337-348 below).

5 2010-2014: ARCHITECTURAL IMPROVEMENTS

78. The 2008-2012 financial crisis prompted further reforms to shore up and complete EMU's architecture.

a Dedicated Euro Area Stability Support

79. As a measure of most immediate urgency in the widening sovereign debt crisis of those years, a euro area financing mechanism was put in place to provide "stability support" to euro area Member States facing serious financing difficulties, as a kind of "firewall" to avoid contagion elsewhere in the euro area. The underlying idea, broadly, was for that mechanism to provide a form of last-resort finance, (i) at interest rates reflecting its own superior credit rating (thus in effect allowing the debtor country to "piggyback" on the superior weighted average credit rating of the euro area as a whole), and (ii) subject to *ad hoc* macroeconomic policy conditionality aimed at restoring the debtor country's access to the financial markets on normal conditions.

80. Under circumstances that can benevolently be described only as creative improvisation, the mechanism was initially established, on June 7, 2010, as a *société anonyme* of Luxembourg law, under the name "European Financial Stability Facility" ("EFSF"), by deed of notary Jacques Delvaux. Under the terms of the "EFSF Framework Agreement", a kind of shareholders' agreement between the euro area Member States governed by ... English law, the EFSF was to borrow on the financial markets with the backing of several (but not joint) guarantees of its members according to a contribution key based on their respective ECB capital subscriptions.

81. The mechanism was subsequently put on firmer ground, but still outside the EU legal framework, by the Treaty Establishing the European Stability Mechanism ("ESM") of February 2, 2012 ("ESM Treaty"), now as a treaty-based international

67. As formulated by Mr. Draghi in his introductory statement at the September 6, 2012 press briefing. *See* the transcript of the ECB's press conference of September 6, 2012, https://www.ecb.europa.eu/press/pressconf/2012/html/is120906.en.html, at p. 1.

organization backed not by guarantees but by capital subscriptions of the euro area Member States. The ESM currently has a subscribed capital of EUR 708.49 billion of which nearly EUR 81 billion has been paid in, and a maximum lending capacity of EUR 500 billion of which EUR 422 billion remains available at the time of writing. We will discuss the structure and *modus operandi* of the EFSF and the ESM in greater detail in Chapter 10.

b Strengthening and Broadening the Stability and Growth Pact

82. The 2008-2012 period of financial crises and successive recessions saw a sharp increase in government deficit and debt ratios in the euro area (*see* paragraph 116, Table 2.2, below). By December 2011, as many as 23 Member States had ended up being subject to the excessive deficit procedure ("EDP") under Article 126 TFEU, including 14 out of the 17 euro area Member States at that time (the exceptions being Estonia, Finland and Luxembourg).[68] A series of EU legislative acts were adopted to address perceived shortcomings in SGP, *i.e.*, five regulations and one directive adopted in November 2011 (commonly but ungracefully referred to as the "Six Pack")[69] and two further regulations adopted in May 2013 (the "Two Pack").[70] A good part of this legislation applies to all Member States but some is specific (or stricter) for euro area Member States.

83. The "Six Pack" and "Two Pack" reforms will be reviewed in more detail in Chapter 8 (*see* paragraphs 586-591 and 594-596 below). In very broad outline, key changes included the following:

(a) In the preventive arm of SGP, Member States with a government debt ratio in excess of 60% or facing *"pronounced risks of overall debt sustainability"* are

68. *Cf.* https://ec.europa.eu/commission/presscorner/detail/en/MEMO_12_7.
69. Regulation (EU) No 1173/2011 of the European Parliament and of the Council of November 16, 2011 on the effective enforcement of budgetary surveillance in the euro area, *OJ* L306, November 23, 2011, p. 1; Regulation (EU) No 1174/2011 of the European Parliament and of the Council of November 16, 2011 on enforcement measures to correct excessive macroeconomic imbalances in the euro area, *ibid.*, p. 8; Regulation (EU) No 1175/2011 of the European Parliament and of the Council of November 16, 2011 amending Council Regulation (EC) No 1466/97 on the strengthening of the surveillance of budgetary positions and the surveillance and coordination of economic policies, *ibid.*, p. 12; Regulation (EU) No 1176/2011 of the European Parliament and of the Council of November 16, 2011 on the prevention and correction of macroeconomic imbalances, *ibid.*, p. 25; Council Regulation (EU) No 1177/2011 of November 8, 2011 amending Regulation (EC) No 1467/97 on speeding up and clarifying the implementation of the excessive deficit procedure, *ibid.*, p. 33; and Directive 2011/85/EU of the Council of November 8, 2011 on the requirements for budgetary frameworks of the Member States, *ibid.*, p. 41.
70. Regulation (EU) No 472/2013 of the European Parliament and of the Council of May 21, 2013 on the strengthening of economic and budgetary surveillance of Member States in the euro area experiencing or threatened with serious difficulties with respect to their financial stability, *OJ* L140, May 27, 2013, p. 1, and Regulation (EU) No 473/2013 of the European Parliament and of the Council of May 21, 2013 on common provisions for monitoring and assessing draft budgetary plans and ensuring the correction of excessive deficit of the Member States in the euro area, *ibid.*, p. 11.

now expected to pursue an annual improvement of their structural budget balance by **more** than 0.5% of GDP. To help Member States maintain their MTO or move toward it at a sufficient pace, an expenditure benchmark is introduced that caps the growth in net government spending: annual government expenditures (excluding certain items) may not grow by more than a reference medium-term rate of potential GDP growth or, in the case of Member States that have not yet reached their MTO, a lower rate to be determined, unless, in both cases, the excess spending is matched by additional discretionary revenue. Also, a more detailed procedure is worked out for monitoring and addressing *"significant deviations"* from a Member State's MTO or the adjustment path toward its MTO.

(b) In SGP's corrective arm, the government debt criterion is operationalized by means of a numerical debt reduction benchmark. Under this benchmark, a government debt ratio in excess of 60% of GDP is considered to diminish sufficiently and approach the 60% level at a satisfactory pace (within the meaning of Article 126(2), first paragraph, (b) TFEU) if it is reduced by 1/20th of the excess *per annum* on average over a three-year period. Euro area Member States under EDP are subject to additional reporting requirements, including the submission of an "economic partnership program" setting out a roadmap of policy measures and structural reforms needed to ensure effective and lasting correction of the excessive deficit.

(c) In both SGP phases, certain requirements may be mitigated or deadlines extended in case of (i) unusual events beyond a Member State's control with a major adverse effect on government finances, or (ii) a severe downturn for the euro area or the European Union as a whole (a "material adverse change" clause of sorts).

(d) Policy surveillance at the EU level is broadened beyond the fiscal area to other sources of possible instability. Thus, a parallel framework is established for the detection, prevention and correction of excessive macroeconomic imbalances, broadly defined to include both internal and external imbalances. The procedure involves the annual screening of possible imbalances by the European Commission using a "scoreboard" of relevant indicators, and an in-depth review of Member States identified as being exposed to imbalances, which may lead to recommendations for preventive action and possibly a procedure for corrective action of excessive imbalances.

(e) For euro area Member States, financial sanctions are introduced or sharpened for failure to take remedial action, or for misrepresentation of government deficit or debt data, in SGP's preventive and corrective phases, as well as for failure to take corrective action to address excessive macroeconomic imbalances under the added macroeconomic surveillance framework. In addition, while not formally a part of the "Six Pack" or "Two Pack" reforms, Regulation (EU) No 1303/2013 allows the Council to suspend part or all of commitments or disbursements from various EU structural and investment funds if a

Member State fails to comply with certain obligations under the EMU fiscal and macroeconomic surveillance frameworks.[71]

(f) The processes for fiscal and macroeconomic surveillance (and certain other processes in the sphere of economic policy coordination) are brought together under a common annual cycle, the "European Semester", with a view to facilitating consistency. For euro area Member States, a common budgetary timeline is established, including, as a key milestone, the submission of a draft central government budget (with a set of metadata) by October 15 of the preceding year for review by the European Commission, which may request revisions if it spots *"particularly serious"* instances of non-compliance with a Member State's fiscal policy obligations under SGP.

(g) A dedicated framework is established for enhanced surveillance of euro area Member States that (i) experience, or are threatened with, serious difficulties in terms of financial stability or sustainability of public finances, with potential adverse spill-over effects elsewhere in the euro area, and/or (ii) request or receive financial assistance from other countries or European or international financial institutions. For euro area Member States in category (ii) in particular, the framework provides rules and procedures for the design and monitoring of macroeconomic adjustment programs, including rules to ensure the consistency of economic policy conditions attached to EFSF/ESM financial assistance with these programs.

(h) General standards are defined for the Member States' national budgetary processes on such matters as accounting, statistics, forecasts, country-specific numerical fiscal rules and medium-term budgetary planning. Euro area Member States are required to set up independent national bodies for reviewing national fiscal policies and monitoring compliance with common fiscal rules.

84. As will further be discussed in Chapter 8, four observations instantly come to mind when looking at the "Six Pack" and "Two Pack" reforms:

(a) These eight legislative acts, which tend to be verbose and together take up some 70 pages in the *Official Journal*, and the many more pages of subsequent guidance have made the EMU fiscal and macroeconomic surveillance frameworks into the labyrinth which they are today. There now appears to be a broad consensus that they are in need of simplification and clearer focus, which is one of the stated objectives of SGP's ongoing reforms. Yet, as it turns

71. Article 23 and Annex III of Regulation (EU) No 1303/2013 of the European Parliament and of the Council of December 17, 2013 laying down common provisions on the European Regional Development Fund, the European Social Fund, the Cohesion Fund, the European Agricultural Fund for Rural Development and the European Maritime and Fisheries Fund and laying down general provisions on the European Regional Development Fund, the European Social Fund, the Cohesion Fund and the European Maritime and Fisheries Fund and repealing Council Regulation (EC) No 1083/2006, *OJ* L347, December 20, 2013, p. 320, amended multiple times and last by Regulation (EU) 2023/45 of February 27, 2023, *OJ* L63, February 28, 2023, p. 1.

out, the inherent complexity of a multi-country configuration, its economic diversity, and the trade-offs presented by today's concurrent economic challenges do not allow substantial simplification and may not even place much virtue in it. The more important issue concerns the efficacy of the decision-making processes to arbitrate competing needs and claims in a manner consistent with the proper functioning and overall stability of the currency union.

(b) As a result of the "Six Pack" and "Two Pack" reforms, the system has evolved from a relatively "soft" form of peer review to a more intrusive form of EU surveillance of national fiscal and economic policies that in some respects might raise questions of border crossing. This is especially the case for the stricter provisions for euro area Member States. EU official thinking seems to be that, in matters of surveillance and coordination of fiscal policies, Article 136(1) TFEU allows the adoption of stricter measures for euro area Member States than could be taken for all Member States under Articles 121 and 126 TFEU.[72]

(c) Pursuant to these reforms, fiscal surveillance evolved from a dominant focus on government deficits to greater attention to government debt sustainability.

(d) The European Commission is placed center stage, as the spider in the surveillance web. Some of the legislative acts even explicitly state the expectation that the Council will, as a rule, follow the Commission's recommendations and proposals or else explain its position publicly, or subject certain Council decisions to "reverse qualified majority voting", meaning that a decision is deemed adopted as proposed by the Commission unless the Council rejects it by qualified majority before some stated deadline (*see* paragraph 579 below).

85. In 2011, both Germany and France (the same pair again) considered that the core elements of a reinforced SGP should be enshrined in the Treaty. When an amendment of the Treaty itself was opposed by the United Kingdom, 25 Member States (including all euro area Member States) eventually signed a separate intergovernmental treaty, *i.e.*, the Treaty on Stability, Coordination and Governance in the Economic and Monetary Union of March 2, 2012 ("TSCG").[73]

TSCG's central part is its Title III (Articles 3 to 8), referred to as the "Fiscal Compact" and binding on the euro area Member States (plus Bulgaria, Denmark and Romania). The substantive rules of the Fiscal Compact correspond in essence to certain key provisions of SGP as meanwhile amended:

72. This interpretation is expressly stated in recital (6) to Regulation 473/2013.

73. For an excellent discussion of the background and content of TSCG, and the legal issues raised by the conclusion of a separate treaty supplementing the Treaty in circumstances where a regular amendment of the Treaty is opposed by certain Member States, *see* P.C. Craig, "The Stability, Coordination and Governance Treaty: Principle, Politics and Pragmatism", *European Law Review*, Vol. 37, 2012, pp. 231-248. We will revisit TSCG in Chapter 8 (*see* paragraphs 592-593 below).

(a) Thus, the Fiscal Compact contains the balanced budget rule, which is deemed to be satisfied when the annual structural balance (cyclically adjusted and net of one-off and temporary measures) is at a Member State's country-specific MTO, with a lower bound of a structural deficit of 0.5% of GDP at market prices (1% if the debt ratio is significantly below 60% and risks to long-term sustainability of public finances are low) (Article 3(1)(a), (b) and (d)).
(b) Temporary deviations from a Member State's MTO or the adjustment path toward it are allowed only in exceptional circumstances (Article 3(1)(c) and (3)(b)) but significant observed deviations otherwise must automatically trigger a correction mechanism (Article 3(1)(e)).
(c) Importantly, these rules must be incorporated in binding and permanent (preferably constitutional) provisions of national law or their full observance throughout the national budgetary process must otherwise be guaranteed. In particular, a correction mechanism for significant deviations must be put in place at the national level on the basis of common principles to be proposed by the European Commission (Article 3(2)).[74]
(d) The Fiscal Compact also integrates the debt reduction benchmark under which Member States with a government debt ratio in excess of 60% of GDP should reduce the excess at an average rate of 1/20th *per annum* as a benchmark (Article 4).
(e) TSCG contemplated that, within at most five years, its substance should be incorporated into the EU legal framework (Article 16). Some of its provisions have meanwhile found their way into EU secondary legislation. As a further step, the European Commission submitted a proposed directive in relation to the Fiscal Compact on December 6, 2017,[75] but nothing came of it. The integration of the remaining substance of the Fiscal Compact into EU law is part of the current reform of SGP (*see* paragraph 612 below).

c Banking Union

86. In the wake of the 2008-2012 financial crisis, several initiatives have been taken, as part of the Banking Union project, notably to reduce risk levels in the banking sector and the risk of contagion spreading from banks to sovereigns (or vice versa). These measures include the establishment of the Single Supervisory Mechanism ("SSM")[76]

74. These principles are set forth in a Communication from the Commission, *Common principles on national fiscal correction mechanisms*, COM(2012) 342 final, June 20, 2012, https://eur-lex.europa.eu/LexUriServ/LexUriServ.do?uri=COM:2012:0342:FIN:En:PDF.
75. Proposal for a Council Directive laying down provisions for strengthening fiscal responsibility and the medium-term budgetary orientation in the Member States, COM(2017) 824 final, December 6, 2017, https://eur-lex.europa.eu/legal-content/EN/TXT/PDF/?uri=CELEX:52017PC0824.
76. *See* Council Regulation (EU) No 1024/2013 of October 15, 2013 conferring specific tasks on the European Central Bank concerning policies relating to the prudential supervision of credit institutions, *OJ* L287, October 29, 2013, p. 63, and Regulation (EU) No 468/2014 of the European Central Bank of April 16, 2014 establishing the framework for cooperation within the Single

and the Single Resolution Mechanism ("SRM"),[77] as well as the further development of the "single rule book" of harmonized capital requirements and other prudential standards. Missing pieces at this time remain the mutualization of deposit insurance (the European Deposit Insurance Scheme) and measures to reduce financial stability risks arising from the banks' sovereign exposures (and their persisting "home bias"). These developments, and those regarding further capital markets integration,[78] are, however, outside the scope of this book.[79]

6 2014-2020: STUBBORN DOWNWARD INFLATION

87. By mid-2013, both the financial crisis and the (second) recession had abated. The euro area economy had bounced back to positive growth, although growth remained sluggish initially and uneven (*see* paragraph 121, Table 2.4, below). The government debt-to-GDP ratio dropped from an average of 93.2 in 2014 to 84.1 in 2019, but again with significant country variations (*see* paragraph 116, Table 2.2, below). After peaking around mid-2011, headline inflation (HICP) began a sustained descent (accentuated by the 2014 drop in oil prices) to well below the ECB's medium-term 2% target (*see* paragraph 114, Table 2.1, below). It was a period marked by downward drifting inflation and perceived deflationary risk. The ECB now shifted its attention to what it saw as a persisting trend decline in inflation.

88. This led to an extended period of monetary easing that was to perdure for more than seven years and that we will review in more detail in Chapter 4 (*see* paragraphs 212-231 below). The already low level of the ECB's policy interest rates (which, in central bank jargon, stood "at the lower bound") prompted a retooling of monetary policy toward the use of "unconventional" (or, more deferentially, "non-standard") tools—forward guidance, close-to-zero or negative policy rates, targeted longer-term

---

Supervisory Mechanism between the European Central Bank and national competent authorities and with national designated authorities (SSM Framework Regulation), *OJ* L141, May 14, 2014, p. 1.

77. *See* Regulation (EU) No 806/2014 of the European Parliament and of the Council of July 15, 2014 establishing uniform rules and a uniform procedure for the resolution of credit institutions and certain investment firms in the framework of a Single Resolution Mechanism and a Single Resolution Fund and amending Regulation (EU) No 1093/2010, *OJ* L225, July 30, 2014, p. 1, amended by Regulation (EU) 2019/877 of May 20, 2019, *OJ* L150, June 7, 2019, p. 226, Regulation (EU) 2019/2033 of November 27, 2019, *OJ* L314, December 5, 2019, p. 1, and Regulation (EU) 2021/23 of December 16, 2020, *OJ* L22, January 22, 2021, p. 1.
78. A plan for further capital markets integration was launched in 2015 and updated in 2020. *See* Communication from the Commission to the European Parliament, the Council, the European Economic and Social Committee and the Committee of the Regions, *Action Plan on Building a Capital Markets Union*, COM(2015) 468 final, September 30, 2015, https://eur-lex.europa.eu/legal-content/EN/TXT/PDF/?uri=CELEX:52015DC0468&from=EN, and *A Capital Markets Union for people and businesses—new action plan*, COM(2020) 590 final, September 24, 2020, https://eur-lex.europa.eu/resource.html?uri=cellar:61042990-fe46-11ea-b44f-01aa75ed71a1.0001.02/DOC_1&format=PDF.
79. For a comprehensive overview of these developments, the reader may wish to refer to Chapters 35 through 38 of *The EU Law of Economic and Monetary Union* (F. Amtenbrink & Chr. Herrmann eds.), Oxford University Press, 2020, pp. 1049-1180.

refinancing operations and, especially, large-scale asset purchases—to move inflation higher:

(a) The ECB had already started to edge its policy rates downward as from November 9, 2011, but in June 2014 it actually moved its deposit facility rate into negative territory. As of June 11, 2014, the ECB reduced the rates on its deposit facility, main refinancing operations and marginal lending facility to −0.10%, 0.15% and 0.40%, respectively. In four steps, these rates were lowered to −0.50%, 0% and 0.25%, respectively, by September 18, 2019, and were maintained at these levels until July 2022.

(b) On June 5, 2014, the ECB announced a first series of "Targeted Longer-Term Refinancing Operations" ("TLTROs") offering banks longer-term funding at favorable rates linked to eligible bank lending to the non-financial businesses and households. These first TLTROs were to be followed by two further series in 2016 and 2019. As many banks were de-leveraging, shedding assets and de-risking their balance sheets during and in the aftermath of the 2008-2012 financial crisis, bank lending (and lending rates) had initially responded hesitantly to lower policy interest rates. TLTROs served to invigorate the bank lending channel, given the importance of bank lending as a source of finance in Europe. Bank uptake of TLTRO funds was substantial.

(c) Importantly, as of the fall of 2014, lagging well behind the Federal Reserve, the ECB turned to "pure play" quantitative easing ("QE") on a larger scale under what became known as the Asset Purchase Program ("APP"). Under APP, the Eurosystem engaged in purchases of various financial instruments subject to an overall monthly cap. APP ended up having four sub-programs or segments, *i.e.*, (i) a third installment of the Covered Bond Purchase Program ("CBPP3") as of October 2014; (ii) an Asset-Backed Securities Purchase Program ("ABSPP") as of November 2014; (iii) a Public Sector Purchase Program ("PSPP") as of March 2015; and (iv) a Corporate Sector Purchase Program ("CSPP") as of June 2016.

89. The overall monthly cap for net purchases under APP (excluding reinvestment of maturing bonds) fluctuated over time: from EUR 60 billion between March 2015 and March 2016 to EUR 80 billion between April 2016 and March 2017, back to EUR 60 billion between April 2017 and December 2017, down to EUR 30 billion between January and September 2018 and to EUR 15 billion between October and December 2018. Net purchases (but not reinvestments) were paused between January and October 2019 but then resumed, much to the chagrin of certain Northern central bank governors, as of November 2019 at the pace of EUR 20 billion, with some subsequent variations (*see* paragraph 97(a) below). Net purchases under APP (but, again, not reinvestments) were eventually discontinued only at the end of June 2022, while reinvestments were reduced as of March 2023 and stopped at the end of June 2023. By mid-2022, the aggregate portfolio of securities acquired under APP had reached EUR

3,265 billion (book value at amortized cost), of which EUR 2,592 billion or about 79.40% in government bonds purchased under PSPP.

90. PSPP has by far been the most prominent APP segment. Government bond purchases under PSPP were made only in the secondary markets so as to steer clear of the monetary financing prohibition of Article 123 TFEU (or at least so as to avoid an obvious transgression of this prohibition). They were subject to limits per issue and per issuer, as well as to the overall monthly cap for APP. Unlike OMT, PSPP was not linked to ESM financial assistance or economic policy conditionality. In broad terms, the monetary policy logic underlying PSPP was to compress yields on government bonds (and hence market interest levels) and to induce portfolio rebalancing in the banking system toward assets with higher returns, notably loans to businesses and households, thereby stimulating investment and consumption and lifting inflation. But PSPP also reduced the cost of government borrowing, including for Member States with weaker deficit and debt statistics, and in this manner indirectly helped to contain widening spreads on government bonds in the euro area.

PSPP has caused a significant proportion of euro area sovereign debt to be parked on the balance sheets of its central banks. By mid-year 2022, the total outstanding government consolidated gross debt for the euro area as a whole (then 19 Member States) stood at about EUR 12,103 billion. At that time, the Eurosystem's aggregate PSPP portfolio holdings were EUR 2,592 billion (book value at amortized cost). If one adds to this the government bonds then held in the PEPP portfolio (*see* paragraph 97(b) below), *i.e.*, some EUR 1,639 billion (again in terms of book value at amortized cost), total euro area government bonds in the Eurosystem's monetary portfolios added up to roughly 35% of outstanding euro area sovereign debt by the middle of 2022.

91. With APP and particularly PSPP, the ECB stretched its monetary policy mandate to, and according to some beyond, its outer boundaries. In a judgment of May 5, 2020, the German Federal Constitutional Court ("BVerfG") contradicted a prior ruling of the European Court of Justice by holding that, by engaging in PSPP as it did, the ECB appears to have acted *ultra vires*. We will further discuss this legal controversy in Chapter 7 (*see* paragraphs 546-551 below).

7 2020-2021: COVID-19

92. Not long after the euro area had substantially recovered from the 2008-2012 financial crisis, the sudden arrival of the COVID-19 pandemic in the early months of 2020 abruptly caused substantial disturbances to economic activity, a sharp contraction in GDP and a deterioration of public finances across the euro area, with economic losses and risks being distributed unevenly among euro area Member States. COVID-19 can be thought of as a mix of large recessionary demand and supply shocks that instantly reduced economic activity and initially pushed down inflation further, with heterogeneous effects across countries and sectors. It required substantial fiscal spending notably on economic relief to businesses and households to protect the economy. In the first months of COVID-19, risk sentiment deteriorated, liquidity dried up and sovereign bond spreads widened considerably. The policy response to COVID-19 was swift and consisted of several layers.

93. ***First***, at the level of national fiscal policies, COVID-19 triggered automatic stabilizers and, in addition, prompted considerable discretionary fiscal spending to provide economic relief to businesses and households (temporary unemployment schemes, tax deferrals and other aid to alleviate cash-flow problems). In the euro area, aggregate discretionary fiscal stimulus in response to COVID-19 was about 4.2% of GDP in 2020 and around the same level in 2021 (including NGEU-funded spending),[80] with significant differences across Member States. By way of comparison, at the height of the global financial crisis in 2009, the overall amount of discretionary stimulus in the European Union amounted to 1.5% of GDP.[81]

94. Unsurprisingly, COVID-19 public spending caused a sharp increase in both the level and geographic dispersion of government deficit and debt ratios (*see* paragraph 116, Table 2.2, below). By the end of 2020, the government deficit ratio increased to 7.1% for the euro area as a whole (up from 0.6% in 2019), with Germany at 4.3% and The Netherlands at 3.7% but France and Belgium at 9.0%, Italy at 9.7% and Spain at 10.1%. Also by 2020 year-end, the government debt ratio had climbed to 97.2% for the euro area (up from 84.1% in 2019), with Germany at 68.7% and The Netherlands at 54.7% but Belgium at 112%, France at 114.6%, Spain at 120.4% and Italy at 154.9%.

95. ***Second***, on March 23, 2020, the Council activated the so-called "general escape clause" of SGP, introduced as part of the "Six Pack" reforms in 2011,[82] to allow temporary relief from the usual fiscal requirements of SGP. Technically, this does not, as is sometimes said, put SGP on hold but it offers greater flexibility in its application by allowing temporary deviations from the adjustment path to the country-specific MTOs and extensions of the deadline for correcting excessive deficits. But clearly, the activation of SGP's escape clause (in combination with greater leniency in the application of State aid rules) gave the Member States more legroom for fiscal support and stimulus in response to COVID-19. It was initially thought that the escape clause might be lifted again in 2022 but this timeframe subsequently moved to the end of 2023.

---

80. *See ECB staff macroeconomic projections for the euro area*, September 2021, p. 12, https://www.ecb. europa.eu/pub/pdf/other/ecb.projections202109_ecbstaff~1f59a501e2.en.pdf. For 2021, aggregate discretionary fiscal stimulus was initially estimated at 4.6% of GDP (*ibid.*), but this estimate appears to have been lowered by half a percentage point in the December 2021 staff projections. *Cf. Eurosystem staff macroeconomic projections for the euro area*, December 2021, p. 13, https://www.ecb.europa.eu/pub/pdf/other/ecb.projections202112_eurosystemstaff~32e481d712.en.pdf.
81. X. Debrun, G. Ferrero *et al.*, *supra*, p. 68.
82. The general escape clause refers to the broader variant of SGP's material adverse change clause. It is defined in terms of a *"severe economic downturn for the euro area or the Union as a whole"*, as distinguished from the narrower formulation in terms of an unusual event beyond a Member State's control and having a major impact on its government finances (Articles 5(1), 6(3), 9(1) and 10(3) of Council Regulation (EC) No 1466/97, as amended, and Articles 3(5) and 5(2) of Council Regulation (EC) No 1467/97, as amended).

96. ***Third,*** several temporary mechanisms were put in place at the EU and euro area levels to provide COVID-related financial support:

(a) At the **EU** level, as will be discussed in more detail in Chapter 9 (*see* paragraphs 642-650 below), certain "solidarity" mechanisms linked to the EU budget were established. These include notably, as the centerpiece of Next-GenerationEU ("NGEU"), a temporary EU-wide Recovery and Resilience Facility ("RRF") to provide up to EUR 672.5 billion (in 2018 prices) in loans and grants to support public investments and reforms made by the Member States for sustainable post-COVID recovery.[83] Three points are of particular interest to our analysis:
   (i) The facility has certain redistributive properties insofar as its grant portion (EUR 312.5 billion in 2018 prices) is allocated according to criteria, particularly in terms of unemployment and growth, that should favor the most vulnerable Member States.[84]
   (ii) In order to fund NGEU support programs, Council Decision (EU, Euratom) 2020/2053 of December 14, 2020 authorizes the European Commission to borrow up to EUR 750 billion (again in 2018 prices) in the capital markets on behalf of the European Union, with the backing of a temporary *ad hoc* increase of the own resources ceilings by 0.6 percentage points.[85]
   (iii) As has become a regular occurrence in matters involving EU or euro area financial support, legal action was brought before the BVerfG challenging Germany's approval of Council Decision 2020/2053 (as required by Article 311 TFEU). Plaintiffs claimed that this would violate their constitutional right to democratic self-determination by impairing the Bundestag's budgetary powers as a matter of German constitutional law, and by exceeding the competences conferred upon the European Union, including by breaching the "no bail-out" clause of Article 125(1) TFEU. By an order of April 15, 2021, the BVerfG dismissed the application for a preliminary injunction while reserving judgment on the merits.[86] In the event, by a judgment of December 6, 2022, the BVerfG declared the complaints unfounded on the merits, albeit with a strong dissenting opinion of Justice Peter Müller.[87] It is a potentially significant

83. *See* Regulation (EU) 2021/241 of the European Parliament and of the Council of February 12, 2021 establishing the Recovery and Resilience Facility, *OJ* L57, February 18, 2021, p. 17, amended by Regulation (EU) 2023/435 of February 27, 2023, *OJ* L63, February 28, 2023, p. 1.
84. Article 11 of Regulation (EU) 2021/241.
85. Articles 5 and 6 of Council Decision (EU, Euratom) 2020/2053 of December 14, 2020 on the system of own resources of the European Union and repealing Decision 2014/335/EU, Euratom, *OJ* L424, December 15, 2020, p. 1.
86. BVerfG, April 15, 2021, ECLI:DE:BVerfG:2021:rs20210415.2bvr054721. An English translation of this order is reproduced on the BVerfG's website at https://www. bundesverfassungsgericht .de/SharedDocs/Entscheidungen/EN/2021/04/rs20210415_2bvr054721en.html.
87. BVerfG, December 6, 2022, ECLI:DE:BVerfG:2022:rs20221206.2bvr054721. For an English translation of this judgment, *see* http://www.bverfg.de/e/rs20221206_2bvr054721en.html.

judgment for the design of EU or euro area financial support mechanisms and we will therefore take a closer look at it in Chapter 9 (*see* paragraphs 670-681 below).

(b) Specifically at the **euro area** level, a new "Pandemic Crisis Support" credit line became available at the ESM in the spring of 2020, offering longer-term loans of up to 2% of a euro area Member State's GDP for COVID-related healthcare expenses. This facility remained available until the end of 2022 but, curiously, was not utilized (*see* paragraph 709 below).

97. *Fourth*, monetary policy action was directed first, following the outbreak of COVID-19, at addressing liquidity tensions and stabilizing volatile financial markets, and then at accommodating fiscal support by preserving favorable financing conditions. As will be discussed further in Chapter 4 (*see* paragraphs 232-242 below), the ECB effectively stepped up monetary easing with a series of additional measures:

(a) On March 12, 2020, the ECB first decided to add a temporary envelope of EUR 120 billion for additional net asset purchases under APP between March and December 2020. "Regular" net purchases under APP continued at the pace of EUR 20 billion until (and including) March 2022. The monthly volume of net purchases was increased to EUR 40 billion in April 2022 and EUR 30 billion in May 2022 and then reduced back to EUR 20 billion in June 2022 before net purchases (but not reinvestments) were discontinued at the end of that month.

(b) When in the early days of COVID-19 the economic outlook deteriorated sharply, the ECB, on March 18, 2020, launched a new temporary asset purchase program, the Pandemic Emergency Purchase Program ("PEPP"), with an initial envelope of EUR 750 billion.[88] This amount was increased by EUR 600 billion in June 2020 and by a further EUR 500 billion in December 2020 to a total of EUR 1,850 billion. Net purchases under PEPP were initially intended to be conducted until the end of 2020, but this time horizon was subsequently extended to March 2022, and net purchases (but not reinvestments) were stopped at the end of that month.

Purchases under PEPP can be conducted flexibly, allowing for fluctuations in the allocation of purchases over time, across asset classes and, significantly, among jurisdictions. Thus, PEPP offers significantly more flexibility than PSPP, which is subject to stricter adherence to the ECB capital subscription key, a monthly APP volume cap, stricter eligibility criteria and purchase limits of 33% for sovereign debt issued by euro area Member States. The flexibility in the geographic allocation of purchases is a significant feature of PEPP. While the allocation of purchases among euro area Member States is

88. *See* Decision (EU) 2020/440 of the European Central Bank of March 24, 2020 on a temporary pandemic emergency purchase programme, *OJ* L91, March 25, 2020, p. 1, amended by Decision (EU) 2020/1143 of July 28, 2020, *OJ* L248, July 31, 2020, p. 24, and Decision (EU) 2021/174 of February 10, 2021, *OJ* L50, February 15, 2021, p. 29.

"guided" as a benchmark by the ECB capital subscription key, the ECB stated, in its unrivaled vocabulary, that *"[a] flexible approach [...] is nonetheless essential to prevent current dislocations in the aggregate euro area yield curve from being translated into further distortions in the euro area risk-free yield curve"*.[89] The underlying monetary logic is that increased heterogeneity among Member States' sovereign yield curves as a result of the differing impact of COVID-19 on their public finances (coming on top of pre-existing differences in fiscal positions) may feed into higher market rates and tightening financing conditions in certain parts of the euro area so as to interfere with the even transmission of the ECB's accommodative monetary policy stance aimed at keeping disinflationary pressures at bay. In other words, PEPP could be used as a tool to contain financial fragmentation in the euro area caused by COVID-19. This is not uncontroversial, as we will see in Chapter 5. The announcement and prompt implementation of PEPP, with its flexible allocation across asset classes, maturities and jurisdictions, appears to have helped to stabilize government bond markets. During PEPP's net purchase phase (which ended in March 2022), geographic selectivity had to be used only intermittently and primarily in the early months at the peak of the crisis.

(c) The ECB also eased the conditions of TLTRO III and conducted a series of additional (non-targeted) longer-term refinancing operations, "Pandemic Emergency Longer-Term Refinancing Operations" ("PELTROs"), at interest rates 25 basis points below its main refinancing rate, to support liquidity conditions in the euro area financial system.

8 2021-2023: THE RETURN OF INFLATION AND UKRAINE

a A Clouded Macroeconomic Landscape

98. When inflation started climbing in the second half of 2021, the ECB for a good while considered this as a "temporary" phenomenon that should not compromise its baseline scenario of a gradual and patient return to monetary policy "normalcy" leaving some national policy space for measured and targeted fiscal stimulus. Given an engrained belief in a trend decline in inflation, the prevailing view at the ECB appeared to be that rising prices were largely due to temporary supply-chain disturbances (such as shipping and seaport bottlenecks and shortages of certain raw materials and semiconductor chips) and pent-up demand in the wake of COVID-19. Even when euro area headline inflation (HICP) had increased to 4.9% in November 2021, the December 2021 staff projections still saw inflation decrease sharply to 3.2% over 2022 and to

89. Recital (5) to Decision (EU) 2020/440.

1.8% in 2023 and 2024.[90] However, toward the end of the year, the tail effects of COVID-19 and rising energy prices and, a few months later, the Ukraine conflict fueled strong upward pressures on inflation.

99. Of course, the ECB could not be blamed for not anticipating that Russian armed forces and mercenaries would engage in a "special military operation" to invade Ukraine (or at least part of it) and set out to destroy its civil and economic infrastructure. At the time of writing, it remained to be seen how the Ukraine conflict (in the broad sense including related Western economic sanctions, trade disruptions and geopolitical tensions) would play out over time. But it seemed inevitable that, at least in the short term, it would have some net upward effect on inflation and public spending, and some net downward effect on GDP, in the euro area, as well as cause volatility in financial, energy and certain commodity markets. In the fall of 2023, the flare-up of the Israel-Palestine conflict and its uncertain consequences further clouded the horizon. This should complicate the euro area's macroeconomic policy mix.

100. Thus, at least in the near term, the tail effects of COVID-19 and the economic fall-out of the Ukraine conflict caused or precipitated a sharp rise in inflation and negatively affected growth. This put an end to the benign alignment of monetary and fiscal policies and de-synchronized them, pushing the euro area economy more in the direction of the textbook trade-off between inflation and growth. It called for monetary tightening (or, as the ECB prefers to characterize it, monetary policy "normalization" after an extended period of monetary easing), alongside appropriate fiscal stimulus to moderate recessionary risks and contain scarring effects on the economic fabric. It is a difficult balancing act. As a theoretical matter, external supply-side cost shocks (such as increases in energy and commodity prices caused by some geopolitical incident) require the monetary authorities to "read the tea leaves". Insofar as inflationary pressures are primarily attributable to such supply-side cost shocks, a central bank may consider them transient and choose not to react, or not to react too quickly or too much, to avoid unnecessary harmful effects on demand, output and employment. But once those pressures begin to infiltrate market expectations and the dynamics of price and wage formation, a more resolute monetary response is needed. In a parallel universe, elected politicians may find it hard to resist the siren song of generous public spending to "protect the people's purchasing power" and restore growth, but this may fuel inflation and work at cross purposes with monetary policy action to contain it. This issue was put in stark terms in the IMF's unusual reprimand of September 27, 2022 regarding the fiscal stimulus plans that the British government under the short-lived leadership of Liz Truss had just unveiled.[91] In the same order of ideas, in the euro area,

90. *Eurosystem staff macroeconomic projections for the euro area*, December 2021, pp. 14-15, https://www.ecb.europa.eu/pub/pdf/other/ecb.projections202112_eurosystemstaff~32e481d712.en.pdf.

91. In public comments of September 27, 2022, the IMF spokesperson observed that *"[g]iven elevated inflation pressures in many countries, including the UK, we do not recommend large and untargeted fiscal packages at this junction, as it is important that fiscal policy does not work at cross purposes to monetary policy"* (https://www.reuters.com/world/uk/imf-says-uk-fiscal-measures-will-likely-increase-inequality-urges-rethink-22-09-27/).

the ECB now repeatedly called upon the Member States to keep fiscal support measures temporary and targeted at the most vulnerable businesses and households so as not to unduly fuel inflationary pressures.

101. In the multi-country setting of the European currency union, these difficulties are compounded by the co-existence of 20 fiscal actors with different economic characteristics, fiscal positions and political priorities, and by the asymmetric fall-out of COVID-19 and, especially, the Ukraine conflict across the euro area Member States. In this changed economic environment, and with the common fiscal rules (SGP) being partially on hold in 2022 and 2023 (*see* paragraph 95 above), Member States may be less able, or less politically inclined, to exercise adequate fiscal discipline in order to stabilize their government deficit and debt ratios. Higher fiscal spending in combination with higher interest rates should be more problematic for Member States with higher borrowing requirements and refinancing needs in respect of pre-existing government debt. This may lead to an increase in the geographic dispersion of government deficit and debt ratios and a widening of sovereign bond spreads, which, when caught in market overreaction, could cause financial fragmentation and further increase borrowing costs for fiscally more fragile Member States. Greater volatility and widening of government bond spreads in the euro area occurred episodically during this period. Yet, given the need to contain inflation, high government deficit and debt ratios could no longer be artificially sustained by an accommodative monetary policy with low policy rates and generous QE. And higher interest rate levels caused by monetary policy tightening will reduce the Member States' fiscal policy space and, in a longer-term perspective, slow down much-needed public and private investments notably in the context of the green transition.

102. In this manner, the return of inflation, coming on the heels of the COVID-19 crisis, has given rise to a double policy trade-off, *i.e.*, (i) in the interaction between monetary and fiscal policies: between inflation control, on the one hand, and output stabilization and investment needs, on the other hand, and (ii) within the monetary policy space: between inflation control, on the one hand, and containing financial fragmentation risk within the euro area and other financial instability risks arising from pulling the monetary brakes after an extended period of monetary easing, on the other hand. These trade-offs now have to be navigated in an environment unsettled by geopolitical tensions and economic uncertainties surrounding such troubling incidents as the Ukraine conflict and an armed conflict in the Middle East and the evermore pressing challenges of climate change.

b Meeting-by-Meeting Monetary Policy Tightening

103. As price pressures broadened across the economy and staff projections in rapid succession made significant upward adjustments to the euro area inflation outlook for 2022 and the following years (*see* paragraph 319, Table 4.3, below), the ECB, hesitantly at first, started a cycle of monetary policy tightening in the summer of 2022. Throughout this process, it repeatedly emphasized, often with reference to the *"elevated level of* *uncertainty"*, that it would follow a *"data-dependent"* and *"meeting-by-meeting"* approach, maintaining *"optionality"*, on the path to *"normalization"* of monetary policy. As will be discussed in greater detail in Chapter 4 (*see* paragraphs 247-298 below), the ECB's monetary policy response thus far essentially unfolded along the four lines described below.

104. ***First***, at its successive monetary policy meetings between the summer of 2022 and the fall of 2023, the ECB lifted its three policy rates in swift steps, *i.e.*, by 50 basis points on July 21, 2022, by 75 basis points on September 8 and October 27, 2022, again by 50 basis points on December 15, 2022 and on February 2 and March 16, 2023, and by 25 basis points on May 4, June 15, July 27 and September 14, 2023. Consequently, by that time, the main refinancing rate had been raised from 0% to 4.50%, the marginal lending rate from 0.25% to 4.75% and the deposit facility rate from –0.50% to 4%—an unprecedented cumulative increase of 4.50% over a time span of 14 months.

Then, at its next monetary policy meeting of October 25-26, 2023, the ECB decided to leave its policy rates unchanged, announcing that, in its current assessment, they had reached levels that, *"maintained for a sufficiently long duration"*, will make a *"substantial contribution"* to a timely return of inflation to its medium-term 2% target.[92] The clear message was that, absent unexpected circumstances, policy rates were now at their peak level and would stay there for a while.

105. ***Second***, net asset purchases under APP and PEPP were discontinued at the end of June 2022 and March 2022, respectively, but, initially, the amounts flowing back on maturing securities in both the APP and PEPP portfolios continued to be fully reinvested, *i.e.*, there was no net reduction of these portfolios—no quantitative tightening ("QT")—for the time being.

Where things stood by the end of June 2022, following the discontinuation of additional net purchases under APP and PEPP, is that the Eurosystem's monetary portfolio contained EUR 3,265 billion of securities purchased under APP and another EUR 1,693 billion of securities purchased under PEPP (both in terms of book value at amortized cost), *i.e.*, about EUR 4.95 trillion in total.[93] These are robust sums by any standard. It invites a closer look into the legal scope of the monetary policy mandate conferred upon the ECB and the judicial control exercised over it—a subject to which we will turn in Chapter 7 (*see*, in particular, paragraphs 523-524 and 526-536 below).

The ECB began phasing out reinvestments in the **APP** portfolio from March 2023 onward. Given the uncertain market effects of QT, the ECB started out cautiously by not reinvesting EUR 15 billion per month on average, *i.e.*, somewhat less than half of the scheduled principal repayments,[94] for an initial period from March through June 2023. It then fully discontinued APP reinvestments as from July 2023. Meanwhile, the ECB continued to fully reinvest maturing securities in the **PEPP** portfolio and for many

92. *See* the ECB's press release of October 26, 2023, https://www.ecb.europa.eu/press/pr/date/2023/html/ecb.mp231026~6028cea576.en.html.
93. The difference with the numbers mentioned in paragraph 90 above is that those in paragraph 105 above include private-sector securities as well.
94. Scheduled principal repayments on securities in the Eurosystem's APP portfolio added up to EUR 130.59 billion in total over the period from March through June 2023.

months repeatedly confirmed its intention to do so *"until at least the end of 2024"*, routinely adding that, in its PEPP reinvestments, it would continue *"applying flexibility"* (read: geographic selectivity) to counter *"risks to the monetary policy transmission mechanism"* (read: financial fragmentation) related to the pandemic. But eventually, on December 14, 2023, the ECB announced that it intended to reduce PEPP reinvestments by EUR 7.5 billion per month on average in the second half of 2024 and to discontinue them altogether at the end of the year.

Still, in both portfolios, the ECB has so far limited itself to a "passive" form of QT, by no longer reinvesting the proceeds from maturing bonds, as distinguished from selling bonds prior to maturity. Given the maturity profile of these portfolios, such merely passive QT would stretch their run-off over a period of almost 10 years. The ECB may at some point accelerate the reduction of these portfolios by sales of unmatured bonds, but no such plan had been announced by the time I put down my pen on Christmas Eve 2023.

106. ***Third***, on July 21, 2022, in response to signs of tensions in the sovereign bond markets,[95] the ECB announced the addition of a new anti-fragmentation instrument to its toolkit, diplomatically called the "Transmission Protection Instrument" ("TPI"). This new tool will allow the Eurosystem to purchase (mostly) public-sector bonds with a remaining maturity between one and 10 years in the secondary markets, without *ex ante* cap, focusing selectively on bonds issued in euro area Member States facing a deterioration of financing conditions disconnected from country-specific economic fundamentals. According to the press release, carefully crafted to link the new instrument to the ECB's monetary policy mandate, TPI can be activated *"to counter unwarranted, disorderly market dynamics that pose a serious threat to the transmission of monetary policy across the euro area"*.[96]

TPI is presented as one of three tools to address financial fragmentation within the euro area. Until the end of 2024, flexible reinvestment of maturing bonds in the PEPP portfolio remains the *"first line of defence"* to counter pandemic-related risks to the monetary policy transmission mechanism. The ECB Governing Council also *"retains discretion"* to activate (the hitherto dormant) OMT for euro area Member States that meet the requisite criteria (*see* paragraph 77 above). I will discuss all this in more detail in Chapter 5 which is devoted in its entirety to the ECB's monetary policy tools for containing financial fragmentation in the euro area.

107. ***Fourth***, on October 27, 2022, as a further step toward "normalizing" financing conditions (and reducing the Eurosystem balance sheet), the ECB increased the pricing of remaining TLTRO III operations by linking their interest rate, as from November 23, 2022, to the average deposit facility rate or main refinancing rate over their remaining

95. For example, following the ECB's June 9, 2022 announcement of its intention to gradually lift policy rates, the yield on 10-year Italian bonds jumped to 4.18% on June 14—then a 240 basis points spread with the yield on 10-year Bunds.
96. *See* the ECB's press release of July 21, 2022, https://www.ecb.europa.eu/press/pr/date/2022/html/ecb.pr220721~973e6e7273.en.html.

term (as opposed to over their entire life), while offering banks three additional voluntary prepayment dates.[97]

c Further SGP Reforms

108. Meanwhile, in 2022 and 2023, the common fiscal rules (SGP) continued to remain in the state of semi-hibernation in which they were put on March 23, 2020 (*see* paragraph 95 above). On February 5, 2020, the Commission had published a review of the strengths and weaknesses of the EMU fiscal and macroeconomic frameworks as amended by the "Six Pack" and "Two Pack" reforms, with a series of questions for public debate on further reforms.[98] Eventually, on November 9, 2022, the Commission outlined its proposed "orientations" for reform, which, aside from streamlining and simplifying the rules and processes, primarily seek to find a proper balance between achieving and maintaining government debt sustainability and the need for structural reforms and strategic investments.[99] The ECOFIN Council considered these orientations on March 14, 2023, noting broad convergence among Member States on key aspects of a revised economic governance framework while also identifying certain issues requiring further clarification and discussion.[100] On April 26, 2023, the Commission then tabled legislative proposals to implement these reforms,[101] and on December 21, 2023, the Council eventually agreed on revised texts for dialogue or consultation with the European Parliament.[102] We will review these ongoing reforms in Chapter 8 (*see* paragraphs 610-622 below).

97. *See* the ECB's press release of October 27, 2012, https://www.ecb.europa.eu/press/pr/date/2022/html/ecb.pr221027_1~c8005660b0.en.html. On the same day, the ECB also decided to reduce the remuneration of minimum reserves from the main refinancing rate to the deposit facility rate. *See* the ECB's separate press release of October 27, 2012 on the subject, https://www.ecb.europa.eu/press/pr/date/2022/html/ecb.pr221027~25d335259c.en.html. On July 27, 2023, the ECB decided to further reduce it to zero. *See* the ECB's press release of July 27, 2023, https://www.ecb.europa.eu/press/pr/date/2023/html/ecb.pr230727~7206e9aa48.en.html.
98. Communication from the Commission to the European Parliament, the Council, the European Central Bank, the European Economic and Social Committee and the Committee of the Regions, *Economic governance review. Report on the application of Regulations (EU) No 1173/2011, 1174/2011, 1175/2011, 1176/2011, 1177/2011, 472/2013 and 473/2013 and on the suitability of Council Directive 2011/85/EU*, COM(2020) 55 final, February 5, 2020, https://eur-lex.europa.eu/legal-content/EN/TXT/PDF/?uri=CELEX:52020DC0055&from=EN.
99. Communication from the Commission to the European Parliament, the Council, the European Central Bank, the European Economic and Social Committee and the Committee of the Regions, *Communication on orientations for a reform of the EU economic governance framework*, COM(2022) 583 final, November 9, 2022, https://economy-finance.ec.europa.eu/system/files/2022-11/com_2022_583_1_en.pdf.
100. *See* the Council's press release of March 14, 2023, https://www.consilium.europa.eu/en/press-releases/2023/03/14/economic-governance-framework-Council-agrees-its-orientations-for-a-reform/.
101. *See* the Commission's press release of April 26, 2023, https://ec.europa.eu/commission/presscorner/detail/en/ip_23-2393.
102. *See* the Council's press release of December 21, 2023, https://www.consilium.europa.eu/en/press/press-releases/2023/12/21/economic-governance-review-council-agrees-on-reform-of-fiscal-rules/pdf.

d Toward a Digital Euro

109. In the past few years, there has been a lot of discussion and analysis on the possible introduction of a euro in digital form. In broad outline, the digital euro (i) would be the electronic equivalent of physical euro banknotes and coins; (ii) would not be some crypto currency but would be issued by Eurosystem central banks and constitute their direct liability to the digital euro user; (iii) would have legal tender status subject to limitations on mandatory acceptance that are consistent with the jurisprudence of the European Court of Justice;[103] and (iv) could be used for person-to-person payments, payments in shops, e-commerce payments and certain government transactions, through various electronic devices (PCs, mobile phones, smartwatch apps, digital wallets).

The digital euro may be upon us, but not instantly. After a two-year study phase, the ECB recently launched a two-year preparation phase as of November 1, 2023, following which it will decide on the further course of action.[104] Secondary legislation will need to be enacted before the ECB can eventually authorize the issue of the digital euro, and the European Commission has meanwhile tabled legislative proposals.[105] Under the current plans, digital euro holdings would not bear interest and would be subject to certain holding limitations that would serve to mitigate financial disintermediation or, in plain English, to limit the outflow of funds on deposit in the banking system. In other words, the digital euro is not intended to become a savings product, which should limit its relevance for monetary policy.

103. This primarily refers to CJEU, January 26, 2021, Joined Cases C-422/19 and C-423,19, *Dietrich & Häring vs. Hessischer Rundfunk*, ECLI:EU:C:2021:63.

104. *See* the ECB's press release of October 18, 2023, https://www.ecb.europa.eu/press/pr/date/2023/html/ecb.pr231018~111a014ae7.en.html.

105. *See* Proposal for a Regulation of the European Parliament and of the Council on the establishment of the digital euro, COM(2023) 369 final, June 28, 2023, https://eur-lex.europa.eu/legal-content/EN/TXT/?uri=CELEX%3A52023PC0369, and Proposal for a Regulation of the European Parliament and of the Council on the provision of digital euro services by payment services providers incorporated in Member States whose currency is not the euro and amending Regulation (EU) 2021/1230 of the European Parliament and the Council, COM(2023) 368 final, June 18, 2023, https://eur-lex.europa.eu/legal-content/EN/TXT/?uri=COM%3A2023%3A0368%3AFIN.

CHAPTER 2

Toward an Optimum Currency Area?

110. One standing at the cradle of EMU once described the euro as *"a political project for our grandchildren"*.[106] These grandchildren are grown-ups by now and will want to take stock. When EMU was launched, the *idée reçue* was that, by eliminating currency risk and reducing cross-border transaction costs, the common currency would foster intra-euro area trade and capital flows which, in turn, would support growth and increase economic convergence, including of income levels (consistent with the aspiration of "shared prosperity" in an "ever closer Union"). Taking exchange rate adjustments off the table as a national policy instrument was expected or hoped to shift political focus to reforms to increase productivity and maintain or improve competitiveness. The currency union would require a measure of discipline and coordination of national fiscal policies which, in combination with a single monetary policy, should lead to greater macroeconomic stability. Twenty-five years later, has the European currency union lived up to these expectations?

111. Prior to the start-up of the currency union and intermittently over the span of its 25-year history, prominent economists expressed skepticism about the longer-term viability of a currency union whose member countries retain substantial fiscal autonomy and which is not backed up by robust centralized budgetary stabilization capacity. As said, Mario Draghi started his famous July 26, 2012 speech by observing that initially the currency union was looked upon as a bumblebee—a mystery of nature in that it should not have flown but did—and that, with the financial crisis, the

106. The phrase was actually used by Jean-Claude Juncker in his June 19, 2019 address at the ECB Forum on Central Banking (*see* fn. 33 above). Mr. Juncker did not then offer any particular explanation for it. But it occurred to me that he must have been paraphrasing the title of a 1930 essay of John Maynard Keynes, *Economic Possibilities for our Grandchildren* (reprinted in J.M. Keynes, *Essays in Persuasion*, New York, W.W. Norton & Co., 1963, pp. 358-373). In this essay, Keynes predicted that, within a hundred years (and absent major wars and population growth), (Western) society would achieve a state of economic bliss in which mankind, now deprived of a good part of its traditional labor, would face the daunting challenge of practicing the art of living.

bumblebee would have to graduate to a real bee. *"And that's what it's doing"*, he added.[107] In the years that followed, it has done so, in some measure.

1 CONVERGENCE AND SYMMETRY

112. A first question that comes to mind is to what extent the European currency union has delivered on the promise of contributing to greater convergence of the economies of its member countries—or, to put the question in less causal terms, to what extent key economic indicators of these countries have shown a converging trend over the life of the currency union and, in particular, its more recent period. In OCA terms, in several respects, the European currency union was not an optimum currency area at its inception. But, according to the "endogeneity" hypothesis of OCA theory, an initially imperfect currency union may by itself generate virtuous dynamics that cause greater trade integration, higher correlation of income and employment and generally more symmetry within the system and, hence, make the currency union "more optimal" over time (*see* paragraph 8 above). Is this what has happened? The evidence is mixed.

113. At the outset, I should note three caveats about the data presented in this section:

(a) The tables that follow do not always cover the same Member States or the same years or time periods, and they sometimes present data for the euro area and the European Union in their varying composition over the years or in their 2022 configuration of, respectively, 19 and 27 Member States. This is sometimes done deliberately, to enhance information content or delete data of lesser relevance, but at other times simply because of limitations in data coverage or quality at source.

(b) In the following pages, I regularly compare data for the euro area and the European Union as a whole. Obviously, these geographies overlap significantly and increasingly so over time: in 1999, the aggregate GDP of the (original) euro area represented 75.10% of that of the then European Union and in 2022, 84.32%. Accordingly, differences between euro area and EU data in fact imply progressively higher differences between euro area and non-euro area Member States. It would have been more rigorous academically to directly compare data for euro area and non-euro area Member States at any given time. But this would have required a labor-intensive breakdown of available data with little added value in terms of informational content. Extracting and checking data was already tedious enough an exercise as it was.

107. *See* the remarks made by Mario Draghi at the Global Investment Conference in London, July 26, 2012, https://www.ecb.europa.eu/press/key/date/2012/html/sp120726.en.html, at p. 1.

(c) As to individual euro area Member States, the data below focus primarily on the euro area's five largest economies, *i.e.*, Germany, France, Italy, Spain and The Netherlands. The "Big Five" should make up a fairly representative group, in terms both of their economic diversity and of their combined weight in the euro area's overall economy. Together, they represented about 85% of the euro area's aggregate GDP in 2002 (with the currency union then counting 12 Member States) and they still stood for around 80% of euro area GDP in 2022 (in the euro area's then configuration of 19 Member States).

a Inflation

114. As to inflation, a critical variable in a currency union, the picture is somewhat pixelated. Table 2.1 below shows, in standard font, the annual rate of change of headline inflation (as measured by the Harmonized Index of Consumer Prices, or "HICP" for short) in the euro area and selected euro area Member States over the period from 1999 to 2022 (jumping intervals of one or several years until 2014). Also shown, in italics, are the corresponding annual changes in a measure of core inflation (*i.e.*, HICP minus energy, food, alcohol and tobacco).

Table 2.1 Euro Area Inflation 1999-2022

	1999	*2003*	*2007*	*2010*	*2012*	*2014*	*2015*	*2016*	*2017*	*2018*	*2019*	*2020*	*2021*	*2022*
EU	1.2	2.0	2.3	2.1	2.6	0.6	0.1	0.2	1.7	1.9	1.5	0.7	2.9	9.2
	–	*1.7*	*1.9*	*1.3*	*1.7*	*0.9*	*1.0*	*0.8*	*1.2*	*1.2*	*1.3*	*1.2*	*1.8*	*4.7*
Euro area	1.1	2.1	2.1	1.6	2.5	0.4	0.2	0.2	1.5	1.8	1.2	0.3	2.6	8.4
	–	*1.8*	*1.9*	*1.0*	*1.5*	*0.8*	*1.1*	*0.8*	*1.0*	*1.0*	*1.0*	*0.7*	*1.5*	*3.9*
Germany	0.6	1.1	2.3	1.1	2.2	0.8	0.7	0.4	1.7	1.9	1.4	0.4	3.2	8.7
	0.5	*0.6*	*1.9*	*0.6*	*1.3*	*1.1*	*1.9*	*1.0*	*1.3*	*1.3*	*1.3*	*0.7*	*2.2*	*3.9*
Netherlands	2.0	2.2	1.6	0.9	2.8	0.3	0.2	0.1	1.3	1.6	2.7	1.1	2.8	11.6
	–	*2.1*	*1.3*	*1.1*	*2.2*	*0.6*	*0.9*	*0.6*	*0.8*	*1.0*	*1.9*	*1.9*	*1.8*	*4.8*
France	0.6	2.2	1.6	1.7	2.2	0.6	0.1	0.3	1.2	2.1	1.3	0.5	2.1	5.9
	0.5	*1.7*	*1.6*	*1.0*	*1.5*	*1.0*	*0.6*	*0.6*	*0.5*	*0.9*	*0.6*	*0.6*	*1.3*	*3.4*
Italy	1.6	2.8	2.0	1.6	3.3	0.2	0.1	–0.1	1.3	1.2	0.6	–0.1	1.9	8.7
	–	*2.5*	*1.8*	*1.6*	*2.0*	*0.7*	*0.7*	*0.5*	*0.8*	*0.6*	*0.5*	*0.5*	*0.8*	*3.3*
Spain	2.2	3.1	2.8	2.0	2.4	–0.2	–0.6	–0.3	2.0	1.7	0.8	–0.3	3.0	8.3
	–	*3.0*	*2.5*	*0.8*	*1.3*	*–0.1*	*0.3*	*0.7*	*1.2*	*1.0*	*1.1*	*0.5*	*0.6*	*3.8*
Portugal	2.2	3.2	2.4	1.4	2.8	–0.2	0.5	0.6	1.6	1.2	0.3	–0.1	0.9	8.1
	–	*3.3*	*2.1*	*0.3*	*1.2*	*0.2*	*0.6*	*0.9*	*1.2*	*0.8*	*0.4*	*–0.2*	*0.2*	*5.0*
Belgium	1.1	1.5	1.8	2.3	2.6	0.5	0.6	1.8	2.2	2.3	1.2	0.4	3.2	10.3
	–	*1.5*	*1.4*	*1.1*	*1.9*	*1.5*	*1.6*	*1.8*	*1.5*	*1.3*	*1.5*	*1.4*	*1.3*	*4.0*
σ	0.65	0.73	0.41	0.45	0.36	0.35	0.40	0.63	0.35	0.39	0.71	0.44	0.79	1.65
	–	*0.86*	*0.38*	*0.38*	*0.37*	*0.50*	*0.52*	*0.41*	*0.32*	*0.23*	*0.52*	*0.63*	*0.64*	*0.60*

Source: Eurostat (online data code PRC_HICP_AIND) (as updated on July 19, 2023). EU of 15 Member States in 1999-2003, 25 in 2004-2006, 27 in 2007-2012, 28 in 2013-2019 and 27 in 2020-2022. Euro area of 11 Member States in 1999-2000, 12 in 2001-2006, 13 in 2007, 15 in 2008, 16 in 2009-2010, 17 in 2011-2013, 18 in 2014 and 19 in 2015-2022. In the last row, **σ** stands for the standard deviation among the inflation readings for the seven euro area Member States selected in the relevant year.

115. These are some takeaways from Table 2.1:

(a) By and large, directional movements were similar and broadly synchronous, but there was significant variability among country rates in most years. Headline inflation dropped precipitously between 2012 and 2015, climbed in 2017 to converge to levels closer to 2% in 2018, then fell off again in 2019-2020, rose significantly in 2021 and jumped off the charts in 2022.
(b) Over the entire 1999-2022 period (including the years jumped in the table), euro area and EU averages for headline inflation track each other relatively closely, *i.e.*, within two decimals, except in 2008-2011 and 2019-2022 when average euro area inflation was more clearly lower than the EU average. Still, the EU average is closer to the ECB's numerical target of 2% in 13 of the 24 years and at equal distance from this target in another four years.
(c) Unsurprisingly, core inflation readings tend to be somewhat less volatile and more slow-moving. Yet, they are generally still strongly correlated with those for headline inflation, with overall high Pearson correlation coefficients, although less so in roughly the first half of the period (when a more pronounced softening of core inflation pointed to underlying disinflationary dynamics).
(d) An interesting thought is this. In a currency union with a single monetary policy, one would ordinarily expect to see a fairly elevated degree of convergence of **nominal** interest rate levels. But, in combination with greater dispersion of country inflation rates, this would produce divergence of **real** interest rates, with the consequence that real rates may end up being comparatively lower in higher-inflation countries, and higher in lower-inflation countries, than is desirable from a monetary policy standpoint. In this manner, during a good part of the currency union's first decade, certain Southern Member States had lower real rates than Germany, which likely fueled domestic demand and credit and may have added to inflationary pressures in those Member States.[108] For a single monetary policy in a multi-country currency union to work well and reasonably evenly, a high degree of convergence of inflation rates across the currency zone is of considerable importance. The increased dispersion of inflation rates in the euro area since 2019 (as illustrated by the σ values in the last row of Table 2.1 above) is a complicating factor.

b Government Deficit and Debt

116. Table 2.2 below looks at how the government deficit-to-GDP and debt-to-GDP ratios—original convergence criteria and continuing SGP benchmarks—evolved over time in the euro area. The numbers in standard font are the deficit ratios, and those in italics are the debt ratios.

108. *Cf.* J. Franks, B. Barkbu *et al.*, "Economic Convergence in the Euro Area: Coming Together or Drifting Apart?", *IMF Working Papers No 18/10*, January 2018, pp. 10-11.

Table 2.2 Euro Area Government Deficit and Debt Ratios 1999-2022

	1999	*2003*	*2007*	*2010*	*2012*	*2014*	*2015*	*2016*	*2017*	*2018*	*2019*	*2020*	*2021*	*2022*	δ *1999/2022*
EU	−1.5 –	−3.1 *66.7*	−0.5 *62.3*	−6.0 *80.4*	−3.7 *85.0*	−2.4 *86.9*	−1.9 *85.1*	−1.4 *84.3*	−0.8 *81.9*	−0.4 *79.8*	−0.5 *77.7*	−6.7 *90.0*	−4.8 *88.0*	−3.4 *84.0*	*+17.3*
Euro area	−1.5 *71.6*	−3.1 *69.4*	−0.6 *66.0*	−6.3 *85.7*	−3.8 *91.1*	−2.5 *93.2*	−2.0 *91.3*	−1.5 *90.5*	−0.9 *88.1*	−0.4 *86.1*	−0.6 *84.1*	−7.1 *97.2*	−5.3 *95.5*	−3.6 *91.6*	*+20.0*
Germany	−1.7 *60.4*	−3.7 *63.5*	0.3 *64.2*	−4.4 *82.0*	0.0 *80.7*	0.6 *75.3*	1.0 *71.9*	1.2 *69.0*	1.3 *65.2*	1.9 *61.9*	1.5 *59.6*	−4.3 *68.7*	−3.7 *69.3*	−2.6 *66.3*	*+5.9*
Netherlands	−0.2 *58.7*	−3.1 *50.0*	−0.2 *43.0*	−5.3 *59.3*	−3.9 *66.2*	−2.3 *67.9*	−1.9 *64.6*	0.1 *61.9*	1.4 *57.0*	1.5 *52.4*	1.8 *48.5*	−3.7 *54.7*	−2.4 *52.5*	0.0 *51.0*	*−7.7*
France	−1.6 *60.5*	−4.0 *64.4*	−2.6 *64.5*	−6.9 *85.3*	−5.0 *90.6*	−3.9 *94.9*	−3.6 *95.6*	−3.6 *98.0*	−3.0 *98.1*	−2.3 *97.8*	−3.1 *97.4*	−9.0 *114.6*	−6.5 *112.9*	−4.7 *111.6*	*+51.1*
Italy	−1.8 *113.3*	−3.2 *105.5*	−1.3 *103.9*	−4.2 *119.2*	−2.9 *126.5*	−3.0 *135.4*	−2.6 *135.3*	−2.4 *134.8*	−2.4 *134.2*	−2.2 *134.4*	−1.5 *134.1*	−9.7 *154.9*	−9.0 *149.9*	−8.0 *144.4*	*+31.1*
Spain	−1.2 *60.8*	−0.4 *47.7*	1.9 *35.8*	−9.5 *60.5*	−11.6 *90.0*	−6.1 *105.1*	−5.3 *103.3*	−4.3 *102.7*	−3.1 *101.8*	−2.6 *100.4*	−3.1 *98.2*	−10.1 *120.4*	−6.9 *118.3*	−4.8 *113.2*	*+ 52.4*
Portugal	−3.0 *55.4*	−5.7 *63.9*	−2.9 *72.7*	−11.4 *100.2*	−6.2 *129.0*	−7.4 *132.9*	−4.4 *131.2*	−1.9 *131.5*	−3.0 *126.1*	−0.3 *121.5*	0.1 *116.6*	−5.8 *134.9*	−2.9 *125.4*	−0.4 *113.9*	*+58.5*
Belgium	−0.6 *115.4*	−1.9 *101.7*	0.1 *87.3*	−4.1 *100.3*	−4.3 *104.8*	−3.1 *107.0*	−2.4 *105.2*	−2.4 *105.0*	−0.7 *102.0*	−0.9 *99.9*	−2.0 *97.6*	−9.0 *112.0*	−5.5 *109.1*	−3.9 *105.1*	*−10.3*
σ	*24.99*	*21.60*	*21.93*	*20.30*	*21.54*	*23.98*	*24.82*	*25.77*	*26.42*	*27.31*	*27.79*	*32.77*	*30.97*	*29.35*	

Source: Eurostat (online data code GOV_10DD_EDPT1) (as updated on April 21, 2023). EU = 27; euro area = 19. Government deficit and debt as measured by ESA 2010. The last row shows the standard deviation (σ) of the government debt ratios of the seven euro area Member States of the sample for the relevant year.

117. As concerns the **government deficit ratio**, the reader will note the following:

(a) The Big Five, *i.e.*, the euro area's five major economies, repeatedly exceeded the 3% deficit benchmark over the 24-year period—France in 17 years (2002-2005, 2008-2016 and 2019-2022), Spain in 14 years (2008-2017 and 2019-2022), Italy in 11 years (2001, 2003-2006, 2009-2011 and 2020-2022), Germany in eight years (2002-2005, 2009-2010 and 2020-2021) and The Netherlands in six years (2003, 2009-2012 and 2020).
(b) The average euro area deficit ratio was marginally higher than the EU average throughout the period (including in the years not shown in the table) but more significantly so in 2020 and 2021.

118. As to the **government debt ratio**, the following points are worth noting for present purposes:

(a) The currency union took off in 1999 with significantly different government debt ratios among its original members. These debt ratios more or less stabilized or trended downward until 2007, increased sharply, to different degrees, between 2008 and 2014, generally decreased between 2015 and 2019, then jumped up in 2020, and edged down again from 2020 peaks in 2021 and 2022.
(b) Still, at the end of 2022, government debt ratios generally stood at significantly higher levels than those prevailing in 1999 and, in the case of Southern Member States (including France, Italy, Spain and Portugal), even than those at the start of the euro area sovereign debt crisis in 2010. Southern Member States saw their debt ratios deteriorate markedly against the euro area average between 2010 and 2020, which resulted in increased divergence of debt ratios within the euro area.
(c) Accordingly, the standard deviation (σ) of the government debt ratios of the seven euro area Member States of our sample increased year by year over the 2010-2020 period. If one looks in particular at the debt ratios of the Big Five (Germany, France, Italy, Spain and The Netherlands), the diverging trend is even more pronounced: the standard deviation (σ) among their debt ratios was 21.29 in 1999, 23.72 in 2007, 23.89 in 2014, 30.37 in 2019, 35.18 in 2021 and 34.00 in 2022.
(d) Remarkably, the government debt ratio for the euro area as a whole has been consistently higher than the EU average, with a margin progressively increasing from 2.6 percentage points in 2000 to 6.1 percentage points in 2012, 7.5 percentage points in 2021 and 7.6 percentage points in 2022.

c Government Investment

119. Table 2.3 below shows the evolution of government investment (general government's share of gross fixed capital formation) as a percentage of GDP over the 1999-2022 period.

Table 2.3 Euro Area Government Investment 1999-2022

	1999	*2003*	*2007*	*2010*	*2012*	*2014*	*2015*	*2016*	*2017*	*2018*	*2019*	*2020*	*2021*	*2022*
EU	3.2	3.3	3.4	3.6	3.2	3.0	3.0	2.8	2.8	2.9	3.0	3.3	3.2	3.2
Euro area	3.2	3.2	3.3	3.5	3.0	2.7	2.8	2.6	2.6	2.7	2.8	3.0	3.0	3.0
Germany	2.4	2.1	2.0	2.4	2.2	2.1	2.1	2.2	2.2	2.4	2.4*	2.7*	2.6*	2.6*
Netherlands	3.8	4.2	3.8	4.2	3.8	3.5	3.6	3.5	3.4	3.4	3.4	3.7	3.4	3.2*
France	3.8	3.9	3.9	4.2	4.0	3.7	3.4	3.4	3.3	3.4	3.7	3.7	3.6	3.7
Italy	2.9	3.1	3.2	3.1	2.6	2.3	2.4	2.3	2.2	2.1	2.3	2.6	2.9	2.7
Spain	3.9	4.2	4.7	4.7	3.1	2.1	2.6	2.0	2.0	2.2	2.2	2.6	2.7	2.8
Portugal	4.9	4.4	3.2	5.3	2.5	2.0	2.3	1.5	1.8	1.8	1.8	2.3	2.6	2.5
Belgium	2.4	2.1	2.0	2.2	2.5	2.6	2.5	2.4	2.4	2.6	2.6	2.7*	2.7*	2.7

Source: Eurostat (online data code GOV_10A_MAIN) (as updated on July 21, 2023). EU = 27; euro area = 19. Numbers marked with an asterisk are provisional values.

120. The data in Table 2.3 prompt the following comments:

(a) Interestingly, average government investment (as a percentage of GDP) in the euro area consistently trails the EU-wide average somewhat over the entire period but the difference widens a little toward the end of the 2010-2012 sovereign debt crisis and in subsequent years.
(b) The government investment share of GDP varies appreciably among euro area Member States. It is often significantly lower in the 2013-2019 period than in the 2000-2009 period, especially in the case of the Southern Member States. Italy comes out below the euro area average every year, as do Spain, Portugal and Belgium since the euro area sovereign debt crisis.
(c) One likely explanation is that, in the aftermath of the sovereign debt crisis, euro area Member States were (forced to be) more cautious to maintain fiscal discipline—and those with higher debt ratios more than others. Predictably, they were politically inclined to do so by applying relatively greater restraint in government investments than in current expenditures on social transfers, general public services and other matters of more immediate electoral visibility. Thus, ironically, public investments were more subdued during much of a period of prolonged monetary easing, while the higher public investments required today, by the deferral of earlier investments and by the needs of the green transition, now face a more restrictive monetary environment and more costly financing conditions. It is one of the key challenges currently facing the monetary/fiscal policy mix and the ongoing reform of SGP.

d Growth

121. Table 2.4 below compares the growth of real GDP at market prices (as a percentage change over the previous year) over the period from 2007 to 2022 in the euro area as a whole (in its varying composition) and selected euro area Member States with GDP growth in the European Union, the OECD and selected non-EU countries.

Table 2.4 Euro Area GDP Growth 2007-2022

	2007	*2008*	*2009*	*2010*	*2011*	*2012*	*2013*	*2014*	*2015*	*2016*	*2017*	*2018*	*2019*	*2020*	*2021*	*2022*
EU	3.0	0.5	–4.3	2.2	1.8	–0.4	0.3	1.8	2.3	1.9	2.7	1.9	1.7	–5.6	5.6	3.4
Euro area	2.9	0.4	–4.4	2.2	1.7	–0.9	–0.3	1.4	2.0	1.9	2.6	1.8	1.6	–6.0	5.4	3.3
Germany	3.0	1.0	–5.7	4.2	3.9	0.4	0.4	2.2	1.5	2.2	2.7	1.0	1.1*	–3.8*	3.2*	1.8*
Netherlands	3.8	2.2	–3.7	1.3	1.6	–1.0	–0.1	1.4	2.0	2.2	2.9	2.4	2.0	–3.9	6.2*	4.3*
France	2.4	0.3	–2.9	1.9	2.2	0.3	0.6	1.0	1.1	1.1	2.3	1.9	1.8	–7.5	6.4*	2.5*
Italy	1.5	–1.0	–5.3	1.7	0.7	–3.0	–1.8	0	0.8	1.3	1.7	0.9	0.5	–9.0	7.0	3.7
Spain	3.6	0.9	–3.8	0.2	–0.8	–3.0	–1.4	1.4	3.8	3.0	3.0	2.3	2.0	–11.3*	5.5*	6.5*
Portugal	2.5	0.3	–3.1	1.7	–1.7	–4.1	–0.9	0.8	1.8	2.0	3.5	2.8	2.7	–8.3	5.5*	6.7*
Greece	3.3	–0.3	–4.3	–5.5	–10.1	–7.1	–2.5	0.5	–0.2	–0.5	1.1	1.7	1.9	–9.0*	8.4*	5.9*
Belgium	3.7	0.4	–2.0	2.9	1.7	0.7	0.5	1.6	2.0	1.3	1.6	1.8	2.3	–5.4*	6.3*	3.2*
OECD	2.7	0.4	–3.4	3.1	2.1	1.4	1.6	2.1	2.6	1.9	2.7	2.4	1.7*	–4.3*	5.7*	2.9*
U.S.	2.0	0.1	–2.6	2.7	1.5	2.3	1.8	2.3	2.7	1.7	2.2	2.9	2.3	–2.8	5.9	2.1*
Canada	2.1	1.0	–2.9	3.1	3.1	1.8	2.3	2.9	0.7	1.0	3.0	2.8	1.9	–5.1	5.0	3.4
Australia	3.6	1.9	2.2	2.5	3.9	2.6	2.6	2.2	2.7	2.3	2.9	2.2	–0.1	2.2	3.6	3.6*
Japan	1.5	–1.2	–5.7	4.1	0	1.4	2.0	0.3	1.6	0.8	1.7	0.6	–0.4	–4.3	2.1	1.0*

Source: Eurostat (online data code NAMA_10_GDP) (as updated on August 9, 2023) and OECD Statistics. EU = 28 until 2019 and 27 as from 2020. Euro area = 13 in 2007, 15 in 2008, 16 in 2009-2010, 17 in 2011-2013, 18 in 2014 and 19 in 2015-2022. Numbers marked with an asterisk are provisional or estimated values.

122. The following general observations can be made on the data presented in Table 2.4:

(a) Over the 16-year period from 2007 to 2022, GDP has generally grown at a notably lower rate in the euro area as a whole than in the OECD (except in 2007, 2008, 2016 and 2022) and in the United States (except in 2007, 2008, 2011, 2016, 2017 and 2022) and even at a somewhat lower rate than in the European Union as a whole (except in 2010 and 2016).

(b) Within the euro area, there were significant differences in GDP growth among member countries, with the Southern Member States (Italy, Spain, Portugal and Greece) generally being subject to greater swings.

123. Table 2.5 below shows how, over the period from 2002 to 2022, GDP *per capita* (at market prices) evolved in selected euro area Member States, including in relation to euro area and EU averages.

Table 2.5 Euro Area GDP per capita 2002-2022

	2002	*2006*	*2010*	*2014*	*2018*	*2019*	*2020*	*2021*	*2022*	*% change 2002/ 2022*	*% change 2014/ 2022*
EU	19,870	23,200	24,900	26,580	30,290	31,310	30,050	32,520	35,280	+77.55	+32.73
Euro area	24,400	27,810	28,850	30,270	33,980	35,000	33,430	35,980	38,760	+58.85	+28.04
Germany	26,950	29,380	31,940	36,150	40,590	41,810*	40,930*	43,480*	46,260*	+71.65	+27.96
Netherlands	31,030	35,760	38,470	39,820	44,920	46,880	45,670	49,650*	54,150*	+74.50	+35.98
France	25,690	29,050	30,690	32,420	35,040	35,980	34,080	36,670*	38,550*	+50.05	+18.90
Italy	23,650	26,590	26,940	26,980	29,580	30,080	27,940	30,230	32,390	+36.95	+20.05
Spain	18,090	22,630	23,040	22,230	25,760	26,440	23,610*	25,500*	27,870*	+54.06	+25.37
Portugal	13,680	15,800	16,990	16,640	19,950	20,840	19,470	20,870*	23,290*	+70.24	+39.96
Belgium	26,440	30,830	33,330	35,950	40,260	41,660	39,830*	43,350*	46,990*	+77.72	+30.70

Source: Eurostat (online data code NAMA_10_PC) (as updated on August 9, 2023). EU = 27; euro area = 12 in 2002 and 2006, 15 in 2010, 18 in 2014 and 19 in 2018-2022. Numbers marked with an asterisk are provisional or estimated values.

124. Key takeaways from Table 2.5 include the following:

(a) Over the entire 2002-2022 period, GDP *per capita* generally grew a little less in the euro area than in the European Union at large.
(b) There is no compelling evidence of significant convergence of GDP *per capita* among the selected euro area Member States. If anything, the gap between the most and the least productive Member States appears to have stagnated or even widened over the past decade.[109] Thus, the coefficient of variation (*i.e.*, the ratio of the standard deviation to the mean) among the Big Five economies was 0.189 in 2002, 0.223 in 2014 and 0.265 in 2022. France, Spain and especially Italy have lagged behind in *per capita* growth.
(c) Technically, convergence of *per capita* GDP or income levels may not be among the more critical OCA conditions, but it is of considerable political importance for the cohesion of the currency union. Anno 2022, the degree of dispersion remains large. Especially in today's challenging and increasingly polarized political environment, it should become more difficult to credibly lay claim to an "ever closer Union" without more visible progress toward "shared prosperity".

e Activity Level and Unemployment

125. Table 2.6 below portrays how, since the earlier years of the currency union, activity, unemployment and youth unemployment rates have evolved in selected euro area Member States, in comparison to euro area and EU averages. Activity rates, *i.e.*, the percentage of economically active persons (persons classified as employed or unemployed, as distinguished from persons outside the labor force) in relation to the total population at working age (15 to 64 years), are shown in bold typeface. Unemployment rates, *i.e.*, the unemployed as a percentage of the labor force, are in standard font. Youth unemployment rates, *i.e.*, the unemployed in the age bracket of 15 to 24 years as a percentage of the active population in the same age group, are italicized.

Table 2.6 Euro Area Activity and Unemployment Rates 2002-2022

	2002	*2006*	*2010*	*2014*	*2018*	*2020*	*2021*	*2022*
EU	**67.7**	**69.3**	**69.7**	**71.2**	**72.8**	**72.4**	**73.6**	**74.5**
	9.6	8.6	10.5	11.0	7.4	7.2	7.1	6.2
	19.6	*18.3*	*22.4*	*24.1*	*16.7*	*17.6*	*16.7*	*14.5*
Euro area	**68.2**	**70.3**	**71.1**	**72.2**	**73.4**	**72.5**	**73.7**	**74.6**
	8.6	8.3	10.3	11.7	8.2	8.0	7.7	6.8
	16.6	*16.8*	*22.0*	*24.2*	*17.5*	*18.1*	*16.8*	*14.6*

109. *Cf.* J. Franks, B. Barkbu *et al.*, *supra*, p. 12, Table 1.

	2002	*2006*	*2010*	*2014*	*2018*	*2020*	*2021*	*2022*
Germany	**71.5**	**74.9**	**75.4**	**76.5**	**77.5**	**77.3**	**78.5**	**79.4**
	8.8	10.3	6.6	4.7	3.2	3.7	3.7	3.1
	9.8	*13.8*	*10.5*	*8.3*	*6.6*	*8.0*	*7.0*	*6.0*
Netherlands	**76.5**	**75.4**	**80.4**	**81.5**	**82.7**	**83.4**	**83.7**	**84.7**
	2.8	5.0	5.0	8.4	4.9	4.9	4.2	3.5
	5.0	*10.0*	*12.4*	*13.8*	*8.9*	*10.6*	*9.3*	*7.6*
France	**69.0**	**69.6**	**71.0**	**72.0**	**72.8**	**72.0**	**73.0**	**73.6**
	-	8.8	9.3	10.3	9.0	8.0	7.9	7.3
	-	*22.0*	*24.7*	*25.7*	*22.0*	*21.5*	*18.9*	*17.3*
Italy	**61.0**	**62.6**	**61.6**	**63.6**	**65.6**	**63.5**	**64.5**	**65.5**
	9.0	6.8	8.5	12.9	10.6	9.3	9.5	8.1
	27.2	*21.8*	*28.0*	*42.7*	*32.2*	*29.8*	*29.7*	*23.7*
Spain	**66.4**	**71.1**	**73.5**	**74.2**	**73.7**	**72.2**	**73.7**	**74.0**
	11.5	8.5	19.9	24.5	15.3	15.5	14.8	12.9
	22.2	*17.9*	*41.5*	*53.2*	*34.3*	*38.3*	*34.8*	*29.8*
Greece	**64.1**	**66.7**	**67.7**	**67.3**	**68.1**	**65.3**	**67.3**	**69.4**
	10.4	9.0	12.9	26.6	19.7	17.6	14.7	12.5
	26.6	*25.0*	*33.6*	*53.0*	*41.2*	*38.0*	*35.5*	*31.4*
Portugal	**72.6**	**73.6**	**71.5**	**71.8**	**74.5**	**73.8**	**75.2**	**76.4**
	5.1	7.8	12.6	14.6	7.2	7.0	6.6	6.0
	11.7	*16.5*	*28.0*	*34.8*	*20.3*	*22.5*	*23.4*	*19.0*
Belgium	**64.1**	**66.5**	**67.7**	**67.8**	**68.6**	**68.4**	**69.7**	**70.5**
	7.5	8.3	8.4	8.7	6.0	5.8	6.3	5.6
	17.7	*20.5*	*22.4*	*23.4*	*16.0*	*15.9*	*18.2*	*16.4*

Source: Eurostat (online data codes TIPSLM60, TPS00203 and TIPSLM80) (as updated on June 20, 2023). EU = 27; euro area = 19 (20 in 2022). Some data are subject to slight variations due to methodological differences.

126. The following points are worth noting:

(a) By and large, average euro area and EU activity and unemployment rates appear to be on a close parallel track, although, since 2011, the average unemployment rate in the euro area has consistently been somewhat higher than the EU average.

(b) Within the euro area, activity rates have generally edged up but to different degrees, with Italy, Greece and Belgium notably lagging behind. Unemployment rates continue to diverge significantly among euro area Member States, with consistently high levels in Spain and Greece and very high youth unemployment rates in Italy, Spain and Greece.

f Foreign Trade

127. As to the effects of the currency union on intra-euro area trade, it is, of course, difficult to disentangle these effects from the broader impact of EU trade integration. In 2020, Paul De Grauwe observed that the currency union may have added some 5% to 20% to intra-euro area trade but that this conclusion is subject to doubt.[110] A 2021 study attempted to estimate the trade impact of the euro using both a gravity equation and a synthetic control method, and looking at bilateral trade flows over the 1990-2015 period among and between the first wave of 12 euro area Member States (Austria, Belgium, Finland, France, Germany, Ireland, Italy, Luxembourg, The Netherlands, Portugal, Spain and Greece) and a second wave of seven subsequent entrants (Slovenia, Cyprus, Malta, Slovakia, Estonia, Latvia and Lithuania) and decomposing data for intermediate and final goods. Under the gravity equation approach, this study found that, after euro adoption, (i) exports among first-wave members increased by 5.4%; (ii) exports from first-wave to second-wave members increased by 4.3%; and (iii) exports from second-wave to first-wave members increased by 6.3%, of which those of final products by 10.6% (which seems consistent with the more downstream position of second-wave members in European production chains due to their lower labor costs).[111]

This invites us to take a deeper dive into the data for euro area foreign trade in goods (for which the most granular data are available) to see how intra-euro area trade of euro area Member States developed in relation to their intra-EU trade and extra-EU foreign trade.

128. Table 2.7 below shows how the exports of goods (volumes in billions of euros) of selected euro area Member States and, for the sake of comparison, certain non-euro area Member States (Sweden and Poland) have evolved over the 21-year period from 2002 to 2022. The numbers in bold typeface refer to exports within (or to) the euro area, those in standard font to exports within the European Union as a whole, and those in italics to exports to the rest of the world (*i.e.*, the world minus the European Union). The final numbers in each country row, between parentheses, are the percentage shares of intra-euro area exports in total exports.

129. In the same way, Table 2.8 below shows the corresponding data for imports of goods (again in billions of euros).

110. P. De Grauwe, *Economics of Monetary Union*, Oxford University Press, 13th ed., 2020, pp. 68 and 89.

111. V. Gunnella, L. Lebastard *et al.*, "The impact of the euro on trade: two decades into monetary union", *ECB Occasional Paper Series No 283*, October 2021, especially pp. 23-25.

Table 2.7 Exports of Goods to Euro Area, European Union and Rest of World 2002-2022

	2002	*2007*	*2012*	*2017*	*2022*	*% change 2002/2022*	*δ 2002/ 2022*
Germany	**286.43**	**427.54**	**409.41**	**471.33**	**601.81**	**+110.10%**	
	360.78	556.94	548.73	664.50	861.43	+138.76%	
	290.47	*407.09*	*541.79*	*617.35*	*714.61*	*+146.01%*	
	(43.98%)	(44.34%)	(37.54%)	(36.76%)	(38.18%)		(-5.80%)
Netherlands	**164.46**	**246.50**	307.59	**329.06**	564.37	**+243.16%**	
	179.88	277.33	346.55	383.37	655.58	+264.44%	
	78.21	*124.56*	*163.54*	*193.71*	*264.39*	*+238.02%*	
	(63.72%)	(61.33%)	(60.30%)	(57.02%)	(61.34%)		(-2.38%)
France	**176.71**	**210.49**	**206.57**	**216.39**	**286.73**	**+62.25%**	
	194.28	234.87	231.18	247.01	328.12	+68.89%	
	156.51	*173.45*	*211.46*	*226.79*	*259.05*	*+65.51%*	
	(50.37%)	(51.55%)	(46.66%)	(45.67%)	(48.83%)		(-1.54%)
Italy	**126.79**	**169.65**	**160.30**	**183.57**	**265.64**	**+109.50%**	
	147.18	203.73	192.91	227.10	328.91	+123.47%	
	121.87	*161.00*	*197.27*	*222.02*	*295.79*	*+142.69%*	
	(47.12%)	(46.51%)	(41.08%)	(40.87%)	(42.56%)		(-4.56%)
Spain	**81.23**	**107.39**	**119.57**	**149.31**	**227.06**	**+179.51%**	
	86.67	116.79	131.75	168.17	252.33	+ 191.11%	
	46.23	*68.02*	*98.04*	*114.92*	*145.31*	*+214.26%*	
	(61.11%)	(58.10%)	(52.03%)	(52.74%)	(57.10%)		(-4.01%)
Portugal	**18.42**	**25.72**	**27.73**	**34.59**	**50.72**	**+175.26%**	
	19.45	27.23	29.73	37.14	55.07	+183.13%	
	7.94	*11.06*	*15.47*	*17.87*	*23.12*	*+191.09%*	
	(67.25%)	(67.18%)	(61.35%)	(62.88%)	(64.85%)		(-2.40%)

Belgium	**140.80** 150.64 *77.91* (61.60%)	**198.12** 215.69 *98.75* (63.00%)	**199.72** 218.54 *128.54* (57.54%)	**217.44** 243.63 *136.95* (57.13%)	**368.11** 410.66 *193.46* (60.93%)	**+161.44%** +172.59% *+148.30%*	(-0.67%)
Sweden	**36.00** 43.62 *42.56* (41.77%)	**52.26** 66.66 *56.50* (42.43%)	**52.02** 66.13 *68.00* (38.78%)	**55.82** 71.59 *63.76* (41.24%)	**76.29** 101.51 *86.44* (40.59%)	**+111.92%** +132.69% *+103.09%*	(-1.18%)
Poland	**27.32** 33.17 *10.32* (62.82%)	**58.71** 74.93 *27.32* (57.41%)	**78.24** 100.19 *44.08* (54.23%)	**118.31** 152.52 *54.86* (57.04%)	**202.18** 258.98 *83.90* (58.96%)	**+639.84%** +680.74% *+712.45%*	(-3.86%)

Source: Eurostat (online data code DS-059268) (as updated on July 14, 2023). EU = 27; euro area = 19. Percentage changes have been computed on the full numbers.

Table 2.8 Imports of Goods from Euro Area, European Union and Rest of World 2002-2022

	2002	*2007*	*2012*	*2017*	*2022*	*% change 2002/2022*	*δ 2002/ 2022*
Germany	**243.68** 307.67 *210.81* (46.99%)	**355.72** 455.98 *313.79* (46.21%)	**403.22** 529.75 *369.10* (44.85%)	**460.49** 640.67 *388.94* (44.72%)	**650.38** 907.90 *586.02* (43.53%)	**+166.89%** +195.08% *+177.98%*	(-3.46%)
Netherlands	**98.23** 109.36 *122.51* (42.36%)	**137.52** 155.47 *203.97* (38.25%)	**151.80** 177.26 *279.55* (33.23%)	**176.85** 207.81 *300.55* (34.78%)	**278.80** 331.16 *524.59* (32.57%)	**+183.82%** +202.81% *+328.18%*	(-9.79%)
France	**199.14** 213.58 *134.62* (57.19%)	**269.42** 294.35 *165.95* (58.53%)	**296.12** 325.91 *198.99* (56.41%)	**320.05** 357.40 *191.22* (58.33%)	**427.08** 477.61 *300.47* (54.88%)	**+114.46%** +123.61% *+123.20%*	(-2.31%)
Italy	**134.78** 151.75 *109.47* (51.59%)	**176.23** 204.32 *169.01* (47.20%)	**164.02** 193.09 *187.20* (43.13%)	**191.62** 230.01 *171.47* (47.72%)	**277.64** 333.98 *321.43* (42.36%)	**+105.99%** +120.09% *+193.61%*	(-9.23%)
Spain	**102.77** 109.15 *65.44* (58.86%)	**151.71** 164.66 *119.39* (53.41%)	**118.77** 131.42 *131.13* (45.23%)	**152.57** 173.50 *138.14* (48.95%)	**206.34** 236.23 232.77 (43.99%)	**+100.76%** +116.41% *+255.68%*	(-14.87%)
Portugal	**30.25** 31.70 *10.75* (71.25%)	**41.81** 43.67 *16.24* (69.76%)	**36.53** 38.61 *17.75* (64.79%)	**48.29** 51.33 *18.35* (69.30%)	**70.57** 75.87 *33.36* (64.60%)	**+133.23%** +139.28% *+210.17%*	(-6.65%)

Belgium	**127.64** 137.23 *72.48* (60.86%)	**178.42** 193.23 *107.06* (59.41%)	**195.71** 212.37 *129.41* (57.26%)	**194.46** 216.33 *146.24* (53.63%)	**316.89** 346.62 *246.28* (53.44%)	**+148.27%** +152.58% *+239.76%*	(-7.42%)
Sweden	**36.32** 44.58 *26.22* (51.29%)	**55.56** 71.30 *40.49* (49.69%)	**60.58** 77.80 *50.17* (47.33%)	**71.46** 90.56 *45.91* (52.36%)	**95.62** 121.87 *70.34* (49.74%)	**+163.27%** +173.38% *+168.22%*	(-1.55%)
Poland	**32.81** 38.51 *19.96* (56.11%)	**72.02** 85.05 *35.85* (59.56%)	**84.96** 100.95 *53.98* (54.83%)	**120.29** 142.63 *64.18* (58.16%)	**194.57** 231.41 *131.12* (53.67%)	**+492.95%** +500.83% *+556.79%*	(-2.44%)

Source: Eurostat (online data code DS-059268) (as updated on July 14, 2023). EU = 27; euro area = 19. Percentage changes have been computed on the full numbers.

130. To complete our data on foreign trade, Table 2.9 below shows the extent to which total euro area imports of goods originated in the selected euro area or other Member State over the 2002-2021 period, *i.e.*, in a sense, how each of these Member States' "market share" of aggregate euro area imports evolved over that period (as a percentage of the total).

Table 2.9 Country Origin of Total Euro Area Imports of Goods 2002-2021

	2002	*2007*	*2012*	*2017*	*2021*	δ *2002/2021*
Germany	14.02	13.88	11.90	12.45	11.84	–2.18
Netherlands	7.46	7.66	8.62	8.40	8.91	+ 1.45
France	8.05	6.84	6.03	6.02	5.33	–2.72
Italy	5.52	5.21	4.48	4.65	4.79	–0.73
Spain	3.69	3.51	3.30	3.74	3.83	+ 0.14
Portugal	0.96	0.73	0.74	0.79	0.83	–0.13
Belgium	5.85	6.12	5.70	5.54	5.64	–0.21
Sweden	1.79	1.79	1.58	1.58	1.53	–0.26
Poland	1.23	1.79	2.20	2.99	3.57	+ 2.34

Source: Data retrieved from Eurostat's Comext data base. Euro area = 19.

131. The following tentative conclusions can be drawn from the above data sets for euro area foreign trade in goods over the 21-year period from 2002 to 2022:

(a) Beyond certain common trends, there are significant differences in the geographic composition, and in the performance over time, of the foreign trade of the selected euro area Member States. There appears to be no appreciable convergence in the shares of intra-euro area trade in total foreign trade.[112]

(b) For the selected Member States, both exports to and imports from the European Union generally increased more than those to or from the euro area over the 2002-2022 period. They sometimes did so by significant margins, especially in the case of Germany, The Netherlands and Italy (and, on the exports side, non-euro area Member States Poland and Sweden). This is most likely due in part to the removal of trade restrictions following the European Union's enlargement to the East in 2004 and 2007.

(c) A similar pattern emerges for trade in goods with the rest of the world (*i.e.*, total worldwide foreign trade minus intra-EU foreign trade), *i.e.*, extra-EU

112. If one looks at the share of intra-euro area exports in total exports of the euro area's Big Five economies (Germany, France, Italy, Spain and The Netherlands) (*see* the percentages between parentheses in Table 2.7 above), the standard deviation (σ) was 7.78 in 2002, 6.52 in 2007, 8.06 in 2012, 7.44 in 2017 and 8.65 in 2022. On the imports side (*see* Table 2.8 above), σ was 6.17 in 2002, 6.87 in 2007, 7.36 in 2012, 7.57 in 2017 and 7.07 in 2022.

trade generally increased more than trade with the euro area, with the exception, on the exports side, of The Netherlands, Belgium and outsider Sweden. Of course, the sharper rise of extra-EU imports in 2021 and especially 2022 is due in part to the higher prices of imported energy and certain commodities in those years.

(d) Accordingly, the Member States' share of their intra-euro area trade in their total worldwide trade in goods (*i.e.*, the percentages between parentheses in Tables 2.7 and 2.8 above) generally trended downward over the 2002-2022 period as a whole. Oftentimes, their euro area share dropped more significantly in the 2008-2012 crisis years, stabilized in the following years and, on the exports side, picked up again toward the end of the period. Except for Germany, the overall 2002-2022 decline is more pronounced on the imports side, notably in the case of Spain, The Netherlands, Belgium and Italy.

(e) The Member States' "market shares" in intra-euro area trade (*see* Table 2.9 above) have been relatively stable, with a somewhat more significant loss over time for France and Germany.

(f) As far as trade in goods is concerned, it is all but obvious how one should derive from the data in Tables 2.7, 2.8 and 2.9 above that the European currency union accelerated trade integration within its geographic perimeter. While, in absolute terms, intra-euro area trade grew considerably, it generally grew at a slower pace than foreign trade with the European Union and the rest of the world.

(g) Still, as concerns the impact of the currency union, these foreign trade data need to be interpreted with caution. Thus, more limited growth of intra-euro area trade may to some degree quite simply reflect limitations on the euro area's "absorption capacity" and its needs for products on offer from euro area sources. In plain terms, there is a limit to the number of BMWs or bottles of Burgundy that euro area consumers will purchase in any given year (as counterintuitive as it may seem). Also, the fact that a euro area Member State saw its intra-euro area exports increase less than its extra-euro area exports, and its euro area "market share" diminish in relative terms, does not necessarily mean that it did not derive net trade benefit from currency union membership. Specifically, Germany traded in a strong currency under regular upward pressure (the German mark) for a relatively weaker currency (the euro) which likely supported its competitiveness in international trade.

g International Competitiveness

132. Unit labor costs often serve as a broad measure of international competitiveness. Table 2.10 below illustrates how real unit labor costs, expressed as an index with base year 2015 (= 100), evolved in selected euro area Member States between 1999 and 2020.

Table 2.10 Euro Area Real Unit Labor Costs 2002-2020

	1999	*2002*	*2007*	*2012*	*2014*	*2017*	*2020*
Germany	98.5	98.8	94.8	98.6	99.0	99.6	99.9
Netherlands	101.3	100.6	98.0	101.9	101.6	99.8	102.5
France	93.8	95.1	96.3	99.1	100.5	100.7	96.4
Italy	94.8	94.8	99.7	100.1	99.5	98.2	97.3
Spain	107.3	104.3	103.7	100.9	100.0	97.8	103.9
Greece	93.9	99.1	103.0	107.2	102.7	98.8	103.2
Portugal	113.2	114.0	110.0	103.8	101.3	100.1	104.7
Ireland	135.2	123.9	137.8	133.8	127.5	99.6	87.2
Belgium	101.0	102.7	100.4	102.4	101.9	98.7	97.2

Source: European Commission, AMECO database (accessed August 14, 2023). Real unit labor costs relative to a competitor group consisting of 37 industrial countries (including notably EU 27, United Kingdom, United States, Canada and Japan), with double export weights (QLCDQ). 2015 = 100.

133. By and large, these data show a fairly stable, slow-moving pattern of real unit labor costs in the majority of cases, but with larger swings in Greece, Portugal and especially Ireland. In these Member States, the 2008-2012 financial crisis marked a break from relatively high pre-crisis levels to lower levels, partly as a result of austerity measures under policy conditionality attached to EFSF/ESM loans. In the case of Greece, Portugal and Spain, unit labor costs tended upward again toward the end of the decade.

134. Table 2.11 below tells the story in terms of the real effective exchange rates ("REER") of selected euro area Member States (and certain non-euro area Member States, *i.e.*, Sweden and Poland) in relation to their euro area trading partners. Here, REER measures a country's price/cost competitiveness relative to its euro area trading partners, using double export weights to capture competition both in their home markets and in export markets elsewhere. Again, the base year for the index is 2015 (= 100), and a rise in the index denotes a **loss** of competitiveness.

Table 2.11 Real Effective Exchange Rates 1999-2022

	1999	*2002*	*2007*	*2012*	*2014*	*2017*	*2019*	*2022*
Germany	107.47	103.84	101.35	98.96	99.44	100.25	100.39	100.79
Netherlands	97.35	102.17	100.03	99.20	100.12	99.42	100.61	104.47
France	104.55	102.59	101.60	100.63	100.21	99.54	99.87	96.36
Italy	97.21	97.89	98.80	100.72	100.18	99.33	97.95	96.63
Spain	92.37	95.03	100.29	101.47	100.96	99.84	99.30	98.85
Greece	97.51	96.30	101.84	105.65	101.32	99.42	97.75	94.72
Portugal	96.50	100.14	102.15	101.14	99.59	100.38	98.82	96.37
Belgium	97.81	97.46	97.25	99.95	99.65	102.29	102.66	104.89

	1999	*2002*	*2007*	*2012*	*2014*	*2017*	*2019*	*2022*
Sweden	112.93	107.23	103.23	108.59	102.30	98.18	89.84	88.90
Poland	85.13	103.15	104.65	102.16	100.99	97.76	96.92	97.47

Source: Eurostat (online data code TIPSER20) (as updated on May 5, 2023). Euro area = 19. 2015 = 100.

135. It appears from these data that, roughly over the first 15 years of the period (until 2013/2014), Germany, France and outsider Sweden saw their competitiveness vis-à-vis euro area trading partners improve, while Italy, Spain, Greece, Portugal and outsider Poland lost euro area competitiveness. Since then, France, Italy, Greece, Portugal and outsiders Sweden and Poland gained competitiveness, while the competitive position of Germany and Spain more or less stabilized and that of The Netherlands and Belgium deteriorated.

h The Euro's Exchange Rate Against the U.S. Dollar

136. Throughout the life of the European currency union thus far, but especially during its first 15 years, the EUR/USD (nominal) exchange rate has been on somewhat of a rollercoaster. In January 1999, the euro made its debut trading at about USD 1.17 but instantly started depreciating to eventually reach an all-time low of 0.82 in October 2000. It regained its 1.17 starting level by October 2003 and moved above that level for an extended period until January 2015, peaking as high as 1.59 in April 2008. From January 2015 onward until this day, the EUR/USD exchange rate virtually continuously fluctuated within a band of 1.0 to 1.25. The euro traded below its initial 1.17 level between January 2015 and August 2017, above 1.17 between August 2017 and May 2018, below 1.17 between June 2018 and July 2020, above 1.17 between August 2020 and September 2021, and again below 1.17 since then (at some point dropping as low as 0.95 in September 2022).

Bearing in mind the recurring turbulences on the foreign exchange markets during the 1971-1993 period (*see* paragraphs 31-33 and 36-38 above), one can easily imagine the kind of tensions that such a volatile EUR/USD trajectory would have produced if the euro area Member States had still been operating an exchange rate system in which their national currencies were interlinked in some snake-type arrangement of fixed but adjustable bilateral central rates, jointly floating against the U.S. dollar and other currencies.

137. Still, even with a single currency and single exchange rate policy, the euro's exchange rate against other currencies, including in particular the U.S. dollar, will inevitably have affected the foreign trade performance and competitiveness of euro area Member States to (somewhat) varying degrees depending on the geographic profile of their foreign trade and notably their exposure to dollar-denominated trade, and the extra-euro area import content of their domestic products for export.

The euro's exchange rate will also affect inflation in the euro area via imports and import prices and their pass-through to production costs and consumer prices. For the euro area as a whole, exchange rate pass-through ("ERPT") to import and consumer prices appears to have diminished since the 1990s and now to be fairly low but not negligible.[113] ERPT will necessarily differ somewhat among euro area Member States (and across sectors) depending on such factors as the (non-euro invoiced) import content of their domestic production and consumption, the degree of import invoicing in euro, and the pricing power of exporters and domestic producers and distributors.[114] While estimates of ERPT to headline inflation generally seem low, some studies suggest that ERPT may be non-linear and, specifically, be larger for more significant exchange rate changes.[115] Also, exchange rate changes may affect inflation through the expectations channel.

138. So far, the ECB (Eurosystem) appears to have adopted a relatively passive exchange rate policy, in the sense that it has not actively pursued particular exchange rate levels for the euro and has only rarely engaged in substantial foreign exchange market interventions. By and large, the euro exchange rate has been one of several variables in the ECB's inflation reaction function. We will revisit this subject in Chapter 3 (*see* paragraphs 158-160 below).

i Business and Financial Cycles

139. A high degree of symmetry of **business cycles** in the euro area, in terms of both synchronicity and amplitude, should obviously be helpful and even critical for the effectiveness of the single monetary policy and for its (directional) alignment with national fiscal policies. Asynchronous business cycles mean that the ECB's monetary policy stance would at any given time be too easy for euro area Member States in a boom phase and/or too strict for those in a bust phase. In a similar vein, significant country differences in the amplitude of a particular business cycle would cause the optimal degree of monetary easing or tightening to differ for different Member States. By the same token, significant disparities in cyclical positions of euro area Member States may also become a source of tension and conflict between the monetary policy stance and national fiscal policies. In blunt terms, significant and persistent disparities in cyclical positions may make Member States worse off under a single monetary policy

113. *See* E. Ortega & Ch. Osbat, "Exchange rate pass-through in the euro area and EU countries", *ECB Occasional Paper Series No 241*, April 2020, pp. 15, 16 (Chart 3) and 17 (Chart 5). According to this study, empirical estimates using simple reduced-form regressions show that, for the euro area, ERPT (of a 1% change in exchange rate) to extra-euro area import prices declined from around 0.8% in 1999 to around 0.3% in 2008 and then broadly stabilized at this level, subject to country variations, and that ERPT to headline inflation (HICP) is even lower for most countries. Given the methodological imperfections of those estimates, the authors caution against their use as rules of thumb and advocate the use of richer dynamic stochastic general equilibrium (DSGE) models to complement the assessment of the impact of exchange rate changes on inflation. *See ibid.*, p. 69.

114. *See ibid.*, pp. 22-37.

115. *Ibid.*, pp. 18-20.

to varying degrees. If one believes in the endogeneity of OCA theory or, more prosaically, in further economic integration aided by the sharing of a common currency, one would expect that business cycles in the euro area should have become more symmetrical over time. Has this hypothesis been confirmed?

140. As to the **synchronicity** of business cycles, it appears that, since the introduction of the euro, business cycles in the different euro area Member States have indeed moved together reasonably well. However, a somewhat different picture emerges when one looks at the **amplitudes** of business cycle fluctuations. While these amplitudes tended to be roughly similar and mild for most of the currency union's first decade, they started to diverge more significantly during and after the 2008-2012 financial crisis, with higher peaks and lower troughs, especially in certain Southern Member States.[116]

141. This pattern of cyclical variance is broadly confirmed by the data in Table 2.12 below, which shows the cyclical dispersion among the euro area's Big Five economies (Germany, France, Italy, Spain and The Netherlands) as measured by the standard deviation (σ) of selected economic indicators.

Table 2.12 Cyclical Dispersion of Big Five Economies 2002-2022

	σ GDP Growth	*σ Output Gap*	*σ Unemployment Rate*	*σ Headline Inflation*	*σ Government Deficit Ratio*
2002	1.03	–	2.51	0.98	1.24
2005	1.08	–	1.49	0.65	2.02
2007	0.83	0.71*	1.27	0.45	1.51
2008	1.04	–	2.10	0.64	1.83
2009	1.05	0.87	4.35	0.44	2.75
2010	1.30	0.52	5.04	0.40	1.96
2011	1.56	1.55	5.81	0.26	2.86
2012	1.50	2.28	6.97	0.42	3.83
2013	0.96	2.52	7.27	0.55	2.41
2014	0.71	2.21	6.72	0.34	2.18
2015	1.06	1.15	5.95	0.41	2.08

116. This substantially corresponds to the conclusion reached by Professor Paul De Grauwe when looking at cyclical movements in GDP (*i.e.*, the cyclical component in GDP growth as distinguished from its trend component) over the period from 1995 to 2014. He found that correlation coefficients were generally on the high(er) side (less so for Germany) but with certain (mainly Southern) Member States experiencing higher variance in the intensity of boom-bust dynamics. *See* P. De Grauwe, *supra*, p. 32, Figure 2.4, and pp. 86-87, Table 4.3. That conclusion is also broadly consistent with the findings of Jeffrey Franks, Bergljot Barkbu *et al.*, who looked at both a concordance statistic, *i.e.*, the fraction of time that countries are in the same phase of their respective cycles (to measure the degree of co-movement between cycles), and the growth differential (to measure amplitude). *See* J. Franks, B. Barkbu *et al.*, *supra*, pp. 14-15 and 30-34.

	σ GDP Growth	*σ Output Gap*	*σ Unemployment Rate*	*σ Headline Inflation*	*σ Government Deficit Ratio*
2016	0.68	0.56	5.29	0.25	2.12
2017	0.47	0.55	4.69	0.30	2.32
2018	0.63	0.23	4.28	0.30	2.00
2019	0.59	0.33	3.97	0.73	2.14
2020	2.95	2.61	4.13	0.49	2.77
2021	1.58	2.03	4.03	0.50	2.36
2022	1.31	1.80	3.56	1.81	2.64

Source: Own calculations from Eurostat data also used in Tables 2.1, 2.2, 2.4 and 2.6 above and from OECD statistics for the output gap (*i.e.*, the deviation of actual GDP from potential GDP as a percentage of potential GDP). * This value entered for 2007 is based on the average for 1997-2007.

142. Table 2.12 above appears to offer the following perspectives on the degree of cyclical convergence among the euro area's Big Five economies:

(a) The dispersion of GDP growth, the output gap and unemployment generally diminished in the years preceding the 2008-2012 financial crisis, increased during and in the immediate aftermath of this crisis, then mostly edged down from 2014 to 2019, significantly increased in 2020 but subsided again in 2021-2022. The dispersion of the government deficit ratio followed a path of its own, remaining at comparatively moderate levels prior to 2008, increasing notably in the 2008-2012 period, crawling within a band of 2 to 2.4 between 2013 and 2019 and moving out of this band again in 2020 and 2022.

(b) In the 2020-2021 crisis years, the dispersion of GDP growth and the output gap exceeded the 2011-2012 peak levels, and that of unemployment and the government deficit ratio remained below 2011-2012 levels (notably so in the case of unemployment).

(c) But, significantly, by the end of 2022, the degree of dispersion of all five indicators stood at higher levels than in 2002 or 2007-2008.

143. The evidence is mixed when one looks at **financial cycles**, *i.e.*, in shorthand, boom-bust cycles of credit and asset prices. Looking at a data set stretching to 2015 Q1, one study found that, in the euro area, synchronicity of financial cycles has tended overall to be lower, and their cyclical amplitude higher, than for business cycles, and that these differences have widened since the introduction of the euro, with significant heterogeneity between "higher-amplitude" Member States (like Greece, Ireland and

Spain) and "lower-amplitude" Member States (including France and especially Germany).[117]

144. Another study looked at longer-term slower-moving GDP fluctuations related to the build-up and correction of macroeconomic imbalances in price competitiveness, current accounts and budget deficits. Using a 1970-2016 data set for the original euro area Member States (except Luxembourg), this study concluded that those longer-term fluctuations were larger and less symmetric (notably in terms of amplitude) than business cycle fluctuations. It also found that the difference had increased over time, particularly in the case of Ireland, Greece, Portugal and Spain, driven primarily by financial variables like credit and housing prices.[118]

145. Finally, the momentum of structural reforms has been uneven among euro area Member States and generally insufficient, as reflected, *inter alia*, in the uneven compliance with country-specific recommendations under SGP, as we will discuss in Chapter 8 (*see* paragraph 604 below).

2 AN INCOMPLETE MONETARY UNION

146. The European currency union did not start out as an optimum currency area and the evidence on subsequent convergence is mixed, as we have seen in previous sections:

(a) Business cycles have become broadly synchronous and movements in key macroeconomic variables are more aligned directionally—a most helpful factor. But there is much less convergence in the amplitude of cyclical fluctuations.
(b) There is no clear evidence of significant convergence of GDP *per capita*, and the gap between the most and the least productive Member States appears to have stagnated or even widened somewhat over the past decade.
(c) Unemployment rates continue to diverge significantly among euro area Member States, with consistently higher levels of unemployment and particularly youth unemployment in certain Southern Member States.
(d) The data reviewed offer no compelling evidence that currency union membership significantly accelerated trade integration within its geographic perimeter.
(e) Among the more worrisome facts are the high levels and high degree of divergence of government debt ratios in recent years and the subdued level of government investments during much of the previous decade.

117. *See* W. Oman, "The Synchronization of Business Cycles and Financial Cycles in the Euro Area", *International Journal of Central Banking*, Vol. 15, 2019, pp. 327-362. In similar vein, *see* J. Franks, B. Bergljot *et al.*, *supra*, pp. 15-17 and 34-38.
118. *See* J.P.C. Hessel, *Financial Factors in the Economic and Monetary Union*, University of Groningen, 2020, pp. 57-106.

147. Of course, much depends on what question is asked. The currency union appears to have contributed to relative stability over a period of intermittent high turbulence. It weathered the 2008-2009 banking crisis, the 2010-2012 sovereign debt crisis, the 2015 near exit of Greece, COVID-19 and, so far, the economic and geopolitical fall-out of a large-scale military conflict on the European continent. One need only imagine, counterfactually, what tensions, conflicts and instability these successive crises would have produced if the Member States had still been operating a snake-type exchange rate system or some looser system of managed currency floating.

148. The currency union's history thus far has not been without significant plot twists:

(a) The tranquil first decade masked fiscal consolidation fatigue, growing macroeconomic imbalances in certain euro area Member States and the build-up of asset bubbles.
(b) In the wake of the 2008-2009 banking crisis, diverging fiscal positions of euro area Member States caused a widening of sovereign bond spreads and, in the event, destabilizing market dynamics and severe fragmentation risk by 2012.
(c) Subsequently, stubbornly low inflation led to an extended period of monetary easing, with monetary policy rates "at the lower bound" and generous quantitative easing, weakening incentives for structural reforms.
(d) With the advent of COVID-19 in the early months of 2020, the ECB maintained and stepped up monetary easing, creating fiscal space for increased public spending in response to the pandemic. Government debt levels increased sharply in 2020, reversing a downward trend in prior years.
(e) When prices started rising in the second half of 2021, the ECB for a good while considered this as a "temporary bump" in the longer-term trend decline in inflation, due to supply-chain disturbances and pent-up demand in the wake of COVID-19. However, toward the end of that year, the tail effects of COVID-19, rising energy prices (Russia had already been throttling gas deliveries to Europe in the fall of 2021) and, a few months later, the Ukraine conflict further fueled a sharp increase in inflation in 2022.

149. The combination of supply-chain disturbances and energy and commodity shocks of those days caused or precipitated a return of inflation, at levels unseen in the history of the European currency union, and adversely affected growth, giving rise to a policy trade-off between price stability and output. This put an end to the prior directional alignment of monetary and fiscal policies: it called for more resolute monetary tightening, alongside appropriate fiscal stimulus to moderate recessionary risks and repair growth. The difficulty is compounded by the asymmetric effects of supply-chain disturbances and energy and commodity shocks across euro area Member States, given differences in the sectoral composition of their economies and in their dependency on imported energy and commodities. Continued fiscal stimulus to different degrees, in conjunction with higher government borrowing costs as a result of monetary tightening, should make the high levels and the geographic dispersion of government debt ratios "stickier". In this changed economic environment, few

Member States may be able, or politically inclined, to exercise adequate fiscal restraint in order to bring their debt ratio down. But high debt ratios can no longer be artificially sustained by an accommodative monetary policy with very low policy rates and generous quantitative easing. The situation presents a latent risk of financial fragmentation, with excessive widening of sovereign bond spreads and, in an adverse scenario, destabilizing market dynamics.

150. The school of economists believing in a long-term trend decline of inflation has not entirely signed out. Surviving adherents may well argue that, at least in Europe, recent inflation is in large measure cost-driven, that cost inflation affects economic sectors differently and with different time lags and, accordingly, will take some time to cascade through the economy and then dissipate again, but that such a drawn-out sequence of cost shocks should not be (mis)taken for a trend increase in underlying inflation. Point taken. But the return of inflation may well prove to be more structural and more lasting than believed (or hoped) by that school of thought (and in the initial official messaging of the ECB and other central banks). This concern is based, *inter alia*, on the following factors:

(a) more volatile and episodically higher energy prices due to political uncertainties and supply-side constraints, including geopolitical tensions, "weaponization" of oil and gas supplies, the perils for crude oil transports in the Strait of Hormuz and the Red Sea, historic underinvestment in oil and gas production capacity and in energy transmission infrastructure, and lagging investment in renewable energy sources;
(b) increased "nearshoring" or "friend-shoring" of supply chains to geographically closer locations with higher wage levels;
(c) increased production costs to meet progressively stricter environmental standards;
(d) more generally, the financing of large-scale public and private investments needed for the green transition and the containment of climate change disruptions; and
(e) unfavorable demographics causing a shrinking of the labor force (the lower birth rates of generations X and Y) and the need to redirect more resources to healthcare and care of the elderly.

151. Higher inflation over a longer time span and possible market dislocations associated with the green transition and climate change should further complicate the euro area's fiscal equations and exacerbate the ECB's monetary policy dilemmas. This should lend urgency to fresh thinking on more effective strategies for risk containment and risk sharing, also in political quarters. The European currency union's checkered history so far reveals the missing elements in its architecture. Back to basics. For a currency union between countries retaining fiscal sovereignty to function properly over time, it needs fiscal rules of the game that achieve a workable mix of risk containment and risk sharing so as to unburden monetary policy and allow it to focus on price stability. Risk containment requires a credible fiscal framework that incentivizes member countries to conduct responsible fiscal policies, keep their debt sustainable and implement structural reforms to address weaknesses in productivity and competitiveness, while also achieving a proper measure of complementarity in the allocation of the burden of adjustment as between deficit and surplus countries. Risk sharing requires some centralized or pooled financial capacity offering stabilization support to help countries overcome asymmetric cyclical fluctuations or external shocks and to bridge imbalances pending structural reforms. Cross-country risk sharing also increases "skin in the game" for all members and diminishes the probability of some partial or total break-up of the currency union.

On both those dimensions—risk containment and risk sharing—the architecture of the European currency union remains incomplete. The question is how, from where we are standing now, it could realistically be completed.

CHAPTER 3

The ECB's Monetary Policy Mandate

152. At tense moments in the brief history of the European currency union, ECB leadership came forward to reassure the financial markets by saying that the ECB *"is ready to do whatever it takes to preserve the euro"*, as Mario Draghi famously did at the Global Investment Conference in London on July 26, 2012. Or that the ECB's commitment to the euro *"has no limits"*, as, almost 10 years later to the day, Isabel Schnabel said in a commencement speech at the Panthéon-Sorbonne University on June 14, 2022.[119] It may be expedient and perhaps even necessary to make statements of this kind from time to time when tensions run high. But an undesirable side effect is that they may further comfort financial markets and politicians in the belief and indeed expectation that the ECB will eventually step in and be able to fix the problem. Overreliance on the capability of monetary policy to keep the economy on a steady course and avert cracks in the currency union may encourage political inaction bias on difficult reforms (which generally needs little encouragement). Yet, monetary policy alone cannot bridge the gap between short-term voter gratification and longer-term prosperity. And, in legal terms, the ECB's ability to act is inexorably limited by the scope of its mandate. This may get lost in translation (although Mario Draghi prefaced his July 26, 2012 message by saying, not once but twice, *"[w]ithin our mandate"*). The ESCB (Eurosystem), with at its core the ECB, has no other powers than those conferred upon it by or pursuant to the Treaties. The ECB can create money out of nothing, *ex nihilo*, but it cannot create additional powers for itself. At least, this is the theory. As we will see, it has been stretched somewhat by the ECB, with the benevolent approval of the European Court of Justice.

---

119. I. Schnabel, "United in diversity – Challenges for monetary policy in a currency union", Commencement speech to the graduates of the Master Program in Money, Banking, Finance and Insurance of the Panthéon-Sorbonne University, Paris, June 14, 2022, https://www.ecb.europa.eu/press/key/date/2022/html/ecb.sp220614~67eda62c44.en.html, at p. 3.

1 THE TREATY MATRIX

a Monetary Policy (Not) Defined

153. The Treaty's rules on the monetary policy mandate are somewhat fuzzy and multi-directional. The core provisions include the following:

(a) The Treaty confers the exclusive competence of monetary policy for the euro area upon the European Union (Article 3(1)(c) TFEU),[120] acting through the ECB and the national central banks of the euro area Member States which, together, constitute the Eurosystem (as a reduced format of the ESCB) (Article 282(1) TFEU).[121]

(b) The Treaty offers no clear definition of monetary policy. It merely refers to a *"single"* monetary policy for the euro area (Article 119(2) TFEU) and, importantly, provides that its *"primary objective"* is to *"maintain price stability"* (Articles 119(2), 127(1), 219(2) and 282(2) TFEU). But the Treaty does not further define what maintaining price stability means. Also, it is the *"primary"*, not the exclusive objective. This then begs the question of what nuance the drafters of these Treaty provisions may have sought to convey with the choice of the word *"primary"*: the main or **principal** objective (*"objectif principal"*, *"obiettivo principale"* or *"hoofddoel"*, as, respectively, in the French, Italian and Dutch versions) or the **controlling** objective (as suggested by *"vorrangige Ziel"* in the German version)?

(c) Protocol (No 4) on the Statute of the European System of Central Banks and of the European Central Bank ("Protocol No 4") contains an open-ended list of policy tools that may be used in the conduct of monetary policy, *i.e.*, open-market and credit operations (Article 18), minimum reserve requirements for banks (Article 19) and *"such other operational methods of monetary control"* as the ECB's Governing Council may approve by majority of two-thirds of the votes cast (Article 20). To what extent does the objective determine or justify the means?

---

120. It should be noted that the exclusivity of a Union competence does not necessarily bar Member State action, but, in such a subject area, Member States may act only insofar as empowered by the Union or for the implementation of Union acts (Article 2(1) TFEU).

121. As noted in the Introduction, this book frequently and almost routinely refers to the monetary policy mandate of the ECB, but this is somewhat of a shortcut. Formally, monetary policy is conducted by the ECB together with the national central banks of the Member States whose currency is the euro, which jointly constitute the Eurosystem, as a reduced format of the European System of Central Banks ("ESCB"). But monetary policy is effectively formulated and directed by the ECB acting through its Governing Council (which consists of the six members of its Executive Board and the governors of the euro area central banks).

Perhaps somewhat confusingly, Article 127(2) TFEU includes the definition and implementation of monetary policy among the basic tasks to be carried out through the ESCB. But Article 139(2)(c) TFEU then says that these provisions do not apply to Member States that have not adopted the euro, and Article 139(3) specifies that the central banks of these Member States are *"excluded from rights and obligations within the ESCB"*.

154. It is sometimes said that EU primary law defines the ESCB's monetary policy mandate by its (primary) objective, tasks and policy instruments. This is an overstatement:

(a) Curiously, the exclusive competence of monetary policy is defined by a "primary", *i.e.*, non-exclusive, objective, and, as we will see, is assigned additional, secondary objectives in relation to other policy areas (*see* paragraph 156 below).
(b) The primary objective of monetary policy, *i.e.*, to maintain price stability, is stated in these broad terms and not otherwise clarified in primary law. In and of itself, such a broadly-worded (non-exclusive) objective does not offer clear and precise guidance as to the substantive scope of that competence.
(c) Elsewhere, the Treaty refers to a *"single"* monetary policy (Article 119(2) TFEU), but this is at best a constraint and does not say anything of substance on what monetary policy is.
(d) The basic tasks of the ESCB are said to include the task *"to define and implement the monetary policy of the Union"* (Article 127(2) TFEU and Article 3.1 of Protocol No 4), but this does not add anything substantively either.
(e) Monetary policy instruments broadly include open market and credit operations (Article 18 of Protocol No 4) and reserve requirements for banks (Article 19). But, as said, Article 20 of Protocol No 4 then adds that the ECB's Governing Council may, by a two-thirds majority, *"decide upon the use of such other operational methods of monetary control as it sees fit"*. This makes the monetary policy toolbox open-ended and, in fact, dependent on an assessment by the very authority vested with the monetary policy mandate as to what this mandate may require.
(f) And the prohibition of monetary financing (Article 123 TFEU) is a constraint, not a definitional element. It merely excludes a particular activity from the permissible scope of the monetary policy mandate.

155. Accordingly, the only real definitional element of monetary policy proffered by EU primary law is an otherwise undefined primary objective of maintaining price stability. The drafters of the relevant Treaty provisions may have assumed that monetary policy is a concept that has a generally accepted and sufficiently precise meaning that is well understood by all. At an elevated level of abstraction, monetary policy could broadly be defined as the set of policy actions that seek to influence or steer the cost and availability of money in the economy. But a simple Google search reveals the multiple variations in official and scholarly definitions that attempt to translate this high-level concept into more operational language. As we will see, the lack of a precise definition may be a source of difficulty when assessing whether particular actions are within the compass of the ESCB's monetary policy mandate and when delineating the respective spheres of the single monetary policy and national economic and fiscal policies.

b Secondary Objectives

156. Things are not made easier by the fact that the Treaty also assigns several secondary objectives to the ESCB or to the ECB specifically:

(a) One such secondary objective, but subordinate (*"[w]ithout prejudice"*) to the primary objective of maintaining price stability, is that the ESCB must *"support the general economic policies in the Union with a view to contributing to the achievement of the objectives of the Union as laid down in Article 3 of the Treaty on European Union"* (Article 127(1) TFEU).[122] This is phrased as an actual obligation (*"shall"*), but the term *"support"* denotes that in these matters the ESCB is not expected to pursue policy objectives or choices of its own but to act in a supporting role, in a play to be written and directed by the competent EU and national authorities. Here, the ESCB is a policy **taker** rather than a policy **maker**.

(b) As another secondary objective, the ESCB must (*"shall"*) also *"contribute"* to the smooth conduct of policies *"pursued by the competent authorities"* regarding banking supervision and *"the stability of the financial system"* (Article 127(5) TFEU). Again, this wording suggests a supporting role for the ESCB rather than an autonomous responsibility or competence to define policy or initiate policy actions.

Here, the Treaty does not expressly subordinate the ESCB's contributory role to banking supervisory and financial stability policies to the primary price stability objective of monetary policy. This could be drafting oversight. But it is also possible and indeed more likely that the authors of these Treaty provisions saw this contributory role as something distinct from the ESCB's monetary policy mandate, with monetary policy proper always being chained to a primary price stability objective. Yet, the two may interact and even conflict, as we will discuss in Chapter 6 (*see* paragraphs 418-440 below).

(c) Still in the prudential area, the Council may confer *"specific tasks"* upon the ECB concerning policies relating to the prudential supervision of financial institutions (other than insurance companies) (Article 127(6) TFEU). The Council has done so by Council Regulation (EU) No 1024/2013 of October 15, 2013, which has assigned certain banking supervisory and macroprudential tasks to the ECB in the framework of the Single Supervisory Mechanism ("SSM").[123]

---

122. In the economic sphere, Article 3(3) TEU lists an idyllic set of objectives such as balanced economic growth and price stability, a highly competitive social market economy aiming at full employment and social progress, a high level of protection and improvement of the environment, and the promotion of scientific and technological advance.

123. Council Regulation (EU) No 1024/2013 of October 15, 2013 conferring specific tasks on the European Central Bank concerning policies relating to the prudential supervision of credit institutions, *OJ* L287, October 29, 2013, p. 63, in particular Articles 4 and 5.

Again, the Treaty does not expressly establish a hierarchy between these tasks and monetary policy. Council Regulation 1024/2013 envisages, perhaps somewhat blissfully, that the ECB should carry out its monetary policy and banking supervisory tasks *"in full separation, in order to avoid conflicts of interest and to ensure that each function is exercised in accordance with the applicable objectives"*.[124] The banking supervisory tasks must be exercised *"without prejudice to and separately from"* the monetary policy tasks and must *"neither interfere with, nor be determined by"* these tasks.[125] Within the ECB, a Chinese wall of sorts is placed between the two functions: (i) a separate internal body, the Supervisory Board, is responsible for the planning and execution of the banking supervisory tasks;[126] (ii) the relevant staff is organizationally separated and subject to separate reporting lines;[127] and (iii) the Governing Council must consider monetary and bank supervisory matters at separate meetings with separate agendas.[128] Curiously, a "Mediations Panel", composed of one member per participating Member State appointed from among the members of the Governing Council and the Supervisory Board, is called upon to resolve, *"in a balanced way, in the interest of the Union as a whole"*, differences of view expressed by competent national authorities in circumstances where the Governing Council objects to a draft decision of the Supervisory Board notably on the ground of monetary policy concerns.[129]

c Specific and General Constraints

157. Additionally, the Treaty subjects the ECB's monetary policy mandate to a number of specific and general constraints:

(a) Under the prohibition of monetary financing, the ECB and national central banks must refrain from extending any credit to, or directly subscribing to any debt securities issued by, an EU institution or a Member State's government sector (Article 123 TFEU). This prohibition is further clarified in Council Regulation (EC) No 3603/93.[130] It is intended to promote sound fiscal policies by keeping governments subject to financial market discipline.

124. Recital (65) to the same Regulation.
125. Article 25(2), first paragraph, of the same Regulation.
126. Article 26 of the same Regulation.
127. Article 25(2), second paragraph, of the same Regulation.
128. Article 25(4) of the same Regulation.
129. Recital (73) and Articles 25(5) and 26(8) of the same Regulation. *See also* Regulation (EU) No 673/2014 of the European Central Bank of June 2, 2014 concerning the establishment of a Mediation Panel and its Rules of Procedure, *OJ* L179, June 19, 2014, p. 72.
130. Council Regulation (EC) No 3603/93 of December 13, 1993 specifying definitions for the application of the prohibitions referred to in Articles 104 and 104b(1) of the Treaty, *OJ* L332, December 31, 1993, p. 1.

(b) The ECB must (*"shall"*) act in accordance with the open market economy principle for the allocation of resources and comply with the other principles set forth in Article 119 TFEU (Article 127(1), *in fine*, TFEU). These *"guiding principles"* include stable prices, sound public finances and monetary conditions, and a sustainable balance of payments (Article 119(3) TFEU).

(c) As is the case for all EU policies and activities, the definition and implementation of monetary policy must *"take into account"* requirements linked to the promotion of a high level of employment (Article 9 TFEU) as well as integrate environmental protection requirements (Article 11 TFEU).

(d) Finally, like other EU institutions, the ECB must in its decision-making observe the principle of proportionality (Article 5(1) and (4) TEU), consistency with other EU policies and actions (Article 7 TFEU) and transparency (Article 15 TFEU). Its legal acts must contain an adequate statement of reasons (Article 296, second paragraph, TFEU).

d Exchange Rate Policy

158. A shared currency requires a single monetary policy for the currency zone but also a single exchange rate policy regarding the currency's external value relationships with other currencies. Like the single monetary policy, the Treaty gears the single exchange rate policy to the "primary" objective of maintaining price stability (Articles 119(2) and 219(1) and (2) TFEU). Competences in matters of exchange rate policy are divided between the ESCB (Eurosystem) and the Council. The ESCB conducts the actual foreign-exchange and other external operations (Article 127(2) TFEU and Article 23 of Protocol No 4) but must do so in a manner consistent with any formal exchange rate agreements which the Council may have concluded with non-euro area States or, absent such arrangements, with *"general orientations"* which the Council may have formulated for exchange rate policy in respect of other currencies (Article 219(1) and (2) TFEU).[131]

Leaving aside ERM II (*see* paragraph 46 above), no formal exchange rate agreement linking the euro and other currencies is currently in place, and the Council has not thus far issued any general orientations in matters of exchange rate policy, which leaves the ECB/Eurosystem a relatively free hand.

159. So far, the ECB does not appear to have pursued a particularly active exchange rate policy. It has not engaged in any significant interventions in the foreign exchange markets except in September and November 2000 in relation to the U.S. dollar and the Japanese yen (for an aggregate amount of EUR 10.21 billion) and in March 2011 in

131. For a more detailed discussion of this division of competences, *see* A. Thiele, "Foreign-Exchange Operations of the ECB and Exchange-Rate Policy", in *The EU Law of Economic and Monetary Union* (F. Amtenbrink & Chr. Herrmann eds.), Oxford University Press, 2020, pp. 699-710, §§23.1-23.22.

relation to the yen (for EUR 700 million).[132] The ECB does not seem to actively target any particular level or zone for the euro exchange rate against other major currencies.

In a series of tweets over the summer of 2019, former U.S. President Donald Trump effectively accused the ECB of manipulating the EUR/USD exchange rate (then in a range of about 1.10 to 1.13). Thus, on September 12, 2019, he tweeted: *"European Central Bank, acting quickly, Cuts Rates 10 Basis Points. They are trying, and succeeding, in depreciating the Euro against the VERY strong Dollar, hurting U.S. exports ... And the Fed sits, and sits, and sits [...]"*. Instants later, at the ECB press briefing, Mario Draghi responded that *"we preserve price stability and we don't target exchange rates, period"*.[133] When the euro dropped below parity with the U.S. dollar between August and October 2022 (for the first time since November 2002), this apparently did not cause great anxiety at the ECB Governing Council's monetary policy meetings of July 20-21, September 7-8 and October 26-27, 2022. In the published minutes of these meetings, it is noted, almost in passing, that the euro's depreciation against the U.S. dollar could or would increase inflationary pressures in particular through the higher cost of dollar-invoiced oil and other commodity imports,[134] but there was no call for or even mention of any foreign exchange interventions.

160. This appears to confirm that the euro's exchange rate is not, in the ordinary course, viewed as a direct policy target but primarily as a variable in the ECB's monetary policy equation aimed at inflation control—and one that would not ordinarily be critical. It seems consistent with empirical evidence of generally low exchange rate pass-through ("ERPT") to headline inflation in the euro area, although there are also some indications that ERPT may be non-linear and higher for larger exchange rate changes (*see* paragraph 137 above). It also suggests that foreign exchange interventions would be considered only exceptionally to deal with disorderly movements.

2 NAVIGATING THE MATRIX

161. Thus, the Treaty lays out a rather diffuse matrix of objectives and constraints that the ECB has to navigate, with significant potential for gray areas, trade-offs and conflicts. Its multidimensional matrix may seem a bit at odds with the "Tinbergen Rule", *i.e.*, the rule of thumb for effective policy according to which *n* independent

132. *See ECB foreign exchange interventions*, https://www.ecb.europa.eu/stats/balance_of_payments_and_external/international_reserves/fx_interventions/html/index.en.html. Since May 2020, the ECB publishes quarterly data on its foreign exchange interventions.

133. *See* the transcript of the ECB's press conference of September 12, 2019, https://www.ecb.europa.eu/press/pressconf/2019/html/ecb.is190912~658eb51d68.en.html, at p. 6. Mr. Trump's tweet was in response to the ECB's announcement of the same day that it lowered its deposit facility rate from –0.40% to –0.50%.

134. *See* the published accounts of the ECB Governing Council's monetary policy meetings of July 20-21, 2022, https://www.ecb.europa.eu/press/accounts/2022/html/ecb.mg220825~162cfabae9.en.html, at p. 9, September 7-8, 2022, https://www.ecb.europa.eu/press/accounts/2022/html/ecb.mg221006~5f7fb03f3.en.html, at pp. 9 and 13, and October 26-27, 2022, https://www.ecb.europa.eu/press/accounts/2022/html/ecb.mg221124~3527764024.en.html, at pp. 2-3.

policy instruments are required to successfully achieve n independent policy targets. The implication would be that each policy instrument should be paired with one policy objective—specifically, the policy objective which it is most effective to influence. But it would appear that the Tinbergen Rule was not uppermost in the minds of the drafters of the relevant Treaty provisions.

162. The drafters of treaties and constitutions tend to write in solemn language about aspirational objectives and exalted principles. It is hard for them to resist the temptation of formulating elevated principles that aspire to an Arcadian world of harmony. Accordingly, the tablets with which the authors of the Treaty descended from their hilltop do not necessarily provide much workable guidance for a monetary authority operating in a complex economic environment. There is little point in submitting those provisions to learned textual exegesis in an attempt to extract detailed guidance from them. They must not be read with excessive reverence for their every word but rather interpreted *potius ut valeat*—in such a manner that they make good sense in relation to what the Treaty seeks to achieve. But generally-worded provisions stating high-level principles lend themselves to opportunistic reading, and this is always a risk.

163. As said, maintaining price stability is the primary objective of the single monetary policy, but **what is "price stability"**? In the absence of a Treaty definition, the ECB has taken it upon itself to define this core element of its own mandate in reference to a symmetric numerical inflation target of 2 % to be achieved over an otherwise undefined and flexible medium-term horizon (*see* paragraphs 172-186 below). In its 2018 judgment in *Weiss*, the Court of Justice of the European Union ("CJEU") ruled, in essence, that this definition does not go beyond the Treaty framework and *"does not appear"* to be flawed by any *"manifest error of assessment"*[135] (*see also* paragraphs 186 and 512 below). Here, the CJEU seemingly applies a judicial standard of marginal review to an EU institution's own definition of the core object of its conferred power—or, in agency terms, to the agent's own interpretation of the very object of its agency.

164. But then the follow-up question is: **what can or must the ECB do to "maintain price stability"**? Since the Treaty does not otherwise define monetary policy and since, under Protocol No 4, the ECB's toolkit is open-ended (*see* paragraphs 153(c) and 154(e) above), how does that—primary but not exclusive—objective determine and limit the actual scope of the ECB's powers for the conduct of monetary policy? To what extent does the end justify the means? To take an extreme example for the sake of argument: could the ECB expand its toolbox to include the imposition of price caps on certain goods or services in the interest of inflation control? Intuitively, few would agree that it could do so, but why not exactly? The objective fits the test. As to the instrument, would a measure of this kind clearly disqualify it as an *"other operational method of monetary control"* within the meaning of Article 20 of Protocol No 4?[136] Or should these

135. CJEU, December 11, 2018, Case C-493/17, *Weiss et al.*, ECLI:EU:C:2018:1000, §56.
136. I may note that, while the French and Italian language versions of Article 20 of Protocol No 4 use an equivalent expression (*"autres méthodes opérationnelles de contrôle monétaire"*, *"altri*

terms be understood to refer only to instruments that operate directly on the cost or supply of money and credit?

165. Let us consider a more realistic example. As we will discuss in Chapter 5, the ECB has engaged in geographically selective secondary market purchases of sovereign bonds to contain excessive widening of sovereign bond spreads within the euro area on the ground that the attendant "financial fragmentation" unduly interferes with the effective pass-through of the monetary policy stance across the euro area (but also, in reality, out of concern that it may threaten the cohesion of the currency union). In its 2015 *Gauweiler* judgment, the CJEU benevolently concluded that actions directed at preserving or restoring the effectiveness of the monetary policy transmission process in the euro area or parts of the euro area can be attached to the Treaty's price stability objective and, accordingly, fall within the compass of the ECB's monetary policy mandate[137] (*see also* paragraphs 344-345, 386-387 and 516-517 below).

Does this jurisprudence tacitly recognize an implied power of the ECB that is derived from its Treaty-conferred price stability mandate and is deemed indispensable for the conferred mandate to be exercised effectively and usefully? But wouldn't such an implied power sit uneasily with the principle of conferral (Article 5(1) and (2) TEU) and weaken its constraining effect? And, absent more precise criteria, wouldn't the CJEU's reasoning make the boundaries of the ECB's monetary policy mandate particularly fluid? There are a good many "bugs" that may slow down, amplify or otherwise interfere with the pass-through of monetary policy through its various transmission channels and sub-channels. For example, country differences in downward wage rigidity may weaken the effective transmission of monetary tightening, but I haven't heard or read anyone suggesting that the ECB could somehow take action to induce greater wage flexibility, subject a monetary policy measure to a condition of that kind, or geographically differentiate monetary policy action according to country differences in wage rigidity. Again, where does one draw the line and on the basis of what criterion exactly?

166. It raises a further question as to the extent to which ECB monetary policy actions can **make incursions into, or produce lateral effects in, other policy areas** that are within the remit of the Member States or other EU institutions. In *Gauweiler* and *Weiss*, the CJEU considered, in essence, that, so long as a measure is principally directed at maintaining price stability (or, to this effect, at preserving the monetary policy transmission mechanism), it falls within the ECB's monetary policy mandate, even if it produces indirect effects in the economic policy sphere (such as protecting the cohesion of the currency union or maintaining viable financing conditions for euro area Member States with higher government debt) and even if those effects are foreseen and knowingly accepted[138] (*see also* paragraphs 388, 523-524, 527(c) and 528(b) below). But how clear, operational and verifiable is the dividing line between a knowingly

metodi operativi di controllo monetario"), the German language version uses a term with a slightly different flavor ("*andere Instrumente der Geldpolitik*").

137. CJEU, June 16, 2015, Case C-62/14, *Gauweiler et al.*, ECLI:EU:C:2015:400, §§48-50.

138. *Gauweiler*, §59, and *Weiss*, §§61-67.

accepted lateral consequence of a monetary policy measure and what effectively becomes a concurrent objective of such a measure? Curiously, in *Weiss*, the CJEU added that *"the authors of the Treaties did not intend to make an absolute separation between economic and monetary policies"*.[139]

In those judgments, technically, the CJEU only addressed the question of whether such cross-over effects in other policy areas would take the ECB's action outside the scope of its monetary policy mandate—and not the question of how possible conflicts with Member States' economic or fiscal policies should be resolved. But one would be inclined to read between the lines that the ECB's monetary policy action and its cross-over effects would stand. Questions remain, however. For example, what about cross-over effects on matters governed by rules or measures under the EMU fiscal or macroeconomic surveillance frameworks? Would the consistency requirement of Article 7 TFEU then place a constraint on cross-over effects that the ECB may knowingly accept in the design of its monetary policy actions?

167. Yet another question is how the ECB must deal with **trade-offs between its primary and secondary objectives**—between monetary policy primarily targeted at maintaining price stability and the EU and national policies which the ECB is supposed to "support", or to which it is supposed to "contribute", under Article 127(1) or (5) TFEU (*see* paragraph 156 above). What to do when a supply-side shock (*e.g.*, some disruption in energy supplies or prices) increases inflation but decreases output and employment? To what extent can the ECB then go easier on inflation control to avoid further depressing economic activity and possibly counteracting fiscal stimulus by Member States? Conversely, if low inflation calls for monetary easing, what is the ECB's margin for "leaning against the wind" by increasing policy rates to counter the build-up of asset bubbles in the interest of preserving financial stability? How much, and in what manner, could or should the ECB modulate its monetary policy actions, in relation to their optimal form and intensity for pursuing its inflation target, in order to support, or at least to minimize adverse effects on, those secondary policy objectives? In weighing different options that all contribute to varying degrees to price stability, must the ECB always choose the option that contributes most to price stability? Or should it be allowed or required, under the relevant Treaty provisions (particularly Article 129 TFEU) and/or the proportionality principle, to choose an imperfect option that mitigates adverse side effects in other policy areas?

168. On the occasion of its 2021 monetary policy strategy review, the ECB observed that, when looking at the Treaty's other (secondary) objectives, it will consider the relevance of these considerations for its (primary) price stability objective as well as its ability to support those other objectives. It added, by way of example, that *"when adjusting its monetary policy instruments, the Governing Council will—provided that two configurations of the instrument set are* ***equally conducive*** *and not prejudicial to price stability—choose the configuration that best supports"* the secondary objectives

139. *Weiss*, §60.

(emphasis added).[140] This suggests that the margin for supporting other policy objectives is limited by a *ceteris paribus* constraint in relation to the price stability objective. But this is nuanced further down on the page (*see* paragraph 183 below), and rigorous priority to inflation control has not always been in evidence in the ECB's actual conduct of monetary policy, as we will see.

169. One would think that, in a proper proportionality assessment, the ECB would first consider the necessity and the suitability or efficacy of particular monetary policy action toward the price stability objective, and then, within any remaining room for maneuvering, choose, design and calibrate the monetary policy instrument(s) in a way that is most supportive to other policy objectives or at least avoids or minimizes adverse side effects in other policy areas—but, in the ECB's words, *"without compromising price stability"*.[141] Yet it remains nebulous terrain. There are many shades of gray between "not compromising" and "optimizing". And to what extent should the containment of adverse effects in other policy areas moderate monetary policy action in relation to its optimal stance for maintaining price stability, if the avoidance or moderation of those effects is properly in the realm of policies within the Member States' competence and the competent authorities have been remiss in taking such action? Does supporting the policies of other competent authorities extend to filling gaps left by inadequate action of these other authorities?

170. We will revisit these and other navigation issues in subsequent chapters, particularly in Chapters 5 and 6. In essence, they all revolve around the degrees of freedom that should be allowed to the ECB in the pursuit of its primary inflation control objective to accommodate other policy concerns. At first blush, the Treaty's multidimensional matrix of objectives and constraints may seem difficult to navigate. But at the same time, the relatively low resolution of the relevant Treaty provisions, on the one hand, and the technical complexity and inherent uncertainties of monetary policy, on the other hand, have in fact offered the ECB considerable leg room. The ECB has created policy space notably by allowing itself a medium-term horizon of unspecified length for maintaining price stability (*see* paragraphs 182-183 below) which affords some time for balancing competing considerations. And in its jurisprudence, principally its *Gauweiler* and *Weiss* judgments, the CJEU has adopted an accommodative or, if you wish, "dovish" reading of the Treaty provisions that allow the ECB significant leeway in the interpretation of the price stability objective, the choice of policy instruments and possible cross-over effects in other policy areas, as we will discuss more fully in Chapter 7 (*see* paragraphs 511-545 below).

171. If all of this is difficult to assess for a central bank with the aid of an abundance of data, and specialized staff and sophisticated models to dissect them, the reader should put herself in the shoes of a judge at the CJEU. The relative lack of black-letter rules in the Treaty and the inherent complexities and uncertainties of the subject matter

140. ECB, *An overview of the ECB's monetary policy strategy*, July 2021, p. 11, https://www.ecb.europa.eu/home/search/review/pdf/ecb.strategyreview_monpol_strategy_overview.en.pdf.
141. *Ibid.*, p. 9.

have led the Court in effect to apply a judicial standard of marginal review to monetary policy actions, including even to issues of competence—to questions as to whether particular policy actions fall within the compass of the ECB's monetary policy mandate. How can the Court effectively control whether or not the ECB has made an error of assessment (manifest or not), or failed its duty of care, without some measure of substantive review of the ECB's underlying analysis? And how could its judges, not schooled in the finer points of monetary theory, confidently identify an error made by the ECB—unless it were so egregious that the ECB would never make it?

And so it was that, in his June 18, 2019 introductory speech at the ECB Forum of Central Banking in Sintra (Portugal), Mario Draghi took a moment to observe that the CJEU has confirmed *"the flexibility embedded in our mandate"* and *"emphasised the broad discretion of the ECB in using all our tools in a necessary and proportionate way to achieve our objective"*.[142]

3 PRICE STABILITY DEFINED

172. Let us now look more closely at how the ECB has articulated its primary objective of maintaining price stability in the formulation of its monetary policy strategy, particularly in its latest monetary policy strategy review of July 2021, which reflects a long stretch on the learning curve since its prior strategy review of 2003.

a A Numerical Inflation Target

173. Price stability could be defined in many ways. Under a common-sense definition, also espoused by the ECB, it can be described in qualitative terms as *"a state in which changes in the general level of prices need not be factored into consumption and investment decisions"*.[143] This echoes the definition given by former Federal Reserve Chairman Alan Greenspan, *i.e.*, *"an environment in which inflation is so low and stable over time that it does not materially enter into the decisions of households and firms"*.[144] This definition has two components, *i.e.*, (i) inflation must be sufficiently low, and (ii) the markets must be reasonably confident that it will remain so over a long enough planning horizon. Monetary policy will have to keep inflation suitably low but also be attentive to keeping market expectations "anchored" in that sense.

174. On October 13, 1998, the ECB's Governing Council defined price stability as a *"year-on-year increase in the Harmonized Index of Consumer Prices (HICP) for the euro*

142. M. Draghi, "Twenty years of the ECB's monetary policy", *in* ECB Forum on Central Banking, June 17-19, 2019, *20 years of European Economic and Monetary Union*, Conference proceedings, p. 32.
143. ECB, *An overview of the ECB's monetary policy strategy*, July 2021, p. 6.
144. A. Greenspan, "Transparency in Monetary Policy", *Federal Reserve Bank of St. Louis Review*, July-August 2002, p. 6.

area of below 2%".[145] This may have suggested a certain indifference of the ECB to inflation rates between 0% and 2%, but on May 8, 2003, as part of its 2003 monetary policy strategy review, the ECB clarified that, within this range, it would aim at an inflation rate *"close to 2% over the medium term"*[146]—the long-time mantra "below but close to 2%". At the ECB press conference of the same day, in response to a question about whether this now implied a pure inflation target, Otmar Issing, the ECB's Chief Economist at that time, responded in the following terms:

> *"Certainly not. [...] This is totally different from what is normally seen as inflation targeting. [...] this 'close to 2%' is not a change, it is a clarification of what we have done so far, what we have achieved—namely inflation expectations remaining in a narrow range of between roughly 1.7% and 1.9%—and what we intend to do in our forward-looking monetary policy".*[147]

175. As part of its monetary policy strategy published on July 8, 2021,[148] the ECB replaced the double-key formulation of its inflation objective (inflation between 0% and 2% and, within this range, close to 2%) with a **straightforward numerical target of 2%**. In this revised definition, the target or benchmark level is marginally higher (2%) than the inflation aim defined in 2003 (below but close to 2%). The ECB considered that the prior double-key formulation may have created some ambiguity about the level of the inflation aim and especially about its (lack of) symmetry, by unduly suggesting stronger policy reactivity to inflation above target.[149]

176. Thus, the ECB has defined price stability as a numerical inflation target in positive territory (initially below but close to 2%, now simply 2%). It views this primarily as a "buffer" to safeguard an effective margin for monetary policy action in response to disinflationary shocks and to avoid policy rates then bumping against their effective lower bound. In this respect, it is more a benchmark than an actual target in the narrow sense. In its 2021 monetary policy strategy review, the ECB (still) considered that the need for such an inflation buffer was reinforced by the further trend decline in the equilibrium real rate of interest and the consequent reduction in the space for conventional policy rate changes in response to disinflationary shocks.[150] Other considerations supporting a positive margin include (i) inflation differences among euro area Member States; (ii) downward nominal wage rigidities; and (iii) a concern over possible positive measurement bias in HICP (implying that the "true" rate of inflation may be lower than the measured level).[151] Significantly, the 2% target or

145. *See* ECB, *A stability-oriented monetary policy strategy for the ESCB*, October 13, 1998, https://www.ecb.europa.eu/press/pr/date/1998/html/pr981013_1.en.html.
146. *See* ECB, *The ECB's monetary policy strategy*, May 8, 2003, https://www.ecb.europa.eu/press/pr/date/2003/html/pr030508_2.en.html.
147. *See* the transcript of the ECB's press "seminar" of May 8, 2003 "on the evaluation of the ECB's monetary policy strategy", https://www.ecb.europa.eu/press/pressconf/2003/html/is030508_1.en.html, at p. 1.
148. *See* ECB, *The ECB's monetary policy strategy statement*, https://ecb.europa.eu/home/search/review/pdf/ecb.strategyreview_monpol_strategy_statement.en.pdf.
149. ECB, *An overview of the ECB's monetary policy strategy*, July 2021, pp. 6-7.
150. *Ibid.*, pp. 2-3 and 6.
151. *Ibid.*, p. 7.

benchmark has always been presented as a buffer to guard against the risk of disinflationary shocks, *i.e.*, to preserve an effective margin for monetary policy action to respond to such shocks. It was not intended, or at least never presented, as an extra margin for monetary easing below 2 % when not needed for responding to disinflationary pressures.

177. The ECB has consistently formulated its inflation benchmark in reference to **headline inflation** as measured by Eurostat's Harmonized Index of Consumer Prices ("HICP").[152] Aside from HICP, the ECB also monitors certain measures of core inflation, among other reasons because volatile components like energy and food prices tend to cause noise in HICP.[153] Understandably, the ECB focuses in the first instance on headline inflation (HICP) insofar as core inflation indices may fail to capture price increases with significant impact on consumer budgets and spending. Yet, the ECB is attentive to core inflation too (and appears to have become more so over the years), especially when, as a result of prolonged or recurring increases in energy and/or food prices, headline and core inflation move significantly out of lockstep for longer periods. A more restrictive monetary policy aimed at controlling headline inflation may then push down core inflation even further. Arguably, this may have happened in the currency union's first decade: as a consequence of episodic energy price hikes, euro area headline inflation averaged 2.35 % between January 1999 and September 2008, while core inflation was on a downward path, softening to 1.7 % on average.[154]

178. Thus, in charting its monetary policy course for controlling inflation, the ECB is guided first and foremost by a numerical benchmark in terms of the evolution of consumer prices. In the early years, the ECB also had a money supply benchmark, in terms of a reference value for the growth rate of M3,[155] but it de-emphasized this

152. As part of the 2021 monetary policy strategy review, the ECB supports the integration, over time, of owner-occupied housing ("OOH") costs (*i.e.*, the housing service costs incurred by homeowners for owning, maintaining and living in their own house) into HICP. Pending completion of the related statistical work, the ECB intends to monitor the (quarterly) stand-alone OOH index as a supplementary source of information. *Ibid.*, pp. 5-6. On the relevance of including OOH costs in HICP, alternative methodological approaches for doing so (notably the net acquisition and rental equivalence approaches) and the roadmap for integrating the OOH index into HICP, *see* M. Eiglsperger, R. Arioli *et al.*, "Owner-occupied housing and inflation measurement", *ECB Economic Bulletin*, 2022, Issue 1, pp. 74-92. *See also* Eurostat, *Owner-occupied housing and the harmonised index of consumer prices—Outcome of the work of the European Statistical System*, Publications Office of the European Union, 2023, 47 pp., https://ec.europa.eu/eurostat/web/products-statistical-working-paper/w/ks-tc-23-001.
153. For a discussion of HICP potential measurement bias, the inclusion of OHH, and measures of underlying inflation considered by the ECB (including HICPXX, Supercore and Persistent and Common Component of Inflation (PCCI)), *see* Ch. Nickel, L.J. Alvarez *et al.*, "Inflation measurement and its assessment in the ECB's monetary policy strategy", Report of the Eurosystem work stream on inflation measurement, *Occasional Paper Series No 265*, September 2021, pp. 29-47, 48-65 and 83-94, respectively.
154. *Cf.* M. Rostagno, C. Altavilla *et al.*, "A tale of two decades: the ECB's monetary policy at 20", *ECB Working Paper Series No 2346*, December 2019, p. 94, Chart 3.1 (Panel A), and pp. 112-113 and 119.
155. The monetary aggregate M3 (broad money) stands for the sum of currency in circulation, overnight deposits, deposits with a term of up to two years or redeemable upon notice of up to

following its 2003 strategy review because of the weak or weakening empirical link between monetary aggregates and inflation.[156] It seems that the intermittent noise on the link between M3 growth and inflation may have been distracting for the markets—and for the ECB itself. Yet, the ECB still monitors various monetary and credit aggregates notably for its assessment of the possible build-up of asset bubbles or other financial imbalances.[157]

b Symmetry

179. In line with public statements made by Mario Draghi on earlier occasions,[158] the ECB in its 2021 monetary policy strategy review stresses that the 2% inflation target is to be viewed as symmetrical, in the sense that the ECB cares as much about significant deviations on either side of the target and regards both as *"equally undesirable"*.[159] Accordingly, monetary policy should *"respond forcefully to large, sustained deviations of inflation from the target in either direction"*, and the 2% target *"should not be interpreted as a ceiling"*.[160] A little later in the explanatory text, the ECB even adds that, given the limited space for lowering policy rates into negative territory, *"[a]n especially forceful or persistent response to negative deviations is warranted"*, and that this may imply *"a transitory period in which inflation is moderately above target"*.[161]

180. On and off, there has been discussion, within the ECB and among academic and other ECB watchers, as to how the ECB should best calibrate and communicate monetary policy reactivity to deviations of inflation on either side of the 2% benchmark. With high inflation in 2022-2023 fresh in our mind, that discussion may have an air of Vienna coffee houses to it, but we must take a longer view. One can see reason in a symmetrical approach insofar as it means that the ECB needs to be attentive to significant deviations from the benchmark in either direction, with the strength of its monetary policy reaction depending on the source, size and persistence of the deviation. For example, in hindsight, the lack of more resolute monetary easing in

three months, repos, money market shares/units, and debt securities with a maturity of up to two years. On December 1, 1998, the ECB set the (initial) reference value for M3 growth at 4.5%. *See* ECB, *The quantitative reference value for monetary growth*, December 1, 1998, https://www.ecb.europa.eu/press/pr/date/1998/html/pr981201_3.en.html.

156. *See* M. Rostagno, C. Altavilla *et al.*, *supra*, pp. 68-69, 80-85 and 105-110.

157. ECB, *An overview of the ECB's monetary policy strategy*, July 2021, pp. 14-15.

158. For example, during the Q&A at the ECB's press briefing of February 6, 2014, Mr. Draghi already spoke of the ECB's *"symmetric attitude"*. *See* the transcript of the ECB's press conference of February 6, 2014, https://www.ecb.europa.eu/press/pressconf/2014/html/is140206.en.html, at p. 10. At the March 10, 2016 press briefing, Mr. Draghi noted as a *"key point"* that the ECB *"is symmetric in the definition of the objective of price stability over the medium term"*. Also, given the medium-term horizon, if inflation were below 2% for a long while, *"it will be above for some time"*—meaning that 2% should not be viewed as a hard cap. *See* the transcript of the ECB's press conference of March 10, 2016, https://www.ecb.europa.eu/press/pressconf/2016/html/is160310.en.html, at p. 9.

159. ECB, *An overview of the ECB's monetary policy strategy*, July 2021, p. 7.

160. *Ibid.*

161. *Ibid.*, p. 10.

2011-2012 (in conjunction with a relatively restrictive stance of fiscal policies in several euro area Member States at that time) allowed softening inflation to drift lower while delaying economic recovery. However, the ECB's observation quoted at the end of the preceding paragraph seems to suggest a kind of "reverse" asymmetry calling for a more forceful monetary policy response, *i.e.*, monetary easing, when inflation dwells **below** target. This view is likely inspired by the perception of a persistent long-term trend decline in the natural or neutral rate of interest, which appears to have been an *idée reçue* at the ECB in the run-up to the 2021 monetary policy strategy review (*see* paragraphs 188-195 below). In that frame of mind, deflationary bias presents a greater risk and is harder to deal with, while upticks in inflation are more readily viewed as transient bumps on a longer-term downward-sloping curve. Yet, elevating stronger reactivity to below-target inflation to a longer-term policy precept raises questions.

181. One question is whether the underlying inflation currents may have shifted. In the second half of 2021, inflation returned with a vengeance (*see* paragraph 300, Table 4.1, below). The ECB's earlier inflation projections were seriously off the mark and had to be significantly revised upward in rapid sequence (*see* paragraph 319, Table 4.3, below). A number of structural factors now seem to point to stronger inflationary pressures over a longer time span (*see* paragraph 150 above).

It raises the question of whether the monetary policy reaction function to inflation readings should not rather lean somewhat more toward the opposite asymmetry of olden days, *i.e.*, to stronger reactivity when there are clear signs of inflation lingering **above** the 2% target for a longer while. Hasn't the ECB itself observed that *"welfare costs of higher inflation [...] increase non-linearly with the level of the target"*?[162] Of course, the ECB needs to remain vigilant to timely respond to more than passing disinflationary developments. But isn't there some "comfort zone" below 2% in which it could be less "activist" when inflation drops below 2%?[163] If costs may escalate more rapidly above 2% inflation while modest shortfalls below this target level are less problematic, why shouldn't monetary policy react more firmly to above-target inflation readings than to moderate below-target inflation? It is a question and one that can be answered only on the basis of empirical data.

c Medium-Term Horizon

182. From the outset, the ECB has taken the position that price stability is to be maintained, *i.e.*, inflation is to be stabilized toward its target level, over a medium-term

162. *Ibid.*, p. 6.

163. In the early years, Otmar Issing, then Chief Economist of the ECB, seemed to think that inflation levels between 1% and 2% constituted such a comfort zone. Speaking at the Bocconi University in Milan on June 10, 2002, he observed that *"most of the problems associated with the lower bound on nominal interest rates could be avoided for rates of inflation as low as 1%"* and that, accordingly, *"the central bank should be vigilant when inflation falls towards an excessively low level, say below 1%"*. The text of this speech may be found at https://www.ecb.europa.eu/press/key/date/2002/html/sp020610.en.html and the quote is from p. 3.

horizon.[164] To my knowledge, the ECB has never in any formal way defined this medium-term horizon as a precise time interval. Such references to time intervals as may be found in this context are often intertwined with the related—but not identical—concepts of the (variable) monetary policy transmission lags or the ECB's projection horizon. Thus, in his May 28, 2001 testimony before the European Parliament's Economic and Monetary Affairs Committee, then ECB President Wim Duisenberg declared that *"we are looking forward one-and-a-half to two years to vouch for the effects of monetary policy measures"*.[165] Speaking at a conference in Frankfurt on September 5, 2008, his successor Jean-Claude Trichet observed, more diplomatically, that the medium term should be understood *"to be at least as long as the average transmission lag for policy actions"*.[166] And, when referring to projected inflation at the end of 2024 at the ECB press conference of September 8, 2022, current ECB President Christine Lagarde hastened to add that the end of 2024 *"is not the medium term but it's the end of our projection exercise"*.[167]

183. The ECB's medium-term policy horizon remains an elastic notion in the sense that its length may vary depending on the nature and size of the shocks to be addressed, the desirable intensity of policy response, the (variable) time lags with which monetary policy actions are transmitted through the economy, and even the need to accommodate other policy concerns than inflation control proper.

Thus, in the explanatory statement on its 2021 monetary policy strategy review, the ECB observes that the medium-term orientation provides flexibility to *"look through temporary shocks that may dissipate of their own accord, thus avoiding unnecessary volatility in activity and employment"*, and, significantly, to cater for *"other considerations relevant to the pursuit of price stability"*, such as financial stability.[168]

The same explanatory statement goes one step further when adding that:

> *"in the presence of an adverse supply shock, the Governing Council may decide to lengthen the horizon over which inflation returns to the target level in order to avoid pronounced falls in economic activity and employment, which, if persistent, could themselves jeopardise medium-term price stability"*,[169]

164. For a general discussion of the medium-term horizon of ECB monetary policy, *see* M. Cecioni, G. Coenen *et al.*, "The ECB's price stability framework: past experience, and current and future challenges", Report of the Eurosystem work stream on the price stability objective, *ECB Occasional Paper Series No 269*, September 2021, pp. 67-74.
165. The transcript of this testimony is reproduced on the ECB's website at https://www.ecb.europa.eu/press/key/date/2001/html/sp010528.en.html and the quote is from p. 6.
166. J.-Cl. Trichet, "Risk and the Macro-economy", Speech at the conference "The ECB and its Watchers X", Frankfurt, September 5, 2008, https://www.ecb.europa.eu/press/key/date/2008/html/sp080905.en.html, at p. 13. In this context, Mr. Trichet added that demand-side shocks call for a shorter policy horizon than supply-side shocks, except when a sequence of supply-side cost shocks over a longer period (such as the energy price increases in the currency union's first decade) become engrained in market expectations.
167. *See* the transcript of the ECB's press conference of September 8, 2022, https://www.ecb.europa.eu/press/pressconf/2022/html/ecb.is220908~cd8363c58e.en.html, at p. 4.
168. ECB, *An overview of the ECB's monetary policy strategy*, July 2021, p. 8.
169. *Ibid.*, p. 11.

thereby ostensibly nuancing too rigorous a conception of the primacy of inflation control by embedding it in a medium-term time frame that, at least in the case of supply shocks, may be stretched to accommodate other policy concerns.

184. In any event, whether medium term may, depending on the circumstances, mean two, three or perhaps even four years, the fact remains that, since 2008, euro area headline inflation has never been close to the ECB's 2% target, except in 2018 (1.8%) (*see* paragraph 300, Table 4.1, below).

d Judicial Seal of Approval

185. In the face of abstract and vague Treaty provisions on the ESCB's monetary policy mandate, the ECB has appropriated considerable legroom by defining price stability as a symmetrical numerical inflation target to be achieved over an otherwise unspecified and variable medium-term horizon. That is understandable in an economic universe that is one of elevated uncertainty. There is no model of everything and the real world is replete with non-linearities and random disruptions—like 9/11, an avoidable Brexit, COVID-19 or Vladimir Putin.

186. As said, in its 2018 judgment in *Weiss*, the CJEU put its seal of approval on the ECB's interpretation of the price stability objective. It ruled, in essence, that the ECB's definition does not go beyond the Treaty framework and *"does not appear"* to be flawed by any *"manifest error of assessment"*.[170] The Court noted that the ECB's approximative formulation of the inflation target (in those days still "below but close to 2%") could properly be justified, *"inter alia"*, by imprecisions in inflation measurement, differences in inflation levels across the euro area and the need of a buffer against the risk of deflation. "Manifest error of assessment" is the standard of what lawyers call "marginal review". Here, curiously, the Court seemingly applied this (lower) standard of review to the ECB's interpretation of the core object, and the Treaty's sole definitional element, of its own monetary policy mandate.

4 THE HOLY GRAIL: THE NATURAL RATE OF INTEREST

187. Thus, the ECB has set for itself a relatively elastic policy rule, *i.e.*, to flexibly and symmetrically pursue a numerical inflation target of 2% over an undefined and possibly variable medium-term horizon. In the highly uncertain economic environment in the wake of COVID-19 and the Ukraine conflict, it has repeatedly added, in statements made since the summer of 2022, that, in the conduct of its monetary policy, it will now *"maintain optionality, data-dependence, gradualism and flexibility"* and follow a *"meeting-by-meeting approach"*, thereby muting forward guidance to the markets (*see* paragraphs 250, 256, 258, 261, 263, 267, 271, 276, 283 and 321 below). It could be and has been argued that good price stabilization performance would require

170. CJEU, December 11, 2018, Case C-493/17, *Weiss et al.*, ECLI:EU:C:2018:1000, §56.

a more articulate policy rule that exhibits a certain inertia over time so as to more firmly anchor market expectations as to inflation or at least as to the ECB's reactivity to inflation developments. But the ECB is certain to counterargue that, given the unusually high degree of uncertainty and fluidity of today's economic environment, this is not the most propitious of times for a more sticky policy rule.

188. Still, one may wonder whether there may be some less visible rules or criteria that guide the ECB's thinking and serve as a more implicit policy compass. Here, the (in)famous **natural rate of interest** (also referred to as the neutral interest rate) springs to mind. It has come up from time to time in ECB statements and publications—although perhaps a little less so in recent times.

189. In her September 26, 2022 testimony before the European Parliament's Committee on Economic and Monetary Affairs, ECB President Christine Lagarde is on record saying that:

> *"I don't know what the exact rate will be, but I can assure you that the Governing Council is determined to reach that point which economists call the neutral interest rate point, which is where monetary policy is neither stimulating nor tightening the economy".*[171]

In a similar vein, at the ECB's July 21, 2022 press briefing, Ms. Lagarde had responded as follows to a question from a journalist:

> *"We are data-dependent, but the ultimate destination of our policy path remains the same, which is to progressively raise interest rates to [a] broadly neutral setting. That's where we want to arrive at. If you are asking me next 'What is the neutral setting?' At this point in time I don't know. What I can observe is that it has changed over the course of the last few years for a reason of factors having to do with demographics, with productivity and all the rest of it. As seen by the markets, it has also significantly adjusted in the last few weeks. So we will cross that bridge when we cross that bridge."*[172]

190. What then is this natural (or neutral) rate of interest? There are nuances in its various definitions but it can broadly be defined as the equilibrium real rate of interest that is consistent with inflation being stable at its target level and the economy operating at its potential.[173] At this equilibrium point, monetary policy is neither accommodative nor contractionary for the economy. The natural interest rate—commonly abbreviated in economic literature as "r^*"—is a bit of a ghost. It is not directly observable in real time, and there is even no universally accepted methodology for measuring it. Estimates of r^* vary and are particularly sensitive to model specifications and assumptions. Yet, at least until recently there appeared to be a broad consensus among economists that r^* has been on a fairly continuous downward path

171. *See* https://www.europarl.europa.eu/cmsdata/254813/ECB%20Hearing%2020220926.EN.pdf, at p. 11.
172. *See* the transcript of the ECB's press conference of July 21, 2022, https://www.ecb.europa.eu/press/pressconf/2022/html/ecb.is220721~51ef267c68.en.html, at p. 10.
173. This corresponds to the definition given in ECB, *An overview of the ECB's monetary policy strategy*, July 2021, p. 2.

for the past two to three decades, with a trend acceleration in the wake of the 2008-2012 financial crisis. Thus, over the past decade and ahead of COVID-19, euro area r^* is generally believed to have dipped to levels close to zero or even into negative territory, with econometric estimates ranging from just over 0% to just shy of –2%, depending on the model used.[174] The trend decline in r^* is broadly common to several advanced economies.[175] Still, there are significant differences in estimated r^* values across euro area Member States.[176]

191. That persistent decline in r^* is believed to be attributable to such factors as (i) a slowdown in productivity growth; (ii) a shift from physical to human capital-intensive industries; (iii) demographic trends (rising life expectancy causing an increase in savings rates); (iv) rising income and wealth levels and inequality (through reduced consumption and increased savings); and, especially since the 2008-2012 financial crisis, (v) increased risk aversion (higher demand for safe and liquid assets). There is considerable ambiguity about how climate change may affect r^* through these and other channels, but current thinking seems to lean to the view that it may have a significant net dampening effect, particularly if the transition to a low-carbon economy were to reduce productivity growth and/or in scenarios involving serious climate-related physical damages.[177] At least until (and including) its 2021 monetary policy strategy review, the *idée reçue* at the ECB was that over the past two decades *"the equilibrium real interest rate in the euro area has fallen significantly"*, and that *"current market expectations suggest that the rate will remain low over the next decade"*.[178]

192. But this is not an immutable law of physics. In recent times, certain forces appear to be at work that may flatten or even bend the downward trend of r^*. These structural factors include (i) the adverse effects of demographic developments on labor supply, with fertility rates sinking further below the 2.1 replacement level and beginning to shrink the labor force, and with the increasing old-age dependency ratio diverting more human resources to care for the elderly; (ii) a certain "deglobalization" due to geopolitical tensions, with increasing "nearshoring" of supply chains to geographically

174. For an overview of various econometric estimates of r^* in the euro area, *see* Cl. Brand, M. Bielecki & A. Penalver, "The natural rate of interest: estimates, drivers, and challenges to monetary policy", *ECB Occasional Paper Series No 217*, December 2018, p. 25, Chart 6, and p. 37, Chart 11; M. Rostagno, C. Altavilla *et al.*, *supra*, p. 124, Chart 3.17; G. Koester, E. Lis *et al.*, "Understanding low inflation in the euro area from 2013 to 2019: cyclical and structural drivers", *ECB Occasional Paper Series No 280*, September 2021, p. 18, Chart A; and F. Panetta, "Small steps in a dark room: guiding policy on the path out of the pandemic", Online speech at the seminar organized by the Robert Schuman Centre for Advanced Studies and Florence School of Banking and Finance at the European University Institute, February 28, 2022, https://www.ecb.europa.eu/press/key/date/2022/html/ecb.sp220228~2ce9f09429.en.html, at p. 16, Chart 16.

175. *See* D. Lodge & J.J. Pérez, "The implications of globalisation for the ECB monetary policy strategy", Report of the Eurosystem work stream on globalization, *ECB Occasional Paper Series No 263*, September 2021, p. 30, Chart 11.

176. *See* Cl. Brand, M. Bielecki & A. Penalver, *supra*, pp. 29-31, Charts A and B.

177. *See* F.P. Mongelli, W. Pointner & J.W. van den End, "The effects of climate change on the natural rate of interest: a critical survey", *ECB Working Paper Series No 2744*, November 2022, especially pp. 6 and 26.

178. ECB, *An overview of the ECB's monetary policy strategy*, July 2021, p. 9.

closer locations with higher wage costs; and (iii) increased production costs associated with stricter environmental regulations and investments in "greener" production technologies and processes, at least part of which are likely to be passed on to consumers. At this point, no one can really predict with a high degree of confidence whether these factors are strong and durable enough to significantly reduce or outweigh those that have been pushing down r^* for several decades. The economic consequences of COVID-19, the Ukraine crisis and climate transition are scrambling the picture. But a future world of continuously low r^* is no longer a sure bet.

193. How then should the level and trajectory of r^* guide or otherwise influence monetary policy? The following considerations may be relevant:

(a) Conventional wisdom has it that the path of r^* over a longer time span is determined by slow-moving, structural factors and that there is little that monetary policy can do to counteract or change these driving forces of r^*, [179] at least not directly. This can be done only by sustained economic policies and structural reforms that support productivity growth, mitigate the adverse economic consequences of population aging and reduce income and wealth inequality.

(b) In theory, r^* could serve as a benchmark for the ECB to assess whether its monetary policy is too tight or too loose. Monetary policy rates that exceed r^* for any significant period suggest that monetary policy is too restrictive and may reinforce deflationary tendencies and, conversely, policy rates falling short of r^* may be too accommodative. The implication is that, in relation to r^*, monetary policy should generally "go with the flow", except as needed to deal with transitory shocks disrupting the inflation path. Thus, the protracted decline of r^*, at least prior to COVID-19, calls for monetary policy to broadly accommodate this decline by monetary easing lest it end up being more restrictive than intended and desirable. And if r^* drops to levels at which policy rates are constrained by the lower bound, then the central bank may have to provide the necessary accommodation by deploying non-standard instruments like asset purchases (quantitative easing). It is possible and even likely that a reasoning along these lines has broadly guided the ECB during much of the 2014-2021 period.

(c) Some may argue that the ECB's concern over the trend decline of r^* has caused it to maintain too high a degree of monetary easing for too long in the final years of the previous decade. It would seem that, until well into 2021, the ECB continued to operate under the assumption of a persistently low r^* due to

179. Like many economic propositions, this view is not universally shared. According to a novel theory advanced by Phurichai Rungcharoenkitkul and Fabian Winkler, the decline in r^* is not primarily due to changes in economic fundamentals beyond monetary policy control but, at least in significant measure, to an informational feedback loop between the inferences which central banks and the financial markets draw from each other's actions and which produce a "hall-of-mirrors effect". *See* Ph. Rungcharoenkitkul & F. Winkler, "The natural rate of interest through a hall of mirrors", *BIS Working Papers No 974*, November 2021, 46 pp.

slow-moving, structural factors that are difficult to reverse in the near future.[180] Accordingly, for a good part of 2021, the baseline policy scenario appeared to be that quantitative easing (net asset purchases) would be continued until sometime in 2022 and would then gradually be diminished before a sluggish lift-off of policy rates in 2023.[181] The credo of a structural trend decline in r^* may well have been a significant factor in leading the ECB to believe, at least for a good while, that the rise in inflation as of the second half of 2021 was likely a "temporary" bump in a low-level trajectory, and to delay policy rate increases until the summer of 2022 (*see* paragraphs 241-242, 247 and 250 below).

(d) Significant differences in r^* levels among euro area Member States (*see* paragraph 190 above) pose challenges for the formulation of a single monetary policy.

194. At the end of the day, estimates of r^* are subject to measurement difficulties and uncertainties, with different models and assumptions producing values that may differ by significant margins. This obviously complicates their use for policy assessments in real time. The difficulty is now compounded by the growing but as of yet ambiguous impact of climate transition on the structural drivers of r^*, and by the fact that a series of recent disruptive developments (including, in short succession, Brexit, increased political divisiveness and a failed *coup d'Etat* in the United States, the rise of populist sentiment in the West, COVID-19, the Ukraine war and tensions in the Middle East) and their uncertain economic consequences have scrambled model assumptions. All this requires serious caution in using r^* estimates as navigation points for monetary policy over shorter time intervals. Still, an analysis of the longer-term trajectory of r^* and the likely impact of various developments on its structural drivers may provide valuable input and guideposts for longer-term monetary policy strategy.

195. At the June 9, 2022 press briefing following the monetary policy meeting of the ECB's Governing Council, Ms. Lagarde expressed some mild exasperation about the recurring focus on r^* (particularly visible in the live video) in the following *cri de coeur*:

> *"The neutral rate: this is a topic that we have deliberately decided not to have on the occasion of this Governing Council meeting. I am sure that we will ad nauseam argue as to whether it is 0.96 or 1.97 or beyond, or below or whatever. Suffice to say that the neutral rate over the course of time for multiple reasons, having to do with productivity, with demographics and all the rest of it, has gone down. But where it stands exactly, we have decided not to discuss it on this Governing Council meeting.*

180. Still in June 2021, the staff's baseline projections for euro area headline inflation (HICP) were 1.9% for 2021, 1.5% for 2022 and 1.4% for 2023. *See Eurosystem staff macroeconomic projections for the euro area*, June 2021, pp. 13-15, https://www.ecb.europa.eu/pub/pdf/other/ecb.projections202106_eurosystemstaff~7000543a66.en.pdf.

181. *Cf.* X. Debrun, G. Ferrero *et al.*, "Monetary-fiscal policy interactions in the euro area", Report of the Eurosystem work stream on monetary-fiscal policy interactions, *ECB Occasional Paper Series No 273*, September 2021, pp. 80-81. In fact, a baseline scenario along those lines subsisted still at the ECB's monetary policy meeting of December 15-16, 2021 (*see* paragraphs 241-242 below).

Believe me, we had plenty to discuss so we saved a little bit for later. To be fair as well, it's not something that we can observe and determine with precision today. It's as you get closer, we will understand better where exactly it stands—and we will debate it. I have no illusion on that."[182]

Ms. Lagarde's ever so gentle impatience about the subject had not dissipated by the ECB's press conference of September 8, 2022, at which she observed that:

"I am not scratching my head around the neutral rate versus the terminal rate versus r and so on and so forth. What we know is that we want to get to that 2% medium-term target".*[183]

And at the ECB's October 27, 2022 press conference, she said that she "thought" that the Governing Council *"had a slight discussion about how not necessarily helpful this evasive neutral rate is".*[184]

196. This would be a fitting quote to end this section, were it not for a question that my attentive dinner companion may bring up at this point. What about "the" or "a" Taylor Rule as a possible policy rule or benchmark? It is a fair question. The Taylor Rule[185] and its variants and offsprings have enjoyed some popularity among economists and central bankers as a benchmark for *ex post* assessment and even *ex ante* guidance of monetary policy. But it too comes with its difficulties. One difficulty is that it is perhaps

---

182. *See* the transcript of the ECB's press conference of June 9, 2022, https://www.ecb.europa.eu/press/pressconf/2022/html/ecb.is220609~abe7c95b19.en.html, at pp. 6-7.
183. *See* the transcript of the ECB's press conference of September 8, 2022, https://www.ecb.europa.eu/press/pressconf/2022/html/ecb.is220908~cd8363c58e.en.html, at p. 9.
184. *See* the transcript of the ECB's press conference of October 27, 2022, https://www.ecb.europa.eu/press/pressconf/2022/html/ecb.is221027~358a06a35f.en.html, at p. 5. The published account of the Governing Council's monetary policy meeting of October 26-27, 2022 briefly reports that a discussion took place on the use of such concepts as the "neutral rate" and the "terminal rate" consistent with inflation returning to target over the medium term, noting that different views were expressed *"on the link between these measures and projection scenarios or on their steady state properties"*. The account then adds that, *"while the difficulty of relying on precise values of these rates was acknowledged"*, the consensus was that, looking ahead, the ECB needed to continue removing monetary accommodation by further policy rate increases. *See* the published account of the ECB Governing Council's monetary policy meeting of October 26-27, 2022, https://www.ecb.europa.eu/press/accounts/2022/html/ecb.mg221124~3527764024.en.html, at p. 13. Interestingly, the published account of the subsequent monetary policy meeting of December 14-15, 2022 reports on a discussion between *"a broad majority of members"* supporting a 50 basis points increase of policy rates and *"[a] large number of members"* initially expressing a preference for a 75 basis points hike. One of the arguments favoring the smaller increase (which was eventually approved) was that *"as interest rates were approaching estimates of a neutral level, the frontloading of interest rate increases and the speed of monetary tightening were becoming less relevant"*, and that, at this point, *"the steadiness of rate hikes and the time over which interest rates remained in restrictive territory mattered more"*. *See* the published account of the ECB Governing Council's monetary policy meeting of December 14-15, 2022, https://www.ecb.europa.eu/press/accounts/2023/html/ecb.mg230119~e522ad4e37.en.html, at p. 13.
185. In broad outline, the Taylor Rule formulaically relates the optimal policy rate to the gap between the actual inflation rate and the target inflation rate and to the output gap, *i.e.*, the percentage deviation of actual GDP from potential GDP. For the original expression of the Taylor Rule, *see* J.B. Taylor, "Discretion versus policy rules in practice", *Carnegie-Rochester Conference Series on Public Policy 39*, 1993, pp. 195-214, especially p. 202, https://doi.org/10.1016/0167-2231(93)90009-L.

too simple, insofar as it does not incorporate several variables that a central bank may find relevant for conducting monetary policy in a complex and dynamic environment.[186] Also, one of the key variables of the Taylor Rule is the so-called "output gap" which is unobservable in real time and notoriously difficult to measure.[187] This said, properly calibrated, the Taylor Rule can be another interesting camera setting to look at the monetary policy stance, also in the euro area.[188] But it is of lesser relevance for the discussion in this book, and I propose to leave it at that.

186. *Cf.* B.S. Bernanke, "The Taylor Rule: A benchmark for monetary policy?", April 18, 2015, https://www.brookings.edu/blog/ben-bernanke/2015/04/28/the-taylor-rule-a-benchmark-for-monetary-policy/.
187. *Cf.* A. Orphanides, "Taylor Rules", *Federal Reserve Board Finance and Economics Discussion Series No 2007-18*, January 2007, pp. 9-11.
188. The perception is that, from 2002 to the onset of the financial crisis in 2008, the ECB's monetary policy rate fell short of the Taylor rate, that these rates were aligned during the financial crisis, and that the policy rate subsequently reverted to significant downward divergence. *Cf.* J. Van Overtveldt, *The Mystic Hand. How Central Banks Shaped the 21st Century Global Economy*, Agate Publishing, Chicago, 2022, pp. 93-94.

CHAPTER 4

From Conventional Monetary Policy to Quantitative Easing and Back to Normalization

1 1999-2007: BY THE TEXTBOOK

197. One would imagine that, for the ECB, the early years must in part have been a time to get organized, establish contacts, collect data, construct and test models and generally find its way in conducting monetary policy for a multi-country currency area—a form of on-the-job learning. Happily, as described in Chapter 1, the currency union's first decade was, by and large, a fairly tranquil period that remained spared of significant disruptions, at least until the summer of 2007. It was a time of generally favorable economic tailwinds. Headline inflation in the euro area evolved within a bandwidth of 2% to 3%, with an average of 2.35% (although a steady increase in energy prices masked a softening of core inflation to below 2%). The financial markets did not appear to worry about sovereign risk, and sovereign bond spreads within the euro area stabilized within a narrow band of around 25 basis points most of the time. Certain clouds were forming at the horizon but markets and policy makers didn't seem to look up too much.

198. In this relatively tranquil first decade, the ECB could conduct a textbook monetary policy based on its policy interest rates, *i.e.*, the main refinancing rate (sometimes referred to as the "repo rate"), the marginal lending rate and the deposit facility rate. It could use conventional policy tools to steer money market rates, specifically interbank overnight lending rates, and, in this manner, the full spectrum of market interest rates in the direction consistent with its monetary policy stance. These policy tools include (i) open market operations in the form of collateralized bank refinancing operations; (ii) standing lending and deposit facilities to provide additional liquidity to, or absorb excess liquidity from, the banking system; and, in an ancillary manner, (iii) minimum reserve requirements for the banking sector.[189]

The ECB's main refinancing rate is the reference rate for regular bank refinancing operations. Its marginal lending rate and its deposit facility rate effectively establish a corridor for interbank overnight lending rates. The reason is that banks should generally be unwilling to borrow in the interbank market at rates in excess of the marginal lending rate and, conversely, to lend excess cash at rates below the deposit facility rate.

The minimum reserve requirement helps to stabilize money market interest rates: its averaging feature over a certain reference period (*see* paragraph 199(c) below) allows banks to temporarily use these reserves when interbank rates are higher, which should dampen the volatility of these rates. It could also serve to create or increase a certain liquidity shortage to be covered by open market operations.

199. In broad outline, monetary policy over the 1999-2007 period (and into the first half of 2008) can be summarized as follows:

(a) In the first two years, the main refinancing rate was increased in several steps from 3% to 4.75% in October 2000, then gradually reduced to 2% by June 2003, and from December 2005 progressively lifted again to 4.25% by the summer of 2008.[190] Except in the early weeks of 1999, the marginal lending and deposit facility rates were consistently set 100 basis points above and below the main refinancing rate, thus producing a relatively wide band or corridor of 200 basis points.
(b) The open market operations consisted primarily of Main Refinancing Operations ("MROs") and, to a lesser extent, Longer-Term Refinancing Operations ("LTROs"). Both involved the allotment of some fixed volume of central bank liquidity to participating banks against eligible collateral, according to a standard tender procedure. MROs were conducted through regular weekly auctions of seven-day funds, then mostly on a variable-rate basis (as of the end of June 2000) but with the main refinancing rate as the minimum bid rate. LTROs were monthly auctions of three-month funds, conducted as pure variable rate tenders without a minimum bid rate. In addition, "finetuning" operations could be conducted on an *ad hoc* basis to deal with unexpected changes in the liquidity needs of the banking sector.

---

189. Operating rules for open market operations, the standing facilities and reserve requirements have been set forth in successive ECB guidelines and recast in Guideline (EU) 2015/510 of the European Central Bank of December 19, 2014 on the implementation of the Eurosystem monetary policy framework, *OJ* L91, April 2, 2015, p. 3, itself amended several times and last by Guideline (EU) 2023/831 of December 16, 2022, *OJ* L104, April 19, 2023, p. 32. The operational framework for steering short-term interest rates is currently being reviewed, as we will discuss in Chapter 6 (*see* paragraphs 479-484 below).

190. Again, please note that these dates refer to the effective dates of the policy rate changes rather than to the dates of the relevant monetary policy decisions of the ECB Governing Council. This is generally the case throughout this book, unless it clearly appears from the context that the date of the monetary policy meeting is intended.

(c) Under the minimum reserve requirement, banks must hold, on deposit in current accounts with central banks, funds corresponding to a certain percentage—initially 2%—of most of their liabilities with a maturity of up to two years. This requirement is to be met on average over a six-week maintenance period, and these reserves were then remunerated at the main refinancing rate.

200. Yet, this first decade did not offer a cloudless sky. Certain problems were fermenting and, with the benefit of hindsight, questions could be asked about the (in)adequacy of monetary policy reactivity to them:

(a) Pre-1999 fiscal consolidation stalled (*see* paragraph 116, Table 2.2, above), and macroeconomic imbalances were building up in certain (especially Mediterranean) Member States that were to become the seedbed of the 2010-2012 euro area sovereign debt crisis. Might monetary policy have been too accommodative, especially in the 2003-2005 time segment?
(b) Should the ECB have raised policy rates more resolutely to check the housing and equity bubbles that were building up in the 2005-2007 period? But could this have been reconciled with the moderate inflation readings of those years (*see* paragraph 114, Table 2.1, above), especially in light of the observation made in subparagraph (c) below?[191]
(c) Over the first decade, headline and core inflation moved somewhat out of lockstep as a consequence of episodic increases in energy prices. While euro area headline inflation (HICP) averaged 2.35% between January 1999 and September 2008, core inflation was on a downward path, softening to 1.7% on average[192] (a prelude to the problem of stubbornly low inflation that was to become a key challenge for monetary policy in much of the second decade). A more restrictive monetary policy might then have pushed down core inflation even further. Subparagraphs (b) and (c) thus offer a first illustration of the kind of policy trade-offs that may arise between inflation control and financial stability considerations, as we will discuss in Chapter 6 (*see* paragraphs 418-440 below).

201. Still, in this first decade, central banking was as Mervyn King, former Governor of the Bank of England, once said it should aspire to be: boring.[193] But this ended in

191. *Cf. also* M. Rostagno, C. Altavilla *et al.*, "A tale of two decades: the ECB's monetary policy at 20", *ECB Working Paper Series No 2346*, December 2019, pp. 132-133. This paper argues that such more resolute monetary policy action would have required earlier and steeper increases in policy rates that would have measurably restrained GDP growth in 2005-2007 and caused a significant shortfall of inflation under its close-to-2% target.
192. *Cf. ibid.*, p. 94, Chart 3.1 (Panel A), and pp. 112-113 and 119.
193. Mr. King started out his April 14, 2000 speech at the 187th Anniversary Banquet of the University of Plymouth by saying that *"our ambition at the Bank of England is to be boring. [...] in our management of the economy [...] our belief is that boring is best"*. The text of this

2008 or, as one might argue, in the summer of 2007. Since then, central banking in the euro area has rarely been boring again. At times, it was even to become too exciting for comfort.

2 2008-2012: CONTAINING THE BANKING AND SOVEREIGN DEBT CRISES

202. In the summer of 2007, the unfolding problems of U.S. subprime mortgage loans and their derivatives began to wash ashore in Europe. On August 9, 2007, BNP Paribas Investment Partners announced that it temporarily suspended cash redemptions from three of its investment funds invested in securities backed by U.S. subprime mortgages, citing its inability to calculate a reliable net asset value for the funds.[194] With signs of interbank markets drying up in between regular weekly MROs, the ECB promptly injected EUR 94.8 billion of liquidity through fixed-rate finetuning operations with full allotment of all bids.[195] It was the early prologue to several years of financial crisis.

203. In the period from 2008 through 2012, the ECB had two successive financial crises on its hand, *i.e.*, the 2008-2009 banking crisis that unfolded in full following Lehman Brothers' filing for bankruptcy on September 15, 2008, and the 2010-2012 sovereign debt crisis resulting from the build-up of tensions in euro area sovereign bond markets triggered by the October 21, 2009 Greek "confessions" (*see* paragraphs 59-74 above). Adding to the complexity of the situation were two recessions which, for the euro area as a whole, stretched from 2008 Q1 to 2009 Q2 and from 2011 Q3 to 2013 Q1, subject to country variations. The ECB's monetary policy response is summarized in the following three subsections.

a Lender of Last Resort

204. The ECB and the national central banks stepped up to their role of lender of last resort to the banking system by making ample central bank liquidity available as needed.

205. In these years, a number of national central banks provided "emergency liquidity assistance" ("ELA") to commercial banks, mostly in Greece, Ireland and Belgium. ELA is a lesser-known channel of central bank finance in which national central banks extend liquidity support, against appropriate collateral, to (supposedly) solvent banks for the purpose of bridging (supposedly) temporary liquidity problems. It is provided under a national central bank's own responsibility, outside the Eurosystem's normal

delightful speech is reproduced at https://www.bankofengland.co.uk-media/boe/files/speech/balancing-the-economic-see-saw.

194. *See* BNP Paribas' press release of August 9, 2007, https://group.bnpparibas/en/press-release/bnp-paribas-investment-partners-temporarily-suspends-calculation-net-asset-funds-parvest-dynamic-abs-bnp-paribas-abs-euribor-bnp-paribas-eonia.

195. *See* M. Rostagno, C. Altavilla *et al.*, *supra*, pp. 144-145.

monetary operations and without risk sharing, but under certain guidelines and procedures designed to give the ECB a measure of oversight and a possibility to object to operations that unduly interfere with its monetary policy.[196] Former ECB President Mario Draghi repeatedly advocated to *"abandon this remnant of national sovereignty in monetary policy"*[197] and to centralize ELA at the Eurosystem level in a process giving the ECB Governing Council the final say.[198]

206. The ECB (Eurosystem) engaged in large-scale liquidity operations to provide a backstop to dysfunctional interbank markets. On October 8, 2008, the ECB announced that starting from the operation to be settled on October 15, the weekly MROs would be carried out through a fixed-rate tender procedure and with **full allotment** at the applicable main refinancing rate[199]—meaning that the volume of central bank liquidity supplied effectively became fully demand-driven.[200] In parallel, LTROs were also switched to full-allotment mode and, as the banking crisis unfolded and tensions built up in the sovereign debt markets, the regular three-month operations were supplemented by operations with longer maturities of six months, one year and even three years.[201]

As a supporting measure, the ECB facilitated access to central bank finance by expanding the list of assets eligible as collateral and by lowering the minimum credit rating for eligible collateral (other than asset-backed securities) from A– to BBB–.[202] The ECB later also lowered the minimum reserve requirement from 2 % to 1 % as of the reserve maintenance period starting on January 18, 2012.[203]

196. These guidelines and procedures were first codified in an agreement of 2013 which was subsequently adapted and expanded. The current version of this agreement, dated November 9, 2020, is reproduced on the ECB's website at https://www.ecb.europa.eu/pub/pdf/other/ecb.agreementemergencyliquidityassistance202012~ba7c45c170.en.pdf?dca797da321228995 6ac24df607eb168.

197. For example, Mr. Draghi did so in his February 26, 2018 testimony before the European Parliament's Committee on Economic and Monetary Affairs, https://www.ecb.europa.eu/pub/pdf/annex/ecb.sp180226_1_transcript.en.pdf, at p. 10.

198. *See, e.g.*, Mr. Draghi's response during the Q&A at the ECB press conference of March 8, 2018, https://www.ecb.europa.eu/press/pressconf/2018/html/ecb.is180308.en.html, at p. 6.

199. *See* the ECB's press release of October 8, 2008, https://www.ecb.europa.eu/press/pr/date/2008/html/pr081008_2.en.html.

200. The fixed-rate full-allotment approach had been "tested" in the summer of 2007, when, on August 9, the ECB conducted a EUR 94.8 billion discretionary finetuning operation at a fixed rate with full allotment of all bids (*see* paragraph 202 above).

201. In fact, the first six-month LTROs had been announced in March 2008. One-year LTROs were carried out in 2009 and 2011, and on December 8, 2011, the ECB decided to conduct two three-year LTROs (with prepayment option after one year).

202. *See* the ECB's press release of October 15, 2008, https://www.ecb.europa.eu/press/pr/date/2008/html/pr081015.en.html. Further technical specifications were announced on October 17 and November 12, 2008, *see* https://www.ecb.europa.eu/press/pr/date/2008/html/pr081017_2.en.html and https://www.ecb.europa.eu/press/pr/date/2008/html/pr081112_1.en.html. Additional measures to increase collateral availability were published on December 8, 2011, *see* https://www.ecb.europa.eu/press/pr/date/2011/html/pr111208_1.en.html.

203. *See* the ECB's press release of December 8, 2011, https://www.ecb.europa.eu/press/pr/date/2011/html/pr111208_1.en.html.

b Policy Rates Toward the Lower Bound

207. Between October 15, 2008 and May 13, 2009, the ECB lowered its main refinancing rate in seven swift steps from 4.25% to 1% and kept it at this level until April 13, 2011. For a brief interval, the ECB increased this rate to 1.25% on April 13, 2011, and then to 1.50% on July 13, 2011, in response to an uptick in inflation rates, but it soon reduced it again to 1.25% on November 9, 2011, and from there, in several steps, to 0% as of March 16, 2016, where it was to stay for over six years.

208. Interestingly, the spread (corridor) between the marginal lending and deposit facility rates around the main refinancing rate was temporarily narrowed from 200 basis points to 100 basis points between October 15, 2008 and January 21, 2009, moved back to 200 basis points between January 21 and May 13, 2009, reduced again to 150 basis points between May 13, 2009 and May 8, 2013 and to 100 basis points between May 8 and November 13, 2013, and from then on kept within a range of 50 to 75 basis points.

c The First Asset Purchase Programs

209. In the summer of 2009, the ECB also put in place a first—modest—asset purchase program, *i.e.*, the first covered bond purchase program ("CBPP1") which ran from July 2009 to June 2010 for a total nominal amount of EUR 60 billion.[204] Subsequently, a sequel, "CBPP2," ran from November 2011 to October 2012 for a nominal amount of EUR 16.4 billion.[205]

210. Then, on May 10, 2010, the ECB launched its Securities Markets Program ("SMP") for secondary market purchases of government and private debt securities in market segments subject to severe tensions.[206] SMP was a temporary program that ran until September 2012 and led to the purchase of some EUR 218 billion of securities, mostly government bonds of Southern euro area Member States. It was an anti-fragmentation instrument *avant la lettre*, and we will revisit it in Chapter 5 in which we will review the ECB's tools to contain financial fragmentation risk associated with excessive widening of sovereign bond spreads (*see*, in particular, paragraphs 332-336 below).

211. Toward the summer of 2011, tensions in the euro area sovereign bond markets flared up again and, in the spring of 2012, became fueled by market concerns over a partial or total break-up of the European currency union. These developments

204. *See* Decision 2009/522/EC of the European Central Bank of July 2, 2009 on the implementation of the covered bond purchase programme, *OJ* L175, July 4, 2009, p. 18 (no longer in force).

205. *See* Decision 2011/744/EU of the European Central Bank of November 3, 2011 on the implementation of the second covered bond purchase programme, *OJ* L297, November 16, 2011, p. 70 (no longer in force).

206. *See* Decision 2010/281/EU of the European Central Bank of May 14, 2010 establishing a securities market programme, *OJ* L124, May 20, 2010, p. 8.

prompted Mario Draghi's famous "whatever it takes" message at the Global Investment Conference in London on July 26, 2012 (*see* paragraph 75 above). Later that summer, the ECB announced that Eurosystem central banks stood ready to engage in outright open market operations, "Outright Monetary Transactions" ("OMT"), to counter excessive widening of sovereign bond spreads due, in particular, to market fears over euro "reversibility". Under this program, Eurosystem central banks could in the secondary markets purchase bonds issued by euro area Member States receiving financial assistance with economic policy conditionality from the EFSF/ESM. No *ex ante* quantitative limits were specified but the liquidity created would be fully "sterilized". OMT, which has remained a dormant instrument so far, is an anti-fragmentation tool *pur sang*, connected to monetary policy by the need to preserve the effective functioning of the monetary policy transmission mechanism. We will discuss it in greater detail in Chapter 5 (*see* paragraphs 337-348 below).

3 2013-2019: STRUGGLING WITH DOWNWARD DRIFTING INFLATION

212. By sometime around mid-2013, both the financial crisis and the (second) recession had abated. The euro area economy bounced back to positive growth, although growth was sluggish initially and uneven (*see* paragraph 121, Table 2.4, above). After peaking around mid-2011, headline inflation began a sustained descent (accentuated by the 2014 drop in oil prices) to well below the ECB's medium-term (then "below but close to") 2% target (*see* paragraph 114, Table 2.1, above). The ECB now shifted its attention to what it saw as a persisting trend decline in inflation. Deflationary risks became its dominant focus.

a Non-standard Monetary Policy

213. This marks the beginning of an extended period of monetary easing that was to perdure for about eight years. The already low level of the ECB's policy interest rates (which, in central bank jargon, approached their "lower bound") prompted a retooling of monetary policy toward the use of "unconventional" (or, in more aseptic terms, "non-standard") tools—forward guidance, policy rates around zero or in negative territory, targeted longer-term refinancing operations and, especially, large-scale asset purchases—to halt the further decline of inflation and push it upward.

214. ***First***, the ECB had already started to edge its policy rates downward as from November 9, 2011 (*see* paragraph 207 above) but in June 2014 it actually moved its deposit facility rate into negative territory. On June 11, 2014, the ECB reduced the rates on its deposit facility, main refinancing operations and marginal lending facility to –0.10%, 0.15% and 0.40%, respectively. In small steps, these rates were lowered to –0.50%, 0% and 0.25%, respectively, by September 18, 2019, and were maintained at these levels until July 2022.[207] Throughout this period, the corridor between the marginal lending and deposit facility rates was kept within a narrower range of 50 to 75 basis points.

215. ***Second***, on June 5, 2014, the ECB announced a first series of "Targeted Longer-Term Refinancing Operations" ("TLTROs") offering banks longer-term funding at favorable rates linked to eligible bank lending to non-financial businesses and households.[208] This first series, TLTRO I (as it became referred to), involved eight quarterly operations, all maturing in September 2018.[209] It was to be followed by two further series, *i.e.*, TLTRO II, starting in June 2016 and involving four operations with a maturity of four years,[210] and TLTRO III, starting in September 2019 and consisting of a series of 10 operations each with a maturity of three years.[211]

During and in the aftermath of the 2008-2012 financial crisis, many banks had been de-leveraging and de-risking their balance sheets by shedding assets and contracting their loan books. As a result, bank lending (and lending rates) had initially responded sluggishly to lower monetary policy rates. TLTROs served to invigorate the bank lending channel, which is of special importance given the prominence of bank

207. In view of the negative deposit facility rate, the ECB introduced a two-tier system for the remuneration of excess reserves held by banks in their current accounts with Eurosystem central banks (as distinguished from funds held in the ECB's deposit facility). These excess reserves are liquidity holdings in excess of the minimum reserve requirements. While such excess reserves on current account would ordinarily be remunerated at the lower of the deposit facility rate or 0%, an amount of up to six times the minimum reserve requirement became exempt from negative interest as of October 30, 2019. *See* the ECB's press release of September 12, 2019, https://www.ecb.europa.eu/press/pr/date/2019/html/ecb.pr190912_2~a0b47cd62a.en.html. The ECB again suspended this two-tier system of remuneration on September 8, 2022 when the deposit facility rate had moved back into positive territory.

     Separate remuneration rules apply to the minimum reserves themselves. These were initially remunerated at the average main refinancing rate over their maintenance period but this remuneration was subsequently reduced to the deposit facility rate as from December 21, 2022 and then to 0% as from September 20, 2023.
208. *See* Decision 2014/541/EU of the European Central Bank of 29 July 2014 on measures relating to targeted longer-term refinancing operations, *OJ* L258, August 29, 2014, p. 11, amended by Decision (EU) 2015/299 of February 10, 2015, *OJ* L53, February 25, 2015, p. 27, and Decision (EU) 2016/811 of April 28, 2016, *OJ* L132, May 21, 2016, p. 129.
209. For a more detailed discussion of TLTRO I, *see* M. Rostagno, C. Altavilla *et al., supra*, pp. 227-230.
210. *See* Decision (EU) 2016/810 of the European Central Bank of April 28, 2016 on a second series of targeted longer-term refinancing operations, *OJ* L132, May 21, 2016, p. 107, amended by Decision (EU) 2016/1974 of October 31, 2016, *OJ* L304, November 11, 2016, p. 7, and Decision (EU) 2019/1312 of July 22, 2019, *OJ* L204, August 2, 2019, p. 123. *See also* M. Rostagno, C. Altavilla *et al., supra*, pp. 258-261.
211. *See* Decision (EU) 2019/1311 of the European Central Bank of July 22, 2019 on a third series of targeted longer-term refinancing operations, *OJ* L204, August 2, 2019, p. 100, amended by Decision (EU) 2019/1558 of September 12, 2019, *OJ* L238, September 16, 2019, p. 2, Decision (EU) 2020/407 of March 16, 2020, *OJ* L80, March 17, 2020, p. 23, Decision (EU) 2020/614 of April 30, 2020, *OJ* L141, May 5, 2020, p. 28, Decision (EU) 2021/124 of January 29, 2021, *OJ* L38, February 3, 2021, p. 93, Decision (EU) 2021/752 of April 30, 2021, *OJ* L161, May 7, 2021, p. 1, and Decision (EU) 2022/2128 of October 27, 2022, *OJ* L285, November 7, 2022, p. 15.

lending as a source of finance in Europe. Bank take-up of TLTRO funds was substantial, especially under TLTRO III.[212]

216. ***Third***, importantly, as of the fall of 2014, lagging well behind the Federal Reserve,[213] the ECB turned to "pure play" quantitative easing ("QE") under what has become known as the Asset Purchase Program ("APP"). Under APP, the Eurosystem engaged in market purchases[214] of various financial instruments subject to an overall monthly cap. APP ended up having four sub-programs or segments, *i.e.*, (i) a third installment of the Covered Bond Purchase Program ("CBPP3") as of October 2014;[215] (ii) an Asset-Backed Securities Purchase Program ("ABSPP") as of November 2014;[216]

212. For the evolution of borrowings by euro area banks under TLTRO I and TLTRO II between May 2016 and June 2019, *see* M. Rostagno, C. Altavilla *et al.*, *supra*, p. 303, Chart 6.19. On TLTRO III and its impact, *see* F. Barbiero, M. Boucinha & L. Burton, "TLTRO III and bank lending conditions", *ECB Economic Bulletin*, 2021, Issue 6, pp. 104-127. Euro area banks participated widely in TLTRO III, with overall take-up reaching about EUR 2.2 trillion by June 2021. *See ibid.*, pp. 105-106, Chart 1.

213. In the United States, the Federal Open Market Committee ("FOMC") had already drastically lowered the target federal funds rate between September 2007 and December 2008, *i.e.*, from 5.25% to a range of 0%-0.25%. With the policy rate then at the lower bound, the FOMC initiated the first 2008-2014 wave of quantitative easing consisting of four asset purchase programs, *i.e.*, three Large-Scale Asset Purchases ("LSAPs") commonly referred to as QE1 (announced in November 2008), QE2 (announced in November 2010) and QE3 (announced in September 2012), and the Maturity Extension Program ("MEP" or "Operation Twist") (announced in September 2011). These programs involved the purchase mostly of longer-dated Treasuries, mortgage-backed securities guaranteed by Fannie Mae, Freddie Mac and Ginnie Mae, and federal agency debt securities. By October 2014, the Federal Reserve's portfolio of these assets stood at USD 4.21 trillion. *See Quarterly Report on Federal Reserve Balance Sheet Developments*, November 2014, p. 5, https://www.federalreserve.gov/monetarypolicy/files/quarterly_balance_sheet_developments_report_201411.pdf. For an interesting overview, *see* K.N. Kuttner, "Outside the Box: Unconventional Monetary Policy in the Great Recession and Beyond", *Journal of Economic Perspectives*, Vol. 32, 2018, pp. 121-146, https://doi.org/10.1257/jep.32.4.121.

214. Central bank purchases of eligible securities under the various APP sub-programs could be made in the primary or secondary markets, except that (i) purchases of securities issued by the government sector or by public undertakings (other than publicly-owned credit institutions) were always confined to the secondary market in view of the monetary financing prohibition of Article 123 TFEU, and (ii) primary market purchases (then limited to reinvestments) were discontinued as of March 2023 (except, under CSPP, for securities of issuers with better climate performance and green bonds).

215. *See* Decision 2014/828/EU of the European Central Bank of October 15, 2014 on the implementation of the third covered bond purchase programme, *OJ* L335, November 22, 2014, p. 22, amended several times and recast by Decision (EU) 2020/187 of February 3, 2020, *OJ* L39, February 12, 2020, p. 6, amended by Decision (EU) 2020/1688 of September 25, 2020, *OJ* L379, November 13, 2020, p. 58.

216. *See* Decision (EU) 2015/5 of the European Central Bank of November 19, 2014 on the implementation of the asset-backed securities program, *OJ* L1, January 6, 2015, p. 4, amended by Decision (EU) 2015/1613 of September 10, 2015, *OJ* L249, September 25, 2015, p. 28, Decision (EU) 2017/102 of January 11, 2017, *OJ* L16, January 20, 2017, p. 55, and Decision (EU) 2017/1361 of May 18, 2017, *OJ* L190, July 21, 2017, p. 24.

(iii) a Public Sector Purchase Program ("PSPP") as of March 2015;[217] and (iv) a Corporate Sector Purchase Program ("CSPP") as of June 2016.[218]

217. The overall monthly volume of net purchases under APP (excluding reinvestment of maturing securities) fluctuated over time: from EUR 60 billion between March 2015 and March 2016 to EUR 80 billion between April 2016 and March 2017, back to EUR 60 billion between April and December 2017, down to EUR 30 billion between January and September 2018 and to EUR 15 billion between October and December 2018. Net purchases were paused between January and October 2019 but then resumed, against the dissenting voice of certain Northern central bank governors,[219] as of November 2019 at the pace of EUR 20 billion (with some subsequent variations discussed in paragraph 237 below). Maturing bonds in the APP portfolio were consistently reinvested, although these reinvestments were distributed over time, in the ECB's words, *"[t]o allow for a regular and balanced market presence"*.[220] Net purchases under APP, but not reinvestments, were eventually discontinued only at the end of June 2022, with reinvestments being scaled down as of March 2023 and stopped altogether at the end of June 2023. By the end of net purchases in June 2022, the Eurosystem's aggregate portfolio of securities acquired under APP had reached EUR 3,265 billion (book value at amortized cost), of which EUR 2,592 billion or about 79.40% in government bonds purchased under PSPP.

b PSPP: A Monetary Experiment

218. PSPP has by far been the most prominent APP sub-program. QE on this scale, targeted at public-sector bonds, has been a monetary experiment for the euro area that deserves a closer look. It is a postmortem insofar as PSPP is now in run-off and unlikely to be reactivated in the near future, but it presents issues that remain relevant. PSPP's principal features are outlined in the following paragraphs.[221]

217. *See* Decision (EU) 2015/774 of the European Central Bank of March 4, 2015 on a secondary markets public sector asset purchase programme, *OJ* L121, May 14, 2015, p. 20, amended several times and recast by Decision (EU) 2020/188 of February 3, 2020, *OJ* L39, February 12, 2020, p. 12.

218. *See* Decision (EU) 2016/948 of the European Central Bank of June 1, 2016 on the implementation of the corporate sector purchase programme, *OJ* L157, June 15, 2016, p. 28, amended by Decision (EU) 2017/103 of January 11, 2017, *OJ* L16, January 20, 2017, p. 20, Decision (EU) 2020/441 of March 24, 2020, *OJ* L91, March 25, 2020, p. 5, Decision (EU) 2022/1613 of September 9, 2022, *OJ* L241, September 19, 2022, p. 13, and Decision (EU) 2024/190 of December 15, 2023 (not yet published in the *Official Journal* on December 24, 2023).

219. The published account of the Governing Council's monetary policy meeting of September 11-12, 2019, diplomatically records that *"[a] number of members assessed the case for renewed net asset purchases as not sufficiently strong"* and noted, among other reservations, that members considered such asset purchases to be *"an instrument of last resort which should only be deployed in the event of more severe contingencies"*. *See* https://www.ecb.europa.eu/press/accounts/2019/html/ecb.mg191010~d8086505d0.en.html, at p. 13.

220. *See* https://www.ecb.europa.eu/mopo/implement/app/html/index.en.html.

221. For a more detailed discussion of PSPP, *see, e.g.*, K. Tuori, "Monetary Policy (Objectives and Instruments)", in *The EU Law of Economic and Monetary Union* (F. Amtenbrink & Chr. Herrmann eds.), Oxford University Press, 2020, pp. 675-686, §§22.179-22.213.

219. ***First***, under PSPP, Eurosystem central banks may, in the secondary markets, purchase a broad range of eligible public-sector debt securities, with a remaining maturity ranging from one (initially two) to 30 years (and 364 days), subject to the overall monthly cap for APP. In the case of newly-issued securities, no purchases are allowed during a certain "black-out" period (of unspecified length) in order to allow the formation of a genuine market price for the securities and to avoid undue interference with primary market price setting.[222] The limitation to secondary market purchases and the black-out period are restrictions aimed at steering clear of the monetary financing prohibition of Article 123 TFEU.

220. ***Second***, the universe of eligible debt securities is broadly defined as to public-sector issuers[223] and their credit quality[224] and may include securities with negative yield to maturity.[225] The relatively low bar as to credit risk, *i.e.*, at least one credit rating of no less than BBB–, may raise eyebrows. Part of the underlying monetary logic seems to have been that, if PSPP purchases were restricted to the highest-grade public-sector bonds, they would in effect substitute cash for cash-equivalent securities, with limited impact on yields. In contrast, more diversified purchases across the risk spectrum should increase the efficacy of PSPP by extracting more credit risk from the markets and hence freeing up more risk-bearing capacity for bank lending and investments.[226] The flipside of the coin is that credit risk will shift to the balance sheets of Eurosystem central banks. Another (more immediate) reason for the lenient credit quality standard, so one may assume, was the concern to avoid excluding bonds issued by certain euro area Member States with higher government debt, including two of the "Big Five", Italy and Spain, whose credit ratings were at or just one or two notches above BBB– in the earlier years of PSPP. Excluding these Member States would have increased the risk of widening government bond spreads and the attendant financial fragmentation.

221. ***Third***, aside from the overall cap on the monthly volume of APP purchases (*see* paragraph 217 above), PSPP purchases are subject to a limit per issue (ISIN), *i.e.*, initially, as a rule, 25 %, subsequently increased to 33 %, and a "concentration" limit per issuer, *i.e.*, as a rule, 33 % of the issuer's outstanding debt in the maturity spectrum

222. Article 4(1) of Decision (EU) 2020/188.
223. Eligible securities generally include euro-denominated marketable debt securities issued by central, regional or local governments of euro area Member States and by certain government agencies, international organizations and multilateral development banks located in the euro area (Article 3(1) of Decision (EU) 2020/188).
224. As a rule, the issuer or guarantor must have a credit quality assessment of at least Credit Quality Step 3 (CQS3) in the Eurosystem's harmonized rating scale, meaning, in practical terms, that it must have at least one credit rating of no less than BBB– with Standard & Poor's or Fitch or no less than Baa3 with Moody's (Article 3(2) of Decision (EU) 2020/188). This does not put the bar very high. In addition, the ECB Governing Council may suspend the minimum credit rating requirement in the case of securities issued or guaranteed by euro area Member States under a European/IMF financial assistance program.
225. Securities with a negative yield to maturity are eligible (Article 3(4) of Decision (EU) 2020/188). Initially, the (then negative) deposit facility rate served as a floor in this respect, but this limitation was dropped, or at least made less binding, in 2017 when purchases of securities with a lower negative yield were allowed *"to the extent necessary"*.
226. *See* M. Rostagno, C. Altavilla *et al.*, *supra*, pp. 243-244.

mentioned above. These limits also partly serve to avoid that the Eurosystem's holdings would constitute a blocking minority at bondholders' assemblies that may be called to approve changes to the terms of the debt or a debt restructuring.

222. ***Fourth***, somewhat in the same philosophy, the ECB accepts *pari passu* treatment with private bondholders on bonds purchased under PSPP.[227] This waiver of any claim to preferred creditor status is intended to remove market concerns about market investors ranking below Eurosystem central banks in the order of repayment upon default of the issuer and being exposed to a higher "haircut" on their bond holdings in a future sovereign debt restructuring of the issuer. Concerns of that kind could reduce investor appetite and attract a higher risk premium on the bonds.

One might think that central bank acceptance of *pari passu* treatment, and hence loss sharing, with market creditors could be an unfavorable element in assessing whether or not PSPP may infringe the monetary financing prohibition of Article 123 TFEU. But in its 2015 *Gauweiler* judgment, the CJEU saw no such difficulty with *pari passu* treatment in respect of bonds that would be purchased under OMT.[228] The CJEU did not specifically address this issue in its 2018 *Weiss* judgment on PSPP (nor did the German Federal Constitutional Court bring it up in its preliminary ruling request).[229] In its 2015 *Accorinti* judgment, the General Court had held that, if Eurosystem central banks had, on the Greek bonds in their monetary portfolio, been plainly exposed to haircuts in the 2012 Greek sovereign debt restructuring, this would have raised an issue under Article 123 TFEU.[230] But, in view of the CJEU's judgment in *Gauweiler*, the General Court backtracked on this in its 2022 *Qi* judgment.[231]

227. Recital (9) to Decision (EU) 2020/188.
228. CJEU, June 16, 2015, Case C-62/14, *Gauweiler et al.*, ECLI:EU:C:2015:400, §§125-126.
229. CJEU, December 11, 2018, Case C-493/17, *Weiss et al.*, ECLI:EU:C:2018:1000.
230. GC, October 7, 2015, Case T-79/13, *Accorinti et al. vs. ECB*, ECLI:EU:T:2015:756. A number of private individuals had brought an Article 340 TFEU action for damages against the ECB for losses which they had suffered on their Greek bond holdings in the 2012 Greek sovereign debt restructuring. Among several other pleas, they claimed that the principle of equal treatment of creditors had been breached by an agreement of February 15, 2012 between Eurosystem central banks and Greece under which Greek bonds acquired under SMP (*see* paragraph 210 above) were swapped for identical bonds with different dates and serial numbers (ISIN codes) so as to effectively exclude them from the debt restructuring. The General Court acknowledged that this swap *"was intended to avoid the involvement of the Eurosystem central banks in the restructuring of the Greek public debt that would mean sacrificing a part of the value of the Greek bonds held in their respective portfolios"*, but considered that *"such unconditional involvement would have been specifically in danger of being classified as intervention having an effect equivalent to that of the direct purchase of State bonds by those central banks, which is prohibited by Article 123 TFEU"* (§114). The General Court repeated this in later cases involving damages claims of private investors in connection with the 2012 Greek sovereign debt restructuring. *See* GC, January 24, 2017, Case T-749/15, *Nausicaa Aanadyomène & Banque d'escompte vs. ECB*, ECLI:EU:T:2017:21, §98, and GC, February 9, 2022, Case T-868/16, *QI et al. vs. European Commission & ECB*, ECLI:EU:T:2022:58, §§109 and 134.
231. In this last judgment, the General Court conceded that, in its *Gauweiler* judgment, the CJEU saw no difficulty in the ECB's acceptance of *pari passu* treatment in respect of bonds to be purchased under OMT, but added that one must not infer from this, *a contrario*, *"an absolute obligation for the ECB to accept, in every case, pari passu treatment with other creditors"* (*QI*, §110). I have given serious consideration to inserting a smiley at this point for an inelegant attempt at face-saving withdrawal.

Most curiously, in the *Accorinti* case, the ECB itself had also raised as a defense that, if the Eurosystem's Greek bond holdings had been subject to the debt restructuring and its haircuts, this would have affected the Eurosystem's financial and functional independence within the meaning of Article 130 TFEU and (even) have *"undermined"* its capacity to refinance banks and operate in the financial markets.[232] Having regard to the size of those bond holdings, the General Court then agreed that this *"would have been likely to affect the financial integrity of the Eurosystem as a whole and, in particular, its capacity to operate in the financial markets and to refinance the credit institutions"*.[233] But this concern was no longer raised in the subsequent *Nausicaa* and *QI* cases. The reasoning of central bankers and judges may evolve under the weight of practical necessities, even in a short time span.

223. ***Fifth***, unlike OMT, PSPP is not linked to ESM financial assistance or any economic policy conditionality.[234]

224. ***Sixth***, in PSPP's original formulation, the distribution of purchases across euro area Member States *"shall be according to the key for subscription of the ECB's capital"* referred to in Article 29 of Protocol No 4.[235] In early 2020, this clause was replaced by less prescriptive wording saying that the allocation of *"cumulative net purchases"* of government bonds across euro area Member States *"shall continue to be* ***guided****, on a* ***stock*** *basis"* (emphasis added) by the ECB capital subscription key.[236]

Still, PSPP has no explicit geographic selectivity feature, in the sense that it does not expressly make allowance for a greater concentration of purchases on bonds issued by certain (higher-debt) Member States.[237] PSPP was plainly aimed at providing across-the-board monetary stimulus to support a return, *i.e.*, a rise, of inflation toward the "below but close to 2%" target (as it was then formulated). Unlike OMT and the later TPI, PSPP is not explicitly directed at containing financial fragmentation, although it should reduce government borrowing costs and indirectly help to counteract the widening of sovereign bond spreads (*see* paragraph 229(b) below). Yet, the less stringent 2020 version of the purchase allocation clause—referring to the ECB capital key as *"guidance"* for *"cumulative"* net purchases *"on a stock basis"*—suggests some margin for temporary deviations of purchase flows from that key. An analysis of the published data for 2015, 2018 and 2020 already shows an upward trend in deviations from the ECB capital key for high-debt Member States including Italy, France, Spain

232. *Accorinti*, §86.
233. *Ibid.*, §93.
234. But this is still indirectly the case for PSPP purchases of bonds issued (or guaranteed) by euro area Member States under a financial assistance program. Article 4(2) of Decision (EU) 2020/188 limits such purchases as a rule to a two-month window following the approval by the ESM Board of Directors (and the IMF Executive Board in case of IMF co-financing) of the next disbursement under the financial assistance program.
235. Article 6(2) of Decision (EU) 2015/774.
236. Article 6(4) of Decision (EU) 2020/188.
237. As we will see, the PEPP framework has similar language to that of Article 6(4) of Decision (EU) 2020/188 but adds an explicit geographic flexibility clause for purchase flows over time (*see* paragraph 240(e) below).

and Belgium.[238] Still, on its website, the ECB reports that PSPP purchases have been conducted in a manner to align each Member State's share in the stock of securities purchased *"as closely as possible"* with its share in the ECB capital key, and that monthly deviations mostly reflected timing differences between repayments and reinvestments and market liquidity conditions and *"largely cancelled each other out"* over time.[239]

Interestingly, in its 2018 *Weiss* judgment, the CJEU considered the allocation of PSPP purchases according to the ECB capital key (then in its original formulation), rather than on the basis of other criteria *"such as, for example, the level of the respective debts of each Member State"*, as one of several helpful features for PSPP to steer clear from the monetary financing prohibition of Article 123 TFEU. In the Court's reasoning, that allocation key does not allow Member States to avoid the consequences of higher public deficits and hence does not diminish their incentive for pursuing sound budgetary policies.[240]

225. ***Seventh***, there is the issue of the allocation among Eurosystem national central banks of the risks associated with (decentralized) monetary asset purchases. SMP purchases, possible OMT purchases and purchases of private-sector securities under APP and PEPP are subject to full risk sharing. In contrast, PSPP purchases are risk-shared only for the 20% quotum consisting of the ECB's own purchases and the purchases of securities issued by international organizations and multilateral development banks. In other words, under PSPP, national central banks purchase government bonds for the most part at their own risk, without redistribution of possible losses within the Eurosystem.

Then ECB President Mario Draghi was quizzed on this issue at the ECB's January 22, 2015 press briefing.[241] Ostensibly in an attempt to de-dramatize the issue, Mr. Draghi first professed surprise at the press attention given to the subject. With a vague reference to Protocol No 4,[242] he stated that full risk sharing would be the default rule in these matters but that the ECB's Governing Council would be *"free to decide what it deems more appropriate according to the circumstances"*. He then proceeded to refer to a number of precedents of risk-allocation decisions in both directions. He differentiated PSPP from both SMP and OMT, explaining that, unlike SMP, PSPP is a *"very large"* program, and that, unlike OMT, PSPP is not geographically selective and targeted at

238. *See* A. Havlik & Fr. Heinemann, "Sliding Down the Slippery Slope? Trends in the Rules and Country Allocations of the Eurosystem's PSPP and PEPP", *Credit and Capital Markets*, Vol. 54, 2021, pp. 190-191, https://doi.org/10.3790/ccm.54.2.173.

239. *See* https://www.ecb.europa.eu/mopo/implement/app/html/pspp-qa.en.html, at Q1.4, Q1.5 and Q1.8 (last accessed on August 20, 2023).

240. CJEU, December 11, 2018, Case C-493/17, *Weiss et al.*, ECLI:EU:C:2018:1000, §140.

241. *See* the transcript of the ECB's press conference of January 22, 2015, https://www.ecb.europa.eu/press/pressconf/2015/html/is150122.en.html, at pp. 4-6.

242. Presumably, Mr. Draghi had Article 32 of Protocol No 4 in mind, under which monetary income accruing to national central banks from Eurosystem monetary operations is pooled and re-allocated among them in proportion to their paid-up shares in the ECB's capital. Under Article 32.4, the ECB's Governing Council may decide that, *"in exceptional circumstances"*, national central banks are to be indemnified for *"specific losses"* arising from Eurosystem monetary operations.

countries *"under stress"* so that full risk sharing is not fundamental for its effectiveness. Accordingly, the ECB had room to *"mitigate the concerns that many countries in the euro area have about the unintended fiscal consequences of potential developments in the future"*—a somewhat muted reference to political concerns over fiscal transfers that may indirectly result from monetary asset purchases in case of sovereign default or debt restructuring.

226. This issue too came up in the subsequent *Weiss* case. One of the questions which the German Federal Constitutional Court ("BVerfG") had referred to the CJEU was whether an ECB decision providing for full risk sharing between national central banks in case of default on bonds purchased might infringe Articles 123 and 125 TFEU and Article 4(2) TEU in circumstances where the resulting losses may require recapitalization of national central banks out of national budgetary resources. In its judgment of December 11, 2018, the CJEU dismissed the question, as phrased, as hypothetical, but noted in passing that *"primary law includes no rules providing for the losses sustained by one of the central banks of the Member States in the course of open market operations to be shared between those central banks"*.[243] In its (in)famous judgment of May 5, 2020, in the same case, the BVerfG inferred from this dictum that such a loss-sharing rule could not be introduced by acts of EU secondary or tertiary law, including ECB decisions, but would require a Treaty amendment.[244] Absent such a Treaty amendment, so the BVerfG considered, any redistribution of losses resulting from open market operations (beyond indemnification of specific losses in exceptional circumstances pursuant to Article 32.4 of Protocol No 4) would breach *"the EU principle of national budgetary autonomy enshrined in Arts. 123 and 125 TFEU"*.[245] To my knowledge, this legal issue has not been fully resolved at the time of writing. It is relevant especially for risk allocation on anti-fragmentation asset purchases that are targeted at bonds of stressed sovereigns (which we will discuss in Chapter 5).

227. Back at the ECB's January 22, 2015 press conference, Mr. Draghi had also confidently observed that, in the event of future losses, *"[b]y and large, most central banks have adequate buffers, so nothing will happen"*.[246] This comment may have been overly optimistic. When, in 2022, the ECB started raising policy rates steeply in response to strong inflationary pressures, the profit-and-loss accounts of Eurosystem central banks were negatively affected by the conjunction of (very) low yields on their large monetary portfolio holdings of bonds acquired in prior years and the increased interest now payable on funds deposited by banks. Some central banks publicly expressed concern that their buffers may become inadequate to absorb projected losses.[247] Paradoxically, central banks of "stronger" economies may be affected more

243. CJEU, December 11, 2018, Case C-493/17, *Weiss et al.*, ECLI:EU:C:2018:1000, §162.
244. BVerfG, May 5, 2020, *Weiss et al.*, ECLI:DE:BVerfG:2020:rs20200505.2bvr085915, §224. For an English translation of this judgment, *see* https://www.bverfg.de/e/rs20200505_2bvr085915en.html.
245. *Ibid.*, §226.
246. *See* the transcript of the ECB's press conference of January 22, 2015, at p. 8.
247. Thus, in a letter of September 9, 2022 to Dutch Finance Minister Sigrid Kaag, Dutch central bank President Klaas Knot noted that the central bank now expected to incur accumulated

than those of "weaker" economies given generally lower yields on government bonds issued by Member States with stronger economic fundamentals.

228. In broad terms, the monetary policy logic underlying PSPP is (was) to compress yields on government bonds (and hence more broadly on market interest levels) and, in this manner, to induce portfolio rebalancing in the banking system toward assets with higher returns, notably loans to businesses and households. This would stimulate investment and consumption, which should lift inflation toward the (then "below but close to") 2% target level. Central bank purchases of government bonds may also counteract deflationary tendencies and push up inflation through other transmission channels. Thus, lower yields on government and other bonds should encourage institutional and private investors to redirect investments toward assets with more attractive risk-return properties. The injection of net additional liquidity into the system should also edge up inflation. And lower interest rates should, *ceteris paribus*, exercise downward pressure on the euro's exchange rate against other currencies and, consequently, increase prices of imported goods. But lifting inflation closer to 2% through the bank lending channel appears to have been the dominant theme in the ECB's official discourse on PSPP.

229. In legal texts and official communications regarding PSPP, there was little or no explicit reference to the easing of **government** borrowing conditions or to counteracting undue widening of sovereign bond spreads with a view to preserving or repairing the monetary policy transmission mechanism.[248] Yet, PSPP may significantly affect these variables as well:

(a) PSPP reduces government bond yields and hence government borrowing costs on new debt (and the refinancing of existing debt), which should widen the Member States' policy space for fiscal stimulus. Thus, one empirical study

losses in the order of EUR 9 billion until 2026 and that, in an adverse scenario, the bank may in time require recapitalization. *See* https://www.dnb.nl/media/3z3k23oj/brief-inzake-kapitaalspositie-dnb-september-2022.pdf.

In market releases of September 21 and December 6, 2022, the Belgian central bank expressed uncertainty as to whether its buffers would suffice to absorb future losses. *See* https://www.nbb.be/doc/ts/enterprise/press/2022/marketrelease_nbb_21092022.pdf and https://www.nbb.be/doc/ts/enterprise/press/2022/cp221206en.pdf. In a further market release of March 29, 2023, the Belgian central bank projected accumulated losses in the amount of EUR 10.8 billion over a five-year time horizon, well in excess of its reserves as at December 31, 2022. *See* https://www.nbb.be/doc/ts/enterprise/press/2023/cp230329en.pdf.

In a press release of March 1, 2023, the German Bundesbank reported that it had to tap about EUR 1 billion of risk provisions for 2022 and that the monetary policy reversal would continue to adversely affect its P&L for a while, but Bundesbank President Joachim Nagel commented that the bank's balance sheet was solid enough to absorb this. Mr. Nagel did not fail to point out that the Bundesbank had repeatedly warned for the financial risks associated with large-scale asset purchases. *See* https://www.bundesbank.de/en/press/press-releases/bundesbank-taps-its-risk-provisions-for-2022-905566.

248. Thus, according to recital (2) to the original Decision (EU) 2015/774 and the later Decision (EU) 2020/188, APP's aims include *"further enhancing the transmission of monetary policy"* (without other specification), *"facilitating credit provision to the euro area economy"* and *"easing borrowing conditions of households and firms"* (with no reference to government borrowing conditions).

estimated that, by extracting duration risk from the market, APP reduced 10-year sovereign bond yields by around 95 basis points by June 2018.[249]

(b) As already mentioned, the less stringent 2020 rewording of PSPP's purchase allocation clause allows some flexibility for (temporary) deviations from the ECB capital subscription key, and such deviations appear to have been made from time to time (and even prior to 2020) for bonds of certain higher-debt euro area Member States (*see* paragraph 224 above). But, even if PSPP purchases are allocated in accordance with the ECB capital key and not geographically selective (*i.e.*, not targeted at bonds issued by fiscally more vulnerable Member States), they should lower government bond yields across the board, including those of higher-debt Member States, and alleviate near-term debt sustainability concerns of these Member States to some degree. Viewed from another angle, purchases of, say, German Bunds will inject euros into the system that are fungible across the euro area and can flow elsewhere in search of better yields, which should eventually compress yield differentials somewhat.

Thus, while the spread between the 10-year Italian Buoni del Tesoro Poliennali ("BTP") and the 10-year German Bund was already on a declining path (from peak levels of around 500 basis points reached in December 2011 and July 2012) before the introduction of PSPP in March 2015, the spread mostly remained below 200 basis points during the net purchase phase of PSPP until June 2022, except (i) between May 2018 and August 2019 when net purchases under APP were reduced or paused (*see* paragraph 217 above); (ii) between March and May 2020 following the outbreak of COVID-19; and again (iii) as of May 2022 after the ECB, on April 14, 2022, had confirmed its expectation to discontinue net purchases under APP in 2022 Q3 and, on June 9, 2022, announced its decision to do so at the end of the month, as well as its intention to start raising policy rates in July.

While the containment of government bond spreads may not have been an explicit concurrent objective of PSPP, it will certainly have been a welcome (and expected) side effect.

230. In the event, PSPP has caused a significant proportion of euro area sovereign debt to be "parked" on the balance sheets of its central banks. At the end of 2022 Q2, total outstanding government consolidated gross debt for the euro area as a whole amounted to EUR 12,102 billion. By the end of June 2022, when net purchases (but not reinvestments of maturing bonds) under PSPP were discontinued, the Eurosystem's aggregate PSPP portfolio holdings (in terms of book value at amortized cost) stood at EUR 2,592 billion. If one adds the government bonds acquired under PEPP (*see* paragraphs 239-240 below), *i.e.*, some EUR 1,639 billion (again in book value at amortized cost) at the end of July 2022, the Eurosystem's total monetary policy

249. *See* F. Eser, W. Lemke *et al.*, "Tracing the impact of the ECB's asset purchase programme on the yield curve", *ECB Working Paper Series No 2293*, July 2019, pp. 6, 37 and 49.

portfolio of government bonds by the summer of 2022 was about EUR 4,231 billion[250] or roughly 35% of euro area outstanding government debt. From a political, economic and legal standpoint, these numbers raise questions as to size and proportionality. Also, at first blush, a neutral observer might be inclined to see this simply as Eurosystem central banks injecting (substantial) additional liquidity to become (large) creditors of their governments and wonder what else this could be than a form of monetization of government debt. In other words, is this consistent with the monetary financing prohibition of Article 123 TFEU?

231. As we will discuss in more detail in Chapter 7 (*see* paragraphs 526-528 and 531-536 below), in its December 11, 2018 judgment in *Weiss*, the CJEU concluded that PSPP falls within the scope of the ECB's monetary policy mandate. It arrived at this conclusion by considering that (i) PSPP aims at raising inflation back to a level below but close to 2%, which can be attached to the primary objective of maintaining price stability that the Treaty assigns to monetary policy;[251] (ii) PSPP's characterization as a monetary policy measure is not called into question by its indirect effects on bank balance sheets and government (re)financing conditions, even if such effects were foreseeable and knowingly accepted;[252] and (iii) purchases of marketable instruments in the financial markets are among the monetary policy tools mentioned in Article 18.1 of Protocol No 4.[253] The Court also found that, under the terms of the program, PSPP purchases do not breach Article 123 TFEU since they are made in the secondary markets under conditions that do not make them equivalent to primary market purchases and that do not lessen the impetus for the Member States concerned to observe budgetary discipline.[254] In its judgment of May 5, 2020 in the same case, the BVerfG broadly, albeit somewhat grudgingly, agreed with this last conclusion, but, discordantly, held that by engaging in PSPP as it did, the ECB appears to have overstepped the boundaries of its monetary policy mandate, *i.e.*, to have acted *ultra vires* (*see* paragraphs 546-551 below).

4 2020-2021: FURTHER MONETARY ACCOMMODATION IN RESPONSE TO COVID-19

232. The sudden arrival of the COVID-19 pandemic in the early months of 2020 caused serious disturbances to economic activity and a sharp contraction in GDP. It necessitated considerable fiscal spending on public health measures and on economic relief to businesses and households. Increased public spending and loss of tax revenue led to a

250. This amount includes government bonds purchased under PSPP and PEPP, but not the residual holdings of government bonds acquired under SMP (which, again in book value at amortized cost, stood at EUR 6.5 billion at the end of 2021 and EUR 2.9 billion at the end of 2022).
251. CJEU, December 11, 2018, Case C-493/17, *Weiss et al.*, ECLI:EU:C:2018:100, §§53-57.
252. *Ibid.*, §§58-67.
253. *Ibid.*, §§68-69. The Court then proceeded to an extensive analysis of the proportionality of PSPP in relation to its monetary policy objective, concluding that it does not infringe the proportionality principle. *Ibid.*, §§71-100.
254. *Ibid.*, §§101-158.

deterioration of public finances that was especially unwelcome for Member States with weaker fiscal positions. In the weeks following the outbreak of COVID-19, risk sentiment worsened, liquidity dried up and sovereign bond spreads widened significantly.

a Monetary Easing for Longer

233. Monetary policy was directed first at addressing liquidity tensions and stabilizing volatile financial markets, and then at preserving favorable financing conditions and accommodating fiscal support in response to COVID-19. The ECB effectively stepped up monetary easing by a series of additional measures.

234. ***First***, the ECB maintained its policy rates at the historically low levels that they had reached since September 18, 2019, *i.e.*, the deposit facility rate at –0.50%, the main refinancing rate at 0% and the marginal lending rate at 0.25%. (In fact, these rates had applied since March 16, 2016, except that the deposit facility rate had been lowered by 10 basis points, from –0.40% to –0.50%, effective September 18, 2019.) Policy rates were kept unchanged at those levels until late July 2022, notwithstanding the fact that headline inflation (HICP) had risen well above the 2% target since the summer of 2021.

235. ***Second***, the ECB launched a series of 11 additional (non-targeted) longer-term refinancing operations, baptized "Pandemic Emergency Longer-Term Refinancing Operations" ("PELTROs"), to support liquidity conditions in the euro area financial system.[255] The first seven PELTROs had tenors diminishing from 16 to eight months, maturing between July and September 2021, and the remaining four had a tenor of approximately 12 months, maturing between March 2022 and January 2023. PELTROs were conducted through fixed-rate tender procedures with full allotment, at interest rates 25 basis points below the main refinancing rate. Also, in several steps, the ECB eased the conditions on its TLTRO III bank refinancing operations (*see* paragraph 215 above) to keep bank credit flowing to the real economy.[256]

236. ***Third***, in April 2020, the ECB temporarily relaxed collateral eligibility conditions in order to ensure adequate availability of collateral for banks to access central bank liquidity. It did so mainly by (i) easing conditions for the use of credit claims, *i.e.*, loans to businesses and households, as collateral; (ii) reducing collateral valuation haircuts; and (iii) "grandfathering" the eligibility of marketable securities that satisfied the minimum credit quality requirement, *i.e.*, generally a credit rating of BBB–, on April 7, 2020, so long as they were not downgraded below credit quality step 5 (CQS5) on the

255. *See* the ECB's press releases of April 30, 2020, https://www.ecb.europa.eu/press/pr/date/2020/html/ecb.pr200430_1~477f400e39.en.html, and December 10, 2020, https://www.ecb.europa.eu/press/pr/date/2020/html/ecb.pr201220~8acfa5026f.en.html.

256. For further details, *see* the ECB's press releases of March 12, 2020, https://www.ecb.europa.eu/press/pr/date/2020/html/ecb.pr200312~39db50b717.en.html, April 30, 2020, https://www.ecb.europa.eu/press/pr/date/2020/html/ecb.pr200430~fa46f38486.en.html, and December 10, 2020, https://www.ecb.europa.eu/press/pr/date/2020/html/ecb.pr201210_1~e8e95af01c.en.html.

Eurosystem harmonized rating scale, *i.e.*, the equivalent of a rating of BB.[257] On December 10, 2020, these measures were extended to June 2022,[258] and on March 24, 2022, the ECB announced that they would progressively be phased out in three steps between July 2022 and March 2024.[259]

237. ***Fourth***, on March 12, 2020, the ECB added a temporary envelope of EUR 120 billion to APP for additional net asset purchases during the period from March to December 2020. Meanwhile, "regular" net purchases under APP continued at the pace of EUR 20 billion until (and including) March 2022. The monthly volume of net purchases was increased to EUR 40 billion in April 2022 and again reduced to EUR 30 billion in May 2022 and back to EUR 20 billion in June 2022, before net purchases (but not the reinvestments of maturing securities) were discontinued at the end of June 2022.

238. ***Fifth***, when in the early weeks the situation deteriorated rapidly, the ECB, on March 18, 2020, launched a new temporary asset purchase program, named the "Pandemic Emergency Purchase Program" ("PEPP").

b PEPP

239. PEPP had a dual purpose. First and foremost, it added a further layer of monetary easing to cushion the severe shock to economic activity caused by COVID-19, by maintaining favorable financing conditions and accommodating fiscal spending, and to help contain perceived additional downside risks to inflation. But it was also intended to serve, if needed, as a tool to contain excessive widening of sovereign bond spreads, as occurred at the outbreak of the pandemic and episodically thereafter.

240. PEPP's framework[260] has been defined in fairly broad terms:

(a) PEPP's initial envelope was EUR 750 billion. This amount was increased by EUR 600 billion in June 2020 and by a further EUR 500 billion in December 2020 to a total of EUR 1,850 billion. Within this overall envelope, the ECB's Executive Board could set the pace and composition of monthly purchases.[261]

(b) Net purchases under PEPP were initially intended to be conducted until the end of 2020 but this time horizon was subsequently extended to March 2022.

---

257. *See* the ECB's press releases of April 7, 2020, https://www.ecb.europa.eu/press/pr/date/2020/html/ecb.pr200407~2472a8ccda.en.html, and April 22, 2020, https://www.ecb.europa.eu/press/pr/date/2020/html/ecb.pr200422~95e0f62a2b.en.html.

258. *See* the ECB's press release of December 10, 2020, https://www.ecb.europa.eu/press/pr/date/html/ecb.mp201210~8c2778b843.en.html.

259. For further details, *see* the ECB's press release of March 24, 2022, https://www.ecb.europa.eu/press/pr/date/2022/html/ecb.pr220324~8b7f2ff5ea.en.html.

260. *See* Decision (EU) 2020/440 of the European Central Bank of March 24, 2020 on a temporary pandemic emergency purchase programme, *OJ* L91, March 25, 2020, p. 1, amended by Decision (EU) 2020/1143 of July 28, 2020, *OJ* L248, July 31, 2020, p. 24, and Decision (EU) 2021/174 of February 10, 2021, *OJ* L50, February 15, 2021, p. 29.

261. Article 5(3) of the same Decision.

Maturing principal repayments on securities in the PEPP portfolio would, however, continue to be reinvested in full until *"at least"* the end of 2022, later extended to 2023 and then to 2024.

(c) PEPP purchases could cover all private-sector and public-sector securities eligible under the various sub-programs of APP[262] (*see* paragraph 216 above). In practice, PEPP purchases have been heavily concentrated on public-sector securities. By the time that net purchases were discontinued at the end of March 2022, these securities represented close to 97% of the aggregate PEPP portfolio (in terms of book value at amortized cost).

(d) Unlike PSPP, PEPP has no purchase limits per issue or per issuer. Nor are the Eurosystem's holdings of public-sector securities acquired under PEPP consolidated with its PSPP's holdings in order to assess PSPP's issue/issuer limits (*see* paragraph 221 above).[263] This effectively makes these PSPP limits partly inoperative since the Eurosystem's aggregate holdings of public-sector securities under both programs may go beyond these limits.

(e) PEPP purchases (including reinvestments) can be conducted in a flexible manner *"allowing for fluctuations in the distribution of purchase flows over time, across asset classes and among jurisdictions"*.[264] While the allocation of cumulative net purchases across euro area Member States is *"guided"*, on a stock basis, by the ECB capital subscription key,[265] this offers some flexibility for geographic differentiation if and when needed to contain excessive widening of sovereign bond spreads. In this sense, PEPP can partially be viewed as an additional anti-fragmentation tool, as we will further discuss in Chapter 5 (*see* paragraphs 350-352 below).

(f) PEPP purchases of private-sector securities are subject to full loss sharing among Eurosystem central banks, while loss sharing on public-sector securities is limited in the same manner as under PSPP[266] (*see* paragraph 225 above).

c The December 15-16, 2021 Monetary Policy Meeting

241. When inflation started climbing in the second half of 2021, spurred by supply chain bottlenecks and rising energy prices, the ECB for a good while considered this as a "temporary" phenomenon that did not compromise its medium-term outlook. At its December 15-16, 2021 monetary policy meeting, the ECB's Governing Council considered that, while inflation (HICP) was rising rapidly and had increased to 4.9% in November 2021, this was driven largely by temporary factors, and that inflation was

262. Article 1(2) of the same Decision. Greek sovereign bonds were also made eligible (Article 3). For public-sector securities, the minimum remaining maturity was shortened to 70 days, with the maximum remaining at 30 years (and 364 days) (Article 2).
263. Article 4 of the same Decision.
264. Article 5(2) and (3) of the same Decision.
265. Article 5(1) of the same Decision.
266. *See* the published account of the ECB Governing Council's monetary policy meeting of March 18, 2020, https://www.ecb.europa.eu/press/accounts/2020/html/ecb.mg200409_1~baf4b2ad06.en.html, at p. 3.

projected to ease in the course of 2022 and to fall back below 2% in 2023 and 2024.[267] There was broad agreement at the meeting that *"substantial monetary policy support was still needed for inflation to stabilise at the Governing Council's inflation target over the medium term"*, and that *"[a] continued high degree of monetary policy support was also deemed necessary to prevent inflation falling below target once the effects of the pandemic [...] had subsided"*.[268]

242. On this basis, the Governing Council then decided to keep policy rates unchanged. Net asset purchases under PEPP would be discontinued at the end of March 2022, but the PEPP reinvestment period was extended by one year until at least the end of 2024. As to APP, it was decided to first increase the monthly pace of APP net purchases to EUR 40 billion in 2022 Q2 and then reduce it to EUR 30 billion in 2022 Q3 and to EUR 20 billion from October 2022 onward *"for as long as necessary to reinforce the accommodative impact"* of the low policy rates and until *"shortly before it starts raising"* these rates.[269] This form of forward rate guidance, "chained" to the duration of net purchases under APP, implied that *"it is very unlikely that we will raise interest rates in the year 2022"*, as ECB President Christine Lagarde confirmed at the December 16, 2021 press briefing.[270]

243. Things were to turn out very differently. In the following two sections, we will review, on a meeting-by-meeting basis, the deliberations of the ECB's Governing Council at its 15 monetary policy meetings over the time span of almost two years between Russia's invasion in Ukraine on February 24, 2022, and December 14, 2023. We will do so mostly with the aid of the published (and redacted) minutes of those meetings and the transcripts of the press conferences following each of these meetings. It makes for lengthy and perhaps somewhat tedious sections but it is important, for purposes of our analysis, to put ourselves in the room with the Governing Council and eavesdrop on its deliberations as it searched for direction in the rapidly changing and at times conflicting incoming data of this highly uncertain period.

5 2022-2023: MONETARY POLICY "NORMALIZATION" IN TIMES OF TURBULENCE

244. By early 2022, the acute phase of COVID-19 had subsided, although the pandemic continued to produce significant tail effects throughout the year. In particular,

267. The December 2021 staff projections saw headline inflation (HICP) decrease to 3.2% over 2022 and to 1.8% in 2023 and 2024. *See Eurosystem staff macroeconomic projections for the euro area*, December 2021, pp. 14-15, https://www.ecb.europa.eu/pub/pdf/other/ecb.projections202112_eurosystemstaff~32e481d712.en.pdf.
268. *See* the published account of the ECB Governing Council's monetary policy meeting of December 15-16, 2021, https://www.ecb.europa.eu/press/accounts/2022/html/ecb.mg220120~7ed187b5b1.en.html, at p. 14.
269. *See* the ECB's press release of December 16, 2021, https://www.ecb.europa.eu/press/pr/date/2021/html/ecb.mp211216~1b6d3a1fd8.en.html.
270. *See* the transcript of the ECB's press conference of December 16, 2021, https://www.ecb.europa.eu/press/pressconf/2021/html/ecb.is211216~9abaace28e.en.html, at p. 6.

supply-chain disruptions, while gradually easing, remained significant in certain sectors, including as a result of China's strict lockdown measures until the end of 2022. The consequent tensions between production bottlenecks and pent-up demand fueled inflationary pressures. And then, at a time of post-pandemic reopening of the economy, Russia launched its attempt to invade Ukraine on February 24, 2022. In the following months, the economic and political fall-out of the Ukraine conflict weighed considerably on business and consumer confidence and, to this day, uncertainties about its consequences, duration and eventual resolution continue to cloud market sentiment and the broader economic outlook for the coming years. As one of its immediate consequences, the conflict intensified inflationary pressures, primarily through supply disruptions and uncertainties and resulting price increases in gas, oil and certain other commodities (wheat, fertilizers and rare metals). Yet, the Putin administration could not claim full credit for the high inflation that befell Europe in 2022 and 2023. Inflationary pressures had been building up since at least 2021, due in part to structural factors (*see* paragraph 192 above) and in part to more circumstantial factors, particularly, as just mentioned, supply-chain disruptions caused by COVID-19 and also the euro's significant depreciation against the U.S. dollar from 2021 Q3 to 2022 Q3 (which notably increased the cost of dollar-invoiced energy and commodity imports). All the same, there is no denying that the Ukraine conflict was a serious negative supply shock in terms of energy and other commodity prices and caused heightened uncertainty. And that the euro area was particularly exposed to the consequences of that conflict given its geographic proximity, the euro area's high dependence on gas and oil imports (including from Russia) and greater vulnerability to movements in international energy prices, and the European Union's more limited geopolitical clout (including as a result of certain political hesitations and dissensions within its membership). And, in the fall of 2023, the hostilities in Israel and the attendant international political tensions were to add a further layer of uncertainty.

245. With inflation surging, growth slowing down and risks of financial instability increasing, these were plainly becoming more treacherous waters for macroeconomic policies to navigate. Those developments put an abrupt end to the environment of low inflation and sluggish growth of prior years in which monetary and fiscal policies were at least directionally aligned toward monetary accommodation and fiscal stimulus. Policy trade-offs now emerged—in the broader monetary/fiscal policy mix, between inflation control, on the one hand, and containing recessionary risks and maintaining public investments, on the other hand, and, within the monetary policy sphere, between inflation control, on the one hand, and limiting financial fragmentation and financial instability risks, on the other hand:

(a) In broad terms, monetary tightening in response to inflationary pressures, by raising policy rates and halting or rolling back asset purchases (quantitative tightening or "QT"), should dampen economic activity and may cause or reinforce recessionary risks.
(b) Not only will monetary tightening increase the cost of financing for businesses and households, but it should also raise government borrowing costs,

which obviously is more burdensome for Member States with higher near-term (re)financing needs. It reduces fiscal policy space for Member States with weaker fiscal positions, including for public investment needs, and may raise or aggravate debt sustainability concerns for those with high government debt.

(c) Yet, Member State governments may feel compelled to varying degrees to increase public spending in order to provide relief for higher energy and other costs of businesses and households and to contain recessionary risks. Fiscal stimulus may sustain and fuel inflationary pressures and work at cross purposes with monetary policy—and, of course, more so as such stimulus is larger, less selective and of longer duration. Increased public spending may also deteriorate Member States' fiscal positions and, especially in the case of higher-debt Member States, expose them to increased risk of market repricing of their sovereign bonds. Widening of sovereign bond spreads may give rise to financial fragmentation within the euro area and, in an adverse scenario, to destabilizing market dynamics. Sovereign bond spreads widened episodically in 2022 and 2023 and sometimes significantly so, especially in the weeks following Russia's invasion of Ukraine on February 24, 2022 and, again, after the ECB's June 9, 2022 announcement of near-term policy rate increases.

(d) Higher interest rate levels should ordinarily increase the interest income of banks (and non-bank financial intermediaries). But the net effect will vary among individual institutions depending, in particular, on the share of assets (loans and holdings of securities) with long(er) interest rate fixation periods, the degree of reliance on short-term funding sources and the extent of hedging of interest rate exposure.[271] The positive effect of higher interest rates on bank earnings may be offset to varying degrees by (i) loss of income due to lower lending volumes; (ii) revaluation losses on the existing stock of lower-yield assets, which may turn into out-of-pocket losses when these assets need to be monetized to meet liquidity needs; (iii) higher loan provisions for increased default risk on loans; and (iv) higher funding costs, in particular on substitute sources of funding when (low-cost) deposits migrate to higher-yielding money market assets. All of these effects are to some degree common to any "pivoting" from an accommodative to a tightening cycle of monetary policy, but it stands to reason that they will be more consequential the lower and longer the prior monetary easing has been and the steeper and less predictable the subsequent monetary tightening is—possibly to the point of causing liquidity tensions and increasing financial instability risks. The difficulties surrounding Silicon Valley Bank and certain other banks that surfaced in March 2023 were brought about in part by such "pivoting" of monetary policy.

271. *Cf.* ECB, *Financial Stability Review*, May 2022, pp. 65 and 67-70, https://www.ecb.europa.eu/pub/pdf/fsr/ecb.fsr202205~f207f46ea0.en.pdf.

246. It all adds up to an inconvenient policy quadrangle—a complex *sudoku*—to which we will return in Chapter 6. For now, I propose to follow, for these final years of our narrative in this chapter, the ECB's own "meeting-by-meeting" approach to review the monetary policy actions taken. Again, this approach may seem a little cumbersome but it reveals better than any other how the ECB's reasoning evolved in real time over this turbulent period and how it struggled to distill direction from the continuous noise of the around-the-clock ticker tape of incoming and sometimes conflicting data. At times, it looked like an advanced game of poker between the financial markets and the ECB, with the markets trying to gauge how the ECB might interpret the data and forming expectations (often colored by wishful thinking) as to the pace, terminal rate and time of reversal of the monetary tightening cycle, and with the ECB trying to read the markets' expectations of its own future actions and then calibrating its messages to steer those expectations. I found it somehow helpful to link this stressful story to the contemplative setting of the floating temple in Kim Ki-duk's movie.[272]

a Spring

247. ***March 9-10, 2022:*** At the ECB Governing Council's monetary policy meeting of March 9-10, 2022, two weeks after Russia had started its attempt to invade Ukraine, it was observed that the ECB was now *"grappling with 'Knightian uncertainty', i.e. a type of uncertainty that was not quantifiable"*.[273] Still, it was broadly agreed that the Ukraine conflict should have an upward effect on inflation and a downward effect on growth and was best characterized as *"yet another negative supply shock"*.[274] With headline inflation (HICP) surprising to the upside, rising from 5.1% in January to 5.8% (later revised to 5.9%) in February 2022, and price pressures spreading, *"[a] large number of members"* advocated *"immediate further steps"*.[275] Yet, the view eventually prevailed that, given the especially high uncertainty created by the Ukraine conflict and its nature of a supply shock (rather than a demand shock), and pending better visibility on the implications of that conflict and the Member States' fiscal policy response, it was preferable to adopt a wait-and-see approach rather than to risk overreacting to the latest inflation readings. It was thought that the ECB *"could afford to be patient"* since medium-term inflation projections still hovered around the 2% target[276] and there were no signs yet of second-round effects through wage growth.[277]

272. "Spring, Summer, Fall, Winter ... and Spring" (2003). As to the references to seasons of the year in the pages that follow, I use the meteorological definition for the Northern Hemisphere.
273. *See* the published account of the ECB Governing Council's monetary policy meeting of March 9-10, 2022, https://www.ecb.europa.eu/press/accounts/2022/html/ecb.mg220407~8e7069ffa0.en.html, at p. 10.
274. *Ibid.*
275. *Ibid.*, at p. 16.
276. The March 2022 ECB staff projections then saw headline inflation (HICP) at 5.1% for 2022, 2.1% for 2023 and 1.9% for 2024. *See ECB staff macroeconomic projections for the euro area*, March 2022, pp. 3 and 19, https://www.ecb.europa.eu/pub/pdf/other/ecb.projections202203_ecbstaff~44f998dfd7.en.pdf.
277. *See* the published account of the ECB Governing Council's monetary policy meeting of March 9-10, 2022, at p. 18. As further justification for this "patient" approach, the Governing Council

248. Accordingly, on March 10, 2022, the ECB announced the following decisions:[278]

(a) The main refinancing rate, the marginal lending rate and the deposit facility rate were maintained at 0%, 0.25% and –0.50%, respectively. It was now specified that any adjustment to these rates would take place *"some time after"* the termination of net purchases under APP (whereas in the earlier formulation, it was said that such net purchases would end *"shortly before"* an increase in policy rates). As a lawyer, I thought that this semantic refinement was too cute to be left unmentioned and be covered by the dust of time.

(b) The schedule of net asset purchases under APP was revised downward to EUR 40 billion for April, EUR 30 billion for May and EUR 20 billion for June 2022, now with a conditional expectation (subject to incoming data) that the ECB would terminate further net purchases *"in the third quarter"* of 2022, while continuing to fully reinvest principal repayments on maturing bonds *"for an extended period of time"* past the date of policy rate lift-off. If one puts subparagraphs (a) and (b) together, the implied forward guidance was that there should be no policy rate increase before sometime in 2022 Q3.

(c) It was confirmed that net asset purchases under PEPP would be discontinued at the end of March 2022 and that proceeds from maturing bonds in the PEPP portfolio would be fully reinvested *"until at least the end of 2024"*.

249. ***April 13-14, 2022*:** By the Governing Council's next monetary policy meeting on April 13-14, 2022, headline inflation (HICP) had further increased to 7.5% (later revised to 7.4%) in March, up from 5.9% in February, mostly due to a steep rise in energy prices, and it was felt that upside risks to the inflation outlook had risen, especially in the near term. Incoming data suggested that the Ukraine conflict would slow economic recovery but not derail it. The labor market had continued to improve and there were differing views within the Governing Council as to the probability of second-round effects on inflation arising from increasing wage costs.[279] While financial markets remained volatile, risk sentiment appeared to have improved somewhat, there had been no liquidity shortages in the euro area banking system and no severe strains in money markets, and sovereign bond spreads had narrowed again.

250. In the meeting, *"some members"* (apparently no longer the *"large number"* of March 9-10, 2022) continued to advocate a more rapid adjustment of monetary policy toward a neutral position and were of the view that the ECB should adapt its inflation narrative to signal a faster policy normalization trajectory. However, the prevailing view was that the circumstances did not warrant an acceleration of restrictive action or

---

may also have found some comfort in the fact that, at that time, financial markets priced in a first policy rate increase of 25 basis points only around the turn of the year. *See ibid.*, at p. 1.

278. *See* the ECB's press release of March 20, 2022, https://www.ecb.europa.eu/press/pr/date/2022/html/ecb.mp220310~2d19f8ba60.en.html.

279. *See* the published account of the ECB Governing Council's monetary policy meeting of April 13-14, 2022, https://www.ecb.europa.eu/press/accounts/2022/hml/ecb.mg220519~c9200dba08.en.html, at p. 11.

a shift in policy guidance from a gradual to a more aggressive tightening.[280] Interestingly, this approach was deemed consistent with the estimated low or even negative level of the natural interest rate in the euro area *"which implied that even relatively small steps might be sufficient to turn the current accommodative monetary policy stance into a restrictive stance"*.[281] On this basis, the ECB held on to the *status quo*, and, in its press release, now explicitly included the message that, in the conduct of monetary policy, it would maintain *"optionality, gradualism and flexibility"*. It also confirmed that incoming data had *"reinforced"* its expectation that net asset purchases under APP would be discontinued in 2022 Q3.[282]

b Summer

251. ***June 8-9, 2022***: By the monetary policy meeting of June 8-9, 2022 (exceptionally held in Amsterdam), headline inflation (HICP) had increased to 8.1 % in May (up from 7.4% in April). Underlying inflation dynamics were seen to be strengthening and broadening. The June 2022 staff projections now estimated headline inflation at 6.8 % in 2022, 3.5 % in 2023 and 2.1 % in 2024.[283] Still, no second-round effects through wages were in evidence at the time. In the sovereign and corporate bond markets, spreads were widening, notably in Italy and Greece, but, despite high volatility and challenging liquidity conditions, spreads had not widened to an excessive degree. It was *"widely acknowledged"* at the meeting that uncertainty remained high and that the transmission of the current inflation shock and its potential persistence into 2023 and 2024 *"needed to be better understood"*.[284]

252. At the same meeting, the Governing Council also engaged in its biannual structured exchange on the interaction between monetary policy and financial stability.[285] It was agreed that the financial stability environment had deteriorated, especially

280. *Ibid.*, at pp. 13-15.
281. *Ibid.*, at p. 15.
282. *See* the ECB's press release of April 14, 2022, https://www.ecb.europa.eu/press/pr/date/2022/html/ecb.mp220414~d1b76520c6.en.html. In the ECB's press release of June 9, 2022, *"data-dependence"* was added to optionality, gradualism and flexibility (*see* https://www.ecb.europa.eu/press/pr/date/2022/html/ecb.mp220609~122666c272.en.html), and its press release of July 21, 2022 included a *"meeting-by-meeting approach"* to policy rate decisions as a further recurring message (*see* https://www.ecb.europa.eu/press/pr/date/2022/html/ecb.mp220721~53e5bdd317.en.html; *see also* paragraphs 256 and 258 below).
283. *See Eurosystem staff macroeconomic projections for the euro area*, June 2022, pp. 19-20, https://www.ecb.europa.eu/pub/pdf/other/ecb.projections202206_eurosystemstaff~2299e41f1e.en.pdf.
284. *See* the published account of the ECB Governing Council's monetary policy meeting of June 8-9, 2022, https://www.ecb.europa.eu/press/accounts/2022/html/ecb.mg220707~d5c3246061.en.html, at p. 14.
285. The July 2021 monetary policy strategy review called for an in-depth assessment of that interaction to be conducted *"at regular intervals"* at the monetary policy meetings of the Governing Council. *See* ECB, *An overview of the ECB's monetary policy strategy*, July 2021, p. 15. In the Governing Council's meeting calendar, this exchange is now on the agenda of the first monetary policy meeting after the release of the ECB's *Financial Stability Review* in May and November of each year.

over the short term, and that monetary policy normalization might affect financial stability *"at different horizons in opposite ways"*.[286] Thus, it was recognized that, when interest rates exit from a prolonged stay at low levels, a change in the monetary cycle could be accompanied by short-term financial stresses and increased financial fragmentation. It was also observed that banks were facing greater credit risk in an environment of lower growth and heightened uncertainty. These developments would need to be *"watched closely"*.[287]

253. Yet, it was clear that the time had come for starting to increase policy rates. Although *"[a] number of members"* initially favored leaving the door open for a larger first increase, consensus was reached to announce the Governing Council's intention to raise policy rates by 25 basis points at its July meeting. For a first increase in 11 years (since July 13, 2011), this was thought to be a proportionate first step in a rate-hiking cycle that needed to be orderly so as to avoid *"unnecessarily surprising the markets and inducing unwarranted volatility"*.[288] Caution prevailed and the Governing Council seemed mindful of the precept once proffered by Mario Draghi that *"in a dark room you move with tiny steps"*.[289] Significantly, in view of the widening of sovereign bond spreads observed in recent months and the increased risk of financial fragmentation associated with monetary policy tightening, members called for work on a possible new anti-fragmentation tool to be accelerated and completed rapidly.[290]

254. Thus, on June 9, 2022, the ECB announced that it *"intended"* to raise its key policy rates by 25 basis points at its July monetary policy meeting, *"expected"* to increase them again in September, and *"anticipated"* a *"gradual but sustained path of further increases"* beyond September.[291] At the press briefing, ECB President Christine Lagarde said that *"it's not just a step; it's a journey"*.[292] The ECB also confirmed that net asset purchases under APP would be discontinued at the end of the month, but the prior messages on the reinvestment of maturing bonds in the APP and PEPP portfolios

286. *See* the published account of the ECB Governing Council's monetary policy meeting of June 8-9, 2022, at p. 16.
287. *Ibid.* The ECB's latest financial stability review had concluded from supervisory data that banks' net interest income could be expected to benefit from higher interest rates in the short run but that rising rates might adversely affect banks with a higher share of fixed-rate assets in the medium term as they would have to pay higher funding costs to cover low-yielding assets. However, interest rate exposure in the euro area banking system appeared moderate on the whole (in part because active hedging of interest rate risk had increased on the expectation of rising interest rates), subject to wide variations across individual banks. *See* ECB, *Financial Stability Review*, May 2022, pp. 65 and 67-70, https://www.ecb.europa.eu/pub/pdf/fsr/ecb.fsr202205~f207f46ea0.en.pdf.
288. *See* the published account of the ECB Governing Council's monetary policy meeting of June 8-9, 2022, at p. 19.
289. *See* the transcript of the ECB's press conference of March 7, 2019, https://www.ecb.europa.eu/press/pressconf/2019/html/ecb.is190307~de1fdbd0b0.en.html, at p. 7.
290. *See* the published account of the ECB Governing Council's monetary policy meeting of June 8-9, 2020, at p. 20.
291. *See* the ECB's press release of June 9, 2022, https://www.ecb.europa.eu/press/pr/date/2022/html/ecb. mp220609~122666c272.en.html.
292. *See* the transcript of the ECB's press conference of June 9, 2022, https://ecb.europa.eu/press/pressconf/2022/html/ecb.is220609~abe7c95b19.en.html, at p. 4.

were substantially maintained, *i.e.*, there was to be no run-off of the existing portfolios—no quantitative tightening ("QT")—for some time to come.

255. *June 15, 2022*: In the days that followed, the ECB's message caused a further widening of the spread between the yields on the 10-year Italian BTP and 10-year German Bund above 200 basis points. It was likely one of the developments that prompted an *ad hoc* meeting of the ECB's Governing Council on June 15, 2022, and a hasty announcement in which the ECB (i) reiterated its message of flexible reinvestment of principal repayments in the PEPP portfolio as may be needed to preserve the functioning of the monetary policy transmission mechanism, and (ii) indicated that the relevant committees and services had been mandated to *"accelerate"* the completion of the design of a new anti-fragmentation instrument.[293]

256. *July 20-21, 2022:* By the next regular monetary policy meeting of the Governing Council on July 20-21, 2022, inflation readings again surprised to the upside, with headline inflation (HICP) rising from 8.1% in May to 8.6% in June. Inflationary pressures, driven by energy and food prices and reinforced by the continued depreciation of the euro against the U.S. dollar,[294] were judged to have broadened and intensified, especially in the short term. Wage growth, by and large, remained contained but, while there was no evidence yet of second-round effects on inflation, the apparent persistence of inflation increased the probability of such effects. There were increasing signs of an economic downturn that could stretch into 2023 but no indication yet of a major recession in the euro area. On the basis of these and other considerations, the Governing Council agreed to lift policy rates not by 25 basis points but by 50 basis points, although *"[s]ome members"* argued in favor of keeping to 25 basis points as had been communicated in June (*see* paragraph 254 above).[295] Given this larger first rate step (*"frontloading"*) and the prevailing *"exceptionally high uncertainty"*, it was also decided to switch to a *"meeting-by-meeting approach"* on policy rate decisions and to abandon specific forward guidance on future rates.[296]

257. At the same meeting, the Governing Council unanimously approved the establishment of a new anti-fragmentation instrument, diplomatically called the "Transmission Protection Instrument" ("TPI"), showing the ECB's readiness to intervene in the bond markets, by purchasing mostly public-sector bonds, to lean against market movements divorced from macroeconomic fundamentals. The underlying reasoning is that excessive widening of (government) bond spreads would impair the proper transmission of monetary policy across the euro area, in particular monetary tightening in response to above-target inflation, in that (i) it would further tighten financing conditions in weaker economies (at the high end of the spreads) over and above what

293. *See* the ECB's press release of June 15, 2022, https://www.ecb.europa.eu/press/pr/date/html/ecb. pr220615 ~ 2aa3900e0a.en.html.
294. Since the end of May 2021, the EUR/USD exchange rate had fallen from about 1.22 to between 1.01 and 1.02 by July 2022.
295. *See* the published account of the ECB Governing Council's monetary policy meeting of July 20-21, 2022, https://www.ecb.europa.eu/press/accounts/2022/html/ecb.mg220825 ~ 162cfabae9.en.html, at p. 16.
296. *Ibid.*, at pp. 16-17.

is appropriate to contain inflation, and, conversely, (ii) it could cause flight-to-safety capital inflows into stronger economies (at the low end of the spreads) that could compress their bond yields below levels needed to control inflation.[297] It was observed that *"a currency union was particularly susceptible to the risk that fragmentation events might degenerate into self-fulfilling debt crises"*.[298] Interestingly, as a tool to mitigate financial fragmentation risk and consequent disruptions in the monetary policy transmission mechanism, TPI was viewed as a parallel instrument to facilitate policy rate normalization and enable the ECB to act more decisively on inflation control.[299] The ECB would now have a freer hand to increase policy rates knowing that, if needed, it could alleviate unduly harsh effects on bond yields and borrowing conditions of fiscally more vulnerable euro area Member States by targeted bond purchases. Curiously, the published account of the meeting records that *"[t]he unity and team spirit among the members of the Governing Council"* in deciding on TPI were *"widely praised"*.[300] This peculiar self-congratulatory note may cause the reader to suspect that unanimity on this subject was atypical or at least unexpected and that praise disguised surprise and relief.

258. Thus, on July 21, 2022, the ECB announced that it lifted its three key policy rates by 50 basis points with effect as of July 27, *i.e.*, its main refinancing rate to 0.50%, its marginal lending rate to 0.75% and its deposit facility rate to 0%.[301] It signaled in general terms that *"further normalisation of interest rates"* at forthcoming meetings would be *"appropriate"*, while also indicating that it would now adopt a *"meeting-by-meeting"* approach to further policy rate decisions. It was a message which, in combination with that of *"data-dependent"* decision-making, could be liable to increase the financial markets' sensitivity to the ticker tape of incoming data and leave them grappling (even) more with the potential implications of these data for the ECB's future rate path. Might it establish a loop in which a meeting-by-meeting approach increases data dependence increases uncertainty increases market volatility?

259. Concomitantly, the ECB announced the addition of TPI as a new anti-fragmentation instrument to its toolkit. TPI was further described in a separate press release of the same day,[302] carefully crafted to link the new instrument to the ECB's monetary policy mandate by emphasizing its purpose to repair dysfunctionalities in the monetary policy transmission mechanism. TPI would allow the Eurosystem to selectively purchase securities (i) in the secondary markets, (ii) with a remaining maturity between one and 10 years, (iii) focusing on public-sector securities, and (iv) issued in

297. *Cf. ibid.*, at p. 5. In similar vein, in a low-inflation environment, excessive widening of bond spreads would impair the proper pass-through of monetary easing by diminishing the easing impulse in countries at the high end of the spreads and by reinforcing it in countries at the low end of the spreads.
298. *Ibid.*
299. *Ibid.*, at pp. 6 and 14.
300. *Ibid.*, at p. 16.
301. *See* the ECB's press release of July 21, 2022, https://www.ecb.europa.eu/press/pr/date/2022/html/ecb.mp220721~53e5bdd317.en.html.
302. *See* the ECB's press release of the same day, https://www.ecb.europa.eu/press/pr/date/2022/html/ecb.pr220721~973e6e7273.en.html.

euro area Member States which, while pursuing sound and sustainable fiscal and macroeconomic policies, are faced with *"a deterioration in financing conditions not warranted by country-specific fundamentals"*. Purchases under TPI are not subject to any pre-determined (or at least pre-announced) cap and could be activated whenever judged necessary by the Governing Council *"to counter unwarranted, disorderly market dynamics that pose a serious threat to the transmission of monetary policy across the euro area"*. We will discuss TPI in more detail in Chapter 5 (*see*, in particular, paragraphs 358-364, 365(c) and 368 below).

c Fall

260. ***September 7-8, 2022***: By the Governing Council's next monetary policy meeting on September 7-8, 2022, there was heightened uncertainty in financial markets about the inflation outlook and the further path of monetary policy. Headline inflation (HICP) in the euro area had reached 9.1% in August, still driven primarily by high energy and food prices but with price pressures spreading across more and more sectors. The September 2022 staff projections for inflation were again significantly revised upward from their June 2022 levels: in the baseline scenario, headline inflation was now projected to average 8.1% in 2022 (up from 6.8%), 5.5% in 2023 (up from 3.5%) and 2.3% in 2024 (up from 2.1%).[303] At the same time, euro area economic growth was slowing down markedly, with the economy now expected to stagnate later in 2022 and in early 2023. This was seen at the Governing Council's meeting as presenting the ECB with an increasingly difficult balancing act of ensuring a timely return of inflation to target while not unnecessarily exacerbating the economic downturn.[304] *"Some members"* preferred to limit a further rate increase to 50 basis points in view of the *"looming risk of recession"* and considering that wage growth remained moderate with little evidence of second-round effects. But a consensus eventually emerged to raise policy rates by 75 basis points. It was noted that even after this increase, *"the key policy rates would remain significantly below the neutral rate"*.[305]

261. Accordingly, on September 8, 2022, the ECB announced that it raised its key policy rates by a further 75 basis points effective as from September 14, *i.e.*, its main refinancing rate to 1.25%, its marginal lending rate to 1.50% and its deposit facility rate to 0.75%.[306] In the press release, the ECB characterized this as a *"major step"* on its normalization path and stated its expectation to raise policy rates further, but without

303. *See ECB staff macroeconomic projections for the euro area*, September 2022, pp. 18-20, https://www.ecb. europa.eu/pub/pdf/other/ecb.projections202209_ecbstaff~3eafaaee1a.en .pdf.

304. *See* the published account of the ECB Governing Council's monetary policy meeting of September 7-8, 2022, https://www.ecb.europa.eu/press/accounts/2022/html/ecb.mg221006 ~a5f7fb03f3.en.html, at p. 14.

305. *Ibid.*, at pp. 14-15.

306. *See* the ECB's press release of September 8, 2022, https://www.ecb.europa.eu/press/pr/date /2022/html/ecb.mp220908~c1b6839378.en.html. Also, with the deposit facility rate now being in positive territory, the ECB suspended the two-tier system for the remuneration of excess reserves. *See* fn. 207 above.

any more specific forward guidance on rates. It would continue to follow a data-dependent, meeting-by-meeting approach. At the same time, the ECB held on to its existing line of continuing reinvestments of maturing bonds in its APP and PEPP portfolios, without any hint at QT in the near term.

262. ***October 26-27, 2022:*** At its monetary policy meeting of October 26-27, 2022, the Governing Council saw that euro area headline inflation (HICP) had risen further to 9.9 % in September. The concern was expressed that fiscal support measures to provide relief from energy price increases should be targeted and temporary lest they fuel inflation.[307] Economic activity had slowed markedly in 2022 Q3 and it *"was argued"* that a technical recession had now become the baseline scenario.[308] Yet, it was *"widely judged"* that the weakening of the economic outlook would not suffice to bring down projected inflation to target. Thus, while *"[a] few members"* favored a rate increase by 50 basis points, *"a very large majority of members"* supported another 75 basis points raise.[309]

263. And so it was that on October 27, 2022, the ECB again lifted its policy rates by 75 basis points with effect as of November 2, *i.e.*, the main refinancing rate to 2%, the marginal lending rate to 2.25% and the deposit facility rate to 1.50%.[310] The press release noted that this new increase marked *"substantial progress in withdrawing monetary policy accommodation"*, but that the Governing Council still *"expected"* to raise interest rates further. At the ECB press briefing that afternoon, Ms. Lagarde confirmed that *"[t]here is still ground to cover"* and that the ECB would decide the future path and pace of policy rate increases meeting by meeting on the basis of the data then available—acknowledging now that the ECB was *"deliberately turning [its] back to forward guidance, which is not helpful in the current circumstances given the level of uncertainty that we have pretty much all around"*.[311] On the same occasion, the ECB announced that, as from November 23, 2022, it would raise the interest rate on TLTRO III operations then outstanding by indexing it to its average deposit facility or main refinancing rate over the remaining term of each such operation (*i.e.*, the period from November 22, 2022 until the maturity date or early repayment date), while opening up three additional windows for banks to prepay part or all of their outstanding borrowings.[312]

307. *See* the published account of the ECB Governing Council's monetary policy meeting of October 26-27, 2022, https://www.ecb.europa.eu/press/accounts/2022/html/ecb.mg221124 ~ 3527764024.en.html, at p. 10.
308. *Ibid.*
309. *Ibid.*, at pp. 15-16.
310. *See* the ECB's press release of October 27, 2022, https://www.ecb.europa.eu/press/pr/date/2022/html/ecb.mp221027 ~ df1d778b84.en.html.
311. *See* the transcript of the ECB's press conference of October 27, 2022, https://www.ecb.europa.eu/press/pressconf/2022/html/ecb.is221027 ~ 358a06a35f.en.html, at p. 4.
312. Further particulars on this measure were given in a separate press release of October 27, 2022, https://www.ecb.europa.eu/press/pr/date/2022/html/ecb.pr221027_1 ~ c8005660b0.en.html. In addition, the ECB announced that minimum reserves which banks are required to hold in their reserve accounts with their national central bank would, as from December 21, 2022, be remunerated at the deposit facility rate, and no longer at the main refinancing rate, so as to align that remuneration more closely with prevailing money market conditions. *See* the ECB's

264. The ECB still maintained its prior message on the continued reinvestment of principal repayments on bonds in the Eurosystem's APP and PEPP portfolios. In the press briefing, however, Ms. Lagarde indicated that the Governing Council would decide the *"key principles"* regarding the future run-off of the APP portfolio (she did not mention the PEPP portfolio) at its December monetary policy meeting *"in advance of the decision to implement and to roll out this reduction"*.[313] Interestingly, Ms. Lagarde also observed that the Governing Council *"did not discuss TPI at all"*.[314] I mention this because the spread between the 10-year Italian BTP and the 10-year German Bund had almost continuously been above 200 basis points since early June 2022, peaking close to 250 basis points on October 7, 2022 but edging down again since then.

d Winter

265. ***December 14-15, 2022:*** At its monetary policy meeting of December 14-15, 2022, the Governing Council had the following incoming data (among multiple other data) to assess:

(a) Euro area headline inflation (HICP) had peaked at 10.6% in October but unexpectedly "softened" a little to 10% in November 2022, mainly on account of lower energy prices. Yet, food inflation had further increased to 13.6% and was expected to continue its upward trend into early 2023, and measures of core inflation remained at high levels. Wage growth was accelerating, with second-round effects on inflation now beginning to appear. In the December 2022 staff projections, those for headline inflation were once again revised upward against those of September 2022, *i.e.*, to 8.4% for 2022 (up from 8.1%), 6.3% for 2023 (up from 5.5%) and 3.4% for 2024 (up from 2.3%), then declining to 2.3% in 2025. Core inflation (HICP excluding energy and food) was now projected at 3.9% in 2022, 4.2% in 2023, 2.8% in 2024, and 2.4% in 2025.[315] Inflation projections were subject to *"an unusual degree of uncertainty, particularly over the medium term"*, and risks to the inflation outlook were seen as primarily on the upside.[316]

(b) The smaller-than-expected increase of the U.S. consumer price index in October had been interpreted in the financial markets as an early sign of easing of inflationary pressures. This had led to a market repricing of policy rate expectations and some easing of financing conditions which, given

separate press release of the same day, https://www.ecb.europa.eu/press/pr/date/2022/html/ecb.pr221027~25d335259c.en.html.

313. *See* the transcript of the ECB's press conference of October 27, 2022, at p. 4.

314. *Ibid.*, at p. 5.

315. *See Eurosystem staff macroeconomic projections for the euro area*, December 2022, pp. 20-23, https://www.ecb.europa.eu/pub/pdf/other/ecb.projections202212_eurosystemstaff~6c1855c75b.en.pdf.

316. *See* the published account of the ECB Governing Council's monetary policy meeting of December 14-15, 2022, https://www.ecb.europa.eu/press/accounts/2023/html/ecb.mg230119~e522ad4e37.en.html, at pp. 12-13.

market sensitivity to macroeconomic news from the United States, had spilled over to the euro area. It was observed at the meeting that this was at odds with the significantly more adverse inflation outlook for the euro area and worked against the ECB's plan to withdraw monetary accommodation, and that, accordingly, this shift in market perception had to be corrected.[317]

(c) Fiscal stimulus in response to higher energy prices and the increased cost of living had been significant[318] and, in view of the fiscal measures included in the governments' draft budgetary plans for 2023, was estimated to rise to 1.9% of GDP in the euro area in 2023.[319] Concern was again expressed at the meeting that the current fiscal response was not sufficiently targeted at the most vulnerable businesses and households, which not only created challenges for public finances but was also likely to exacerbate inflationary pressures and require stronger monetary policy action to control inflation.[320]

(d) Average real GDP growth in the euro area had slowed down considerably to 0.3% in 2022 Q3 and was projected to contract slightly in 2022 Q4 and 2023 Q1, remain subdued at 0.5% for 2023 and rebound to 1.9% in 2024.[321] It was observed that a recession would likely be short-lived and mild and could not be counted on to dampen inflationary pressures to a significant degree.[322]

(e) As part of the Governing Council's regular biannual consideration of the interrelation between monetary policy and financial stability, it was agreed that financial stability conditions in the euro area had further deteriorated since the previous review of May 2022. It was noted in particular that sudden liquidity needs of non-bank financial institutions might amplify market volatility. Still, euro area banks were seen to have *"comfortable levels"* of capital that should help reduce the possible negative side effects of monetary tightening.[323] It was thought that insufficient or delayed monetary policy reactivity to inflation might simply defer repercussions on financial stability

317. *Ibid.*, at pp. 1 and 13.
318. *Cf.* ECB, *Financial Stability Review*, November 2022, p. 21, Chart 1.4, panel (b), https://www.ecb.europa.eu/pub/pdf/fsr/ecb.fsr202211~6383d08c21.en.pdf. This diagram shows, for 17 euro area Member States, the widely varying but generally elevated shares of non-targeted energy and war-related fiscal measures as at October 31, 2022.
319. *See* the published account of the ECB Governing Council's monetary policy meeting of December 14-15, 2022, at p. 4.
320. *Ibid.*, at p. 10.
321. *See Eurosystem staff macroeconomic projections for the euro area*, December 2022, at pp. 5-8.
322. *See* the published account of the ECB Governing Council's monetary policy meeting of December 14-15, 2022, at p. 14.
323. *Ibid.* In fact, the ECB's latest financial stability review found that, while the solvency and leverage ratios of euro area banks had declined in the first half of 2022, they remained at robust levels, with the average Common Equity Tier 1 (CET1) ratio of significant banks standing at 15%. *See* ECB, *Financial Stability Review*, November 2022, pp. 63-64. Yet, this report also noted that, while the growth outlook had deteriorated and the share of underperforming loans had continued to rise, provisioning coverage ratios for non-performing and underperforming loans had not followed (*ibid.*, pp. 51-52). The report saw signs of increasing credit risks (*ibid.*, p. 55) and a probability of higher loan provisioning costs in 2023 due to the further weakening of the macroeconomic outlook (*ibid.*, pp. 59-61).

and likely increase them.[324] At this point, the published account of the meeting adds, without any further detail, that the Governing Council discussed potentially disorderly market reactions to *"various shocks, including different scenarios of quantitative tightening and adverse changes in fiscal policy"*.[325] Unsurprisingly, the document remains discreet on the scenarios considered and the ECB's possible response.

266. In light of these developments, *"[a] large number of members"* initially favored a further rate increase of 75 basis points, and some held on to this position. However, *"a broad majority"* supported a raise by 50 basis points, but with a clear message that interest rates would still have to rise *"significantly"*—a message intended to produce an upward shift in market expectations as to the future rate path.[326] Interestingly, it was observed in this respect that, *"as interest rates were approaching estimates of a neutral level"*, the steepness (*"frontloading"*) and speed of rate increases mattered less than their steadiness and the time period over which rates would remain in restrictive territory.[327] In parallel, it was decided to start a "passive" phase of QT as of March 2023 by reducing reinvestment of principal repayments in the APP portfolio initially by EUR 15 billion per month until (and including) June 2023. *"Some members"* advocated a faster pace of reduction or even an outright termination of APP reinvestments, but it was feared that too fast a pace of reduction could rekindle bond market fragmentation and make further policy rate increases more difficult.[328]

267. Thus, on December 15, 2022, the ECB announced that it raised its three key policy rates by a further 50 basis points effective December 21, *i.e.*, the main refinancing rate to 2.50 %, the marginal lending rate to 2.75 % and the deposit facility rate to 2 %.[329] The press release also pushed back on market hopes of a near-term "pivot" by stating the Governing Council's judgment that rates *"will still have to rise significantly at a steady pace to reach levels that are sufficiently restrictive to ensure a timely return of inflation to the 2% medium-term target"*, and by adding that *"[k]eeping interest rates at restrictive levels"* would *"over time"* reduce inflation by dampening demand and guard against the risk of a persistent upward shift in inflation expectations. But the press release otherwise confirmed the data-dependent and meeting-by-meeting approach to future policy rate decisions.

268. In the same announcement, the ECB also shared broad indications on its plan for an initial "passive" phase of QT. As of March 2023, the Eurosystem would start reducing its **APP** portfolio *"at a measured and predictable pace"* by not reinvesting a certain amount of principal repayments on maturing bonds (but not yet by selling

324. *See* the published account of the ECB Governing Council's monetary policy meeting of December 14-15, 2022, at p. 14.
325. *Ibid.*
326. *Ibid.*, at pp. 15-16.
327. *Ibid.*, at p. 16.
328. *Ibid.*, at pp. 17-18.
329. *See* the ECB's press release of December 15, 2022, https://www.ecb.europa.eu/press/pr/date/2022/html/ecb.mp221215~f3461d7b6e.en.html.

bonds prior to maturity). In an initial period of four months, that amount would be EUR 15 billion per month on average (*i.e.*, roughly half of the scheduled principal repayments in that period). The subsequent pace of APP portfolio reduction would be determined later and be subject to regular reassessment *"to ensure it remains consistent with the overall monetary policy strategy and stance, to preserve market functioning, and to maintain control over short-term money market conditions"*. In addition, the press release signaled that the review of the ECB's operational framework for steering short-term interest rates, to be carried out by the end of 2023 (*see* paragraphs 479-484 below), would provide information on the endpoint of the *"balance sheet normalisation process"*. Still, the ECB confirmed its intention to fully reinvest maturing bonds in the **PEPP** portfolio until at least the end of 2024.

269. ***February 1-2, 2023:*** By the next monetary policy meeting of February 1-2, 2023, headline inflation (HICP) had further subsided to 8.5% (subsequently revised to 8.6%) in January, down from 10.6% in October, 10.1% in November and 9.2% in December 2022, due mainly to the decline in energy prices, but core inflation had not come down from its December 2022 level and still stood at 5.2% in January. It was acknowledged at the meeting that risks to the inflation outlook had become *"more balanced, especially in the near term"*.[330] Yet, in the published account of the meeting, the Governing Council is seen struggling to come to grips with several factors of uncertainty:

(a) The decline in energy prices seemed to be driven in some measure by the mild weather conditions over the winter, and it was unclear whether the lower level of energy prices would persist given the *"exceptionally high degree of global uncertainty"*.[331] Among other factors, the reopening of the Chinese economy following the relaxation of COVID-19 restrictions might well increase demand for, and prices of, natural gas and other commodities.[332] Different views were expressed as to the speed and extent of the pass-through of decreasing energy prices to core inflation.[333]

(b) There was also considerable uncertainty about the dampening effect that monetary tightening may thus far have had on inflation dynamics, given that monetary policy transmission lags tend to be long and variable. But it was noted that bank lending to businesses had declined sharply over recent months and that broader financing conditions had tightened overall since the December meeting.[334]

(c) Wage growth had been accelerating, and, while it was *"widely"* agreed that there was no evidence of a wage-price spiral yet, it was also argued that ongoing wage growth was inconsistent with the 2% inflation target.[335]

330. *See* the published account of the ECB Governing Council's monetary policy meeting of February 1-2, 2023, https://www.ecb.europa.eu/press/accounts/2023/html/ecb.mg230302~009d06dd5a.en.html, at p. 13.
331. *Ibid.*, at p. 9.
332. *Ibid.*, at pp. 8, 12 and 13.
333. *Ibid.*, at pp. 11-12.
334. *Ibid.*, at pp. 12 and 14.
335. *Ibid.*, at p. 12.

(d) It was agreed, at the level of principle, that national fiscal support measures to alleviate the impact of high energy prices should be rolled back in line with the decline in energy prices lest they drive up medium-term inflationary pressures and necessitate a stronger monetary policy response to control inflation. *"Several members"* believed that current fiscal policies were already working against monetary policy efforts to restore price stability.[336]

(e) Market data (specifically, the euro area overnight index swap forward curve) suggested that, in recent weeks, financial markets had revised their policy rate expectations downward and were now pricing in material rate cuts as of 2024. It was felt that these market expectations implied a more optimistic view than the inflation trajectory reflected in the December 2022 staff projections (*see* paragraph 265(a) above) and were *"somewhat at odds"* with the message that the Governing Council had intended to convey on December 15, 2022, to the effect that interest rates would need to stay at restrictive levels for a while in order for inflation to return to target.[337] One might think that the wordsmithing that had gone into the relevant (first) paragraph of the December 15, 2022 press release (*see* paragraph 267 above) had perhaps somewhat obfuscated that message.

270. In the end, there was *"broad support"* for raising policy rates again by 50 basis points and for communicating the Governing Council's "intention" to increase them by another 50 basis points at its March meeting, although *"reservations were expressed"* regarding this last message.[338] But the prevailing view was that further increases were required for policy rates to enter restrictive territory, that concerns of overtightening were premature, that current policy rates were *"barely consistent with the range of estimates for the neutral rate"*, and that the Eurosystem's large bond portfolio was still providing substantial accommodation.[339]

271. Accordingly, on February 2, 2023, the ECB announced that it would increase its three key rates by 50 basis points with effect as of February 8, *i.e.*, its main refinancing rate to 3%, its marginal lending rate to 3.25% and its deposit facility rate to 2.50%.[340] By way of a partial return of forward guidance on rates, the press release added that the Governing Council *"intends"* to raise policy rates by another 50 basis points at its next monetary policy meeting in March and would then evaluate the subsequent path of its monetary policy. The press release qualified this message by repeating that *"[i]n any*

336. *Ibid.*, at p. 13.
337. *Ibid.*, at pp. 1 and 17.
338. *Ibid.*, at pp. 16-17.
339. *Ibid.* Interestingly, it was also observed that there continued to be merit in "frontloading" rate increases *"given the still substantial distance to the prospective terminal rate"*. *Ibid.*, at p. 17. In other words, according to some view deemed worth recording in the published account of the meeting, there was some target terminal rate level "substantially" higher than the current policy rates. Curiously, this message was not clearly picked up by the financial markets when the meeting minutes were published on March 2, 2023.
340. *See* the ECB's press release of February 2, 2023, https://www.ecb.europa.eu/press/pr/date/2023/html/ecb.mp230202~08a972ac76.en.html.

event", the Governing Council would continue to follow a data-dependent and meeting-by-meeting approach to future policy rate decisions. It also repeated, *verbatim*, the December 15, 2022 message that *"[k]eeping interest rates at restrictive levels will over time reduce inflation"* (*see* paragraphs 267 and 269(e) above).

272. In the same press release, the ECB clarified its *modus operandi* for the gradual phase-out of reinvestments in the Eurosystem's APP portfolio as from March 2023 (*see* paragraph 268 above), with further particulars set out in a separate press release of the same day.[341]

e ... And Spring

273. ***March 15-16, 2023:*** The spring of 2023 started out ominously. A good 10 days into March, market anxiety flared up over the difficulties, in rapid succession, at Silicon Valley Bank, Signature Bank and First Republic Bank in the United States. By mid-March, closer to home, dark clouds were packing around Crédit Suisse. Predictably, loud voices were quick to claim that, as they purportedly had previously warned, aggressive monetary tightening was bound to break something somewhere at some point, and that it was now urgent for central banks to rein in monetary tightening. Of course, market anxiety over bank safety, whether or not objectively justified, tends to be highly contagious and presents an elevated risk of triggering destabilizing market dynamics. Central banks must then stand ready to take early and resolute action to calm down fears when soothing messages about the robustness of the banking system fail to do so. And continued heightened vigilance is required as the initial incidents may ripple through the system with varying time lags. In any event, the market developments of those days blurred the policy outlook by intensifying risks of financial instability and more severe credit contraction. It was in those unsettled circumstances, a mere few days into an incipient crisis of uncertain scope and duration, that the ECB's Governing Council had to consider its further course of action at its scheduled monetary policy meeting of March 15-16, 2023. As the Governing Council congregated in Frankfurt, Crédit Suisse stock fell by some 14% on March 15.

274. In February, headline inflation (HICP) had slightly edged down to 8.5% (from 8.6% in January), with a decline in energy prices being offset by a further increase in

341. *See* the ECB's press release of the same day, https://www.ecb.europa.eu/press/pr/date/2023/html/ecb.pr230202~1a4ecbe398.en.html. The reduced reinvestments, *i.e.*, reinvestments corresponding to the flow-back of principal repayments on maturing bonds less EUR 15 billion per month, would be carried out according to the following criteria: (i) they would be allocated across APP sub-programs in proportion to the principal repayments in each sub-program; (ii) within PSPP, they would be allocated among euro area Member States and supranational issuers *pro rata* their respective shares of principal repayments; (iii) in the private-sector sub-programs (ABSPP, CBPP3 and CSPP), primary market purchases would be phased out, except for corporate issuers with better climate performance and for green bonds; and (iv) corporate bond purchases would be tilted more strongly toward issuers with better climate performance. The green touches of items (iii) and (iv) are in line with earlier ECB announcements in the wake of its 2021 monetary policy strategy review (*see* paragraph 476 below).

food prices. Underlying price pressures remained strong and core inflation (HICP minus energy and food) had climbed to 5.6% (up from 5.2% in January). At the meeting of the Governing Council, it was noted that wage pressures had strengthened and were taking over from energy as the main driver of underlying inflation.[342] It was also observed, for the first time, that the *"significantly more dynamic"* increase in corporate profit margins in sectors with constrained supply and resurgent demand played a role in fueling inflationary pressures and *"warranted constant monitoring and further analysis on an equal footing with developments in wages"*.[343] More generally, if core inflation might be approaching a turning point, this could not yet be seen in hard data.[344] The March 2023 staff macroeconomic projections, which had been finalized before the new financial market tensions, now saw average euro area headline inflation at 5.3% in 2023 (down from 6.3% in the December 2022 projections), 2.9% in 2024 (down from 3.4%) and 2.1% in 2025 (down from 2.3%), and core inflation at 4.6% in 2023 (**up** from 4.2% in the December 2022 projections), 2.5% in 2024 (down from 2.8%) and 2.2% in 2025 (down from 2.4%).[345] The published account of the meeting records that members expressed *"a range of views"* on the upside and downside risks affecting these baseline inflation projections and that it was considered that, in view of the uncertainty associated with current financial market turbulence, there was no need for the Governing Council to communicate *"its own collective balance of risks to price stability from the range of risk factors"*.[346]

275. In the end, *"a very large majority"* of the members agreed to raise policy rates by a further 50 basis points, in line with the intention announced on February 2, 2023 (*see* paragraph 271 above), while *"[s]ome members"* preferred to put policy rate increases on hold until financial market tensions had subsided.[347] It would seem from the published account of the meeting that the Governing Council (or at least the majority of its members) was not overly alarmed by the ongoing financial market tensions. It was recognized that these tensions imparted additional uncertainty to the economic and inflation outlook and that, if persisting at high levels, could tighten credit conditions more strongly than expected and accelerate disinflation.[348] But it was felt that, absent a significant deterioration of the situation, the current tensions were

342. *See* the published account of the ECB Governing Council's monetary policy meeting of March 15-16, 2023, https://www.ecb.europa.eu/press/accounts/2023/html/ecb.mg230420~e8043d2d3d.en.html, at p. 11.
343. *Ibid.*, at pp. 6 and 12.
344. *Ibid.*, at p. 11.
345. *See ECB staff macroeconomic projections for the euro area*, March 2023, pp. 7 and 19-21, https://www.ecb.europa.eu/pub/pdf/other/ecb.projections202303_ecbstaff~77c0227058.en.pdf.
346. *See* the published account of the ECB Governing Council's monetary policy meeting of March 15-16, 2023, at p. 13.
347. *Ibid.*, at pp. 15-16. At the press conference following the meeting, ECB President Christine Lagarde mentioned that the rate increase had been decided *"in rather record time"*, with only *"three or four"* members wishing to take *"a bit more time"* to see how things unfolded. *See* the transcript of the ECB's press conference of March 16, 2023, https://www.ecb.europa.eu/press/pressconf/2023/html/ecb.is230316~6c10b087b5.en.html, at p. 5.
348. *See* the published account of the ECB Governing Council's monetary policy meeting of March 15-16, 2023, at pp. 8, 10 and 15.

unlikely to fundamentally alter the Governing Council's assessment of the inflation outlook.[349] It was *"recalled"* that, in any event, the ECB had *"liquidity instruments"* at hand in its toolkit to address liquidity strains in the banking sector, which allowed it *"to look through the recent volatility in financial market variables to set interest rates in accordance with its price stability objective"*.[350]

Here, the Governing Council circled back to the old "separation principle" between the monetary policy stance aimed at inflation control, on the one hand, and liquidity provision to preserve the proper functioning of the money markets (whatever the interest rate level is), on the other hand. We will take a closer look at this principle in Chapter 6 (*see* paragraphs 421-425 below). But now, the Governing Council boldly affirmed that this principle calls *"for the monetary policy stance to be assessed independently of risks related to financial stability"*.[351] It was also felt that there was no *"fundamental"* trade-off between the objectives of price stability and financial stability and that both were complementary in that *"safeguarding financial stability supported an orderly transmission of monetary policy and the achievement of price stability over the medium term"*.[352] Yet, toward the end of the meeting, it was suggested that, while the Governing Council should refrain from communicating specific expectations for the future policy rate path, a message should be conveyed to the effect that *"had the recent market turmoil not occurred, the Governing Council would have expressed the expectation that it would increase rates further"*.[353] This seems to be in partial contradiction with the earlier affirmation that the monetary policy stance is to be determined independently from financial stability risks.

276. Thus, on March 16, 2023, the ECB announced that, with inflation being projected *"to remain too high for too long"*, it kept to its earlier intention and raised its key policy rates by a further 50 basis points effective March 22, *i.e.*, the main refinancing rate to 3.50%, the marginal lending rate to 3.75% and the deposit facility rate to 3%.[354] The press release itself did not give any concrete indication as to the future rate path. It stated that the high level of uncertainty reinforces the importance of data-dependent policy rate decisions, and now added that these decisions will be determined by the Governing Council's assessment of (i) the inflation outlook in light of incoming economic and financial data; (ii) the dynamics of underlying inflation; and (iii) the strength of monetary policy transmission. At the press conference of the same day, ECB President Christine Lagarde observed that, if the ECB's baseline were to persist notwithstanding current uncertainties, *"we have a lot more ground to cover"*[355]—which seems to put a more Jesuitic spin on the message discussed at the Governing Council's meeting (*see* paragraph 275, *in fine*, above). As concerns the prospects of inflation

349. *Ibid.*, at p. 15.
350. *Ibid.*
351. *Ibid.*, at p. 14.
352. *Ibid.*, at p. 15.
353. *Ibid.*, at p. 16.
354. *See* the ECB's press release of March 16, 2023, https://www.ecb.europa.eu/press/pr/date/2023/html/ecb.mp230316~aad5249f30.en.html.
355. *See* the transcript of the ECB's press conference of March 16, 2023, at p. 4.

returning to the 2% target, Ms. Lagarde otherwise noted that *"[w]e are seeing some slight improvement in certain areas but frankly, not a lot"*.[356]

277. In parallel, the March 16, 2023 press release emphasized that the Governing Council *"stands ready to respond as necessary"* to preserve price stability and financial stability in the euro area, and that the ECB's toolkit is *"fully equipped"* to provide liquidity support to the euro area financial system if needed and to safeguard the smooth transmission of monetary policy. When asked at the press conference about a possible conflict between the objectives of price stability and financial stability, Ms. Lagarde repeated, six times in the span of a few minutes, that there is no trade-off between these objectives and that both are being addressed separately with their respective instruments,[357] which again echoes the separation principle. In response to another question at the press conference, Ms. Lagarde observed that *"it could well be the case"* that TPI could be activated when banking tensions compromise monetary policy transmission but that this had not yet been debated within the Governing Council.[358] Yet, it would seem unlikely that Ms. Lagarde, a seasoned international lawyer having held several ministerial positions in the French Government for six years and served as the IMF's Managing Director for eight years, would venture such a possibility, even in tentative terms, if there hadn't in fact been some preliminary consideration of the idea on the upper office floors of the ECB's twin towers in Frankfurt.

278. ***May 3-4, 2023*****:** By the next monetary policy meeting of the ECB's Governing Council on May 3-4, 2023, the situation had evolved as follows:

(a) No banking or broader financial crisis had erupted (yet) in the wake of the difficulties at Silicon Valley Bank, certain other U.S. banks and Crédit Suisse. Ms. Isabel Schnabel could reassure the meeting that measures of systemic stress, volatility and market liquidity as well as sovereign bond spreads had reverted to close their levels prior to the failure of Silicon Valley Bank.[359]

(b) The inflation readings prompted much discussion at the meeting on the inflation outlook and the dynamics of underlying inflation. Annual headline inflation (HICP) was estimated at 7% in April 2023, after having dropped from 8.5% in February to 6.9% in March. Core inflation in April stood at 5.6%, *i.e.*, the same level as in February and slightly down from 5.7% in March. Food price inflation in April remained elevated at 13.6%, against 15% in February and 15.5% in March. While energy prices had come down, other inflation components were higher than expected in the ECB staff macroeconomic projections of March 2023. And inflation was still being fueled by the

356. *Ibid.*, at p. 7.
357. *Ibid.*, at pp. 6-7.
358. *Ibid.*, at p. 8.
359. *See* the published account of the ECB Governing Council's monetary policy meeting of May 3-4, 2023, https://www.ecb.europa.eu/press/accounts/2023/html/ecb.mg230601~9d35f80dee.en.html, at p. 1. In fact, the spread between the 10-year Italian BTP and the 10-year German Bund had consistently dwelled below 200 basis points since early March 2023.

unfolding pass-through of past energy cost increases and supply-chain bottlenecks.[360]

(c) It was noted that underlying price pressures remained strong and pointed to increased persistence and that there was no robust evidence yet of a turning point in underlying inflation.[361] Interestingly, it was also cautioned that, historically, there was no stable predictive relationship between headline inflation and core inflation (or other indicators of underlying inflation) one to two years ahead, and that it should not be surprising that, after the earlier surge in energy prices, core inflation would decline only with a significant lag.[362] The concern was expressed that, as high inflation perdures, it would fuel a trend in wage increases that would be out of line with productivity growth and become inconsistent with the ECB's inflation target. Wages had increased significantly which, in conjunction with weaker labor productivity growth, implied a notable increase in unit labor costs.[363] There were signs that increasing wage pressures together with higher profit margins could be causing a wage-profit-price spiral with wages chasing higher prices and profits chasing higher wages (and other input costs).[364] In partial conclusion, the latest developments as to the level and momentum of core inflation were *"broadly seen as worrisome"* and a *"source of concern"*.[365]

(d) As to monetary policy transmission, there was now clearer evidence that the earlier policy rate increases were being transmitted forcefully at the level of financing and monetary conditions in the euro area. In particular, the bank credit channel saw higher lending rates, tighter credit standards and declining loan demand. In real terms, the contraction of loans to businesses as a percentage of GDP was similar to that observed in 2008 and 2011.[366] Beyond this first stage of transmission, however, the lags and strength of the pass-through of monetary tightening to the real economy remained uncertain, with the transmission of much of the impact of prior rate increases still pending.

(e) All in all, given the inflation outlook, the still strong dynamics of underlying inflation and the remaining uncertainties about the speed and strength of monetary policy transmission to the real economy, the sense in the room was that the conditions were not in place to *"declare victory"*.[367]

279. Accordingly, the ECB's Governing Council decided to raise the three key policy rates by 25 basis points with effect as of May 10, *i.e.*, the main refinancing rate to 3.75%, the marginal lending rate to 4% and the deposit facility rate to 3.25%. A

360. *Ibid.*, at p. 8.
361. *Ibid.*, at p. 9.
362. *Ibid.*, at p. 10.
363. *Ibid.*
364. *Ibid.*, at pp. 10-11.
365. *Ibid.*, at pp. 9 and 13.
366. *Ibid.*, at p. 12.
367. *Ibid.*, at p. 14.

"number of members" initially favored an increase by 50 basis points, but *"almost all members"* eventually ended up supporting the more standard size of rate increment of 25 basis points notably because of the uncertainties surrounding the speed and strength of monetary policy transmission. The cumulative increase of policy rates by 350 basis points since July 2022 must mean that rates were *"getting closer to their destination"*, and much of the impact of the rate increases so far was still in the pipeline. At the same time, it was felt that the new rate increase should be messaged in such a way as (i) to avoid this smaller increase being misinterpreted as signaling an imminent pause in the monetary tightening cycle, and (ii) to make clear that, once policy rates had reached their peak level, they would need to stay there for a while.[368] These messages were reflected in the ECB's press release of May 4, 2023[369]—the second more clearly than the first, but ECB President Christine Lagarde made sure to state point (i) more explicitly at the ECB press briefing of the same day.[370]

280. *"[S]aving a little bit of optionality just in case"*, as Ms. Lagarde put it,[371] the ECB also stated its "expectation" that the reinvestment of maturing securities in the Eurosystem's **APP** portfolio would be fully discontinued as of July 2023. At the Governing Council's meeting, switching to (somewhat) higher gear on QT was viewed as being consistent with (i) the current monetary policy stance and the need to reduce excess liquidity; (ii) the desirability of recreating monetary policy space for future situations in which policy rates would again approach the lower bound; and, lo and behold, (iii) the principle of proportionality. The Governing Council felt comforted by the smooth market absorption of the ongoing first phase of non-reinvestment of EUR 15 billion per month on average (*see* paragraph 268 above), notwithstanding the turbulences of the Silicon Valley Bank episode and the relative frontloading of government bond issuance in 2023. The Council was also reassured by its perception that markets had largely priced in the switch to full APP run-off as of the summer. It did not appear to be overly concerned about the simultaneous significant decline in excess liquidity resulting from TLTRO repayments.[372] At the May 4, 2023 press briefing, Ms. Lagarde observed that the switch to full run-off would reduce the APP portfolio by *"roughly"* EUR 25 billion per month on average[373] and that its actual tightening impact should not be *"material"*.[374] Hypothetically, with such a purely "passive" QT (letting securities

368. *Ibid.*, at pp. 14-15.
369. *See* the ECB's press release of May 4, 2023, https://www.ecb.europa.eu/press/pr/date/2023/html/ecb.mp230504~cdfd11a697.en.html.
370. *See* the transcript of the ECB's press conference of May 4, 2023, https://www.ecb.europa.eu/press/pressconf/2023/html/ecb.is230504~f242392c72.en.html, at p. 4 (*"based on the information we have today, we have more ground to cover and we are not pausing—that's extremely clear"*) and p. 8 (*"given our baseline, the findings that we have, the data that we can analyse today, our judgement in the room is that we are not pausing, that applies to today, based on what we see we determine that we have more ground to cover"*).
371. *Ibid.*, at p. 6.
372. *See* the published account of the ECB Governing Council's monetary policy meeting of May 3-4, 2023, at pp. 16-17. In particular, banks were to repay about EUR 477 billion on TLTRO III operations at the end of June 2023.
373. *See* the transcript of the ECB's press conference of May 4, 2023, at p. 6.
374. *Ibid.*, at p. 9.

mature without reinvesting the proceeds, as distinguished from selling securities prior to maturity), it would take well over 10 years for the APP portfolio to run down to zero. But on May 4, 2023, there was no hint yet of moving to "active" QT. And the ECB again confirmed its intention to continue full reinvestment in the **PEPP** portfolio *"until at least the end of 2024"*.

f Toward the End of a Cycle

281. At its monetary policy meetings in the summer of 2023, the ECB's Governing Council was confronted with the heightened ambiguities of a tightening cycle approaching its peak.

282. ***June 14-15, 2023*:** By the monetary policy meeting of June 14-15, 2023, the economic data increasingly presented shades of gray:

(a) No banking crisis or broader financial market turmoil had set in following the difficulties surrounding Silicon Valley Bank, certain other U.S. banks and Crédit Suisse in March, and signs of systemic stress had abated. By and large, financial market conditions had normalized across market segments. The phasing-out of APP reinvestments appeared to have been absorbed smoothly by the market and sovereign bond spreads had narrowed.[375]

(b) Annualized headline inflation (HICP) had continued to decline from 7% in April to 6.1% in May, food price inflation had diminished from 13.6% in April but remained very high at 12.5%, and core inflation (HICP minus energy and food) had edged down from 5.6% in April to 5.3% in May. Yet, the inflation outlook for 2023-2025 had not brightened: the June 2023 staff macroeconomic projections for the euro area now expected headline inflation to average 5.4% in 2023 (up from 5.3% in the March 2023 projections), 3% in 2024 (up from 2.9%) and 2.2% in 2025 (up from 2.1%), and core inflation to reach 5.1% in 2023 (up from 4.6% in the March 2023 projections), 3% in 2024 (up from 2.5%) and 2.3% in 2025 (up from 2.2%).[376]

(c) As to underlying inflation dynamics, the Governing Council concluded that indicators of underlying price pressures remained strong, although *"some*

375. However, in her introductory review of financial market developments at the meeting, Ms. Isabel Schnabel cautioned that sovereign bond spreads remained sensitive to fundamentals, *"as illustrated by the response to recent shifts in rating outlooks"*. *See* the published account of the ECB Governing Council's monetary policy meeting of June 14-15, 2023, https://www.ecb.europa.eu/press/accounts/2023/html/ecb.mg230713~f7e54fdb87.en.html, at p. 1. Ms. Schnabel was presumably referring to recent rating decisions of Fitch which, on March 10, 2023, had affirmed Belgium's sovereign rating at AA– but revised its outlook to negative, and, on April 28, 2023, had downgraded France from AA to AA–.

376. *Eurosystem staff macroeconomic projections for the euro area*, June 2023, pp. 6 and 14-17, https://www.ecb.europa.eu/pub/pdf/other/ecb.projections202306_eurosystemstaff~6625228e9f.en.pdf.

showed tentative signs of softening".[377] Recent data suggested that core inflation might have stabilized, but the fact that core inflation readings had repeatedly been higher than projected gave pause and pointed to greater persistence. There was no persuasive evidence yet that underlying inflation had reached a turning point, and it would likely take some time before underlying inflation measures took a steady downward path.[378] Wage pressures and, in some sectors, profit margins had overtaken energy and food as the main drivers of inflation. Wage pressures in particular continued to be strong in relation to subdued growth in productivity, although there were signs that they had started to moderate in several euro area Member States and there was currently no evidence of significant second-round effects or a wage-price spiral.[379] Interestingly, it was noted that the projected decline of inflation toward 2% in the medium term was based on the assumption that wage pressures would gradually subside and that profit margins would shrink again (*i.e.*, that businesses would in part absorb higher labor costs through lower profit margins). Given the continued shortage of skilled labor, this suggests a narrow path to getting close to the 2% target by 2025.[380]

(d) At the meeting, Governing Council members *"generally concurred"* that policy rates were now in restrictive territory, although it remained unclear at which point they would become sufficiently restrictive. As to the timing and efficacy of monetary policy transmission, the Governing Council saw evidence that its tighter monetary policy stance was being transmitted forcefully into weaker credit dynamics, with higher lending rates, tighter financing conditions and lower loan demand, and was also beginning to gradually reach the real economy. But it also noted that inflation was responding with different lags across euro area Member States.[381]

283. On the basis of these data and considerations, the Governing Council decided to raise policy rates by a further 25 basis points, *i.e.*, the main refinancing rate to 4%, the marginal lending rate to 4.25% and the deposit facility rate to 3.50%, with effect as of June 21, 2023. This decision was supported by *"[a] very broad consensus"*, although some members had initially advocated a raise by 50 basis points. But the Governing Council saw merit in keeping to a data-dependent, meeting-by-meeting approach *"in an uncertain environment, particularly as rates were moving closer to a possible peak level"*. Yet, it was also believed *"essential"* to communicate that monetary policy still had *"more ground to cover"* to bring back inflation to target in a timely manner.[382] At the June 15, 2023 press conference, ECB President Christine Lagarde took this message to

377. *See* the published account of the ECB Governing Council's monetary policy meeting of June 14-15, 2023, at p. 6.
378. *Ibid.*, at pp. 10 and 16.
379. *Ibid.*, at pp. 11 and 16.
380. *Ibid.*, at pp. 11-12.
381. *Ibid.*, at p. 16.
382. *Ibid.*, at p. 17.

heart, stating repeatedly that *"we have ground to cover"*, *"we're not at destination"* and *"[t]he journey to get there is not over"*.[383] She added that, absent a material change to its baseline, the ECB would very likely increase rates again at its July meeting.[384] In response to questions about possible pausing or skipping of rate increases, she affirmed that *"we are not thinking about pausing"* and even, probably somewhat hyperbolically, that *"we have not discussed it at all and we have not begun thinking about it"*.[385]

284. The Governing Council further confirmed that reinvestments under APP would be discontinued at the end of June 2023, while also re-affirming its intention to continue reinvestments under PEPP *"until at least the end of 2024"*. At the June 15, 2023 press conference, Ms. Lagarde suggested that there is currently *"no plan"* to go any further in reducing the Eurosystem's APP and PEPP portfolios beyond APP's passive run-off.[386]

285. Interestingly, at the Governing Council's meeting, the sentiment was expressed that the ECB should stress that national fiscal policies should be tightened so as to dampen demand and support the disinflation process.[387] In the published monetary policy statement, this ended up more diplomatically as a call to governments to promptly roll back support measures related to the energy crisis and to design fiscal policies in such a manner as to make the economy more productive and gradually reduce high public debt.[388]

286. ***July 26-27, 2023*:** At its monetary policy meeting of July 26-27, 2023, the ECB's Governing Council continued its cautious approach to reaching final altitude in its monetary tightening cycle in light of fresh incoming data:

(a) As to developments in the financial markets, the inversion of the euro area yield curve had deepened, with higher short-term rate expectations and with term premium remaining compressed due to the stock effect of the Eurosystem's large monetary policy portfolio of bond holdings.[389] The decline in liquidity following the substantial TLTRO III repayments in June and the start of full run-off of the APP portfolio as of July 2023 had not so far produced upward pressure on money market rates.[390] Sovereign bond spreads were close to their levels in late 2021, before the start of the monetary policy tightening cycle.[391] Euro area risk-free yields and asset prices had (again)

383. *See* the transcript of the ECB's press conference of June 15, 2023, https://www.ecb.europa.eu/press/pressconf/2023/html/ecb.is230615~3de9d68335.en.html, at pp. 4 and 7.
384. *Ibid.*, at pp. 4 and 5.
385. *Ibid.*, at pp. 4 and 7.
386. *Ibid.*, at p. 9.
387. *See* the published account of the ECB Governing Council's monetary policy meeting of June 14-15, 2023, at p. 18.
388. *See* the transcript of the ECB's press conference of June 15, 2023, at p. 2.
389. *See* the published account of the ECB Governing Council's monetary policy meeting of July 26-27, 2023, https://www.ecb.europa.eu/press/accounts/2023/html/ecb.mg230831~b04764f45f.en.html, at p. 2.
390. *Ibid.*, at p. 3.
391. *Ibid.*, at p. 2.

shown significant sensitivity to U.S. economic developments, and this was seen to present a challenge for euro area monetary policy insofar as financial markets appeared to expect a directionally similar interest rate path for both currency zones while *"economic activity in the euro area had decoupled from the more positive developments in the United States"*.[392]

(b) Euro area headline inflation (HICP) had gone down further from 6.1% in May to 5.5% in June. Energy inflation had dropped to 5.6%, and food price inflation had slowed from 12.5% in May to 11.6% in June but obviously remained at an excessive level. Core inflation had edged up from 5.3% in May to 5.5% in June, with opposite movements in (non-energy) industrial goods inflation, which had decreased from 5.8% to 5.5% (reflecting easing supply-chain bottlenecks, weaker demand and stronger global competition), and in services inflation, which had risen from 5.0% to 5.4% (reflecting, among other factors, increased spending on tourism).[393] It was noted that there was no material surprise in the latest inflation readings which was itself seen as *"good news"* after the prior sequence of upward surprises.[394]

(c) While inflation momentum had decreased overall, it remained uncertain how underlying inflation dynamics would eventually play out. The following developments were noted (among others):

  (i) Food price developments remained a major source of uncertainty. In this respect, Russia's recent withdrawal from the Black Sea Grain Initiative and extreme weather conditions in parts of Europe were seen as additional upside risks.[395]

  (ii) The labor market remained robust and its resilience in the face of weakening growth was *"puzzling"*.[396] Yet, while wage growth in 2023 Q1 had been somewhat higher than expected, by and large, incoming data were consistent with the June 2023 projections of a turnaround and lower wage growth in 2024.[397] Some doubt was expressed as to whether one of the key assumptions of these projections, *i.e.*, that increased labor costs would partly be absorbed by a reduction of corporate profit margins, would hold in view of the strong profit growth observed in 2022 and into 2023.[398] But there were currently *"no discernible indications"* of strengthening second-round effects causing wage-price spirals.[399]

392. *Ibid.*, at pp. 1 and 14.
393. *Ibid.*, at p. 5.
394. *Ibid.*, at p. 10.
395. *Ibid.*, at p. 11.
396. *Ibid.*, at p. 9.
397. *Ibid.*, at p. 11.
398. *Ibid.*, at p. 12.
399. *Ibid.*, at pp. 13 and 15.

(iii) The appreciation of the euro against the U.S. dollar and in nominal effective terms over the past months should lower import prices and eventually reduce inflationary pressures.[400]

(iv) The greater fiscal restraint reflected in the national budget plans for 2024 and the additional adjustments requested by the European Commission should also support the disinflation process.[401]

(d) As to monetary policy transmission, there was now clear evidence that monetary policy tightening was being transmitted strongly into broader financing conditions. There had been another sharp drop in loan demand in 2023 Q2, with corporate loan demand even having fallen below its level at the height of the 2008-2010 financial crisis.[402] Unsurprisingly, the tightening of financing conditions appeared to most strongly affect sectors depending more heavily on debt financing, including housing, construction, the automotive industry and capital goods.[403] Yet, various doubts and concerns were voiced around the table—the ambivalence that increases in proximity to the end of a tightening cycle:

(i) On the one hand, it was felt that economic activity had declined less than could have been expected in response to the substantial monetary tightening so far. But, on the other hand, concern was expressed about a high risk of stronger than expected monetary policy transmission in view of the sharp increase in bank lending rates and weak credit growth.[404]

(ii) The contrast between the downturn in activity in the industrial sector and the still positive growth in the services sector (as well as the fact that the U.S. manufacturing sector appeared to be holding up better than in the euro area) raised doubts as to the extent to which the euro area slowdown could be attributed to monetary tightening or to the residual effects of the 2020-2022 supply shocks.[405] While monetary policy transmission was working well in its "first leg", *i.e.*, the pass-through to financing conditions, it was important to achieve a better understanding of its functioning in the "second leg", *i.e.*, the transmission from financing conditions to the real economy.[406]

(iii) Accordingly, there remained uncertainty about both the current degree of restrictiveness of monetary policy and the degree that might ultimately be required.[407]

400. *Ibid.*, at pp. 2 and 7.
401. *Ibid.*, at p. 10.
402. *Ibid.*, at p. 6.
403. *Ibid.*, at p. 16.
404. *Ibid.*
405. *Ibid.*, at pp. 9 and 16.
406. *Ibid.*, at p. 16.
407. *Ibid.*, at p. 15.

(e) Finally, while the time horizon for returning inflation to the 2% target had already slipped from 2024 Q4 to 2025, it was believed important not to further extend it beyond 2025.[408]

287. While a *"preference"* was initially expressed for pausing rate increases, the Governing Council eventually agreed, unanimously, to raise policy rates by a further 25 basis points—without hinting at further rate increases but also without signaling that it was about to pause rate increases or that a peak level had been reached.[409] The Governing Council wished to adopt a perfect poker face on what it might do, or not do, next.

Accordingly, on July 27, 2023, the ECB announced that it would again lift policy rates by 25 basis points, *i.e.*, the main refinancing rate to 4.25%, the marginal lending rate to 4.50% and the deposit facility rate to 3.75%, with effect as of August 2, 2023. Thus, in a time span of 12 months, the ECB's key rates had now been raised in nine steps by a cumulative 4.25%.

Significantly, public communication of this decision left out the almost ritual mention of there remaining "more ground to cover". The official press release now stated that the ECB's policy rates will be *"**set** at sufficiently restrictive levels for as long as necessary"* to achieve a timely return of inflation to the 2% medium-term target[410]—to be contrasted with the expression used in the May 4 and June 15, 2023 communiqués, *i.e.*, that policy rates will be *"**brought** to levels sufficiently restrictive"* to achieve that result and will then be *"kept at those levels for as long as necessary"* (emphasis added). Lest this tweak in formulation be lost in translation, Ms. Lagarde, at the July 27, 2023 press conference, noted that the *"slight change of verb"* was not *"just random or irrelevant"*.[411] She then helpfully clarified the underlying message, namely that the ECB's future assessment of the data *"will actually tell us **whether** and how much ground we have to cover"* (emphasis added) and that, accordingly, at the September and subsequent monetary policy meetings, *"we might hike and we might hold"* and this decision may vary from one meeting to another.[412] In other words, at this juncture, there may or may not be more ground to cover. But Ms. Lagarde was very clear in ruling out a rate cut anytime soon.[413]

408. *Ibid.*, at pp. 16-17.
409. *Ibid.*, at p. 17.
410. *See* the ECB's press release of July 27, 2023, https://www.ecb.europa.eu/press/pr/date/2023/html/ecb.mp230723~d80cfcf24.en.html.
411. *See* the transcript of the ECB's press conference of July 27, 2023, https://www.ecb.europa.eu/press/pressconf/2023/html/ecb.is230727~e0a11feb2e.en.html, at p. 4.
412. *Ibid.*, at pp. 4, 6, 8 and 9.
413. *Ibid.*, at p. 6: *"that is a definite no!" Cf.* the published account of the ECB Governing Council's monetary policy meeting of July 26-27, 2023, at p. 19: *"It was felt that the word 'set' was consistent with preserving optionality, which, however, did not include the possibility of a rate cut at the September meeting"*. A most curious instance of wordsmithing indeed.

288. With the APP portfolio being in full (passive) run-off mode since the beginning of July, the Governing Council again confirmed its intention to continue to reinvest maturing securities in the PEPP portfolio *"until at least the end of 2024"*. At the July 27, 2023 press conference, Ms. Lagarde observed that the Governing Council had not discussed an accelerated shrinking of either portfolio.[414]

289. Finally, I may note that the Governing Council also decided to further reduce the remuneration of minimum reserves from the deposit facility rate to 0% as of the beginning of the reserve maintenance period starting on September 20, 2023.[415] At the Governing Council's meeting, certain members had proposed to raise the minimum reserve requirement back to 2%, as it had been before January 18, 2012 (*see* paragraph 206 above). But this proposal was not accepted, and, interestingly, *"caution was expressed against using the minimum reserve ratio as an active instrument for adjusting the monetary policy stance"*.[416]

290. ***September 13-14, 2023***: At the September 13-14, 2023 monetary policy meeting of the ECB's Governing Council, key data on the dashboard included the following:

(a) Euro area inflation readings continued to soften somewhat. Headline inflation (HICP) had edged down from 5.5% in June to 5.3% in July but stalled at the same level in August (later revised to 5.2%) due to an increase in energy prices. Food price inflation continued to decline from its March peak but still stood at almost 10% in August. Core inflation (*i.e.*, HICP less energy and food) decreased from 5.5% in July to 5.3% in August.

(b) As to the inflation outlook, the September 2023 staff macroeconomic projections now saw headline inflation at 5.6% for 2023 (up from 5.4% in the June 2023 projections), 3.2% for 2024 (up from 3%) and 2.1% for 2025 (down from 2.2%), and core inflation at 5.1% for 2023 (the same level as in the June 2023 projections), 2.9% for 2024 (down from 3%) and 2.2% for 2025 (down from 2.3%).[417] It was noted at the meeting that, according to these projections, headline inflation would reach the 2% target only in 2025 Q4.[418] It was

414. *See* the transcript of the ECB's press conference of July 27, 2023, at p. 5.
415. *See* the ECB's separate press release of July 27, 2023 on this subject, https://www.ecb.europa.eu/press/pr/date/2023/html/ecb.pr250727~7206e9aa48.en.html. *Cf.* fn. 312 above.
416. *See* the published account of the ECB Governing Council's monetary policy meeting of July 26-27, 2023, at p. 18.
417. *See ECB staff macroeconomic projections for the euro area*, September 2023, pp. 17-21, https://www.ecb.europa.eu/pub/pdf/other/ecb.projections202309_ecbstaff~4eb3c5960e.en.pdf.
418. *See* the published account of the ECB Governing Council's monetary policy meeting of September 13-14, 2023, https://www.ecb.europa.eu/press/accounts/2023/html/ecb.mg231012~2f3d803d32.en.html, at p. 15.

also observed that the projections were based on a number of *"benign assumptions"*, including declining energy prices, and that, if they had been updated since their August 22, 2023 cut-off date to reflect the intervening increase in oil prices[419] and depreciation of the euro, inflation would no longer return to target by the end of 2025.[420] Such indeed is the fragility of inflation projections – and the significant degree of dependency of inflation outcomes on extraneous factors over which monetary policy has little or no control.

(c) While underlying price pressures remained strong, most indicators of underlying inflation were now *"more clearly on a moderately declining path"*.[421] Among the developments discussed at the meeting on this subject, the following seem particularly noteworthy:

   (i) Measures of inflation momentum in recent months were significantly lower than annual inflation rates, although more so for goods inflation than for services inflation.[422]

   (ii) Wage pressures had remained elevated in 2023 Q2 and, although there were some tentative signs that they were approaching their peak, there was no hard evidence yet of a turnaround in wage dynamics. Given the seasonal pattern of wage setting, a clearer direction should emerge only in 2024 Q1.[423]

   (iii) GDP growth broadly stagnated over the first half of the year and was expected to remain subdued in the coming months due to the increased impact of monetary tightening and weakening euro area exports. The September 2023 staff projections now estimated real GDP growth at 0.7% for 2023 (down from 0.9% in the June 2023 projections), 1% for 2024 (down from 1.5%) and 1.5% for 2025 (down from 1.6%).[424] The economic slowdown should support the disinflationary process but the data did not offer enough comfort that this would be sufficient to return inflation to target in a timely manner.[425] It was observed that the current projections implied a "sacrifice ratio", *i.e.*, the cost of reducing inflation in terms of loss of output and employment, that was *"remarkably favourable"*.[426]

419. Oil prices rose sharply following the concomitant announcement by Saudi Arabia and Russia, on September 5, 2023, that they would extend voluntary cuts in the production of oil by 1.3 million barrels a day in total until the end of 2023 (subject to monthly review), on top of earlier production cuts and the quota reductions agreed by OPEC+ in October 2022.
420. *Ibid.*, at p. 11.
421. *Ibid.*, at p. 16.
422. *Ibid.*, at p. 3.
423. *Ibid.*, pp. 4, 12 and 16.
424. *See ECB staff macroeconomic projections for the euro area*, September 2023, pp. 4-6.
425. *See* the published account of the ECB Governing Council's monetary policy meeting of September 13-14, 2023, at p. 11.
426. *Ibid.*, at p. 10.

(d) As to monetary policy transmission, there was now *"ample"* evidence of monetary policy tightening being transmitted *"strongly"* to broader financing conditions, and even more so than expected.[427] Several observations were made on this subject:

(i) There had been a further weakening of credit dynamics, which likely reflected a combination of weaker loan demand and tighter credit supply by banks (as a result notably of higher bank funding costs due to the migration of overnight deposits to term deposits and alternative savings products and to the run-off of TLTROs). Weak lending and the reduction in the Eurosystem balance sheet caused monetary and credit aggregates to decelerate sharply over the past three months.[428]

(ii) It was noted that the pass-through of policy rate increases varied significantly among Member States depending on such factors as the size of the construction sector, the extent of home ownership and the respective shares of fixed-rate and floating-rate mortgages.[429]

(iii) In her introductory review of financial market developments, Isabel Schnabel observed that nominal longer-term yields had hovered around 3% since October 2022, which suggested that the impact of monetary policy tightening was lagging at the longer end of the curve.[430]

(iv) It was felt that a significant part of the pass-through of monetary policy tightening was still in the pipeline, but different views were expressed as to whether the pass-through so far had been stronger than, or rather in line with, historical patterns, and whether it could still increase or would now rather recede over time.[431]

(v) Market inflation expectations—an important channel of monetary policy transmission—had broadly remained anchored since mid-2022, which the Governing Council saluted as a great achievement of its monetary policy decisions.[432]

(e) While the uncertainty surrounding the inflation outlook remained *"exceptionally high"*,[433] it was felt that the monetary policy cycle had now reached a stage where the risks of tightening too much or too little had become more balanced and the choice between further raising policy rates and pausing was *"a close call"*.[434]

427. *Ibid.*, at p. 16.
428. *Ibid.*, at p. 14. In particular, on an annualized basis, loans to households had declined by 0.8% over the past three months, which was the strongest contraction on record in the history of the currency union, and M3 had contracted by 1.5%. *See ibid.*, at pp. 6-7, and the transcript of the ECB's press conference of September 14, 2023, https://www.ecb.europa.eu/press/pressconf/2023/html/ecb.is230914~686786984a.en.html, at p. 3.
429. *See* the published account of the ECB Governing Council's monetary policy meeting of September 13-14, 2023, at p. 15.
430. *Ibid.*, at p. 2.
431. *Ibid.*, at pp. 15 and 16. *Cf. also ibid.*, at p. 10.
432. *Ibid.*, at pp. 13 and 16.
433. *Ibid.*, at pp. 8 and 15.
434. *Ibid.*, at p. 16.

291. On this basis, the Governing Council decided to raise policy rates once more by 25 basis points, *i.e.*, the main refinancing rate to 4.50%, the marginal lending rate to 4.75% and the deposit facility rate to 4%, with effect as of September 20, 2023. This decision was backed by *"a solid majority"* of the governors, although *"[s]ome"* would have preferred to pause.[435] Thus, in 10 successive steps, the ECB had lifted policy rates by a cumulative 4.50% over a time span of 14 months.

292. The ECB's press release of September 14, 2023, repeated that, while inflation continues to decline, it *"is still expected to remain too high for too long"*. But, significantly, it now omitted any mention of there remaining "more ground to cover", and instead contained the following novel sentence:

> *"[b]ased on its current assessment, the Governing Council considers that the key ECB interest rates have reached levels that, maintained for a sufficiently long duration, will make a substantial contribution to the timely return of inflation to the target"*.[436]

This clearly suggests that, in the ECB's current assessment, policy rates had reached or were close to peak level and would likely stay there for a while. At the press briefing of the same day, President Lagarde observed that the message did not imply *"that we are now at peak"* but then conceded that *"it's obvious that the focus is probably going to move a bit more to the duration"*.[437] On this last point, she denied that the Governing Council had discussed any particular length of time.[438]

293. Ms. Lagarde also mentioned that the Governing Council had not discussed any acceleration of APP's run-off through outright sales of securities prior to their maturity, nor any end date for the continuing reinvestments under PEPP.[439]

294. ***October 25-26, 2023***: By the Governing Council's next monetary policy meeting, held on October 25-26, 2023 in Athens, the balance of considerations more clearly tilted toward pausing further policy rate increases:

435. *Ibid.*, at pp. 17-18.
436. *See* the ECB's press release of September 14, 2023, https://www.ecb.europa.eu/press/pr/date/2023/html/ecb.mp230914~aab39f8c21.en.html. The press release also repeated the July 27, 2023 messages to the effect that the Governing Council's future decisions will ensure that those rates will be *"set at sufficiently restrictive levels for as long as necessary"*, and that the Governing Council will continue to follow a data-dependent approach in determining *"the appropriate level and duration of restriction"*. At the press conference, Ms. Lagarde finessed the message by drawing attention to the word *"levels"* (a hint at possible separate tweaks to policy rates?) and the words *"substantial contribution"* (which she characterized somewhat enigmatically as *"heavy words"*), and by stressing the words *"sufficiently long duration"*, *"sufficiently restrictive levels"* and *"as long as necessary"*. *See* the transcript of the ECB's press conference of September 14, 2023, https://www.ecb.europa.eu/press/pressconf/2023/html/ecb.is230914~686786984a.en.html, at p. 4.
437. *Ibid.*, at p. 6.
438. *Ibid.*, at pp. 5-6.
439. *Ibid.*, at p. 5.

(a) Year-on-year headline inflation (HICP) had dropped significantly from 5.2% in August to 4.3% in September. The decline was broad-based but attributable in part to base effects, *i.e.*, the diminishing effect of the sharp rises in energy and food prices in the second half of 2022.[440] Food inflation remained high but had decreased from 10% in August to 8.8% in September, and core inflation (*i.e.*, HICP less energy and food) from 5.3% to 4.5%. Most measures of underlying inflation had continued to ease and appeared past their peak levels.[441]

(b) There was again considerable discussion about the inflation outlook and underlying inflation dynamics:

  (i) The short-term growth outlook had weakened and there was some discussion as to whether this was still consistent with a "soft landing" scenario.[442]

  (ii) Heightened geopolitical tensions, including those in the Middle East, could reduce confidence levels and drive up oil and gas prices in the near term, although price increases and effects on futures prices had so far been limited. But, as a general matter, energy prices have become less predictable.[443]

  (iii) The unemployment rate was at a historical low of 6.4% in August but job creation slowed in line with the cooling economy. Negotiated wage growth remained robust in 2023 Q3, but there were only limited signs of second-round effects and no evidence of any wage-price spirals so far. However, the outlook for wage growth and hence unit labor costs remained highly uncertain and would only gradually crystallize in the course of 2024.[444]

  (iv) The Member States' draft budgetary plans for 2024 overall reflected a significant reduction in fiscal support compared to 2023, but more so on account of diminished energy cost relief than on account of austerity measures. It was also observed that recent reductions in government debt ratios were due more to the effects of high inflation than to policy-driven fiscal consolidation.[445]

  (v) The financial markets now appeared to expect a first 25 basis points rate cut only in September rather than June 2024.[446]

440. It was noted that, *ceteris paribus*, such base effects should cause headline inflation to decline further in the near term but that energy-related base effects should produce a temporary rebound of inflation by the turn of 2023. *See* the published account of the ECB Governing Council's monetary policy meeting of October 25-26, 2023, https://www.ecb.europa.eu/press/accounts/2023/html/ecb.mg231123~40c9631bc7.en.html, at p. 10.

441. *Ibid.*, at pp. 5 and 10.

442. *Ibid.*, at p. 8.

443. *Ibid.*, at pp. 3, 7, 10 and 12.

444. *Ibid.*, at pp. 4, 5, 10 and 11.

445. *Ibid.*, at pp. 4 and 9.

446. *Ibid.*, at pp. 2 and 16.

(vi) In view of these and other considerations, there were differing views on the overall balance of risks for inflation, which some saw as still being tilted to the upside and others as more balanced.[447]

(c) On monetary policy transmission, the following developments were noted:

(i) Monetary policy tightening continued to be transmitted strongly to broader financing conditions (as reflected notably in higher lending rates, tighter credit standards and reduced loan demand) and was increasingly affecting the real economy (particularly investments and the housing sector).[448]

(ii) Now, at the end of the tightening cycle, long-term interest rates had been rising since the summer, mostly under the influence of U.S. developments. Different views were expressed on the desirability of higher long-term rates in the euro area—between those nervous about potentially excessive tightening and increased debt sustainability concerns for certain euro area Member States, and others welcoming the additional tightening effects.[449]

(iii) It was widely felt that, on the whole, monetary policy transmission *"was working well and was strong yet gradual and orderly"*.[450] But there remained uncertainty about how much pass-through might still be in the pipeline (and could possibly lead to over-tightening)—the ambiguities of the "last mile" in the monetary tightening cycle.[451]

295. On this basis, the Governing Council decided to leave its policy rates unchanged, *i.e.*, the main refinancing rate at 4.50%, the marginal lending rate at 4.75% and the deposit facility rate at 4%. The October 26, 2023 press release repeated the September 14 message to the effect that, in the Governing Council's current assessment, these rates now *"are at levels* (instead of *"have reached levels"*) *that, maintained for a sufficiently long duration, will make a substantial contribution"* to a timely return of inflation to the 2% medium-term target.[452]

At the press conference of October 26, 2023, President Lagarde confirmed that the timing of a possible rate cut had not been discussed and that such a discussion would be *"absolutely premature"*.[453]

The press release also reiterated the ECB's intention to continue reinvestments under PEPP *"until at least the end of 2024"*. There was *"broad agreement"* in the

447. *Ibid.*, at pp. 11-12.
448. *Ibid.*, at pp. 6 and 13-14.
449. *Ibid.*, at pp. 1 and 12-13.
450. *Ibid.*, at p. 14.
451. *Ibid.*, at pp. 14-15.
452. *See* the ECB's press release of October 26, 2023, https://www.ecb.europa.eu/press/pr/date/2023/html/ecb.mp231026~6028cea576.en.html.
453. *See* the transcript of the ECB's press conference of October 26, 2023, https://www.ecb.europa.eu/press/pressconf/2023/html/ecb.is231026~c23b4eb5f0.en.html, at pp. 4-5.

Governing Council that this was consistent with its decision to put policy rates on hold and that a discussion of an early termination of PEPP reinvestments was premature.[454]

296. *December 13-14, 2023*: And so we arrive at the ECB Governing Council's monetary policy meeting of December 13-14, 2023, the last in this chapter's narrative.[455] Key developments on the Council's dashboard included the following:

(a) Both headline inflation (HICP) and core inflation (*i.e.*, HICP excluding energy, food, alcohol and tobacco) had softened further over the past two months to an estimated annual rate of 2.4% and 3.6%, respectively, in November. The decline varied significantly across sectors (energy −11.5%, food +6.9%) but was broad-based. The December staff macroeconomic projections now estimated headline inflation at 5.4% for 2023 (down from 5.6% in the September 2023 projections), 2.7% for 2024 (down from 3.2%) and 2.1% for 2025 (the same level as in the September 2023 projections), and core inflation at 5.0% for 2023 (down from 5.1%), 2.7% for 2024 (down from 2.9%) and 2.3% for 2025 (up from 2.2%).[456]

(b) As to underlying inflation dynamics, domestic price pressures remained high due primarily to a combination of strong wage growth and diminishing productivity, resulting in rising unit labor costs. At the press conference of December 14, 2023, ECB President Christine Lagarde stressed that, in the coming months, the ECB would be very attentive to wage developments, as data come in from the upcoming wage-setting cycle, and to the extent to which labor cost increases will be absorbed by reduced corporate profit margins.[457] One of the assumptions embedded in the December 2023 inflation projections is that wage increases will in part be "buffered" by profit margins.[458]

(c) The prior policy rate increases continued to be transmitted strongly into broader financing conditions, as reflected in higher lending rates, tighter loan supply and subdued loan demand. However, market rates dropped markedly since the Governing Council's October 25-26, 2023 monetary policy meeting,

454. *See* the published account of the ECB Governing Council's monetary policy meeting of October 25-26, 2023, at p. 17.

455. For this meeting, our (official) sources were limited to the ECB's press release of December 14, 2023 and the transcript of the press conference of the same day. When, on December 24, 2023, I put down my pen, the official minutes of the Governing Council's meeting had not yet been published.

456. *See Eurosystem staff macroeconomic projections for the euro area*, December 2023, pp. 18-26, especially p. 22, Table 4, https://www.ecb.europa.eu/pub/pdf/other/ecb.projections202312_eurosystemstaff~9a39ab5088.en.pdf.

457. *See* the transcript of the ECB's press conference of December 14, 2023, https://www.ecb.europa.eu/press/pressconf/2023/html/ecb.is231214~df8627de60.en.html, at pp. 5, 7 and 8.

458. *See Eurosystem staff macroeconomic projections for the euro area*, December 2023, p. 23.

and indeed below the rates assumed in the December 2023 staff projections,[459] due to intervening market repricing on the expectation of more rapid disinflation and swifter policy rate cuts in 2024.

297. On this basis, unsurprisingly, the Governing Council decided to keep its key policy rates unchanged, *i.e.*, the main refinancing rate at 4.50%, the marginal lending rate at 4.75% and the deposit facility rate at 4%. Concomitantly, the ECB's press release reproduced *verbatim* the messages set forth in the October 26, 2023 press release, *i.e.*, that, on the basis of its current assessment, the Governing Council considers that these policy rates *"are at levels that, maintained for a sufficiently long duration, will make a substantial contribution"* to a timely return of inflation to the 2% medium-term target and that its future decisions *"will ensure that its policy rates will be set at sufficiently restrictive levels for as long as necessary"*.[460] But no other tangible indication was given as to this "duration" or the timing of future policy rate decreases.

At the press conference, Ms. Lagarde mentioned that rate cuts had not been discussed *"at all"*, and that there is *"a whole plateau"* between hiking and cutting.[461] She added that *"we don't think that it's time to lower our guard"*, that there *"is still work to be done"* and that *"this can very much take the form of holding"*.[462] In this connection, interestingly, she specifically called attention—not once but twice—to the fact that the ECB's inflation outlook was *"conditioned"* on the interest rate path embedded in the December 2023 staff projections, *i.e.*, the market data before their cut-off date of November 23, 2023[463] (*see* paragraph 296(c) above). The intervening decrease in market rates, insofar as it reflects overly optimistic market expectations of rapid disinflation and a swifter rate-cutting cycle, could itself slow down the disinflationary process and keep inflation higher. The other critical factor that Ms. Lagarde referred to in relation to the future policy rate path was the evolution of wages and corporate profits (read: a slowdown of wage growth and a sufficient degree of absorption of wage increases by corporate profit margins) over the coming months (*see* paragraph 296(b) above). Since these data would become available only over the course of 2024 Q1 (and would then require a careful reading of the tea leaves), one would be tempted to read between the lines that, absent unexpected developments, policy rate cuts before (late)

459. The December 2023 staff projections, with cut-off date November 23, 2023, had used, as technical assumptions, three-month Euribor rates of 3.6% for 2024, 2.8% for 2025 and 2.7% for 2026, and 10-year government bond yields of 3.2% for 2024, 3.3% for 2025 and 3.4% for 2026. *See ibid.*, p. 8.
460. *See* the ECB's press release of December 14, 2023, https://www.ecb.europa.eu/press/pr/date/2023/html/ecb.mp231214~9846e62f62.en.html.
461. *See* the transcript of the ECB's press conference of December 14, 2023, at p. 5.
462. *Ibid.*, at p. 7.
463. *Ibid.*, at pp. 4-5 and 7. *See* fn. 459 above.

spring 2024 seem unlikely. In any event, in content and tone, the ECB's message again appeared more cautious than that of the Federal Reserve just one day earlier (which had clearly hinted at near-term rate cuts).

298. Contrary to repeated earlier statements, the Governing Council also announced that it now intends to phase down reinvestments in the PEPP portfolio, by EUR 7.5 billion per month on average, over the second half of 2024 and to discontinue them altogether at the end of the year. At the press conference, Ms. Lagarde dismissed any link with possible policy rate cuts, saying that the PEPP decision should be viewed on a stand-alone basis, something operating *"on the back burner"*, and that now seemed a good moment to do this given that there is little financial fragmentation.[464]

6 THE ECB'S TRACK RECORD

299. It has fallen to the ECB to define and conduct an essential part of macroeconomic policy, *i.e.*, monetary policy and indeed a single monetary policy, for a subset of now 20 Member States in an incomplete EMU, in which (i) the degree of economic convergence and symmetry continues to fall short of academic OCA standards in several respects, as we discussed in Chapter 2; (ii) Member States retain a substantial measure of autonomy to pursue national fiscal policies, which, notwithstanding increased surveillance at EU level, has left a legacy of divergent fiscal positions; and (iii) there is no robust centralized budgetary mechanism for (quasi-)automatic stability support. The conduct of a single monetary policy in such a configuration is a very complex task, especially in a challenging and fluid economic and political environment. The women and men at the ECB need our nuanced judgment and constructive criticism. Nothing less will do. This is a good time to pause on our journey and jot down some first thoughts or questions on the ECB's track record.

a An Elusive Inflation Target

300. If one looks at the ECB's track record purely in terms of its medium-term 2% target for headline inflation (HICP), it appears from Table 4.1 below that, over the 15 years since 2008, year-to-year headline inflation in the euro area has never been close to the 2% target, except in 2018 (1.8%). And the inflation outcome for 2023 (given a 12-month average rate of change of 5.9% in November) should not be close either. But this obviously does not tell the entire story.

464. *Ibid.*, at p. 5.

Table 4.1 Euro Area Inflation (HICP) 2008-2022

	2008	*2009*	*2010*	*2011*	*2012*	*2013*	*2014*	*2015*	*2016*	*2017*	*2018*	*2019*	*2020*	*2021*	*2022*
Euro area	3.3	0.3	1.6	2.7	2.5	1.4	0.4	0.2	0.2	1.5	1.8	1.2	0.3	2.6	8.4
Germany	2.8	0.2	1.1	2.5	2.2	1.6	0.8	0.7	0.4	1.7	1.9	1.4	0.4	3.2	8.7
Netherlands	2.2	1.0	0.9	2.5	2.8	2.6	0.3	0.2	0.1	1.3	1.6	2.7	1.1	2.8	11.6
France	3.2	0.1	1.7	2.3	2.2	1.0	0.6	0.1	0.3	1.2	2.1	1.3	0.5	2.1	5.9
Italy	3.5	0.8	1.6	2.9	3.3	1.2	0.2	0.1	−0.1	1.3	1.2	0.6	−0.1	1.9	8.7
Spain	4.1	−0.2	2.0	3.0	2.4	1.5	−0.2	−0.6	−0.3	2.0	1.7	0.8	−0.3	3.0	8.3
Big Five σ	0.64	0.44	0.40	0.26	0.42	0.55	0.34	0.41	0.25	0.30	0.30	0.73	0.49	0.51	1.81

Source: Eurostat (online data code PRC_HICP_AIND) (as updated on July 19, 2023). Euro area = 15 (2008), 16 (2009-2010), 17 (2011-2013), 18 (2014) and 19 (2015-2022).

301. One might in retrospect wonder whether the ECB should not have taken more resolute action to check the build-up of housing and equity bubbles in 2005-2007 (*see* paragraph 200(b) above) or whether it did not overreact to inflationary signals by raising policy rates on April 13 and July 13, 2011 (*see* paragraph 207 above). But the more pressing question is whether the ECB did not subsequently engage in substantial monetary easing for too long before shifting to a monetary tightening cycle in 2022. Did it underestimate the return of inflationary pressures by characterizing them as "transitory" until the end of 2021? Did the ECB shift gear too late by terminating net purchases under PEPP and APP only at the end of March and June 2022, respectively, and by lifting policy rates only as of July 2022? Was it then pressed to catch up too rapidly and/or too much by raising policy rates by as much as a cumulative 4.50 % over a time span as short as 14 months? Did this rapid shift cause strains and increase instability risks in the financial system?

b Monetary Easing for Too Long?

302. What gives the most pause are the scale and duration of monetary easing since 2013-2014, at a time when the 2008-2012 financial crisis and the 2011 Q3 - 2013 Q1 recession had subsided. Policy rates in proximity of zero, TLTROs and, especially since the spring of 2015, large-scale asset purchases (QE) were deployed to counter disinflationary pressures—a monetary policy stance that was to perdure until 2022.

303. The ECB's own assessment, as part of its 2021 monetary policy strategy review, is that its deployment of these unconventional monetary policy measures since 2014 *"has made a significant contribution to countering disinflationary pressures, dispelling deflation concerns and averting a more pronounced downward drift in inflation expectations".*[465] The ECB's monetary easing may have lifted inflation in 2017-2018 from its very low 2014-2016 levels but inflation dropped again significantly in 2019 and 2020. While the ECB may have averted a deeper decline in inflation, it remains that it has failed to stabilize euro area inflation close to its 2 % target level over that extended period of monetary easing, except in 2018 (1.8 %).

304. Two considerations may help to put the long 2013-2021 monetary easing in perspective:

(a) In the aftermath of the 2010-2012 euro area sovereign debt crisis, euro area Member States by and large tended to apply relatively greater fiscal restraint, partly of their own volition and partly as a result of the reinforced common fiscal rules or the policy conditionality attached to EFSF/ESM stability support. This was reflected in generally more moderate public spending,

465. ECB, *An overview of the ECB's monetary policy strategy*, July 2021, p. 4.

including on public investments (*see* paragraph 119, Table 2.3, above), and in a decrease of the average euro area government debt ratio from 93.2 in 2014 to 84.1 in 2019 (with Germany and The Netherlands standing out in terms of budget surpluses and debt reduction) (*see* paragraph 116, Table 2.2, above). In a sense, stronger monetary easing had to make up for a relative shortfall in counter-cyclical fiscal stimulus. This echoes Mario Draghi's words when, in his June 18, 2019 farewell address at the ECB Central Banking Forum in Sintra (Portugal), he spoke of an *"unbalanced macroeconomic policy-mix in the euro area"* in which *"[o]ver the last 10 years, the burden of macroeconomic adjustment has fallen disproportionately on monetary policy"*.[466]

(b) Another factor was inherent in a particular strand of monetary analysis. For a long while (and in some measure still today among the more obdurate adherents of the doctrine), the *idée reçue* at the ECB was that the natural (or neutral) rate of interest (r^*) is on a long-term trend decline due to slow-moving, structural factors. It was inferred from this premise that, over longer periods, monetary policy should "go with the flow" and broadly accommodate this decline lest it be too restrictive and fuel deflationary bias (*see* paragraphs 188-195 above). This line of thinking may have underestimated underlying changes in the structural determinants of inflation.

305. Aside from issues of efficacy, the question remains whether the scale and duration of monetary easing from 2013 through 2019 in pursuit of higher inflation, as extended in COVID-19 years 2020 and 2021, could, from a proportionality perspective, be fully justified in relation to its real and potential side effects. This question arises in particular for the later years of monetary easing, especially given monetary policy transmission lags. Thus, zealous monetary easing for such an extended period is bound in some measure to have (i) facilitated private borrowing and debt accumulation; (ii) sustained a suboptimal allocation of resources by lowering financing costs for sub-productive or sub-competitive activities and keeping them afloat for longer; (iii) encouraged greater risk-taking in search for higher yields, contributed to the build-up of bubbles in the equity and housing markets, and increased banks' appetite for higher-yield/higher-risk lending (including consumer finance); (iv) eroded retirement savings and, in a sense, caused an intergenerational shift to younger generations at borrowing age; (v) anchored market expectations that this was the "new normal"; and (vi) allowed inflationary undercurrents to gain strength. In this manner, long monetary easing may eventually have necessitated a steeper reversal of the monetary policy stance and at the same time have contributed to vulnerabilities that have complicated such a reversal, as we will further discuss in the next subsection.

466. M. Draghi, "Twenty years of the ECB's monetary policy", in *ECB Forum on Central Banking*, June 17-19, 2019, *20 years of European Economic and Monetary Union*, Conference proceedings, p. 34.

c Too Hesitant a Shift to Monetary Tightening?

306. There would never have been a right time for COVID-19 but it came at a particularly inopportune moment in the monetary policy cycle. The acute phase of COVID-19 in 2020 and roughly the first half of 2021 admittedly made it an inauspicious time for monetary tightening. In order to maintain favorable financing conditions and accommodate fiscal support, the ECB kept policy rates unchanged at levels close to zero, launched additional longer-term refinancing operations on a full-allotment basis (PELTROs), continued net purchases under APP, and added PEPP as a further layer of QE (*see* paragraphs 233-240 above). When inflationary pressures increased in 2021, the ECB for a good while viewed them as transient, as a blip in a downward-sloping curve—still in line with the credo of a long-term trend decline in r^*. Thus, even after the annual rate of headline inflation (HICP) in the euro area had jumped from 0.9% in January to 4.9% in November 2021, the ECB at its monetary policy meeting of December 15-16, 2021 considered that *"[a] continued high degree of monetary support was also deemed necessary to prevent inflation falling below target once the effects of the pandemic [...] had subsided"* (*see* paragraph 241 above). And, at the December 16, 2021 press conference, ECB President Christine Lagarde stated that *"it is very unlikely that we will raise interest rates in the year 2022"* (*see* paragraph 242 above). In fairness, the ECB was not alone in its perception of a transitory rise in inflation. In the United States, the statements following the successive Federal Open Market Committee ("FOMC") meetings of April 27-28, June 15-16, July 27-28, September 21-22 and November 2-3, 2021 all referred to elevated inflation as *"largely reflecting transitory factors"*[467]—but, interestingly, this reference to transitory factors was dropped in the statement issued following the FOMC's December 14-15, 2021 meeting.[468]

307. And so it was that, in 2022, the ECB started its policy "normalization" process, at first in gingerly steps. The Eurosystem discontinued net asset purchases under PEPP at the end of March and those under APP at the end of June 2022 but initially held off on any reduction of its considerable QE portfolios (by then some EUR 4.9 trillion in total) and continued to fully reinvest maturing securities. It was only at its December 14-15, 2022 monetary policy meeting that the ECB decided to start shrinking the Eurosystem's APP portfolio as of March 2023 *"at a measured and predictable pace"* by reducing reinvestment of principal repayments from maturing securities by a modest EUR 15 billion per month. Eventually, APP reinvestments were halted entirely at the end of June 2023 but without any hint at "active" shrinking of the APP portfolio through sales

467. These FOMC statements and minutes may be found at https://www.federalreserve.gov/monetarypolicy/fomccalendars.htm. The November 3, 2021 statement became a little more cautious by referring to *"factors that are expected to be transitory"*. *See* https://www.federalreserve.gov/monetarypolicy/files/monetary20211103a.1pdf.

468. *See* https://www.federalreserve.gov/monetarypolicy/files/monetary20211215a.&.pdf.

of securities prior to maturity (*see* paragraphs 266, 268, 272 and 280 above). And the ECB continued to fully reinvest maturing securities in the PEPP portfolio and kept repeating that it would do so *"until at least the end of 2024"*. Meanwhile, average year-to-year headline inflation (HICP) in the euro area had sharply increased from 5.1% in January to 8.1% in May 2022. At long last, on June 9, 2022, the ECB announced its intention to raise policy rates by 25 basis points at its July meeting, with the expectation of a *"gradual but sustained path"* of further rate increases (*see* paragraphs 253-254 above). The modest first step of 25 basis points, raised to 50 basis points at the July 21-22, 2022 meeting, reflected caution to avoid *"unnecessarily surprising the markets and inducing unwarranted volatility"*. In the event, inflation dynamics would cause the ECB to adopt a rate increase trajectory—a cumulative increase by an unprecedented 4.50% over a time span of 14 months between July 2022 and September 2023—that most likely was significantly faster and steeper than what the ECB may initially have had in mind.

308. The sequence of events just summarized prompts the question of whether the ECB was too late in shifting gear. One thought that comes to mind is that the delay in monetary tightening may have given inflationary pressures time to strengthen, broaden and become more embedded and, consequently, may eventually have necessitated a steeper rate-hiking trajectory. Also, any significant reversal from a monetary easing cycle to one of monetary tightening comes with a certain risk of destabilizing one or more financial market segments. It stands to reason that this risk increases as (i) the prior monetary easing has been longer and deeper; (ii) the subsequent tightening is steeper; and (iii) the reversal is more abrupt. And then there is the difficult question of navigating to the proper altitude and from there to a proper landing approach. Given the uncertain lags of monetary policy transmission through its different channels and sub-channels, a steeper tightening cycle may run a greater risk of overshooting and hurting the economy. This judgment becomes harder and harder as one advances in the rate-hiking cycle. In blunt terms, it then comes down to the question of which policy error is worst or, put differently, most difficult and costly to repair: overshooting in monetary tightening or having allowed inflationary pressures and expectations to further seep through the economy and solidify?

d Questions About Quantitative Easing and Quantitative Tightening

309. Looking again at the trajectory of euro area inflation over the past 10 years (*see* paragraph 300, Table 4.1, above), one may wonder whether the ECB's version of QE really worked as intended and did so effectively. At first blush, one might think that the first wave of QE, *i.e.*, APP over the 2014-2018 period, did not succeed very well in durably bending the inflation curve upward. Or is this to some extent an optical illusion in that APP did prevent further disinflation and, given transmission lags, may even have nourished inflationary pressures that were to surface later? In particular, the combination with the second wave of QE, *i.e.*, the reactivation of APP and the addition of PEPP between late 2019 and mid-2022, raises the question of whether the ECB's extended QE may have added fuel to a smoldering fire of subjacent inflationary pressures that eventually began to break into the open in 2021. The ECB's own assessment, as part of its 2021 monetary policy strategy review, is that its deployment of such unconventional monetary policy tools since 2014 *"has made a significant contribution to countering disinflationary pressures, dispelling deflation concerns and averting a more pronounced downward drift in inflation expectations"*.[469] But might it have over-contributed in its later years?

310. There is some discussion among economists over how and how well QE works. In a January 16, 2014 discussion at the Brookings Institution, then Federal Reserve Chairman Ben Bernanke wisecracked that *"the problem with QE is it works in practice but it doesn't work in theory"*.[470] Still, one would expect that QE, if of sufficient scale and properly messaged, should in some measure stimulate the economy and counteract disinflationary pressures notably by (i) effectively swapping liquidity for longer-dated less liquid assets (bonds and other securities); (ii) extracting credit and duration risk from the financial markets, thereby freeing up more risk-bearing capacity for bank lending and investments; (iii) sustaining or increasing demand for the government bonds and other securities eligible for QE purchases, which should help to keep bond yields and, hence, government and corporate borrowing costs down; and (iv) inducing banks and investors to rebalance their portfolios toward loans and assets offering higher returns.

311. Of course, once policy rates were approaching their lower bound in 2013-2014, the ECB did not have an abundance of other options to counter disinflationary pressures. It should then have seemed sensible to consider larger-scale asset purchases, as the Federal Reserve had conducted since the end of 2008 when its target federal funds rate had dropped to the lower bound—and as the ECB itself had experimented with, albeit not on a macroeconomically relevant scale, with CBPP1, CBPP2 and SMP between 2009 and 2012 (see paragraphs 209-210 above). And, to be fair, in the first wave of QE from 2014 to 2018, there appeared to be some positive correlation between APP and inflation: after APP had been rolled out and scaled up between October 2014 and March 2017, inflation picked up significantly in 2017-2018, and, conversely, when APP net purchases were scaled down as of April 2017 and especially as of January 2018 and then paused from January to October 2019, inflation

469. ECB, *An overview of the ECB's monetary policy strategy*, July 2021, p. 4.
470. The relevant video clip may be found at https://www.cnbc.com/amp/2014/01/16/bernanke-cracks-wise-the-best-qe-joke-ever.html.

again fell back significantly in 2019-2020 (*see* paragraph 300, Table 4.1, above). Still, if QE is or can be an effective tool for countering disinflationary pressures, the neutral observer will be left with certain questions, including (i) whether the ECB should not have stepped up asset purchases earlier, in 2012 or 2013 (rather than discontinuing CBPP2 and SMP); (ii) whether it was right in reducing and then pausing APP net purchases between April 2017 and October 2019; and (iii) whether, in contrast, the second wave of QE between 2020 and 2022 was not too generous for too long.

312. This brings us to the even more nebulous terrain of QT. Net asset purchases under APP were discontinued at the end of June 2022, after those under PEPP had been halted at the end of March 2022, but, at first, principal repayments on securities in both these portfolios continued to be reinvested in full. It was only as of March 2023 that the Eurosystem cautiously started a "passive" phase of QT on its APP portfolio (which then stood at EUR 3,251 billion) by no longer reinvesting a portion of principal repayments (initially a modest EUR 15 billion per month or 0.46%), *i.e.*, by allowing a portion of maturing securities to "roll off" without replacing them. When it appeared that market absorption of this reduction was smooth and that the markets were largely pricing in a total reinvestment stop as of the summer, the ECB fully discontinued APP reinvestments at the end of June 2023 (which should reduce the APP portfolio by roughly EUR 25 billion per month on average) (*see* paragraph 280 above). But there was no hint yet at any "active" QT by selling securities prior to maturity. And, in parallel, the ECB kept saying that principal repayments in the PEPP portfolio would continue to be fully reinvested *"until at least the end of 2024"*, until at long last, on December 14, 2023, it announced its intention to phase down PEPP reinvestments, by EUR 7.5 billion per month on average, in the second half of 2024 and to discontinue them altogether at the end of this year (*see* paragraph 298 above). Here, the obvious question is whether the ECB should not have initiated QT earlier and more vigorously given the build-up of inflationary pressures in 2021 and 2022 and given likely transmission lags.

313. QT is largely uncharted territory and there is not a whole lot of intelligence or empirical evidence about how exactly it works through the financial system. In the United States, after a first episode of QT between the fall of 2017 and the fall of 2019, the Federal Reserve again shifted to QT as of June 2022, also in a "passive" mode, *i.e.*, (primarily) by limiting reinvestment to principal repayments exceeding certain pre-specified caps.[471] When asked about the monetary policy impact of this measure at the Federal Reserve's press conference on May 4, 2022, Chairman Jerome Powell offered a tentative estimate, *i.e.*, the equivalent of one 25 basis points rate increase over the course of one year, but hastened to add that this estimate came *"with very wide*

471. *See* FOMC, *Plans for Reducing the Size of the Federal Reserve's Balance Sheet*, May 4, 2022, https://www.federalreserve.gov./monetarypolicy/policy-normalization.htm.

uncertainty bands—very wide. We don't really know".[472] The uncertainty as to the market reception and broader effects of QT is likely a key factor explaining why both the Federal Reserve and the ECB have thus far adopted a circumspect approach, proceeding gradually and at a pre-announced pace.

314. QE and QT are a bit of a quagmire. Ample QE to push up low inflation, especially over a longer time span, will load high volumes of low-yielding securities onto central bank balance sheets. This has been the case for the Eurosystem, whose pre-QT combined APP and PEPP portfolios stood at about EUR 4.96 trillion at the end of February 2023, and even more so for the Federal Reserve whose pre-QT aggregate holdings of U.S. Treasuries, federal agency debt securities and agency mortgage-backed securities added up to some USD 8.47 trillion at the end of March 2022.[473] In this manner, central banks have in fact extracted a significant quantum of interest rate risk (as well as default risk) from the financial markets and taken it on their own books. This exposes central banks to losses when inflationary pressures require them to raise policy rates, as illustrated by the expected losses announced by, among others, the Dutch and Belgian central banks in 2022 and 2023 (*see* paragraph 227 above). Conventional wisdom has it that, technically, central banks cannot default and can operate with negative equity. But the question is whether there is not some less tangible limit to the extent to which central banks can expand their balance sheets and accumulate losses.

315. Or consider the matter from the angle of sovereign debt. As said, aggregate government bond holdings in the Eurosystem's monetary portfolios represented roughly 35 % of total outstanding euro area sovereign debt by mid-2022 (*see* paragraph 230 above). How much more could be added? Could it go up to, say, 45 % %? 55 %? Are there limits to how much sovereign debt could be gobbled up by this black hole and for how long? Wouldn't the financial markets at some point begin to wonder, as in the tale of Hans Christian Andersen, whether the emperor has any clothes on? In other words, wouldn't this at some stage raise street credibility issues? Could it at some point cause financial markets to lose faith in the central banks' capacity to take resolute action when needed? Or could it negatively affect the market valuation of sovereign debt given the overhang of such debt in central bank portfolios that central banks may choose or need to offload at some juncture? And does not all this raise serious questions under the Treaty prohibition on the monetization of government debt (Article 123 TFEU) ? At any rate, common sense would suggest that large-scale QE should at some stage be followed by an adequate measure of QT to allow central banks to unload and

472. *See* the transcript of Chairman Powell's press conference of May 4, 2022, https://www.federalreserve.gov/mediacorner/files/FOMCpresconf20220504.pdf, at pp. 19-20. One year later to the day, when asked about the tightening impact of the proposed full reinvestment stop on APP at the ECB's press conference of May 4, 2023, ECB President Christine Lagarde did not wish to commit to any specific number but noted that the impact was *"not material"*. *See* the transcript of this conference, https://www.ecb.europa.eu/press/pressconf/2023/html/ecb.is230504~f242392c72.en.html, at p. 9.

473. *See Federal Reserve Balance Sheet Developments*, May 2022, p. 2, https://www.federalreserve.gov/monetarypolicy/files/balance_sheet_developments_report_202205.pdf.

free up capacity for future action.[474] But it also stands to reason that this should be done cautiously with an eye toward the market's capacity to absorb the corresponding liquidity extraction. QT may be trickier than QE, and "active" QT trickier than merely "passive" QT. It is one of the issues addressed in the review of the ECB's operational framework for monetary policy (*see* paragraphs 479-484 below).

e More Conservative than the Federal Reserve?

316. The reader might wonder whether the ECB is or has been more conservative or, if you wish, more cautious or hesitant than the Federal Reserve in the conduct of monetary policy.[475] The next question is whether this is good or bad or, in the end, even matters that much at all. From a mere visual inspection of the time series of monetary policy actions over the past 25 years, it would appear that the ECB has generally been more cautious, or less aggressive, than the Federal Reserve, both in changing policy rates and in scaling up and then rolling back QE:

(a) During the period from January 1, 1999 through December 24, 2023, the ECB changed policy rates 58 times (15 times since January 1, 2014) and the Federal Reserve 71 times (25 times since 2014). The ECB changed rates by 50 basis points or more on 17 occasions, the Federal Reserve on 25 occasions. The Federal Reserve went much deeper earlier in lowering rates as of 2008 and was a few months quicker in raising them in 2022.

(b) Table 4.2 below shows significant differences in the timing and scale of QE. The Federal Reserve's much earlier start of QE as of the end of 2008 is not entirely surprising insofar as the target federal funds rate had already been decreased precipitously to the lower bound by then (with a target range of 0% to 0.25% as of December 16, 2008). A stand-out difference is in the scale of QE, at least in absolute terms. In relative terms, as a percentage of cumulative GDP over the relevant period, the numbers are a good deal closer. Also, the Federal Reserve started QT in June 2022, *i.e.*, nine months earlier, and at a somewhat higher pace, than the ECB.

Table 4.2 Quantitative Easing: ECB Versus Federal Reserve

	ECB	*Federal Reserve*
2008-2014	–[(a)]	USD 4,219 bn[(b)] *(4.40% of 2009-2014 GDP)*

474. This at least was one of the reasons noted by the ECB's Governing Council for deciding on a full reinvestment stop on APP as of July 2023. *See* the published account of the ECB Governing Council's monetary policy meeting of May 3-4, 2023, https://www.ecb.europa.eu/press/accounts/2023/html/ecb.mg230601~9d35f80dee.en.html, at p. 16.
475. For one of the more sensible discussions of this subject, *see* P. De Grauwe, *supra*, pp. 168-173.

	ECB	*Federal Reserve*
2014-2018	EUR 2,623 bn[(c)] *(4.83% of 2014-2018 GDP)*	–
2020-2022	EUR 2,360 bn[(d)] *(6.59% of 2019-2021 GDP)*	USD 4,630 bn[(e)] *(7.04% of 2019-2021 GDP)*

Source: ECB, *APP History of cumulative purchase breakdowns* and *History of monthly net purchase under the PEPP*, and Federal Reserve, *Quarterly Reports on Federal Reserve Balance Sheet Developments* and *Federal Reserve Balance Sheet Developments*.

Notes: (a) The table does not report CBPP1, CBPP2 and SMP as QE since these asset purchase programs were conducted on too modest a scale to have much macroeconomic relevance and, in the case of SMP, since this program was more an anti-fragmentation instrument than one of monetary easing (and its liquidity effect was largely "sterilized") (*see* paragraphs 332-336 below). (b) Cumulative holdings of U.S. Treasuries, federal agency debt securities and agency mortgage-backed securities on October 29, 2014. (c) Cumulative APP holdings at the end of February 2020. (d) Cumulative incremental APP holdings at the end of June 2022 + cumulative PEPP holdings at the end of March 2022. (e) Incremental holdings of U.S. Treasuries, federal agency debt securities and agency mortgage-backed securities acquired between February 26, 2020 and March 30, 2022.

(c) Still, at the end of the day, there is no denying that, over the 2008-2014 period, the ECB was considerably slower than the Federal Reserve in lowering policy rates and then moving to large-scale asset purchases. While over the course of 2008, the Federal Reserve reduced the target federal funds rate in seven swift steps from 4.25% to a range of 0% to 0.25% by the end of that year, the ECB first increased its main refinancing rate from 4% to 4.25% in July and then decreased it in three steps to 2.5% by December 2008. It then slowly reduced it in small steps to 0.25% in November 2013 and eventually to 0% in March 2016. In the interval, it had even lifted policy rates twice by 25 basis points, in April and July 2011, in response to a temporary uptick in inflation due in part to an increase in oil prices. And the ECB turned to full-throttle QE only at the end of 2014 or, perhaps more accurately, in March 2015 with the launch of PSPP. It seems clear that, in that period, more conservative or "hawkish" voices in the ECB's Governing Council were wary of too fast a pace of monetary easing and regarded asset purchases, particularly of sovereign bonds, as a contingency tool of last resort to be deployed only in a genuinely adverse scenario. While by no means silenced, hawkish voices seem to have become somewhat more subdued on this matter in later years.

317. At this point in time, one should not probably make too much of differences in institutional temperament between the ECB and the Federal Reserve. The Federal Reserve's somewhat greater monetary policy reactivity to business cycle movements (the output gap) may to some extent be inherent in the broader definition of its monetary policy mandate which includes promoting maximum employment alongside stable prices,[476] while the ECB's mandate has a primary focus on maintaining price stability. The ECB's greater caution may also be explained in part by the recurring need for the ECB, in Europe's incomplete EMU, to look in the rear mirror for signs of undue widening of sovereign bond spreads that may scramble monetary policy transmission and, in an adverse scenario, trigger destabilizing market dynamics that threaten the cohesion of the currency union. But more often than not a key explanatory factor for different monetary policy reactivity may be found in differences in the economic circumstances of the moment. Thus, for example, the ECB's initially somewhat slower and more moderate response to surging inflation in 2022 can be attributed in part to different inflation dynamics: in the euro area, inflationary pressures were at first driven mainly by supply-side disturbances, particularly tensions and high prices in the energy markets, while in the United States, they were due more to demand-driven overheating.

f No Model of Everything

318. One's judgment is all too easily colored by hindsight. In real time, models are imperfect and offer no crystal ball. The ECB looks at a wealth of data and uses sophisticated stochastic and other models and simulations for its analysis and forecasting of relevant developments. Yet, these data are incomplete, have time lags and may be conflicting. The number of variables or moving parts is large and they may interact in diffuse and unpredictable ways. Oftentimes, risks are not measurable with any degree of precision, and some occur purely randomly. It is simply very hard for the ECB to confidently distill from all this an unequivocal vision as to the direction and strength of monetary policy actions, and its conclusions will inevitably be subject to a significant margin of error. Our narrative of the ECB Governing Council's monetary policy meetings from March 2022 through December 2023 in the previous sections abundantly illustrates a central bank's real-time difficulties in conducting monetary policy in a fluid economic environment and the hesitations that come with this task.

319. Table 4.3 below irreverently shows how the baseline inflation outlook of the quarterly macroeconomic projections of the ECB/Eurosystem staff evolved over the short time span from March 2021 to December 2023. The numbers in standard font are the projections for headline inflation (HICP), and the numbers in italics those for core inflation (HICP excluding energy and food). On these most critical indicators for monetary policy, the table does not suggest a very steady hand, not even in the months preceding Russia's military aggression against Ukraine, and it raises questions as to model reliability.

476. According to Section 2A of the Federal Reserve Act of 1913, the Board of Governors of the Federal Reserve System and the FOMC *"shall maintain long run growth of the monetary and credit aggregates commensurate with the economy's long run potential to increase production, so as to promote effectively the goals of maximum employment, stable prices, and moderate long-term interest rates"*.

Table 4.3 Inflation Projections 2021 Q1–2023 Q4

	March 2021	*June 2021*	*Sept. 2021*	*Dec. 2021*	*March 2022*	*June 2022*	*Sept. 2022*	*Dec. 2022*	*March 2023*	*June 2023*	*Sept. 2023*	*Dec. 2023*
2021	1.5% *1.0%*	1.9% *1.1%*	2.2% *1.3%*	2.6% *1.4%*	–	–	–	–	–	–	–	–
2022	1.2% *1.1%*	1.5% *1.3%*	1.7% *1.4%*	3.2% *1.9%*	5.1% *2.6%*	6.8% *3.3%*	8.1% *3.9%*	8.4% *3.9%*	–	–	–	–
2023	1.4% *1.3%*	1.4% *1.4%*	1.5% *1.5%*	1.8% *1.7%*	2.1% *1.8%*	3.5% *2.8%*	5.5% *3.4%*	6.3% *4.2%*	5.3% *4.6%*	5.4% *5.1%*	5.6% *5.1%*	5.4% *5.0%*
2024	–	–	–	1.8% *1.8%*	1.9% *1.9%*	2.1% *2.3%*	2.3% *2.3%*	3.4% *2.8%*	2.9% *2.5%*	3.0% *3.0%*	3.2% *2.9%*	2.7% *2.7%*
2025	–	–	–	–	–	–	–	2.3% *2.4%*	2.1% *2.2%*	2.2% *2.3%*	2.1% *2.2%*	2.1% *2.3%*
2026	–	–	–	–	–	–	–	–	–	–	–	1.9% *2.1%*

Source: Quarterly ECB/Eurosystem staff macroeconomic projections for the euro area.

320. In his (virtual) speech at the Frankfurt Euro Finance Summit on July 4, 2022, Bundesbank President Joachim Nagel candidly observed that *"past projections underestimated the actual path of inflation on multiple occasions"* and that *"[i]t may be the case that our models are not capturing the currently exceptionally strong price dynamics in full"*.[477] At the ECB press briefing of September 8, 2022, ECB President Christine Lagarde also admitted to forecasting errors, while adding that these were errors made by all forecasters.[478] Models need constant improvement, particularly if they produce projections that turn out to be widely off the mark on a critical variable. But it remains, of course, that models can never capture everything.

g More Articulate Policy Guidance?

321. A final thought to conclude this long chapter. In the face of a fairly diffuse Treaty matrix of objectives and constraints, and confronted with a highly uncertain and challenging environment, the ECB has set itself an open-ended navigation course for its monetary policy, *i.e.*, to flexibly and symmetrically pursue a headline inflation target of 2% over an otherwise undefined and variable medium-term horizon. Since the spring of 2022, the ECB has added (with occasional variations in the wording) that, in pursuing this course, it will maintain "optionality, data dependence, gradualism and flexibility" and follow a "meeting-by-meeting approach". And since the spring of 2023, the ECB has offered further guidance by clarifying that its reaction function going forward will be determined by its assessment of: (i) the inflation outlook in light of the incoming economic and financial data; (ii) the dynamics of underlying inflation; and (iii) the strength of monetary policy transmission (*see* paragraph 276 above)—none of which is particularly revealing or unexpected. This all makes for a relatively vague policy rule that leaves a wide measure of discretion. Of course, there is no denying that the years 2020-2023 have been unusually turbulent with, in short succession, COVID-19, supply chain disruptions, the Ukraine conflict, tensions and volatility in the energy market, increased geopolitical frictions, occasional stresses in the banking market and the non-bank financial sector, and the hostilities in the Middle East. In such an environment of "everything everywhere all at once", as the ECB's Fabio Panetta characterized it,[479] it would seem to make good sense for the ECB to be flexible and avoid pre-committing to any specific policy path.

322. Yet, it is in the end a question of degree and balance. Higher uncertainty and complexity do not inevitably require higher discretion. Markets need a measure of visibility on the future direction of monetary policy, especially in times of significant

477. J. Nagel, "Where is monetary policy headed?", Virtual speech at the Frankfurt Euro Finance Summit, July 4, 2022, https://www.bundesbank.de/en/press/speeches/where-is-monetary-policy-headed--894058, at p. 3.

478. *See* the transcript of the ECB's press conference of September 8, 2022, https://www.ecb.europa.eu/press/pressconf/2022/html/ecb.is220908~cd8363c58e.en.html, at p. 8.

479. F. Panetta, "Everything everywhere all at once: responding to multiple global shocks", Speech at The ECB and its Watchers XXIII Conference, Frankfurt, March 22, 2023, https://www.ecb.europa.eu/press/key/date/2023/html/ecb.sp230322_2~af38beedf3.en.html.

economic fluidity. The ECB's message of a data-dependent, meeting-by-meeting approach will leave financial markets trying to interpret the continuous ticker tape of incoming data and to guesstimate how monetary policy may respond to this or that possibly ephemeral development. Market expectations about the monetary policy path may become volatile, unstable and/or simply wrong, as appears to have been the case on several occasions in recent years. It has at times led to a somewhat bizarre interaction between the ECB and the financial markets in which the ECB reads the markets' interpretation of its possible intentions and may feel bound to correct this interpretation—a hot-and-cold game of sorts. This may only add to the complexity of the puzzle.

One also wonders whether a low-resolution policy rule, especially when combined with the lack of specific forward guidance and a repeated emphasis on a data-dependent meeting-by-meeting approach, may not stretch monetary policy transmission lags, particularly at the longer end of the interest curve. Could this be one of the reasons why, as Isabel Schnabel observed at the ECB's monetary policy meeting of September 13-14, 2023, nominal longer-term yields had hovered around 3% since October 2022 notwithstanding the successive policy rate increases since July 2022?[480]

323. It could be (and has been) argued that good stabilization performance would require clearer, more articulate policy guidance that exhibits a certain inertia over time so as to more firmly steer market expectations as to inflation and the ECB's reactivity to inflation developments. Of course, a central bank could not rigidly adhere to some Taylor-type or other formulaic policy rule, and any reasonable policy guidance will need to leave a significant margin for judgment in light of new incoming data. But thoughtful and credible guidance on a baseline monetary policy path, including its conditionality, over a time span of several quarters could provide a benchmark for market expectations and help to reduce volatility.

324. There are various ways for a central bank to provide more visibility on its expectations and intentions as to the likely course of monetary policy going forward. In the United States, every quarter the FOMC publishes (on a no-name basis) the expectations of its members (the seven members of the Federal Reserve's Board of Governors and the presidents of the 12 regional federal reserve banks) as to the most likely levels of GDP growth, unemployment and inflation for the current and next two years and over the longer run, with a "dot plot" showing their views of the corresponding federal funds rate (midpoint of target range or target level).[481] One would not easily see the members of the ECB Governing Council submitting to such dotplotting, and this may not be a great loss since dot plots of this kind have, in the end, limited information value. But there are other ways. Happily, in some of its recent meetings, the ECB has been more forthcoming in offering guidance about the further course of monetary

480. *See* the published account of the ECB Governing Council's monetary policy meeting of September 13-14, 2023, at p. 2.

481. *See, e.g., Summary of Economic Projections*, March 22, 2023, https://www.federalreserve.gov/monetarypolicy/files/fomcprojtabl20230322.pdf, at p. 2, Table 1, p. 4, Figure 2, and p. 15, Figure 5.

policy in the near term. Thus, notwithstanding its official insistence on a meeting-by-meeting approach and reluctance to give specific forward rate guidance, the ECB has from time to time provided various clues as to, for example, the remaining distance to its terminal rate, the prospect of pausing, the need for policy rates to linger for a while in restrictive territory, and its judgment that the projected decline of headline inflation to 2.2% in 2025 *"is not satisfactory and it's not timely"*.[482] It would seem a relatively modest step for the ECB to put indications of that kind together in a more articulate statement of its baseline monetary policy scenario for the near term and its key underlying assumptions.

482. *See* the transcript of the ECB's press conference of June 15, 2023, https://www.ecb.europa.eu/press/pressconf/2023/html/ecb.is230615~3de9d68335.en.html, at p. 7.

CHAPTER 5

Monetary Policy and Financial Fragmentation

1 FINANCIAL FRAGMENTATION IN A CURRENCY UNION

325. In Chapter 1, we discussed how the semi-fixed exchange rate arrangements among European currencies that preceded the European currency union repeatedly gave rise to tensions when markets perceived exchange rates to be misaligned, and how these difficulties were from time to time compounded by the pull-up effect of the German mark when it served as the refuge currency for a weakening U.S. dollar. These tensions subsided when European currencies were proclaimed to be "irreversibly" replaced by a single currency. But financial markets cannot be stopped from pricing risk on the basis of their own risk assessments. Inevitably, currency union or not, they will at some point become concerned about, and price in higher risk for, a country's worsening economic fundamentals or deviant fiscal behavior. While in a currency union markets can no longer target misaligned exchange rates, they can and do shift their attention to government bonds and may require higher risk premiums for member countries whose poor economic performance and/or out-of-line fiscal policies could present a higher risk of sovereign default or debt rescheduling or even compromise continued currency union membership. In a sense, speculation against national currencies then gives way to speculation against government bonds.

326. This is not just an innate penchant for speculation or other whim of the financial markets. There is some financial logic to it. In a simplified version of reality, when country *X* has a currency of its own, the risk of default on government bonds issued in its national currency is technically limited by its ability to issue the necessary currency at maturity. But, aside from duration risk, bondholders face exchange rate risk, and country *X*'s poor macroeconomic policies will exert downward pressure on its currency. When, now as a member of a currency union, country *X* issues bonds in the common currency, it no longer has the ability to issue currency as needed to avoid default. Exchange rate risk is now subdued and limited to exchange rate variations of the common currency against relevant third currencies, **except** if markets begin to perceive redenomination risk, *i.e.*, the risk of country *X*'s currency union exit and return to a national currency of lesser value. In an incomplete monetary union, in which member countries retain significant economic and fiscal policy autonomy and there is no robust centralized budgetary stabilization capacity, perceived flaws in country *X*'s economic and fiscal policies increase its credit risk and push up its cost of borrowing, possibly, in an adverse scenario, to the point of spilling over into perceived redenomination risk.

327. Differential assessment of sovereign risk will be reflected in higher yields on government bonds of "weaker" economies and lower yields on those of "stronger" economies, and this spread may widen and become detached from underlying economic fundamentals as risk aversion and flight-to-safety dynamics increase. Unlike with exchange rate tensions, the widening of government bond spreads is not contained by any mechanism of reciprocal intervention obligations and will invariably be mostly to the detriment of the weaker economies at the higher end of the spreads. Excessive widening of spreads, when more than momentary, will cause a fragmentation of the interest rate curve among currency union member countries as government bond yields serve as a benchmark for pricing corporate bonds and bank lending to businesses and households. Such financial fragmentation will interfere with the proper pass-through and hence the effectiveness of the single monetary policy across the euro area. Excessive widening of government bond spreads may get caught in destabilizing market dynamics fueled by fears of default or currency union exit and cut off a member country from access to the financial markets on viable terms.

328. Thus far, this more extreme scenario occurred only once, *i.e.*, during the more acute phase of the euro area sovereign debt crisis in the second half of 2011 and the spring and summer of 2012. But in subsequent years, government bond spreads between high-debt and low-debt euro area Member States episodically widened to a degree causing concern. If one looks at the evolution of the spread between the 10-year Italian BTP and the 10-year German Bund (which is oftentimes considered a benchmark spread or, in a sense, the canary in the coal mine for problematic widening of government bond spreads), this spread: (i) rose above 200 basis points in June 2011, peaked above 500 basis points around the turn of the year and again in July 2012, and then fell back below 200 basis points by February 2014; (ii) again increased above 200 basis points in May 2018, peaking above 300 basis points in November 2018 before dropping below 200 basis points toward the end of August 2019; (iii) widened to more than 200 basis points between March and May 2020 at the outbreak of COVID-19, peaking at 275 basis points on March 17, 2020; (iv) rose again above 200 basis points in May 2022 and especially following the ECB's June 9, 2022 announcement of gradual policy rate increases, peaked at around 250 basis points on October 7 and then fell below 200 basis points in November 2022; and (v) rose moderately again above this level in the second half of December 2022 and in early January 2023 and since then remained mostly below 200 basis points throughout 2023.[483]

329. Financial fragmentation arising from excessive widening of sovereign bond spreads is an immanent risk of a multi-country currency union in which economic and fiscal policies and their financing are for the most part decentralized at the member country level, as has been and largely still is the case in Europe's incomplete EMU. In the European currency union, (i) economic and fiscal policies substantially remain national competences, subject to a measure of coordination and surveillance at the EU level; (ii) there is no sufficiently robust centralized budgetary stabilization capacity; (iii) the Treaty prohibits the monetization of government debt (Article 123 TFEU) and contains a "no bail-out" clause (Article 125 TFEU); and (iv) there is no form of common "backstop" on national debt, aside from the EFSF/ESM rescue loan mechanism. On and off, containing financial fragmentation became a serious concern of the ECB—especially during the 2010-2012 euro area sovereign debt crisis, in the initial months after the outbreak of COVID-19 in 2020, and again when the ECB shifted to a monetary tightening cycle in the summer of 2022.

The ECB (Eurosystem) has mostly addressed financial fragmentation risk by engaging in, or at least announcing, geographically selective asset purchases, principally purchases of government bonds, targeted at euro area Member States at the high end of the spreads, *i.e.*, the Member States with more vulnerable economies and weaker fiscal positions. These programs, which will be reviewed in this chapter, include the Securities Market Program ("SMP"), the Outright Monetary Transactions ("OMT") initiative, the Pandemic Emergency Purchase Program ("PEPP") (in part), and the Transmission Protection Instrument ("TPI"). Interestingly, the ECB did not legitimize these targeted asset purchases primarily on the basis of its distinct responsibility for contributing to the stability of the financial system under Article 127(5) TFEU. It has instead sought to attach those purchases to its monetary policy mandate by the need to safeguard the proper functioning of the monetary policy transmission mechanism, which would be distorted by excessive widening of government bond spreads and the resulting fragmentation of the interest rate curve among euro area Member States. As we will see, the European Court of Justice has, helpfully, given its blessing to this reasoning in its 2015 *Gauweiler* judgment (*see* paragraphs 344-346 below).

330. Those anti-fragmentation asset purchase programs are to be distinguished from the quantitative easing ("QE") programs that are aimed at across-the-board monetary easing to counter disinflationary pressures, *i.e.*, the Asset Purchase Program ("APP") and "mainstream" PEPP. In this classification, PEPP is somewhat of a hybrid or dual-purpose program, *i.e.*, (i) its "mainstream" role is (was) to provide further monetary easing to check expected additional disinflationary pressures from COVID-19 (a monetary policy stance objective), and (ii) the flexible allocation of purchases and reinvestments across asset classes, maturities and, especially, geographies allows it to

483. *See* https://www.borsaitaliana.it/obbligazioni/spread/italia/btp-bund.en.htm.

be used to contain financial fragmentation, as occurred mostly in the early months following the outbreak of COVID-19 (a monetary policy transmission objective) (*see* paragraphs 350-352 below). But APP and "mainstream" PEPP were in the first instance aimed at plainly providing monetary stimulus or accommodation in circumstances where policy rates were at the lower bound. Thus, the Public Sector Purchase Program ("PSPP"), APP's main sub-program, is geographically "neutral" in the sense that purchases are allocated substantially in accordance with the ECB capital subscription key, without express allowance for a greater concentration of purchases on more vulnerable Member States (although, from time to time, purchase flows deviated somewhat from the ECB capital key in favor of higher-debt Member States) (*see* paragraph 224 above). Yet, while not explicitly directed at containing financial fragmentation, large-scale QE purchases of government bonds reduced government borrowing costs across the board, including for euro area Member States with weaker government deficit and debt ratios, and, in this manner, indirectly helped to dampen spreads on government bonds (*see* paragraph 229 above).

331. This chapter will take a closer look at the ECB's anti-fragmentation asset purchase programs. To an outside observer, geographically selective central bank purchases of assets, particularly government bonds, aimed at containing excessive widening of bond spreads raise several questions, including (but not limited to) the following:

(a) Can such targeted asset purchases properly be characterized as monetary policy in the first place? Is the ECB's stated goal of preserving or restoring the proper functioning of the monetary policy transmission mechanism solid enough justification for bringing such purchases within the scope of its monetary policy mandate?
(b) Could the characterization of those purchases as monetary policy be compromised when they effectively serve the concurrent objective of preserving the cohesion of the currency union and avoiding exit by one or several members?
(c) What then is the dividing line between (i) ESM stability support (which may take the form, *inter alia*, of government bond purchases) to euro area Member States that *"are experiencing, or are threatened by, severe financing problems"* when such support is needed *"to safeguard the financial stability of the euro area as a whole and of its Member States"* (as the ESM's purpose is defined in Article 3 of the ESM Treaty), and (ii) central bank asset purchases selectively targeted at government bonds issued by euro Member States facing stressful financing conditions so as to contain excessive widening of sovereign bond spreads that distorts the proper functioning of the monetary policy transmission mechanism but could also become destabilizing for the currency union?
(d) Are geographically selective asset purchases consistent with the supposed "singleness" of monetary policy as contemplated by Article 119(2) TFEU? Wouldn't this "singleness" of monetary policy stand in the way of differentiating monetary policy actions to address specific country circumstances?

(e) Couldn't such purchases conflict with the ECB's primary mandate of inflation control, especially in an environment of higher inflation? Would consistency then require that the additional liquidity injected by those purchases be systematically sterilized by liquidity-absorption operations?
(f) Could such purchases legitimately be conditioned on, or linked to, economic or fiscal policy commitments of the relevant euro area Member State while remaining within the compass of the monetary policy mandate?
(g) Wouldn't central bank purchases of government bonds become (even more) problematic under the monetary financing prohibition of Article 123 TFEU when targeted at Member States struggling to maintain access to the financial markets on viable terms?
(h) And when all these questions are answered, how could the ECB confidently identify actionable financial fragmentation? At which point does the widening of sovereign bond spreads become excessive or unwarranted? When it is out of line with underlying economic fundamentals? How must the ECB determine when financial markets are effectively mispricing sovereign risk, *i.e.*, in fact, conclude that the markets are wrong? Also, at which point does an unwarranted widening of sovereign bond spreads present a genuine risk for effective monetary policy transmission? Or is this not really a separate question insofar as monetary policy transmission must be deemed to be distorted when sovereign bond spreads widen beyond the level warranted by economic fundamentals?

2 THE SECURITIES MARKET PROGRAM

332. During the 2008-2012 financial crisis, government deficit and debt levels increased to different degrees among euro area Member States (*see* paragraph 116, Table 2.2, above) as a result, notably, of bank rescue operations and a certain desynchronization of business cycles.[484] The October 21, 2009 Greek "confessions" served as a wake-up call that made the financial markets and the rating agencies increasingly attentive to differences in sovereign risk within the euro area. This caused a widening of sovereign bond spreads to the detriment of euro area Member States with weaker fiscal positions, and, as part of an adverse feedback loop that became referred to as the "bank-sovereign doom loop", the higher sovereign bond yields in these Member States depressed their bond prices which, in turn, negatively affected bank balance sheets (given the "home bias" of bank holdings of sovereign bonds).

333. Then, on May 10, 2010, the ECB launched its Securities Markets Program ("SMP").[485] It did so over the opposition of then Bundesbank President Axel Weber and

484. *Cf.* F. Gori, "Fostering cyclical convergence in the euro area", *OECD Economics Department Working Papers No 1697*, January 3, 2022, p. 6, Figure 1.
485. *See* the ECB's press release of May 10, 2010, https://www.ecb.europa.eu/press/pr/date/2010/html/pr100510.en.html, and Decision 2010/281/EU of the European Central Bank of May 14, 2010 establishing a securities market programme, *OJ* L124, May 20, 2010, p. 8. For a fuller

amid some speculation that ECB President Jean-Claude Trichet was trying to protect French banks from losses on their Greek bond holdings.[486] SMP was a temporary program for the purchase of government and private debt securities in market segments subject to severe tensions. It was an anti-fragmentation tool *avant la lettre*. Its stated aim was to ensure depth and liquidity in dysfunctional market segments, and it was justified by reference to:

> *"current exceptional circumstances in financial markets, characterised by severe tensions in certain market segments which are hampering the monetary policy transmission mechanism and thereby the effective conduct of monetary policy oriented towards price stability in the medium term".*[487]

334. SMP purchases were not formally conditioned on particular policy actions to be taken by the relevant euro area Member State,[488] although there were persistent rumors that, on occasion, the ECB may have used SMP as a lever to extract or enforce policy or reform commitments from Member States. Thus, in a letter marked "secret" dated November 19, 2010, to the Irish Minister of Finance and in two letters marked "strictly confidential" dated August 5, 2011, to the Spanish and Italian Prime Ministers,[489] the

discussion of SMP, *see, e.g.*, K. Tuori, "Monetary Policy (Objectives and Instruments)", in *The EU Law of Economic and Monetary Union* (F. Amtenbrink & Chr. Herrmann eds.), Oxford University Press, 2020, pp. 655-665, §§22.117-22.147, and A.A. Smith, "The European Central Bank's Securities Market Programme", *Journal of Financial Crises*, 2020, pp. 369-381.

486. *Cf.* W. Reuter, "ECB Buying Up Greek Bonds: German Central Bankers Suspect French Intrigue", *Spiegel International*, May 31, 2010, https://www.spiegel.de/international/europe/ecb-buying-up-greek-bonds-german-central-bankers-suspect-french-intrigue-a-697680.html. The reality is that, over the years, Eurosystem central banks earned significant income (interest payments and amortized discount) on SMP purchases of Greek bonds. *See* the ECB's letter of October 10, 2017 to Nikolaos Chountis, member of the European Parliament, https://www.ecb.europa.eu/pub/pdf/other/ecb.mepletter171010Chountis.en.pdf? ca00752c61bdb4df6c227f4f3c62b98a.The euro area Member States returned a good part (but not all) of this gain to Greece. This, in fact, became a negotiating chip in the discussions on the financial assistance programs for Greece and the related policy conditionality. Thus, the Eurogroup announced on November 27, 2012 that income accruing on SMP bonds as from 2013 (but not earlier income) would be passed on to Greece in a phased manner and conditional upon Greece's implementation of the agreed reform measures. *See* https://www.consilium.europa.eu/uedocs/cms_data/docs/pressdata/en/ecofin/133857.pdf. On June 27, 2015, the Eurogroup effectively halted these payments given the deadlock in the negotiations over a further program. *See* https://www.consilium.europa.eu/en/press-releases/2015/06/27/eurogroup-statement-greece/. Then, on June 22, 2018, as part of the medium-term debt relief package, the Eurogroup agreed that the SMP profit of 2014 and the profit as from 2017 would be returned to Greece in semi-annual instalments starting in 2018, subject to continued compliance with agreed policy conditions. *See* https://www.consilium.europa.eu/en/press/press-releases/2018/06/22eurogroup-statement-on-greece-22-june-2018/#: ~ text = The%20Eurogroup%20welcomes%20the%20commitments,strategy%20by%20the%20Greek%20authorities.

487. Recital (2) to Decision 2010/281/EU. Recital (3) also refers to the need to *"restore an appropriate monetary policy transmission mechanism"*.

488. Yet, when stating that the ECB's Governing Council will decide on the scope of the purchases, recital (4) to Decision 2010/281/EU immediately adds that the Governing Council has *"taken note"* of the Member States' commitment to meet their fiscal targets under excessive deficit procedures and the additional commitments of some *"to accelerate fiscal consolidation and ensure the sustainability of their public finances"*.

489. These letters were subsequently reclassified for release and may be found at, respectively, https://www.ecb.europa.eu/press/html/irish-letters.en.html; https://www.ecb.europa.eu/ecb/access_to_documents/document/correspondence/shared/data/ecb.dr.cor20110805Zapa

ECB remarkably insisted on receiving commitments on fairly specific national policy actions and reforms (*see* paragraph 505 below). None of these letters contained any express reference to SMP, but, in a press release of August 7, 2011, then ECB President Jean-Claude Trichet welcomed the announcement by Spain and Italy of certain fiscal measures and structural reforms and indicated that the ECB will now *"actively implement"* SMP.[490]

335. SMP was to run until September 2012 (when it was effectively replaced by the OMT initiative discussed below) and led to the purchase of government bonds for an aggregate nominal amount of about EUR 218 billion, including Greek bonds (EUR 33.9 billion), Portuguese bonds (EUR 22.8 billion), Spanish bonds (EUR 44.3 billion), Irish bonds (EUR 14.2 billion) and Italian bonds (remarkably EUR 102.8 billion).[491] Interestingly, the SMP's liquidity effect was largely "sterilized" by weekly liquidity-absorption operations until June 2014.[492]

336. SMP was not directly challenged before the European Court of Justice ("CJEU"), but SMP's relationship with the ECB's monetary policy mandate came up indirectly in several Article 340 TFEU damages claims which private parties brought against the ECB before the General Court for loss that they had incurred in the 2012 Greek sovereign debt restructuring. Under a February 15, 2012 agreement with Greece, Eurosystem central banks had swapped Greek government bonds that they had acquired under SMP against identical bonds with different dates and serial numbers (ISIN codes) which effectively excluded them from the debt restructuring. Among several other pleas, the applicants claimed that this breached a general principle of equal treatment of creditors. In the 2015 *Accorinti* case[493] and the 2017 *Nausicaa* case,[494] the General Court considered that Eurosystem central banks were not in a position comparable to that of other creditors because they had acquired their bonds in the exercise of their monetary policy mandate—but without any substantive examination as to whether SMP could properly be characterized as monetary policy. In the 2022 *Qi* case,[495] the General Court engaged in some further analysis of this question and, with reference to the CJEU's judgments in *Gauweiler* and *Weiss*, concluded that SMP purchases were in the realm of monetary policy.

---

tero.en.pdf; and https://www.ecb.europa.eu/ecb/access_to_documents/document/pa_document/shared/data/ecb.dr.par2021_0001lettertoItalian PrimeMinister.en.pdf.

490. *See* Statement of the President of the ECB of August 7, 2011, https://www.ecb.europa.eu/press/pr/date/2011/html/pr110807.en.html.

491. Click "History of SMP holdings per issuer" at https://www.ecb.europa.eu/mopo/implement/app/html/index.en.html.

492. These took the form of finetuning operations by way of quick tenders to collect one-week fixed-term deposits.

493. GC, October 7, 2015, Case T-79/13, *Accorinti et al. vs. ECB*, ECLI:EU:T:2015:756, §§88-90.

494. GC, January 24, 2017, Case T-749/15, *Nausicaa Anadyomène & Banque d'escompte vs. ECB*, ECLI:EU: T:2017:21, §§111-113.

495. GC, February 9, 2022, Case T-868/16, *Qi et al. vs. European Commission & ECB*, ECLI:EU:T:2022:58, §§168-170 and 173-174.

3 OUTRIGHT MONETARY TRANSACTIONS

a "Whatever It Takes"

337. Between 2010 and 2012, several euro area Member States—Ireland, Greece, Portugal, Spain and Cyprus—became subject to severe financial stress and eventually required financial assistance. This, in combination with successive downgrades of sovereign credit ratings (*see* paragraph 65, Table 1.1, above), the Franco-German agreement on "private sector involvement" ("PSI") at the October 18-19, 2010 Deauville summit (*see* paragraph 74 above) and a growing sense of inevitability of a Greek sovereign debt restructuring, caused tensions in the sovereign bond markets to flare up in 2011. In the spring of 2012, they became fueled by market concerns over a partial or total break-up of the European currency union (redenomination risk). It was then that Mario Draghi, speaking at the Global Investment Conference in London on July 26, 2012, said that *"we think the euro is irreversible"* and proclaimed that *"[w]ithin our mandate, the ECB is ready to do whatever it takes to preserve the euro. And believe me, it will be enough"*.[496] At the end of his speech, he made the link with monetary policy in another short sentence: *"To the extent that the size of these sovereign premia hampers the functioning of the monetary policy transmission channel, they come within our mandate"*.[497] Since that fateful summer, the containment of excessive widening of sovereign bond spreads and the consequent financial fragmentation has from time to time *de facto* become a parallel objective of ECB monetary policy.

338. With ECB policy rates then already being at the low end (and not being amenable to geographic differentiation anyway), the ECB had to find another way of compressing bond spreads. Selectively buying government bonds in the secondary markets, targeting those of euro area Member States at the high end of the spreads, must have seemed an obvious answer. On the legal side, there were concerns about whether this would fit within the compass of the ECB's monetary policy mandate. The ECB then chose to perfect the justification given almost casually for SMP (*see* paragraph 333 above). If monetary policy is to be "single" for the euro area (as the Treaty requires), then the ECB's monetary policy mandate must extend to such action as is needed to ensure the effective pass-through of its single monetary policy stance throughout the euro area. Excessive sovereign bond spreads cause fragmentation of bond markets and interest rates, and hence interfere with the even transmission of monetary policy. If there is not enough space left for lowering policy rates much further, then the ECB must be able to take alternative action to compress market spreads, including by buying sovereign bonds, to safeguard the singleness of monetary policy. This reasoning has become a common theme in the ECB's successive asset purchase programs. But it is at the very core of its justification of asset purchase programs that are explicitly aimed at

496. Verbatim of the remarks made by Mario Draghi at the Global Investment Conference in London on July 26, 2012, https://www.ecb.europa.eu/press/key/date/2012/html/sp120726.en.html, at p. 2.
497. *Ibid.*, at p. 3.

containing financial fragmentation and, to this end, offer flexibility in the allocation of bond purchases across geographies, *i.e.*, OMT, PEPP (in part) and TPI.

b Key Features

339. Thus, on August 2, 2012, the ECB announced a new program under which the Eurosystem may engage in outright open market operations to counter excessive widening of sovereign bond spreads. The program was reportedly adopted with near unanimity, with a single dissenting voice of then Bundesbank President Jens Weidmann. General features of the new program, by the name of "Outright Monetary Transactions" ("OMT"), were published in a succinct press release on September 6, 2012,[498] which was not particularly rich in detail.

340. OMT's broadly formulated framework includes the following elements:

(a) OMT's stated purpose is *"to address severe distortions in government bond markets which originate from, in particular, unfounded fears on the part of investors of the reversibility in the euro"*,[499] with a view to *"safeguarding an appropriate monetary policy transmission and the singleness of the monetary policy"*. OMT purchases would be triggered by excessive widening of sovereign bond spreads caused by destabilizing market dynamics driven *"in particular"* by perceived but *"unfounded"* redenomination risk, *i.e.*, the risk of euro exit of one or more Member States which would then revert to a national currency of likely lesser value.

(b) To this effect, Eurosystem central banks may in the secondary markets purchase bonds issued by euro area Member States that are subject to *"strict and effective"* economic policy conditionality under a financial assistance program from the EFSF/ESM.[500]

(c) The underlying idea is that OMT purchases would complement EFSF/ESM stability support by focusing on the shorter end of the yield curve, *i.e.*, on government bonds with a remaining maturity between one and three years.

(d) There would be no *ex ante* quantitative limits on OMT purchases but the additional liquidity created would be fully sterilized.

(e) For bonds purchased under OMT, the ECB would not claim preferred creditor status ("PCS") but accept *pari passu* treatment with private bondholders.

---

498. *See* the ECB's press release of September 6, 2012, https://www.ecb.europa.eu/press/pr/date/2012/html/pr120906_1.en.html. For a more detailed discussion of OMT, *see, e.g.*, K. Tuori, *supra*, pp. 665-675, §§22.148-22.178.

499. This phrase is taken from Mr. Draghi's introductory statement at the ECB's September 6, 2012 press briefing, as memorialized in the published transcript of this press conference, https://www ecb.europa.eu/press/pressconf/2012/html/is120906.en.html, at p. 1.

500. The September 6, 2012 press release specifies that this may take the form of either a full macroeconomic adjustment program or a precautionary program (under an Enhanced Conditions Credit Line), so long as they include the possibility of EFSF/ESM primary market purchases.

341. Economic policy conditionality attached to EFSF/ESM financial assistance was presented as a key eligibility condition for OMT, and it was stated in the September 6, 2012 press release that OMT purchases would (not "could") be discontinued if the euro area Member State in question did not comply with such conditionality. Apparently, the ECB's insistence on continued compliance with policy conditions was at least partly motivated by its frustration over Silvio Berlusconi's government having walked back on its policy commitments of the summer of 2011 (*see* paragraph 334 above).

342. At our summertime dinner table, my guests will likely be puzzled by several questions regarding the link between OMT and EFSF/ESM stability support and its economic policy conditionality:

(a) Why should Eurosystem central banks purchase a Member State's government bonds in circumstances in which that Member State receives stability support from the EFSF or the ESM given that, under the terms of their constituent instruments, these institutions could themselves provide such support by subscribing to government bonds issued by that Member State or purchasing them in the secondary market?[501] Is it because of some unique monetary policy angle that is sometimes but not always present in EFSF/ESM stability support cases? If so, why should OMT purchases be restricted to these cases in the first place? Or is it mostly a matter of added central bank firepower or rapidity of execution? In any event, these parallel interventions add sharp relief to the question of why such bond purchases should be characterized as monetary policy when made by Eurosystem central banks but, under the CJEU's *Pringle* judgment, as economic policy when carried out by the EFSF/ESM.[502] At the end of the day, why should government bond purchases to compress out-of-line bond yields of a Member State under financial stress not simply be left to a euro area stability support mechanism like the ESM?

(b) The reader may also wonder whether economic policy conditionality would not weaken the link between government bond purchases under OMT and their stated monetary policy objective of safeguarding or restoring the proper functioning of the monetary policy transmission mechanism. In the ECB's logic, it falls within its monetary policy mandate and responsibility to act when the proper functioning of the monetary policy transmission mechanism is impaired. Why then should its intervention be linked to EFSF/ESM stability support and conditioned on the Member State's compliance with related

501. *See* Article 2(1)(b) of the EFSF Framework Agreement and Articles 17 and 18 of the ESM Treaty, respectively.

502. A mere few months after the announcement of OMT, the CJEU, in its judgment of November 27, 2012 in the *Pringle* case, ruled that a stability support mechanism like the ESM aimed at preserving the cohesion of the currency union is an instrument not of monetary policy but of economic policy and hence within the competence of the Member States. *See* CJEU, November 27, 2012, Case C-370/12, *Pringle*, ECLI:EU:C:2012:756, §§52-60 and 93-98. *See also* paragraphs 514 and 690 below.

economic policy conditionality? One would think that, so long as the impairment of the monetary policy transmission mechanism subsists, a Member State's failure to comply with EFSF/ESM economic policy conditionality would not leave monetary policy transmission any less in need of repair and that discontinuation of OMT purchases would not serve to improve it. There is a certain ambivalence in, or tension between, justifying bond purchases as monetary policy action by the need to preserve or repair the monetary policy transmission mechanism, on the one hand, but then conditioning such action on the existence of, and continued compliance with, policy conditionality related to fiscal restraint or economic reforms, on the other hand.

343. Ironically perhaps, the OMT program has not so far been applied in practice. Its mere announcement appears to have sufficed at the time. But the ECB has kept OMT on the books, as one of several possible tools to address financial fragmentation risk (*see* paragraphs 365(a) and 366 below).

c The *Gauweiler* Case

344. Although OMT has thus far remained in a dormant state as a virtual program, it was challenged before the German Federal Constitutional Court ("BVerfG") which then referred several questions as to OMT's consistency with EU law to the CJEU for a preliminary ruling.

In its 2015 *Gauweiler* judgment, the CJEU first accepted the ECB's rationale for bringing OMT within the scope of monetary policy, on the basis of the following considerations:

(a) Disruptions in monetary policy transmission channels would impair the effective pass-through of monetary policy actions in parts of the euro area and undermine the singleness of monetary policy. Measures aimed at ensuring the proper functioning of the monetary transmission mechanism can therefore be attached to the ECB's monetary policy mandate.[503]
(b) Open-market purchases of marketable financial instruments are a monetary policy instrument authorized by Article 18.1 of Protocol No 4. Remedying disruptions in the monetary policy transmission mechanism localized in particular government bond markets entails geographically selective bond purchases. And no Treaty provision requires the ESCB to operate in the financial markets *"by means of general measures that would necessarily be applicable to all the States of the euro area"*.[504]

503. CJEU, June 16, 2015, Case C-62/14, *Gauweiler et al.*, ECLI:EU:C:2015:400, §§46-50. The General Court also confirmed this in its 2022 *Qi* judgment. *See* GC, February 9, 2022, Case T-868/16, *Qi et al. vs. European Commission & ECB*, ECLI:EU:T:2022:58, §§101 and 174.
504. *Gauweiler*, §§54-55.

(c) Neither the fact that OMT purchases may have indirect effects on the stability of the currency union nor the fact that they are made conditional upon compliance with EFSF/ESM macroeconomic adjustment programs means that they should be recharacterized as economic policy measures.[505]

345. The Court then proceeded to an assessment of the proportionality of OMT in relation to its stated monetary policy objective:

(a) The Court (summarily) considered the ECB's analysis underlying OMT, *i.e.*, that excessive widening of sovereign bond spreads, due in part to perceived redenomination risk, may give rise to financial fragmentation that undermines the monetary policy transmission mechanism. It held that *"it does not appear"* that this analysis is *"vitiated by a manifest error in assessment"*.[506] This is not called into question by the fact that that analysis is contested since *"questions of monetary policy are usually of a controversial nature"* (*sic*), and the ECB must be allowed *"broad discretion"* in assessments of this kind.[507] In the end, the ECB could *"legitimately take the view"* that selective bond purchases as contemplated by OMT would be suitable to achieve the objective of restoring the monetary policy transmission mechanism and the singleness of monetary policy.[508]

(b) The Court also found that OMT does not *"manifestly"* go beyond what is necessary to achieve that objective, having regard notably to (i) the fact that the actual implementation of OMT will be *"dependent upon an in-depth assessment of the requirements of monetary policy"*, and that the ECB had not deemed activation of OMT justified in prior years (in other words, that the ECB had not been an easy grader in applying OMT thus far);[509] (ii) the limited potential scale of OMT given that OMT purchases are reserved to Member States under EFSM/ESM stability support, that they are focused on government bonds at the short end of the maturity spectrum, and that Eurosystem central banks may resell the bonds at any time;[510] and (iii) the fact that the ECB *"weighed up the various interests in play"* so as to prevent disadvantages that would be manifestly disproportionate to OMT's objectives[511]—a consideration which, curiously, is put forward without any further explanation.

346. Furthermore, the CJEU concluded that OMT would not violate the monetary financing prohibition of Article 123 TFEU:

505. *Ibid.*, §§51-52 and 59-64.
506. *Ibid.*, §74.
507. *Ibid.*, §75. *Cf. also ibid.*, §68.
508. *Ibid.*, §80.
509. *Ibid.*, §§83-84.
510. *Ibid.*, §§85-87.
511. *Ibid.*, §91.

(a) The Court observed that OMT purchases would be made in the secondary markets under conditions that would not make them equivalent to primary market purchases and that would not lessen the impetus of the Member State concerned to follow a sound budgetary policy. This the Court inferred from certain OMT design features including the fact that (i) the relevant Member State would have no *ex ante* certainty that a particular quantity of its bonds would be purchased, or held to maturity, by the ESCB; (ii) OMT could not be implemented in such a way as to harmonize government bond yields irrespective of differences in underlying fundamentals; and (iii) OMT purchases would be linked to an EFSF/ESM macroeconomic adjustment program.[512]

(b) Also, the Court did not take issue with the ESCB's exposure to loss as a result of the acceptance of *pari passu* treatment: it saw this as a risk inherent in the purchase of bonds in the secondary markets, which is an operation authorized by Article 18.1 of Protocol No 4 without being made conditional upon the ESCB having PCS.[513] The Court did not expressly consider whether PCS might be a rule of customary international law (this is most likely not the case but the Court did not address this point).

347. In its June 21, 2016 judgment on the merits,[514] the BVerfG unenthusiastically went along with the CJEU's preliminary ruling, but not without expressing its misgivings about perceived shortcomings in the CJEU's judicial review. It criticized the CJEU notably for (i) accepting that OMT pursues a monetary policy objective without reviewing indications that evidently (*"offensichtlich"*) point to the contrary, such as the selectivity of OMT purchases, the parallelism with EFSF/ESM support programs, and the fact that OMT purchases are not allowed in case of the Member State's non-compliance with EFSF/ESM economic policy conditions, irrespective of the effects on the monetary policy transmission mechanism;[515] (ii) uncritically accepting the objectives of the measure as asserted by the ECB, allowing it a wide margin of assessment and, in this manner, leaving it considerable leeway to define the actual scope of the competence conferred on it by the Treaty;[516] and (iii) not addressing the issue whether the independence granted to the ECB by Article 130 TFEU and the consequent reduction in democratic legitimation of its acts should not require a restrictive interpretation of its mandate and a stricter judicial review of its acts.[517]

348. While in the end not taking issue with the September 6, 2012 policy statement on OMT, the BVerfG held that, going forward, the Bundesbank may participate in OMT's implementation only if the parameters set forth in that policy statement are satisfied as

512. *Ibid.*, §§93-121.
513. *Ibid.*, §§123-126.
514. BVerfG, June 21, 2016, ECLI:DE:BVerfG:2016:rs20160621.2bvr272813. An English translation of this judgment may be found on the BVerfG's website at https://www.bverfg.de/e/rs20160621_2bvr272813en.html.
515. *Ibid.*, §182.
516. *Ibid.*, §§183-186.
517. *Ibid.*, §§187-189.

well as a number of additional parameters which the BVerfG eagerly inferred from the CJEU's analysis, notably its proportionality assessment and its review under Article 123 TFEU. In the BVerfG's reading, these parameters specifically include the following conditions: (i) the volume of purchases must be fixed *ex ante*; (ii) neither the purchases nor their volume may be pre-announced; (iii) a pre-defined gray period must be observed between the issue date of the government bonds and their purchase in the secondary market so as to avoid interference with issue pricing; (iv) purchases must be limited to government bonds of Member States that still have market access; (v) bonds purchased should not as a rule be held to maturity except if there are monetary policy reasons for doing so; and (vi) purchases are to be reduced or discontinued, and bonds purchased are to be resold, when continued intervention becomes unnecessary.[518] Furthermore, the German Federal Government and the Bundestag are under a duty to monitor the implementation of OMT in order to avoid the Bundestag's budgetary autonomy being compromised by the volume and risk of OMT purchases.[519] In light of all these conditions, one might be inclined to think that any future activation of OMT is unlikely to be a walk in the park. But, at the end of the day, none of these conditions should be vastly problematic, with the possible exception of condition (iv).

4 THE PANDEMIC EMERGENCY PURCHASE PROGRAM

349. Let me start this section with a brief parenthesis on the Public Sector Purchase Program ("PSPP") that was launched in 2015 as part of APP. As discussed in Chapter 4 (*see* paragraphs 218 *et seq.* above), PSPP was a QE program *pur sang* and had no explicit anti-fragmentation purpose or geographic selectivity feature. Its primary aim was to exercise downward pressure on sovereign bond yields and hence market interest rates so as to check disinflationary pressures and lift inflation closer to 2%. Yet, by reducing government bond yields across the board, PSPP indirectly helped to curb the widening of sovereign bond spreads among euro area Member States. Also, as previously noted (*see* paragraph 224 above), the key for the allocation of PSPP purchases among jurisdictions was tweaked in early 2020 to loosen the tie with the ECB capital subscription key somewhat. Perhaps this was done in part to validate occasional deviations from the ECB capital key in PSPP purchase flows in 2015, 2018 and 2020 in favor of bonds of certain higher-debt Member States including Italy, France, Spain and Belgium. But, all in all, PSPP should not be classified as an anti-fragmentation tool.

350. In contrast, the Pandemic Emergency Purchase Program ("PEPP") announced on March 18, 2020 offers explicit geographic flexibility. The sudden outbreak of COVID-19 in the early months of 2020 initially caused a sharp widening of sovereign bond spreads in the euro area. By then, the financial markets had become sensitive to signs of

518. *Ibid.*, §206. *Cf. also ibid.*, §§195, 199 and 202-204.
519. *Ibid.*, §220.

significant widening of sovereign bond spreads. At one of her first ECB press conferences, on March 12, 2020, ECB President Christine Lagarde had stated that closing sovereign bond spreads was not the mission of the ECB.[520] Instant market reaction caused the already widening spread between the 10-year Italian BTP and the 10-year German Bund to jump by some 40 basis points. This prompted Ms. Lagarde to swiftly correct her statement in a CNBC interview, saying that high spreads impair monetary policy transmission and that the ECB was *"fully committed to avoid any fragmentation"*—a comment which the ECB judged necessary to add as a footnote to the published transcript of its March 12, 2020 press briefing.[521]

351. As indicated in Chapter 4 (*see* paragraph 240(e) above), PEPP serves in part to contain financial fragmentation risk caused by the pandemic. While, as a rule, the allocation of cumulative net purchases under PEPP among euro area Member States is *"guided"*, *"on a stock basis"*, by the ECB capital subscription key,[522] the PEPP framework explicitly offers flexibility for the geographic differentiation of purchase flows over time.[523] The addition of this express flexibility clause suggests that adherence to the ECB capital key is less stringent than under PSPP (even in the less prescriptive 2020 reformulation of its purchase allocation rule). The underlying monetary logic, once again, is that of preserving the proper functioning of the monetary policy transmission mechanism: increased heterogeneity among Member States' sovereign yield curves as a result of the differing impact of COVID-19 may feed into higher market rates and tightening financing conditions in certain parts of the euro area so as to interfere with the proper transmission of the ECB's then accommodative or "dovish" monetary policy stance aimed at maintaining favorable financing conditions and keeping disinflationary pressures at bay.

352. The announcement and prompt implementation of PEPP, with its flexible allocation across asset classes, maturities and jurisdictions, appears to have helped to stabilize the markets. By and large, the use of PEPP as an anti-fragmentation tool has remained relatively moderate so far:

(a) During PEPP's net purchase phase (*i.e.*, from the end of March 2020 until and including March 2022), geographic differentiation from the ECB capital key occurred intermittently but remained limited overall. In a March 31, 2022 speech, ECB Chief Economist Philip Lane observed that capital key deviations

520. *See* the transcript of the ECB's press conference of March 12, 2020, https://www.ecb.europa.eu/press/pressconf/2020/html/ecb.is200312~f857a21b6c.en.html, at p. 8.
521. *Ibid.*, at p. 11. In the CNBC interview (and the statement reproduced in the footnote to the transcript), Ms. Lagarde added that the ECB *"will use the flexibility embedded in the asset purchase programme, including within the public sector purchase programme"*. The reference to PSPP must probably be linked to the more flexible formulation of the allocation of PSPP purchases in relation to the ECB capital subscription key (*see* paragraph 349 above).
522. Article 5(1) of Decision (EU) 2020/440 of the European Central Bank of March 24, 2020 on a temporary pandemic emergency purchase programme, *OJ* L91, March 25, 2020, p. 1, amended by Decision (EU) 2020/1143 of July 28, 2020, *OJ* L248, July 31, 2020, p. 24, and Decision (EU) 2021/174 of February 10, 2021, *OJ* L50, February 15, 2021, p. 29.
523. Article 5(2) and (3) of the same Decision.

peaked in the early weeks of PEPP but self-corrected over time.[524] A closer look at the published data confirms that, during PEPP's net purchase phase, cumulative deviations from the ECB capital key were the most significant in the period from March to June 2020 and then receded.[525] In terms of the stock of securities held at the end of March 2022, the largest upward percentage deviations from the capital key were recorded for Italy (+ 9%), Spain (+ 5%) and Belgium (+ 3%).[526]

(b) Net purchases under PEPP were discontinued at the end of March 2022 but proceeds from maturing bonds in the PEPP portfolio continued to be fully reinvested. For a long while, the ECB repeatedly confirmed that this would go on *"until at least the end of 2024"*, but on December 14, 2023, it announced its plan to phase down these reinvestments in the second half of 2024 and discontinue them altogether at the end of the year (*see* paragraph 298 above). Geographic differentiation has been applied episodically during this reinvestment-only phase.[527]

5 THE TRANSMISSION PROTECTION INSTRUMENT

a Financial Fragmentation in a High-Inflation Environment

353. By now, the reader will have spotted a potential conflict between anti-fragmentation asset purchases and inflation control that goes to the heart of the monetary policy mandate. No such conflict is apparent in an environment of **low inflation**: inflation (significantly) below the 2% benchmark calls for monetary easing, and, in these circumstances, anti-fragmentation government bond purchases and the attendant liquidity injection would be at least directionally consistent with such a monetary policy stance in terms of the primary price stability objective. But this happy constellation no longer exists in a **high-inflation** environment, such as that prevailing in 2022-2023, which calls for a more restrictive monetary policy and higher policy rates:

524. Ph. Lane, "Monetary policy during the pandemic: the role of the PEPP", Speech at the Paris School of Economics, March 31, 2022, https://www.ecb.europa.eu/press/key/date/2022/html/ecb.sp220331 ~ b11d74f249.en.html, at p. 7, Chart 6.

525. *See* B. Böninghausen, L.F. Brennan *et al.*, "The pandemic emergency purchase programme —an initial review", *ECB Economic Bulletin*, 2022, Issue 8, p. 101, Chart 4.

526. *See* C. Birkholz & Fr. Heinemann, "Magnitudes and Capital Key Divergence of the Eurosystem's PSPP/PEPP Purchases-Update April 2023", *ZEW Expert Brief No 2*, April 4, 2023, pp. 6-7, especially Figure 3 at p. 7.

527. For example, between June 22 and July 22, 2022, PEPP portfolio holdings of German public-sector securities fell by EUR 14.27 billion, while those of Spanish and Italian public-sector securities rose by EUR 5.91 billion and EUR 9.76 billion, respectively. Click the spreadsheet *History of public sector securities cumulative purchase breakdowns under the PEPP* at https://www.ecb.europa.eu/mopo/implement/pepp/html/index.en.html. Such episodic selectivity resulted by the end of January 2023 in a further overweighting of Spain's and Italy's shares in relation to the ECB capital key. *See* C. Birkholz & Fr. Heinemann, *supra*, p. 8, Figure 4, p. 10, Table 1, and p. 14, Figure A1.

(a) The consequent rise in interest rate levels and government borrowing costs presents a higher risk of causing or fueling a widening of government bond spreads to the detriment of euro area Member States with weaker economic fundamentals and higher pre-existing government debt. Market yield differentials may become divorced from underlying economic fundamentals and then impair proper pass-through of the monetary policy stance—now in the sense that too high a dose of restriction will come to apply to "weaker" Member States at the high end of the spreads and, in case of flight-to-safety capital flows, too low a dose to "stronger" Member States at the low end of the spreads. In an adverse scenario, this may set in motion destabilizing market dynamics that could even degenerate into a sovereign debt crisis, as occurred in 2011-2012 in different circumstances. The concern is not entirely academic insofar as, at the end of 2022, government debt ratios in the euro area generally stood at higher levels, and with greater divergence between Northern and Southern euro area Member States, than in 2010 (*see* paragraph 116, Table 2.2, above).
(b) Yet, central bank asset purchases to contain financial fragmentation risk will inject additional liquidity into the system, and now, in a high-inflation environment, this runs counter to the more restrictive monetary policy stance that is required strictly from a price stability standpoint. Unless the additional liquidity could somehow be re-absorbed or "sterilized" within the medium-term horizon, above-target inflation gives rise to an apparent conflict between the ECB's primary objective of inflation control and the parallel objective of containing financial fragmentation.
(c) Moreover, if higher inflation coincides with a slow-down of growth and recessionary risk (as in recent times), that conflict is exacerbated by a bi-directional macroeconomic policy mix as national fiscal authorities will be inclined to increase public spending and disinclined (or simply unable) to reduce government debt, neither of which will help to contain widening bond spreads.

354. In Europe's incomplete EMU, the conflict between inflation control and containment of financial fragmentation is bound to arise from time to time in a higher-inflation environment. Resolute monetary tightening to control inflation will increase financial fragmentation risk and financial fragmentation will disturb the proper pass-through of that monetary policy stance. The containment of financial fragmentation becomes a prerequisite for effective monetary tightening and resolute policy rate increases but, by the same token, anti-fragmentation asset purchases will inject additional liquidity into the system. The ECB will have to weigh its options, between (i) moderating monetary policy rate increases to keep fragmentation risk at bay, or (ii) adopting a steeper rate path but standing ready to engage in anti-fragmentation asset purchases, in the hope that these can be limited or at least that their liquidity impact can be sterilized sometime somehow. One could see that option (ii) would ordinarily be viewed as more consistent, or less inconsistent, with a monetary policy mandate primarily focused on price stability.

355. Thus, following the ECB's June 9, 2022 announcement of its intention to begin a cycle of gradual policy rate increases as of July (*see* paragraph 254 above), government bond spreads started widening.[528] Seemingly alarmed by this development, the ECB's Governing Council then held an *ad hoc* meeting on June 15, 2022. In a statement issued after this meeting, the ECB reiterated its *"pledge [...] to act against resurgent fragmentation risks"*, noting that COVID-19 *"has left lasting vulnerabilities in the euro area economy which are indeed contributing to the uneven transmission of the normalisation of our monetary policy across jurisdictions"*.[529] The statement continued by saying that, with this in mind, the ECB will *"apply flexibility"* (read: geographic selectivity if and when needed) in reinvesting maturing bonds in its PEPP portfolio. More importantly, it added that the ECB had mandated the relevant Eurosystem committees and its own services *"to accelerate the completion of the design of a new anti-fragmentation instrument"*.[530] This hasty announcement of anti-fragmentation measures momentarily calmed the waters somewhat.

356. In her June 28, 2022 address at the ECB Forum on Central Banking in Sintra (Portugal), ECB President Christine Lagarde observed, in reference to the ECB's forthcoming anti-fragmentation tool, that:

> *"[i]n the past, the ECB has made use of separate instruments to target inflation and to preserve the functioning of the monetary policy transmission mechanism. Measures to preserve transmission could be used at any level of interest rates—so long as they were designed not to interfere with the monetary policy stance.*
>
> *At times when inflation fell too low, it made sense to shift from 'separation' to 'combination' so that all tools reinforced the required policy easing. [...] But with high inflation now being the main challenge, there are merits in separating policy tools again.*
>
> *Preserving policy transmission throughout the euro area will allow rates to rise as far as necessary. In this sense, there is no trade-off between launching this*

528. The spread between the 10-year Italian BTP and the 10-year German Bund widened to around 240 basis points on June 14, 2022. It then fell back briefly below 200 basis points in the days following the ECB's June 15 announcement. As of July 11, 2022, it widened again above 200 basis points, continued mostly to fluctuate in a band of 200 to 250 basis points for the remainder of the year and started to narrow below 200 basis points as of early January 2023.
529. *See* the ECB's press release of June 15, 2022, https://www.ecb.europa.eu/press/pr/date/2022/html/ecb.pr220615~2aa3900e0a.en.html. The reader will note the curious use of the lawyers' term "jurisdictions".
530. *Ibid.* The phrase echoes an observation made at the Governing Council's monetary policy meeting of June 8-9, 2022 (*see* paragraph 253 above). It suggests that committee work had been going on for a while and neared completion but now needed a final push to land swiftly. Lawyers will be familiar with this tone of message in their communications with clients at the proximity of, or past, deadlines. Interestingly, at the ECB's press conference of July 21, 2022, Ms. Lagarde noted that the new instrument *"has been developed in record time by our teams"*. *See* the transcript of this press conference, https://www.ecb.europa.eu/press/pressconf/2022/html/ecb.is220721~51ef267c68.en.html, at p. 11.

new tool and adopting the necessary policy stance to stabilise inflation at our target. In fact, one enables the other."[531]

357. Here, Ms. Lagarde appears to circle back to the "separation principle" of earlier times to which Jean-Claude Trichet referred on several occasions during his term of office.[532] Broadly, the separation principle distinguishes between the use of standard measures (in particular policy rates) to deliver price stability in the medium term and the use of non-standard measures to address occasional dysfunctionalities or instability in financial markets or market segments. In a similar vein, Ms. Lagarde's statement suggests the parallel use of separate tools for two distinct objectives, *i.e.*, (i) the use of "mainstream" tools, particularly policy rates, for inflation control in line with the primary price stability objective of monetary policy, and (ii) the use of non-standard tools, **irrespective** of the prevailing interest rate level, to repair "bugs" in monetary policy transmission channels. There is perhaps a subtle shift in Ms. Lagarde's use of the separation principle that probably only lawyers would care about. Whereas originally the principle was used to distinguish monetary policy actions from actions taken by the ECB in its separate contributory role to the stability of the financial system (Article 127(5) TFEU), the blend of the separation principle in Ms. Lagarde's statement serves to distinguish two lines of action **within** the monetary policy mandate, *i.e.*, the use of standard tools for inflation control proper and the use of non-standard tools for safeguarding monetary policy transmission. We will revisit the separation principle in Chapter 6 (*see* paragraphs 421-425 below).

b Key Features

358. In the event, on July 21, 2022, the ECB decided to raise its key policy rates by 50 basis points (rather than by 25 basis points as signaled on June 9) as the first step on its rate increase path. Concomitantly, the ECB announced the addition of a new anti-fragmentation instrument to its toolkit, diplomatically called the "Transmission Protection Instrument" ("TPI") (*see* paragraphs 256-259 above). A summary term sheet of TPI was published in a separate press release on the same day.[533] At the ECB's press briefing that afternoon, Ms. Lagarde conceded that this term sheet did not contain all particulars, adding with remarkable candor that certain elements *"are best kept*

531. Chr. Lagarde, "Price stability and policy transmission in the euro area", Speech at the ECB Forum on Central Banking 2022, Sintra, Portugal, June 28, 2022, https://www.ecb.europa.eu/press/key/date/2022/html/ecb.sp220628~754ac25107.en.html, at p. 6.

532. *See, e.g.*, Mr. Trichet's comment on the subject in the Q&A segment of the ECB's March 3, 2011 press conference, https://www.ecb.europa.eu/press/pressconf/2011/html/is110303.en.html, at p. 5. This was not the first time that Mr. Trichet had mentioned such a principle. For example, at the ECB's press conference of September 6, 2007, he distinguished the ECB's primary mandate, *i.e.*, the delivery of price stability, from its responsibility for the proper functioning of the money market, adding even that these two responsibilities *"do not influence each other"*. *See* the transcript of the ECB's press conference of September 6, 2007, https://www.ecb.europa.eu/press/pressconf/2007/html/is070906.en.html, at pp. 4-5.

533. *See* the ECB's press release of July 21, 2022, https://www.ecb.europa.eu/press/pr/date/2022/html/ecb.pr220721~973e6e7273.en.html.

unpublished, undisclosed, uncommented upon" (*sic*).[534] While this is not very surprising, it is, of course, most intriguing.

359. According to the July 21, 2022 term sheet, the Eurosystem may engage in secondary market purchases of (mostly) public-sector bonds issued in euro area Member States facing a *"deterioration in financing conditions that is not warranted by country-specific fundamentals"* when such purchases are necessary *"to counter unwarranted, disorderly market dynamics that pose a serious threat to the transmission of monetary policy across the euro area"*. It will be for the ECB's Governing Council to determine, on a case-by-case basis, whether these conditions are met (*see* paragraph 361 below).

360. TPI purchases will focus on marketable public-sector debt securities[535] with a remaining maturity between one and 10 years, without any *ex ante* cap on the monthly or overall volume of such purchases. According to the published account of the Governing Council's monetary policy meeting of July 20-21, 2022, *"[t]he scale of TPI purchases would depend on the severity of the risks facing policy transmission"*.[536] At the ECB's July 21, 2022 press briefing, Ms. Lagarde observed that *"the ECB is capable of going big for that"*.[537] Also, the Eurosystem accepts *pari passu* treatment with private bondholders, *i.e.*, waives any claim to PCS, on the bonds purchased under TPI.

361. Still, according to the July 21, 2022 term sheet, TPI purchases will be activated by a decision of the ECB's Governing Council on the basis of a broad assessment covering the following areas:

(a) The Governing Council will determine the relevant Member State's eligibility according to criteria aimed at assessing whether it pursues *"sound and sustainable fiscal and macroeconomic policies"*, including notably in terms of (i) compliance with the common fiscal framework, specifically: not being subject to an excessive deficit procedure ("EDP")[538] or not being assessed as having failed to take effective action in response to a Council recommendation under Article 126(7) TFEU; (ii) the absence of severe macroeconomic

534. *See* the transcript of the ECB's press conference of July 21, 2021, https://www.ecb.europa.eu/press/pressconf/2022/html/ecb.is220721~51ef267c68.en.html, at p. 9.

535. However, the July 21, 2022 press release leaves open the possibility of purchases of private-sector securities *"if appropriate"*.

536. *See* the published account of the ECB Governing Council's monetary policy meeting of July 20-21, 2022, https://www.ecb.europa.eu/press/accounts/2022/html/ecb.mg220825~162cfabae9.en.html, at p. 6.

537. *See* the transcript of the ECB's press conference of July 21, 2022, at p. 6.

538. This particular criterion was somewhat academic initially since no euro area Member State was under EDP on July 21, 2022 and, in fact, no EDP had then been opened since the outbreak of COVID-19. On March 23, 2020, the Council of Ministers had activated the general escape clause of the Stability and Growth Pact, which had not yet been lifted in the summer of 2022 (*see* paragraph 95 above). Likewise, no excessive imbalance procedure was pending (or indeed had ever been initiated) at that time.

imbalances, specifically: not being subject to an excessive imbalance procedure or not being assessed as having failed to take corrective action recommended by the Council under Article 121(4) TFEU; (iii) a trajectory of government debt that is sustainable; and (iv) sound and sustainable macroeconomic policies, specifically: compliance with the country-specific recommendations *"in the fiscal sphere"* under the European Semester and with the commitments made in the Member State's recovery and resilience plans for the Recovery and Resilience Facility (*see* paragraphs 645 *et seq.* below).

Thus, it would seem that euro area Member States may be found eligible for TPI purchases on the basis of a broad *ex ante* assessment of their compliance with **existing** commitments under the EMU fiscal and macroeconomic surveillance frameworks, and that TPI purchases would not come with additional policy conditionality. Still, at first blush, those cumulative eligibility criteria appear to put a relatively high bar, especially for the Member States with weaker fiscal positions that are the most likely to find themselves at the high end of widening sovereign bond spreads.[539] But, at the July 21, 2022 press briefing, Ms. Lagarde clarified that these criteria are indicative and not exclusive and that the Governing Council retains discretion in making its eligibility determination.[540] The term sheet itself notes that those criteria serve as *"an input into the Governing Council's decision-making and will be dynamically adjusted to the unfolding risks and conditions to be addressed"*. One might wonder whether the ECB's measure of discretion in assessing country eligibility for TPI purchases opens up the possibility for the ECB to discreetly put pressure on governments to step up their policy or reform efforts (as appears to have happened previously under SMP, *see* paragraph 334 above).

(b) The Governing Council will make a comprehensive assessment of *"market and transmission indicators"* to evaluate whether diverging financing conditions have become disconnected from country-specific fundamentals and whether disorderly market dynamics pose a serious threat to the monetary policy transmission mechanism. In the same logic, purchases under TPI will be discontinued once remaining interest rate differences are judged to reflect country fundamentals or upon a *"durable"* improvement in monetary policy transmission.

Unsurprisingly, the relevant indicators and criteria are not specified or at least not published—undoubtedly to keep elbow room and avoid giving the

539. According to the European Commission's autumn 2023 forecast, (i) eight euro area Member States are expected to have a government deficit ratio in excess of 3% in 2023 (Belgium, France, Italy, Latvia, Malta, Slovakia, Slovenia and Spain), nine in 2024 (the same plus Finland) and also nine in 2025 (the same less Slovenia and plus Estonia), and (ii) six euro area Member States are projected to have a government debt ratio in excess of 100% in 2023 and 2024 (Belgium, France, Greece, Italy, Portugal and Spain) and five still in 2025 (the same less Portugal). *See* European Commission, *European Economic Forecast—Autumn 2023, European Economy Institutional Papers No 258*, November 2023, pp. 45 (Graph I.2.45), 48 (Graph I.2.51), 187 (Table 34) and 190 (Table 40).

540. *See* the transcript of the ECB's press conference of July 22, 2022, at pp. 5 and 7.

markets a series of orange and red lights to get nervous about. Also, it may not be easy to reliably determine when and to what extent a Member State's market financing conditions are out of line with economic fundamentals, *i.e.*, when and to what extent financial markets are effectively mispricing sovereign risk in relation to underlying fundamentals. The actual trigger points for TPI purchases, and the yardsticks for their quantum and duration, seem to leave significant scope for judgment, as we will discuss later (*see* paragraphs 369-381 below).

(c) Finally, the Governing Council will make a proportionality assessment, *i.e.*, a judgment as to whether the activation of purchases under TPI is proportionate in relation to the achievement of the ECB's primary price stability objective. This seemingly deferential nod to the proportionality principle seems to imply a tacit admission that the concrete need for action to contain financial fragmentation (and its effects on liquidity) will be balanced against what would be optimal for inflation control—and hence that circumstances could arise in which the former may prompt a temporary deviation from the latter (as is recognized under the separation principle).

362. Aside from this reference to a proportionality assessment, the July 21, 2022 term sheet contains a separate short paragraph on the interaction between TPI and the ECB's monetary policy stance. This paragraph goes in particular to the issue of the consistency of TPI purchases and the consequent liquidity injection with a more restrictive monetary policy stance. Here, the term sheet does not expressly commit to (fully) sterilize the liquidity impact of TPI purchases within a medium-term horizon. It indicates instead that, to avoid interference with the monetary policy stance, the Governing Council will *"address"* the implications of TPI purchases for the scale of the Eurosystem's aggregate monetary policy portfolio of debt securities and for the amount of excess liquidity. TPI purchases will be carried out in such a way as not to cause any *"persistent impact on the overall Eurosystem balance sheet"* and on the monetary policy stance. At the July 21, 2022 press briefing, Ms. Lagarde added that she was *"not going to go through the details of exactly which mechanism, sterilisation or otherwise, we would be using"*, and that *"[t]hese are practical matters that certainly have been discussed, have been agreed"*.[541] Yet, the published account of the Governing Council's monetary policy meeting of July 20-21, 2022 does not shed any further light on this.

363. Neither the term sheet of July 21, 2022, nor the transcript of that afternoon's press briefing, nor the published account of the July 20-21, 2022 monetary policy meeting specifically address how losses arising from TPI purchases would be allocated within the Eurosystem. Might one therefore assume that TPI purchases are subject to full loss sharing, as was the case for SMP purchases and would also be the case for possible OMT purchases? At least at some point, the ECB appeared to hold the view that loss sharing was the default mode under Article 32.4 of Protocol No 4, but this view is not

541. *Ibid.*, at p. 6.

necessarily shared by the CJEU and most certainly not by the BVerfG (*see* paragraphs 225-226 above).

364. Overall, a key takeaway from the July 21, 2022 announcement is that the (published) TPI terms leave a considerable margin of discretion to the ECB's Governing Council in determining when and where the instrument should be activated and for how much and how long. Ms. Lagarde repeatedly emphasized the Governing Council's discretion at the July 21, 2022 press briefing (using such terms as *"entire discretion"* and even *"in sovereignty"*).[542] TPI also appears to have an open architecture. In the published account of the Governing Council's monetary policy meeting of July 21-22, 2022, ECB Chief Economist Philip Lane is on record as observing that:

> *"The TPI [is] a monetary policy tool to address a wide variety of shocks that could lead to fragmentation and ultimately to transmission impairments. The TPI's specific design features, as well as the safeguards for complying with the monetary financing prohibition and the principle of proportionality, would be decided on by the Governing Council in the light of the specific shocks that needed to be addressed in any given situation".*[543]

6 CHOICE OF INSTRUMENT

365. TPI is now one of three instruments in the ECB's toolbox to address financial fragmentation:

(a) **OMT**, announced in the summer of 2012 in response to perceived "redenomination risk", *i.e.*, the risk of euro exit of one or more Member States, has been lying idle thus far. In its July 21, 2022 term sheet on TPI, the ECB dusted off OMT, saying that the Governing Council *"retains discretion"* to conduct OMT *"for countries that fulfill the requisite criteria"*. OMT would allow the Eurosystem to purchase government bonds in the secondary markets, at the shorter end of the yield curve, in the case of euro area Member States receiving ESM financial assistance under economic policy conditionality.

(b) **PEPP** is a temporary instrument linked to the economic fallout of COVID-19. While net purchases under PEPP were discontinued at the end of March 2022, the proceeds from maturing securities in the PEPP portfolio continue to be reinvested for the time being—but the ECB meanwhile announced its intention to phase down PEPP reinvestments in the second half of 2024 and discontinue them altogether at the end of the year. According to the July 21, 2022 term sheet, *"PEPP reinvestment flexibility"* (read: the possibility of geographically selective reinvestments) remains the *"first line of defence"* to

542. *Ibid.*, at pp. 5, 7 and 11.
543. *See* the published account of the ECB Governing Council's monetary policy meeting of July 21-22, 2022, at p. 6.

counter pandemic-related risks to the monetary policy transmission mechanism.

(c) **TPI** appears as the broader and more permanent instrument for leaning against bond market movements that are out of line with economic fundamentals and present tangible risks to effective monetary policy transmission.

The boundaries between these three anti-fragmentation tools may not seem razor-sharp in every respect, and one would suspect that the ECB does not want them to be too precise. But we should still make an attempt to distinguish their possible uses.

366. ***First***, **OMT**'s stated purpose is to address "*severe distortions in government bond markets*" that originate "*in particular*" from undue market perception of redenomination risk, *i.e.*, "*unfounded fears on the part of investors of the reversibility in the euro*" (*see* paragraph 340(a) above). Also, OMT purchases are linked to ESM stability support and the economic policy conditionality that comes with it (*see* paragraphs 340(b) and 341 above). Euro area Member States may be hesitant to call on ESM financial assistance precisely because of its (additional) policy conditionality and perhaps also because of a certain stigma attached to ESM life support. The austerity measures and reforms that were imposed by the Troika as part of EFSF/ESM financial assistance notably to Greece (*see* paragraphs 72 above and 716 below) have become a byword of iniquity in the Mediterranean Basin, especially (but not exclusively) in the eyes of populist political parties. Member States will naturally favor "cov-lite" and less conspicuous alternatives like PEPP and TPI (even if the ECB's broad discretion in assessing country eligibility for TPI offers it some leverage for discreet insistence on certain national policy measures). Accordingly, the very availability of PEPP and especially TPI may push OMT to the sidelines as *ultimum remedium*—and, by the same token, contribute to marginalizing ESM stability support in its current forms.

367. ***Second***, **PEPP** is a temporary and finite program to address the economic and financial fall-out of COVID-19, including financial fragmentation that may arise in this context. This places two limitations on the use of PEPP as an anti-fragmentation tool:

(a) PEPP being a temporary emergency program established in response to the "*specific, extraordinary and acute economic crisis*" caused by the spread of COVID-19,[544] its use as an anti-fragmentation tool, including in its post-March 2022 reinvestment phase, should be directed at countering financial fragmentation risks linked to the pandemic. But with the economic impact of COVID-19 gradually subsiding, to what extent could any excessive widening of sovereign bond spreads still primarily be attributed to COVID-19 rather than to subsequent developments such as the Ukraine conflict, recurring energy market tensions or indeed monetary policy tightening in response to higher inflation? What is due to the virus, what to Vladimir Putin and what to the ECB's steep policy rate increases since the summer of 2022? How to

544. Recital (3) to Decision (EU) 2020/440 of the European Central Bank of March 24, 2020 on a temporary pandemic emergency purchase programme.

disentangle the effects of these and other developments? Questions as to the continued legitimacy and proportionality of using PEPP as an anti-fragmentation instrument already came up during the ECB Governing Council's deliberations at its monetary policy meeting of December 15-16, 2021. At this meeting, it was broadly agreed that the pandemic's acute phase in economic terms was coming to an end, that PEPP had delivered on its dual objective of offsetting COVID-19's negative impact on the inflation outlook and of staving off unwarranted market fragmentation caused by the pandemic, and that therefore net asset purchases under PEPP could be carried out at a lower pace in the first quarter of 2022 and discontinued at the end of that quarter. Still, the prevailing view was that it was desirable to extend PEPP's reinvestment horizon until at least the end of 2024, with continued flexibility to adjust reinvestments across time, asset classes and geographies, in order to maintain the ECB's ability to counter future market fragmentation in the unpredictable course of the pandemic. But the observation was made around the table that:

> *"the PEPP's flexibility was targeted at the specific pandemic shock and might not be proportionate if risks to the transmission of monetary policy and market fragmentation arose in other contexts. It was recalled that the PEPP had been designed to address a symmetric shock that could give rise to asymmetric consequences."* [545]

(b) As said, net purchases under PEPP were discontinued at the end of March 2022 and PEPP then entered a transitory phase of mere reinvestment of maturing bonds. For many months, the ECB repeatedly confirmed its intention to fully reinvest principal repayments on bonds *"until at least the end of 2024"* before beginning to roll off the PEPP portfolio. But on December 14, 2023, it announced its intention to phase down reinvestments, by EUR 7.5 billion per month on average, in the second half of 2024 and to discontinue them entirely at the end of the year. Thus, as from April 2022, PEPP purchases have been limited to reinvestment of the flow-back on maturing bonds, to be reduced by EUR 7.5 billion per month in the second half of 2024 and to zero at the end of the year. Accordingly, the flow-back that would become available at any given time in the near term, even if fully used for anti-fragmentation reinvestments, should be relatively limited given that the PEPP portfolio consists predominantly of longer-term public-sector securities (which still had a remaining weighted average maturity of 7.34 years at the end of November 2023).[546] Moreover, for anti-fragmentation purposes, one should presumably look primarily at the flow-back originating from the Member States at the lower end of the yield spreads, *i.e.*, as a rule, the

545. *See* the published account of the ECB Governing Council's monetary policy meeting of December 15-16, 2021, https://www.ecb.europa.eu/press/accounts/2022/html/ecb.mg220120~7ed187b5b1.en.html, at p. 16.

546. *See* "Bimonthly breakdown of public sector securities under the PEPP" at https://www.ecb.europa.eu/mopo/implement/pepp/html/index.en.html.

stronger economies.[547] Consequently, in the limited time left to it, PEPP may have only modest firepower as an anti-fragmentation tool.

368. ***Third***, in view of (i) the limitations on OMT and PEPP identified above and (ii) TPI's broadly-defined framework and more permanent nature, one would expect that **TPI** should eventually become the workhorse in the ECB's anti-fragmentation toolkit. It would not, however, be surprising if the ECB wanted to hold off on activating TPI for as long as it could and, in the remaining months of 2024, preferred to continue using the lighter and more discreet tool of PEPP reinvestments for smaller-scale earlier-stage interventions for as long as it could broadly justify this.

7 TRIGGER POINTS FOR INTERVENTION

369. A difficult question is to identify the proper trigger points for anti-fragmentation asset purchases. When does a widening of sovereign bond spreads become "excessive" or "unwarranted" in relation to underlying economic fundamentals, and when does this unduly interfere with effective monetary policy transmission? Or is this, in the end, really one and the same question, *i.e.*, must a widening of bond spreads be deemed to unduly interfere with proper monetary policy transmission once it has become excessive in reference to economic fundamentals? We will, in this section, discuss these issues primarily in reference to TPI.

370. In her June 14, 2022 commencement speech at the Panthéon-Sorbonne University, Isabel Schnabel, a member of the ECB's Executive Board, linked actionable financial fragmentation to both a divergence from economic fundamentals and a threat of financial instability, saying that *"[p]ut simply, fragmentation reflects a sudden break in the relationship between sovereign yields and fundamentals, giving rise to non-linear and destabilising dynamics"*.[548] In a similar vein, in her June 28, 2022 address at the 2022 ECB Forum on Central Banking in Sintra, ECB President Christine Lagarde defined unwarranted fragmentation as a situation in which *"spreads in some countries respond in a rapid and disorderly way to an underlying change in risk-free rates, over and above what would be justified by economic fundamentals"*, with repricing being *"exacerbated and distorted by destabilising market dynamics"*.[549]

547. Also, flow-back from maturing bonds of the stronger economies may well be desynchronized from episodes of excessive widening of sovereign bond spreads and the need to purchase bonds of Member States at the high end of the spreads. But this should presumably be a problem of lesser importance insofar as the ECB has allowed itself a measure of intertemporal flexibility for reinvestments in order to smooth out purchase flows.

548. I. Schnabel, "United in diversity – Challenges for monetary policy in a currency union", Commencement speech to the graduates of the Master Program in Money, Banking, Finance and Insurance of the Panthéon-Sorbonne University, Paris, June 14, 2022, https://www.ecb.europa.eu/press/key/date/2022/html/ecb.sp220614~67eda62c44.en.html, at p. 3.

549. Chr. Lagarde, "Price stability and policy transmission in the euro area", Speech at the ECB Forum on Central Banking 2022, Sintra, Portugal, June 28, 2022, https://www.ecb.europa.eu/press/key/date/2022/html/ecb.sp220628~754ac25107.en.html, at p. 5.

Accordingly, in both Ms. Schnabel's and Ms. Lagarde's definitions, excessive financial fragmentation appears to have two prongs, *i.e.*, (i) sovereign bond yields, and hence the spreads between them, have moved out of line with "economic fundamentals", and (ii) the misalignment unfolds in some abrupt and disorderly manner, giving rise to, or being caught in, destabilizing market dynamics. This definition may well be narrower than what financial markets have come to expect in terms of ECB reactivity to widening government bond spreads.

a Misalignment with Economic Fundamentals

371. The first prong of this definition appears to exclude differences in sovereign bond yields and spreads that properly reflect differences in economic fundamentals. In an incomplete monetary union between countries that retain substantial economic and fiscal sovereignty, sovereign bond yields should naturally differ somewhat in view of differences in credit risk due to differences in the members' economic characteristics and performance, their domestic or external imbalances, their economic and fiscal policies, and their debt levels. One would expect that such yield differences will tend to be lower among advanced economies operating in a relatively integrated market and having broadly synchronous business cycles. Also, those underlying differentiating factors generally tend to be slow-moving and, in a rational market environment, should not ordinarily cause abrupt changes in bond yields that threaten financial stability.

Even "natural" yield differentials that reflect broadly correct market pricing of economic fundamentals may interfere somewhat with an even transmission of the single monetary policy stance across the euro area. But the ECB seems to suggest that this is a fact of life in Europe's incomplete EMU in which a single monetary policy contends with 20 government bond yield curves, and that it could or should not do anything about it so long as yield differentials are broadly aligned with economic fundamentals. When, on March 12, 2020, Ms. Lagarde observed that closing sovereign bond spreads is not the mission of the ECB (*see* paragraph 350 above), she was after all right in a literal sense insofar as the ECB is not in the business of harmonizing sovereign bond yields irrespective of differences in economic fundamentals.

372. Yet, when are market sovereign bond yields misaligned with underlying "economic fundamentals"? When are the financial markets effectively mispricing sovereign bonds? Or, in plain terms, when are the markets wrong? Judging financial markets wrong is not an obvious matter, and it requires superior knowledge than the collective wisdom of those supposedly sophisticated markets.[550]

373. Noting that, in EMU's first decade, sovereign bond spreads stabilized within a narrow band of around 25 basis points, Ms. Schnabel in her June 14, 2022 Sorbonne speech observed that there is a broad consensus to the effect that during that period markets *"systematically underpriced sovereign risk"* in view of the domestic and

550. I am the first to concede that it is somewhat awkward to use the words "financial markets" and "wisdom" in the same sentence.

external imbalances that were building up in several Member States.[551] Of course, if Ms. Schnabel is right, such market underpricing of sovereign risk caused a compression rather than a widening of sovereign bond spreads—an artificial conflation rather than a fragmentation of financing conditions. One would think that the ECB should presumably be somewhat less worried about such a reverse fact pattern, at least so long as the markets do not, by some accident or epiphany, suddenly realize their error and overreact in the opposite direction (as happened in the 2010-2012 sovereign debt crisis). But an undue compression of sovereign bond yields in relation to economic fundamentals is distortive as well insofar as, at any given monetary policy stance, it keeps government borrowing costs of deficit countries lower than they should be and, in this manner, mutes a normal constraint on public spending. However, this distortion could not be remedied by selective government bond purchases or other monetary actions.

374. The assessment of a possible misalignment of market sovereign bond yields with economic fundamentals is all but straightforward. A few initial thoughts:

(a) Financial markets primarily focus on sovereign risk in the narrower sense of the probability of sovereign default or debt restructuring over the relevant investment horizon. As said, the risk of sovereign default generally tends to be low in advanced economies. It is not correlated in a linear fashion with a deterioration of economic fundamentals which ordinarily is a slow-moving process, and this correlation should be weaker at the shorter end of the maturity spectrum.

(b) Membership of the European currency union may affect this correlation in several ways:

  (i) The optics of the currency union should *prima facie* be broadly favorable. Markets could to some degree rationally expect (as they ostensibly did during much of its first decade) that, if sovereign default risk is generally limited in advanced economies, this should be the case *a fortiori* for EU Member States sharing a fairly integrated market, having passed the convergence tests for admission to the currency union and being subject to a measure of fiscal discipline imposed by the EMU fiscal and macroeconomic surveillance frameworks.

  (ii) Yet, in the currency union, participating Member States are deprived of a national currency and monetary policy of their own. They can no longer let their currency depreciate or print money when needed. This, in combination with the Treaty prohibition on monetary financing (Article 123 TFEU) and its "no bail-out" clause (Article 125 TFEU), should strengthen the link between sovereign risk and economic fundamentals.

551. I. Schnabel, *supra*, at p. 4.

(iii) In the same order of ideas, a credible common fiscal framework and robust centralized stability support mechanisms should weaken that correlation.

(c) The Member States' fiscal positions should be a key economic fundamental. Circling back to Ms. Schnabel's statement, an observation that gives pause is that, between 1999 and 2010, the government debt-to-GDP ratios of Southern euro area Member States generally stood at significantly lower levels, and diverged less from those of Germany and The Netherlands, than in 2019-2022 (*see* paragraph 116, Table 2.2, above).

375. Clearly, sovereign bond spreads widened considerably during the 2010-2012 sovereign debt crisis in the euro area and especially so from mid-2011 onward, in particular to the detriment of the Southern euro area Member States. It is commonly acknowledged that this widening of spreads went well beyond what could be ascribed to normal repricing of sovereign risk in light of deteriorating economic fundamentals of the relevant Member States, and that it was aggravated by negative market sentiment caused by (i) market uncertainty, liquidity shortages and greater risk aversion in the wake of the global financial crisis; (ii) rising concerns over debt sustainability of certain Member States, particularly following Greece's October 21, 2009 "confessions", the Franco-German agreement on "private sector involvement" ("PSI") at their October 18-19, 2010 Deauville summit (*see* paragraph 74 above) and discussions about Greece's sovereign debt restructuring; and, in the spring and summer of 2012, (iii) fears of a partial or total break-up of the European currency union (redenomination risk).

376. One empirical study looked at credit default swaps ("CDS") of that period and found that CDS spreads then widened beyond what could be explained on the basis of country-specific fiscal positions and other fundamentals, which points to market overreaction—although the study left open the possibility that the difference could in some measure be due to expectations of future deterioration in fiscal positions.[552]

Another study related the observed widening of spreads in 2010-2011 to a number of variables reflecting economic fundamentals and to a time dummy variable intended to capture time-dependent effects unrelated to fundamentals.[553] The authors found a significant positive correlation between the spreads and the economic fundamentals, particularly the government debt-to-GDP ratio and the ratio of government debt to total tax revenues, *i.e.*, the higher these ratios, the higher the spreads. They also noted that this relationship was non-linear, in the sense that the marginal increase in the spreads becomes higher as those ratios increase. Importantly, the authors concluded that a significant portion of the increases in spreads is attributable to time effects

552. J. Aizenman, M. Hutchison & Y. Jinjarak, "What is the risk of European sovereign debt defaults? Fiscal space, CDS spreads and market pricing of risk", *Journal of International Money and Finance*, Vol. 34, 2013, pp. 37-59, https://doi.org/10.1016/j.jimonfin.2012.11.011.

553. P. De Grauwe & Y. Ji, "Self-fulfilling crises in the Eurozone: An empirical test", *Journal of International Money and Finance*, Vol. 34, 2013, pp. 15-36, https://doi.org/10.1016/j.jimonfin.2012.11.003. *See also* P. De Grauwe, *Economics of Monetary Union*, Oxford University Press, 13th ed., 2020, pp. 116-117.

unrelated to changes in fundamentals, suggesting that they were associated with changes in market sentiment. Specifically, they found that factors unrelated to deteriorating fundamentals accounted for a significant part (but still less than 40%) of the spread variation in the case of Greece, about half in the case of Portugal and Ireland, and most of the spread variation in the case of Spain.

377. But the question remains how, by what metrics, the ECB could reliably determine in real time whether and to what extent the financial markets are mispricing sovereign risk in relation to underlying macroeconomic fundamentals. In order to disentangle economic fundamentals and a residual component of market overreaction as determinants of sovereign risk premiums, all relevant fundamental factors would need to be properly accounted for. This is challenging, especially in a fluid market environment. Central bankers (and economists alike) sometimes present this in terms of distinguishing between fundamentals-driven and beliefs-driven (re)pricing of sovereign risk. But who can tell in real time when and in what measure market expectations or fears are exaggerated? OMT is supposed to address government bond market distortions originating in particular from *"unfounded fears"* of euro exit(s) (*see* paragraph 340(a) above). How could anyone confidently diagnose such fears as unfounded at any particular point in time—except on the basis of political conviction or commitment?

b Destabilizing Market Dynamics

378. At first blush, the second prong of the ECB's financial fragmentation definition seems more straightforward: the widening of sovereign bond spreads must be caught in destabilizing, self-reinforcing market dynamics. Passing market volatility would not be enough. Here, in her June 14, 2022 commencement speech, Ms. Schnabel offered as examples the market volatility that arose amid the French presidential elections in 2017 and during a period of political uncertainty in Italy in 2018.[554] In their June 2022 speeches, both Ms. Schnabel and Ms. Lagarde referred to some abrupt or rapid disorderly market process. But how is one supposed to distinguish in real time between mere passing volatility and its more serious variant?

379. Surely, few would argue that the ECB's monetary policy mandate extends to "arbitraging" away sovereign bond yield differentials whenever it believes these to be out of line with economic fundamentals. Market mispricing somehow must get caught in destabilizing dynamics. But where does one draw the line? And should not the ECB be allowed to intervene at an earlier stage, upon the first signs of market disruption, when it perceives a serious risk of instability down the line? Wouldn't cost efficiency considerations favor anticipatory action before destabilizing dynamics gather momentum and become more difficult to control?

In a (virtual) speech at the Frankfurt Euro Finance Summit on July 4, 2022, Bundesbank President Joachim Nagel acknowledged that it is *"virtually impossible to establish for sure whether or not a widened spread is fundamentally justified"*. In a

554. I. Schnabel, *supra*, at p. 5.

rebuttal to the advocacy of swift action, he added that since, *"for good reason"*, monetary policy pursues a medium-term inflation target, it must not be driven by what are often very short-lived price movements in the financial markets. Accordingly, *"unusual monetary policy measures to combat fragmentation can be justified only in exceptional circumstances"*.[555]

380. Overall, the ECB's two-pronged definition of excessive financial fragmentation lacks high resolution. One may be inclined to suspect that the judgmental nature of the first prong may lead to *de facto* dominance of the second prong so as to effectively narrow the assessment to one of destabilization risk in sovereign bond markets. In any event, it is not surprising that the ECB did not establish or at least not publish any "hard" criteria. It should much prefer a facts-and-circumstances approach and would not wish to extend an open invitation to the financial markets to test any pre-announced red lines.

c Undue Interference with Monetary Policy Transmission

381. And then there is still the question of whether excessive widening of sovereign bond spreads must be deemed in and of itself to unduly interfere with the effective functioning of the monetary policy transmission mechanism, or whether undue interference with monetary policy transmission constitutes an additional separate condition for activating anti-fragmentation asset purchases. It is not obvious why this should be a separate condition. Logically, since sovereign bond yields serve as the benchmark for determining financing conditions in the wider economy, changes in sovereign bond yields that for any significant lapse of time go beyond the level warranted by economic fundamentals inevitably undermine the even transmission of the monetary policy stance, especially when caught in disorderly or destabilizing dynamics. In his July 4, 2022 speech, however, Joachim Nagel clearly considered a finding of impairment of the monetary policy transmission mechanism as a separate condition for activating anti-fragmentation asset purchases, in addition to observed bond spreads being fundamentally unjustified.[556] But this is the voice of the Bundesbank—one that cannot be suspected of giving up easily on guardrails in these matters.

8 LEGITIMACY AND PROPORTIONALITY

382. At our summertime dinner table, the reader and I are still left with several questions as to the legitimacy and proportionality of the Eurosystem's recourse to geographically selective sovereign bond purchases as a tool for containing financial

555. J. Nagel, "Where is monetary policy headed?", Speech at the Frankfurt Euro Finance Summit, July 4, 2022, https://www.bundesbank.de/en/press/speeches/where-is-monetary-policy-headed--894058, at pp. 5-6.
556. *Ibid.*, at p. 6.

fragmentation in the euro area. How comfortably do purchases of that kind fit within the Treaty-conferred monetary policy mandate as essentially defined by the primary objective of maintaining price stability? Are they really compatible in spirit with the Treaty's prohibition of monetary financing? And don't they raise issues of moral hazard and proportionality?

Yet, in Europe's incomplete EMU, it is a fact of life that sovereign bond yields may from time to time become misaligned with underlying economic fundamentals, and that the consequent unwarranted widening of sovereign bond spreads may cause a fragmentation of financing conditions within the euro area that interferes with proper monetary policy transmission and, in an adverse scenario, may get caught in destabilizing market dynamics and eventually produce tectonic stresses within the currency union. It happened before and it may happen again. These risks cannot be left unattended. The further question then is whether such financial fragmentation could effectively be contained by some alternative mechanism that has fewer undesirable side effects, and is legally safer, than geographically selective government bond purchases by central banks.

a A Question of Ends and Means

383. Are anti-fragmentation asset purchases really monetary policy? Buying and selling securities in the financial markets is without any doubt among the permissible techniques for carrying out monetary policy (Article 18.1 of Protocol No 4). But this does not necessarily make them monetary policy. It all depends on the use to which a particular tool is put, and open-market purchases of financial instruments may serve different purposes. The question remains whether geographically selective government bond purchases to counteract excessive widening of spreads between bond yields actually serve a genuine monetary policy purpose within the Treaty's relatively vague job description of monetary policy.

384. Significantly, the ECB itself has not primarily or even explicitly linked such anti-fragmentation asset purchases to one of its secondary Treaty missions, such as that of supporting the general economic policies in the European Union (Articles 119(2), 127(1) and 282(2) TFEU) or that of contributing to the smooth conduct of policies relating to the stability of the financial system (Article 127(5) TFEU). Instead, the ECB has attached those asset purchases to its monetary policy mandate and its primary price stability objective by the need to safeguard or repair the proper functioning of the monetary policy transmission mechanism, *i.e.*, to restore the effective pass-through of its single monetary policy stance across geographies in the face of fragmentation of sovereign bond yields and its knock-on effects on market interest rates more broadly.

385. One could see how this reasoning plays out in a situation in which euro area inflation below the 2 % target calls for monetary easing, as was the case for much of the 2013-2020 period. Excessive widening of sovereign bond spreads then obstructs proper pass-through of monetary easing impulses in Member States at the high end of the spreads, while risk aversion may at the same time divert capital to Member States at the lower end of the spreads and push their interest rate level too low. Transposing this line of reasoning to a fact pattern in which high inflation requires a more restrictive monetary policy, as in 2022-2023, one would then argue that unwarranted widening of sovereign bond spreads distorts monetary policy transmission because monetary tightening impulses are unduly amplified in Member States at the high end of the spreads and because flight-to-safety market dynamics may unduly mute those impulses in Member States at the lower end of the spreads.

386. In its 2015 *Gauweiler* judgment on OMT, the CJEU accepted the transmission-based justification in a few short paragraphs that merit quotation in full:

> *"First, the objective of safeguarding the singleness of monetary policy contributes to achieving the objectives of that policy inasmuch as, under Article 119(2) TFEU, monetary policy must be 'single'.*
>
> *Secondly, the objective of safeguarding an appropriate transmission of monetary policy is likely both to preserve the singleness of monetary policy and to contribute to its primary objective, which is to maintain price stability.*
>
> *The ability of the ESCB to influence price developments by means of its monetary policy decisions in fact depends, to a great extent, on the transmission of 'impulses' which the ESCB sends out across the money market to the various sectors of the economy. Consequently, if the monetary policy transmission is disrupted, that is likely to render the ESCB's decisions ineffective in a part of the euro area and, accordingly, to undermine the singleness of monetary policy. Moreover, since disruption of the transmission mechanism undermines the effectiveness of the measures adopted by the ESCB, that necessarily affects the ESCB's ability to guarantee price stability. Accordingly, measures that are intended to preserve that transmission mechanism may be regarded as pertaining to the primary objective laid down in Article 127(1) TFEU."*[557]

387. These abstract considerations have become the bedrock of the ECB's justification for the proposition that anti-fragmentation sovereign bond purchases fall within the compass of its monetary policy mandate. Reduced to its bare core, the Court's underlying reasoning seems to be that the ECB's monetary policy competence implies the power to remove obstacles to its intended effects. But can it be said that the Treaty-conferred monetary policy mandate generally extends to the removal of obstacles to its effective exercise? Does this reasoning not to some degree reflect a confusion of ends and means? To use a simplistic metaphor, cooking requires an oven in good operating condition but would this make repairing the oven part of cooking? What are the boundaries of this reasoning? We will return to the Court's reasoning and its verbal expression in Chapter 7 (*see* paragraphs 516-524 below).

557. CJEU, June 16, 2015, Case C-62/14, *Gauweiler et al.*, ECLI:EU:C:2015:400, §§48-50. The Court elaborated somewhat on this reasoning in its subsequent proportionality assessment of OMT. *See ibid.*, §§72-73 and 76-78.

b What Lies Beneath the Surface: Parallel Objectives

388. Mustn't we look more deeply into the policy agendas? Insofar as anti-fragmentation asset purchases serve to contain destabilizing market dynamics driven by fears of currency union exit—as is a stated objective of OMT (*see* paragraph 340(a) above)—, this raises another question as to whether such purchases are squarely within the realm of monetary policy. In its 2012 *Pringle* judgment, the CJEU held that ESM financial support to safeguard the financial stability of the euro area (which may also take the form of government bond purchases) is *"clearly distinct"* from the objective of maintaining price stability and therefore cannot be characterized as a monetary policy measure".[558] In its 2015 *Gauweiler* ruling, the Court acknowledged that the stability of the euro area *"is a matter of economic policy"* but then pulled OMT onto dry ground in a single sentence saying that *"a monetary policy measure cannot be treated as equivalent to an economic policy measure merely because it may have indirect effects on the stability of the euro area"*.[559] But how must one distinguish an intended indirect effect from a concurrent or indeed even primary objective of a particular policy action? In fact, if one looks at the circumstances in which OMT was announced in the turbulent summer months of 2012, there can be little doubt that the primary concern then was to calm market fears of a partial or total break-up of the currency union—and not, in the first instance, to ensure the proper transmission of the ECB's lowered monetary policy rates (*see* paragraphs 75-77 above).

389. Fast forward to geographically selective PEPP reinvestments or possible TPI (or OMT) purchases in a high-inflation environment such as that of 2022-2023. Isn't part of the real rationale, a parallel objective, now to give the ECB a freer hand for, and reduce resistance to, the necessary policy rate increases by having backup tools ready to curb destabilizing movements in sovereign bond markets that may be triggered by such policy rate increases? This was said in so many words by ECB President Christine Lagarde in her June 28, 2022 address in Sintra, when she observed that TPI *"will allow rates to rise as far as necessary"* (*see* paragraph 356 above), and at the July 20-21, 2022 monetary policy meeting of the ECB's Governing Council (*see* paragraph 257 above). But isn't this tantamount to saying that the monetary policy mandate encompasses action to remove impediments to the optimal conduct of monetary policy that derive from supposedly exaggerated market concerns about perceived weaknesses in a Member State's fiscal positions or policies? In more graphic terms, is it the proper task of the ECB, as monetary policy authority, to provide governments of euro area Member States that have vulnerable fiscal positions and are perhaps delinquent on structural reforms with some form of anesthetic to assuage the consequences of monetary tightening on their borrowing conditions? More generally, does the ECB's monetary policy mandate extend to open market operations to repair "bugs" in monetary policy transmission that originate in (market overreaction to) weaknesses in national fiscal choices and policies?

558. CJEU, November 27, 2012, Case C-370/12, *Pringle*, ECLI:EU:C:2012:756, §56.
559. *Gauweiler*, §§51-52.

390. From a broader philosophical perspective, it stands to reason that financial fragmentation risk should be avoided or remedied in the first place by responsible fiscal policies and structural reforms at national level, properly reviewed and coordinated under the EMU fiscal and macroeconomic surveillance frameworks, and perhaps, if government debt remains unsustainable, by sovereign debt restructuring as *ultimum remedium*. True, in the real world, asymmetric shocks, policy impact lags and political frictions may disrupt patient logic and ignite fear-driven market dynamics. It makes good sense, in a currency union, to have some centralized mechanism to take out or mitigate this fear factor—to "cage the chimp". But the question is: is this a proper task for monetary policy?

c Possible Conflict with Inflation Control

391. Another consideration relevant to the (un)suitability of geographically differentiated asset purchases by central banks for this task is the potential for conflict with inflation control. In a low-inflation environment calling for monetary easing, the injection of additional liquidity by such purchases is at least directionally consistent with that monetary policy stance. But the opposite is true when high inflation requires monetary tightening. Additional central bank liquidity injection would now be at cross-current with the anti-inflationary direction of monetary policy required by the primary objective of price stability.

The ECB has attempted to rationalize this apparent conflict by referring to a "separation principle" which distinguishes the use of mainstream monetary policy tools (particularly policy rates) for inflation control proper and the separate application of non-standard tools (such as asset purchases) to address market dysfunctionalities that cause "bugs" in monetary policy transmission (*see* paragraphs 356-357 above and 421-425 below). In this reasoning, there is no real conflict or trade-off between the two lines of action, and the second is complementary to the first, insofar as the proper functioning of the monetary policy transmission mechanism is a prerequisite to the effective pass-through of the monetary tightening needed to contain inflation.

Sure, but this is no Houdini vanishing act that makes the friction disappear. Monetary tightening still increases financial fragmentation risk and anti-fragmentation asset purchases still inject additional liquidity at a time of monetary tightening. In practical terms, one way to mitigate this conflict would be for the additional liquidity to be sterilized (as was done in the case of SMP, *see* paragraph 335 above), within the same medium-term horizon that the ECB has given itself to achieve its inflation target. But then the question is how such liquidity re-absorption could effectively be structured so as not to interfere with the desired anti-fragmentation effects of the asset purchases or cause other distortions.

d The Monetary Financing Prohibition

392. Central bank purchases of government debt, even if confined to the secondary markets, sit somewhat uneasily with the prohibition of government debt monetization of Article 123 TFEU. One would think that anti-fragmentation purchases could be especially problematic in this respect given that they are targeted at Member States struggling to maintain access to the financial markets on viable terms. But the CJEU was not troubled by this in the case of OMT. In its 2015 *Gauweiler* judgment, it found that OMT purchases would steer clear of the monetary financing prohibition because they would be made in the secondary markets under conditions that would not make them equivalent to primary market purchases and that would not lessen the impetus of the Member State concerned to follow a sound budgetary policy. The Court based this conclusion on certain OMT design features including the fact that (i) the relevant Member State would have no *ex ante* certainty that a particular quantity of its bonds would be purchased, or held to maturity, by the ESCB (Eurosystem); (ii) OMT could not be implemented in such a way as to harmonize government bond yields irrespective of differences in underlying fundamentals; and (iii) OMT purchases would be linked to EFSF/ESM stability support and related economic policy conditionality[560] (*see also* paragraph 346 above and paragraphs 533, 534(a) and 535(a) and (b) below).

e Economic Policy Conditionality

393. This brings us to yet another legal question on how anti-fragmentation asset purchases fit into the monetary policy mandate. OMT purchases would be tied to ESM financial assistance and its economic policy conditionality (*see* paragraphs 340(b), 341 and 342(b) above), and TPI purchases would be subject to a prior assessment of the relevant Member State's "good standing" in relation to its policy commitments under the EMU fiscal and macroeconomic surveillance frameworks and its recovery and resilience plans (*see* paragraph 361(a) above). Is this nexus with commitments in the sphere of fiscal policies and structural reforms consistent with monetary policy focused on inflation control or, to this effect, the proper functioning of the monetary policy transmission mechanism? If indeed effective inflation control requires the repair of bugs in monetary policy transmission, why should central bank intervention then be made dependent at all on compliance with economic policy conditions?

394. In its 2015 *Gauweiler* judgment, the CJEU held that the fact that OMT purchases are made conditional upon full compliance with economic policy commitments attached to EFSF/ESM stability support did not alter its earlier conclusion that OMT falls within the realm of monetary policy.[561] With reference to the ECB's secondary mission to support the general economic policies in the Union, the Court noted that said condition served to ensure that monetary policy action did not work against the

560. *Gauweiler*, §§93-121.
561. *Ibid.*, §§57-65.

effectiveness of those policies. It further observed that this condition is consistent with the ECB's obligation under Article 127(1) *jo.* 119(3) TFEU to act in accordance with the guiding principle that public finances must be sound. On an even more slippery slope, the Court went on to say that government bond purchases subject to economic policy conditionality may be regarded as economic policy when undertaken by the ESM, and as monetary policy when conducted by the ESCB (Eurosystem), and that the difference of objective is decisive in this dual characterization, *i.e.*, safeguarding the stability of the euro area for the former and maintaining price stability for the latter.

These abstract considerations are not very compelling. Perhaps a better justification for linking anti-fragmentation asset purchases to compliance with (existing) economic policy conditions would be the need to prevent moral hazard.[562] But it would still not be entirely persuasive in a monetary policy context. At the end of the day, if central bank asset purchases are monetary policy because they are required to preserve or restore the monetary policy transmission mechanism, it is not logically coherent for such purchases to be made conditional on current or future compliance with national policy commitments in the economic or fiscal spheres. In the cold light of day, monetary policy actions stand or fall with their need as a matter of monetary logic and should not be made dependent on action or inaction of Member States in other policy spheres.

f Moral Hazard and Proportionality

395. Anti-fragmentation government bond purchases by central banks have or may have undesirable side effects:

(a) They may create moral hazard by offering a safety net to reform-wary governments and by comforting political inaction bias. And the very existence of anti-fragmentation asset purchase programs may lead governments—and financial markets—to expect that, when push comes to shove, central banks will stand ready to step in and ensure that governments maintain access to financial markets on viable terms. As said, economic policy conditionality may mitigate moral hazard concerns but is more difficult to reconcile with monetary policy logic.

(b) Also, as discussed, anti-fragmentation purchases inject additional liquidity into the system, which may work against an anti-inflationary monetary policy stance. And sterilizing such additional liquidity within a reasonably short time span may be easier said than done and interfere with defragmentation.

(c) Furthermore, Eurosystem bond purchases load additional government debt onto central bank balance sheets, specifically government debt of Member

562. Indeed, later in the *Gauweiler* judgment, the Court considered OMT's link with EFSF/ESM economic policy conditionality a helpful factor in support of OMT's consistency with the monetary financing prohibition of Article 123 TFEU insofar as, in order to steer clear of this prohibition, government bond purchases must not lessen *"the impetus of the Member States concerned to follow a sound budgetary policy"*. *Ibid.*, §§109 and 120.

States under financial stress. This increases central bank exposure to (i) interest rate risk in case of subsequent upward movement in interest rates (including as a result of policy rate increases that may be needed for inflation control), and (ii) risk of sovereign default or debt restructuring (given acceptance of *pari passu* treatment). Interest rate risk may be mitigated to some degree by the fact that the bonds purchased would be those of Member States at the high end of the yield spreads. In contrast, default risk should be higher on bonds issued by Member States under financial stress that will typically have more fragile fiscal positions or other underlying vulnerabilities.

396. Accordingly, even if one assumes that anti-fragmentation bond purchases serve a legitimate monetary policy objective and are an effective instrument to attain this objective, the question remains whether that objective could not be achieved by some more limited and targeted action that avoids or mitigates undesirable side effects.

9 ALTERNATIVE APPROACHES

397. Could one think of an alternative instrument that would adequately contain financial fragmentation with fewer or milder side effects and that, importantly, would raise fewer legal doubts as to its consistency with the ECB's monetary policy mandate and the prohibition of monetary financing?

a Activating the ESM's Primary and/or Secondary Market Facilities

398. One fairly obvious thought that comes to mind would be to take anti-fragmentation asset purchases outside of the central bank perimeter and monetary policy sphere and entrust them instead to some separate EU or intergovernmental fund. Here, the ESM would be a prime candidate as it (i) is an existing and fully operational structure; (ii) is specifically authorized by its constituent treaty to grant stability support to euro area Member States by purchasing their government bonds in the primary or secondary markets (Articles 17 and 18 of the ESM Treaty); and (iii) has plausible firepower left, *i.e.*, at the time of writing, some EUR 422 billion (EUR 354 billion after deducting the planned EUR 68 billion backstop credit line to the Single Resolution Board) in uncommitted financing capacity (*see* paragraph 734 below).

399. ESM stability support is reserved for euro area Member States in, or threatened by, *"severe financing problems"* when such support is *"indispensable to safeguard the financial stability of the euro area as a whole and of its Member States"* (Article 3 of the ESM Treaty jo. Article 136(3) TFEU). This should capture the typical fact pattern necessitating anti-fragmentation interventions, although it is possible that the ECB may have a somewhat broader scope of application in mind for TPI (including possibly in market segments other than government bonds). ESM support is also subject to *"strict conditionality"* (again as stipulated by the same treaty provisions) but this should not necessarily be read as requiring incremental *ad hoc* policy conditionality. In my opinion, this condition could be met by compliance with existing policy commitments under the various EU frameworks (*see* paragraphs 740-742 below), mutatis mutandis as in the case of TPI (*see* paragraph 361(a) above).

400. One must assume that the ECB and the Eurogroup have considered this possibility when looking at TPI and for some reason have preferred to structure TPI as a monetary policy tool in the hands of Eurosystem central banks. One may speculate that there have been several possible reasons for this choice, including (i) the intended broader scope of application of TPI; (ii) the need to balance the circumstances, size and duration of TPI purchases in relation to monetary policy requirements and constraints at any given time; (iii) the deeper pocket and greater rapidity of execution of Eurosystem central banks; and (iv) reluctance in certain political quarters to involve the ESM.

b Interest Stabilization Mechanism

401. One could think of a different mechanism. Perhaps this is the time to dust off an old idea of Friedrich Heinemann who in 2012 proposed a form of interest subsidy mechanism.[563] Professor Heinemann's proposal is based on the simple observation that any episode of market anxiety causing excessive widening of sovereign bond spreads leads to losers and winners among euro area Member States: higher-risk Member States, with bond yields at the high end of the spreads, suffer an unwarranted increase in government borrowing costs, while, conversely, Member States with higher creditworthiness, at the low end of the spreads, derive a windfall gain from lower government borrowing costs caused by flight-to-safety market dynamics. Accordingly, Professor Heinemann would establish a form of normalized interest rate corridor within which sovereign bond yields could be considered justified by underlying fundamentals. Member States whose bond yields are driven above the upper limit would, from some centralized fund, receive temporary interest subsidies to cover excess interest expenditures on new borrowings, subject to credible conditionality linking the continuing flow of interest subsidies to ongoing fiscal policy conditions and structural reforms. Member States that are fortunate to see their bond yields drop below the lower limit would contribute part of their windfall interest savings on new borrowings to the fund. Importantly, the proposed interest subsidy scheme would be an interest **stabilization** mechanism, triggered by unwarranted deviations from macroeconomic fundamentals, and not an interest **equalization** mechanism.

402. With all that has happened since 2012, one could consider updating Professor Heinemann's idea in the following respects:

563. *See* Fr. Heinemann, "FIRE for the Euro: A Superior Way to Bond Market Stabilization", *Jahrbücher für Nationalökonomie und Statistik*, Vol. 232, 2012, pp. 702-709, https://doi.org/10.1515/jbnst-2012-0609.

(a) Since the upper and lower limits of the interest rate corridor are intended to be the outer bounds of a zone in which sovereign bond yields may be deemed to be broadly aligned with underlying economic fundamentals, the corridors would not only have to be differentiated among euro area Member States but they would also have to be reset from time to time to capture changes in fundamentals and market developments. Admittedly, this would not be an easy process and it would be a challenge to keep politics at bay. Key criteria would have to be pre-agreed. Happily, interest rate corridors should not need to be reset too frequently given that economic fundamentals tend to be slow-moving and that the bandwidth of the corridors should provide some flexibility.

(b) As a rule, interest subsidies under the scheme should not be made subject to **additional** policy conditionality, but only to an eligibility assessment that looks to the relevant Member State's "good standing" in terms of its existing policy commitments under the EMU fiscal and macroeconomic surveillance frameworks. Indeed, the interest subsidy is merely supposed to cover the increment in government borrowing costs that is attributable to market over-reaction, *i.e.*, to negative market dynamics disconnected from economic fundamentals. Logically, this should not justify incremental policy conditionality.

(c) In order for contributions to the fund to more or less match interest subsidies paid out of the fund, government bond market turbulences would over time have to cause broadly equal gains and losses under the interest rate corridors. Looking at debt-weighted average government bond yields, Professor Heinemann found that gains and losses were symmetrical in the 2010-2012 euro area sovereign debt crisis. But this is by no means a law of physics given differences in the amounts and timing of (re)financing needs among euro area Member States. An institution like the ESM would need to backstop the fund for asymmetries in the volumes and timing of contributions and subsidies.

(d) Again, it would be safest, legally, for such an interest subsidy mechanism to be set up and managed outside of the Eurosystem perimeter and monetary policy sphere because its nexus with monetary policy proper is too tenuous. The ESM would seem an obvious choice for this given its *raison d'être*, governance structure, capital backing and know-how notably in funding strategies. The mechanism could be hosted and operated by the ESM, as a facility created pursuant to Articles 19 and 24 of the ESM Treaty or, alternatively, be established separately by an intergovernmental agreement between the euro area Member States, with the ESM managing and backstopping the facility. This second variant would probably be preferable, given that the first variant may sit uneasily with the ESM's core mission of loan-based stability support (*see* paragraph 739 below).

403. To sum up, a non-monetary anti-fragmentation mechanism of the kind just described would broadly offer the following advantages over targeted government bond purchases by Eurosystem central banks:

(a) Such a mechanism should be on firmer legal ground and not raise doubts as to its consistency with the monetary policy mandate or the prohibition of monetary financing.
(b) It should not inject significant net additional liquidity into the system and would hence be broadly neutral for the monetary policy stance.
(c) It would not load additional government debt onto the balance sheets of the Eurosystem central banks (or the ESM).
(d) Proper eligibility criteria looking to a Member State's compliance with common fiscal rules and existing policy and reform commitments should avoid or minimize moral hazard.
(e) The scheme would involve a form of fiscal transfer between euro area Member States but the usual political sensitivity about inter-country fiscal transfers should be blunted by the fact that here the transfers would be limited to windfall interest savings of the most creditworthy Member States, caused by flight-to-safety dynamics, that are the counterpart of unwarranted extra interest costs of less creditworthy Member States, caused by market overreaction.

404. But there would be relative disadvantages as well:

(a) Defining and updating interest rate corridors reflecting "normal" zones of sovereign bond yields that can be considered to be in line with underlying economic fundamentals remains an approximative exercise for the reasons discussed earlier (*see* paragraphs 371-377 above). This would also be true, *mutatis mutandis*, for anti-fragmentation bond purchases by central banks, except that central banks could act and adjust in a more flexible *ad hoc* manner with a somewhat greater degree of freedom. Also, in an intergovernmental setting like the ESM, that exercise would be vulnerable to political interference to which more discreet asset purchases by central banks would be exposed to a lesser degree.
(b) The quantitative equivalence of interest subsidies and contributions over time is a source of uncertainty and would require empirical testing. But backstopping by the ESM (and its flexible funding) should allow to bridge any shortfalls over a longer period.
(c) Another comparative disadvantage of an interest stabilization mechanism is that it would not operate instantly to contain an excessive widening of sovereign bond spreads in the secondary markets (and its knock-on effects on other market interest rates) but focus instead on neutralizing the impact of

such market turbulences on government (re)financing costs going forward. Yet, one would expect that this effect and the "forward guidance" conveyed by the interest rate corridors would likely dampen future market overreaction.

CHAPTER 6

Monetary Policy Trade-Offs

405. It is instructive to relate the fairly diffuse matrix of high-level policy objectives and constraints in which the Treaty embeds the ECB's monetary policy mandate, as described in Chapter 3, to certain real-life trade-offs that the single monetary policy faces (i) in its interactions with national fiscal policies; (ii) in the ECB's role to contribute to financial stability; and (iii) in dealing with the challenges of climate transition. This chapter is also a good place for a short discussion of (iv) certain choices that must be made in the ongoing review of the ECB's operational framework for steering short-term interest rates.

1 THE MACROECONOMIC POLICY MIX

406. Let us pause first for a brief refresher from the textbooks. Economists generally teach that monetary and fiscal policies have or should have broadly complementary roles in macroeconomic stabilization, with monetary policy focusing primarily on price stability and fiscal policy on output stabilization. This seems straightforward enough when inflation and output/employment move in the same direction, as is typically the case for demand-driven cyclical changes. In this fact pattern, monetary and fiscal policies are directionally aligned: in the boom phase, rising inflation and an overheating economy require monetary tightening and fiscal restraint, while in the bust phase, disinflationary pressures and sluggish or negative growth call for monetary easing and fiscal stimulus. Such a directional alignment still leaves questions of proper policy mix and dosage but at least it avoids the sharper conflicts as to the positive or negative sign of the policy response.

407. In contrast, when inflation and output/employment move in opposite directions, frictions and trade-offs arise, at least in the shorter term.[564] This is typically the case for

564. Of course, one could say that, in the circle of (economic) life, there should be no long-term trade-off between inflation and output/employment: booming activity will, at some point,

supply-side shocks (like a surge in energy prices) that may concurrently produce higher inflation and depress output/employment and hence "desynchronize" monetary and fiscal policies. Of course, supply-side shocks may be relatively mild and/or short-lived and their effects may fizzle out within a medium-term horizon. But if this is considered unlikely and they begin infiltrating market inflation expectations, the monetary authority may need to take restrictive monetary policy action, at some cost in terms of depressing demand and output. At the same time, fiscal stimulus to preserve output/employment may contribute to upward price pressures and, in this manner, counteract the effort at monetary tightening. And increased government borrowing costs induced by higher monetary policy rates may reduce fiscal policy space, especially in the presence of a high level of pre-existing sovereign debt.

408. If all of this may be complicated enough in a single-country setting, these frictions and conflicts are multiplied in the euro area's configuration of 20 sovereign States sharing a common currency, in which a single monetary policy interacts with 20 national fiscal policies in what remains an incomplete EMU with relatively "soft" common fiscal rules and without a robust common budgetary stabilization capacity. In such a configuration, the degree of symmetry within the system is a critical factor. We have seen in Chapter 2 that the euro area still offers a mixed picture when it comes to the convergence of key macroeconomic variables. Happily, business cycles have become fairly synchronous, albeit with differences in amplitude, but financial cycles appear to be less symmetric (*see* paragraphs 139-144 above). There are different degrees of vulnerability to external shocks due to the heterogeneity of country characteristics, including differences in such factors as a country's product portfolio, dependency on imported energy and exposure to climate change. Other relevant sources of heterogeneity across euro area Member States derive from differences in their fiscal capacity to smooth the business cycle and absorb external shocks, which in turn arise from differences in the architecture of their fiscal systems, notably in the size and effectiveness of automatic stabilizers,[565] and from differences in policy space for (discretionary) fiscal action as a result, in particular, of the level and maturity profile of their sovereign debt.

409. Thus, the ECB's single monetary policy has to contend with different national fiscal policies reflecting different national policy preferences, needs and constraints. This is bound in greater or lesser measure to produce asymmetries and dysfunctionalities in the monetary-fiscal policy mix across the euro area. In the abstract, one would like to think that fiscal policy should ordinarily be the workhorse for output/

cause prices and costs to rise, which will, at some point, depress demand and output, which will, at some point, diminish prices and costs, which will, at some point, stimulate demand and output again. But, outside the timeless realm of Heraclitus' *panta rhei*, contemporary politics have little patience for such perpetual self-correcting cycles and their intermittent disruptions.

565. Automatic stabilizers can broadly be defined as those built-in components of government revenues and expenditures that smooth the economic cycle (progressive taxes, unemployment benefits, ...) without need for discretionary fiscal action. The size of these automatic stabilizers varies significantly among euro area Member States. *See* X. Debrun, G. Ferrero *et al.*, "Monetary-fiscal policy interaction in the euro area", Report of the Eurosystem work stream on monetary-fiscal interactions, *ECB Occasional Paper Series No 273*, September 2021, pp. 40-42.

employment stabilization, leaving monetary policy to focus primarily on price stability. In Europe's incomplete EMU with significant country heterogeneity, this casting of fiscal policy would seem to make even more sense because, unlike the single "one-size-fits-all" monetary policy, national fiscal policies can cater to country-specific needs. In fact, given the singleness of monetary and exchange rate policies, fiscal policy is the main policy instrument left to euro area Member States for addressing macroeconomic imbalances at the country level. The workhorse casting of fiscal policy implies that it should generally be counter-cyclical, and this should especially be the case when monetary policy becomes constrained as policy rates approach the lower bound. In this casting, difficulties arise when some euro area Member States see their fiscal policy space narrowed by concerns over the sustainability of their sovereign debt or, conversely, are too conservative in using the fiscal headroom that they have. And the situation in which inflation and output/employment move in opposite directions is always inherently difficult but even more so in a relatively heterogeneous multi-country setting in which member countries retain a substantial measure of fiscal autonomy. It is through this lens that we will now briefly look at the interaction of monetary and fiscal policies in the euro area over roughly the past 15 years.

410. In the early phase of the 2008-2012 financial crisis, monetary and fiscal policies were broadly aligned in providing stimulus. By 2010, there were signs that the economy had bottomed out, and with tensions now developing in the sovereign bond markets and rating agencies proceeding to a series of downgrades of sovereign credit ratings (*see* paragraph 65, Table 1.1, above), concerns over government credit standing and financial market access led several euro area Member States to turn to greater fiscal restraint. The overall euro area fiscal stance became contractionary and remained so until (and including) 2013,[566] notwithstanding low or even negative GDP growth (*see* paragraph 121, Table 2.4, above). Such pro-cyclical fiscal policies in effect counteracted the moderate stimulus provided by an accommodative monetary policy. In April and July 2011, the ECB briefly raised its policy rates, each time by 25 basis points, in response to a temporary uptick in inflation, before cautiously lowering them again as from November 2011 (*see* paragraph 207 above).[567] In those years, the combination of restrained fiscal policies and the ECB's initial hesitation to proceed to more resolute monetary easing arguably contributed to prolonging the (second) recession from 2011 Q3 to 2013 Q1 and nurturing disinflationary trends.

566. *See* M. Rostagno, C. Altavilla *et al.*, "A tale of two decades: the ECB's monetary policy at 20", *ECB Working Paper Series No 2346*, December 2019, p. 316, Chart 6.30. This appears to have been consistent with *"l'air du temps"*. At the G-20 summit of June 26-27, 2010, advanced economies committed to fiscal plans that would cut their government deficits at least in half by 2013 and stabilize or reduce their government debt-to-GDP ratios by 2016. *See The G-20 Toronto Summit Declaration*, June 26-27, 2010, §10 and Annex I, §9, https://www.oecd.org/g20/summits/toronto/g20-declaration.pdf.

567. In an interview not long ago, Klaas Knot, President of the Dutch central bank, acknowledged that in 2011 the ECB should *"probably have paid a little bit more attention"* to low levels of core inflation before raising its policy rates in response to increasing oil prices. *See* M. Arnold, "Leading ECB policymaker hints at sharp climb to peak rates", *Financial Times*, December 26, 2022, https://www.ft.com/content/87ca91ac-02cb-42ed-9c64-b274ac078103.

411. The euro area fiscal stance turned broadly neutral only in 2014 and remained so in the following years. By then, the ECB had switched to resolute monetary easing, with policy rates now at or close to 0 % and large-scale asset purchases (quantitative easing), which it was to maintain for an extended period stretching into the first part of 2022. The ECB's *leitmotiv* was to counter stubborn disinflationary pressures, with inflation drifting well below the (then "below but close to") 2 % target (*see* paragraph 114, Table 2.1, above). While fiscal policies overall remained insufficiently counter-cyclical, monetary easing probably also contributed to restoring moderate GDP growth prior to the outbreak of COVID-19 (*see* paragraph 121, Table 2.4, above). In his June 18, 2019 farewell address at the ECB Central Banking Forum in Sintra (Portugal), outgoing ECB President Mario Draghi had the following to say on the subject:

> *"But fiscal policy should play its role. Over the last 10 years, the burden of macroeconomic adjustment has fallen disproportionately on monetary policy. We have even seen instances where fiscal policy has been pro-cyclical and countered the monetary stimulus.*
>
> *If the unbalanced macroeconomic policy-mix in the euro area in part explains the slide into disinflation, so a better policy mix can help bring it to a close. Monetary policy can always achieve its objective alone, but especially in Europe where public sectors are large, it can do so faster and with fewer side effects if fiscal policies are aligned with it."*[568]

412. Properly decoding Mr. Draghi's words is, at times, an exercise akin to biblical exegesis. Ostensibly, he was saying here that, over the 2011-2019 period, more counter-cyclical fiscal policies would have better supported monetary policy in its quest to vanquish disinflationary pressures. Or, giving only a slightly different twist to the same message, one could read it as suggesting that monetary policy wouldn't have had to go so low for so long if fiscal policies had properly done their part of macroeconomic stabilization. But wouldn't this be tantamount to saying that greater monetary activism had to make up for relative fiscal passivity—that, in part, monetary policy had in effect to fill in for inadequate national fiscal policies in providing stimulus to the economy? And how should this weigh in the assessment of the legitimacy and proportionality of the ECB's long monetary easing, particularly its asset purchases, over the 2014-2021 period?

413. In 2020, the outbreak of COVID-19 caused a sharp downturn in economic activity (*see* paragraph 121, Table 2.4, above) and, in that and the following year, a considerable increase in government deficits across the euro area due to increased public spending on social transfers, other economic relief for businesses and households and public health measures, and to loss of tax revenue (*see* paragraph 116, Table 2.2, above). It was then widely believed that macroeconomic policies should remain supportive for some time in order to limit the economic scarring effects of the pandemic and ensure a sustained economic recovery. On the monetary policy side, the prevailing

568. M. Draghi, "Twenty years of the ECB's monetary policy", *ECB Forum on Central Banking*, June 17-19, 2019, *20 years of European Economic and Monetary Union*, Conference proceedings, p. 34.

view at the ECB, until deeply into 2021, was that the inflation outlook remained subdued and that monetary policy could and should remain accommodative, thereby preserving favorable financing conditions and leaving adequate policy space for fiscal support. In the words of one contemporaneous ECB paper, the idea was to provide *"a clear signal to governments not to underspend relative to the scale of the* [CoViD-19] *shock or withdraw fiscal stimulus too early out of fear that borrowing costs will tighten prematurely"*.[569]

414. Thus, in the macroeconomic policy mix of 2020-2021, fiscal policy seemed to move more center stage, with monetary policy in a more supporting role to maintain favorable financing conditions. Monetary and fiscal policies now acted in tandem, which seemed fine so long as inflation and the medium-term inflation outlook remained muted, as they did in 2020. But in 2021, both began to rise significantly. While in December 2020, baseline projections for headline inflation (HICP) still stood at 1% for 2021, 1.1% for 2022 and 1.4% for 2023,[570] by December 2021, they had been revised upward to 2.6%, 3.2% and 1.8%, respectively (*see* paragraph 319, Table 4.3, above), and year-on-year inflation had reached 4.9% in November 2021. Yet, as late as at its December 15-16, 2021 monetary policy meeting, the ECB's Governing Council still decided (i) to leave its policy rates unchanged at levels closely around zero; (ii) to discontinue net purchases under PEPP at the end of March 2022 but to continue to fully reinvest maturing bonds in the PEPP portfolio until at least the end of 2024; and (iii) to gradually reduce net purchases under APP to a monthly pace of EUR 20 billion by October 2022 while then maintaining them at this level until *"shortly before it starts raising the key ECB interest rates"*—thereby signaling that it did not currently plan to increase policy rates in 2022 or at least not before the very end of 2022 (*see* paragraph 242 above). The ECB likely took comfort in baseline projections that then saw inflationary pressures gradually subsiding over the course of 2022, with headline inflation dropping again below 2% in 2023, within its medium-term horizon. But a prominent theme in its messaging remained the desirability of maintaining favorable liquidity conditions and an ample degree of monetary accommodation. It is open to argument whether these decisions still reflected a proper balancing of the primary objective of seeing to price stability and the secondary objective of supporting fiscal policies. Available economic research may then have provided good support for characterizing inflationary pressures as transient, but even then, could expected inflation well above 2% for two consecutive years, 2021 and 2022, properly be viewed as a mere blip in the curve that did not call for stronger monetary policy reactivity?

415. As from early 2022, developments triggered by Russia's attempt at invading Ukraine produced a serious negative supply shock, in the form of surging energy and commodity prices, and adversely affected market sentiment. The economic fall-out of the Ukraine conflict, coming on top of remaining pandemic-related supply chain

569. X. Debrun, G. Ferrero *et al.*, *supra*, pp. 71-72.
570. *See Eurosystem macroeconomic projections for the euro area*, December 2020, pp. 14-16 and 21, https://www.ecb.europa.eu/pub/pdf/other/ecb.projections202012_eurosystemstaff~bf8254a.en.pdf.

disturbances and the economic slowdown in China (due in part to its strict lockdown measures until the end of the year), stalled post-COVID-19 economic recovery in the euro area and now put inflation and output/employment squarely on opposite tracks. The sharp increase in inflation, driven by energy and food prices but soon spreading more widely throughout the economy, eventually forced the ECB to switch more firmly to monetary tightening in the summer by starting a series of policy rate increases and discontinuing net purchases under APP as of July 2022 (*see* paragraphs 253-254, 256 and 258 above). Concomitantly, euro area Member States mostly stepped up fiscal support to provide relief for high energy costs and to contain recessionary risks. With larger-scale fiscal stimulus now risking to fuel upward pressures on prices that monetary policy was seeking to contain, the ECB repeatedly appealed to euro area Member States to calibrate fiscal policies to "targeted, temporary and tailored" measures addressing the most pressing needs, to be attentive to the need of gradually bringing down high government debt ratios, and, as of February 2023, to "promptly" roll back energy-related support measures in line with declining energy prices.[571] In her September 26, 2022 testimony before the European Parliament's Committee on Economic and Monetary Affairs, ECB President Christine Lagarde distinguished such targeted fiscal measures, which she said may be helpful and needed, from across-the-board fiscal stimulus that may work at cross-purposes with monetary policy, adding that, at that point in time, the vast proportion of national fiscal measures fell in the latter category, which is *"not necessarily conducive to a well-coordinated fiscal and monetary policy"*.[572]

416. In such an environment of high inflation and recessionary risks, there are negative cross effects in both directions. While fiscal stimulus may fuel inflationary pressures that monetary policy seeks to contain, tighter monetary policy will raise financing costs, including government borrowing costs, which may further depress demand and output and reduce fiscal policy space, especially for countries with higher

571. Thus, an explicit paragraph to this effect, with varying nuances, was included in the ECB's monetary policy statements of June 9, 2022 (https://www.ecb.europa.eu/press/pressconf/2022/html/ecb.is220609~abe7c95b19.en.html, at p. 2), July 21, 2022 (https://www.ecb.europa.eu/press/pressconf/2022/html/ecb. is220721~51ef267c68e.en.html, at p. 2), September 8, 2022 (https://ecb.europa.eu/press/pressconf/2022/html/ecb.is220908~cd8363c58e.en.html, at p. 2), October 27, 2022 (https://ecb.europa.eu/press/pressconf/2022/html/ecb.is221027~358a06a35f.en.html, at p. 2), December 15, 2022 (https://ecb.europa.eu/press/pressconf/2022/html/ecb.is221215~197ac630ae.en.html, at p. 2), February 2, 2023 (https://ecb. europa.eu/press/pressconf/2023/html/ecb.is230202~4313651089.en.html, at p. 2), March 16, 2023 (https://ecb.europa.eu/press/pressconf/2023/html/ecb.is230316~6c10b087b5.en.html, at p. 2), May 4, 2023 (https://ecb. europa.eu/press/pressconf/2023/html/ecb.is230504~f242392c72.en.html, at p. 2), June 15, 2023 (https://ecb.europa.eu/press/pressconf/2023/html/ecb.is230615~3de9d68335.en.html, at p. 2), July 27, 2023 (https://ecb.europa.eu/press/pressconf/2023/html/ecb.is230727~e0a11feb2e.en.html, at p. 2), September 14, 2023 (https://www.ecb.europa.eu/press/pressconf/2023/html/ecb.is230914~686786984a.en.html, at p. 2), October 26, 2023 (https://www.ecb.europa.eu/press/pressconf/2023/html/ecb.is231026~c23b4eb5f0.en.html, at p. 2), and December 14, 2023 (https://www.ecb.europa.eu/press/pressconf/2023/html/ecb. is231214~df8627de60.en.html, at p. 2).
572. Testimony of September 26, 2022 before the European Parliament's Committee on Economic and Monetary Affairs, https://www.europarl.europa.eu/cmsdata/254813/ECB%20Hearing%2020220926.EN.pdf, at p. 5.

debt levels. It may cause a widening of government bond spreads which may at some point give rise to financial fragmentation and interfere with proper monetary policy transmission. This may in turn prompt central banks to engage in anti-fragmentation bond purchases but, as discussed in Chapter 5, asset purchases of this kind come with problems of their own, notably by injecting additional liquidity into the system at a time of high inflation (unless this additional liquidity could somehow be sterilized). In theory, therefore, such asset purchases should be viewed as temporary stopgap measures, to be used sparingly, especially in a high-inflation environment. But if destabilizing market dynamics were to set in, market and political realities may dictate otherwise.

417. In Europe's incomplete EMU, there is no obvious solution (other than goodwill and common sense) for resolving the kind of frictions and conflicts between monetary and fiscal policies that are bound to arise from time to time, particularly in a high-inflation/low-growth environment. In the current institutional set-up, it is difficult to see how any effective two-way arbitrage mechanism on the proper macroeconomic policy mix could be put in place beyond the level of non-binding dialogue. The difficulty essentially derives from the fact that (i) on the one hand, the ECB's monetary policy mandate is first and foremost focused on inflation control and (rightfully) firewalled from political interference, and (ii) on the other hand, the euro area Member States retain a substantial measure of autonomy over their fiscal policies (except in the coercive phase of an excessive deficit procedure or in back-against-the-wall situations in which they have no choice but to accept economic policy conditions in exchange for institutional financial support), and, within its own mandate, the ECB must tread carefully when seeking to press its fiscal policy preferences or to condition monetary policy actions on particular fiscal measures. Tensions could be mitigated by a better alignment of national fiscal policies within the EMU coordination and surveillance processes that would not focus one-dimensionally on fiscal discipline of Member States individually but also look more broadly to defining a coherent euro area fiscal stance in which euro area Member States with more fiscal policy space accept a share of responsibility for overall balance by providing more fiscal stimulus when needed, as we will discuss in Chapter 8. Tensions could be alleviated as well by more robust centralized stabilization support, as will be discussed in Chapters 9 and 10. Both remain difficult propositions politically, although recent developments suggest that positions have become less frozen than they used to be, as we will see.

2 MONETARY POLICY AND FINANCIAL STABILITY

a Back to the Treaty

418. The Treaty itself does not expressly confer upon the ECB/ESCB any direct, first-line responsibility for safeguarding financial stability. Under Article 127(1) TFEU, the ESCB must *"support"* the general economic policies in the Union with a view to contributing to the achievement of the Union's objectives set forth in Article 3 TEU, but, while this provision refers to a broad range of objectives and aspirations, the stability of the financial system is not expressly mentioned among them (although it could, of course, be considered a prerequisite for those objectives and aspirations). Nor does Article 119 TFEU expressly refer to financial stability as an objective or guiding principle for the Member States' and the Union's actions with which the ESCB is expected to comply as well under Article 127(1), *in fine*, TFEU. Under Article 127(5) TFEU, the ESCB must *"contribute"* to the smooth conduct of the policies pursued *"by the competent authorities"* relating to the prudential supervision of credit institutions and the stability of the financial system. This rather suggests a supporting role for the ESCB, not a primary responsibility or autonomous competence. Finally, Article 127(6) TFEU authorizes the Council to confer *"specific tasks"* upon the ECB concerning policies relating to the prudential supervision of financial institutions (other than insurance companies). On this basis, the ECB has been given certain supervisory and macroprudential tasks in the framework of the Single Supervisory Mechanism for the banking sector.[573] But this is it.

419. There is a general (albeit rarely well-articulated) expectation that central banks ultimately stand guard for the stability of the financial system, at least in the sense that they must be ready to step in by providing the necessary liquidity when the system is threatened by severe disruptions. If the authors of the Treaty provisions on EMU were aware of this, they did not express it in the most felicitous terms. A central bank's "lender-of-last-resort" responsibility to the financial system is a direct, self-standing task that seems hard to squeeze into the apparently narrower supporting role defined by Article 127(5) TFEU, *i.e.*, that of *"contribut[ing] to the smooth conduct of policies pursued by the competent authorities relating to [...] the stability of the financial system"*. Given that the delineation of the Union's powers is governed by the principle of conferral (Article 5(1) and (2) TEU), that is a little annoying. *Faute de mieux*, the proper functioning of the monetary policy transmission mechanism would again have to come to the rescue by attaching lender-of-last-resort operations to the monetary policy mandate. In this line of reasoning (which now appears to be favored by the ECB), it is argued that safeguarding financial stability must be subsumed under the ECB's monetary policy mandate insofar as a reasonable measure of financial stability, in particular a minimum degree of orderly functioning of the money markets, is a prerequisite for the effectiveness of monetary policy aimed at price stability and its proper pass-through via the monetary policy transmission mechanism. It is certainly probable that severe money market dysfunctions will impair monetary policy transmission. But then, so would a major blackout of Europe's interconnected power grid.

420. Let us circle back to Article 127(5) TFEU for a moment. Interestingly, this provision does not expressly subordinate the ESCB's contributory role to financial stability policies to the primary price stability objective of monetary policy—in contrast to Article 127(1) TFEU which provides that the ESCB's support of general economic

573. *See*, in particular, Articles 4 and 5 of Council Regulation (EU) No 1024/2013 of October 15, 2013 conferring specific tasks on the European Central Bank concerning policies relating to the prudential supervision of credit institutions, *OJ* L287, October 29, 2013, p. 63.

policies is *"[w]ithout prejudice to the objective of price stability"*. This could be drafting oversight. But it is also possible and indeed likely that the authors of these Treaty provisions saw the ESCB's contributory role to financial stability policies as something distinct from its monetary policy mandate, with monetary policy proper always being chained to a primary price stability objective. A somewhat similar—but not identical—reasoning is implicit in the "separation principle" that has episodically been advanced in ECB statements. It is not identical insofar as this principle, as it has evolved and is now mostly understood, serves to separate two complementary but distinct lines of action **within** the monetary policy mandate, as discussed below.

b The Separation Principle

421. The "separation principle" was once characterized by former ECB President Jean-Claude Trichet as a *"clear"* principle that is *"strictly applied"*.[574] Surely, this is in the eye of the beholder. Under this principle, broadly speaking, standard monetary policy tools, and in particular policy rates, are used to ensure price stability, *i.e.*, for inflation control, while non-standard tools like atypical forms of liquidity provision and asset purchases separately address dislocations in the money markets, irrespective of the interest rate level and the inflation outlook and, hence, the monetary policy stance directed at inflation control. To my knowledge, the first "official" statement of a principle of this kind was made at the ECB's press conference on September 6, 2007. With reference to the ECB's urgent liquidity provision in response to the tensions surrounding certain BNP Paribas investment funds in August 2007 (*see* paragraph 427 below), Mr. Trichet distinguished the ECB's *"primary mandate"* of delivering price stability from its *"important"* separate responsibility for the proper functioning of the money markets. He explained that the ECB does not *"mix the two responsibilities"* which *"do not influence each other"*, and that one should not *"confuse the appropriate functioning of the money market and the monetary policy stance"*, adding that *"at whatever level of interest, the market has to function"*.[575] This early formulation of the principle may suggest that the ECB's responsibility to safeguard the functioning of the money markets, or financial stability more broadly, is or was viewed as distinct from its monetary policy mandate proper. But in later statements, it became attached to the monetary policy mandate by the need to safeguard the monetary policy transmission mechanism.[576]

574. J.-Cl. Trichet, "The ECB's response to the crisis", Speech at the WDR Europa-Forum, Berlin, May 26, 2011, https://www.ecb.europa.eu/press/key/date/2011/html/sp110526.en.html, at p. 5.

575. *See* the transcript of the ECB's press conference of September 6, 2007, https://www.ecb.europa.eu/press/pressconf/2007/html/is070906.en.html, at pp. 4-5.

576. *See, e.g.*, J.-Cl. Trichet, "Monetary policy in uncertain times", Speech at the Bank of Finland 200th Anniversary Conference, Helsinki, May 5, 2011, https://www.bis.org/review/r110509c.pdf, at pp. 3-4, and transcript of the ECB's press conference of August 4, 2011, https://www.ecb.europa.eu/press/pressconf/2011/html/is110804.html, at p. 5.

422. According to Patrick Honohan, former Governor of the Central Bank of Ireland and, in this capacity, member of the ECB's Governing Council from September 2009 to November 2015, *"[o]ne likely reason that the separation principle gained traction and survived so long is that it helped to avoid or defuse potential conflict between hawks and doves among ECB decision makers"*.[577] The same author considers the principle as *"seductive but analytically flawed"* and criticizes it for delaying the ECB's recourse to larger-scale asset purchases for macroeconomic stabilization when the financial crisis in the euro area deepened in 2011-2012.[578] Eventually, a short while later, the separation principle went dormant as inflation continued to decline way below 2%, and, with policy rates now reaching the lower bound, larger-scale asset purchases became necessary to provide monetary easing and counter disinflationary pressures.

423. The return of inflation in recent years appears to have resuscitated the separation principle. Let me repeat here the instructive quote from the observations which ECB President Christine Lagarde made in her June 28, 2022 address at the annual ECB Forum on Central Banking in reference to the Transmission Protection Instrument then on the drawing board:

> *"[i]n the past, the ECB has made use of separate instruments to target inflation and to preserve the functioning of the monetary policy transmission mechanism. Measures to preserve transmission could be used at any level of interest rates—so long as they were designed not to interfere with the monetary policy stance.*
>
> *At times, when inflation fell too low, it made sense to shift from 'separation' to 'combination' so that all tools reinforced the required policy easing. [...] But with high inflation now being the main challenge, there are merits in separating policy tools again.*
>
> *Preserving policy transmission throughout the euro area will allow rates to rise as far as necessary. In this sense, there is no trade-off between launching this new tool and adopting the necessary policy stance to stabilise inflation at our target. In fact, one enables the other."*[579]

The minutes of the ECB Governing Council's monetary policy meeting of March 15-16, 2023 also report an exchange on the separation principle amidst increased financial market tensions following the collapse of Silicon Valley Bank. It was said that this principle required the monetary policy stance to be assessed independently from financial instability risks and that the ECB had other instruments at hand to address liquidity strains. It was also *"felt"* that *"[a]ll in all"* there is no *"fundamental"* trade-off between the price stability and financial stability objectives and that these objectives are complementary inasmuch as safeguarding financial stability supports an orderly transmission of monetary policy and the achievement of price stability over the

577. P. Honohan, "Real and Imagined Constraints on Euro Area Monetary Policy", *Peterson Institute for International Economics Working Paper No 18-8*, August 2018, p. 4. *Cf. also ibid.*, p. 12.
578. *Ibid.*, pp. 11 and 15-17.
579. Chr. Lagarde, "Price stability and policy transmission in the euro area", Speech at the ECB Forum on Central Banking 2022, Sintra, Portugal, June 28, 2022, https://www.ecb.europa.eu/press/key/date/2022/html/ecb.sp220628~754ac25107.en.html, at p. 6.

medium-term.[580] And at the ECB press briefing of March 16, 2023, Ms. Lagarde repeatedly stressed that there is no trade-off between the two objectives which are being addressed separately with their respective instruments.[581] These comments were likely intended in part to push back on market speculation that financial market tensions would prompt a pause in, or even a reversal of, monetary policy tightening at that time.

424. Thus, as its formulation has evolved over the years, the separation principle must not (or no longer) be understood to distinguish monetary policy and liquidity provision to preserve financial stability as two separate mandates. The latter is now subsumed under the former as a means to safeguard proper monetary policy transmission. The principle rather refers to the separate use of different instruments to serve distinct but complementary monetary policy purposes, *i.e.*, the primary purpose of inflation control and the ancillary purpose of ensuring the proper functioning of the monetary policy transmission mechanism.

425. At first blush, this may all seem fine and even alluring as an academic proposition, but, upon closer look, it raises questions:

(a) In case of below-target inflation, how strict or exclusive can the instrumental separation be? Must policy rates then be solely determined by the optimal strategy to push up inflation to target in the medium term? Does this imply that policy rates could not temporarily be increased, "lean against the wind", to defuse the build-up of asset bubbles that may present serious financial instability risks? Or, to echo Patrick Honohan's criticism (*see* paragraph 422 above), that non-standard tools like asset purchases should not be used to counter disinflationary pressures, especially when policy rates are at the lower bound (as indeed occurred during the 2014-2021 period)? Surely, today, the ECB would not (or no longer) deny either. Thus, it would seem that the separation principle does not, or at least not fully, apply in a low-inflation environment.

(b) In case of above-target inflation, the separation principle seems to make more sense. Yet, in the real world, friction may then arise between the supposedly complementary monetary policy purposes. Policy rate increases that are objectively desirable for inflation control may cause or exacerbate financial instability risks in one or more market segments that, in turn, may at some point come to interfere with proper monetary policy pass-through. But the deployment of non-standard tools like asset purchases for purposes of financial stabilization would inject additional liquidity into the system and, in this manner, fuel inflationary pressures, at cross-current with the restrictive

580. *See* the published account of the ECB Governing Council's monetary policy meeting of March 15-16, 2023, https://www.ecb.europa.eu/press/accounts/2023/html/ecb.mg230420~e8043d2d3d.en.html, at pp. 14-15.

581. *See* the transcript of the ECB's press conference of March 16, 2023, https://www.ecb.europa.eu/press/pressconf/2023/html/ecb.is230316~6c10b087b5.en.html, at pp. 6-7.

monetary policy stance. Which objective then counts most? Should policy rate increases that would be optimal for inflation control be moderated or spread in time to mitigate financial instability risks and, if so, in what circumstances and to what extent? Should asset purchases be deferred as long as possible and/or the additional liquidity sterilized so as to minimize interference with the monetary policy stance? The ECB would most likely respond, so I suspect, that these frictions cannot be arbitrated on the basis of an abstract once-and-for-all ranking of priorities but should be resolved on a case-by-case basis, in a "data-dependent manner" in light of all the relevant facts and circumstances.

c Systemic Crises

426. It seems broadly accepted, within the fellowship of central banks and in scholarly opinion, that, upon the occurrence of systemic liquidity shocks or other severe stresses in the financial system, a central bank could and should step in as "lender of last resort" and provide the necessary liquidity notably to preserve the functioning of the money markets. But what are the boundaries of this broad consensus view? What fact patterns may properly trigger lender-of-last-resort interventions and in what measure?

427. Let us consider a seemingly straightforward example. On August 9, 2007, against the backdrop of the unfolding U.S. subprime mortgage crisis, BNP Paribas Investment Partners announced that it temporarily suspended cash redemptions from three of its investment funds invested in securities backed by U.S. subprime mortgages, citing its inability to calculate a reliable net asset value for these funds.[582] With signs of interbank markets quickly drying up in a jittery market environment, the ECB promptly injected EUR 94.8 billion of liquidity through fixed-rate full-allotment finetuning operations.[583] To my knowledge, this intervention was uncontroversial (to the extent that anything can be uncontroversial in monetary policy matters). An abrupt confidence shock that causes interbank markets to instantly dry up, leaving banks in need of liquidity unable to raise funds in these markets, leaves little choice. But not all fact patterns are equally clear—and, on closer inspection, even the example just mentioned may not have been that straightforward a case for instantaneous crisis intervention.

428. There could be a moral hazard issue. If the financial markets come to expect that the central bank will intervene in any event to accommodate liquidity dry-outs and avert financial crises, this could distort incentives for sound risk analysis and pricing and encourage the markets to engage in bolder risk-taking. It is a risk reminiscent of the infamous "Greenspan put". Financial markets must not become too confident that the central bank stands ready to swiftly step in at the first signs of market stress, short of

582. *See* BNP Paribas' press release of August 9, 2007, https://group.bnpparibas/en/press-release/bnp-paribas-investment-partners-temporarily-suspends-calculation-net-asset-funds-parvest-dynamic-abs-bnp-paribas-abs-euribor-bnp-paribas-eonia.
583. *See* M. Rostagno, C. Altavilla *et al.*, *supra*, pp. 144-145.

major financial market dislocations. And, in that sense, central banks must not become *"the markets' best friends"*, as Mohamed El-Erian, former chair of President Obama's Global Development Council, once put it.[584] If financial exuberance causes turbulence, it does not flow from natural law that the central bank should be responsible for shielding lenders and investors from the consequences of their financial decisions. But this logic does not withstand practical necessities in case of serious systemic risk.

429. The reader and I may almost forget this these days but, in a longer time perspective, serious financial instability should not be a pressing issue most of the time. In the words of Ben Bernanke, Timothy Geithner and Henry ("Hank") Paulson, *"[u]sually, turmoil in financial markets burns itself out. Markets adjust, firms fail and life goes on"*.[585] And *"policymakers shouldn't overreact to every air pocket in the market or setback for a big bank as if it's the precursor to a catastrophe"*.[586] But once it becomes clear that a crisis is genuinely systemic, *"policymakers need to do everything in their power to quell it, regardless of the political ramifications, regardless of their ideological convictions"* and even *"regardless of what they've said or promised in the past"*.[587]

430. In this sense, the central bank may, as a lender of last resort, be the guarantor of **liquidity** to keep the financial system afloat in case of systemic shocks. But, in the ECB's own words, monetary policy is not *"responsible for guaranteeing* ***financial stability****"* (emphasis added).[588] It is a firefighting responsibility—not a direct responsibility for preventing fires. Monetary policy is not subservient to financial stability, in the sense that it must not be expected to systematically tighten when financial imbalances build up, nor to systematically loosen when financial imbalances materialize.[589]

d Pre-crisis Build-Up of Financial Imbalances

431. But, of course, not all fact patterns are equally acute. What about smoldering fires that present a risk of turning ablaze and causing serious damage at some point? This brings us to a broader field of interaction between monetary policy and financial stability beyond the narrow area of genuine lender-of-last-resort crisis situations, *i.e.*, containing a **pre-crisis** build-up of financial imbalances that **may** turn systemic—or, if you wish, the crisis-prevention arm of financial stability action.

584. M. El-Erian, "Central banks are now the markets' best friends", *The Guardian*, January 10, 2020, https://www.theguardian.com/business/2020/jan/10/central-banks-are-now-the-markets-best-friends.
585. B.S. Bernanke, T.F. Geithner & H.M. Paulson, *Firefighting: the Financial Crisis and its Lessons*, London, Profile Books, 2019, p. 1.
586. *Ibid.*, p. 8.
587. *Ibid.*
588. ECB, *An overview of the ECB's monetary policy strategy*, July 2021, p. 12, https://www.ecb.europa.eu/home/search/review/pdf/ecb.strategyreview_monpol_strategy_overview.en.pdf.
589. *Ibid.*

432. It is uncontroversial that macroprudential policies (and microprudential supervision) should be the first in line to keep the build-up of financial imbalances in check. But what if such policies are ineffective in containing financial instability risks or are simply lacking (as is still largely the case for certain non-bank financial intermediaries and crypto markets)? To what extent can or must the central bank then be expected to step in? Would this not involve a transfer to the ECB of shared responsibility in policy areas in which, under Article 127(5) TFEU, it is supposed only to *"contribute to the smooth conduct"* of policies within the competence of other—national or EU—authorities? True, when macroprudential policies fail to adequately contain financial instability risks, it may be welfare-enhancing for the central bank to intervene. But, under the Treaty, competences do not arise simply because they make good sense or because other authorities fail to act or to solve the problem. And the further question, again, is how much focus on inflation control can be sacrificed for pre-crisis financial stabilization interventions? Given the ECB's Treaty mandate, to what extent may preemptive financial stabilization action detract from the primary objective of maintaining price stability?

433. Another thought that comes to mind is that monetary policy instruments, especially the standard tools, may be too blunt for dealing efficiently with financial market distortions, insofar as oftentimes these problems are concentrated in particular market segments or geographic areas, and monetary policy action would have broader wingspan and macroeconomic effects. For example, intuitively one would think that, in the case of excesses in housing credit, a tightening of loan-to-value ratios (or, perhaps more judiciously, loan-to-income or debt-service-to-income ratios) in this market segment would dampen excessive credit with less overall output losses than an across-the-board increase in monetary policy rates.[590] Furthermore, financial imbalances often develop differently along national boundaries as a consequence of continued segregation of financial market segments (*e.g.*, residential real estate) or different regulations. This should make it less efficient to address them with an area-wide instrument. We will revisit these and other operational difficulties associated with the use of monetary policy tools for preemptively addressing financial stability issues later in this subsection (*see* paragraph 437 below).

434. As an abstract proposition, it stands to reason that monetary policy actions directed at inflation control should be designed in such a way as to avoid or minimize adverse impact on financial stability variables insofar as this can be done without detracting from the proper monetary policy stance, *i.e.*, at broadly identical effects for inflation control—*ceteris paribus*. For example, in 2014, in a low-inflation environment calling for monetary easing, the ECB launched TLTROs (*see* paragraph 215 above). Unlike the prior LTROs, TLTROs were "targeted" in the sense that longer-term bank refinancing at favorable rates was now linked to the volume of eligible bank loans to

590. *Cf.* U. Albertazzi, E. Assouan *et al.*, "The role of financial stability considerations in monetary policy and the interaction with macroprudential policy in the euro area", Report of the Eurosystem work stream on macroprudential policy, monetary policy and financial stability, *ECB Occasional Paper Series No 272*, September 2021 (revised June 2023), p. 31.

(non-financial) businesses and households. Bank investments in government bonds were excluded, in part because the aim was to incentivize bank lending to the real economy, but also in part because large bank holdings of (mostly domestic) government bonds had been a factor in the bank-sovereign "doom loop" of the 2008-2012 financial crisis. The ECB also specifically excluded housing loans to households from the pool of TLTRO-eligible bank loans[591] to avoid fueling the build-up of a bubble in residential real estate—or, as then ECB President Mario Draghi put it at the ECB's June 5, 2014 press briefing, to avoid TLTRO funds being spent *"on sectors that are already experiencing or are just coming out of a bubbly-ish situation"*.[592]

435. Yet, outside the *ceteris paribus* setting just discussed, potential or actual trade-offs between inflation control and financial stability concerns may and do arise, especially (but not only) when business or financial cycles are asynchronous (*see* paragraph 437(b) and (c) below):

(a) Suppose that a housing or equity bubble builds up in a period of subdued inflation well below 2 % that calls for monetary easing. This is not hard to imagine: asset bubbles have an inconvenient habit of prospering in periods of easier money and lower interest rates. Should the ECB then temporarily tighten monetary policy to cool off those rising asset prices, or at least pause or moderate further monetary easing action in order not to fuel further exuberance in asset pricing? At the risk of inflation drifting further below 2 % and requiring more forceful monetary action down the line to restore inflation to its target level? One could see that a number of variables would enter the equation, including notably the current distance of inflation from its medium-term 2 % target, the direction and strength of prevailing inflation dynamics, the degree and duration of pro-cyclical monetary tightening that would be needed to contain the asset bubble, the characteristics of the bubble and, critically, its potential systemic risk, *i.e.*, the probability that, if left unchecked, it could burst into a broader financial crisis that would exacerbate disinflationary pressures and might be even harder and costlier to deal with. When balancing these competing considerations, what flexibility does the ECB have for deviating from the optimal monetary policy path for inflation control in order to take preemptive action to contain financial instability risks? In the end, if some troubling financial imbalance is building up while inflation is (moderately) below the 2 % benchmark, couldn't it make good sense for the ECB to "lean against the wind"[593] for a while by (moderately) tightening

---

591. Article 1(3) of Decision 2014/541/EU of the European Central Bank of July 29, 2014 on measures related to targeted longer-term refinancing operations, *OJ* L258, August 29, 2014, p. 11, amended by Decision (EU) 2015/299 of February 10, 2015, *OJ* L53, February 25, 2015, p. 27, and Decision (EU) 2016/811 of April 28, 2016, *OJ* L132, May 21, 2016, p. 129.

592. *See* the transcript of the ECB's press conference of June 5, 2014, https://www.ecb.europa.eu/press/pressconf/2014/html/is140605.en.html, at p. 7. *Cf. also* U. Albertazzi, E. Assouan *et al.*, *supra*, pp. 54-55.

593. The expression "lean against the wind" is authentic monetary jargon. It is often used in discussions over whether the monetary authority should "lean" or "clean", *i.e.*, whether (or to

monetary policy so as to counter the build-up of a financial imbalance which, if not contained at a sufficiently early stage, may develop into a more serious financial stability issue that could complicate future monetary policy?

(b) Or consider instead a fact pattern in which credit is booming, housing and equity prices are surging and headline inflation is rising above the 2 % target. Could or should the ECB now moderate or delay monetary tightening in order to mitigate debt-servicing problems for overstretched borrowers and prevent asset bubbles from deflating too abruptly and causing financial instability? In the same order of ideas, at a time of higher inflation, could or should the ECB go slower on policy rate increases to avoid that higher government borrowing costs put the more highly-leveraged Member States into difficulty and trigger an excessive widening of sovereign bond spreads?

436. These are difficult judgment calls to make. Under a conservative legal reading of the ECB's monetary policy mandate and its primary focus on maintaining price stability, they raise questions as to the legitimacy and proportionality of ECB actions that bend the monetary policy path for preemptive action to contain risks to financial stability. Yet, when all is said and done, wouldn't we all want the ECB to have a reasonable measure of flexibility in making those calls? As a general proposition, it could make good economic sense for the ECB, within its medium-term policy horizon (and the bounds of its elasticity), to temporarily deviate from a monetary policy path focusing one-dimensionally on the inflation target, (i) in a low-inflation environment, by "leaning against the wind" for a while to deflate asset bubbles that present a serious risk of financial instability and disruptive effects down the line, or (ii) in a high-inflation environment, by adopting a pre-announced gradual approach to policy rate increases to mitigate debt service and refinancing issues.

437. In any event, aside from the policy and legal issues, it remains that preemptive action to contain potentially serious risks to financial stability presents operational difficulties and uncertainties:

(a) It may be difficult to identify and properly diagnose incipient financial imbalances that pose longer-term financial instability risks. By way of illustration, Table 6.1 below shows the evolution of key European and U.S. stock indexes between 2013 and 2023, broken down into three periods, *i.e.*, (i) the period from November 2013 (after the ECB had cut its deposit facility rate and main refinancing rate to 0% and 0.25%, respectively, *i.e.*, a level comparable to the FOMC's then target range of 0%-0.25% for the federal funds rate) to February 2020 (moments before the outbreak of COVID-19); (ii) the period from February 2020 to June 2022 (following the ECB's June 9, 2022 announcement of its plan to start a cycle of policy rate increases and a few months into the Ukraine conflict); and (iii) the period from June 2022 to March 2023

what extent) it should take preemptive action (tighten) to moderate bubbles in progress or rather clean up (loosen) when the bubble bursts.

(on the eve of the March 8, 2023 press release that triggered market anxiety over Silicon Valley Bank).

Table 6.1 European and U.S. Stock Indexes 2013-2023

	November 30/31, 2013-February 14, 2020	*February 14, 2020 -June 9, 2022*	*June 9, 2022-March 7, 2023*
Euro Stoxx 50	+ 24.43 %	–3.03 %	+ 14.88 %
DAX	+ 46.13 %	+ 3.30 %	+ 9.58 %
CAC 40	+ 41.56 %	+ 4.76 %	+ 15.42 %
Dow Jones Industrial	+ 82.44 %	+ 9.77 %	+ 1.80 %
S&P 500	+ 87.27 %	+ 18.86 %	–0.78 %
NASDAQ Composite	+ 178.01 %	+ 20.78 %	–1.90 %

Source: Own calculations from data at https://www.boerse-frankfurt.de/equities/indices.

What to make of this? In these data, can the ECB (or anyone else for that matter) confidently recognize emerging asset bubbles in the (generally less exuberant) euro area and distinguish "risky" bubbles from "benign" bubbles that pose no systemic risk and/or will gradually subside of their own accord? And the fog may thicken as one looks at fluctuations over shorter time intervals.

(b) Financial cycles tend to stretch over much longer periods than any plausible definition of the medium-term horizon of monetary policy. Their peak-to-peak length may vary between eight years and as many as 20 years and the average trough-to-peak build-up time between five and seven years.[594] And leaning-against-the-wind monetary policy is unlikely to be sustainable over any significant period of time.
(c) Financial cycles are oftentimes asynchronous and of varying length across euro area Member States and among market segments. This tends to make one-size-fits-all monetary policy too blunt an instrument to effectively address financial imbalances. It confirms that more targeted macroprudential policies should be first in line to counteract country-specific or sector-specific financial imbalances.
(d) Such (limited) empirical analysis as has been done on the matter suggests that the costs of monetary policy leaning, in terms of deviation of inflation from target and in terms of output/employment, generally outweigh the benefits in

594. *See* U. Albertazzi, E. Assouan *et al.*, *supra*, pp. 77 and 80.

terms of financial stabilization.[595] This again suggests that, if the ECB feels compelled by circumstances to lean against the wind nonetheless, it would be best to do so only for a limited time span so as not to de-anchor inflation expectations, and only when inflation is not too far off-target.

438. In the explanatory memorandum regarding its 2021 monetary policy strategy review, the ECB confirmed that macroprudential (and microprudential) policies should be the first line of defense against the build-up of financial instability risks.[596] It also acknowledged that financial stability considerations should be taken into account in monetary policy analysis in view of price stability risks generated by financial crises, but that *"it is important to avoid the misperception that monetary policy is responsible for guaranteeing financial stability"*.[597] In particular, the ECB noted that it *"does not conduct systematic policies of either "leaning against the wind" (whereby monetary policy is systematically tightened when systemic risk builds up) or of "cleaning" (whereby monetary policy is systematically loosened when systemic risk materialises)"*. Instead, it follows a flexible approach whereby *"[a]ny monetary policy reaction to financial stability concerns will depend on prevailing circumstances and will be guided by the implications for medium-term price stability"*.[598] In the same document, the ECB also indicated that its monetary and financial analysis now includes *"a more systematic evaluation of the longer-term build-up of financial vulnerabilities and imbalances and their possible implications for the tail risks to output and inflation"*,[599] and that the interaction between monetary policy and financial stability is considered at the monetary policy meetings of its Governing Council *"drawing on the Financial Stability Review and other relevant material"*.[600]

e To Sum Up

439. To sum up these thoughts on the relationship between monetary policy and financial stability:

(a) The Treaty itself does not expressly confer upon the ESCB any lead responsibility for guarding the stability of the financial system. It requires the ESCB to *"contribute"* to the smooth conduct of policies pursued *"by the competent authorities"* in the interest of the stability of the financial system (Article

595. *Ibid.*, pp. 82-83. *See also, e.g.*, L.E.O. Svensson, "Cost-Benefit Analysis of Leaning Against the Wind: Are Costs Larger Also with Less Effective Macroprudential Policy?", *IMF Working Paper No 16/3*, January 2016, 74 pp.
596. ECB, *An overview of the ECB's monetary policy strategy*, July 2021, p. 12.
597. *Ibid.*
598. *Ibid.*
599. *Ibid.*, p. 14.
600. *Ibid.*, p. 15. The subject is specifically addressed (at least) twice a year at the Governing Council's monetary policy meetings following release of the ECB's bi-annual *Financial Stability Review* in May and November.

127(5) TFEU) and contemplates that *"specific tasks"* may be assigned to the ECB in the area of prudential supervision of financial institutions (Article 127(6) TFEU) (as has happened under the Single Supervisory Mechanism). But in the ECB's *modus operandi*, self-standing actions to safeguard financial stability (other than under its banking supervisory tasks) have mostly been subsumed under its monetary policy mandate by the need to preserve the proper functioning of the monetary policy transmission mechanism.

(b) Since the 2008-2012 financial crisis, financial stability concerns have appeared more prominently on the ECB's radar screen, and there is broad consensus that the ECB should be attentive to them.

(c) Attention to financial stability does not necessarily cause significant frictions or trade-offs with the primary price stability objective of monetary policy. It is uncontroversial that, in the design and conduct of monetary policy actions aimed at the desired effect on inflation, the ECB should make reasonable efforts to avoid or minimize adverse side effects on financial stability. This does not alter the hierarchy of objectives. It is about mitigating side effects on financial stability insofar as this can be accommodated without detracting from inflation control requirements, at least in a medium-term perspective. It presupposes the absence of significant conflicts between price stability and financial stability concerns.

(d) It seems broadly accepted that, when the financial system is hit by severe disruptions of systemic proportions, the ECB should as "lender of last resort" stand ready to provide the necessary liquidity to keep the system afloat, irrespective of the monetary policy stance directed at inflation control. Again, a possible legal justification is that this task can be attached to the monetary policy mandate by the need to avoid dislocation of the monetary policy transmission mechanism. In crisis situations of this kind, the trade-off between price stability and financial stability is, in a sense, a false trade-off. But then the question is: how bad must things have become? If the fire is not yet ablaze but ominously smoldering, what is the central bank's scope for firefighting? Moral hazard ("Greenspan put") issues have to be considered.

(e) Difficult judgment calls arise in respect of emerging financial imbalances outside of a present or imminent threat of systemic crisis. In particular, in a **low-inflation** environment calling for monetary policy easing, a difficult question is in what circumstances and to what extent the ECB may deviate from the optimal monetary policy path to lift the inflation level by engaging in pro-cyclical monetary tightening, "leaning against the wind", to halt or slow down the build-up of some financial imbalance. Preemptive action of this kind is not unproblematic as it raises legal and cost-benefit issues. Clearly, macroprudential policies should be the first in line to prevent or remedy financial imbalances. As to monetary policy, a tentative and admittedly broad conclusion could be that "leaning against the wind" should be justified only if (i) the ECB reasonably believes that the growing financial imbalance, if left unchecked, poses a genuine threat to monetary policy transmission and price stability in the medium term, and (ii) "leaning" is as short-lived and limited as possible.

(f) Conversely, in an environment of **higher inflation**, the question may arise to what extent the ECB could or should temper or slow down policy rate increases in order to avoid that too steep an upward rate path could cause financial stability issues in one or more market segments, notably by abruptly deflating asset bubbles and/or giving rise to debt servicing or refinancing difficulties. Risks of this kind are likely to be higher upon switching to a monetary tightening cycle after an extended period of pronounced monetary easing, as occurred in 2022. In fact patterns of this kind, one would think that the better approach would ordinarily be one of a gradual and sufficiently clearly scripted rate increase path.

(g) In Chapter 5, we have discussed financial fragmentation risk which can be thought of as a particular species of financial instability risk, and indeed one to which the European currency union, as part of an incomplete EMU, is particularly vulnerable. We have seen how excessive widening of sovereign bond spreads may become caught in destabilizing market dynamics. Here again, trade-offs may arise in particular in a **higher-inflation** environment calling for monetary policy tightening. Monetary tightening may trigger or aggravate financial fragmentation, but monetary action to contain financial fragmentation, by moderating policy rate increases and/or conducting anti-fragmentation asset purchases, could fuel inflationary pressures. It is once more a balancing act. Depending on the strength of inflationary pressures, anti-fragmentation asset purchases may be the lesser evil, but one would think that in this case the ECB should ordinarily be expected, insofar as possible, to minimize interference with its monetary tightening stance by sterilizing the additional liquidity injected.

440. In light of the fact patterns just described, there broadly appears to be merit in the separation principle, subject to certain nuances. To put all this in a simplified matrix, it should generally be preferable:

(a) to reserve conventional monetary policy tools for inflation control and, in particular, to keep policy rates glued to the inflation target, but with some tolerance (i) in a low-inflation environment, for temporary and limited "leaning against the wind" to contain the build-up of financial imbalances that could present systemic risk, and (ii) in a high-inflation environment, for a measure of caution and gradualism in the upward rate path, especially after a long period of monetary easing, to mitigate risks to financial stability;

(b) to apply non-standard tools like special liquidity provision schemes and asset purchases (i) in a low-inflation environment, to support monetary easing when policy rates are constrained by the lower bound, and (ii) to contain financial instability risks but subject, in a high-inflation environment, to proper measures to minimize interference with the (then more restrictive) monetary policy stance, including, insofar as possible, sterilization of additional liquidity injected.

3 THE GREENING OF MONETARY POLICY

441. There is no escaping the ubiquitous subjects of climate change and the green transition. More and more central banks are considering how to integrate these dimensions in their monetary policy analysis and actions and are putting their toe in the water with early initiatives. So is the ECB.

a The Treaty Revisited

442. It is useful at the outset to circle back to the provisions of the Treaty that may be relevant to the question of how the ECB should factor in environmental considerations in the formulation and conduct of monetary policy. Unsurprisingly, these provisions set forth only high-level principles that, by and large, leave a broad margin for interpretation and inference.

443. ***First***, the Treaty mandates the ECB to define and conduct a single monetary policy for the euro area with the primary objective of maintaining price stability (Articles 119(2), 127(1) and (2), and 282(1) and (2) TFEU). Thus, to state the obvious, if climate-related developments pose a threat to price stability, or, by extension, to the proper functioning of the monetary policy transmission mechanism, in the euro area, it is incumbent on the ECB to factor this in when charting and implementing monetary policy.

444. ***Second***, subject (*"[w]ithout prejudice"*) to the objective of maintaining price stability, the ECB must *"support"* the general economic policies in the European Union with a view to contributing to the achievement of the Union's objectives (Articles 119(2), 127(1) and 282(2) TFEU), which include *"a high level of protection and improvement of the quality of the environment"* (Article 3(3) TEU). The ECB has read into these provisions a mission to *"support the green transition of the economy in line with the EU's climate neutrality objectives"*.[601] Here, the Treaty wording and context suggest that the ECB acts in a supporting role, in a play to be written and directed by the competent EU and national authorities. At first blush, it would seem that not much more can be inferred from this than that, in the design and conduct of its monetary policy actions, the ECB must have due regard to the climate-related policies of those competent authorities and seek to accommodate, or at least avoid inconsistencies with, these policies where it can reasonably do so without detracting from the monetary policy stance that is then required by the price stability objective.

601. *See* the ECB's press release of July 4, 2022, https://www.ecb.europa.eu/press/pr/date/2022/html/ecb.pr220704~4f48a72462.en.html.

445. ***Third***, as discussed in the previous section, the ECB must also *"contribute"* to the smooth conduct of policies pursued by the competent EU and national authorities in relation to banking supervision and the stability of the financial system (Article 127(5) TFEU). These include the policies pursued by the ECB's banking supervisory arm in the exercise of the specific tasks conferred on it under the Single Supervisory Mechanism (Article 127(6) TFEU). In the banking sector, prudential standards and supervision have a role to play in the area of climate change and the green transition in particular by ensuring that banks properly reflect climate risks in their loan pricing, bad-debt provisions and capital buffers. As to how monetary policy should interact with those policies, one would think that the reasoning outlined at the end of the preceding paragraph should apply *mutatis mutandis*.

446. ***Fourth***, environmental protection requirements must be *"integrated"* into the definition and implementation of EU policies and activities, *"in particular with a view to promoting sustainable development"* (Article 11 TFEU). This should also apply to the definition and conduct of monetary policy for the euro area, but again one may wonder whether, in substance, this would require much more than what was said in paragraph 444 above.

447. ***Fifth***, the ECB must act in accordance with *"the principle of an open market economy with free competition, favouring an efficient allocation of resources"* (Articles 119(2) and 127(1) TFEU). This is intriguing. We will consider shortly whether this should be read as imposing a form of market neutrality on monetary policy actions that would stand in the way of, or otherwise limit, differential treatment of "green" and "brown" assets (*see* paragraphs 465-471 below).

b Europe's Green Réveil

448. Since those Treaty provisions were committed to paper, mitigating climate change and ensuring an orderly and timely green transition have moved up high on the EU policy agenda. This has been the case notably since the European Commission's December 11, 2019 communication on the "European Green Deal".[602] In line with the Paris Agreement of December 12, 2015, the European Union has committed to achieve climate neutrality by 2050 by reducing EU-wide greenhouse gas emissions[603] to "net zero" by that year, with an intermediate target of reducing net emissions by at least 55%, compared to 1990 levels, by 2030. These targets are now codified in Regulation

602. Communication from the Commission to the European Parliament, the European Council, the Council, the European Economic and Social Committee and the Committee of the Regions, *The European Green Deal*, COM(2019) 640 final, December 11, 2019, https://eur-lex.europa.eu/resource.html?uri=cellar.b828d165-1c22-11ea-8c1f-01aa75ed71a1.0002.02/DOC_1&format=PDF.

603. This term refers to gases released in the earth's atmosphere that produce a greenhouse effect. Carbon dioxide (CO_2) makes up the vast majority of these gases. I will henceforth use the more familiar abbreviation CO_2 for convenience, although it is somewhat of a shortcut.

(EU) 2021/1119, the so-called "European Climate Law",[604] which requires the *"relevant"* EU institutions and the Member States to take the necessary measures to enable the collective achievement of the climate neutrality objective *"taking into account the importance of promoting both fairness and solidarity among Member States and cost-effectiveness in achieving this objective"*.[605] In its "Fit for 55" communication of July 14, 2021, the European Commission presented a package of EU legislative and policy actions, in the fiscal and regulatory sphere, for attaining the 2030 intermediate target.[606] Then, on May 18, 2022, the Commission submitted its "REPowerEU Plan" to accelerate the green transition, notably by increasing the 2030 target share for renewables from 40% to 45%, with a view, in particular, to reducing dependency on Russian fossil fuels.[607] There is and will be more, and it is certain that further plans and laws in this subject area, quite probably with catchy titles, will continue to flow from the pens of the EU institutions.

449. I should open a short parenthesis on a point regarding the European Climate Law that is of some relevance to our discussion. Articles 2(2), 4(1) and 5(1) and (3) of Regulation (EU) 2021/1119 are addressed to the *"relevant Union institutions"*, a term not otherwise defined, and the question arises whether the ECB is directly bound by these provisions as one of such *"relevant"* institutions. This was probably not specifically intended by the drafters of this regulation (if they considered the issue at all). The ECB is not an institution with relevant legislative or policy-making competence in this subject area. Also, from an institutional standpoint and under Article 130 TFEU, it would be questionable if EU secondary legislation could expand or modify the scope of the ECB's Treaty mandate when not specifically contemplated by the Treaty (as in Article 127(6) TFEU).[608]

604. Articles 2(1) and 4(1) of Regulation (EU) 2021/1119 of the European Parliament and of the Council of June 30, 2021 establishing the framework for achieving climate neutrality and amending Regulations (EC) No 401/2009 and (EU) 2018/1999 ("European Climate Law"), *OJ* L243, July 9, 2021, p. 1.

605. Article 2(2) of Regulation (EU) 2021/1119. This provision echoes point I.5 of the conclusions of the European Council meeting of December 12, 2019 which stated that *"[a]ll relevant EU legislation and policies need to be consistent with, and contribute to, the fulfilment of the climate neutrality objective while respecting a level playing field"* (https://consilium.europa.eu/media/41768/12-euro-final-conclusions-en.pdf, at p. 2).

606. Communication from the Commission to the European Parliament, the Council, the European Economic and Social Committee and the Committee of the Regions, *"Fit for 55": delivering the EU's 2030 Climate Target on the way to climate neutrality*, COM(2021) 550 final, July 14, 2021, https://eur-lex.europa.eu/legal-content/EN/TXT/PDF/?uri=CELEX:52021DC0550&from=EN. The proposed measures relate in particular to carbon pricing (strengthening and extending the scope of the Emissions Trading System ("ETS") and a carbon border adjustment mechanism), energy taxation, stricter CO_2 performance standards for cars, more sustainable aviation and maritime fuels, a new Social Climate Fund and enhancements to other budgetary funds.

607. Communication from the Commission to the European Parliament, the European Council, the Council, the European Economic and Social Committee and the Committee of Regions, *REPowerEU Plan*, COM(2022) 230 final, May 18, 2022, https://eur-lex.europa.eu/resource.html?uri=cellar:fc930f14-d7ae-11ec-a95f-01aa75ed71a.1-0001.02/DOC_1&format=PDF.

608. In the same sense, *see* F. Elderson, "The European Climate Law and the European Central Bank", Speech at the Lustrum Symposium of the Dutch Financial Law Association, Amsterdam, December 1, 2022, https://www. ecb.europa.eu/press/key/date/2022/html/ecb.sp221201_1~435e6ea81a.en.html, at pp. 2-3, and "Monetary policy in the climate and nature crises:

450. Achieving the European Union's climate objectives will necessitate a large-scale effort at "decarbonizing" the economy by shifting the energy mix from fossil fuels (oil, natural gas and coal) to renewable energy sources and by increasing energy efficiency across the board. This, in turn, will require substantial private and public investments, which, over the period from 2022 to 2030, have been estimated at an **additional** EUR 466 billion on average per year for Fit-for-55 needs[609] and a further EUR 33 billion on average per year (EUR 300 billion in total for the 2022-2030 period) for REPowerEU needs.[610] One would think that mobilizing and reallocating capital on this considerable scale will need to be accommodated by policy actions across a broad policy spectrum.

c Possible Implications for Monetary Policy

451. The green transition and the attendant environmental and fiscal policy actions will inevitably have implications for, and produce interactions with, monetary policy. What could these implications and interactions be, specifically in the euro area? The subject matter is still very much under study but set out below are some of the broader considerations to contextualize the relevant issues.

452. ***First***, as a starting point, the burden of mitigating climate change and ensuring an orderly green transition, with at its core the financing of the necessary investments and reforms, primarily falls on EU and national environmental and fiscal policies. Current thinking is that a critical line of action will be appropriate carbon pricing through an expanded and improved EU Emissions Trading System ("ETS") and properly calibrated national taxes that put an increased cost on CO_2 emissions. The resulting revenue could in some measure serve to cover increased public expenditures on (i) public investments in transmission and transport infrastructure (including such things as loading points for e-cars, to give an uncontroversial example); (ii) subsidies to redirect investment flows to low-carbon assets and stimulate green innovation and energy efficiency (properly framed by EU State aid rules); and (iii) climate-related social

preserving a '*Stabilitätskultur*'," Speech at the Bertelsmann Stiftung, Berlin, November 22, 2023, https://www.ecb.europa.eu/press/key/date/2023/html/ecb.sp231122~e12db02da3.en.html, at p. 1.

609. This amount has been computed by the ECB staff on the basis of Commission estimates and converted to 2022 prices. *See* F. Panetta, "Investing in Europe's future: The case for a rethink", Speech at Istituto per gli Studi di Politica Internazionale, Milan, November 11, 2022, https://www.ecb.europa.eu/press/key/date/2022/html/ecb.sp221111~9dfd501542.en.html, at p. 6, Chart 3. *Cf.* Communication from the Commission to the European Parliament, the European Council, the Council, the European Economic and Social Committee and the Committee of the Regions, *Towards a green, digital and resilient economy: our European Growth Model*, COM(2022) 83 final, March 2, 2022, p. 4, https://eur-lex.europe.eu/legal-content/EN/TXT/PDF/?uri=CELEX:52022DC0083.The estimated amount only partly includes investment needs for transport infrastructure and does not include investments to make existing assets more resilient to physical climate change, increased costs due to extreme weather events or investments for wider environmental protection objectives beyond climate.

610. *See* Commission staff working document, *Implementing the REPowerEU action plan: investment needs, hydrogen accelerator and achieving the bio-methane targets*, SWD(2022) 230 final, May 18, 2022, p. 15, https://eur-lex.europa.eu/legal-content/EN/TXT/PDF/?uri=CELEX:52022CS0230&from=EN.

transfers such as unemployment benefits in respect of job losses in carbon-intensive businesses and transfers to compensate higher energy costs for low-income households. In parallel, distortionary taxes and environmentally harmful subsidies will need to be withdrawn. On the regulatory side, a wide range of environmental standards need to be (re)set to improve climate performance and energy efficiency.

453. Aside from its inherent complexity and uncertainties, this process presents difficult policy challenges at several levels:

(a) An inherent political difficulty for policy actions in this subject area is the "tragedy of the horizon", *i.e.*, the difficulty of politically legitimizing visible short-term costs for less visible longer-term gains, including in terms of minimizing economic scarring effects and other ill effects caused by climate change. This time inconsistency problem may deprioritize and discourage green public expenditures and investments. It will likely be more acute for Member States whose fiscal policy space is limited by high government deficit and debt ratios. Then again, as Isabel Schnabel, member of the ECB's Executive Board, pointedly observed, the tragedy of the horizon is increasingly turning into *"a tragedy of having too little time to act"*.[611]
(b) Policy actions will necessitate a fairly high degree of coordination and alignment at the EU level, especially given their effects on intra-EU trade and investment flows and their cross-border spill-over effects more generally. This will in turn require broad support from Member States with different political and economic stakes in the matter. That suggests an elevated risk of suboptimal compromises and hesitant progress.
(c) The burden of climate change adjustment is spread unevenly among Member States given differences, in particular, in their existing energy mix and dependency on fossil fuel imports, additional green investment needs and their exposure to physical climate risks. Thus, estimates of additional private and public investment needs for the 2021-2030 period vary significantly across the euro area, ranging from around 7% of GDP annually for Portugal, to almost 3% for Belgium, close to 2% for Italy and below 1% for The Netherlands, Germany and Finland, with the share of public investments varying widely as well.[612]

454. These differences, in combination with those in the Member States' fiscal policy space, raise the question of whether government expenditures and debt in respect of green investments should in some measure be exempted from, or treated more

611. I. Schnabel, "From green neglect to green dominance?", Speech at the online seminar organized as part of the Cleveland Fed Conversations on Central Banking, March 3, 2021, https://ecb.europa.eu/press/key/date/2021/html/ecb.sp210303_1 ~ f3df48854e.en.html, at p. 1.

612. *See* M. Delgado-Téllez, M. Ferdinandusse & C. Nerlich, "Fiscal policies to mitigate climate change in the euro area", *ECB Economic Bulletin*, 2022, Issue 6, pp. 86 (Chart 4, panel b) and 87 (Chart 5).

leniently under, the fiscal rules of the Stability and Growth Pact—a question to which we will return in Chapter 8 (*see* paragraphs 608(d) and 609 below).

They also provide a compelling argument for more financing from EU budgetary resources. Thus, the (EU-wide) Recovery and Resilience Facility of NextGenerationEU (*see* paragraphs 645-650 below) has a strong focus on investments and reforms supporting the green transition: each Member State must dedicate at least 37% of the expenditures of its recovery and resilience plan to such measures.[613] By the end of summer 2023, estimated expenditures on climate-related measures in adopted plans added up to a total of EUR 204 billion or about 40% of plan allocations.[614] It is a significant step but still limited in size and duration in relation to overall needs. This observation has prompted several (semi-)official[615] and scholarly[616] ideas and proposals for additional and/or more permanent climate-related EU funding schemes.

455. ***Second***, it is highly uncertain how climate change and the transition to a low(er)-carbon economy will affect inflation and output/employment, and hence the proper monetary policy stance, in the euro area over the medium term and longer time intervals. This will critically depend on such factors as (i) the nature, timing and effectiveness of EU and national environmental and fiscal measures; (ii) technological developments; (iii) the sales strategy of, and possible market manipulation by, fossil fuel producers, especially OPEC+ and Russia; and (iv) random developments ("non-linearities") like extreme weather events, a possible collapse of the Thwaites ("Doomsday") Glacier and Russian politics. It is obviously very hard to reliably capture all of these and other relevant variables and their interactions in a comprehensive model. One is left with a tentative analysis of different scenarios under alternative assumptions that will inevitably produce a relatively wide range of outcomes.

613. *See* recital (23), Articles 16(2)(b)(i), 18(4)(e) and 19(3)(e), and Annex V, point 2.5, of Regulation (EU) 2021/241 of the European Parliament and of the Council of February 12, 2021 establishing the Recovery and Resilience Facility, *OJ* L57, February 18, 2021, p. 17, amended by Regulation (EU) 2023/435 of February 27, 2023, *OJ* L63, February 28, 2023, p. 1.

614. *See* Report from the Commission to the European Parliament and the Council on the implementation of the Recovery and Resilience Facility: Moving forward, COM(2023) 545 final, September 25, 2023, pp. 38-39, https://commission.europa.eu/system/files/2023-09/COM_2023_545_1_EN_0.pdf.

615. *See, e.g.*, Communication from the Commission to the European Parliament, the European Council, the Council, the European Economic and Social Committee and the Committee of the Regions, *A Green Deal Industrial Plan for the Net-Zero Age*, COM(2023) 62 final, February 1, 2023, pp. 10-13, https://eur-lex.europa.eu/legal-content/EN/TXT/PDF/?uri=CELEX:52023DC0062. In this communication, the Commission announced that, for the mid-term review of the 2021-2027 Multiannual Financial Framework as of the summer of 2023, it would propose a "European Sovereignty Fund" to support critical and emerging technologies relevant to the green transition and digital transformation. *Ibid.*, p. 13. Eventually, on June 20, 2023, the Commission proposed to establish a "Strategic Technologies for Europe Platform" (its acronym "STEP" may well have driven the rather bland choice of name for the initiative) to reinforce and leverage existing EU instruments for financially supporting investments in critical technologies. *See* the Commission's press release of June 20, 2023, https://ec.europa.eu/commission/presscorner/detail/en/ip_23_3364.

616. *See, e.g.*, L. Abraham, M. O'Connell & I. Arruga Oleaga, "The legal and institutional feasibility of an EU Climate and Energy Security Fund", *ECB Occasional Paper Series No 313*, March 2023, 39 pp.

456. Not long ago, the IMF stated the expectation that, with a properly balanced policy package, the green transition should not, by 2030, lead to a material increase of euro area inflation above the baseline.[617] In a similar vein, Fabio Panetta, a member of the ECB's Executive Board, has argued that appropriate public policies should be capable of containing inflationary pressures arising from the green transition and could even produce a *"divine coincidence"* between decarbonization and price stability.[618] In both cases, the assumption of timely, effective and properly aligned public policies reflects a certain degree of optimism. Also, the real-world price effects of the adjustments along the transition path are all but straightforward. It does not require exceptional imagination to expect that, in the earlier years of the process, the green transition may well produce net inflationary pressures, possibly in combination with subdued growth, as a result of, among other factors, higher carbon pricing, stricter environmental standards and higher demand for, and/or lower supply of, inputs used in green technologies (including such critical minerals as copper, nickel, cobalt and lithium). Concomitantly, volatility and episodically high levels of fossil fuel prices in an initial phase might scramble inflation expectations. Furthermore, monetary tightening in response to higher inflation, as occurred at a critical time in 2022-2023, may delay or discourage the necessary green investments by increasing their cost of financing and bleakening their risk-return profile. More generally, the shifts and unknowns surrounding climate change and the green transition may cause a heightened sense of uncertainty in businesses and households, weighing on investment and consumption. In any event, it seems likely that the uncertainties associated with green transition dynamics and physical climate events will require even more flexibility in monetary policy and subject it to a greater margin of error.

457. Surely, there could be no forgiveness in this earthly life for failing to write something about the potential impact of climate change on the natural rate of interest (r*) (*see* paragraphs 188-195 above). Although, unsurprisingly, economic literature is not unanimous on the subject, the majority sentiment seems to be that eventually, climate change is likely to have a net dampening effect on r*.[619] If so, this may reduce a central bank's policy space for providing monetary accommodation by lowering policy rates. Still, the net effect could go the other way, especially in an initial phase.

458. ***Third***, as said, the green transition involves a large-scale reallocation of capital—equity and debt—toward renewable energy sources and green technologies, including already between now and 2030 (*see* paragraph 450 above). This involves both private and public investments in substantial amounts. Given the size of private

617. IMF, *World Economic Outlook: Countering the Cost-of-Living Crisis*, October 2022, p. 80, Figure 3.4, panel 4.
618. F. Panetta, "Greener and cheaper: could the transition away from fossil fuels generate a divine coincidence?", Speech at the Italian Banking Association, Rome, November 16, 2022, https://www.ecb.europa.eu/press/key/date/2022/html/ecb.sp221116~c1d5160785.en.html, especially at pp. 7 and 9-11.
619. *See* F.P. Mongelli, W. Pointner & J.W. van den End, "The effects of climate change on the natural rate of interest: a critical survey", *ECB Working Paper Series No 2744*, November 2022, especially pp. 5-6 and 21-26. *Cf. also* F. Elderson, "Monetary policy in the climate and nature crises: preserving a *'Stabilitätskultur'*", at p. 2.

investments needed and the relatively limited time span for their roll-out, the shift of private capital will require policy support in various forms, including such measures as (i) fiscal incentives and State subsidies; (ii) climate-related disclosure standards to enable the financial markets (and the rating agencies) to properly (re)price climate performance and risks; and (iii) prudential rules to ensure that banks adequately reflect climate risks in their lending standards, bad-debt provisions and capital buffers. Again, EU and national policies in the spheres of State aid, taxation, securities regulation and prudential standards stand first in line to support that reallocation of private capital and keep this process orderly. But the question is whether and how monetary policy should accommodate the reallocation of capital from fossil fuels and "brown" production processes to renewable energy sources and "green" technologies. This is the issue that we will consider in subsections d. and e. below.

d The Proper Role of Monetary Policy

459. The ECB's monetary policy mandate is essentially determined by the primary objective of maintaining price stability (Articles 119(2), 127(1) and 282(2) TFEU). As a theoretical proposition, if particular climate-related developments demonstrably pose a significant threat to price stability in the near to medium term, the use of monetary policy tools to address this risk should, in principle, fall within the ECB's monetary policy mandate. Under the ECB's broad interpretation of this mandate, this would likewise be the case when climate-related developments distort the proper functioning of the monetary policy transmission mechanism in one or several of its channels. One could even argue that the ECB should be able to take anticipatory or preemptive action to prevent dysfunctionalities of that kind from developing into full-fledged disruptions and causing greater harm to price stability down the line. The question then is: what, in practical terms and in terms of verifiable criteria, are the boundaries of this abstract and potentially broad reasoning?

460. Climate-related concerns also come into play in the ECB's additional mission to *"support"*, but without prejudice to its price stability objective, the general economic policies in the European Union with a view to contributing to the achievement of the Union's objectives (Articles 119(2), 127(1) and 282(2) TFEU), which include *"a high level of protection and improvement of the quality of the environment"* (Article 3(3) TEU). Accordingly, any climate-related action of the ECB on this basis is subject to a dual limitation, *i.e.*, (i) it may not be inconsistent with the proper pursuit of the price stability objective, and (ii) the ECB can only act in support of, and in line with, climate-related policies set by the competent authorities—as a "policy taker", not a "policy maker".

461. As a matter of principle, maintaining price stability is the controlling objective of monetary policy and climate-related concerns that clearly conflict with that objective must yield in the conduct of monetary policy. Thus, as a rule, when inflation rises well above the 2% target for longer than a brief interval, the ECB should tighten monetary policy, even if this has the effect of raising financing costs for green investments.

The medium-term horizon which the ECB has given itself for the pursuit of its 2 % inflation target may offer a modicum of flexibility—but probably not a whole lot in relation to climate change. There is a certain "tragedy of the horizon" here too insofar as the implementation of the green transition in terms of planning and investments will ordinarily stretch over a longer time span, while monetary policy actions are bound by a medium-term horizon and vary over the business cycle.

462. Absent any (clear) conflict or trade-off with its price stability mandate, the ECB could and should calibrate its monetary policy actions to accommodate climate policy objectives or at least to avoid or minimize adverse interferences with these objectives, insofar as reasonably possible without harming the effectiveness of monetary policy as it is directed at controlling inflation over a medium-term horizon.

Not long ago, Frank Elderson, a member of the ECB's Executive Board, summed it up in the following terms:

> *"To put this in less legalistic and more pragmatic terms: whenever we have a choice between two instruments—or calibrations of instruments—that are equally conducive to price stability, we choose the one that is most supportive of the EU's general economic policies, including the climate neutrality objective".*[620]

Accordingly, there should, for example, be no problem in expanding the pool of eligible assets under the collateral framework to include green(er) assets.[621] As we will see, however, upgrading the collateral status of green assets by lowering standard valuation haircuts, or excluding or limiting collateral eligibility of brown assets, on environmental policy grounds (rather than as a matter of risk management on the basis of differences in intrinsic risk characteristics of the assets) may be more problematic under a market neutrality concept (*see* paragraphs 466-467 below).

Likewise, when low inflation calls for monetary easing and the already low level of policy rates causes the ECB to proceed to asset purchases (quantitative easing), including and even overweighting green(er) bonds in the desirable volume of asset purchases (or reinvestments) may be fine—subject again to possible market neutrality concerns (*see* paragraphs 468-469 below).

463. Questions arise in the inevitable gray areas between those general principles, where the ECB may be seen as compromising to some degree on the desirable scope, intensity or timing of monetary policy actions for the purpose of inflation control in order to accommodate climate-related concerns. For example, when its overall monetary policy stance is restrictive in response to inflationary pressures, could the ECB in

620. F. Elderson, "Policymakers as policy takers – accounting for climate-related and environmental factors in banking supervision and monetary policy", Speech at the Peterson Institute for International Economics, Washington, April 21, 2023, https://www.ecb.europa.eu/press/key/date/2023/html/ecb.sp230421~489cd977e0.en.html, at p. 4.

621. For example, on September 22, 2020, the ECB announced that, as of January 1, 2021, sustainability-linked bonds (*i.e.*, bonds with coupons linked to certain sustainability performance standards) become eligible as collateral for central bank credit operations and, subject to other program-specific eligibility criteria, for asset purchases under APP and PEPP. *See* the ECB's press release of September 22, 2020, https://www.ecb.europa.eu/press/pr/date/2020/html/ecb.pr200922~482e4a5a90.en.html.

its liquidity provision to banks nevertheless charge a preferential (*i.e.*, lower) rate on amounts corresponding to onward green loans made by the banks, so as to soften the impact of that monetary tightening on financing costs for green investments? Aside from raising questions of market neutrality, this would seem borderline under a strict reading of the ECB's monetary policy mandate. But the ECB is somewhat at an advantage in gray zones, in that it is ordinarily difficult for it to be caught on a "manifest error of assessment", which, by and large, is the judicial standard applied by the European Court of Justice in reviewing the conduct of monetary policy (*see* paragraphs 510 *et seq.* below).

464. As said, the burden of adjustment to climate change is spread unevenly among euro area Member States due, among other factors, to differences in their existing energy mix, their degree of dependency on fossil fuel imports and their geographic exposure to the physical risks of climate change. Thus, as to this last factor, it is believed that, in an initial phase, Mediterranean countries are more exposed to physical climate risks (extreme weather events like droughts, storms and floods), with possible damages being several times larger than in Northern Europe.[622] The different burden of adjustment is reflected in significant country differences in the additional private and public investments needed over the coming years for improving resilience against climate risks and for the green transition (*see* paragraph 453(c) above) and will likely translate into further differences in public spending. This lack of symmetry across the euro area, in combination with differences in existing government deficit and debt positions, may well increase financial fragmentation risk and hence the probability of central bank anti-fragmentation interventions.

e Market Neutrality

465. Under Articles 119(2) and 127(1) TFEU, the ECB must act in accordance with *"the principle of an open market economy with free competition, favouring an efficient allocation of resources"*. As these Treaty provisions are formulated, the ECB must do so both in the exercise of its price stability mandate and when acting in support of the general economic policies in the Union with a view to contributing, *inter alia*, to the objectives of environmental protection and improvement. But what could this mean more specifically? One question here is whether those Treaty provisions should be read to imply some binding "market neutrality" requirement, in terms of non-interference with the free market price discovery and resource allocation mechanism, and, if so, how this should be defined in operational terms. Another question is how binding this requirement would be in relation to the ECB's concurrent duty under Article 11 TFEU to integrate environmental protection requirements in the definition and conduct of monetary policy. Which of those two requirements weighs more heavily in case of conflict? Let us consider, by way of illustration, how they may come into play in the

622. *See* F. Drudi, C. Holthausen *et al.*, "Climate change and monetary policy in the euro area", Report of the Eurosystem workstream on climate change, *ECB Occasional Paper Series No 271*, September 2021, pp. 27 and 117.

ECB's collateral policy and in its asset purchases (including reinvestments) under such monetary policy programs as APP and PEPP.

466. A word on the ECB's **collateral policy** first. A core monetary policy activity consists of providing liquidity to banks by way of credit operations which, under Article 18.1 of Protocol No 4, must be secured by *"adequate collateral"*. Collateral policy, in terms of defining eligible assets and their valuation, has traditionally been viewed essentially as a risk management function aimed at ensuring adequate coverage of financial risks related to fluctuations in the market value of the assets, the credit risk (risk of default) of their issuers, and the time needed for the monetization of the assets.[623] On occasion, risk management considerations have yielded in some measure to monetary policy needs. Thus, at the outbreak of COVID-19, the ECB adopted a package of temporary collateral easing measures (including by relaxing eligibility conditions and reducing valuation haircuts by a linear 20%) to ensure sufficient availability of collateral for access to the central bank refinancing window and counter the tightening of financing conditions across the euro area[624] (*see* paragraph 236 above).

The ECB's policies on collateral eligibility and haircuts could influence decisions by banks to hold certain financial assets more than others and, in this manner, affect the market pricing of these assets. Insofar as those policies would be based on considerations other than the intrinsic risk characteristics of the assets—in particular insofar as they would reflect climate-related policy choices to favor green assets and/or disfavor brown assets—, they would provide non-market incentives or disincentives for banks to hold these assets and may raise questions under a common sense conception of market neutrality. But, as said, it appears that, traditionally, the ECB has viewed collateral policy mostly as a matter of risk management based on relevant risk characteristics of the assets.[625]

467. As one of the steps which it announced on July 4, 2022 *"to incorporate climate change in its monetary policy operations"*, the ECB indicated that it would, as of 2022, consider climate change risks when reviewing haircuts applied to corporate bonds used as collateral, and that it expects to introduce, before the end of 2024, limits to the share of eligible securities issued by (non-financial) companies with large CO_2 footprint (*see* paragraph 475 below). These measures are said to be aimed at reducing climate-related financial risks in Eurosystem credit operations.

Of course, climate-related risks may affect the value and risk profile of financial assets to varying degrees. Yet, as it is, the ECB's collateral framework is based on the

623. For an overview of the ECB's methodology for calibrating haircuts, *see* M. Adler, G. Camba-Méndez *et al.*, "The valuation haircuts applied to eligible marketable assets for ECB credit operations", *ECB Occasional Paper Series No 312*, March 2023, pp. 12-24.

624. *See* the ECB's press release of April 7, 2020, https://www.ecb.europa.eu/press/pr/date/2020/html/ecb. pr200407~2472a8ccda.en.html. *See also* the ECB's press release of April 22, 2020 on "grandfathering" the eligibility of assets subject to rating downgrades, https://www.ecb.europa.eu/press/pr/date/2020/html/ecb.pr200422_1~95e0f62a2b.en.html.

625. In this respect, the ECB has followed a residual risk equivalence approach in which haircuts are set so as to broadly equalize the expected loss in an adverse scenario across asset classes. *See* M. Adler, G. Camba-Méndez *et al.*, *supra*, pp. 5 and 11.

market prices of the assets, to which various markdowns and haircuts are then applied to properly reflect the relevant financial risks from the standpoint of the collateral holder (and with the possibility of mark-to-market adjustments and margin calls). One would assume that climate-related risks would already in good part be priced into market values and captured by haircut methodology. Under a strict notion of market neutrality, any incremental markdowns, haircuts or other limitations for climate-related risks would seem warranted only insofar as needed to correct some failure of market pricing or haircut methodology to fully capture such risks. An assumption underlying such incremental corrections would be that the ECB knows better than the markets which, given the still limited empirical evidence on the correlation between climate-related and financial risks, is not an obvious proposition. But any additional markdowns or haircuts going beyond risk management corrections of this kind, whether or not expressly in the pursuit of an environmental agenda, may raise an issue of market neutrality—and, more mundanely, of double-counting of risks.[626] On December 20, 2022, however, the ECB announced, as part of the outcome of a periodic review of its collateral framework, that its haircut schedule appears to offer adequate protection for climate-related financial risks, without the need for additional adjustments (*see* paragraph 475 below).

468. Let us now briefly consider the Eurosystem's **asset purchases** under monetary policy programs from the vantage point of market neutrality—a perspective which tilts our focus to purchases of private-sector securities. The discussion is presently largely hypothetical since, among existing monetary policy purchase programs, (i) OMT is still dormant and exclusively concerns public-sector securities; (ii) APP became limited to reinvestments as of July 2022 and is now in run-off since July 2023; (iii) PEPP has only a modest component of private-sector securities and has been limited to reinvestments since April 2022, with reinvestments now expected to be phased down in the second half of 2024 and discontinued at the end of this year; and (iv) TPI had not yet been activated at the time of writing and is focused on public-sector securities. But there is merit in hypothetical discussions too.

One would think that at least for purchases of corporate debt securities a plain-vanilla market-neutral approach would be for central banks to purchase bonds simply in proportion to the volume or market value of outstanding bonds. This approach appears to have broadly guided the Eurosystem's purchases of private-sector securities under APP and PEPP until 2021 (subject to applicable eligibility criteria). One recent study found that this has caused the CSPP segment of the APP portfolio to contain a relatively large proportion of bonds issued by companies in the manufacturing, utility, automobile and transportation sectors which tend to be the more CO_2-intensive sectors.[627] In other words, that classical allocation key has *de facto* tilted the Eurosystem's CSPP portfolio toward brown(er) rather than green(er) corporate bonds. This should not entirely be surprising insofar as companies in those sectors tend

626. *Ibid.*, p. 30.
627. *See* M. Papoutsi, M. Piazzesi & M. Schneider, "How unconventional is green monetary policy?", March 30,. 2022, pp. 7-12, https://web.stanford.edu/~piazzesi/How_unconventional_is_green_monetary_policy.pdf.

to be capital-intensive, oftentimes are more leveraged (in part on the strength of higher levels of tangible fixed assets that can serve as collateral), and, as a result, have been relatively overrepresented in the European bond landscape. This particular market feature arguably hampers an optimal allocation of resources, at least from the vantage point of the green transition. Yet, does this reflect some market failure or imperfection that warrants central bank purchases of a higher than proportional share of green(er) securities? If bond markets (and rating agencies) inadequately price the higher climate-related risks of issuers with larger CO_2 footprint (higher and more volatile energy costs, increased costs associated with stricter environmental standards, stranded assets, *etc.*), this could properly be characterized as a market imperfection. But even if this were the case, the question would then be whether this should not in the first instance be remedied by proper market disclosure standards (and perhaps appropriate issue or issuer labels) rather than by central banks purchasing a lower proportion of brown(er) securities, and a higher proportion of green(er) securities, in relation to market capitalization.

469. Still, when the ECB and other Eurosystem central banks do engage in asset purchases for monetary policy purposes, to what extent could they then favor or disfavor securities on climate-related grounds, by overweighting securities serving to finance green investments and underweighting those for financing brown investments or, more broadly, by underweighting those of issuers with larger CO_2 footprint or poor climate performance? One could see a reasoning along the following lines:

(a) In terms of consistency with the ECB's monetary policy mandate, portfolio choices of that kind should be fine so long as they are neutral to the desired monetary policy outcome for price stability (inflation control). One could expect that this first test should not ordinarily present significant problems, at least so long as such portfolio choices do not affect the overall volume of purchases as determined on monetary policy grounds.

(b) As concerns the market neutrality test derived from the open market economy principle, those portfolio choices should not be problematic either insofar as they reflect risk management decisions based on the intrinsic risk characteristics of the securities. One could not reasonably deny central banks the possibility to apply risk management standards when purchasing assets in the conduct of monetary policy (unless the relevant monetary policy purpose requires otherwise, as in the purchase of higher-risk government bonds for anti-fragmentation purposes).

(c) The harder question is whether a market neutrality requirement would stand in the way of favoring green(er) over brown(er) securities on climate policy grounds beyond risk management considerations. As said, the ECB considers it part of its secondary mission of supporting the general economic policies in the Union that it should support the green transition in line with the Union's climate neutrality objectives (*see* paragraph 444 above). Yet, as Articles 119(2) and 127(1) TFEU are worded, the open market economy principle from which the market neutrality requirement is derived, applies also when the ECB is acting under its secondary mission.

The question then becomes how this principle should properly be understood, and how it should be balanced against the general provisions of Article 11 TFEU and the European Climate Law. Article 11 TFEU calls, in general terms, for environmental protection requirements to be integrated into the definition and implementation of the Union's policies and activities. The European Climate Law requires *"relevant"* EU institutions to take the necessary measures to enable the achievement of the climate neutrality objective (*see* paragraph 448 above). From a strictly legal standpoint, one would be inclined to think that the open market economy principle, which the Treaty states specifically in respect of the ECB's mandate, would as *lex specialis* prevail over the general principle stated in Article 11 TFEU. It should also prevail over secondary legislation like the European Climate Law, even if the ECB were deemed to be a *"relevant"* EU institution for these purposes which, as said, is doubtful (*see* paragraph 449 above).

470. In EU primary law, the open market economy principle is a broad concept, without any explicit reference to market neutrality, a notion that as such is absent from the Treaty. Also, the added wording in Article 127(1) TFEU—*"favouring an efficient allocation of resources"*—should offer some defense against an interpretation equating the open market economy principle with a narrow variant of market neutrality. It should allow some scope for a plausible argument to the effect that, in the design of its monetary policy actions, the ECB should be able to address market imperfections that hamper efficient resource allocation, at least so long as this does not conflict with the monetary policy stance directed at inflation control. One would expect the European Court of Justice to be sympathetic to such a reasoning.

Still, the ECB should tread cautiously in this area, as the ECB or at least some at the ECB appear to be aware. In another speech not very long ago, Isabel Schnabel had the following to say on the subject:

> *"In view of such market failures, it seems appropriate to replace the **market neutrality principle** by a **market efficiency principle**.*
>
> *Such a principle would explicitly recognise that a supposedly 'neutral' market allocation may be suboptimal in the presence of externalities. It would allow us to acknowledge that market failures may drive a wedge between market prices on the one hand and efficient asset values that internalise externalities on the other.*
>
> *Nevertheless, in line with the provisions of the Treaties, considering climate externalities under the market efficiency principle would need to be consistent with maintaining a functioning price discovery mechanism. Furthermore, monetary policy implementation in line with the market efficiency principle would need to remain without prejudice to our primary mandate of safeguarding price stability."*[628]

628. I. Schnabel, "From market neutrality to market efficiency", Speech at the ECB DG-Research Symposium "Climate change, financial markets and green growth", Frankfurt, June 14, 2021, https://www.ecb.europa.eu/press/key/date/2021/html/ecb.sp210614 ~ 162bd7c253.en.html, at p. 5.

471. Yet, there may be some wisdom in a market neutrality rule for central banking, *i.e.*, in the notion that, as a rule, central banks should not concern themselves or seek to interfere with the market allocation of resources. Central banks are not in the business of steering the market's resource allocation choices. This rule may be crumbling under the weight of contemporary public opinion that central banks should play an active role in addressing climate change. But central banks should, as always, hold firm in the face of market expectations and be prepared to resist political pressures for greater climate activism that could eventually detract from their primary focus on inflation control. Playing into expectations will fuel further expectations. Absent express and unequivocal primary law support for market neutrality, not much censorship is likely to come from the Court of Justice. It will essentially come down to a question of ECB self-censure.

f A More Activist ECB

472. In recent years, in addition to its efforts to reduce its own organizational CO_2 footprint, the ECB has become somewhat more "activist" in the field of climate change and the green transition. It now has a "climate agenda"[629] and has put in place various work streams notably to analyze and model the macroeconomic impact of climate change and mitigation policies on inflation and output, to assess climate-related financial risks for the Eurosystem balance sheet, to review options for monetary policy actions to support the green transition, to examine the potential role of central banks in scaling up green finance, to map climate risks for financial stability and appropriate macroprudential policy responses, and to integrate the assessment of climate-related exposures and risk management capabilities of banks into bank supervisory processes.[630]

473. As more specifically concerns monetary policy, on July 8, 2021, as part of its broader 2021 monetary policy strategy review, the ECB presented an "action plan" to progressively integrate climate change considerations in its monetary policy in a more systematic manner.[631] And on July 4, 2022, it announced certain further steps pursuant

629. *See ECB climate agenda 2022*, July 4, 2022, https://www.ecb.europa.eu/press/pr/date/2022/html/ecb. pr220704_annex ~ cb39c2dcbb.en.pdf. For an overview of the ECB's ongoing initiatives and plans regarding climate change and the green transition, reference is made to its web page on the subject at https://www.ecb.europa.eu/ecb/climate/html/index.en.html.
630. In January 2021, the ECB announced the establishment of a "climate change center" as an internal unit to steer and coordinate the various work streams on climate-related issues. *See* the ECB's press release of January 25, 2021, https://www.ecb.europa.eu/press/pr/date/2021/html/ecb.pr210125_1 ~ 3fc4ebb4c6.en.html.
631. *See* the ECB's press release of July 8, 2021 and the attached "road map", https://www.ecb.europa.eu/press/pr/date/2021/html/ecb.pr210708_1 ~ f104919225.en.html?form = MY015V.

to this action plan.[632] The ECB's climate-related actions thus far in the monetary policy sphere are summarized in the following paragraphs.[633]

474. ***First***, the ECB has stepped up its efforts at incorporating climate-related variables and data in its macroeconomic modeling and forecasting. This obviously makes eminent sense but it is a particularly difficult task, in view notably of the complex interactions and "non-linearities" in climate change and green transition dynamics and the limited availability of historic empirical data over sufficiently representative time periods.

475. ***Second***, with regard to its collateral framework for bank liquidity provision, the ECB announced on July 4, 2022, that (i) as of 2022, it assesses climate-related risks when reviewing haircuts applied to corporate bonds; (ii) before the end of 2024 (subject to technical prerequisites being in place and after prior test runs), it expects to limit the share of securities issued by companies with a large CO_2 footprint; and (iii) upon implementation of the Corporate Sustainability Reporting Directive ("CSRD"),[634] as rolled out over the coming years, it will only accept as collateral securities issued by companies complying with CSRD (in the case of companies and securities within the scope of CSRD). Ostensibly to avoid any suspicion of interference with monetary policy, the ECB clarified that these measures will *"ensure that ample collateral remains available, allowing monetary policy to continue to be implemented effectively"*.[635]

As to item (i), interestingly, the ECB announced on December 20, 2022, that, as part of its broader review of the risk control framework for credit operations, it had not so far found empirical evidence that pointed to the need for changes to its haircut schedule to capture climate-related financial risks not already covered by its current (updated) schedule.[636] This approach and conclusion are reassuring in light of the concern expressed earlier (*see* paragraph 467 above).

476. ***Third***, also on July 4, 2022, the ECB announced that it will *"gradually decarbonise"* the corporate bond holdings in the Eurosystem's monetary policy portfolios *"on a path aligned with the goals of the Paris Agreement"*.[637] This somewhat ornate expression effectively means that the Eurosystem will over time increase the portfolio weight of corporate bonds issued by companies with better climate performance, and consequently diminish the relative share of those issued by companies with poor climate performance, by tilting new purchases and reinvestments of bonds in its

632. *See* the ECB's press release of July 4, 2022, https://www.ecb.europa.eu/press/pr/date/2022/html/ecb.pr220704~4f48a72462.en.html.
633. For a more detailed discussion, *see* J. Aubrechtová, E. Heinle *et al.*, "Enhancing Climate Resilience of Monetary Policy Implementation in the Euro Area, *ECB Occasional Paper Series No 318*, June 2023, 39 pp.
634. Directive (EU) 2022/2464 of the European Parliament and of the Council of December 14, 2022 amending Regulation (EU) No 537/2014, Directive 2004/109/EC, Directive 2006/43/EC and Directive 2013/34/EU, as regards corporate sustainability reporting, *OJ* L322, December 16, 2022, p. 15.
635. *See* the ECB's press release of July 4, 2022.
636. *See* the ECB's press release of December 20, 2022, https://www.ecb.europa.eu/press/pr/date/2022/html/ecb.pr221220_1~ca6ca2cc09.en.html.
637. *See* the ECB's press release of July 4, 2022.

monetary policy portfolios toward issuers in the former category.[638] This portfolio rebalancing is based on the issuers' "climate scores", which are a composite of three sub-scores looking at past CO_2 emissions, objectives to reduce future CO_2 emissions and the quality of CO_2 disclosures.[639] This benchmarking is or was applied to all additional purchases and reinvestments of corporate bonds in the CSPP sub-program of APP and in PEPP since October 1, 2022. Again to avoid interference with the prevailing monetary policy stance, the ECB was careful to specify that *"[t]he overall volume of corporate bond purchases will continue to be determined solely by monetary policy considerations"*.[640]

This measure is presently of limited consequence since under APP (including CSPP), net purchases were discontinued at the end of June 2022 and reinvestments at the end of June 2023, and, under PEPP, net purchases were halted at the end of March 2022. Reinvestments in the PEPP portfolio are expected to continue until the end of 2024 (and at a reduced pace in the second half of 2024), but holdings of corporate bonds in this portfolio are relatively modest (about EUR 46 billion in book value at amortized cost at the end of November 2023). While PEPP offers reinvestment flexibility across asset classes, flow-back from maturing securities before the end of 2024 should be limited (given the longer maturities of the securities), and the ECB may want to maintain adequate firepower for anti-fragmentation reinvestments in government bonds (*see* paragraphs 367(b) and 368 above).

The ECB has committed to publish climate-related information on the Eurosystem's monetary and non-monetary securities portfolios once every year, and it did so for the first time in March 2023.[641]

477. This "decarbonization" approach has not formally been extended to the Eurosystem's much larger purchases and reinvestments of public-sector bonds under PSPP and PEPP. One likely reason is the lack of a reliable and agreed methodology for climate-scoring government bonds. Yet, the PSPP and PEPP portfolios contain a certain

638. *See* Decision (EU) 2022/1613 of the European Central Bank of September 9, 2022 amending Decision (EU) 2016/948 on the implementation of the corporate sector purchase programme, *OJ* L241, September 19, 2022, p. 13, and Decision (EU) 2024/190 of the European Central Bank of December 15, 2023 amending Decision (EU) 2016/948 on the implementation of the corporate sector purchase programme (not yet published in the *Official Journal* by December 24, 2023). *See also* the ECB's press release of September 19, 2022, https://www.ecb.europa.eu/press/pr/date/2022/html/ecb.pr220919 ~ fae53c59bd.en.html. The ECB decided on "stronger" tilting of this kind during the partial reinvestment phase under APP from March through June 2023 (before APP reinvestments were discontinued at the end of June 2023). *See* the ECB's press release of February 2, 2023, https://www.ecb.europa.eu/press/pr/date/2023/html/ecb.pr230202 ~ 1a4ecbe398.en.html.

639. Particulars of this climate scoring methodology are to be found in the dedicated FAQ segment on the ECB's website at https://www.ecb.europa.eu/mopo/implement/app/html/ecb.faq_cspp_climate_change.en.html.

640. *See* the ECB's press release of September 19, 2022.

641. *See* the ECB's press release of March 23, 2023, https://www.ecb.europa.eu/press/pr/date/2023/html/ecb.pr230323 ~ 05efc3cf49.en.html. The first report on the carbon footprint of the monetary portfolios (*Climate-related financial disclosures of the Eurosystem's corporate sector holdings for monetary policy purposes*, March 2023, 28 pp.) is published at https://www.ecb.europa.eu/pub/pdf/other/ecb.climate_related_financial_disclosures_eurosystem_corporate_sector_holdings_monetary_policy_purposes2023 ~ 9eae8df8d9.en.pdf.

amount of "green bonds" issued by public-sector entities. Interestingly, Frank Elderson has floated the idea to increase the weight of EU supranational green bonds at the expense of domestic government bonds when there is no clear monetary policy rationale for preferring the latter.[642]

478. Also, the ECB has not so far taken the step, in its TLTRO III program or some new targeted refinancing facility for banks, of offering preferential interest or other terms on bank refinancing linked to onward green loans by banks. Various calls have been made for such "green" TLTROs or other dual-rate formulas of bank refinancing, notably to incentivize bank lending for energy-saving housing renovations.[643] While it appears that an approach of that kind is not entirely off the table, there should be legal hesitations about whether such green refinancing at preferential terms can be reconciled with the ECB's monetary policy mandate in a high-inflation environment calling for monetary tightening or indeed with a narrow reading of the market neutrality principle (*see* paragraph 463 above).

4 SHRINKING THE EUROSYSTEM BALANCE SHEET

479. On December 15, 2022, the ECB announced that it would review its operational framework for steering short-term interest rates by the end of 2023, which, upon completion, would allow it to provide further information on the endpoint of the Eurosystem's *"balance sheet normalisation process"* (*see* paragraph 268 above). This timing will likely not be met and the review should stretch some time into 2024. No other official communications had been made about the content of this review by the time I put down my pen on December 24, 2023, but speeches given in the course of 2023 by Executive Board member Isabel Schnabel[644] and Chief Economist Philip Lane,[645] two authoritative voices in the subject area, provide useful clues.

480. The link with central bank balance sheet reduction is not fortuitous. A key concern is that the reduction ("normalization") of the Eurosystem balance sheet may at some point weaken the Eurosystem's capability to steer money market interest rates, and the question then is how, operationally, monetary control over short-term interest rates could most effectively be preserved.

As shown in Table 6.2 below, the Eurosystem balance sheet has been bloated by a large volume of monetary assets as a consequence of generous monetary easing in the

642. F. Elderson, "The European Climate Law and the European Central Bank", at p. 5.
643. *See, e.g.,* "R.I.P. TLTROs, long live green dual rates", Open letter to the European Central Bank's Governing Council, June 1, 2022, https://www.positivemoney.eu/wp-content/uploads/2022/06/Open-Letter-ECB-Green-TLTROs-June-2022.pdf.
644. *See* I. Schnabel, "Back to normal? Balance sheet size and interest rate control", Speech at an event organized by Columbia University and SGH Macro Advisors, New York, March 27, 2023, https://www.ecb.europa.eu/press/key/date/2023/html/ecb.sp230327_1~1fe4adb3a9b.en.html.
645. *See* Ph. Lane, "Central bank liquidity: a macroeconomic perspective", Speech at the ECB Conference on Money Markets, Frankfurt, November 9, 2023, https://www.ecb.europa.eu/press/key/date/2023/html/ecb.sp231109~fd9153a89f.en.html.

previous decade, which resulted in ample excess liquidity in the banking system and large central bank reserve holdings by commercial banks. That volume of monetary assets has begun to diminish as a result mostly of the (p)repayment of TLTRO III loans and should continue to decline now that the APP portfolio is in (passive) run-off (with reinvestments phased down as of March 2023 and fully discontinued as of July 2023) and the PEPP portfolio will likewise go in (passive) run-off as of the second half of 2024 (with reinvestments initially phased down and then discontinued altogether at the end of the year). The shrinking of the Eurosystem balance sheet, especially if it were to be accelerated, may at some point reduce liquidity close to or below bank liquidity needs and their demand for central bank reserves. This may cause volatility in money market rates and diminish central bank capability to steer them toward the deposit facility rate. The question is how best to avoid or minimize this partial loss of monetary control.

Table 6.2 Eurosystem Monetary Assets and Central Bank Reserves (Millions of Euros)

	December 31, 2021	*December 31, 2022*	*December 22, 2023*
Bank refinancing[(a)]	2,201,882	1,324,347	404,787
Monetary securities portfolio[(b)]	4,713,403	4,937,179	4,701,284
Total	6,915,285	6,261,526	5,106,071
% of total assets	80.74%	78.70%	74.00%
Central bank reserves[(c)]	4,293,938	3,998,889	3,649,649

Source: ECB, Annual report 2022, Annex C1, https://www.ecb.europa.eu/pub/pdf/annrep/ecb.ar2022~8ae51d163b.en.pdf, and Weekly consolidated financial statement of the Eurosystem as at December 22, 2023, https://www.ecb.europa.eu/press/pr/wfs/2023/html/ecb.fst231128.en.html.
Notes: [(a)] Liquidity provision to euro area commercial banks under the various monetary policy lending instruments (asset item 5). [(b)] Securities acquired under monetary policy asset purchase programs such as APP and PEPP (asset item 7.1). [(c)] Reserves (including minimum reserves) held by euro area commercial banks with Eurosystem central banks (notably on current accounts or in the deposit facility) (liability item 2).

481. Prior to the 2008-2012 financial crisis, the Eurosystem supplied a fixed volume of liquidity that more or less matched commercial bank demand, mostly through weekly auctions of seven-day funds on a fixed-allotment basis (*see* paragraph 199(b) above). In this manner, it managed to steer money market rates close to the main refinancing rate, in the middle of the band ("corridor") between the deposit facility rate and the marginal lending rate.

During and after the financial crisis, the Eurosystem switched regular bank refinancing operations (weekly MROs and three-month LTROs) to full-allotment modus, meaning in effect that the volume of liquidity supplied became fully demand-driven (*see* paragraph 206 above). As from 2014, the Eurosystem proceeded to three successive series of TLTROs and to large-scale asset purchases under APP and, as of 2020, PEPP (*see* paragraphs 215-217 and 237-240 above). These operations injected a substantial volume of liquidity into the system and left commercial banks with much larger reserve balances than they had previously held. This ample supply of liquidity effectively pushed money market rates toward the deposit facility rate, *i.e.*, the floor of the "corridor". It also reduced the volume of reserves intermediated via the interbank market,[646] and, with a large volume of liquidity held by non-bank intermediaries without access to the central banks' deposit facility, the short-term rate (€STR) at times traded below the deposit facility rate—the floor that became "leaking".[647] But, overall, the excess reserves in the system allowed the ECB to steer money market rates and more or less anchor them to the deposit facility rate.

482. In 2022-2023, the time came for reducing or "normalizing" the Eurosystem balance sheet. Surplus liquidity is now beginning to melt off as a result of the (p)repayment of TLTRO III loans and, to a lesser extent, the gradual (passive) run-off of the APP portfolio (and soon the PEPP portfolio). The question arises whether this process could be accelerated, notably by a more rapid reduction of the APP and PEPP portfolios, without unduly weakening monetary policy control over money market rates. This risk arises when surplus liquidity declines to a level close to bank liquidity needs, at which point bank liquidity demand may produce upward pressure on money market rates. It is uncertain when this point may be reached, essentially because of the lack of visibility on the extent of commercial bank demand for reserves. This demand is bound to be on an upward trajectory due to such factors as (i) the general increase in size of the banking system; (ii) bank regulatory developments, including the banks' need for high-quality liquid assets (HQLA) to comply with the liquidity coverage ratio (LCR) under Basel III; (iii) the relative shortage of "safe assets" (due in part to the fact that central bank purchases of government bonds reduced the "free float" of safe assets); (iv) a greater risk aversion in light of the elevated level of political and economic uncertainty; and, especially in the current environment of monetary tightening, (v) the risk of outflows of customer deposits to higher-yielding savings products.[648] But it is hard to predict the quantum of bank demand for reserves with a sufficient degree of confidence. This, presumably, would make it difficult to return to the pre-2008 system of auctioning off some fixed supply of bank reserves.

483. In light of the foregoing, there are various approaches that the Eurosystem could take toward ensuring adequate liquidity supply and maintaining an adequate measure of control over money market rates (*i.e.*, keeping them in the vicinity of the deposit facility rate), and each such approach comes with different implications for the volume of the Eurosystem's monetary asset portfolio and the scope for reducing it. One could, in the abstract, think of three broad strategies:

(a) One approach would be to continue to maintain a sizable stock of excess reserves in the system and hence to limit the further reduction of the existing monetary asset portfolio. Disadvantages of this approach include (i) the

646. *See* I. Schnabel, *supra*, p. 3 and slide 8.
647. *Ibid.*, p. 5 and slide 13.
648. *Ibid.*, p. 4, and Ph. Lane, *supra*, pp. 11-12.

uneven distribution of the corresponding reserves which tend to be more concentrated with a limited number of larger banks and in money centers (with the risk that liquidity shortages might still arise in other corners of the banking system);[649] (ii) certain distortions caused by large central bank holdings of government bonds (including the consequent interest rate exposure of central banks and the reduction of safe assets available in the market); and (iii) the fact that this approach goes against the desirability of shrinking the monetary asset portfolio so as to free up space for future anti-deflationary or anti-fragmentation asset purchases.

(b) An alternative approach would consist of ensuring an elastic supply of liquidity through fixed-rate full-allotment bank refinancing operations, while proceeding with the reduction of the monetary asset portfolio. This requires that banks find their way back to the central bank refinancing window. A possible disadvantage is the risk of undersupplying liquidity insofar as the sum of individual bank bids may fall short of collective bank liquidity needs.[650]

(c) As an intermediate option, approach (b) could be combined with maintaining some "structural" monetary asset portfolio that would be considerably smaller than in approach (a) and serve as a kind of liquidity buffer.

484. One would suspect that, in its review, the ECB will be inclined toward approach (b) or (c). Related more technical issues that appear to be (or to have been) under consideration include: (i) the possible narrowing of the spread (currently 50 basis points since September 2019) between the main refinancing rate and the deposit facility rate; (ii) a possible increase of the 1% minimum reserve requirement; and (iii) allowing certain non-bank financial intermediaries some form of access to the deposit facility (with items (ii) and (iii) now seeming less likely).

649. I. Schnabel, *supra*, p. 6 and slide 15.
650. *Ibid.*, p. 8.

CHAPTER 7

Central Bank Independence, Accountability and Judicial Control

485. We have reached the point where, in light of the narrative in previous chapters, we can take a closer look at certain institutional issues that are of special importance to the proper conduct of monetary policy in the European currency union, *i.e.*, the independence of the ECB and its accountability, and the appropriate measure of judicial control over the ECB's monetary policy actions.

1 CENTRAL BANK INDEPENDENCE AND ACCOUNTABILITY

486. In the later part of the twentieth century, at the time of the original design of EMU, a broad consensus had developed to the effect that the efficacy of inflation control is best served by entrusting monetary policy to an independent central bank shielded from the short-termism and public spending bias of politics. For Germany in particular, the ECB was to be an avatar of its trusted Bundesbank in the euroverse. Accordingly, the Treaty and its Protocol No 4 confer a high degree of institutional, operational and financial autonomy on the ECB. Looking at various indices of central bank independence, several studies have ranked the ECB at or near the top of the league in independence among G20 central banks, with higher scores than, notably, the Federal Reserve.[651]

a Independence from Politics

487. Article 130 TFEU[652] is the core provision ringfencing the ECB and the national central banks from EU and national politics: in the performance of their tasks, they may

651. *See* R. Dall'Orto Mas, B. Vonessen *et al.*, "The case for central bank independence: A review of key issues in the international debate", *ECB Occasional Paper Series No 248*, October 2020, p. 29, Table 2.
652. Article 130 TFEU is repeated in Article 7 of Protocol No 4 and restated in broader terms in Article 282(3) TFEU in respect of the ECB.

neither seek nor take instructions from EU institutions or agencies or from Member State governments, which in turn may not seek to influence the members of the decision-making bodies of the ECB or the national central banks. This provision is, in a sense, backed up by the monetary financing prohibition of Article 123(1) TFEU, under which the ECB and national central banks must refrain from extending any credit to, or directly subscribing to any debt securities issued by, an EU institution or a Member State's government sector. Article 123(1) TFEU takes one of the textbook subjects for political pressure and lobbying off the table. The autonomy of the ECB in particular is protected in several of its key aspects, as we will briefly review in the following paragraphs, especially with regard to the conduct of monetary policy.

488. ***First***, the Treaty confers and defines the monetary policy mandate and envelops it in a "bubble" of EU primary law, *i.e.*, the Treaty and its Protocol No 4. Thus, the Treaty itself mandates the ESCB—in fact, provisionally (so long as there are Member States that have not adopted the euro) in its reduced format of the Eurosystem, *i.e.*, the ECB together with the national central banks of the euro area Member States[653]—to define and conduct the single monetary policy for the euro area,[654] an exclusive EU competence,[655] with a primary focus on maintaining price stability.[656] It is an exclusive mandate. National authorities of the euro area Member States (other than their central banks) no longer have any competence in matters of monetary policy. But, in addition, even other EU institutions (other than the Court of Justice) by and large have no say in the matter. EU primary law allows other EU institutions to adopt secondary legislation or take other measures in the realm of monetary policy only in a limited number of matters that are mostly of lesser importance to the actual conduct of monetary policy proper.

489. Thus, in the monetary policy space, the Treaty comprehensively lists a number of specific matters for which EU secondary legislation may establish certain implementing rules for the relevant provisions of the Treaty or Protocol No 4 or on which they may amend Protocol No 4. By and large, these matters concern technical, organizational or procedural aspects rather than the substantive content of monetary policy, as shown in Table 7.1.

653. Reference is made to the transitional provisions set forth in Articles 139(2) and (3) and 141 TFEU and Articles 42 to 47 of Protocol No 4.

654. Articles 127(1) and (2) and 282(1) TFEU and Article 3.1 of Protocol No 4. Under Article 12.1 of Protocol No 4, the actual formulation of monetary policy falls to the Governing Council of the ECB, while the implementation of this policy is partly decentralized to the national central banks of the euro area Member States. *Cf. also* Articles 9.2 and 14.3 of Protocol No 4. On the decentralized implementation of monetary policy within the Eurosystem, *see, e.g.*, J. Langner, "ESCB/Eurosystem/National Central Banks", in *The EU Law of Economic and Monetary Union* (F. Amtenbrink & Chr. Herrmann eds.), Oxford University Press, 2020, pp. 396-401, especially pp. 400-401, §§15.18-15.20.

655. Articles 3(1)(c) and 119(2) TFEU.

656. Articles 119(2), 127(1) and 282(2) TFEU.

Table 7.1 Scope of EU Secondary Legislation in the Monetary Policy Space

	Council	*European Parliament and Council under Ordinary Legislative Procedure*	*European Council* [(c)]
Implementing Treaty provisions	Art. 125(2) (definitions for the application of Arts. 123-125); Art. 128(2) (denominations and technical specifications for euro coins); Art. 138 (common positions and unified representation in international forums); Art. 219 (exchange rate arrangements with third currencies)	Art. 133 (measures for the use of the euro)	
Implementing Protocol No 4 [(a)]	Art. 4(a) (limits and conditions for national authorities to consult the ECB on draft legislation); Art. 5.4 (persons subject to statistical reporting requirements); Art. 19.2 (basis for minimum reserves and maximum permissible ratios); Art.20.2 (scope of new operational methods of monetary control insofar as imposing obligations on third parties); Art. 28.1 (limits and conditions for ECB capital increases); Art. 29.2 (statistical data for the ECB capital subscription key);		

	Council	*European Parliament and Council under Ordinary Legislative Procedure*	*European Council* [c]
	Art. 30.4 (limits and conditions for further calls of foreign reserve assets); Art. 34.3 (limits and conditions for ECB fines)		
Amending Protocol No 4 [b]		Art. 5.1-5.3 (collection of statistical information); Art. 17 (accounts for financial intermediaries and collateral); Art. 18 (open market and credit operations); Art. 19.1 (minimum reserve requirements); Art. 22 (clearing and payment systems); Art. 23 (operations with third countries and international organizations); Art. 24 (administrative and staff operations); Art. 26 (financial accounts); Art. 32 (calculation and allocation of monetary income); Art. 33.1(a) (allocation of ECB net profit to general reserve fund); Art. 36 (staff)	Art. 10.2 (ECB Governing Council voting rules)

Notes: [a] Article 129(4) TFEU and Article 41 of Protocol No 4. The Council acts either on a proposal of the European Commission, after consulting the European Parliament and the ECB, or on a recommendation of the ECB, after consulting the European Parliament and the Commission.

Notes to Table 7.1 (cont.)

[b] Article 129(3) TFEU and Article 40.1 of Protocol No 4. Here, the European Parliament and the Council act either on a proposal of the Commission, after consulting the ECB, or on a recommendation of the ECB (adopted by unanimous decision of its Governing Council), after consulting the Commission.

[c] Article 40.2 of Protocol No 4. An amendment of Article 10.2 of Protocol No 4 requires a unanimous decision of the European Council, acting either on a unanimous recommendation of the ECB, after consulting the European Parliament and the Commission, or on a recommendation of the Commission, after consulting the European Parliament and the ECB. Such an amendment takes effect only upon approval by the Member States in accordance with their constitutional requirements.

490. But outside these circumscribed areas, EU secondary legislation could not alter or restrict the ECB's monetary policy mandate or prescribe binding rules for its conduct. For example, the Council could not set a numerical inflation target for the ECB to pursue, nor require it to favor green bonds in its asset purchases for monetary policy purposes or to link bank liquidity provision to green onward lending—unless, arguably, under the so-called "flexibility clause" of Article 352 TFEU. Of course, otherwise, the ECB generally remains subject to EU secondary legislation that does not concern monetary policy nor interfere with its independent conduct.[657]

491. The conferral of an (i) exclusive monetary policy mandate, (ii) by the Treaty itself, (iii) with a primary focus on price stability, (iv) ringfenced from political interference, and (v) in a legal bubble largely shielded from substantive requirements or restrictions under EU secondary legislation, are strong features of ECB independence in the conduct of monetary policy. But, as we have discussed in previous chapters, this has been diluted to some degree by (i) the Treaty's somewhat diffuse matrix of secondary objectives and constraints, including the ECB's duty to *"support"* economic policies, *"contribute to"* the conduct of policies for the stability of the financial system, and *"integrate"* environmental protection requirements; (ii) the prudential responsibilities conferred upon the ECB under the Single Supervisory Mechanism; (iii) the fact that, in the aftermath of the 2008-2012 financial crisis, inadequate national fiscal policies shifted a greater part of the burden of macroeconomic adjustment to monetary policy under circumstances that arguably required the ECB to go "lower for longer"; and (iv) smoldering financial fragmentation risks originating in sovereign debt markets that episodically prompted the ECB to announce or engage in geographically selective asset purchases. Each of these factors presents risks for central bank independence, because they may give rise to difficult policy trade-offs of the kind we have discussed in Chapters V and VI, and because they create expectations in financial markets, political circles and public opinion that may put pressure on the ECB to digress from the

657. *Cf.* CJEU, July 10, 2003, Case C-11/00, *Commission vs. ECB*, ECLI:EU:C:2003:395. In this case, the Court annulled an ECB decision that had set up separate internal procedures for fraud prevention and control distinct from the general system for EU institutions established by Regulation (EC) No 1073/1999 of the European Parliament and of the Council of May 25, 1999 concerning investigations conducted by the European Anti-Fraud Office (OLAF) (meanwhile replaced by Regulation (EU, Euratom) No 883/2013 of September 11, 2013). In particular, the Court rejected an ECB plea that this general system conflicts with ECB independence (§§130-145).

optimal monetary policy path for inflation control. "Mission creep" is always risky for the core mission. This is recognized, with regard to national central banks, in Article 14.4 of Protocol No 4 which allows the ECB's Governing Council, by a two-thirds majority of the votes cast, to oppose national central banks taking on additional functions that interfere with the objectives and tasks of the ESCB.

492. *Second*, EU primary law leaves the ECB a large measure of instrument independence to conduct monetary policy. Protocol No 4 contains an open-ended list of broadly-worded instruments that may be used, *i.e.*, (i) open-market and credit operations;[658] (ii) minimum reserve requirements for banks (subject to such rules as the Council may establish to define their basis and maximum permissible ratios);[659] and (iii) *"such other operational methods of monetary control"* as the ECB's Governing Council may itself approve by majority of two-thirds of the votes cast (subject to possible Council rules defining the scope of such methods if they impose obligations on third parties).[660] Also, the ECB has rule-making powers in matters of monetary policy.[661]

493. *Third*, EU primary law protects the personal independence of members of the decision-making bodies of the ECB, specifically the (six) members of its Executive Board and the other members of its Governing Council, *i.e.*, the governors of the national central banks of the euro area:

(a) Thus, the ECB's President and the (five) other members of its Executive Board are appointed by the European Council for a one-off fixed term of eight years.[662] They can be removed from office only if they no longer fulfill the conditions required for the performance of their duties or are found to have engaged in serious misconduct, and only by the European Court of Justice upon application of the ECB's Governing Council or Executive Board.[663] These provisions should reduce any inclination these officers may have to lend a sympathetic ear to political pleas or pressures for fear of removal from office or in the hope of re-appointment. Still, as the world turns, they might harbor ambitions for appointment to high political office after their term of office with the ECB, and one would imagine that their agreements with the ECB or the ECB's internal rules contain cool-off or other clauses restricting near-term post-ECB positions that require political support.

658. Article 18 of Protocol No 4.
659. Article 19 of Protocol No 4. The Council has set broad framework rules for minimum reserve requirements in Council Regulation (EC) No 2531/98 of November 23, 1998 concerning the application of minimum reserves by the European Central Bank, *OJ* L318, November 27, 1998, p. 1, amended by Council Regulation No (EC) 134/2002 of January 22, 2002, *OJ* L24, January 26, 2002, p. 1. Article 4 of this Regulation allows the ECB to set the minimum reserve requirement anywhere in a range of 0% to ... 10%, which is not particularly constraining.
660. Article 20 of Protocol No 4.
661. Article 132(1) TFEU and Article 34.1 of Protocol No 4. *Cf. also* Article 282(4) TFEU.
662. Article 283(2), second and third paragraphs, TFEU and Article 11.2, first and second paragraphs, of Protocol No 4.
663. Article 11.4 of Protocol No 4.

(b) In a similar vein, the statutes of national central banks must provide that their governors are appointed for a minimum term of five years.[664] These governors can likewise be removed only on the narrow grounds just mentioned, and the governor concerned or the ECB's Governing Council can appeal a decision to this effect before the European Court of Justice for violation of the Treaties or any rule of law relating to their application.[665] To my knowledge, the Court has so far been called upon once to adjudicate such a matter when it annulled a decision of the Anti-Corruption Office of Latvia suspending the governor of the Latvian central bank on charges of having accepted a bribe. The Court did so on the ground that Latvia had failed to adduce evidence establishing sufficient indications that the governor concerned had engaged in serious misconduct capable of justifying his removal from office.[666]

494. ***Fourth***, EU primary law ensures a substantial degree of organizational and financial independence of the ECB. The ECB is an EU institution established by the Treaty—not an EU agency that would be subject to the *Meroni* doctrine.[667] It has separate legal personality,[668] its own governing bodies, its own staff, and its own self-financed budget separate from the EU budget. We will take a closer look at relevant aspects of the ECB's financial autonomy in the next subsection (*see* paragraphs 497-500 below).

495. The above core elements of central bank independence are engraved in the stone tablets of the Treaty and its Protocol No 4. They cannot be reduced or altered without a Treaty amendment, which, even under the simplified procedure of Article 48(6) TEU, effectively requires the consent of all Member States (including those not participating in the currency union). Pursuant to Article 129(3) TFEU, certain more technical provisions of Protocol No 4 may be amended by the European Parliament and the Council, under the ordinary legislative procedure, but, by and large, these provisions do not go to the heart of central bank autonomy in the conduct of monetary policy (*see* paragraph 489, Table 7.1, above). In that sense, one could say that the core features of ECB independence have a higher degree of fixity than the (pre-1999) statutes of the national central banks of the future euro area—including the coveted statute of the Bundesbank—and those of most central banks outside of the euro area, which generally could be changed by the parliamentary majority of the day.

664. Article 14.2, first paragraph, of Protocol No 4.
665. Article 14.2, second paragraph, of Protocol No 4.
666. CJEU, February 26, 2019, Joined Cases C-202/18 and C-238/18, *Rimsevics and ECB vs. Latvia*, ECLI: EU:C:2019:139.
667. In broad outline, the *Meroni* doctrine stands in the way of delegating powers involving the exercise of significant policy discretion to institutions or agencies not established by the Treaties themselves. This doctrine is based on an early judgment of the European Court of Justice, *i.e.*, CJEU, June 13, 1958, Case C-10/56, *Meroni vs. High Authority*, ECLI:EU:C:1958:8. It has been clarified in the Court's later judgment in the short-selling case, *i.e.*, CJEU, January 22, 2014, C-270/12, *United Kingdom vs. Parliament and Council*, ECLI:EU:C:2014:18, §§41-55.
668. Article 282(3) TFEU and Article 9.1 of Protocol No 4.

496. The key features of ECB independence appear to command broad societal acceptance and do not seem to be the subject of significant controversy. While politicians and the media may criticize ECB policy actions (and seemingly do so with increasing frequency in recent years), direct challenges to the ECB's independence remain rare. In the United States, former President Donald Trump during his term of office not only sent numerous tweets calling for faster rate cuts by the Federal Reserve but also repeatedly threatened to remove the Chairman of the Federal Reserve and (unsuccessfully) nominated several close political allies and/or outspoken critics of the Federal Reserve (including a former economic adviser sympathetic to the gold standard) for seats on its Board.[669] Even aside from the bizarre aspects of such comportment, overt political interference of this kind has (so far) remained unthinkable in the euro area.

b Financial Autonomy

497. The ECB's financial resources consist of (i) the contributions to its capital made by the national central banks; (ii) the income generated by its activities; and (iii) its loss reserves—but to the exclusion of any grants from the EU budget:

(a) The ECB's share capital is subscribed by the national central banks of the EU Member States according to a key based on each Member State's share in the total population and GDP of the European Union and recalculated at five-year intervals.[670] At the time of writing, the ECB's share capital stood at EUR 10.82 billion.[671] Capital payments are called by the ECB's Governing Council,[672] by a qualified majority vote,[673] and, again at the time of writing, a total amount of EUR 8.92 billion had been paid up, *i.e.*, EUR 8.85 billion by euro area central banks and EUR 74.01 million by non-euro area central banks.[674] With

669. For a chronological survey of Mr. Trump's interventions in 2017-2019, *see* R. Dall'Orto Mas, B. Vonessen *et al.*, *supra*, pp. 37 and 57, Table 11.
670. Article 29 of Protocol No 4.
671. The ECB's share capital was initially set at EUR 5 billion by Article 28.1 of Protocol No 4. On May 8, 2000, the Council authorized the ECB's Governing Council to increase the capital by a further EUR 5 billion (Council Regulation (EC) No 1009/2000 of May 8, 2000 concerning capital increases of the European Central Bank, *OJ* L115, May 16, 2000, p. 1). The Governing Council did so in one go in December 2010 (Decision 2011/20/EU of the European Central Bank of December 13, 2010 on the increase of the European Central Bank's capital, *OJ* L11, January 15, 2011, p. 53).In addition, the ECB's capital increases automatically upon accession of new Member States to the European Union in accordance with Article 48.3 of Protocol No 4. Upon Brexit, the capital was kept steady by redistributing the Bank of England's share among the remaining central banks.
672. Article 28.3 of Protocol No 4.
673. A qualified majority requires votes cast in favor that represent at least two-thirds of the subscribed capital and at least half of the shareholders, with the votes of Executive Board members being zero-weighted. *See* Article 10.3 of Protocol No 4.
674. Central banks of non-euro area Member States are currently required to pay up 3.75% of their capital subscription as a contribution to the ECB's operational costs. *Cf.* Article 47 of Protocol No 4. They are neither entitled to any share of the ECB's distributable profits nor liable to fund any of its losses.

EUR 10.82 billion of subscribed capital and a balance sheet total of EUR 698.85 billion on December 31, 2022, *i.e.*, a ratio of about 1.55%, the ECB appears thinly capitalized, but capital is ordinarily of lesser relevance for central banks. The capital may be increased by a qualified majority vote of the ECB's Governing Council, but subject to the limits and conditions to be defined by the Council.[675]

(b) The ECB's annual net profit (if any) is distributed to its shareholders, except for an amount, to be determined by the ECB's Governing Council, that is allocated to a general loss reserve. This allocation is subject to an annual cap of 20% of the net profit and an overall cap of 100% of the capital.[676] The loss reserve stood at EUR 6.63 billion on December 31, 2022, after a deduction of EUR 1.62 billion to absorb 2022 losses.

(c) Any net loss incurred by the ECB may be offset, sequentially, against its loss reserve (as occurred in 2022) and, if the Governing Council so decides, against the monetary income ("seigniorage") allocated to the national central banks for the relevant financial year.[677]

(d) The ECB also counts its revaluation accounts (*i.e.*, unrealized gains on gold, foreign currency instruments, non-held-to-maturity securities and certain other instruments) among its financial buffers inasmuch as they serve as a first cushion to absorb valuation losses caused by future unfavorable developments in exchange rates and asset prices. These revaluation accounts stood at EUR 36.48 billion on December 31, 2022.

498. In connection with this last point, it should be noted that, under the ECB's accounting policies, securities acquired for monetary policy purposes (including those purchased under APP and PEPP) are, like held-to-maturity securities, carried at amortized cost (subject to an annual impairment test) and not marked to market.[678] The ECB's monetary securities portfolio was recorded in the balance sheet at EUR 457.27 billion on December 31, 2022, *i.e.*, 65.43% of the balance sheet total (and 9.26% of the aggregate monetary securities portfolio of the Eurosystem), while its market value was then estimated at EUR 397.95 billion, *i.e.*, a negative difference of EUR 59.31 billion.[679] One would think that loss on these securities would have to be recognized upon their sale prior to maturity, *i.e.*, if quantitative tightening ("QT") were to be accelerated beyond its current "passive" phase of mere non-reinvestment of maturing

675. Article 28.1 of Protocol No 4.
676. Article 33.1(a) of Protocol No 4.
677. Article 33.2 of Protocol No 4.
678. *See* Annual Accounts of the ECB 2022, pp. 34 and 45, https://www.ecb.europa.eu/pub/pdf/annrep/ecb.annualaccounts2022~ee9329bf6f.en.pdf. *Cf.* Article 9(4) and (5) of Decision (EU) 2016/2247 of the European Central Bank of November 3, 2016 on the annual accounts of the European Central Bank, *OJ* L347, December 20, 2016, p. 1, amended by Decision (EU) 2017/2239 of November 16, 2017, *OJ* L320, December 6, 2017, p. 18, Decision (EU) 2019/2215 of November 28, 2019, *OJ* L332, December 23, 2019, p. 168, and Decision (EU) 2021/2040 of November 11, 2021, *OJ* L419, November 24, 2021, p. 1.
679. *See* Annual Accounts of the ECB 2022, p. 46.

securities in the APP portfolio. "Active" QT would crystallize the loss, but I don't expect that this has been one of the reasons why the ECB has thus far held off on "active" QT.

499. The ECB is a not-for-profit institution, in the sense that its purpose is to carry out public-interest tasks and not to maximize profit or indeed to earn any profit. The risk of loss is inherent in the conduct of monetary policy. The treatment of central bank losses has become a topical subject, now that the "normalization" of monetary policy and the attendant rise in policy rates (including the deposit facility rate) as of 2022 causes a transitional mismatch between a central bank's higher interest expenses on funds deposited by banks and its interest income from low-yield securities purchased under prior quantitative easing ("QE") programs in a low-inflation environment. It is an uneasy paradox: in order to counter disinflationary pressures, QE asset purchases have in fact shifted part of the risk of future interest rate increases caused by monetary policy tightening from the financial markets to the central banks. In other words, by engaging in large-scale asset purchases in a low-interest environment, Eurosystem central banks have effectively extracted interest rate risk from the financial markets and taken it on their books. And the paradox is sharpened by the fact that this risk may hit national central banks of fiscally conservative Member States (like Germany and The Netherlands) harder due to the lower coupons on their sovereign bonds.

500. As a result, the ECB incurred a loss of EUR 1.62 billion in 2022, which was absorbed by its loss reserve. Several national central banks in the euro area also reported a loss for the financial year 2022 and announced that they expect to incur further losses in the coming financial years (*see* paragraph 227 above). The question arises what is to be done if accumulated losses deplete existing financial buffers or even the share capital. Technically, central banks could continue to operate at a loss, even with negative equity, and simply carry forward losses on their books. But conventional wisdom is that such a state of affairs should not perdure lest it harm the market credibility and independence of central banks. As said, in the case of the ECB, when losses exceed the existing loss reserve, its Governing Council could, *"if necessary"*, decide to set off the excess against monetary income that would otherwise be allocated to the national central banks.[680] The Council could also authorize the ECB's Governing Council to further increase the capital, in which case the Governing Council could do so by qualified majority decision.[681] Presently, there is no mechanism for the ECB's losses to be covered through the EU budget.

If push came to shove, wouldn't the European Union have an obligation under the Treaty to maintain a functioning ECB capable of performing the tasks conferred upon it by the Treaty? And, likewise, wouldn't the Member States have a similar responsibility under the Treaty to keep their national central banks in working order? One could imagine that any significant recapitalization of the ECB, or of national central banks, might give rise to difficult political discussions that could put central bank independence to the test. But it may not come to this insofar as, in the cycle of

680. Article 33.2 of Protocol No 4.
681. Article 28.1 of Protocol No 4.

monetary life, central bank losses should eventually come to pass—even if they have assumed considerable proportions lately due to the sharp monetary tightening following an extended period of monetary easing with large-scale QE asset purchases.

c Accountability and Control

501. The scope of the monetary policy mandate delegated to the ECB (ESCB/Eurosystem), its weight in the overall macroeconomic policy mix and its considerable economic and social (including redistributive) effects across society would lead one to expect a commensurate level of accountability and control over how this mandate is carried out. But aside from firewalling the ECB from political interference, the Treaty and Protocol No 4 have relatively little to say on the subject. The ECB must submit an annual report to the other EU institutions, including on monetary policy in the prior and current year, the ECB's President must present this report to the Council and the European Parliament *"which may hold a general debate on that basis"*, and he or she and the other Executive Board members may, at the request of the European Parliament or on their own initiative, be heard by the competent committees of the Parliament.[682] But, given the ECB's high degree of independence, as protected by EU primary law, there is little that the political authorities can do, legally, to change the course of monetary policy, aside from expressing their displeasure.

502. From the vantage point of democratic legitimacy, there is an obvious tension between delegating a considerable part of macroeconomic policy to a "technocratic" institution, under a broadly-worded mandate, and the relative lack of control by electorally accountable political authorities. One could be forgiven for thinking that it almost feels like extending Montesquieu's *trias politica* to central banking as an independent fourth branch.

One may be tempted in this context to inquire about the level of trust in the ECB in public opinion, and perhaps this merits a short digression. According to periodic Eurobarometer surveys, "net trust" in the ECB (*i.e.*, the number of respondents ticking the box "Tend to trust" minus those ticking the box "Tend not to trust") was at its highest in 2007, dropped precipitously as from 2008 and even into negative territory between 2011 and 2018, edged up again as from 2017 and moved back into positive territory as from 2019.[683] In its 2021 Annual Report, the ECB noted that the latest Eurobarometer survey indicated that 47% of the respondents tended to trust the ECB,

682. Article 284(3) TFEU and Article 15.3 of Protocol No 4.
683. *See* European Commission, *Standard Eurobarometer 98 Winter 2022-2023*, *Public opinion in the European* Union, February 2023, pp. 101-102, https://europa.eu/eurobarometer/surveys/detail/2872. *See also* I. Schnabel, "The importance of trust for the ECB's monetary policy", Speech at the Hamburger Institut für Sozialforschung, December 16, 2020, https://www.bis.org/review/r201218c.pdf, 16 pp., especially p. 3, Figure 1, and S. Bergbauer, N. Hernborg *et al.*, "Citizens' attitudes towards the ECB, the euro and Economic and Monetary Union", *ECB Economic Bulletin*, 2020, Issue 4, pp. 80-103, especially p. 81, Chart 1.

which compared favorably to prior crisis episodes.[684] It is perhaps somewhat surprising that the ECB found this statistic important enough to mention in its annual report, and even more surprising that it added that *"[t]hese improvements indicate that the citizens recognise the work done by the ECB in responding to the pandemic crisis and improving its communication practices to citizens"*. This reading may be somewhat aspirational. Over the 2006-2022 period, the ECB's trust index closely tracks that of the European Parliament and the European Commission but, as from 2009, is almost consistently somewhat lower.[685]

But it is also true, and in the end perhaps more significant, that, in recent years, the ECB has made a commendable effort at transparency—in its appearances before the European Parliament (the ECB President now attends quarterly hearings at the European Parliament's Committee on Economic and Monetary Affairs) and national parliaments, in responding to written questions from members of the European Parliament, in its press briefings, in publishing accounts of its Governing Council's monetary policy meetings, in the abundant explanatory material on its website and in its numerous publications and speeches. There is a whole lot that we now know or can know about the ECB's policies and analysis—except perhaps for the real bedroom secrets.

503. The relative absence of political control should place greater weight on effective judicial control by the European Court of Justice. Yet, the broad wording and lack of precision of many of the Treaty's and Protocol No 4's provisions on monetary policy, in combination with the technical complexity and judgmental nature of monetary policy questions, leave the ECB with a fairly broad margin of judgment in carrying out its mandate, while at the same time making substantive judicial review more difficult. By and large, the Court has so far been accommodative, "dovish", in judging the ECB's monetary policy actions, applying a standard of (infra-)marginal review, as we will discuss further in a subsequent section of this chapter (*see* paragraphs 510 *et seq.* below). Arguably, for judicial control to be effective, the Court might have to move up the intensity of its review by a notch.

d Political Neutrality

504. One would also think that the high degree of political independence of the ECB in the conduct of monetary policy should hold it to a certain duty of political neutrality or restraint in matters that fall within the remit of other EU or national authorities. It is not merely, or not even in the first instance, a question of acting *ultra vires*. The ECB's political independence and credibility may be put at risk when it enters the domain of

684. *ECB Annual Report 2021*, p. 113, https://www.ecb.europa.eu/pub/pdf/annrep/ecb.ar2021~14d7439b2d.en.pdf. Yet, 39% of the respondents tended not to trust the ECB at that time. According to the subsequent Eurobarometer winter 2022-2023 survey, those tending to trust then represented 46%, and those tending not to trust 38%, producing a constant positive net margin of 8%. *See Standard Eurobarometer 98 Winter 2022-2023*, p. 100.
685. *Ibid.*, pp. 101-102.

political decision-making and arbitrage in policy matters outside the proper domain of monetary policy.

505. By way of illustration, it is all but obvious that, during the 2008-2012 financial crisis, the ECB should have taken it upon itself to address letters, marked "secret" or "highly confidential", to certain euro area governments to insist on certain measures of fiscal restraint and structural reforms. Letters of this kind that have meanwhile become public include a letter of November 19, 2010 to Irish Minister of Finance Brian Lenihan,[686] a letter of August 5, 2011 to Spanish Prime Minister José Luis Rodriguez Zapatero,[687] and a letter of the same date to Italian Prime Minister Silvio Berlusconi.[688] Interestingly, prior to the leakage of this last letter in the press, the association

686. This letter, marked "secret", was reclassified for publication four years later and, together with certain prior correspondence, can be found at https://www.ecb.europa.eu/press/html/irish-letters.en.html. The letter starts out with the observation that the provision of emergency liquidity assistance ("ELA") by Eurosystem central banks to Irish financial institutions *"may interfere with the objectives and tasks of the Eurosystem and may contravene the prohibition of monetary financing" (sic!)*. This is a surprisingly candid statement and the point is fair enough. But the letter then subjects continued provision of ELA to those institutions to certain conditions, including a request from the Irish Government for financial support with a commitment *"to undertake decisive actions in the areas of fiscal consolidation, structural reforms and financial sector restructuring, in agreement with the European Commission, the International Monetary Fund and the ECB"*.

687. This letter, marked "strictly confidential" and reclassified for release in December 2014, is reproduced at https://www.ecb.europa.eu/ecb/access_to_documents/document/correspondence/shared/data/ecb.dr.cor20110805Zapatero.en.pdf. In this letter, the ECB summons the Spanish Government urgently to take a number of measures which the ECB considers *"essential"*, *i.e.*, (i) a series of further measures to improve the functioning of the labor market, including (1) measures to ensure an effective decentralization of wage negotiations at company level, (2) *"bold and exceptional steps"* to ban inflation-adjustment clauses, (3) action to encourage wage moderation in the private sector, and (4) changes to labor-market regulations to speed up the reintegration of unemployed into the labor force; (ii) *"bold measures"* ensuring the sustainability of public finances, including *"additional structural fiscal consolidation measures for the remainder of 2011 of above 0.5% of GDP as a minimum"*; and (iii) further product market reforms in the energy sector, the rental housing market and the services industry.

688. This letter, co-signed by Jean-Claude Trichet and Mario Draghi, was also marked "strictly confidential" but was soon leaked in the Italian press. It can be found at https://www.ecb.europa.eu/ecb/access_to_documents/document/pa_document/shared/data/ecb.dr.par2021_0001lettertoItalianPrimeMinister.en.pdf. In particularly stern terms, the letter urges the Italian Government to take immediate action on a number of measures considered *"essential"*, *i.e.*, (i) measures to enhance growth, including (1) a *"comprehensive, far-reaching and credible reform strategy"* for the full liberalization of professional services and of local public services *"through large scale privatizations"*, (2) decentralization of collective wage bargaining at company level, and (3) a *"thorough review"* of the rules on the hiring and dismissal of employees; and (ii) *"immediate and bold measures"* ensuring the sustainability of public finances, including (1) additional fiscal measures to achieve a better-than-planned budget deficit in 2011, a net borrowing of 1% in 2012 and a balanced budget in 2013, mainly through expenditure cuts and savings in the pension system and the cost of public employees, (2) the introduction of a rule requiring slippages from deficit targets to be automatically compensated by horizontal cuts in discretionary expenditures, and (3) tighter controls on borrowing and expenditures by regional and local governments. Remarkably, the letter requests that these measures be taken as soon as possible by means of decree-laws and then ratified by the Italian Parliament by the end of September 2011, and even adds that *"[a] constitutional reform tightening fiscal rules would also be appropriate"*.

Generazione Attiva had applied to the ECB for access to the document, which the ECB denied in a letter of September 7, 2011, saying that disclosure would not be in the public interest and would cause:

> *"pregiudizio all'efficacia dei messaggi della stessa Bce ai governi degli stati membri, in quanto strumento atto a promuovere un contesto favorevole al ripristino della fiducia degli investitori dei mercati finanziari, elemento di primaria importanza ai fini di una fluida conduzione della politica monetaria"*.[689]

Thus, the ECB then considered such "messages" to euro area governments as an intrinsically confidential tool to promote a favorable context for restoring confidence in the financial markets—element of first importance for the proper pass-through of monetary policy. Here again, the ECB attached its forays into broader territory to the needs of proper monetary policy transmission.

506. These admonitions go beyond the kind of *"opinions"* which Article 127(4), second paragraph, TFEU allows the ECB to submit to national authorities *"on matters in its fields of competence"*, and appear to cross the line into fairly concrete demands for fiscal measures and economic reforms. I don't know whether the ECB may have pursued this kind of *correspondance intime* in more recent years, but I would rather assume it has not. In a similar vein, it is not plainly clear that the ECB should have become involved, as a member of the so-called "Troika" alongside the European Commission and the IMF, in negotiations on the economic policy conditionality attached to EFSF/ESM financial assistance (*see* paragraphs 714-718 below)—except insofar as its involvement was limited to an advisory role on aspects of monetary policy (or bank supervision). Likewise, it would give pause if the ECB were to subject its monetary purchases of sovereign bonds to economic or fiscal policy conditions, unless, arguably, such conditionality is limited to compliance with existing policy conditions attached to EFSF/ESM financial assistance, like in the case of OMT (*see* paragraphs 340(b), 341 and 342(b) above), or with existing policy commitments under the EMU fiscal and macroeconomic surveillance frameworks, as broadly seems to be the intention in the case for TPI (*see* paragraph 361(a) above).

e Market Credibility

507. The interaction between central banks and financial markets is a complicated affair. A central bank's market credibility is important for the proper conduct of monetary policy in several ways. One side of the story is that financial markets—not unlike politicians—tend to prefer easy, accommodative monetary policy and like to believe that the central bank will stand ready to avert or fix any serious financial crisis. The corresponding test of central bank market independence and credibility is its ability to withstand financial market expectations and pressures and to avoid that

689. Excerpts from this letter, including that quoted above, are reproduced in "Bce.'La lettera all'Italia deve rimanere segreta'", *Contropiano*, September 9, 2011, https://contrapiano.org/news/politica-news/2011/09/09/bce-la-lettera-allitalia-deve-rimanere-segreta-03293.

monetary policy becomes effectively constrained by market credos that detract from the proper price stability trajectory—to avoid that central banking becomes entrapped by a "Greenspan put".

508. Market credibility is also important to enable a central bank, by formal or informal forward guidance, to steer market expectations of inflation nearer to the level that the central bank seeks to achieve, or at least to avoid market expectations becoming anchored in the wrong direction. Getting the markets' inflation expectations right is a monetary job more than half done. One could see this as a salutary form of market manipulation. The efficacy of this policy tool obviously depends on the central bank's "street credibility", which in turn depends on the clarity and consistency of its messaging to the markets and on its track record of making good on its guidance and achieving its price stability objective.

509. One may sometimes be left wondering about the degree of the ECB's street credibility. The ECB has articulated its primary price stability objective in terms of a numerical target for headline inflation, to be pursued symmetrically and over a medium-term horizon (*see* paragraphs 172 *et seq.* above). But this general policy rule is somewhat diluted by (i) ambiguities about symmetry and the apparent elasticity of the medium term (*see* paragraphs 179-184 above); (ii) the occasional need to contain financial fragmentation and recurring trade-offs with secondary policy objectives and constraints (as discussed in Chapters V and VI); (iii) the ECB's recent (over)emphasis on a "data-dependent", "meeting-by-meeting" approach in light of the need of "flexibility" and "optionality" (*see* paragraphs 103 and 321 above), which is an open invitation to financial markets to interpret the continuous ticker tape of incoming data between monetary policy meetings of the ECB's Governing Council and to read the tea leaves as to how the ECB might respond to them; and (iv) the ECB's less than stellar track record in coming close to its inflation target in the past decade (*see* paragraph 300 above). It again raises the question of the desirability of a policy rule of higher resolution and constancy and more articulate forward guidance (*see* paragraphs 321-324 above). Clearly, the ECB does not throw dice. Neither do well-informed financial markets—or at least they will do so to a lesser degree when properly informed and guided. Still, in the interaction between financial markets and the ECB in recent years, dice appear to have been rolling more often, and with noisier clicks, than may be desirable. Unjustified volatility may be avoided or reduced by a better market understanding of the ECB's expectations and intentions as to the likely course of monetary policy in the near term. Clarity and understanding are generally positively correlated.

2 JUDICIAL REVIEW OF MONETARY POLICY

510. As discussed in Chapter 3, the Treaty classifies monetary policy for the euro area as an exclusive competence of the Union, to be conducted by the ECB *"together with"* the national central banks of the euro area Member States (the ESCB in its reduced format of the Eurosystem). But the Treaty does not substantively define the monetary policy mandate delegated to the ECB (Eurosystem) otherwise than by (i) holding it to the *"primary"* (but not exclusive) objective of maintaining price stability; (ii) referring to the "singleness" of monetary policy for the euro area; (iii) providing, in its Protocol No 4, an open-ended list of general operational techniques; and (iv) prohibiting monetary financing of EU and national public-sector entities. The Treaty also blurs the picture somewhat by holding the ECB's (Eurosystem's) actions to a number of broadly-worded secondary objectives and constraints. It is time now to consider more systematically how the European Court of Justice ("CJEU") has reviewed ECB monetary policy actions in light of these low-resolution provisions of EU primary law.[690]

a The Price Stability Objective

511. The Treaty has not defined the abstract notion of maintaining price stability. As said, the ECB has taken it upon itself to express this objective as a medium-term and symmetrical numerical target for headline inflation. Initially, in 1998, it defined this target as a year-on-year increase in headline inflation (HICP) below 2%. In 2003, it clarified that, within this 0% to 2% range, it would aim at an inflation rate *"close to 2% over the medium term"*. Eventually, as part of its July 2021 monetary policy strategy, the ECB replaced the double-key formulation of its inflation target (inflation between 0% and 2% and, within this range, close to 2%) with a straightforward numerical target of 2% (*see* paragraphs 173-177 above).

512. In its 2018 judgment in *Weiss*, the CJEU pronounced its *nihil obstat* on the ECB's interpretation of the price stability objective of its monetary policy mandate. The Court considered that *"[i]t does not appear"* that the ECB's (2003) definition of the price stability objective—in those days still "below but close to 2%" over the medium term—goes beyond the Treaty framework or is flawed by any *"manifest error of assessment"*.[691] The Court noted that the ECB's approximate formulation of the inflation target could properly be justified, *"inter alia"*, by imprecisions in inflation measurement, differences in inflation levels within the euro area and the need for a buffer against deflationary risks. "Manifest error of assessment" is a judicial standard of what many lawyers would call "marginal review". It is typically reserved for judicial review of legal acts in the **exercise** of competences that involve appraisal of complex factual or technical matters and/or a measure of policy discretion, for which a court of law should not substitute its own assessment. But in *Weiss*, curiously, the CJEU seems to apply this lower standard of review even to how the ECB itself understands the price stability objective that is the Treaty's core definitional element of its very competence—which, so one might have imagined, should be a question of law subject to full review.

690. The more hurried reader may switch to a more condensed version of this section in J. Meyers, "Thoughts on the Monetary Policy Mandate of the European Central Bank", *Liber Amicorum Xavier Dieux*, Larcier, Brussels, 2022, pp. 1209 *et seq.*, especially pp. 1227-1239.
691. CJEU, December 11, 2018, Case C-493/17, *Weiss et al.*, ECLI:EU:C:2018:1000, §56.

b Boundaries of Monetary Policy and Cross-Over Effects in Other Policy Areas

513. Absent clear Treaty definitions and given inevitable cross-over effects, the precise delineation of the respective spheres of monetary policy and economic and fiscal policies is not particularly straightforward. Yet, the distinction is legally important because monetary policy for the euro area is an exclusive EU competence (Article 3(1)(c) TFEU), delegated to the ECB (Eurosystem) (Article 282(1) TFEU), while economic and fiscal policies mostly remain an exclusive competence of the Member States, subject to a measure of coordination and surveillance at EU level (Articles 2(3) and 5(1)TFEU) and subject to certain areas of shared competence (Article 4(2) TFEU). Questions of delineation have come to the forefront in particular with regard to the ECB's sovereign bond purchases and have given rise to two important CJEU judgments, each time on a preliminary ruling request from the German Federal Constitutional Court (Bundesverfassungsgericht or "BVerfG" for short). One is the 2015 judgment in *Gauweiler* concerning OMT, the hitherto dormant anti-fragmentation instrument (*see* paragraphs 337-343 above),[692] and the other is the 2018 *Weiss* judgment concerning PSPP, the more "pure play" QE program now in run-off (*see* paragraphs 218-231 above). We will consider them in chronological sequence, thus starting with the most criticizable and ending with the most controversial—but not before stepping back briefly to the CJEU's 2012 *Pringle* judgment.[693]

514. In ***Pringle***, the CJEU had held that the establishment of the European Stability Mechanism ("ESM") does not encroach upon the European Union's exclusive competence of monetary policy for the euro area. It arrived at this conclusion by considering that (i) the ESM's objective is to safeguard the stability of the euro area as a whole, which is *"clearly distinct"* from the primary objective of maintaining price stability;[694] (ii) at the level of instruments, the granting of financial assistance to a Member State (which, spoiler alert, may also take the form of purchases of sovereign bonds) *"clearly does not fall within monetary policy"*;[695] and (iii) ESM financial assistance serves to complement the EU framework for closer coordination and surveillance of the Member States' economic and fiscal policies.[696] The Court concluded that these three features place ESM financial assistance in the realm of economic policy, not monetary policy.[697] It added that such a mechanism cannot be treated as equivalent to a monetary policy measure for the sole reason that it may have indirect effects on the stability of the **euro**[698] (which, in the eyes of the Court, is apparently something else than the ESM's objective of safeguarding the stability of the **euro are**a as a whole).

692. CJEU, June 16, 2015, Case C-62/14, *Gauweiler et al.*, ECLI:EU:C:2015:400.
693. CJEU, November 27, 2012, Case C-370/12, *Pringle*, ECLI:EU:C:2012:756.
694. *Ibid.*, §56.
695. *Ibid.*, §57.
696. *Ibid.*, §58.
697. *Ibid.*, §59.
698. *Ibid.*, §56.

515. Given that, under Article 18 of the ESM Treaty, the ESM's financial assistance may take the form of secondary market purchases of sovereign bonds,[699] a question that comes to mind is how such asset purchases could be characterized as economic policy when made by the ESM and as monetary policy when carried out by the ECB. This dual characterization is especially challenging when the ECB purchases sovereign bonds in factual circumstances comparable to those in which the ESM might also be called upon to do so under the ESM Treaty, *i.e.*, where, under OMT, PEPP or TPI, the ECB engages in geographically selective purchases of sovereign bonds targeted at euro area Member States experiencing more difficult (costly) access to the financial markets following an excessive widening of sovereign bond spreads. At first blush, this may remind one of Erwin Schrödinger's thought experiment on the quantum theory paradox in which Mr. Schrödinger's cat was simultaneously dead and alive. In its 2015 *Gauweiler* judgment, the CJEU sought to address this apparent paradox for OMT, and in its 2018 *Weiss* judgment, for PSPP. *Gauweiler* should be the more difficult case conceptually since it concerned geographically selective bond purchases for anti-fragmentation purposes, while *Weiss* related to across-the-board QE purchases for purposes of monetary easing.

516. In particular, in ***Gauweiler***, the difficulty of the exercise was compounded by several factors:

(a) OMT is not "pure play" QE aimed at countering disinflationary pressures but is first and foremost intended as an anti-fragmentation tool to counter excessive widening of sovereign bond spreads due to destabilizing market dynamics driven by fears of a total or partial break-up of the currency union. This imports a clear *Pringle*-type dimension of preserving the cohesion or stability of the euro area.
(b) Such anti-fragmentation action implies geographic differentiation of sovereign bond purchases within the euro area, which *prima facie* seems to sit uneasily with the singleness of monetary policy for the currency union.
(c) Sovereign bond purchases under OMT would be targeted at euro area Member States at the high end of the spreads, which have lost or are close to losing access to market finance on viable terms. By creating additional secondary market demand for their sovereign bonds, OMT purchases would depress their sovereign bond yields and hence reduce the cost of future government borrowings. This may raise questions notably under the Treaty's monetary financing prohibition, which we will consider separately in a later subsection (*see* paragraphs 533-536 below).
(d) OMT bond purchases would be linked to EFSF/ESM financial assistance and its economic policy conditionality.
(e) Finally, the actual terms of OMT were not yet set forth in any formal legal act but only in a succinct ECB press release of September 6, 2012, that is not

699. At the time of writing, the ESM had not yet effectively used this tool—but it is in the toolbox provided in its constituent treaty.

particularly rich in detail,[700] and in (unpublished) draft legal acts considered by the ECB's Governing Council when approving the press release.[701]

517. The above factors would not seem particularly helpful to confidently characterizing OMT as monetary policy action within the ECB's mandate. But, in its 2015 *Gauweiler* judgment, the CJEU wriggled itself out of this conundrum essentially by adopting the following reasoning:

(a) Holding on to the line of *Pringle*, the Court started out by affirming that, in determining whether a measure falls within the perimeter of monetary policy, *"it is appropriate"* to refer *"principally"* to the objective of that measure.[702]

(b) The Court then accepted the ECB's now familiar reasoning to the effect that disruptions in the monetary policy transmission mechanism, such as those caused by excessive widening of sovereign bond spreads, are likely to render monetary policy less effective in parts of the euro area and, consequently, to undermine the singleness of monetary policy, which *"necessarily"* affects the ECB's ability to ensure price stability. Therefore, measures aimed at safeguarding the proper functioning of the monetary policy transmission mechanism *"may be regarded as pertaining to"* the primary objective of maintaining price stability.[703]

(c) Again circling back to *Pringle*, the Court was not troubled by the fact that OMT *"might also"* contribute to the stability of the euro area, *"which is a matter of economic policy"*, but which here it put in the category of *"indirect effects"* that do not render a monetary policy measure equivalent to an economic policy measure.[704]

(d) Turning to the geographic selectivity of OMT, the Court noted that open-market purchases of marketable financial instruments are a permissible instrument of monetary policy under Article 18.1 of Protocol No 4, that OMT aims to remedy disruptions in the monetary policy transmission mechanism localized in particular government bond markets, and that, under the circumstances, such selectivity would not, *"of itself"*, take the instrument outside the realm of monetary policy. Not *"of itself"*? The Court then added, perhaps in unnecessarily general terms, that no Treaty provision requires the ECB *"to operate in the financial markets by means of general measures that would necessarily be applicable to all the States of the euro area"*.[705]

---

700. *See* the ECB's press release of September 6, 2012, https://www.ecb.europa.eu/press/pr/date/2012/html/pr120906_1.en.html.
701. The Court mentions these drafts in *Gauweiler*, §71, but I have not seen them.
702. *Gauweiler*, §46.
703. *Ibid.*, §§48-50. These paragraphs are quoted in full in paragraph 386 above. The Court elaborates on this reasoning in its proportionality assessment later in the judgment. *See ibid.*, §§72-78.
704. *Ibid.*, §§51-52.
705. *Ibid.*, §§54-55. *Cf. also*, in the proportionality assessment, *ibid.*, §89.

(e) The Court saw no reason to recharacterize asset purchases under OMT as a measure of economic policy on the ground that they are made conditional on compliance with macroeconomic adjustment or precautionary programs attached to EFSF/ESM financial assistance. The Court considered this consistent with (i) the ECB's Treaty obligation to support the general economic policies in the European Union; (ii) the need to ensure that OMT purchases would not work against the effectiveness of the Member States' economic policies; and (iii) the ECB's duty, under Article 127(1) *jo.* Article 119(3) TFEU, to abide by the guiding principle that public finances must be sound. In the eyes of the Court, the latter consideration appears to legitimize conditionality aimed at preventing that monetary policy measures like OMT asset purchases act *"as an incentive to Member States to allow their financial situation to deteriorate"*. [706] Here, the Court appears to say that monetary policy measures may be subject to economic policy conditionality if needed to guard against "moral hazard". The Court further observed that a Member State's compliance with EFSF/ESM economic policy conditionality would not be a sufficient condition for triggering OMT purchases but that these would be strictly conditional on the existence of disruptions of the monetary policy transmission mechanism *"or"* the singleness of monetary policy.

(f) This then led the Court further down a slippery slope as it went on to say that, while secondary market purchases of government bonds subject to economic policy conditionality could be regarded as falling within economic policy when made by the ESM, this should not equally be the case when such purchases are made by the ECB under a program like OMT, and that the difference between the objectives of the ESM and those of the ECB is decisive in this regard.[707]

518. The Court's reasoning in *Gauweiler* is also relevant, *mutatis mutandis*, for the assessment of anti-fragmentation asset purchases under PEPP and TPI. But it prompts several critical questions.

519. ***First***, at a level of pure reason, the objective for which a competence is conferred does not, in and of itself, define the substantive scope and content of this competence. This is even less so here since (i) the Treaty has made price stability a "primary", not an exclusive, objective of monetary policy, has not defined what price stability really means, and has embedded it in a somewhat diffuse matrix of secondary objectives and constraints, and (ii) the price stability objective has effectively been defined, and adapted over time, by the ECB, the very institution entrusted with the mandate to maintain it. An objective of this kind is a tenuous basis for tracing the boundaries of a

---

706. *Ibid.*, §§57-61. Later in the judgment, the Court considered OMT's link with ESM economic policy conditionality a helpful factor for OMT's consistency with the monetary financing prohibition of Article 123(1) TFEU (*see* paragraph 535(a) below).

707. *Ibid.*, §§62-64.

competence, or distinguishing it from adjacent competences, with any degree of precision.

520. *Second*, the Court benevolently accepted that actions directed at restoring the effectiveness of the monetary policy transmission mechanism in the euro area or parts of the euro area can be attached to the Treaty's price stability objective and hence fall within the compass of the ECB's monetary policy mandate.[708] This abstract reasoning, of almost Kantian *reine Vernunft*, has become the bedrock of the ECB's justification for anti-fragmentation sovereign bond purchases. From a legal standpoint, it gives pause for several reasons:

(a) Dissected to its bare core, the underlying logic appears to be that the ECB's monetary policy competence implies the power to remove impediments to proper monetary policy transmission across the euro area, *i.e.*, to its effective exercise as a single monetary policy. This seems close to recognizing an implied power of the ECB that is derived from its Treaty-conferred price stability mandate and is deemed indispensable for the conferred competence to be exercised effectively and usefully. But wouldn't such an implied power sit uneasily with the principle of conferral stated in Article 5(1) and (2) TEU and weaken its constraining effect? The application of the international law doctrine of implied powers in the EU legal sphere is somewhat controversial. This has not stopped the Court from applying it from time to time in various areas, and it seems—implicitly—to do so in *Gauweiler*. My own view on the subject is that the introduction of Article 352 TFEU (the so-called "flexibility clause") should have put an end to the praetorian development of implied powers derived merely from the objectives set out in the Treaties and now confines the Court to the narrower (and politically less sensitive) variant of implied powers that are derived from, and substantively connected with, a particular competence or task conferred by the Treaties and are indispensable for its effective exercise.[709] This seems to fit the line of reasoning in *Gauweiler*. But one could see why the Court would prefer to stay away from overtly taking the implied powers track and its ambiguities.

(b) A conferred competence cannot generally extend to the removal of just any and all obstacles to its effective exercise. There must be some substantive connection with such competence that is genuine and relevant, and, in *Gauweiler*, the Court saw this link in the proper functioning of the monetary policy transmission mechanism. But this is a broad concept, and how changes to monetary policy settings flow through to the economy and eventually to inflation is a complex process with many channels and sub-channels. In the

708. The General Court later adopted this reasoning in relation to central bank purchases of Greek sovereign bonds under SMP. *See* GC, February 9, 2022, Case T-868/16, *Qi et al. vs. European Commission & ECB*, ECLI:EU:T:2022:58, §§101 and 174.

709. This substantially corresponds to how implied powers theory was applied by the Court in CJEU, July 9, 1987, Joined Cases 281, 283-285 and 287/85, *Germany vs. Commission*, ECLI:EU:C:1987:351, §§27-30, especially §28.

real world, there are a wide variety of "bugs" and "hiccups" that, in some channel or sub-channel, may obstruct the proper pass-through of the desired monetary policy stance and diminish its effectiveness. The Court has not articulated more precise criteria to determine what kind of bugs, at what level or sub-level in the transmission process, may justify central bank reactivity and in what circumstances, and the absence of such criteria makes the boundaries of the ECB's monetary policy mandate particularly fluid. Also, many of those bugs are country-specific and originate in, and could (should) be addressed by, national economic or fiscal policies, which raises the issue of monetary policy incursions into national policy areas (*see* paragraphs 523-524 below).

(c) In a sense, the Court's reasoning on the proper functioning of the monetary policy transmission mechanism turns the Treaty requirement of the singleness of monetary policy upside down by allowing, or at least opening the door for, geographic differentiation of monetary policy actions in the name of sufficiently preserving the singleness of the monetary policy stance.

521. ***Third***, the Court did not address the conflict that may arise between central bank asset purchases to repair the monetary policy transmission mechanism and the proper monetary policy stance required for inflation control. In a low-inflation environment that calls for monetary easing, the additional liquidity injected by such asset purchases is at least directionally consistent with that monetary policy stance. But the opposite is true when high inflation requires monetary tightening. Unless somehow sterilized, additional liquidity injection would now work against the anti-inflationary direction of monetary policy required by the primary objective of price stability. This issue did not come up in *Gauweiler* probably because the judgment was rendered at a time of monetary easing in response to below-target inflation and, moreover, the OMT announcement contemplated that the additional liquidity would be fully sterilized (*see* paragraph 340(d) above). But the conflict may arise for anti-fragmentation asset purchases under PEPP or TPI in today's high-inflation environment (*see* paragraphs 362 and 391 above).[710]

522. ***Fourth***, the Court readily accepted that OMT's link with EFSF/ESM stability support and its economic policy conditionality did not disqualify OMT as monetary policy (*see* paragraph 517(e) above). But can a monetary policy measure really be linked to economic or fiscal policy conditions while remaining within the compass of the monetary policy mandate and, if so, to what extent? Several forms of conditionality may need to be distinguished:

(a) The ECB could make eligibility for a particular measure, here sovereign bond purchases, subject to an ***ex ante*** assessment of a Member State's good standing under **existing** policy conditions and commitments pursuant to the

710. The July 21, 2022 press release on TPI does not unequivocally commit to (fully) sterilize the liquidity impact of TPI purchases (*see* paragraph 362 above).

EMU fiscal and macroeconomic surveillance frameworks, as, by and large, appears to be the case for TPI (*see* paragraph 361(a) above). This could arguably be justified in some measure by the consistency requirement of Article 7 TFEU. But even then, what does a Member State's compliance or non-compliance with existing economic or fiscal policy conditions intrinsically have to do with the need for monetary policy action to control inflation or repair the monetary policy transmission mechanism? If the inflation level or the transmission mechanism needs fixing for monetary policy reasons, why should this be conditional on a Member State's compliance with policy commitments in other areas? Even this "softer" form of economic policy conditionality weakens the link with pure monetary policy logic.

(b) OMT takes this one step further by reserving sovereign bond purchases to Member States receiving EFSF/ESM financial assistance under a macroeconomic adjustment (or precautionary) program and subjecting such purchases to **continued** compliance with such policy conditionality (which the ECB has helped to design as part of the Troika).

(c) Surely, the line could or should be drawn where the ECB would condition asset purchases (or indeed any other monetary policy action) on a Member State's compliance with **additional** policy conditions of its own in the economic or fiscal policy spaces. But even on this point, the *Gauweiler* judgment is somewhat ambiguous in that it appears to suggest that the ECB's duty, under Article 127(1) *jo.* Article 119(3) TFEU, to abide by the principle of sound public finances justifies conditions that prevent the relevant monetary policy measure *"from acting as an incentive to Member States to allow their financial situation to deteriorate"*[711] (*see* paragraph 517(e) above). This could be read to cover all manner of sin in terms of fiscal policy conditions.

523. ***Fifth***, this brings us to the broader issue of cross-over effects in other policy areas, particularly in matters of economic and fiscal policies that are within the remit of the Member States. Applying its "teleological" criterion of finality, the Court considers a measure's principal objective as the determinative factor for its characterization as monetary or economic policy. If the measure is principally directed at maintaining price stability (or, to this effect, at restoring the proper functioning of the monetary policy transmission mechanism), then it is monetary policy. In the Court's reasoning, the circumstance that it may also produce "indirect effects" in the economic or fiscal policy sphere is then of no consequence at the level of the measure's characterization as monetary policy. At a separate level, as part of its proportionality assessment, the ECB would have to weigh such indirect effects, and, insofar as possible, seek to calibrate its monetary policy actions in such a way as to minimize harmful effects in other policy areas (although this is a point which the Court did not yet fully articulate in *Gauweiler*).

711. *Gauweiler*, §61.

524. The Court's reasoning on cross-over effects (the Court itself refers somewhat diminutively to *"indirect effects"*) remains fairly abstract. Several questions are left without clear answers:

(a) It may not be straightforward to distinguish a cross-over effect of a monetary policy measure in the economic policy area from a concurrent or even controlling policy objective, especially not when that cross-over effect is anticipated and indeed intended. OMT, which was at issue in *Gauweiler*, is a case in point. When conceived in the summer of 2012, this asset purchase program was not in the first instance aimed at monetary easing for inflation control purposes. In the words of then ECB President Mario Draghi, it was meant to *"enable us to address severe distortions in government bond markets which originate from, in particular, unfounded fears on the part of investors of the reversibility of the euro"*.[712] OMT was supposed to contain destabilizing market dynamics driven by speculation of a total or partial break-up of the currency union and was originally intended to deliver on Mr. Draghi's "whatever it takes" promise of July 26, 2012 to preserve the euro (*see* paragraph 337 above). Yet, as the Court said, the stability of the euro area is a matter of economic policy.[713] Sure, such destabilizing market movements would disturb the monetary policy transmission mechanism and pose potentially serious challenges for price stability in the euro area, as Mr. Draghi hastened to add. But wouldn't any distortions in government bond markets serious enough to pose a threat to the cohesion of the currency union have such consequences? What then is the dividing line between the two competence spheres?

(b) In *Gauweiler* and subsequently also in *Weiss*, the Court only addressed the question of whether cross-over effects of monetary policy measures in economic or fiscal policy areas would disqualify such measures as falling in the realm of monetary policy—and not the question of how possible conflicts with Member States' economic and fiscal policies should be resolved. One would be tempted to read between the lines of these judgments that, if the measure is found to qualify as monetary policy, it will stand in its entirety as being *intra vires* and prevail over conflicting national measures. However, under the narrower variant of the implied powers doctrine (*see* paragraph 520(a) above), implied powers may not encroach on the exclusive competences of Member States. On this basis, Member States (or, exceptionally, private persons having *locus standi*) could arguably seek partial annulment of a monetary policy measure (especially one based on the need to repair monetary policy transmission) on the ground that, and insofar as, it makes incursions into policy matters for which the Member States hold exclusive competence. Under established jurisprudence of the Court, partial annulment

712. *See* the transcript of the ECB's press conference of September 6, 2012, https://www.ecb.europa.eu/press/pressconf/2012/html/is120906.en.html, at p. 1.

713. *Pringle*, §56, and *Gauweiler*, §51.

would be possible only if the terms challenged could be severed from the remainder of the measure without altering its substance.[714] This would essentially be a facts-and-circumstances question. As concerns economic policy conditions attached to a monetary policy measure, the conflict problem should generally not arise if these conditions merely reflect or refer to conditions already resulting from existing commitments or binding provisions of EU law.

525. I must pause here briefly to clarify a point, lest the reader suspect me of overindulging in Jesuitic legal reasoning oblivious to practical necessities. For the avoidance of doubt, I am not saying that asset purchases or other actions to contain financial fragmentation may not be necessary in the European currency union, nor that OMT was ill-advised under the circumstances in which it came about. In the first half of 2012, excessive widening of sovereign bond spreads was feeding through to corporate bond yields and bank lending rates, producing distortions throughout the yield curve, and became caught in destabilizing market dynamics increasingly driven by market fears of a partial or total break-up of the currency union. Conventional monetary policy was losing its capability to steer interest rates and, by the summer of that year, action became badly needed.[715] In the circumstances of that time, OMT emerged as the practical solution. As said, upon closer analysis, it is questionable whether OMT falls within the scope of the monetary policy mandate conferred by the Treaty. But there was at least an arguable case in that sense, and urgent situations may arise in which legally fragile action is clearly preferable to inaction. The Court is likely to have been conscious of this. But the point remains that, in a longer-term perspective, it makes sense to move anti-fragmentation asset purchases to firmer legal ground by taking them outside the monetary policy perimeter and lodging them in a mechanism like the ESM, in line with *Pringle* (*see* paragraphs 397-404 above).

526. Three-and-a-half years later, in ***Weiss***, the CJEU had to consider whether PSPP falls within the ECB's monetary policy mandate, again in response to a preliminary ruling request from the BVerfG. It was, at least conceptually, a more straightforward question insofar as PSPP is "pure play" QE: it was plainly aimed at providing monetary stimulus to contain disinflationary pressures and support a rise of inflation closer to the 2% target at a time when this could no longer be achieved by lowering policy rates, then at their lower bound. Unlike OMT and the later TPI, PSPP was not specifically directed at containing financial fragmentation (although, by reducing government borrowing costs across the board, it should indirectly have helped to contain the widening of sovereign bond spreads). PSPP purchases were, in principle, allocated

714. *Cf.* K. Lenaerts, I. Maselis & K. Gutman, *EU Procedural Law*, Oxford University Press, 2014, p. 413, §7.220.

715. For a description of this episode by a then member of the ECB's Executive Board, *see* B. Coeuré, "Outright Monetary Transactions, one year on", Speech at the conference "The ECB and its OMT Programme" organized by the Centre for Economic Policy Research, the German Institute for Economic Research and KfW Bankengruppe, Berlin, September 2, 2013, https://www.ecb.europa.eu/press/key/date/2013/html/sp130902.en.html, at pp. 2-4.

across euro area Member States according to the ECB capital subscription key, without any express geographic selectivity feature.[716]

527. Unsurprisingly, the CJEU found that PSPP remains within the compass of monetary policy. It based this conclusion essentially on the following considerations:

(a) Holding on to the "teleological" criterion of *Pringle* and *Gauweiler*, the Court considered it appropriate to refer *"principally"* to the objective of a measure when determining whether or not it is monetary policy. The primary objective of monetary policy is to maintain price stability, and, while the Treaty defines this objective only in an abstract manner, the Court found no fault with the ECB's concrete expression of it as a level of inflation below but close to 2% (as it was then formulated) over the medium term (*see* paragraph 512 above). Consequently, PSPP's stated objective, *i.e.*, to raise inflation back to that level over the medium term, can be attached to the primary objective of monetary policy set out by the Treaty.[717]

(b) The Court added that purchasing marketable instruments in the financial markets is among the monetary policy tools contemplated by EU primary law, *i.e.*, Article 18.1 of Protocol No 4.[718]

(c) Again in line with *Pringle* and *Gauweiler*, the Court held that PSPP's characterization as a monetary policy measure is not called into question by its—considerable—cross-over effects on bank balance sheets and government (re)financing conditions, even if such effects were foreseeable and indeed knowingly accepted.[719]

528. Given PSPP's clear focus on inflation control, its lack of explicit geographic selectivity and the absence of economic policy conditionality (or any link with ESM stability support), the Court's reasoning in *Weiss* involved less wriggling than in *Gauweiler*. But I should add two further comments:

(a) The Court's analysis summarized in paragraph 527(a) above puts a question mark over the continuation of QE asset purchases when inflation started climbing significantly above 2% as from the fall of 2021, *i.e.*, over the continued net purchases under APP and PEPP until the end of June and March 2022, respectively, but also over the continued reinvestments of maturing bonds under APP until the end of June 2023 and those under PEPP until this

716. As noted in paragraph 224 above, however, a 2020 amendment to Decision (EU) 2015/774 substituted a less stringent formulation of this allocation key which suggests some margin for temporary deviations of purchase flows from that key. A 2021 analysis of published data shows an upward trend in such deviations for high-debt Member States, including Italy, France, Spain and Belgium, in 2015, 2018 and 2020.

717. *Weiss*, §§53-57.

718. *Ibid.*, §§68-69.

719. *Ibid.*, §§58-67.

day, and possibly even over the absence so far of any resales of bonds prior to maturity.

(b) When addressing PSPP's cross-over effects in other policy areas (*see* paragraph 527(c) above), the Court curiously, and unnecessarily, observed, with reference to Article 127(1) TFEU, that *"the authors of the Treaties did not intend to make an absolute separation between economic and monetary policies"*.[720] This dictum surely must not be taken too literally. These are mutually exclusive competences and, consequently, must be capable of clear distinction. Where they are not, workable criteria must be developed. A purely teleological approach looking at abstract objectives may not suffice.

c Proportionality

529. Like all other EU institutions, the ECB must abide by the principle of proportionality in the exercise of its competences.[721] This principle requires, in short, that the ECB's actions be suitable for attaining their monetary policy objective(s) and do not go beyond what is necessary for doing so. It places the ECB under a duty of care, on a reasonable efforts basis, to weigh the scope and efficacy of its actions against their foreseeable consequences and side effects, to consider whether its objective(s) cannot be achieved by more limited action and, insofar as reasonably possible, to calibrate the chosen measure in such a way as to avoid or minimize undesirable collateral effects. This, in a nutshell, is the theory. Lawyers often take great pleasure in finessing it. Both in *Gauweiler* and *Weiss*, the CJEU has been "accommodative" in reviewing OMT and PSPP, respectively, under the proportionality principle.

530. As a general matter, the Court considered that, when designing and implementing measures of this kind, the ECB engages in analysis and forecasts, and makes complex assessments and technical choices, for which it must be allowed *"broad discretion"*.[722] These are the standard circumstances that require the Court to stand back and limit its review to censuring manifest errors of assessment and procedural flaws. The Court must still review whether the ECB has *"carefully and impartially"* examined the relevant elements of the situation and properly stated the reasons for its decision,[723] but the Court cannot be expected to determine substantive issues of monetary analysis. In fact,

> *"given that questions of monetary policy are usually of a controversial nature* [sic!] *and in view of the ESCB's broad discretion, nothing more can be required of the ESCB apart from that it use its economic expertise and the necessary technical means at its disposal to carry out that analysis with all care and accuracy"*.[724]

---

720. *Ibid.*, §60.
721. Article 5(1) and (4) TEU.
722. *Gauweiler*, §68, and *Weiss*, §73.
723. *Gauweiler*, §69.
724. *Gauweiler*, §75, and *Weiss*, §91.

531. Thus, in *Gauweiler* and *Weiss*, the CJEU reviewed whether OMT and PSPP are suitable to achieve their stated objective and do not *"manifestly"* go beyond what is necessary for this purpose. In both cases, the Court by and large confined itself to a benign review of the *prima facie* plausibility of the ECB's stated reasons and explanations, without much substantive probing and, occasionally, with some apparent contradiction in its considerations:

(a) In *Gauweiler*, the Court considered that, under economic conditions *"such as described by the ECB"*, the ECB could *"legitimately take the view"* that OMT is *"appropriate"* for its stated purpose.[725] It then focused primarily on the fact that, notwithstanding the absence of any *ex ante* quantitative limit on OMT purchases, the potential scale of the program should be limited by several of its features, curiously mentioning even its geographic selectivity as one of these features[726] (to be contrasted with subparagraph (b)(ii) below).

(b) In *Weiss*, the Court referred notably to (i) the fact that, with policy rates then being at their lower bound and the ECB already conducting purchases of private-sector securities, it does not appear that the objective of countering deflationary risks could have been achieved by any other more limited type of action than PSPP;[727] (ii) the absence, in PSPP, of geographic selectivity, which ensures that PSPP purchases will not serve to meet the specific financing needs of certain euro area Member States;[728] (iii) the minimum credit quality requirements for eligible sovereign bonds, which prevent banks from offloading higher-risk bonds on central banks;[729] (iv) the temporary nature of PSPP and the relatively short periods for which it had been extended (by the time of the judgment);[730] (v) the size limitations resulting from the monthly APP volume cap and the purchase limits per issuer and issue, although the Court also acknowledged that the efficacy of PSPP may require that bonds be purchased in large volume and held in portfolio *"on a lasting basis"*, with reinvestment of maturing bonds;[731] and (vi) the fact that it is *"not apparent"* that a program of more limited size or shorter duration would have been capable of bringing about the changes in inflation *"as effectively and rapidly"* as PSPP.[732]

(c) In both *Gauweiler* and *Weiss*, the Court observed that the ECB *"has weighed up the various interests in play"* so as to effectively prevent disadvantages from arising upon implementation of the program that would be *"manifestly"* disproportionate to its objective.[733] In *Gauweiler*, the Court did not elaborate

725. *Gauweiler*, §§85-89.
726. *Ibid.*, §89.
727. *Weiss*, §§80-81.
728. *Ibid.*, §82.
729. *Ibid.*, §83.
730. *Ibid.*, §§84-86.
731. *Ibid.*, §§87-90.
732. *Ibid.*, §92.
733. *Gauweiler*, §91, and *Weiss*, §93.

on this point, while in *Weiss*, it then described how in PSPP the risk of loss on the bonds purchased is mitigated and allocated within the Eurosystem.[734]

532. The Court's proportionality review in *Gauweiler* and *Weiss* leaves me with the following thoughts:

(a) Clearly, the design and implementation of monetary policy measures involve technical and often complex analysis of many variables, an abundance of evolving data and a good deal of uncertainties, "non-linearities" and unknowns, and this is the case *a fortiori* in a currency union of 20 sovereign States within an incomplete EMU. This inevitably requires specialized knowledge but also a significant measure of judgment and a certain margin of discretion (and error) on the part of the ECB. This complicates effective judicial review, particularly at the level of the proportionality assessment. The Court has stood back and appears to have limited its review mostly to a *prima facie* appraisal of common sense plausibility of the ECB's stated reasons, without substantive probing of the merits of the underlying analysis or opposing views. But how, in this approach, could the Court ever find the ECB's reasoning to fall short of *prima facie* plausibility? How could its judges, not schooled in the finer points of monetary theory or econometric analysis, ever confidently recognize an error in the ECB's assessment—unless the error were so egregious that the ECB would never make it in the first place? In other words, wouldn't such a marginal review necessarily tend to be deferential to the ECB's analysis and hence largely symbolic?

(b) Thus, by and large, the Court's proportionality assessment remained deferential to the ECB's stated reasoning and somewhat disengaged—and more so in *Gauweiler* than in *Weiss*. And several of the considerations advanced in *Weiss* do not appear to have been independently fact-checked or critically tested. As to the PSPP's temporary nature (*see* paragraph 531(b)(iv) above), the Court glossed over the fact that, by the time of its December 11, 2018 judgment, PSPP had already been in operation for three years and nine months.[735] As to PSPP's size (*see* paragraph 531(b)(v) above), the Court did not consider, or at least not mention, that, by the time of its judgment,

734. *Weiss*, §§94-99.

735. Nor did the Court consider that PSPP would go on after the judgment, as in fact it did for several more years. It is possible that the Court took some comfort in the ECB's June 14, 2018 announcement that it expected to reduce the monthly pace of net purchases under APP from EUR 30 billion to EUR 15 billion as of October 2018 and to discontinue APP net purchases (but not reinvestments) at the end of December 2018 (*see* the ECB's press release of June 14, 2018, https://www.ecb.europa.eu/press/pr/date/2018/html/ecb.mp180614.en.html). This was mentioned in the opinion of Advocate General Melchior Wathelet (*see* Opinion of Advocate General Wathelet of October 4, 2018 in Case C-493/17, ECLI:EU:C:2018:815, §104) but not in the Court's judgment which, curiously, referred only to PSPP's extension until the end of **2017** (*see Weiss*, §85).

aggregate Eurosystem PSPP holdings already stood close to EUR 2.1 trillion,[736] *i.e.*, almost 45 % of the Eurosystem's consolidated balance sheet as at November 30, 2018,[737] and about 21 % of total euro area government debt outstanding at that time.[738] As to the efficacy of PSPP asset purchases to increase below-target inflation (*see* paragraph 531(b)(vi) above), the evidence was really mixed as monthly headline inflation readings were significantly below the 2 % target from March 2015 through December 2016 and dropped again below target between March 2017 and April 2018.[739] It is possible that those considerations of the Court were based on information in the written and oral observations of the ECB in the course of the proceedings and not updated by the time of the judgment. But the question here is: leaving aside any substantive probing of the monetary analysis underlying the ECB's actions, should the Court be expected to engage in basic fact-checking in some measure?[740]

(c) The *Weiss* judgment shows the pitfalls of assessing the proportionality of an ongoing program of which the duration, size and effects continued to evolve. Would the Court have struggled more in its proportionality assessment if PSPP had come before it two years later? Or if new questions were referred to it now, prompted for example by the ECB's failure to accelerate the run-off of the PSPP portfolio by outright sales of securities prior to maturity?

(d) One would think that judicial review of proportionality should go beyond a perfunctory assessment of whether or not the measure at issue appears to be overreaching in terms of size or duration. One might expect that it would also look at whether, in the choice and design of the instrument used, the ECB has duly considered likely side effects of the measure and possible ways to mitigate them. An analysis of this kind is mostly lacking in *Gauweiler* where the Court was content to merely observe, without further particulars, that the ECB *"weighed up the various interests in play"* so as to prevent disproportionate disadvantages, and in *Weiss*, that analysis was fragmentary (*see* paragraph 531(c) above). Arguably, the Court should or could do little more than to check whether, in the choice and design of a measure, the ECB has effectively considered the collateral effects that are at issue in the proceedings

736. Specifically, total PSPP holdings were EUR 2,096,584 million at the end of November 2018. *See* "History of cumulative purchase breakdowns under APP" at https://www.ecb.europa.eu/mopo/implement/app/html/index.en.html.

737. The consolidated balance sheet total of the Eurosystem stood at EUR 4,660,299 million as at November 30, 2018. *See* "Consolidated financial statement of the Eurosystem 30 November 2018" at https://www.ecb.europa.eu/press/pr/wfs/html/index.en.html.

738. EUR 9,991,467.6 million at the end of 2018, according to Eurostat's data base, online data code GOV_10DD_EDPT1 (as updated on October 23, 2023).

739. Monthly headline inflation (HICP), annual rate of change, from Eurostat's data base, online data code PRC_HICP_MANR (as updated on September 29, 2023).

740. In his opinion in *Weiss*, Advocate General Wathelet engaged in a more articulate proportionality assessment, including by reviewing the minutes of the successive monetary policy meetings of the ECB's Governing Council—but again without clear indications of critical fact-checking. *See* Opinion of Advocate General Wathelet of October 4, 2018 in Case C-493/17, §§124-152.

and possibilities to mitigate them and has done so without clear "red card" errors or omissions. But this assessment should be clearly summarized in the judgment.

d No Monetary Financing

533. In both *Gauweiler* and *Weiss*, the BVerfG also asked the CJEU to consider whether the Eurosystem's secondary market purchases of government bonds under OMT and PSPP, respectively, may be in breach of the Treaty prohibition of monetary financing, *i.e.*, the monetization of government debt. While Article 123(1) TFEU expressly prohibits direct subscription of government bonds by central banks at primary market level, it does not, or at least not expressly, exclude subsequent central bank purchases of such bonds in the secondary market. However, the CJEU held that such secondary market purchases would nevertheless be caught by the Article 123(1) prohibition if (i) they became the *de facto* equivalent of primary market subscriptions, or (ii) they unduly diminished the Member States' incentive to pursue sound budgetary policies.[741] The Court reviewed OMT and PSPP under each of these two "anti-avoidance" tests.

534. In the Court's reasoning, in order not to fail the **first** test, central bank purchases may not be carried out in a manner that gives the financial markets, *i.e.*, prospective subscribers of the bonds in the primary market, a high degree of certainty that the bonds will be purchased by central banks within a time period and on conditions that allow market operators in effect to subscribe for the bonds as intermediaries for the central banks.[742] This seems to be a narrow and somewhat curious formulation of the first test. Perhaps the true underlying concern is (or should be) that market visibility on the timing and volume of subsequent central bank purchases of the bonds must not be such as to distort the pricing of the bonds at the time of issuance and, in effect, to allow the issuer to place debt in a higher volume and/or at a lower interest rate.

In any event, the Court cleared both OMT and PSPP under this first test:

(a) In *Gauweiler*, the Court summarily observed that according to drafts submitted and statements made by the ECB ... in the course of the proceedings, the ECB intended not to purchase bonds under OMT within some "black-out" period after issuance and not to pre-announce the timing or volume of purchases.[743] Redeeming virtue was found in opaqueness.

(b) In *Weiss*, the Court likewise took comfort in the fact that several PSPP program features limited foreseeability of PSPP purchases, including (i) a black-out period of uncertain duration;[744] (ii) the uncertain volume of PSPP purchases within the disclosed overall and variable monthly APP volume

741. *Gauweiler*, §§94-101, and *Weiss*, §§102-107.
742. *Gauweiler*, §104, and *Weiss*, §§109-110.
743. *Gauweiler*, §§105-106.
744. *Weiss*, §§114-116.

cap;[745] (iii) the broad spectrum as to the types and maturities of eligible public-sector debt securities;[746] and (iv) the purchase limits per issuer and per issue.[747]

535. The Court derived the **second** "anti-avoidance" test, *i.e.*, the requirement not to diminish the Member States' incentive to pursue sound budgetary policies, from the aim of Article 123(1) TFEU that appears in preparatory work for the Treaty of Maastricht, and from the ESCB's obligation to support the general economic policies in the Union.[748]

Again, both OMT and PSPP were cleared under this second test:

(a) In *Gauweiler*, the Court let OMT pass under this test, considering, in essence, that (i) the beneficiary Member State could not chart its budgetary policies on any *ex ante* certainty that a particular quantity of its bonds would be purchased, or held to maturity, by the Eurosystem;[749] (ii) OMT would not be implemented in such a way as to harmonize government bond yields across the euro area irrespective of country differences in underlying macroeconomic fundamentals;[750] and (iii) OMT purchases would be linked to EFSF/ESM financial assistance and be conditional upon full compliance with macroeconomic adjustment programs attached to such financial assistance.[751] Consideration (iii) seems to imply that, in the eyes of the Court, anti-fragmentation asset purchases may be harder to defend under Article 123(1) TFEU if they came without economic policy conditionality. Yet, at the same time, such conditionality would be more difficult to reconcile with the monetary policy logic of such purchases (*see* paragraph 522 above).

(b) Interestingly, also in *Gauweiler*, the Court was not troubled by the ECB's acceptance of *pari passu* treatment with other bondholders and the consequent exposure to loss on the bonds purchased in the event of sovereign default or debt restructuring. The Court considered that this would not weaken the program's built-in incentives for the Member State to pursue sound budgetary policies. It also observed that the risk of loss is inherent in de purchase of bonds, which is an operation authorized by Article 18.1 of Protocol No 4 without being conditional upon the ECB's having preferred creditor status.[752] Curiously, in its *Accorinti* judgment a few months later, the

745. *Ibid.*, §§118-120.
746. *Ibid.*, §§121-123.
747. *Ibid.*, §§124-126.
748. *Gauweiler*, §§100 and 109.
749. *Ibid.*, §§112-114 and 116-118.
750. *Ibid.*, §113.
751. *Ibid.*, §120.
752. *Ibid.*, §§123-126. In its subsequent judgment in the same case, the BVerfG does not appear to share this view, noting that, in the oral hearing, the ECB representative declared that the ECB would not approve a debt cut. *See* BVerfG, June 21, 2016, ECLI:DE:BVerfG:2016:rs20160621.2bvr272813, §204. An English translation of this judgment may be found at http://www.bverfg

General Court considered that *pari passu* treatment would have raised an issue under Article 123(1) TFEU,[753] but, with reference to the *Gauweiler* decision, it halfheartedly backtracked on this in its 2022 *Qi* judgment[754] (*see* paragraph 222 above).

(c) In *Weiss*, the Court noted a number of PSPP features that should keep Member States on their toes for maintaining budgetary discipline, including (i) uncertainties as to future bond purchases and the continuity of the program;[755] (ii) overall volume limitations and purchase limits per issuer and per issue;[756] and (iii) credit quality requirements.[757] Remarkably, the Court now considered the allocation of PSPP purchases according to the ECB capital subscription key, rather than on the basis of less neutral criteria such as *"for example"* government debt levels, as a helpful feature in this respect because that allocation key does not allow Member States to avoid the consequences of a deterioration in their budgetary positions.[758] This seems to imply *a contrario* that geographic selectivity deviating from the ECB capital key (as is an intrinsic feature of anti-fragmentation asset purchases) may rather be unhelpful in steering clear from the monetary financing prohibition of Article 123(1) TFEU. But the Court did not address this point in its Article 123 analysis in *Gauweiler*.

536. Finally, in *Weiss*, the Court further held that neither the absence of an obligation for the central banks to resell the government bonds prior to maturity[759] nor the acquisition of such bonds at a negative yield to maturity[760] suffice to establish a breach of Article 123(1) TFEU.

.de/e/rs20160621_2bvr272813en.html. I recall that, likewise, former Bundesbank President Jens Weidmann repeatedly expressed a contrary view to that espoused by the CJEU.

753. As a matter of fact, the question had also come up in the contemporaneous proceedings before the General Court in the *Accorinti* case, in which private individuals challenged the exclusion from the 2012 Greek sovereign debt restructuring of government bonds originally acquired by Eurosystem central banks under SMP and then swapped for identical bonds with different dates and serial numbers. In that case, discordantly, the ECB raised as a defense that, if Eurosystem bond holdings had been subject to the debt restructuring and its haircuts, this would have been inconsistent with the Eurosystem's financial and functional independence under Article 130 TFEU. Having regard to the size of those holdings, the General Court agreed that this would have been likely to affect the financial integrity of the Eurosystem but, in addition, held that an unconditional involvement in the debt restructuring *"would have been specifically in danger of being classified as intervention having an effect equivalent to that of the direct purchase of State bonds by those central banks, which is prohibited by Article 123 TFEU"*. *See* GC, October 7, 2015, Case T-79/13, *Accorinti et al. vs. ECB*, ECLI:EU:T:2015:756, §§86, 93 and 114.

754. *See* GC, February 9, 2022, Case T-868/16, *Qi et al. vs. European Commission & ECB*, ECLI:EU:T:2022:58, §110.

755. *Weiss*, §§132-136.

756. *Ibid.*, §§138-141.

757. *Ibid.*, §§142-143.

758. *Ibid.*, §140.

759. *Ibid.*, §§149-152.

760. *Ibid.*, §§154-157.

e Statement of Reasons

537. Under Article 296, second paragraph, TFEU, legal acts of EU institutions must state the reasons on which they are based, and so must those of the ECB. I should say a word on how the CJEU has applied this requirement to the ECB's decisions in monetary affairs. It is a favorite topic of lawyers—oftentimes used as *ultimum remedium* when other arguments fall short. Both in *Gauweiler* and (more elaborately so) in *Weiss*, the Court was fairly magnanimous on the subject.[761] It considered that, so long as the decisions themselves clearly express their essential objective, they need not address *"every relevant point of fact and law"* nor state specific reasons for *"each of the technical choices made"*. Also, when assessing the adequacy of the statement of reasons, the Court must have regard not only to the wording of the decision but also *"to the context and the whole body of legal rules governing the matter in question"*. In this respect, the Court could look at contemporaneous public statements made by the ECB, as the author of the act, as supplementing the statement of reasons, including in its press release, in the ECB President's introductory statement and Q&A at the press conference, in the (published) account of the Governing Council's monetary policy meeting and even, in *Weiss*, in studies published in the ECB's *Economic Bulletin*.[762]

538. The Court's reasoning on the requisite statement of reasons is broadly consistent with its earlier jurisprudence on the matter in the case of acts of general application (as distinguished from those addressed to individuals).[763] It should apply *a fortiori* to **policy** decisions (a further distinction not expressly made by the Court in *Gauweiler* or *Weiss*). For measures of this kind, so long as the measure's core rationale is stated in the act itself, I am not troubled by the Court looking at contemporaneous public statements of the ECB to confirm and complete its understanding of a measure's reasons. But, in my view, these statements would need to (i) be institutionally attributable to the ECB *qualitate qua*; (ii) be substantially contemporaneous with the relevant act; (iii) be public; and (iv) specifically address the circumstances and content of the relevant act. I would think that this should not generally extend, for example, to articles published in the ECB's *Economic Bulletin* (although this bulletin is produced under the responsibility of the ECB's Executive Board) nor to the (frequent) speeches of members of the ECB's Executive Board at various fora—and this may be for the better to avoid consistency issues.

f Dovish Judicial Review

539. In partial summary, it appears from the discussion of the *Gauweiler* and *Weiss* judgments in the preceding subsections that the CJEU's control over the manner in which the ECB understands and carries out its monetary policy mandate has been

761. *See Gauweiler*, §§70-71, and *Weiss*, §§31-42.
762. *Weiss*, §40.
763. *Cf.* K. Lenaerts, I. Maselis & K. Gutman, *supra*, pp. 378-380, §7.170.

broadly accommodative or, in monetary jargon, "dovish". The CJEU has, by and large, applied a form of "marginal" review, effectively leaving the ECB considerable leeway in defining the scope and boundaries of monetary policy and in choosing, designing and applying its monetary policy tools.

540. ***First***, faced with the scarcity of other definitional elements in the Treaty, the Court has delineated monetary policy principally by reference to its primary (but not exclusive) objective of maintaining price stability. And, absent a Treaty definition of this objective, it has readily accepted the ECB's operational definition, in terms of a medium-term inflation target of (close to) 2%, as not going beyond the Treaty framework and not being impaired by a manifest error of assessment.

541. ***Second***, characterizing policy actions "principally" on the basis of their objective, the Court has shown significant tolerance for cross-over effects of monetary policy actions in neighboring spheres of economic and fiscal policies, even if these effects were anticipated and knowingly accepted. It has not critically examined in any depth whether a measure's stated objective could properly be considered its controlling objective, and it has readily qualified cross-overs into other policy spheres as *"indirect effects"* without looking more closely into whether they might in reality constitute concurrent objectives. In this respect, the Court appears to derive some comfort from its belief that the Treaty did not intend to establish *"an absolute separation"* between monetary and economic policies.

542. ***Third***, as to the question of whether the ECB could, within its monetary policy mandate, link particular measures to economic policy conditions, the Court has accepted in *Gauweiler* that OMT purchases could be reserved for Member States under EFSF/ESM financial assistance and be conditional upon continued compliance with economic policy conditionality attached to such assistance. It has done so by a reasoning that appears to leave the door ajar for the broader possibility of the ECB subjecting its anti-fragmentation asset purchases to additional policy conditionality of its own.

543. ***Fourth***, in order to legitimize central bank asset purchases directed at containing financial fragmentation as being within the compass of monetary policy and to reconcile their geographic selectivity with the singleness of this policy, the Court has accepted that actions aimed at ensuring the proper pass-through of the monetary policy stance through the various transmission channels *"may be regarded as pertaining to the primary objective"* of monetary policy. In this manner, the Court appears to have made the proper functioning of the monetary policy transmission mechanism a parallel criterion for attaching central bank actions to the monetary policy mandate. This criterion may be capable of broader application to other measures beyond anti-fragmentation asset purchases. In the real world, there are a wide variety of "bugs" and "hiccups", in the web of channels and sub-channels of monetary policy transmission, that may obstruct the proper pass-through of the desired monetary policy stance and diminish its effectiveness. The Court has not (yet) articulated more precise criteria to determine what kind of bugs, and at what level, may justify monetary policy reactivity and in what circumstances, and the absence of such criteria makes the boundaries of the ECB's monetary policy mandate fluid. Also, the Court has not addressed the possible conflict that may arise between central bank (anti-fragmentation) asset purchases and inflation control, notably in a high(er)-inflation environment.

544. ***Fifth***, in its proportionality review of the ECB's monetary policy actions, the Court has allowed the ECB *"broad discretion"* in its analysis and choices and essentially confined judicial control to censuring manifest errors of assessment. These are the kinds of errors that the ECB is unlikely to make—or that the Court may not be able to recognize or authoritatively establish for that matter. By and large, the Court has limited itself to a benign review of the *prima facie* plausibility of the ECB's stated reasons, without substantive probing of the underlying analysis or opposing views and, apparently, without much fact-checking of its own. Also, it does not appear from the actual judgments in *Gauweiler* and *Weiss* that the Court has looked very closely into the question of whether, in the choice and design of its measures, the ECB has properly weighed possible harmful collateral effects and considered possibilities for mitigating them.

545. ***Sixth***, the Court has accepted that the Eurosystem's secondary market purchases of government bonds do not constitute monetization of government debt prohibited by Article 123(1) TFEU so long as those purchases cannot *de facto* be equated with direct subscriptions and do not unduly diminish a Member State's incentive to pursue sound fiscal policies. These are two relatively lenient tests that the Court has applied with a measure of benevolence. This has put the bar low enough for selective anti-fragmentation bond purchases to pass.

g Meanwhile in Karlsruhe ...

546. In the *Gauweiler* case, the BVerfG went along with the CJEU's interpretative ruling, albeit somewhat grudgingly[764] (*see* paragraphs 347-348 above). But, in its notorious judgment of May 5, 2020, in the *Weiss* case,[765] the BVerfG overtly challenged the CJEU's reasoning on the consistency of PSPP with the ECB's monetary policy mandate and its related proportionality review. This controversial part of the BVerfG's judgment invited a lot of polemic and hyperbole in the media. One seasoned commentator even described it as *"an act of legal secession"*, which *"[f]uture historians may mark [...] as the decisive turning point in Europe's history, towards disintegration"*.[766] One of the BVerfG's justices, Peter Huber, found it necessary to speak to journalists in an attempt to nuance the judgment, saying that *"[w]ir wollen also mehr EuGH, wir*

764. *See* BVerfG, June 21, 2016, ECLI:DE:BVerfG:2016:rs20160621.2bvr272813. An English translation of this judgment is reproduced on the BVerfG's website at https://www.bverfg.de/e/rs20160621_2bvr272813en.html.
765. *See* BVerfG, May 5, 2020, ECLI:DE:BVerfG:2020:rs20200505.2bvr085915. For an English translation of this (lengthy) judgment, *see* http://www.bverfg.de/e/rs20200505_2bvr085915en.html.
766. M. Wolf, "German court decides to take back control with ECB ruling", *Financial Times*, May 12, 2020, https://www.ft.com/content/37825304-9428-11ea-af4b-499244625ac4.

wollen, dass er seinen Job besser macht".[767] If this comment was intended to assuage the BVerfG's criticism of the CJEU's judgment, it may actually have come out the wrong way. It is somewhat ironical that, in the event, the BVerfG chose to rebel against the CJEU's more reasoned judgment on the more straightforward PSPP program, and not against the CJEU's earlier, more elliptical judgment on the legally more criticizable OMT program.

547. Thus, in the more inflammatory sections of the May 5, 2020 judgment, the BVerfG took issue with the CJEU's reasoning on the consistency of PSPP with the monetary policy mandate and its proportionality.[768] It held that it was not bound by the CJEU's preliminary ruling on this subject because, in essence, the CJEU had fallen short of properly exercising its mandate of effective judicial control, conferred by Article 19(1), first paragraph, second sentence, TEU, by issuing a ruling which, allowance being made for a certain margin of error (*"Fehlertoleranz"*, *sic*!), interprets the Treaties in a manner that is no longer comprehensible (*"nicht mehr nachvollziehbar"*) and is objectively arbitrary (*"objektiv willkürlich"*). But on what grounds did the BVerfG reach such a conclusion of Wagnerian harshness?

548. In broad outline, the BVerfG considered that in its assessment of PSPP, the CJEU (i) had not reviewed the genuineness and strength of PSPP's link to the price stability objective more closely but had essentially taken the ECB's word for it; (ii) had not sufficiently examined whether PSPP's foreseeable economic and budgetary effects did not reflect the pursuit of other objectives that encroach upon the Member States' economic and fiscal competences; (iii) had not properly weighed the proportionality of PSPP in view of its collateral effects notably on bank balance sheets, fixed-income pension schemes and savings; and (iv) had left the ECB too wide a measure of discretion, effectively allowing it to self-define and expand its monetary policy mandate, including possibly to an extent that would require amendment of the Treaty. Its own assessment of these issues then led the BVerfG to conclude that, by adopting PSPP as it did, the ECB appears to have acted *ultra vires*. It ruled that the Bundesbank should discontinue further participation in PSPP (and, in consultation with the ESCB, gradually dispose of its existing portfolio of bonds purchased under PSPP) unless, within three months, the ECB re-issued its PSPP decision with a proper balancing of the above considerations.

549. In contrast, the BVerfG accepted that in the case of PSPP, no manifest breach or circumvention of the monetary financing prohibition of Article 123(1) TFEU could be ascertained in view of certain features of PSPP.[769] Here, the BVerfG singled out two particular features, *i.e.*, the 33% purchase limit per issuer and the allocation of PSPP purchases in accordance with the ECB capital subscription key, as crucial safeguards

767. Quoted in several German newspapers, including in the *Handelsblatt* of May 13, 2020, https://www.handelsblatt.com/finanzen/geldpolitik/gegenwehr-verfassungsrichter-verteid igt-ezb-urteil-gegen-kritik/25825784.html.
768. *See* BVerfG, May 5, 2020, §§116-178.
769. *Ibid.*, §§180-221.

(*"entscheidenden 'Garantien'"*).[770] If this last feature were a genuine red line, it would not bode well for PEPP (given its greater flexibility in the allocation of purchases across geographies) and especially not for TPI (given its inherent geographic selectivity as an anti-fragmentation instrument *pur sang*).

550. The BVerfG's judgment of May 5, 2020, did not mark the end of the world as we know it. The BVerfG appears to have backed down somewhat since then. By an order of April 29, 2021,[771] it dismissed petitions for orders of execution under its May 5, 2020 judgment as inadmissible on procedural grounds. The BVerfG noted on this occasion that, at its meeting of June 3-4, 2020, the ECB's Governing Council had addressed proportionality issues in respect of PSPP,[772] and that, after exchanges with the President of the Bundesbank and reviewing certain documents received from the ECB, the Bundestag had concluded on July 2, 2020 that the ECB's proportionality assessment now met the requirements of the May 5, 2020 judgment.

551. Still, on June 9, 2021, the European Commission, indefatigably, announced that it had initiated Article 258 TFEU infringement proceedings against Germany for the BVerfG's alleged disregard of the primacy of EU law. But in a further plot twist, on December 2, 2021, the Commission closed the proceedings after having received *"very strong commitments"* from Germany recognizing the primacy of EU law and the final and binding nature of CJEU decisions, affirming that the legality of EU acts cannot be made subject to the examination of constitutional complaints before the German courts but can only be reviewed by the CJEU, and pledging to use *"all means at its disposal"* to avoid future repetition of an *ultra vires* finding by its (supposedly independent) judiciary.[773] In this manner, the parties (wisely?) avoided that a thorny issue ended up again with the CJEU.

h Effective Judicial Review

552. Undeniably, the CJEU has so far been accommodative, "dovish", in its judicial review of the ECB's monetary policy actions. One may speculate that the Court has been guided by a certain pragmatism or, if you wish, *raison d'Etat*, cognizant of the fact that in Europe's incomplete EMU, political and market realities have placed a heavy responsibility of macroeconomic stabilization on monetary policy and that, realistically, this requires a flexible, dynamic interpretation of the monetary policy mandate. Or more simply the fact that, absent ready alternatives, the urgency of the problem

770. *Ibid.*, §§216-217.

771. BVerfG, April 29, 2021, ECLI:DE:BVerfG:2021:rs20210429.2bvr165115. For an English translation of this order, *see* http://www.bverfg.de/e/rs20210429_2bvr165115en.html.

772. The minutes of this meeting indeed contain a fairly lengthy (and studied) section setting forth broader considerations regarding the efficacy and proportionality of asset purchases as a monetary policy tool. *See* the published account of the ECB Governing Council's monetary policy meeting of June 3-4, 2020, https://www.ecb.europa.eu/press/accounts/2020/html/ecb.mg200625~fd97330d5f.en.html, at pp. 13-16.

773. *See* the Commission's press release of December 2, 2021, https://ec.europa.eu/commission/presscorner/detail/en/inf_21_6201.

made imperfect action preferable to inaction. Yet, given the low resolution of the relevant Treaty provisions, the vast scope and impact of monetary policy, especially as it has evolved over the past decade, and the fact that it is carried out by an independent institution shielded from political directions and control by Article 130 TFEU, it is entirely legitimate to ask whether the CJEU should not hold monetary policy actions to a higher degree of judicial review. In an environment of increased public debate over the ECB's monetary policy actions, it is helpful and necessary that the CJEU is seen to exercise a measure of effective judicial control over this mandate and, accordingly, that the ECB is not perceived as having *carte blanche* to define its own mandate subject only to judicial censure of egregious transgressions that it is too smart to commit. But one has to approach the subject with a humble heart, in the knowledge that in this area, next to central banking, fewer jobs are more difficult than that of the judges of the CJEU. There are no obvious fixes. The CJEU is effectively the Union's supreme constitutional court and no such court can escape the occasional need to balance the rule of law and *raison d'Etat* in matters of broad societal import.

553. I should open a short parenthesis here on the Court's broader jurisprudence on the proper—marginal—scope of judicial review of acts of EU institutions in matters involving the assessment of complex factual situations requiring the exercise of judgment. The Court's time-honored position has been that, in such matters, the judiciary must refrain from substituting an assessment of its own for that of the competent institution but must instead confine itself to reviewing whether, in the exercise of its margin for judgment, the institution has, as a fundamental procedural guarantee, observed its obligation to carefully and impartially examine all of the relevant aspects of the situation at hand.

Let us consider, by way of illustration, how the Court applied this approach in its May 4, 2023 judgment in *Crédit Lyonnais*, on appeal from a judgment of the General Court that had partially annulled a decision of the ECB in a bank supervisory matter.[774] The Court derived from the proposition stated in the preceding paragraph, as *"settled case-law"*, that the judiciary:

> *"must, inter alia, establish not only whether the evidence relied on is factually accurate, reliable and consistent but also whether that evidence contains all the relevant information which must be taken into account in order to assess a complex situation and whether it is capable of substantiating the conclusions drawn from it"*.[775]

It added that, insofar as the analysis of the institution (here, the ECB) involves projections of future effects *"that may or may not occur"*, such analysis may be based on scenarios so long as these are not *"implausible in the light of the available information"*.[776]

774. CJEU, May 4, 2023, Case C-389/21 P, *ECB vs. Crédit Lyonnais*, ECLI:EU:C:2023:368.
775. *Ibid.*, §56.
776. *Ibid.*, §§92-93. In subsequent paragraphs, the Court spoke of *"manifestly implausible"* (§§94 and 101) and *"wholly implausible"* (§96).

These appear to be plausibly serious tests. But it seemed that the Court gave with one hand and took away with the other. It also found that the General Court had exceeded the permissible scope of judicial review by basing its partial annulment of the ECB's decision on the General Court's own assessment of certain facts and risks without confining itself to establishing a manifest error in the ECB's assessment.[777] Here, the Court drew a very thin line. How are the European courts supposed to identify a clear error in the ECB's assessment without taking a fresh look at the relevant facts and circumstances themselves and forming a view as to what they mean? Put in these terms, the Court's thin line may be invisibly thin. But it all may be a common sense question of degree: the European courts should not embark on an analysis of their own but stick to reviewing the ECB's decision within its four corners. Still, could this mean that the courts may not refer to or consider information external to the decision when reviewing the *prima facie* validity of the assessment made in this decision?

In *Crédit Lyonnais*, the dispute concerned the treatment of certain exposures in the calculation of an individual bank's leverage ratio, a pure bank supervisory question. One would think that *a fortiori* the Court would not be inclined to go any further in the case of general policy decisions like those in the monetary policy sphere where the ECB must be allowed a measure of discretion to make policy choices on the basis of its assessment of complex and partly uncertain economic data.

554. In his opinion in *Weiss*, Advocate General Melchior Wathelet put the issue squarely when writing that the Court could not be criticized for limiting the scope of judicial review in monetary policy affairs as it has done *"since a more in-depth analysis would no longer be legal, but, in the present case, would be economic, and this falls outside the technical competence of the court"*.[778] Surely a candid observation, but two important nuances are in order:

(a) One should distinguish questions regarding the **scope** of the monetary policy mandate (and its delineation against other policy spheres) from questions regarding the manner of **exercise** of that mandate (including its proportionality assessment). A standard of "marginal" review (which, aside from procedural flaws, censures only manifest errors of appraisal and clear transgressions of the limits of discretion) may indeed be appropriate for the second type of questions. But full judicial review should be brought to bear on questions of the first kind.

(b) As particularly concerns questions of the second type, of course, monetary policy analysis is often technical and complex and sometimes even arcane. It rests on theories and involves the use of models which, in all of their

777. *See*, in particular, *ibid.*, §§65-74.

778. *See* Opinion of Advocate General Wathelet of October 4, 2018 in Case C-493/17, §117. In addition, in his footnote 91, the Advocate General refers, without comment, to certain authors who also rely on the necessary independence of the ECB to justify the limited scope of judicial review. I amicably disagree. It is precisely the ECB's independence from political direction and control that places greater weight on effective judicial review.

sophistication, leave many uncertainties and unknowns. And monetary theory is not entirely free from doctrinal disagreements. The actual conduct of monetary policy requires difficult judgments that are subject to a significant margin of error. One could not reasonably expect the Court to wade deeply into substantive probing of the validity of the ECB's monetary analysis, and the Court must not trespass on the ECB's margin of judgment by substituting its own policy views. In principle, marginal review is indeed the customary standard of judicial control in matters of this kind. Yet, even marginal review must not become "inframarginal" and be overly deferential to the ECB's explanations. The Court could and should kick the tires of the ECB's decisions by asking common sense questions as to their factual basis, the factors considered and the consistency of the reasoning. The Court's lack of technical expertise should not in and of itself be a reason for a hands-off approach. Technical complexity is not unique to monetary policy and arises in other matters in which the Court may lack expertise of its own but which it must nevertheless adjudicate. If really needed, the Court could, on its own motion, order witness testimony or expert reports.[779]

555. It would seem that the Court could strengthen its review of monetary policy actions in several respects:

(a) It would be desirable for the Court to clarify the pixelated dividing line between the respective spheres of monetary policy and economic and fiscal policies. It should pause to carefully consider the cross-over effects of monetary policy actions into other policy areas and not dismiss them too quickly as unavoidable *"indirect effects"*. The Court could examine more closely whether they appear to be genuine secondary effects or instead reflect some concurrent or even primary objective. In a similar vein, when reviewing a monetary policy measure, the Court could also look more critically at any link with economic or fiscal policy conditionality, from the dual vantage point of undue intrusions in these policy areas and consistency with the stated monetary policy logic of the measure.

(b) Insofar as the effective functioning of the monetary policy transmission mechanism is to serve as a parallel criterion for attaching central bank asset purchases or other non-standard actions to the monetary policy mandate, this reasoning is in need of more precise criteria to determine what kind of "bugs" in the transmission mechanism may justify monetary policy reactivity and in what circumstances. For example, what about country-specific bugs that derive from national economic or fiscal policy choices or indeed are caused by deficiencies in these national policies? The Court should also address the potential conflict that may arise between such transmission repair action and

779. Articles 66 and 70 of the Rules of Procedure of the Court of Justice.

the monetary policy stance aimed at inflation control, notably in a higher-inflation environment.

(c) The proportionality assessment is a particularly difficult area for judicial review. Still, within the bandwidth of marginal review, it should be possible for the Court to move up a notch in the scale. It could do so by not taking the reasons proffered by the ECB at face value but by more systematically reviewing whether those reasons are *prima facie* plausible, coherent, rest on credible analysis and are capable of substantiating that the relevant measure is suitable and necessary for pursuing the stated objective. The Court could also review more closely whether, in the choice and design of the instrument, proper consideration has been given to minimizing adverse collateral effects.

(d) The Court could articulate sharper tests that would need to be met in order for secondary market purchases of government bonds to steer clear of prohibited monetization of government debt. This is especially relevant for defining the permissible use of this tool as an anti-fragmentation instrument. Presumably, the Court could focus here on some criterion of destabilizing market dynamics that disconnect sovereign bond yields from underlying macroeconomic fundamentals (*see* paragraphs 369 *et seq.* above).

556. In the monetary policy sphere, the ECB's margin for judgment does not only or even predominantly derive from the technical complexity of the subject. It derives first and foremost from the **policy** nature of the choices to be made and from the inevitable uncertainties regarding their future effects and their *ex ante* assessment. Still, it is incumbent on the judiciary to review that these decisions are not based on materially incorrect facts, implausible projections or inconsistent reasoning, and that the ECB has engaged reasonable efforts to consider all relevant information. There is oftentimes merit in brevity. One would not ordinarily look forward with keen anticipation to reading longer judgments. But this subject area may be among the exceptions.

557. All this said, I concur with the Court's characterization of **PSPP** as monetary policy in its 2018 *Weiss* judgment insofar as PSPP, as a form of across-the-board QE not linked to economic policy conditionality, is a—non-conventional—technique of monetary easing. But substantively, I continue to struggle with the Court's reasoning in its 2015 *Gauweiler* judgment that placed **OMT** within the compass of the ECB's monetary policy mandate. It is conceptually and legally more of a stretch to classify OMT or other anti-fragmentation asset purchases as monetary policy. Geographically selective asset purchases to counter excessive widening of sovereign bond spreads and contain financial instability and even redenomination risk, *i.e.*, the risk of euro exit, are not monetary policy proper. They are something else, *i.e.*, by the reasoning of the 2012 *Pringle* judgment, economic policy. It is at this level, by some euro area stability mechanism based on Article 136(3) TFEU, outside the perimeter of monetary policy, that this problem could be addressed on firmer legal ground (*see* paragraphs 397-404 above). By ruling as it did in *Gauweiler*, the Court may have acted wisely and with statesmanship under the circumstances, given the potentially destabilizing consequences of an *ultra vires* ruling. But it did so at the cost of a questionable legal reasoning.

Chapter 8

EMU Fiscal and Macroeconomic Surveillance Rules

558. The EMU fiscal and macroeconomic surveillance frameworks have over time become a complex web of rules and procedures for the review and coordination of the Member States' economic and fiscal policies. They have evolved considerably over the course of the past 25 years on what has been a continuous learning curve, and one significant further reform is in progress at the time of writing. These frameworks apply in good part to all EU Member States but also include a subset of specific provisions for euro area Member States, as we will see. This chapter attempts to provide a synthesis of their key features and challenges, focusing on the aspects most relevant in the context of the currency union. It is hard to condense this elaborate rule book and its current reform into a chapter of manageable size. The Commission's own "vade mecum" on the (pre-reform) fiscal rules is over 90 pages in its latest (2019) edition,[780] and its "compendium" on the macroeconomic imbalance procedure is over 120 pages.[781]

1 ALIGNING NATIONAL ECONOMIC AND FISCAL POLICIES IN AN INCOMPLETE EMU: A RUBIK'S CUBE

559. In today's European currency union, a single currency, exchange rate policy and monetary policy co-exist with a plurality of national economic and fiscal policies of 20 fairly diverse euro area Member States. Under the Treaties, these Member States keep a substantial degree of autonomy over their economic and fiscal policies, subject to a measure of "coordination" at the EU level. By the same token, they retain, as a matter

780. European Commission, *Vade Mecum on the Stability & Growth Pact, European Economy Institutional Papers No 101*, April 2019, 95 pp.
781. European Commission, *The Macroeconomic Imbalance Procedure. Rationale, Process, Application: A Compendium, European Economy Institutional Papers No 39*, November 2016, 126 pp.

of principle, sole and final responsibility for their public finances: (i) neither the Union nor the other Member States are co-liable for their debts or may bail them out (Article 125 TFEU); (ii) neither the ECB nor national central banks may finance their governments (Article 123 TFEU); and (iii) there are no robust budgetary mechanisms at EU level for (quasi-)automatic stability support transfers to Member States.

560. Being deprived of exchange rate adjustment and monetary policy as macroeconomic stabilization instruments under their control, and given limited financial transfer mechanisms at the EU level, euro area Member States now depend more heavily on economic and fiscal policies to stabilize their economies in response to cyclical fluctuations or external shocks, and to do so in a manner that strikes the proper political balance between competing claims of their domestic constituencies. While this necessitates an adequate measure of autonomy in the conduct of these policies, currency union membership simultaneously requires Member States to submit to a degree of discipline and coordination of those policies in order to avoid undue interference with the single monetary policy and to contain the build-up of excessive sovereign debt or trade imbalances that may produce adverse spill-over effects elsewhere in the currency zone and, in the event, strain the currency union and compromise continued currency union membership. To reconcile a proper degree of national economic and fiscal autonomy with common rules of the game to contain risks to the currency union is a difficult proposition. The evolving EMU fiscal and macroeconomic surveillance frameworks have over the years struggled with this challenge, with mitigated success.

561. It is in fact a particularly complex Rubik's Cube and one that may well be impossible to solve fully in an incomplete EMU. The task at hand may be described more as finding an imperfect combination of the parts that is workable and adequately efficient. It must navigate difficult substantive challenges of an economic and political nature, as well as legal issues as to the scope and coercive nature of the kind of common rules that can be put in place.

562. In the fiscal policy space, common rules of the game must avoid both undue fiscal largesse and undue fiscal restraint, especially when pro-cyclical:

(a) Excessive and/or indiscriminate fiscal stimulus may interfere with a restrictive monetary policy stance in an environment of higher inflation, as it did at times in 2022 and 2023. It may also over time cause the build-up of high and eventually unsustainable levels of government debt. High and diverging levels of government debt in the system may constrain monetary policy to a more accommodative stance than is desirable for inflation control and/or require geographically selective asset purchases to counter excessive widening of sovereign bond spreads, financial fragmentation and its attendant risks for the cohesion of the currency union.

(b) In contrast, undue fiscal restraint, like the pro-cyclical fiscal restraint observed by several Member States in the aftermath of the 2010-2012 euro area sovereign debt crisis, dampens growth and weighs on public investments. It may shift the burden of macroeconomic adjustment disproportionately to monetary policy and require stronger and/or longer monetary easing, as arguably happened in the euro area during much of the 2013-2019 period.

563. Finding the right macroeconomic policy mix between monetary and fiscal policies may be difficult enough in a single-country setting, especially when inflation and output/employment move in opposite directions. These difficulties are compounded in a multi-country currency union in which a single monetary policy has to contend with a plurality of national fiscal policies that need to address different economic and political circumstances. The potential for tensions and conflicts increases with the degree of country heterogeneity and hence the lack of symmetry within the system. As we discussed in Chapter 2, the evidence as to growing convergence among euro area economies is mixed. While business cycles have broadly become more synchronous across the euro area, there remain appreciable country differences in cyclical amplitudes. In other words, movements in key macroeconomic variables have tended to become more aligned directionally but their actual values have continued to differ significantly—and generally more so in periods of stress like the 2008-2012 and 2020-2022 years. By and large, developments in the euro area do not offer uncontroverted evidence in support of the endogeneity hypothesis of OCA theory (*see* paragraph 146 above).

564. Also, the interaction between the single monetary policy and national fiscal policies will vary from one Member State to another because of differences in a myriad of ingrained or slow-moving country characteristics (such as the degree of dependency on fossil fuel imports, wage bargaining practices, the importance of automatic budgetary stabilizers, the upstream or downstream location in production chains, fixed or floating rate housing loans, *et cetera*). Such differences in structural country characteristics will inevitably differentiate the pass-through of the single monetary policy through the various channels and sub-channels of monetary policy transmission.

565. More broadly, national policies may cause excessive external imbalances that produce negative spill-over effects elsewhere in the euro area and may eventually strain the cohesion of the currency union. Common rules of the game must not be confined to addressing deviations in fiscal positions but must address broader imbalances and deal with their outward spillovers. Modeling cross-border effects of national policies is a difficult and, to varying degrees, conjectural exercise.

566. Common rules of the game will likely be short on substantive one-size-fits-all rules—simply, in large part, because in reality one size fits few or none. Instead, those rules mostly provide a framework of criteria and processes that lead to country-specific adjustments. Yet, country focus must not detract from an overall euro area perspective: whether country fiscal positions or imbalances are excessive or otherwise deviant should be determined in part in reference to the macroeconomic stability of the euro area as a whole, or at least one would like to think that this should be so in a currency union. In a sense, a single euro area monetary policy stance should as its counterpart have a broadly coherent aggregate euro area fiscal stance—an overall view of what is fiscally desirable for the euro area in its entirety. And the sum of country-specific adjustments should be consistent with that aggregate view. If the euro area as a whole requires moderate fiscal stimulus, country-specific adjustments should not add up to a neutral or restrictive fiscal stance.[782] This seems obvious but it is actually hard to figure out with much precision, and it touches upon the thorny issue of the allocation of the burden of adjustment.

567. The preceding paragraphs raise the politically sensitive issue of the allocation of the adjustment burden among euro area Member States. There is first the classical issue of (a)symmetry in the allocation between "deficit" and "surplus" countries. One may be inclined to think that common rules of the game should primarily focus on avoiding and remedying excessive public spending, government debt and trade deficits—and this seems to have been the dominant focus of the EU rules for many years. But fiscal restraint and trade surpluses may not always be the unequivocal virtues they appear to be, especially not in a currency union of diverse economies. A (larger) Member State's fiscal conservatism or sizable and persistent trade surpluses may produce negative spill-over effects elsewhere in the euro area notably by making it more difficult for its euro area trading partners to correct their current account deficits. And when euro area inflation is too low, a Member State's persistent fiscal conservatism may also complicate monetary policy action aimed at countering disinflationary pressures. From a consolidated euro area angle, it may well make good sense for that Member State to use some of its fiscal space to promote higher real wage growth and otherwise stimulate domestic demand so as to ease the burden of adjustment on its euro area trading partners. This will especially be the case in circumstances in which other euro area Member States would otherwise face unrealistically large or counterproductive adjustments to rebalance their trade accounts or reduce their sovereign debt. But one can easily see how politically contentious discussions on the (re)allocation of the burden of adjustment and related claims for more symmetry could become.[783]

782. An inconsistency of this kind was spotted by the European Court of Auditors for 2017 and 2018. *See* European Court of Auditors, *Audit of the Macroeconomic Imbalance Procedure (MIP)*, Special Report No 03/2018, January 23, 2018, p. 29, §50, https://www.eca.europa.eu/Lists/ECADocuments/SR18_03/SR_MIP_EN.pdf.

783. By way of illustration, the textbook example of a fiscally conservative Member State with recurring trade surpluses has traditionally been Germany. In 2016, the European Commission proposed that the Council in its country-specific policy recommendations call on Germany to *"[a]chieve a sustained upward trend in public investment [...] by using the available fiscal space and prioritising expenditure"* (COM(2016) 326 final, May 18, 2016, p. 6, https://eur-lex.europa.eu/legal-content/EN/TXT/PDF/?uri = CELEX: 52016DC0326). The Council's recommendation of July 12, 2016 deleted the all too explicit reference to using available fiscal space and prioritising expenditure and replaced it with the phrase *"while respecting the medium term objective"* (*OJ* C299, August 18, 2016, p. 19, at p. 22). A year later, noting that Germany's current account surplus had increased further in 2015, stayed broadly at the same level in 2016 and was expected to remain elevated, the Commission proposed that the Council call on Germany to take action in 2017 and 2018 to *"[u]se fiscal policy to support domestic demand and achieve a sustained upward trend in investment"* (COM(2017) 505 final, May 22, 2017, p. 7, https://commission.europa.eu/system/files/2017-D5/2017-european-semester-country-specific-recommendations-commission-recommendations-germany.pdf). In the Council's recommendation to Germany of July 11, 2017, this subdued formulation was subtly rephrased to *"[w]hile respecting the medium-term objective, use fiscal and structural policies to support*

568. Another side of the symmetry issue is that the national policies of the larger economies (notably the Big Five) and the imbalances to which they may give rise naturally tend to produce larger spill-over effects within the euro area. Accordingly, as a theoretical matter, one would expect that the common rules of the game should pay closer attention to those imbalances and may require relatively stronger remedial action from larger economies. Size matters in Europe's incomplete EMU, in ways that may not have been fully explored in academic literature. Conversely, imbalances in smaller economies should generally affect euro area equilibria less significantly, while at the same time, because of their limited weight in euro area price indicators, these smaller economies are also more likely to find themselves having to live with a single monetary policy stance that is less than optimal for their needs. Thus, due to the greater outward spill-overs of their national economic and fiscal policies, larger economies could be expected to submit to relatively greater limitations and adjustments in the interest of the overall macroeconomic stability of the euro area. But this does not make the political discussions on (a)symmetry in the allocation of the burden of adjustment any easier, especially not when the larger economies have imbalances of opposite sign (as has often been the case among the Big Five).

569. In the past few years, the euro area economy entered a zone of higher turbulence with (i) high and geographically diverse inflation; (ii) simmering recessionary risks; (iii) high and diverging government debt levels; (iv) substantial public and private investment needs to make up for the "investment gap" of the prior decade and to address climate change and the green transition, digital transformation and the rebuilding of defense capabilities; (v) geopolitical tensions and risks of disruptions to international trade and investment flows; and (vi) a particularly elevated degree of uncertainty as to how these processes will interact and play out over time. It is in these unforgiving circumstances that the common fiscal rules are now undergoing further revision, as we will discuss in the final section of this chapter (*see* paragraphs 607 *et seq.* below).

2 TREATY RULES AND LIMITATIONS

a The Treaty's General Provisions

570. In the European Union, economic and fiscal policies remain, as a rule, within the exclusive competence of the Member States, subject to the limitations and carve-outs provided by the Treaty. Except as provided in Article 4 TFEU, economic and fiscal policies are not competences shared between the Union and the Member States within the meaning of Article 2(2) TFEU. But the Treaty subjects those national policies to a measure of "coordination" at the EU level, as outlined below.

---

potential growth and domestic demand as well as to achieve a sustained upward trend in investment" (*OJ* C261, August 9, 2017, p. 18, at p. 22). One can sense how political sensitivities on the subject brought the higher art of diplomacy to bear on the formulation of non-binding recommendations.

571. The more general Treaty provisions on economic policy coordination include the following:

(a) Under Article 2(3) TFEU, Member States are under an obligation to coordinate their economic policies *"within arrangements as determined by this Treaty, which the Union shall have competence to provide"*. Article 5(1), first paragraph, TFEU repeats the Member States' obligation to coordinate their economic policies *"within the Union"*, adding that *"[t]o this end, the Council shall adopt measures, in particular broad guidelines for these policies"*.
(b) Perhaps somewhat more ambiguously, Article 119(1) TFEU provides that *"the activities of the Member States and the Union shall include, as provided in the Treaties, the adoption of an economic policy which is based on the close coordination of Member States' economic policies [...] and on the definition of common objectives"*. Under Article 119(3), *"[t]hese activities of the Member States and the Union"* must comply with certain *"guiding principles"*, including stable prices, sound public finances and a sustainable balance of payments.
(c) Circling back to the Member States' economic policies, Article 120 TFEU requires Member States to conduct these policies *"with a view to contributing to the achievement of the objectives of the Union"* defined in Article 3 TEU and *"in the context of the broad guidelines"* set out in a recommendation by the Council. Under Article 121(1) TFEU, they must regard their economic policies *"as a matter of common concern"* and coordinate them *"within the Council"*.

572. After these somewhat meandering and low-resolution provisions, Article 121 TFEU continues by requiring the Council to prepare, upon a recommendation from the European Commission, a draft of *"broad guidelines of the economic policies of the Member States and the Union"*, to report to the European Council and, on the basis of the European Council's conclusion, to adopt a recommendation setting out those broad guidelines. Article 121 then outlines a *"multilateral surveillance"* process in which the Council, on the basis of reports from the Commission, monitors economic developments in each of the Member States and in the Union. If a Member State's economic policies are inconsistent with the broad guidelines or *"risk jeopardising the proper functioning of economic and monetary union"*, the Commission *"may"* address a warning to that Member State and, on a recommendation from the Commission, the Council *"may"* follow up with *"the necessary recommendations"*.

573. Article 126 TFEU addresses the subject of excessive fiscal imbalances—at least those with negative sign—with greater specificity and establishes what is commonly referred to as the "excessive deficit procedure" or "EDP":

(a) Member States are placed under an affirmative obligation to avoid *"excessive government deficits"*—a term which, perhaps counterintuitively, is understood to cover excessive government **debt** as well.

(b) The Commission is tasked with monitoring the Member States' budgetary situation and government debt with a view to identifying *"gross errors"*. This curious formulation of what the Commission is supposed to look out for is then particularized as examining compliance with budgetary discipline *"on the basis of"* the two fiscal convergence criteria that served (and continue to serve) as tests for admission to currency union membership (*see* paragraph 49(b) above).

(c) These fiscal benchmarks are that (i) a Member State's actual or planned government deficit may not exceed 3 % of GDP (at market prices), unless this ratio has declined *"substantially and continuously"* to a level close to 3 %, or, alternatively, the excess is *"exceptional and temporary"* with the ratio remaining close to 3 %; and (ii) its government debt may not exceed 60 % of GDP (at market prices), unless this ratio is *"sufficiently diminishing"* and *"approaching"* 60 % *"at a satisfactory pace"* (Article 126(2), first paragraph, TFEU). Interestingly, the numerical values of these two ratios are actually specified in Protocol No 12 on the excessive deficit procedure, annexed to the Treaties, and this Protocol may be replaced by *"appropriate provisions"* adopted by the Council, acting unanimously and after consulting the European Parliament and the ECB (Article 126(14), second paragraph, TFEU).

(d) When a Member State fails either (or both) of these fiscal criteria, a process unfolds in which, sequentially:
   (i) the Commission draws up a report and, if it considers that an excessive deficit *"exists or may occur"*, addresses an *"opinion"* to the Member State concerned;
   (ii) upon a proposal from the Commission, the Council must then decide *"after an overall assessment"* whether an excessive deficit exists and, if it so decides, it must, on a recommendation from the Commission, address *"recommendations"* to the Member State to remedy the situation within some specified period;
   (iii) absent *"effective action"* by the Member State within this time frame, the Council *"may"* publish its recommendations;
   (iv) if a **euro area** Member State *"persists"* in failing to implement these recommendations, the Council *"may"* summon (*"give notice to"*) that Member State to take, by a specified deadline, such *"deficit reduction"* measures as the Council deems necessary; and
   (v) so long as the euro area Member State in question fails to comply with that summons, the Council *"may"* impose, and further intensify, one or more economic sanctions, including by requiring additional market disclosures for the issuance of government bonds, by *"inviting"* the European Investment Bank to *"reconsider"* its lending policy toward that Member State, and by imposing a non-interest-bearing deposit and outright fines *"of an appropriate size"*.

b The Treaty's Euro Area-Specific Provisions

574. While the Treaty provisions summarized in the preceding subsection generally apply to all Member States, the Treaty also contains or contemplates certain euro area-specific rules:

(a) The final coercive steps of EDP set forth in Article 126(9) and (11) TFEU, outlined in paragraph 573(d)(iv) and (v) above, apply only to euro area Member States, and not, under Article 139(2)(b) TFEU, to Member States "with a derogation".

(b) The Treaty of Lisbon of December 13, 2007 has added a second paragraph to Article 5(1) TFEU saying, in broad terms, that *"[s]pecific provisions"* on economic policy coordination shall apply to euro area Member States. To this effect, the Lisbon Treaty has further added Article 136(1) and (2) TFEU which mandate the Council (with only representatives of euro area Member States entitled to vote) to adopt, *"in accordance with the relevant provisions of the Treaties"*, measures specific to euro area Member States to strengthen the coordination and surveillance of their *"budgetary discipline"* and to set out economic policy guidelines for them that are compatible with those adopted for the Union as a whole. Article 136 has served as a basis for euro area-specific provisions of EU secondary legislation on the fiscal and macro-economic surveillance frameworks, including two regulations as part of the 2011 "Six Pack" reforms and the two regulations of the 2013 "Two Pack" reforms (*see* paragraphs 590 and 594-596 below).

(c) Article 137 TFEU and Protocol No 14 on the Euro Group, also added by the Lisbon Treaty, give a nod of recognition to the Eurogroup, *i.e.*, the meeting of ministers of the euro area Member States, as a forum for informal discussions on *"questions related to the specific responsibilities they share with regard to the single currency"*. Undeniably, the Eurogroup has *de facto* become an important actor in euro area governance. But, legally, it is an instrument of intergovernmental coordination without any competence of its own in the EU legal order.

In its 2016 *Mallis* judgment, the European Court of Justice held that the Eurogroup could neither be equated with a configuration of the Council within the meaning of Article 16(6) TEU nor be classified as a body, office or agency of the European Union within the scope of Article 263 TFEU, with the consequence that the acts of the Eurogroup are not subject to legality review and possible annulment by the Court.[784] In its 2018 *Chrysostomides* judgment, however, the General Court considered that, since the Eurogroup is formally recognized by Article 137 TFEU and Protocol No 14 and intended to contribute to one of the Union's stated objectives, it could still be viewed as an

784. CJEU, September 20, 2016, Joined Cases C-105/15 P to C-109/15 P, *Mallis et al. vs. European Commission and ECB*, ECLI:EU:C:2016:702, §61.

institution of the Union whose acts are attributable to the Union and may engage its non-contractual liability under Article 340, second paragraph, TFEU.[785] But on appeal, the Court of Justice overruled the General Court's judgment on this point.[786]

The Court's conclusions regarding the standing and actions of the Eurogroup in the EU legal order should apply *a fortiori* for the Euro Summits, *i.e.*, informal meetings of the Heads of State or Government of the euro area Member States, which are not mentioned in the Treaties but have been established by Article 12 of the separate Treaty on Stability, Coordination and Governance in the Economic and Monetary Union of March 2, 2012 to discuss matters relevant to the currency union, including *"strategic orientations for the conduct of economic policies to increase convergence in the euro area"*.

c Euro Area-Specific Provisions in Separate International Agreements

575. Certain matters pertaining to the coordination and surveillance of national economic and fiscal policies more specifically in the euro area are dealt with in two separate international agreements outside or on the periphery of the EU legal framework:

(a) The Treaty on Stability, Coordination and Governance in the Economic and Monetary Union ("TSCG") just mentioned is an intergovernmental agreement concluded on March 2, 2012 in response to the euro area sovereign debt crisis of those years, to which all Member States are now parties.[787] It strengthens and supplements the EU rules and processes (as they then existed) regarding budgetary discipline, coordination of economic policies, and euro area governance matters. TSCG essentially builds on the existing EU organizational set-up and procedures, and it abounds with qualifiers stressing that its provisions are without prejudice to, and must be interpreted and applied in a manner consistent with, applicable rules of EU law. TSCG's key section is Title III (Articles 3 to 8), entitled and commonly referred to as the "Fiscal Compact", which is binding on all euro area Member States and, on an opt-in basis, on Bulgaria, Denmark and Romania. We will discuss the Fiscal Compact later in this chapter (*see* paragraph 593 below).

TSCG's provisions were originally intended as amendments to the Treaty but, when this was opposed by the United Kingdom, a separate intergovernmental agreement between a "coalition of the willing" was

785. GC, July 13, 2018, Case T-680/13, *Chrysostomides vs. Council et al.*, ECLI:EU:T:2018:486, §§109-114.

786. CJEU, December 16, 2020, Joined Cases C-597/18 P, C-598/18 P, C-603/18 P and C-604/18 P, *Council vs. Chrysostomides et al.*, ECLI:EU:C:2020:1028, §§87-90.

787. TSCG was originally signed by all then Member States except the United Kingdom and the Czech Republic. Croatia signed up on March 17, 2018 and the Czech Republic eventually on April 3, 2019.

viewed as an interim solution and stepping stone toward later incorporation into the Treaty or EU secondary legislation. Thus, Article 16 TSCG calls for the necessary steps to be taken, within at most five years from TSCG's entry into effect (on January 1, 2013), to incorporate its substance into the EU legal framework. In fact, there was already at the outset a fair degree of substantive commonality between some of TSCG's provisions and those contained in EU secondary legislation on the subject, as just amended by the "Six Pack" reforms, and certain other provisions were subsequently integrated into EU law by the "Two Pack" regulations (*see* paragraph 593(a) and (d) below). The integration of certain additional elements of the Fiscal Compact into the EU legal framework is being addressed in the current reforms of the EU common fiscal rules (*see* paragraph 612 below).

(b) The other separate international agreement is the Treaty Establishing the European Stability Mechanism concluded on February 2, 2012 between the euro area Member States only ("ESM Treaty"). Also in response to the euro area sovereign debt crisis of those days, the ESM Treaty set up a dedicated euro area financing mechanism for extending stability support in various forms to euro area Member States. As will be further discussed in Chapter 10, ESM stability support comes with economic policy conditionality, and this raises questions as to the interaction between such policy conditions and the EU competences and rules on the coordination and surveillance of national economic and fiscal policies (*see* paragraphs 577(c), 580, 715(b) and 717-718 below).

d Four More Observations

576. At this juncture, four further observations need to be made regarding the core legal framework for the coordination of national economic and fiscal policies outlined above.

577. ***First***, as a rule, economic and fiscal policies remain exclusive competences of the Member States, with the Union's competence being limited to "coordination" of these policies. But questions remain about the precise objectives, scope and enforceability of policy coordination at the Union level:

(a) It is not always crystal clear from the relevant Treaty provisions precisely which **objective(s)** such coordination must pursue or focus on. In its seminal 1997 Luxembourg Resolution on economic policy coordination, the European Council stated that the *"basic reason"* for closer EU surveillance and coordination of economic policies among euro area Member States is that, to the extent that national economic developments have an impact on inflation prospects in the euro area, they will influence monetary conditions in that area.[788] This suggests a focus on national economic policies and developments insofar as they affect inflation. Then again, Article 136(1)(a) TFEU, added by the 2007 Lisbon Treaty, refers to euro area-specific measures to strengthen the coordination and surveillance of *"budgetary discipline"* (*see* paragraph 574(b) above).

(b) Nor, in general, is the Treaty particularly articulate in defining the **substantive scope** of the Union's coordination competence, the extent to which its coordination measures may weigh in on or bend the priorities and conduct of national policies, and the degree of coercion that may be applied in this respect. It would seem in any event that EU action regarding coordination of the Member States' economic policies must adhere to the principle of subsidiarity stated in Article 5(3) TEU. In the 1997 Luxembourg Resolution, the European Council confirmed that enhanced economic policy coordination within the euro area must observe this principle and *"respect the prerogatives of national governments in determining their structural and budgetary policies"*.[789]

(c) In its 2012 *Pringle* judgment, the European Court of Justice observed that *"Articles 2(3) and 5(1) TFEU restrict the role of the Union in the area of economic policy to the adoption of coordinating measures"*, and then added that this does not extend to the establishment of a stability support mechanism like the ESM.[790] It did so notwithstanding the fact that economic policy conditions attached to ESM stability support constitute an essential aspect of this mechanism. On this subject, the Court noted, perhaps somewhat perfunctorily, that such policy conditionality *"does not constitute an instrument for the coordination of the economic policies of the Member States, but is intended to ensure that the activities of the ESM are compatible with, inter alia, Article 125 TFEU and coordinating measures adopted by the Union"*[791] (*see also* paragraph 580 below).

(d) When addressing the tools of coordination, the Treaty speaks mostly in terms of guidelines (even "broad" guidelines) and recommendations—soft-law tools that are not legally binding—with the single exception of the final phase of EDP for which Article 126(9) and (11) TFEU authorizes the Council to summon a euro area Member State to take particular corrective action and to

788. *See* Resolution of the European Council of December 13, 1997 on economic policy coordination in Stage 3 of EMU and on Treaty Articles 109 and 109b, §I.1, https://www.europarl.europa.eu/summits/lux1_en. htm#annex1.

789. *Ibid.*, §I.3. This was repeated in the Council's March 20, 2005 report to the European Council, *Improving the implementation of the Stability and Growth Pact*, Annex II to the Presidency Conclusions of the European Council of March 22-23, 2005, p. 23, https://data.consilium.europa.eu/doc/document/ST-7619-2005-REV-1/en/pdf. The subsidiarity principle was also expressly acknowledged in subsequent secondary legislation, including, in the "Six Pack" reforms, in recital (20) to Regulation 1174/2011, recital (27) to Regulation 1176/2011 and recital (28) to Directive 2011/85.

790. CJEU, November 27, 2012, Case C-370/12, *Pringle*, ECLI:EU:C:2012:756, §64.

791. *Ibid.*, §111.

impose economic sanctions if this Member State fails to comply (*see* paragraph 573(d)(iv) and (v) above). This naturally begs the question of whether, absent such an express Treaty empowerment, coercive action could be taken to enforce measures of policy coordination in other circumstances. Over the years, the fiscal and macroeconomic surveillance frameworks developed by EU secondary legislation have become more elaborate and, especially for the euro area, more intrusive. They have, at least on paper, become more constraining, with several provisions being backed up by financial penalties—on paper because, while the Member States' compliance record has been mixed, financial penalties have mostly remained a dead letter (*see* paragraphs 590 and 605(c) below). But the question remains.

578. ***Second***, those questions arise in particular with regard to Article 136 TFEU added by the Lisbon Treaty (*see* paragraph 574(b) above). Specifically, Article 136(1) mandates the Council to adopt euro area-specific measures in order to *"strengthen the coordination and surveillance of [...] budgetary discipline"* of euro area Member States and to set out *"economic policy guidelines"* specifically for euro area Member States. Does Article 136(1) merely offer a legal basis for differentiating coordination measures for the euro area but still within the compass of the Treaty's other provisions on the coordination of the Member States' economic and fiscal policies? Or can Article 136(1) be read to authorize measures that go beyond those contemplated by these provisions, including Articles 121 and 126 TFEU, and extend to substantive measures that are legally binding?

At first blush, the wording of Article 136(1) seems to support the narrower interpretation in that it requires the Council to act *"in accordance with the relevant provisions of the Treaties"* and *"in accordance with the relevant procedure from among those referred to in Articles 121 and 126"*. Article 136(1)(b) also speaks of economic policy *"guidelines"*, adding that they must be *"compatible"* with those adopted for the Union as a whole. Moreover, it would seem somewhat counterintuitive that a Treaty provision would convey broad authority on the Council to adopt, for a subset of Member States, measures of a different kind and legal nature than those contemplated by other Treaty provisions, at least without saying so expressly and indicating boundaries. And, absent clear Treaty wording, could binding Council measures narrow the space within which euro area Member States can exercise their supposedly exclusive competence for economic and fiscal policies, and in effect shift policymaking authority in these areas to the Union? Nevertheless, EU institutions appear to have espoused, at least implicitly, the more dynamic interpretation of Article 136(1).[792]

---

792. A more explicit hint at the more dynamic interpretation is to be found in recital (6) to "Two Pack" Regulation 473/2013, which says that the Treaty *"allows the adoption of specific measures in the euro area which go beyond the provisions applicable to all Member States"* and refers to *"reinforced coordination and surveillance"*. *Cf.* also J.-P. Keppenne, "EU Fiscal Governance on the Member States: The Stability and Growth Pact and Beyond", in *The EU Law of Economic and Monetary Union* (F. Amtenbrink & Chr. Herrmann eds.), Oxford University Press, 2020, pp. 845-846, §28.104.

579. ***Third***, the Treaty provisions reflect the notion that it is incumbent on the Member States themselves to coordinate their economic policies *"within the Council"*—within arrangements and guidelines discussed and adopted at Council meetings (*see* paragraph 571 above). They give policy coordination a distinct flavor of peer dialogue and review and put the Council, as a forum for political deliberation, center stage in the process.[793] Both as an institutional and as a practical matter, however, the European Commission has over time assumed an increasing role in reviewing national economic and fiscal policies, proposing Council measures, monitoring their implementation and generally managing the process.

Remarkably, certain Council voting features have strengthened the Commission's hand. Thus, for certain decisions (such as the decision to hold a Member State in excessive deficit), the Council must act on a proposal from the Commission which, under Article 16(4) TEU *jo.* Article 238(2) TFEU and Article 238(3) TFEU, lowers the qualified majority threshold for Council voting. Under a kind of voting pact set forth in Article 7 TSCG, the euro area Member States have committed to *"support"* proposals and even recommendations made by the Commission when it considers a euro area Member State to be in breach of the deficit criterion under EDP unless a qualified majority of euro area Member States is opposed to the Commission's proposal or recommendation. Taking matters one step further, "Six Pack" regulations—EU secondary legislation!—have introduced so-called "reversed qualified majority voting" ("RQMV") for certain Council decisions under EDP and the excessive imbalance procedure: under RQMV, Commission proposals are deemed adopted by the Council unless a qualified majority[794] of the Council rejects the proposal by some specified deadline. More broadly, the "Six Pack" reforms have added a kind of "comply or explain" rule for Council decisions in the preventive and corrective arms of SGP, under which the Council *"is expected to, as rule, follow the recommendations and proposals of the Commission or explain its position publicly"*.[795]

There have episodically been tensions and conflicts between (euro area) Member States and the Commission over the proper balance of powers in EMU decision-making, including occasional attempts to limit the Commission's margin of discretion by more precise criteria.

580. ***Fourth***, unsurprisingly, the hybrid architecture of EMU governance with its mixture of EU rules and procedures and intergovernmental building blocks (the

---

793. In its 1997 Luxembourg Resolution on economic policy coordination (*see* fn. 788 above), the European Council referred in this respect to *"[t]he defining position of the ECOFIN Council at the centre of the economic coordination and decision-making process"* (§I.6).

794. In a single case, a simple majority suffices to reject the Commission's recommendation. *See* Article 6(2), fifth paragraph, of Council Regulation (EC) No 1466/97 of July 7, 1997 on the strengthening of the surveillance of budgetary positions and the surveillance and coordination of economic policies, as amended by Article 1(9) of Regulation (EU) No 1175/2011 of November 16, 2011.

795. Article 2-ab(2) of Council Regulation (EC) No 1466/97 of July 7, 1997, as inserted by Article 1(4) of Regulation (EU) No 1175/2011 of November 16, 2011, and Article 2a(1), second paragraph, of Council Regulation (EC) No 1467/97 of July 7, 1997 on speeding up and clarifying the implementation of the excessive deficit procedure, as inserted by Article 1(3) of Council Regulation (EU) No 1177/2011 of November 8, 2011.

Eurogroup, Euro Summits, TSCG and the ESM Treaty) has been the subject of much discussion and some discomfort among politicians and legal scholars. Yet, it is all not as bad as it may look. While there have been occasional frictions and dissonant notes, operationally, the two sets of institutions, rules and procedures have, by and large, been made to work together reasonably satisfactorily. The integration of the intergovernmental components into a unified EU architecture may be a desirable longer-term objective, but it does not, in my view, rise to the level of a short-term priority given the abundance of more pressing matters.

The economic policy conditionality attached to ESM stability support is a case in point. In its 2012 *Pringle* judgment, the Court considered that such conditionality does not constitute an instrument of coordination of the Member States' economic policies (*see* paragraph 577(c) above). Still, this leaves questions as to the interaction of ESM policy conditionality with EU policy coordination measures, the role of the Commission and the ECB in the negotiation of ESM policy conditions, and available judicial remedies under EU law. As we will discuss in Chapter 10, these questions have for the most part been addressed in the Court's 2016 judgment in *Ledra*, by "Two Pack" Regulation 472/2013 and by further clarifications added to the amended ESM Treaty (*see* paragraphs 596 and 717-718 below).

3 EMU'S EVOLVING FISCAL AND MACROECONOMIC SURVEILLANCE FRAMEWORKS: A LEARNING CURVE

a In the Beginning

581. In the run-up to the European currency union and in its first decade, the prevailing concern was to avoid fiscal profligacy and free-riding behavior by Member States and to maintain budgetary discipline by continued compliance with the fiscal convergence criteria that served (and still serve) as tests for admission to currency union membership (*see* paragraph 573(c) above). These criteria are anchored in the now familiar reference values of 3% for the government deficit ratio and 60% for the government debt ratio, set forth in Protocol No 12, and the initial focus was predominantly on the deficit criterion.

582. The original Stability and Growth Pact ("SGP") consisted of a European Council resolution of June 17, 1997 and the initial versions of Council Regulations (EC) Nos 1466/97 and 1467/97 of July 7, 1997—all in all, a mere 13 pages in the *Official Journal*:

(a) The **European Council resolution of June 17, 1997**[796] sets forth a series of (political) commitments and guidelines on the implementation of SGP, including notably the Member States' commitment to pursue budgetary positions *"close to balance or in surplus"* as a medium-term objective. This

796. Resolution of the European Council of June 17, 1997 on the Stability and Growth Pact, *OJ* C236, August 2, 1997, p. 1.

was believed at the time to allow Member States to deal with normal cyclical fluctuations while observing the 3% cap on the government deficit ratio.

(b) On the basis of what is now Article 121 TFEU, **Council Regulation (EC) No 1466/97**[797] deals with what is commonly referred to as the "preventive arm" of SGP. It offers particulars on the EU surveillance procedure aimed at preventing Member States' fiscal positions from evolving too far out of line with the fiscal convergence criteria. To this end, Member States must submit, and update on an annual basis, medium-term plans—called "stability programs" for euro area Member States and "convergence programs" for other Member States. In this program, each Member State must present the medium-term objective for its budgetary position (which must be close to balance or in surplus and include a "safety margin" to avoid an excessive deficit), the corresponding adjustment path for its government deficit or surplus and expected trajectory of its government debt ratio, the underlying economic assumptions, and the fiscal and other economic policy measures (to be) taken to achieve these targets. The Council, with the support of the European Commission and the Economic and Financial Committee, then reviews and monitors each program in a process in which the Council (i) opines on the program and may invite the Member State concerned to strengthen it; (ii) in case of significant divergence from the medium-term budgetary objective or adjustment path, issues an "early warning" recommendation to the Member State to take the necessary adjustment measures; and (iii) if such divergence persists or worsens, recommends to the Member State to take *"prompt corrective measures"*.

(c) As to the "corrective arm" of SGP, **Council Regulation (EC) No 1467/97**[798] implements Article 126 TFEU by providing further particulars on EDP:
   (i) It clarifies when an excess of the government deficit ratio over 3% can be considered *"exceptional and temporary"*. In particular, it defines "exceptional" by reference to either an *"unusual event"* beyond the Member State's control with a major impact on its government finances or a *"severe economic downturn"*.
   (ii) It establishes time limits for the various steps in EDP.
   (iii) It sets rules for the financial sanctions that may be imposed on euro area Member States in the final phase of EDP, *i.e.*, a non-interest-bearing deposit equal to 0.2% of GDP plus one-tenth of the deficit's excess over 3% but capped overall at 0.5% of GDP, which, *"as a rule"*, will be converted into a fine when the excessive deficit has not been corrected within two years.

797. Council Regulation (EC) No 1466/97 of July 7, 1997 on the strengthening of the surveillance of budgetary positions and the surveillance and coordination of economic policies, *OJ* L209, August 2, 1997, p. 1.
798. Council Regulation (EC) No 1467/97 of July 7, 1997 on speeding up and clarifying the implementation of the excessive deficit procedure, *OJ* L209, August 2, 1997, p. 6.

b 2005 Reforms

583. In the early years of the currency union, pre-1999 fiscal consolidation stalled, probably due in some measure to consolidation fatigue at a political level, and the government deficit ratios edged up again (*see* paragraph 116, Table 2.2, above). Few Member States achieved the medium-term objective of a budgetary position "close to balance or in surplus", and several became subject to EDP.[799] This was partly due also to the fact that, as formulated, this balanced budget rule may have put the bar too high for a good number of Member States: such a uniform standard did not fit real-world economic and fiscal heterogeneity among Member States very well, and it was formulated in nominal rather than structural terms (which made things harder during cyclical downturns). In the spring of 2005, the Council reached an agreement on a series of changes to SGP[800] which were endorsed by the European Council of March 22-23, 2005 and then reflected in Council Regulations (EC) Nos 1055/2005 and 1056/2005 of June 27, 2005.

584. Council Regulation (EC) No 1055/2005[801] made changes in the preventive arm of SGP, including mainly the following:

(a) The medium-term budgetary objective ("MTO") is differentiated among the Member States—in the words of recital (5), *"to take into account the diversity of economic and budgetary positions and developments as well as of fiscal risk to the sustainability of public finances, also in the face of prospective demographic changes"*. Country-specific MTOs need no longer be close to balance or in surplus (subject to subparagraph (b) below) but must still include a "safety margin" with respect to the 3% deficit ratio, ensure rapid progress toward sustainability and, *"taking this into account, [...] allow room for*

799. Offenders, in an advanced stage of EDP, at some point even included France and Germany, which gave rise to a curious legal dispute. The European Commission had proposed that, pursuant to Article 126(8) and (9) TFEU, the Council formally determine that Germany and France had failed to take effective action in response to earlier Council recommendations, and summon each of them to take the necessary deficit reduction measures by some specified deadline. At a meeting of November 25, 2003, the Council was unable to take these decisions for lack of the requisite qualified majority and decided instead to hold EDP in abeyance in view of certain policy commitments offered by Germany and France. The Commission then challenged the Council's inaction before the European Court of Justice. The Court held that the Commission's annulment action was inadmissible insofar as it concerned the Council's inability to adopt the proposed decisions, but suggested that the Commission could institute an action for failure to act under Article 265 TFEU. In contrast, the Court annulled the Council's decision to hold EDP in abeyance on the basis of policy commitments other than those initially recommended by the Council. *See* CJEU, July 23, 2004, Case C-27/04, *Commission vs. Council*, ECLI:EU:C:2004:436.

800. *See* the Council's March 20, 2005 report to the European Council, *Improving the Implementation of the Stability and Growth Pact*, Annex II to the Presidency Conclusions of the European Council of March 22-23, 2005, pp. 21-38, https://data.consilium.europa.eu/doc/document/ST-7619-2005-REV-1/en/pdf.

801. Council Regulation (EC) No 1055/2005 of June 27, 2005 amending Regulation (EC) No 1466/97 on the strengthening of the surveillance of budgetary positions and the surveillance and coordination of economic policies, *OJ* L174, July 7, 2005, p. 1.

budgetary manoeuvre, considering in particular the needs for public investment". MTOs could be revised every four years, or earlier in case of major structural reforms.

(b) For euro area and ERM II Member States, MTOs are to be set in a range between a deficit of 1% of GDP and balance or surplus, now in structural terms, *i.e.*, cyclically adjusted and net of one-off and temporary measures. The shift in focus to a structural budget benchmark makes theoretical sense insofar as compliance with a deficit limit in nominal terms may lead to pro-cyclical tightening in a downturn. MTOs could then be differentiated within that range on the basis of the Member States' government debt ratio and potential growth, the underlying idea being that MTOs should ordinarily move up in the range as Member States have higher government debt and/or lower growth potential.[802]

(c) As concerns the adjustment path to attain their respective MTOs, euro area and ERM II Member States are expected to pursue an annual improvement of their structural balance by 0.5% of GDP as a benchmark—but possibly more in economic good times and less in bad times.

(d) Temporary deviations from the MTO or the adjustment path may be allowed for major structural reforms with direct long-term cost-saving effects (including certain pension reforms).

585. In SGP's corrective arm, **Council Regulation (EC) No 1056/2005**[803] notably made the following changes:

(a) It broadens the notion of "severe economic downturn", for the purpose of assessing whether a government deficit in excess of 3% of GDP can be deemed "exceptional", by allowing the Commission and the Council to consider that this is the case when the excess results from negative annual GDP volume growth or from a cumulative loss of output over a *"protracted period"* of very low annual GDP volume growth relative to its potential.

(b) It clarifies the "all other relevant factors" to be considered by the European Commission in its Article 126(3) TFEU report following a Member State's breach of one or both of the fiscal convergence criteria.

(c) It extends several deadlines for Council decisions and Member States' corrective actions under EDP.

(d) It specifies that a Member State in excessive deficit will, as a benchmark, be required to achieve a minimum annual improvement of its structural balance of at least 0.5% of GDP.

---

802. *Cf.* the Council's March 20, 2005 report to the European Council, *Improving the Implementation of the Stability and Growth Pact*, p. 28.

803. Council Regulation (EC) No 1056/2005 of June 27, 2005 amending Regulation (EC) No 1467/97 on speeding up and clarifying the implementation of the excessive deficit procedure, *OJ* L174, July 7, 2005, p. 5.

c The 2011 "Six Pack" Reforms

586. The 2008-2012 financial crisis, including the banking crisis, the euro area sovereign debt crisis and two recessions, saw a sharp increase in government deficit and debt ratios in the euro area (*see* paragraph 116, Table 2.2, above). By 2011, as many as 23 Member States had ended up in excessive deficit, including 14 of the then 17 euro area Member States (the exceptions being Estonia, Finland and Luxembourg). In a reform commonly (and inelegantly) referred to as the "Six Pack", five regulations and one directive—all in all 47 pages in the *Official Journal*—were adopted in November 2011 to address perceived shortcomings in the EMU framework for economic and fiscal policy coordination. The summary below focuses on the provisions most relevant for euro area Member States.

587. In the preventive arm of SGP, significant further changes were made by **Regulation (EU) No 1175/2011**,[804] including, in particular, the following:

(a) The formulation and monitoring of the Council's broad economic policy guidelines pursuant to Article 121(2) TFEU, the submission and assessment of the Member States' stability programs in SGP's preventive arm, the new process of surveillance of macroeconomic imbalances (*see* paragraph 589 below) and certain other work streams in the sphere of economic policy coordination are now embedded in the so-called "European Semester". The European Semester is an annual surveillance cycle with a common timetable, stretching from November of each year to early summer of the following year, aimed at improving the consistency of policy analysis and recommendations and resulting in a single set of country-specific recommendations ("CSR") by the Council. The European Semester does not encompass the steps in SGP's corrective arm (EDP) which follow an *ad hoc* time sequence of their own.

(b) The content of the stability programs to be submitted by the Member States is detailed in several respects and, significantly, must now include information on implicit liabilities in respect of population aging and contingent liabilities (like State guarantees) with potentially large budgetary impact. The programs must be based on the most likely macro-fiscal scenario, or one that is more prudent, and must explain the most significant differences between this scenario and the Commission's forecasts.

(c) For the assessment of a Member State's progress toward its MTO, an additional government expenditure benchmark is introduced. Under this complementary and supposedly more readily observable benchmark, the annual growth of government expenditures (excluding interest, expenditures on EU programs fully matched by EU funds and non-discretionary changes in

804. Regulation (EU) No 1175/2011 of the European Parliament and of the Council of November 16, 2011 amending Council Regulation (EC) No 1466/97 on the strengthening of the surveillance of budgetary positions and the surveillance and coordination of economic policies, *OJ* L306, November 23, 2011, p. 12.

unemployment benefits) should not exceed a reference medium-term rate of potential GDP growth, or a lower rate in the case of Member States falling short of their MTO, unless the excess is covered by discretionary revenue measures. In other words, this new benchmark sets the (estimated) medium-term rate of potential output growth as a kind of speed limit on the growth of primary government expenditure in excess of additional discretionary revenue.

(d) Member States with a government debt ratio in excess of 60% of GDP or (indeed curiously "or") facing *"pronounced risks of overall debt sustainability"* should pursue a more vigorous adjustment path toward their MTO by seeking an annual improvement of their structural balance by **more** than 0.5% of GDP.

(e) Each MTO is now to be revised every three (instead of four) years but, as before, may be adjusted in the interval in case of structural reforms with a major impact on the sustainability of public finances. In addition, temporary deviations from an MTO or the related adjustment path may still be allowed for major structural reforms with direct long-term cost-saving effects (including certain pension reforms) but now also in case of a material adverse change, *i.e.*, either an unusual event beyond the Member State's control with a major impact on its government finances or a severe economic downturn for the euro area or the Union as a whole (*i.e.*, here not just the Member State in question).

(f) The surveillance process is worked out in greater detail and based on the notion of *"significant deviations"* from the MTO or the related adjustment path. Whether such a deviation is "significant" depends on an overall assessment which should in particular include the following numerical criteria: (i) when looking at the change in the structural balance in the case of a Member State falling short of its MTO, a deviation of at least 0.5% of GDP in a single year or at least 0.25% of GDP on average per year in two consecutive years, and (ii) when looking at government expenditures, a deviation with a total impact on the government balance of at least 0.5% of GDP in a single year or cumulatively over two consecutive years.

588. Council Regulation (EU) No 1177/2011[805] made a number of changes in SGP's corrective arm. The most relevant for present purposes is an increased focus on the level and evolution of government debt and its sustainability (also reflected in Regulation 1175/2011 for the preventive arm, *see* paragraph 587(d) above). It had become apparent that, with declining growth, it was no longer possible to rely on policing the government deficit ratio to stabilize or reduce the debt ratio. In particular, Council Regulation 1177/2011 operationalized the debt criterion by a numerical debt

805. Council Regulation (EU) No 1177/2011 of November 8, 2011 amending Regulation (EC) No 1467/97 on speeding up and clarifying the implementation of the excessive deficit procedure, *OJ* L306, November 23, 2011, p. 33.

reduction benchmark under which a government debt ratio in excess of 60% of GDP will be deemed to be *"sufficiently diminishing"* and approaching 60% *"at a satisfactory pace"* (within the meaning of Article 126(2), first paragraph, (b) TFEU) if the excess decreases, as a benchmark, at an average pace of 1/20th *per annum* over a three-year period. However, recital (14) to the Regulation takes pains to stress that non-compliance with this benchmark should not in and of itself be sufficient to hold a Member State in excessive deficit but that this would require consideration of the full range of relevant factors. It adds that, in particular, consideration of *"the effect of the cycle and the composition of the stock-flow adjustment on debt developments"* may avoid a finding of excessive deficit on the basis of the debt criterion.

589. In parallel with the deepening of fiscal surveillance under SGP, **Regulation (EU) No 1176/2011**[806] broadened multilateral surveillance to other macroeconomic imbalances in accordance with a process integrated in the European Semester:

(a) For purposes of this macroeconomic imbalance procedure ("MIP"), "imbalances" are broadly defined in Article 2 as *"any trend giving rise to macroeconomic developments which are adversely affecting, or have the potential adversely to affect, the proper functioning of the economy of a Member State or of the economic or monetary union, or of the Union as a whole"*. It is hard to think of a more open-ended formulation. And "excessive imbalances" are then defined as *"severe imbalances, including imbalances that jeopardise or risk jeopardising the proper functioning of the economic and monetary union"*. It is noteworthy that the elevation of imbalances to the category of excessive imbalances is triggered in particular by negative spill-over effects that (may) threaten the proper functioning of EMU. And recital (17) to Regulation 1176/2011 focuses on current account imbalances, saying that the need for policy action is *"particularly pressing"* in Member States suffering persistently large current account deficits and loss of competitiveness, but also that Member States accumulating large trade surpluses should *"aim to"* identify and implement measures to strengthen domestic demand and growth potential.

(b) The process is kicked off in November of each year by an "alert mechanism report" ("AMR") in which the Commission identifies Member States that it considers *"may be affected by, or may be at risk of being affected by, imbalances"* (in the unrivaled wording of Article 3(3)). The Commission does so with the aid of a "scoreboard" of relevant indicators (with indicative threshold values serving as alert levels) as a non-exclusive filtering tool.[807] As

806. Regulation (EU) No 1176/2011 of the European Parliament and of the Council of November 16, 2011 on the prevention and correction of macroeconomic balances, *OJ* L306, November 23, 2011, p. 25.

807. This scoreboard currently includes 14 "headline" indicators and 28 "auxiliary" indicators. *See* https://ec.europa.eu/eurostat/web/macroeconomic-imbalances-procedure/indicators. Recital (14) to Regulation 1176/2011 exhorts the Commission not to draw conclusions from *"an automatic reading"* of the scoreboard but to consider *"all pieces of information"* as part of a comprehensive analysis.

a further step, the Commission then proceeds to an "in-depth review" ("IDR") of Member States that emerge from this screening as affected by imbalances or being at risk of becoming so.

(c) If imbalances are found to exist on the basis of an IDR, the Council, upon a recommendation from the Commission, may address the necessary recommendations for preventive action to the Member State concerned. Alternatively, if an IDR points to excessive imbalances, the Commission may recommend that the Council open an excessive imbalance procedure ("EIP") which involves enhanced surveillance of a corrective action plan (and, in the case of euro area Member States, the—theoretical—possibility of sanctions for inadequate action). The Commission has never thus far recommended initiation of an EIP and considers, on the basis of Article 121(4) TFEU, that it retains full discretion to recommend or not to recommend such action.[808]

(d) Interestingly, in its Articles 1(3) and 6(3), Regulation 1176/2011 expressly acknowledges, with reference to Article 152 TFEU and Article 28 of the Charter of Fundamental Rights of the European Union, that policy recommendations issued pursuant to this Regulation must respect the role of the social partners, national practices for wage formation and the right of collective bargaining and collective action.[809]

590. For euro area Member States, **Regulations (EU) Nos 1173/2011**[810] and **1174/2011**[811] expanded the system of financial sanctions to enhance enforcement of SGP and MIP, respectively. Thus, Regulation 1173/2011 added financial sanctions for certain instances of a Member State's failure to take remedial action in the preventive arm of SGP (interest-bearing deposit of 0.2% of GDP) or in earlier phases of EDP (non-interest-bearing deposit or fine of 0.2% of GDP), as well as for intentional or seriously negligent misrepresentation of government deficit or debt data (variable fine up to 0.2% of GDP). Regulation 1174/2011 introduced financial sanctions for non-compliance in the EIP phase of MIP (interest-bearing deposit or annual fine of 0.1% of GDP). No such fines have thus far effectively been imposed for instances of substantive non-compliance with SGP (or MIP in the absence of any EIP).[812] To my knowledge,

808. *See* the Commission's replies to the special report of the European Court of Auditors, *Audit of the Macroeconomic Imbalance Procedure (MIP)*, Special Report No 03/2018, January 23, 2018, p. 17, https://www.eca.europa.eu/Lists/ECADocuments/SR18_03/SR_MIP_EN.pdf.

809. Similar express references of this kind are to be found in the "Two Pack" Regulations, in particular in Articles 1(4) and 7(1), fourth and fifth paragraphs, of Regulation 472/2013 and Article 1(2) of Regulation 473/2013.

810. Regulation (EU) No 1173/2011 of the European Parliament and of the Council of November 16, 2011 on the effective enforcement of budgetary surveillance in the euro area, *OJ* L306, November 23, 2011, p. 1.

811. Regulation (EU) No 1174/2011 of the European Parliament and of the Council of November 16, 2011 on enforcement measures to correct excessive macroeconomic imbalances in the euro area, *OJ* L306, November 23, 2011, p. 8.

812. Curiously, the Council "cancelled" a fine of EUR 358.73 million on Portugal, and one of EUR 2.16 billion on Spain, for failure to take effective action in the corrective arm of SGP. It did so following a reasoned request of these Member States under Article 6(4) of Regulation

fines for statistical misreporting were applied on two occasions[813]—as improbable as it may seem that Member States could be found to have done so intentionally or by serious negligence.

591. Finally, **Council Directive 2011/85/EU**[814] established certain general standards for the Member States' national budgetary processes on such matters as public accounting systems and statistics, macroeconomic and budgetary forecasts, country-specific numerical fiscal rules, and medium-term budgetary planning with a planning horizon of at least three years.[815]

d The 2012 Treaty on Stability, Coordination and Governance in the Economic and Monetary Union

592. As said, in 2011, both Germany and France considered that certain core elements of the reinforced SGP should be enshrined in the Treaty. When an amendment of the Treaty itself was opposed by the United Kingdom, 25 Member States (including all euro area Member States at that time) eventually signed a separate intergovernmental treaty, *i.e.*, the Treaty on Stability, Coordination and Governance in the Economic and Monetary Union of March 2, 2012 ("TSCG"). Meanwhile, all Member States have become parties to TSCG. TSCG was intended as an intermediate step pending integration of its substance into the EU legal framework by the end of 2017 (*see* paragraph 575(a) above). Several of its provisions have since been incorporated into EU secondary legislation (*see* paragraph 593(a) and (d) below). As a further step, the Commission submitted a proposed directive in relation to the Fiscal Compact on December 6,

1173/2011 and in view of further policy commitments made by them. *See* Council Implementing Decision (EU) 2017/2350 of August 9, 2016 on imposing a fine on Portugal for failure to take effective action to address an excessive deficit, *OJ* L336, December 16, 2017, p. 24, and Council Implementing Decision (EU) 2017/2351 of August 9, 2016 on imposing a fine on Spain for failure to take effective action to address an excessive deficit, *ibid.*, p. 27.

813. *See* Council Decision (EU) 2015/1289 of July 13, 2015 imposing a fine on Spain for the manipulation of deficit data in the Autonomous Community in Valencia, *OJ* L198, July 28, 2015, p. 19 (fine of EUR 18.93 million, which Spain unsuccessfully challenged before the Court of Justice, *see* CJEU, December 20, 2017, Case C-521/15, *Spain vs. Council*, ECLI:EU:C:2017:982), and Council Implementing Decision (EU) 2018/818 of May 28, 2018 imposing a fine on Austria for the manipulation of debt data in Land Salzburg, *OJ* L137, June 4, 2018, p. 23 (fine of EUR 28.82 million).

814. Council Directive 2011/85/EU of November 8, 2011 on requirements for budgetary frameworks of the Member States, *OJ* L306, November 23, 2011, p. 41.

815. On this subject, reference should be made also to Council Regulation (EC) No 479/2009 of May 25, 2009 on the application of the Protocol on the excessive deficit procedure annexed to the Treaty establishing the European Community, *OJ* L145, June 10, 2009, p. 1, amended by Council Regulation (EU) No 679/2010 of July 26, 2010, *OJ* L198, July 30, 2010, p. 1, and by Commission Regulation (EU) No 2020/2014 of March 7, 2014, *OJ* L69, March 8, 2014, p. 101. Regulation 479/2009 replaced a 1993 regulation that had itself been amended several times. It is not considered to be part of the "Six Pack" but defines certain terms for purposes of Protocol No 12, the data on government deficit and debt that Member States have to report to Eurostat, and related quality controls.

2017,[816] but nothing came of it. The integration of remaining elements of the Fiscal Compact into the EU legal framework is being addressed again in the current reform of the common fiscal rules (*see* paragraph 612 below).

593. TSCG strengthened and supplemented the EU rules and processes (as they then existed) on certain matters regarding budgetary discipline, coordination of economic policies and euro area governance matters. Its key section is Title III (Articles 3 to 8), entitled and commonly referred to as the "Fiscal Compact", which is binding on all euro area Member States and, on an opt-in basis, on Bulgaria, Denmark and Romania.

Relevant provisions of the Fiscal Compact include the following:

(a) The Member States commit to keep their general government budgetary position balanced or in surplus. This balanced budget rule is deemed to be satisfied when the annual structural balance (cyclically adjusted and net of one-off and temporary measures) is at or close to a Member State's country-specific MTO, with a lower bound of a structural deficit of 0.5% of GDP at market prices (1% if the debt ratio is significantly below 60% and risks to long-term sustainability of public finances are low) (Article 3(1)(a), (b) and (d)). Temporary deviations from a Member State's MTO or the adjustment path toward it are allowed only in exceptional circumstances (Article 3(1)(c)), *i.e.*, either an unusual event beyond the Member State's control and having a major impact on its fiscal position or a severe economic downturn (Article 3(3)(b)). The provisions just summarized substantially mirror those of EU secondary legislation, except that the –0.5% lower bound is stricter than the benchmark –1% tolerance of Council Regulation 1466/97, as amended by Council Regulation 1055/2005 (*see* paragraph 584(b) above).

(b) The balanced budget commitment is to be backed up by a correction mechanism at the national level that is triggered automatically by observed significant deviations from a Member State's MTO or the adjustment path toward it (Article 3(1)(e)). The national correction mechanisms must be based on common principles to be proposed by the European Commission (Article 3(2)).[817]

(c) Importantly, the rules set out in subparagraphs (a) and (b) above must be "internalized" in the Member States' legal order, *i.e.*, they must be reflected in binding and permanent—preferably constitutional—provisions of national law or their full observance throughout the national budgetary process must otherwise be guaranteed (Article 3(2)).

816. Proposal for a Council Directive laying down provisions for strengthening fiscal responsibility and the medium-term budgetary orientation in the Member States, COM(2017) 824 final, December 6, 2017, https://eur-lex.europa.eu/legal-content/EN/TXT/PDF/?uri=CELEX:52017PC0824.

817. These principles are set forth in a Communication from the Commission, *Common principles on national fiscal correction mechanisms*, COM(2012) 342 final, June 20, 2012, https://eur-lex.europa.eu/LexUriServ/LexUriServ.do?uri=COM:2012:0342:FIN:En:PDF.

(d) Other provisions of the Fiscal Compact are less memorable insofar as they have meanwhile been incorporated in EU secondary legislation. Thus, it includes the numerical debt reduction benchmark (Article 4) that in parallel had been reflected in Article 2(1a) of Council Regulation 1467/97, inserted by "Six Pack" Council Regulation 1177/2011 (*see* paragraph 588 above). The requirement that Member States subject to EDP submit an "economic partnership program" (Article 5) subsequently found its way into Article 9 of "Two Pack" Regulation 473/2013, and the Member States' obligation of advance reporting on their debt issuance plans (Article 6) into Article 8 of the same Regulation (*see* paragraph 595(b) and (c) below).

e The 2013 "Two Pack" Reforms

594. In 2013, this train of reforms was supplemented, solely for euro area Member States, by "Two Pack" Regulations (EU) Nos 472/13 and 473/13 of May 21, 2013, which are summarized below, in reverse order.

595. The principal changes made by **Regulation (EU) No 473/2013**[818] include the following:

(a) A common timeline for the preparation and review of national budgets is added at the back end of the European Semester. By October 15 of each year, Euro area Member States must submit to the European Commission and the Eurogroup a draft budgetary plan for the forthcoming year that is to be consistent with applicable CSR and, as the case may be, Council opinions on economic partnership programs. The Commission will review each draft plan and, if it identifies instances of *"particularly serious non-compliance"* with SGP budgetary policy obligations, request that a revised draft be submitted.
(b) Euro area Member States must give the Commission and the Eurogroup prior notice of their national debt issuance plans.
(c) Euro area Member States in EDP are subject to more stringent reporting requirements and closer monitoring and must notably present an "economic partnership program", *i.e.*, a roadmap laying out the policy measures and structural reforms needed to achieve an effective and lasting correction of their excessive deficit.

818. Regulation (EU) No 473/2013 of the European Parliament and of the Council of May 21, 2013 on common provisions for monitoring and assessing draft budgetary plans and ensuring the correction of excessive deficit of the Member States in the euro area, *OJ* L140, May 27, 2013, p. 11.

596. Regulation (EU) No 472/2013[819] established an enhanced surveillance process for euro area Member States that (i) experience, or are threatened with, serious difficulties with respect to their financial stability or the sustainability of their public finances, with potential adverse spill-over effects elsewhere in the euro area, and/or (ii) request or receive financial assistance from other countries or from European or international financial institutions like the EFSF/ESM and the IMF. In particular, for Member States in category (ii), Regulation 472/2013 sets forth rules and procedures for the design and monitoring of macroeconomic adjustment programs, including rules to ensure the consistency of economic policy conditions attached to EFSF/ESM financial assistance with these programs (*see* paragraph 715(b) below).

f 2013-2020: Continuous Learning

597. After the spring of 2013, further bricks were added to the edifice. **Regulation (EU) No 1303/2013** provided another tool for enforcing key provisions of the EMU fiscal and macroeconomic surveillance frameworks: its Article 23 allows the Council, on a proposal of the Commission, to suspend part or all of payments or commitments out of various EU structural and investment funds (the so-called "ESI Funds") when a Member State fails to take certain actions under SGP or MIP.[820] Several years later, a similar clause was included in **Regulation (EU) 2021/241** in respect of financing from the Recovery and Resilience Facility of NextGenerationEU: under Article 10, the Council may put disbursements or commitments on hold in certain instances of non-compliance with SGP or MIP.[821]

598. As the dust settled following the 2011-2013 reforms, the rule book was further clarified and supplemented by various guidance and other "soft law" texts, which will need to be revised again to reflect the ongoing reform of SGP. The most relevant of these documents include the following:

(a) five successive versions of a set of guidelines (also referred to as "code of conduct") for the implementation of SGP in both its preventive arm and EDP,

819. Regulation (EU) No 472/2013 of the European Parliament and of the Council of May 21, 2013 on the strengthening of economic and budgetary surveillance of Member States in the euro area experiencing or threatened with serious difficulties with respect to their financial stability, *OJ* L140, May 27, 2013, p. 1.

820. Article 23 and Annex III of Regulation (EU) No 1303/2013 of the European Parliament and of the Council of December 17, 2013 laying down common provisions on the European Regional Development Fund, the European Social Fund, the Cohesion Fund, the European Agricultural Fund for Rural Development and the European Maritime and Fisheries Fund and laying down general provisions on the European Regional Development Fund, the European Social Fund, the Cohesion Fund and the European Maritime and Fisheries Fund and repealing Council Regulation (EC) No 1083/2006, *OJ* L347, December 20, 2013, p. 320, amended multiple times and last by Regulation (EU) 2023/435 of February 27, 2023, *OJ* L63, February 28, 2023, p. 1.

821. Article 10 of Regulation (EU) 2021/241 of the European Parliament and of the Council of February 12, 2021 establishing the Recovery and Resilience Facility, *OJ* L57, February 18, 2021, p. 17, amended by Regulation (EU) 2023/435 of February 27, 2023, *OJ* L63, February 28, 2023, p. 1.

of which the latest version was agreed by the Economic and Financial Committee on May 15, 2017 and endorsed by the Council on May 18, 2017;[822]

(b) three successive versions of a similar set of guidelines (or "code of conduct") for the implementation of the "Two Pack" regulations, of which the latest version is dated September 30, 2016;[823]

(c) a "commonly agreed position" on the flexibility built into SGP in respect of the annual fiscal adjustment toward the MTO, structural reforms and government investments, which was adopted by the Economic and Financial Committee on November 27, 2015 and endorsed by the Council on February 12, 2016[824] (*see* paragraph 599 below);

(d) two opinions of the Economic and Financial Committee of November 29, 2016, endorsed by the Council on December 6, 2016, one on the expenditure benchmark in SGP's preventive arm[825] and the other on the methodology for assessing effective action under EDP;[826]

(e) the Commission's "vade mecum" on SGP,[827] of which the latest (2019) edition is accompanied by an interesting paper on certain numerical examples and technical aspects intended for specialists in national administrations;[828] and

(f) the Commission's "compendium" on MIP.[829]

599. Among these elaborate texts, I should single out the "commonly agreed position" on the margin of flexibility for modulating national adjustment efforts in the preventive arm of SGP (*see* paragraph 598(c) above):

(a) The document establishes a benchmark "matrix" for the annual fiscal adjustment in structural terms (*i.e.*, cyclically adjusted and net of one-off and other

822. *Specifications on the implementation of the Stability and Growth Pact and Guidelines on the format and content of Stability and Convergence Programmes*, May 15, 2017, 61 pp., https://data.consilium.europa.eu/doc/document/ST-9344-2017-INIT/en/pdf.
823. *Specifications on the implementation of the Two Pack and Guidelines on the format and content of draft budgetary plans, economic partnership programmes and debt issuance reports*, September 30, 2016, 48 pp., https://ec.europa.eu/economy_finance/economic_governance/sgp/pdf/coc/2014-11-07_two_pact_coc_amended_en.pdf.
824. *A commonly agreed position on flexibility within the Stability and Growth Pact: flexibility for cyclical conditions, structural reforms and investment*, reproduced as Annex 5 to the SGP code of conduct referred to in fn. 822 above, pp. 53-61.
825. *Improving the predictability and transparency of the SGP: A stronger focus on the expenditure benchmark in the preventive arm*, November 29, 2016, 7 pp., https://data.consilium.europa.eu/doc/document/ST-14814-2016-INIT/en/pdf.
826. *Improving the assessment of effective action in the context of the excessive deficit procedure—A specification of the methodology*, November 29, 2016, 18 pp., https://data.consilium.europa.eu/doc/document/ST-14815-2016-INIT/en/pdf.
827. European Commission, *Vade Mecum on the Stability & Growth Pact, European Economy Institutional Papers No 101*, April 2019, 95 pp.
828. *Numerical examples and technical aspects for "hands-on" experts*, 2019, 66 pp., https://economy-finance.ec.europa.eu/system/files/2019-04/numerical_examples_and_technical_aspects_for_hands_on_experts_-_2019_edition.pdf.
829. European Commission, *The Macroeconomic Imbalance Procedure. Rationale, Process, Application: A Compendium, European Economy Institutional Papers No 39*, November 2016, 126 pp.

temporary measures) toward the MTO. Starting from a benchmark effort of 0.5% of GDP as a baseline (*see* paragraphs 584(c) and 587(d) above), this matrix differentiates the required adjustment effort depending on (i) cyclical conditions (measured primarily by the output gap, *i.e.*, actual growth relative to potential growth) and (ii) the level and sustainability risk of government debt.[830]

(b) The agreed position also operationalizes SGP's structural reform and investment clauses by defining the conditions under which (i) major structural reforms may justify temporary deviations from a Member State's MTO or the adjustment path toward it,[831] and (ii) public investments may be considered equivalent to major structural reforms for these purposes.[832]

g 2020-2023: The General Escape Clause Activated

600. Following the outbreak of COVID-19, the Council, meeting by video conference on March 23, 2020, agreed to activate the so-called "general escape clause" of SGP to give the Member States more space for fiscal support and stimulus in response to the pandemic.[833] The general escape clause is the broader variant of the "material adverse change" clause and is triggered by a *"severe economic downturn in the euro area or the Union as a whole"*[834] (as distinguished from the narrower "unusual event" variant defined in terms of an unusual event beyond a Member State's control that has a major impact on its government finances). The clause offers possibilities for relief from SGP's usual fiscal requirements by allowing temporary deviations from MTOs or the related adjustment path in SGP's preventive arm, and by extending deadlines for corrective action and/or adopting a revised fiscal trajectory for Member States in EDP.

601. Of course, the common fiscal rules could not be kept in this state of semi-hibernation for an extended period of time. It was initially thought that the general escape clause might be lifted again in 2022 but this timeframe subsequently moved to the end of 2023. Yet, given the perceived shortcomings of the existing rule book and the challenges of the changed economic environment, it was also broadly acknowledged that it would not be desirable to simply resume full application of the current rule book at that time. Accordingly, a parallel process of further reform of the common fiscal rules was initiated. By early 2023, it became increasingly clear that political agreement might not be reached in time to complete the legislative process in 2023 (as indeed turned out to be the case) and also that, if and when eventually agreed, the reforms would need

830. *See* the document referenced in fn. 824 above, pp. 53-55.
831. *Ibid.*, pp. 55-57.
832. *Ibid.*, pp. 57-61.
833. *See Statement of EU ministers of finance on the Stability and Growth Pact in light of the COVID-19 crisis*, March 23, 2020, https://www.consilium.europa.eu/en/press/press-releases/2020/03/23/statement-of-eu-ministers-of-finance-on-the-stability-and-growth-pact-in-light-of-the-covid-19-crisis/.
834. *See* Articles 5(1), 6(3), 9(1) and 10(3) of Council Regulation 1466/97, as amended, and Articles 3(5) and 5(2) of Council Regulation 1467/97, as amended.

some run-in period. This would imply that the existing rule book would in principle continue to apply for some time into 2024. The Commission then announced a bridging approach in which, for a transitional period as of the spring of 2023, it would incorporate into the surveillance cycle some broadly agreed elements of the reform orientations insofar as consistent with current legislation.[835]

4 ISSUES AND ONGOING REFORMS

a Taking Stock

602. Several thoughts come to mind as one looks at how the EMU fiscal and macroeconomic surveillance frameworks have evolved and performed over their relatively brief history up to COVID-19.

603. ***First***, the rules have become more comprehensive, sophisticated and nuanced. But this has come with disadvantages:

(a) After several iterations, the rule book ended up quite complex. There is nothing intrinsically wrong with complexity insofar as this is unavoidable to deal with complex realities. But when a rule book has become a labyrinth for all but the cognoscenti, it does not facilitate transparency or buy-in.

(b) The intricate corpus of rules and exceptions, the fact that numerical benchmarks are not necessarily dispositive, and the complex and inevitably judgmental nature of the economic assessments to be made create a significant margin of judgment and hence political arbitrage. Examples are the "structural reform clause", the "investment clause" and the "unusual events clause". These clauses notably allow temporary deviations from a Member State's adjustment path toward its MTO (*see* paragraphs 584(d), 587(e) and 599(b) above). While they have been applied only episodically,[836] their potentially broad scope invites political bargaining. To politicians these clauses must be what the apple has been to Eve. Italy in particular has repeatedly benefited from each of them for a variety of reasons.[837]

835. *See* the Commission's press release of March 8, 2023, https://ec.europa.eu/commission/presscorner/detail/en/ip_23_1410, and Communication from the Commission to the Council, *Fiscal policy guidance for 2024*, COM(2023) 141 final, March 8, 2023, pp. 2 and 6-9, https://eur-lex.europa.eu/legal-content/EN/TXT/PDF/?uri=CELEX:52023DC0141.

836. *See* Communication from the Commission to the European Parliament, the Council, the European Central Bank, the European Economic and Social Committee and the Committee of the Regions, *Economic governance review. Report on the application of Regulations (EU) No 1173/2011, 1174/2011, 1175/2011, 1176/2011, 1177/2011, 472/2013 and 473/2013 and on the suitability of Council Directive 2011/85/EU*, COM(2020) 55 final, February 5, 2020, p. 10, https://eur-lex.europa.eu/legal-content/EN/TXT/PDF/?uri=CELEX:52020DC0055&from=EN.

837. Thus, Italy was allowed temporary deviations from the adjustment path toward its MTO in 2015 and 2016 for structural reforms; in 2016 for public investments; in 2016, 2017 and 2018 for exceptional expenditures caused by the influx of refugees and migrants; in 2017 for

(c) Certain key fiscal rules are anchored in variables that are unobservable in real time. Thus, in the agreed "matrix", the benchmark annual fiscal adjustment toward a Member State's MTO varies with the cyclical position as measured by the output gap (*see* paragraph 599(a) above). The output gap is the difference between actual output (GDP) and potential output (*i.e.*, the level of output that can be sustained over the medium term with stable inflation) as a percentage of potential output. Also, the additional government expenditure benchmark for assessing a Member State's progress toward its MTO is defined in relation to a reference medium-term rate of potential GDP growth (*see* paragraph 587(c) above). Potential output (and hence the output gap) and potential GDP growth must be estimated, and these estimates may vary from year to year and are subject to a significant margin of error, especially in the proximity of a recession.[838]

604. ***Second,*** the results obtained in the euro area since the 2011-2013 reforms and prior to the outbreak of COVID-19 in the early months of 2020 appear to be less than stellar. Over this period, the Member States' record of compliance with the various rules and recommendations has varied considerably across different rules and jurisdictions.[839] This mixed record casts doubt about the efficacy of several aspects of the revised frameworks. Let us briefly consider some of the key statistics:

(a) **Government deficit ratios** (in nominal terms) generally edged down and remained below the 3 % threshold over the 2013-2019 period except, notably, that France and Spain breached this threshold in several years (*see* paragraph

investments to protect against seismic risks; and in 2019 for expenditures related to the collapse of the Morandi bridge in Genoa and on a prevention plan to limit hydrogeological risks due to exceptionally adverse weather conditions. *See* the Commission (DG ECFIN)'s *Assessment of the 2015 Stability Programme for Italy*, May 27, 2015, pp. 17-18, https://ec.europa.eu/economy_finance/economic_governance/sgp/pdf/20_scps/2015/12_it_scp_en.pdf; *Assessment of the 2016 Stability Programme for Italy*, May 26, 2016, pp. 7 and 18-20, https://ec.europa.eu/economy_finance/economic_governance/sgp/pdf/20_scps/2016/12_it_scp_en.pdf; *Assessment of the 2018 Stability Programme for Italy*, May 23, 2018, p. 16, https://economy-finance.ec.europa.eu/system/files/2018-05/12_it_assessment_of_2018_sp.pdf; and *Assessment of the 2019 Stability Programme for Italy*, June 5, 2019, p. 20, https://economy-finance.ec.europa.eu/system/files/2019-06/12_it_sp_assessment_0.pdf.

838. *See* M. Ademmer, J. Boysen-Hogrefe *et al.*, "Schätzung von Produktionspotenzial und -lücke: Eine Analyse des EU-Verfahrens und mögliche Verbesserungen", *Kieler Beiträge zur Wirtschaftspolitik*, No 19, February 2019, especially pp. 49-101. Interestingly, this study shows particularly significant revisions to potential growth estimates for Italy and Spain over the 2005-2017 period. *Ibid.*, p. 52, Figures 3.1-3 and 3.1-4.

839. For a more granular overview, I should refer the reader to the "compliance tracker" kept by the secretariat of the European Fiscal Board which documents the Member States' compliance with, and deviations from, four numerical SGP benchmarks, *i.e.*, (i) the (nominal) government deficit ratio; (ii) the government debt ratio and related debt reduction benchmark (*see* paragraph 588 above); (iii) the structural balance rule (*see* paragraphs 584(b) and 593(a) above); and (iv) the government expenditure benchmark (*see* paragraph 587(c) above). This data base may be accessed via the link at https://commission.europa.eu/business-economy-euro/economic-and-fiscal-policy-coordination/european-fiscal-board-efb_en#compliance-tracker.

116, Table 2.2, above). But, by and large, these were years of relatively moderate government deficits, due in part to a measure of (pro-cyclical) fiscal restraint by several euro area Member States in the aftermath of the 2010-2012 euro area sovereign debt crisis, as well as to generous monetary easing that provided alternative stimulus and helped to keep government borrowing costs down (*see* paragraphs 68 and 410-411 above).

(b) During the same period, **government debt ratios** mostly came down significantly from 2012-2013 peak levels, except in the case of France and Italy. But they still ended up in 2019 at relatively high levels, in excess of 90% in seven of the then 19 euro area Member States and substantially so in Greece, Italy and Portugal, with a higher degree of divergence between Southern Member States (France, Italy, Spain, Portugal and Greece) and certain Northern Member States (Germany, The Netherlands and Finland) (*see* paragraph 116, Table 2.2, above). In fact, by the end of 2019, government debt ratios of 14 out of the then 19 euro area Member States stood at mostly significantly higher levels, and with greater divergence between North and South, than those prevailing at the start of the currency union in 1999—with Southern Member States losing ground in particular during and after the 2010-2012 sovereign debt crisis. Remarkably also, over the entire 1999-2019 period, the average euro area government debt ratio was consistently higher than that for the European Union as a whole, with a margin that progressively widened from under 3 to over 6 percentage points.

(c) Again in the 2013-2019 period, **government investments** (as a percentage of GDP) broadly continued to decline from pre-2012 levels (*see* paragraph 119, Table 2.3, above) and remained well below levels seen in the United States and Japan.[840] One likely explanation is that, in the aftermath of the euro area sovereign debt crisis, euro area Member States were more cautious to maintain a measure of fiscal discipline, and those with higher debt ratios more so than others—probably (i) partly under the influence of closer SGP surveillance; (ii) because financial markets (and rating agencies) had become more attentive to fiscal performance and related SGP benchmarks; and (iii) in some cases as a result of policy conditionality attached to EFSF/ESM financial support. In these circumstances, unsurprisingly, Member States would find it politically more expedient to cut back on government investments rather than on current expenditures for social transfers, general public services or other matters of more immediate electoral relevance. The "investment clause", which so far has been applied only on a few occasions, has hardly been an effective tool for countering this trend.

(d) Over the same period, only a few euro area Member States achieved a **structural balance position** in line with, or close to, their MTOs, *i.e.*, in most cases, a structural deficit of no more than 0.5% of GDP (or 1% if the

840. *See* N. Arnold, R. Balakrishnan *et al.*, "Reforming the EU Fiscal Framework: Strengthening the Fiscal Rules and Institutions", *IMF Departmental Paper No DP/2022/014*, September 2022, p. 7, Figure 5.

government debt ratio was significantly below 60 % and risks to the long-term sustainability of public finances were low) (*see* paragraph 593(a) above).[841] Several Member States missed their MTOs by a fairly wide margin and repeatedly failed to achieve the required annual fiscal adjustment effort to narrow the gap. Table 8.1 shows the structural budget balance (as a percentage of potential GDP) for each of the euro area's "Big Five" economies, as well as Portugal and Belgium, for the period from 2014 to 2022 and the Commission's autumn 2023 forecasts for the years 2023 to 2025.

Table 8.1 Structural Budget Balance 2014-2025

	2014-2018 average	*2019*	*2020*	*2021*	*2022^p*	*2023^p*	*2024^p*	*2025^p*
Germany	1.1	0.9	–2.7	–3.0	–2.4	–1.7	–1.1	–1.0
Netherlands	0.0	0.8	–1.0	–1.9	–1.1	–0.5	–1.3	–1.4
France	–2.8	–3.5	–5.1	–5.7	–4.9	–4.7	–4.4	–4.5
Italy	–1.4	–1.9	–4.8	–8.5	–9.1	–6.1	–5.1	–5.2
Spain	–2.0	–3.8	–4.0	–4.1	–4.7	–4.5	–3.5	–3.7
Portugal	–	–0.9	–1.6	–1.4	–0.9	0.0	–0.1	–0.3
Belgium	–2.2	–3.0	–5.6	–4.8	–3.8	–4.7	–4.5	–4.6

Source: European Commission, *European Economic Forecast—Spring 2023, European Economy Institutional Paper No 200,* May 2023, p. 178, Table 40 (entries for 2014-2018 and 2019), and *European Economic Forecast—Autumn 2023, European Economy Institutional Paper No 258,* November 2023, p. 189, Table 39 (remaining entries).

(e) As to the **government expenditure benchmark**, the European Fiscal Board's compliance tracker[842] shows that, over the 2013-2019 period, Germany complied in six out of seven years, The Netherlands in five years, Portugal in four years, Belgium in three years, Italy and Spain in two years, and France in only one year.

(f) The degree of actual implementation of **CSR** under the European Semester was, on the whole, moderate to low.[843] This applies also to the MIP segment of CSR.[844]

841. During this period, most euro area Member States had an MTO of –0.5% of GDP most of the time but some were at –1% in certain years, *i.e.*, Germany and Ireland in 2019, The Netherlands in 2017, 2018 and 2019, Finland in 2013, 2014, 2018 and 2019, Latvia in each of the years 2014-2019, Lithuania and Malta in each of the years 2015-2019, and Slovakia, Luxembourg and Estonia in all of the years.
842. *See* fn. 839 above.
843. *See* European Court of Auditors, *The European Semester—Country Specific Recommendations address important issues but need better implementation*, Special Report No 16/2020, September 3, 2020, pp. 22-24, §§34-37, https://www.eca.europa.eu/en/publications/SR20_16.
844. *See* A. Bénassy-Quéré & G. Wolff, *How has the macroeconomic imbalances procedure worked in practice to improve the resilience of the euro area?*, Study prepared at the request of the European Parliament's Committee on Economic and Monetary Affairs, March 2020, pp. 14-16,

(g) All in all, the record of compliance of euro area Member States over the 2013-2019 period has varied across the different fiscal benchmarks and across jurisdictions. Compliance with the (nominal) deficit and debt ratios was generally better than with the structural budget balance and government expenditure benchmarks.[845] And compliance was on average significantly lower for, in descending order, Belgium, Spain, Italy and France, and appeared to be strongly negatively correlated with higher government debt ratios.[846]

605. ***Third***, as the common rule book has become more complex and intrusive and its record of compliance has been mixed, its actual enforcement at the EU level has remained all but vigorous:

(a) Notwithstanding stubbornly high levels of government debt in certain (mainly Southern) Member States, no euro area Member State was in EDP by early 2020.
(b) Under MIP, no EIP has ever been initiated so far (*see* paragraph 589(c) above).
(c) Thus far, no fines have effectively been imposed on any Member State, except two modest fines for statistical transgressions (*see* paragraph 590 above). Fines appear to be *"a custom [m]ore honour'd in the breach than the observance"* (Hamlet, Act I, Scene IV)—perhaps even in the sense probably intended by Shakespeare: a rule that is more honorably ignored than applied.

606. ***Fourth***, the rule book remains focused primarily on preventing and remedying excessive budgetary deficits, government debt and other imbalances with negative sign. It has been much less effective in causing Member States that are in good standing under the fiscal benchmarks but pursue unduly conservative fiscal policies and/or run persistent external surpluses, to use more of their fiscal place so as to mitigate negative spill-over effects elsewhere in the euro area and facilitate macroeconomic stabilization of the euro area as a whole. In that sense, the rule book is asymmetrical. This constrains the ability to centrally steer a consolidated euro area fiscal stance that would be the counterpart of the single monetary policy stance and reduce frictions in the macroeconomic policy mix.

---

https://www.europarl.europa.eu/RegData/etudes/STUD/2020/645710/IPOL_STU(2020)645710_EN.pdf. Interestingly, this study also found that, over the 2013-2018 period, there was no significant correlation between CSR implementation rates and the improvement of imbalances. *Ibid.*, p. 17. *See also* European Court of Auditors, *Audit of the Macroeconomic Imbalance Procedure (MIP)*, Special Report No 03/2018, January 23, 2018, pp. 20-21, §33, https://www.eca.europa.eu/Lists/ECADocuments/SR18_03/SR_MIP_EN.pdf.

845. *See* M. Larch, J. Malzubris & S. Santacroce, "Numerical Compliance with EU Fiscal Rules: Facts and Figures from a New Database", *Intereconomics*, Vol. 58, 2023, p. 36, Figure 3, https://doi.org/10.2478/ie-2023-0008.

846. *Ibid.*, p. 35, Figure 2.

b A Catch 22?

607. In 2022 and 2023, the common fiscal rules remained in the state of semi-hibernation in which they were put when the general escape clause was activated on March 23, 2020 following the outbreak of COVID-19 (*see* paragraph 600 above). But they cannot be kept on the back burner for much longer and the current plan is to lift the escape clause at the end of 2023. Yet, simply returning to the pre-COVID-19 rule book would not appear to be a viable option given its existing shortcomings and, more importantly, because several of its features seem ill-suited to the changed realities of the post-pandemic economic environment.

608. In the realm of public finances, those changed realities, as seen now in these final days of 2023, include the following:

(a) **Government deficit ratios** (in nominal terms) should come down from the 2020-2021 peak levels in the short term due to the post-pandemic bounce-back of economic activity and the phasing-out of pandemic-related public expenditures.[847] Energy market uncertainties (and hence the possible continuation or resumption of public aid to alleviate the impact of high energy costs on businesses and households) remain one of several risk factors in this equation. In the medium term, upward pressures on government deficits are likely to derive from (i) a slowdown of economic activity, including as a result of monetary tightening in response to higher inflation; (ii) increased interest expenditures on additional government debt and on the refinancing of outstanding government debt as it matures, also due to monetary tightening;[848] (iii) higher public expenditures on pensions and healthcare, and lower tax revenue, caused by population aging; (iv) expenditures in relation to climate change and the green transition; and (v) increased spending on defense and intelligence capability in response to the various security threats posed notably by Russia.

As to item (ii), it is true that higher market interest rates feed into the cost of servicing outstanding government debt only progressively over time given that government debt is usually issued on a fixed-rate basis and with longer maturities. Still, as is shown in Table 8.2, in many euro area Member States around 50 % of outstanding central government debt at the end of 2022 had a remaining maturity of less than five years, with a significant component maturing in 2023.

847. *See* European Commission, *European Economic Forecast—Autumn 2023, European Economy Institutional Paper No 258*, November 2023, p. 187, Table 34.
848. *Cf. ibid.*, Table 35.

Table 8.2 Remaining Maturity of Euro Area Central Government Debt at the End of 2022 (Millions of Euros)

	Total	*< 1 Year*	*1 Year to 5 Years*
Germany	2,563,080.7	544,623.9 (21.24%)	832,097.4 (32.46%)
Netherlands	480,065.0	–	–
France	2,950,049.0	457,346.7 (15.50%)	1,001,331.9 (33.94%)
Italy	2,756,969.4	619,293.2 (22.46%)	857,765.1 (31.11%)
Spain	1,502,543.0	211,224.3 (14.05%)	512,723.5 (34.12%)
Portugal	272,585.7	57,733.2 (21.17%)	66,127.4 (24.26%)
Belgium	577,640.0	76,189.4 (13.19%)	130,727.9 (22.63%)

Source: Eurostat (online data code GOV_10DD_RMD) (as updated on June 19, 2023). Maturity profile of Dutch government debt not reported.

(b) The **structural budget balance** of most euro area Member States worsened significantly from pre-pandemic levels and several of them saw the gap with their respective MTOs widen further (*see* paragraph 604(d), Table 8.1, above). While structural budget balances are now generally projected to improve to varying degrees in 2023-2025, projected imbalances (and hence their distance to MTOs) remain problematic for several Member States, including Italy, Belgium, France and Spain and, realistically, could probably not be bridged within a time span of a few years.

(c) While they have declined somewhat from 2020-2021 peak levels, **government debt ratios** in a number of euro area Member States remain elevated and well above pre-pandemic levels, with a historically high degree of divergence within the euro area (*see* paragraph 116, Table 2.2, above). These ratios are currently projected to further improve somewhat in 2023-2025 (except in certain smaller Member States).[849] But, in a higher interest rate environment with subdued growth, the interest-growth rate differential should be less favorable for significant debt reduction. The high government debt levels in several euro area Member States, including in particular Italy, France, Spain and Belgium, raise concerns about sustainability in the medium term.[850] They limit the ability of these Member States to finance the necessary additional public investments (*see* subparagraph (d) below). They also

849. *Ibid.*, p. 190, Table 40.

850. In its latest Debt Sustainability Monitor, the Commission found eight euro area Member States (Italy, France, Spain, Belgium, Greece, Portugal, Croatia and Slovakia) to be at high fiscal sustainability risk in the medium term and six others (Austria, Slovenia, Malta and even

present a latent risk of excessive widening of sovereign bond spreads and attendant financial fragmentation, especially so long as interest rates remain at higher levels.

(d) Substantial **public investments** will be required over an extended period (i) to make up for insufficient public investments in the 2013-2019 period (*see* paragraphs 119-120 and 604(c) above) and (ii) to address the needs of the green transition (*see* paragraph 450 above), greater energy independence, resilience against climate change and restoring credible defense capability. Some part of these public investments will be co-financed out of EU budgetary funds (as will be discussed in Chapter 9) but the (larger) balance will need to be funded out of national budgetary resources, *i.e.*, some combination of cuts on other public expenditures, increased fiscal revenue and additional government debt. This will be a challenge, especially for Member States that are already heavily indebted. Such investments may be given favorable treatment under the common fiscal rules and excluded from fiscal adjustment calculations, but the related government debt still bears interest and must eventually be repaid or refinanced. As German Finance Minister Christian Lindner and finance ministers of 10 other fiscally more conservative Member States wrote in a joint op-ed that was published on June 15, 2023 in several European newspapers:

> *"As far as the capital markets are concerned, debt is debt. Capital markets are not interested in the motives for taking on debt, however worthy they may be."*[851]

609. In the end, one of the key challenges or perhaps the key challenge today is how the need to contain government debt and, in particular, to effectively and credibly reduce excessive government debt to levels that are sustainable in the medium term can in a realistic manner be reconciled with the need of substantial public investments. The current rule book largely failed to deliver on this during an extended period of low inflation and ultra-low interest rates. Paradoxically, the revised rule book will now have to solve this equation in a higher inflation environment with significantly higher interest rates—all while de-constraining monetary policy from pressures to go lower on policy rates than is desirable for inflation control and/or to engage in (legally questionable) geographically targeted government bond purchases to contain financial fragmentation. Given the limitations on EU budgetary transfers and the difficulties and risks associated with sovereign debt restructuring, that question bears all the hallmarks of a catch-22—and one that is prone to reignite slumbering disputes between "hawks" and "doves" among euro area Member States. Yet, the above quote from Christian

Germany, The Netherlands and Finland) at medium risk. *See* European Commission, *Debt Sustainability Monitor 2022, European Economy Institutional Paper No 199*, April 2023, pp. 43-58.

851. The full text of this op-ed is reproduced on the website of the German Federal Ministry of Finance at https://www.bundesfinanzministerium.de/Content/EN/Standardartikel/Press_Room/Namensartikel/2023-06-15-reform-of-european-fiscal-rules.html.

Lindner is not entirely *à propos*. The cost of a euro borrowed must be measured against the future returns that it produces. Accordingly, when applying the common fiscal rules to the curious cash-based accounting of government budgets, proper allowance must be made for government expenditures on productive investments.

c Toward Further Reforms

610. In a December 2020 Article IV staff report, the IMF observed that then was an opportune time to consider a fundamental reform and simplification of SGP.[852] The report also noted the European Commission's response that it was open to rethinking these rules before the general escape clause was lifted but that, *"given how potentially contentious a possible reform could be"*, the Commission considered that prospects were dim for reaching an agreement on a comprehensive reform soon.[853] On February 5, 2020, the Commission had published a review of the strengths and weaknesses of the fiscal and macroeconomic surveillance frameworks as amended by the "Six Pack" and "Two Pack" reforms, with a series of questions for public debate on further reforms.[854] Eventually, on November 9, 2022, the Commission outlined its proposed "orientations" for reform.[855] The ECOFIN Council considered these orientations on March 14, 2023, noting broad convergence among Member States on key aspects of a revised economic governance framework while also identifying several issues requiring further clarification and discussion.[856]

611. On April 26, 2023, the Commission then tabled legislative proposals to implement these reforms,[857] *i.e.*, (i) a draft regulation replacing Council Regulation (EC) No 1466/97 on the preventive arm of SGP;[858] (ii) another draft regulation amending

852. IMF Country Report No 2020/324, *Euro Area Policies. Staff Report for the 2020 Article IV Consultation with Member Countries*, December 3, 2020, p. 22, §39, https://www.imf.org/en/Publications/CR/Issues/2020/12/21/2020-Consultation-on-Common-Euro-Area-Policies-Press-Release-Staff-Report-and-Statement-by-49979.

853. *Ibid.*, p. 23, §42.

854. Communication from the Commission to the European Parliament, the Council, the European Central Bank, the European Economic and Social Committee and the Committee of the Regions, *Economic governance review. Report on the application of Regulations (EU) No 1173/2011, 1174/2011, 1175/2011, 1176/2011, 1177/2011, 472/2013 and 473/2013 and on the suitability of Council Directive 2011/85/EU*, COM(2020) 55 final, February 5, 2020, 20 pp., https://eur-lex.europa.eu/legal-content/EN/TXT/PDF/?uri=CELEX:52020DC0055&from=EN.

855. Communication from the Commission to the European Parliament, the Council, the European Central Bank, the European Economic and Social Committee and the Committee of the Regions, *Communication on orientations for a reform of the EU economic governance framework*, COM(2022) 583 final, November 9, 2022, 27 pp., https://economy-finance.ec.europa.eu/system/files/2022-11/com_2022_583_1_en.pdf.

856. *See* the Council's press release of March 14, 2023, https://www.consilium.europa.eu/en/press-releases/2023/03/14/economic-governance-framework-Council-agrees-its-orientations-for-a-reform/.

857. *See* the Commission's press release of April 26, 2023, https://ec.europa.eu/commission/presscorner detail/en/ip_23-2393.

858. Proposal for a Regulation of the European Parliament and of the Council on the effective coordination of economic policies and multilateral budgetary surveillance and repealing

Regulation (EC) No 1467/97 on SGP's corrective arm;[859] and (iii) a draft directive amending Council Directive 2011/85/EU on requirements for the Member States' budgetary frameworks.[860] Outlined below are the key elements of these proposed reforms, including relevant changes made in the texts agreed by the Council on December 21, 2023 ahead of its discussions with the European Parliament (*see* paragraph 621 below). It should be noted at the outset that these reforms focus on SGP (while also containing certain provisions on the interface between SGP and MIP).

612. ***First***, the stated objectives of the reforms ambitiously include (i) bringing down high government debt ratios onto a sustainable path in a gradual and realistic manner and then keeping them at prudent levels; (ii) supporting structural reforms and strategic investments; (iii) moving toward a more risk-based surveillance framework that differentiates between Member States according to the seriousness of their government debt and other economic challenges; (iv) streamlining and simplifying the framework notably by integrating fiscal trajectories and reform and investment commitments into a "holistic" surveillance architecture; (v) focusing more on a medium-term planning horizon within the annual cycle of the European Semester; (vi) increasing "national ownership" of the adjustment efforts; and (vii) improving *ex post* enforcement. According to the Commission, its proposed reforms along these lines incorporate the substance of the Fiscal Compact into EU law further to Article 16 TSCG[861] (*see* paragraph 575(a) above).

613. ***Second***, the reference values of 3% and 60% for the government deficit and debt ratios, respectively, set forth in Protocol No 12 to the Treaties, would be maintained. Sentiment about reviewing the 60% government debt threshold for having become outdated did not prevail. However, the Commission proposes to abandon the current numerical debt reduction benchmark, under which a government debt-to-GDP ratio in excess of 60% is considered *"sufficiently diminishing and approaching the reference value at a satisfactory pace"* (within the meaning of Article 126(2), first paragraph, (b) TFEU) if it declines at a pace of 1/20th of the excess *per annum* on average over a three-year period (*see* paragraphs 83(b) and 588 above). At current government debt levels, this particular benchmark is broadly viewed as requiring an unrealistic effort from the more heavily indebted Member States and as unduly constraining growth and investment in the post-pandemic environment.

Council Regulation (EC) No 1466/97, COM(2023) 240 final, April 26, 2023, https://economy-finance.ec.europa.eu/system/files/2023-04/COM_2023_240_1_EN.pdf. Its seven annexes may be found at https://economy-finance.ec.europa.eu/system/files/2023-04/COM_2023_240_1_EN_annexe_proposition.pdf.

859. Proposal for a Council Regulation amending Regulation (EC) No 1467/97 on speeding up and clarifying the implementation of the excessive deficit procedure, COM(2023) 241 final, April 26, 2023, https://economy-finance.ec.europa.eu/system/files/2023-04/COM_2023_241_1_EN.pdf.

860. Proposal for a Council Directive amending Directive 2011/85/EU on requirements for budgetary frameworks of the Member States, COM(2023) 242 final, April 26, 2023, https://economy-finance. ec.europa.eu/system/files/2023-04/COM_2023_242_1_EN.pdf.

861. COM(2023) 240 final, pp. 3-4, and COM(2023) 241 final, pp. 3-4.

The Commission proposals contain no alternative numerical or easily measurable standard for assessing proper government debt reduction, although public debt sustainability would be a critical factor in setting and monitoring country-specific net expenditure trajectories (*see* paragraph 615 below). This was to become a contentious issue in the following months as Germany and certain other fiscally conservative Member States continued to advocate the need for some common quantitative debt reduction benchmark that could be less onerous than de 1/20th rule but would be transparent and apply to all Member States with excess debt. Further discussions on this subject would finally lead to the inclusion of alternative numerical "safeguards" in the text agreed by the Council on December 21, 2023 (*see* paragraph 621(a) below).

614. ***Third***, the Commission proposals envisage a differentiated approach toward each Member State that would take into account the heterogeneity of fiscal positions and challenges and be based on country-specific multi-annual adjustment trajectories. Government net expenditure would henceforth serve as the core operational indicator for defining and monitoring these country-specific adjustment paths. Government net expenditure is defined as government expenditure net of interest expenditure on government debt, discretionary revenue measures, expenditures on EU programs fully matched by revenue from EU funds, and cyclical elements of unemployment benefits. In its March 14, 2023 conclusions, the Council included the definition of this expenditure aggregate in the list of items requiring further clarification and discussion,[862] and, in the text agreed by the Council on December 21, 2023, *"one-offs and other temporary measures"* have also been excluded from the definition of net expenditure. Defined in this manner as (nationally financed) net primary government expenditure, this indicator should not be affected by the operation of automatic budgetary stabilizers or by changes in expenditures outside the direct control of government, and should provide room for counter-cyclical stabilization. It would not rely on variables, like the output gap and potential GDP growth, that are unobservable in real time (*see* paragraph 603(c) above).

615. ***Fourth***, the cornerstone of the surveillance process in SGP's preventive arm would now be "national medium-term fiscal-structural plans" which the Member States would submit for review by the Commission and endorsement by the Council and which would be monitored via annual progress reports. These plans should set out both a multi-annual trajectory for government net expenditure over the plan horizon and the fiscal measures, structural reforms and public investments to address the main challenges identified in the European Semester. For Member States with a government deficit ratio above 3% or a public debt ratio above 60%, the Commission would provide prior guidance by establishing country-specific "technical trajectories" for government net expenditure. These reference trajectories would have to ensure that (i) the government deficit ratio is brought and maintained below 3%; (ii) the public debt ratio is put on a *"plausibly downward path"* (not "plausible downward path", although this may be a drafting quirk) or remains *"at prudent levels"*, as the case may be; (iii) the

862. *See* the Council's press release of March 14, 2023, §7.

fiscal adjustment effort is properly distributed over the adjustment period[863] (a safeguard against undue backloading); and (iv) as a rule, the growth of government net expenditure remains on average below medium-term output growth over the plan horizon.[864] National plans presenting a higher net expenditure trajectory than the Commission's technical trajectory must offer *"sound and verifiable*[865] *economic arguments"* for the difference.

In the discussions that followed, several Member States appeared to be uneasy to varying degrees about the latitude given to the Commission in setting net expenditure trajectories and implied debt reduction scenarios in bilateral interactions with the Member States. Aside from broader issues of even-handed treatment, one of the worries about such "bilateralism" turns on doubts about the Commission's effective negotiating leverage to drive a hard bargain with larger Member States like France and Italy—or indeed Germany for that matter. To assuage these and other concerns about bilateralism, certain counterweights have been added in the agreed December 21, 2023 text, including, in particular, a "debt sustainability safeguard" and a "deficit resilience safeguard" (*see* paragraph 621 (a) below), as well as a clause providing that the Council will establish the methodology for the plausibility assessment of the projected decline of the government debt ratio.

616. ***Fifth***, in the Commission's proposals, the national medium-term fiscal-structural plans must present a net expenditure trajectory covering a period of *"at least"* four years. The adjustment period, *i.e.*, the period over which the fiscal adjustment is carried out, is likewise minimum four years but may be extended by maximum three years if the Member State commits to a package of eligible reforms and investments that are time-bound, frontloaded and verifiable and, among other conditions, ensure that the overall level of (nationally financed) public investments over the lifetime of the plan is higher than their medium-term level before the plan.

The combination of an original adjustment period of *minimum* four years and a possible extension of *maximum* three years was a bit curious. This has been clarified in the agreed December 21, 2023 text: the plan horizon would be four or five years (depending on the regular term of the national legislature), and the adjustment period four years, subject still to extension by maximum three years. Both the June 15, 2023 joint op-ed of the finance ministers of fiscally more conservative Member States[866] and a July 5, 2023 opinion of the ECB[867] critically observed that such a time horizon is long and stretches beyond a typical electoral cycle. Or, in less diplomatic language: with an adjustment period of four and potentially up to seven years, how could a newly-elected

863. To this effect, the Commission proposal specifies that the fiscal adjustment effort over the plan horizon should be at least proportional to the total effort over the entire adjustment period. The text agreed by the Council on December 21, 2023 adds that the effort should be *"linear as a rule"*.
864. This last item (iv) is dropped in the agreed December 21, 2023 text.
865. *"Verifiable"* has been replaced by *"data-driven"* in the December 21, 2023 text.
866. *See* fn. 851 above.
867. *See* Opinion of the European Central Bank of July 5, 2023 on a proposal for economic governance in the Union, p. 5, https://www.ecb.europa.eu/pub/pdf/legal/ecb.leg_con_2023_20.en.pdf?31aa0f5c814f93218 959c568105a6690.

government with a political agenda of its own and taking office sometime during that period, effectively be held to implement fiscal policy and reform commitments agreed by the preceding government? In the Commission's proposal, a Member State may request to submit a revised medium-term fiscal-structural plan if *"objective circumstances"* prevent the implementation of the original plan or ... following a change of government. The December 21, 2023 text clarifies that, in the latter case, the newly-appointed government may in any event submit a revised plan covering a new period of four or five years (and not merely the remaining term of the initial plan). It is another kind of "tragedy of the horizon": multi-annual adjustment trajectories are intrinsically vulnerable to changes in government. This risk cannot be avoided but it can be reduced by keeping the adjustment periods shorter and aligning them to regular electoral cycles.

Also, Member States may still be allowed temporary deviations from their net expenditure path under escape clauses that broadly correspond to the current country-specific unusual events clause and the general escape clause.

617. ***Sixth***, in SGP's corrective arm, a government debt ratio in excess of 60% would now be considered to be *"sufficiently diminishing and approaching the reference value at a satisfactory pace"* (within the meaning of Article 126(2), first paragraph, (b) TFEU) if a Member State respects its net expenditure path. Accordingly, a debt-based EDP, *i.e.*, an EDP for breach of the debt criterion, would henceforth focus on departures from a Member State's net expenditure path. Also, a finding of a substantial public debt challenge in the Commission's latest Debt Sustainability Monitor[868] would, as a rule, be a key factor for opening a debt-based EDP. At the insistence of Germany and certain other Member States, an alternative numerical EDP trigger has been included in the agreed December 21, 2023 text (*see* paragraph 621(b) below).

618. ***Seventh***, once found to be in excessive deficit, a Member State would have to implement a corrective net expenditure path which (i) in the case of a deficit-based EDP, is consistent with an annual fiscal adjustment[869] of at least 0.5% of GDP as a benchmark for the years in which the government deficit ratio is expected to exceed 3%; (ii) puts the government debt ratio on a *"plausibly downward path"* or keeps it at a prudent level, as the case may be; and (iii) ensures that the average fiscal adjustment effort over the first three years is not below the average over the entire adjustment period (again to thwart political temptations of backloading).

619. **Eighth**, still in SGP's corrective arm, the proposed reform seeks to "de-constrain" the effective use of fines for euro area Member States by ... lowering their amount and

---

868. This classification corresponds to the Commission's assessment of high fiscal sustainability risk over the medium term on the basis of its Debt Sustainability Analysis ("DSA") toolkit. *Cf.* European Commission, *Debt Sustainability Monitor 2022, European Economy Institutional Paper No 199*, April 2023, pp. 20-22. The Commission's DSA includes a baseline projection for the debt trajectory over 10 years, complemented by additional deterministic projections under alternative fiscal, macroeconomic and financial assumptions, as well as stochastic debt projections covering a broad range of possible shocks. For further particulars on this methodology, *see* European Commission, *Fiscal Sustainability Report 2021, European Economy Institutional Paper No 171*, April 2022, pp. 58-86.

869. In the agreed December 21, 2023 text, it is specified that a structural adjustment is intended.

reinforcing their incentive effect. Thus, fines would accumulate at the rate of maximum 0.05% of GDP for successive six-month periods until effective action is taken in response to a Council notice under Article 126(9) TFEU, up to a maximum amount of 0.5% of GDP in the aggregate.[870]

d A Landing Zone

620. On December 8, 2023, after several months of exchanges and notwithstanding *"significant"* progress made in *"intense"* discussions in the preceding weeks and days, the ECOFIN Council still failed to reach an overall agreement on revised compromise texts submitted by the then Spanish Presidency.[871] But Council chair Nadia Calviño expressed the hope to *"finalise this in the coming days and weeks, so that we can find a political agreement before the end of the year"*.[872] In plainer English: the Member States had reached a landing zone. Then, on December 21, 2023, political agreement was reached on revised texts.[873]

621. The agreed December 21, 2023 texts are close to the Spanish Presidency compromise texts. The principal changes to the Commission proposals notably include the following:

(a) In SGP's preventive arm, numerical benchmarks are added as "safeguards" to serve as a common denominator and ensure a measure of predictability of the adjustment efforts (subtitle: to rein in bilateralism between the Commission and the individual Member States). These safeguards are introduced in the design phase of the Member States' medium-term fiscal-structural plans and specifically at the level of the technical trajectories which the Commission must set out for Member States with government deficit and/or debt ratios above the 3% and 60% reference values (*see* paragraph 615 above). Thus, under a "debt sustainability safeguard", the technical trajectory would have to ensure that the projected government debt ratio declines by at least 0.5%

870. This cap is dropped in the agreed December 21, 2023 text.
871. The Spanish Presidency's compromise texts of the three Commission proposals are to be found at https://www.consilium.europa.eu/media/68693/st15874-re01-en23.pdf, https://www.consilium.europa.eu/media/68694/st15876-re01-en23.pdf, and https://www.consilium.europa.eu/media/68695/st15396-re01-en23.pdf.
872. *See* https://www.consilium.europa.eu/en/meetings/ecofin/2023/12/08/.
873. *See* the Council's press release of December 21, 2023, https://www.consilium.europa.eu/press/press-releases/2023/12/21/economic-governance-review-council-agrees-on-reform-of-fiscal-rules/pdf. Technically, the agreement consists of a mandate for negotiations with the European Parliament on the proposed regulation regarding SGP's preventive arm (which is subject to the ordinary legislative procedure) and an agreement in principle on the other two proposals, *i.e.*, the proposed regulation regarding SGP's corrective arm and the proposed directive on requirements for national budgetary frameworks, with a view to consulting the European Parliament. The revised texts may be found at https://data.consilium.europa.eu/doc/document/ST-15874-2023-REV-4/en/pdf, https://data.consilium.europa.eu/doc/document/ST-15876-2023-REV-4/en/pdf, and https://data.consilium.europa.eu/doc/document/ST-15396-2023-REV-4/en/pdf.

of GDP *per annum* on average so long as the debt ratio remains between 60% and 90%, and by at least 1% of GDP *per annum* on average so long as the debt ratio exceeds 90%. In addition, a "deficit resilience safeguard" should ensure that fiscal adjustment is continued until the relevant Member State achieves a safety margin, "common resilience margin", of 1.5% of GDP in structural terms below the 3% reference value, as a fiscal buffer to facilitate counter-cyclical actions and for public investments and reforms. This margin would need to be achieved by an annual improvement in the structural primary balance of 0.4% of GDP (or 0.25% of GDP if the adjustment period is extended).

(b) In SGP's corrective arm, the Commission must prepare an Article 126(3) TFEU report to trigger a debt-based EDP when a Member State's government debt ratio exceeds 60%, its headline deficit is not close to balance or in surplus and the observed deviations from its net expenditure path exceed 0.3% of GDP annually or 0.6% of GDP cumulatively.

(c) Also in SGP's corrective arm, the benchmark adjustment effort in a corrective net expenditure path under a deficit-based EDP (*i.e.*, an annual structural adjustment of at least 0.5% of GDP) could now be adapted to take into account the increase in interest payments in the years 2025, 2026 and 2027.

622. In any event, one of the three proposals, *i.e.*, the draft regulation replacing Council Regulation (EC) No 1466/97 on SGP's preventive arm, is subject to the ordinary legislative procedure in which the European Parliament acts as co-legislator, while the other two proposals only require consultation with the Parliament. The SGP reforms are a legislative priority and timing is becoming sharp, also given that elections for the Parliament will be held on June 6 to 9, 2024 and the last plenary session of the outgoing Parliament is scheduled at the end of April. Interinstitutional negotiations (so-called "trilogues") will take place to facilitate smooth completion of the legislative process on the draft regulation regarding SGP's preventive arm and will need to iron out certain concerns reflected in the amendments contained in the December 15, 2023 report of the European Parliament's Committee on Economic and Monetary Affairs.[874] But it seemed possible at the time of writing that the SGP reforms would land closely to the December 21, 2023 texts.

874. *See* the report of the European Parliament's Committee on Economic and Monetary Affairs, A9-0439/2023, December 15, 2023, 70 pp., https://www.europarl.europa.eu/doceo/document/A-9-2023-0439_EN.pdf.

CHAPTER 9
Centralized Stability Support and the EU Budget

1 REASON AND POLITICS

a The Case for Centralized Stabilization Capacity

623. Let me first recap some of the earlier general considerations. A multi-country currency union in which a single currency, under a single monetary policy, is shared by a number of economically more or less diverse countries that retain a substantial measure of sovereignty in economic and fiscal matters, is an intrinsically complex and potentially unstable configuration. It stands to reason that such a currency union is not sustainable if its member countries are left unfettered freedom in the conduct of their national economic and fiscal policies. Differences in productivity and competitiveness, dissimilarities in national political preferences, temptations of profligate public spending and political inaction bias on structural reforms may give rise to persistent imbalances within the currency zone. Excessive public deficit and debt levels may eventually cause dislocations in government bond markets and, in an adverse scenario, trigger destabilizing market dynamics that may threaten the cohesion of the currency union, as happened in the 2010-2012 euro area sovereign debt crisis. High and diverging government debt levels may constrain the common monetary policy and "entrap" it in a relatively more accommodative stance than is desirable for maintaining price stability, and/or prompt geographically targeted asset purchases to contain financial fragmentation. Clearly, the continued cohesion of a multi-country currency union will require a common fiscal framework to maintain responsible fiscal conduct and keep government deficit and debt levels sustainable over time. We discussed in Chapter 8 the difficult brick-by-brick process of constructing such a framework and its continuing and partly unavoidable tensions and limitations in Europe's unfinished EMU.

624. Yet, currency union member countries do need adequate fiscal space to counter cyclical downturns and external shocks and to finance public investments and support structural reforms—regardless of the sins of the fathers and the fiscal positions that they may have inherited from them. Now being deprived of exchange rate adjustment and monetary policy tools of their own, these countries are left to economic and fiscal policies to address those needs. Economic policy coordination and common fiscal rules must not unduly compress their reduced fiscal space for doing so. But even if they don't, country differences in the timing or amplitude of business cycles, asymmetric effects of external shocks (for example, in the case of an oil shock, due to differences in the degree of dependency on imported fuels), and, more generally, differences in economic characteristics, structural reform needs and fiscal architecture will cause the fiscal positions of member countries to diverge to a greater or lesser degree. From time to time, member countries with weaker fiscal positions may be faced with a higher market risk premium on their government bonds and be forced into pro-cyclical fiscal restraint to avoid credit rating downgrades and maintain financial market access on viable terms. This is what happened to some extent in the euro area during and in the aftermath of the 2008-2012 financial crisis, resulting in an overall insufficiently counter-cyclical fiscal policy stance that was detrimental to public investment and growth. A policy configuration of this kind may also shift too much of the weight of macroeconomic stabilization to monetary policy, requiring stronger monetary easing for longer to make up for the relative shortfall of fiscal stimulus, as former ECB President Mario Draghi observed in his June 18, 2019 farewell address at the ECB Central Banking Forum (*see* paragraphs 304(a) and 411 above).

625. This issue becomes more pressing now that considerable public investments and structural reforms are needed to maintain competitiveness and a reasonable level of growth, at a time when current and projected inflation appears to leave less room for significant monetary accommodation in the short to medium term. While such investments and reforms vary from one country to another, a common theme is that substantial public spending will need to be directed notably (i) toward addressing the effects of climate change and supporting the transition to a low(er)-carbon economy; (ii) given unfavorable demographic trends (and considering the shrinking population at working age and the diversion of human resources to care of the older generations), toward funding educational, (re)training and activation programs to maintain a sufficient influx of human resources into the labor market in terms of both numbers and skills; (iii) toward rebuilding adequate defense capability; and (iv) toward closing the investment gap left by public under-investment in the previous decennium.

626. Monetary policy must not be burdened with the task of filling the gaps in the macroeconomic policy mix and become entrapped in a more accommodative stance than is required for inflation control. Anti-fragmentation sovereign bond purchases are sub-optimal and should at best be a temporary stop-gap measure. And sovereign debt restructuring (especially if involving nominal haircuts) is intrinsically problematic in a currency union and should remain genuinely exceptional in the euro area, as *ultima ratio*, particularly in view of the damage done to balance sheets of banks and other financial intermediaries and because it is bound to feed market oversensitivity to sovereign risks and a "who's next?" syndrome. It is clear, at least as a theoretical matter, that some well-designed central stability support mechanism(s) of sufficient size will need to be part of the equation.

627. Again, for a currency union between countries retaining fiscal sovereignty to function properly over time, it needs fiscal rules and mechanisms that achieve a workable mix of both risk containment and risk sharing so as to unburden monetary policy and allow it to focus on price stability. **Risk containment** requires a credible fiscal framework that prompts member countries to conduct responsible fiscal policies, keep their government finances sustainable, and implement structural reforms to address weaknesses in productivity and competitiveness and support the green transition. **Risk sharing** requires some centralized or pooled fiscal capacity notably to help member countries overcome asymmetric shocks or to support structural reforms and bridge imbalances pending such reforms. Cross-country risk sharing should also increase "skin in the game" for all members and diminish the probability of some partial or total break-up of the currency union.

b The Transfer Union Controversy

628. The academic case for centralized stabilization capacity is clear and compelling, the political case much less so. Several euro area Member States have repeatedly expressed reservations or outright objections against the European currency union becoming a "transfer union" or against financing mechanisms that were seen to imply inter-country transfers within the European Union or the euro area. A euro area budgetary transfer mechanism on any significant scale was a long-time red line for several Member States, including Germany and certain other fiscally conservative Member States. During the 2008-2012 financial crisis, it was a dividing line between Northern and Southern euro area Member States—roughly between "creditor" and "debtor" countries. In the negotiations on the 2021-2027 Multiannual Financial Framework, Germany showed signs of leaning toward French ideas on a euro area budgetary instrument with stabilization properties. But then the "New Hanseatic League", a loose coalition of eight smaller Member States under the *de facto* leadership of The Netherlands, became the clearest voice in opposing an instrument of that kind and in moving the needle instead in the direction of a conditional reform-delivery instrument, as we will discuss later in this chapter (*see* paragraphs 651-663 below).

629. A constitutional issue has been looming large in the background of these political discussions. In Germany, an EU or euro area financial transfer mechanism presents issues of constitutional import. Issues of this kind also arise in certain other euro area Member States but I single out Germany for the intensity and impact of the constitutional issue in this leading euro area economy. Under established jurisprudence of the German Federal Constitutional Court, the Bundesverfassungsgericht ("BVerfG"), Germany could not, as a constitutional matter, adhere to any EU or international arrangement that could entail significant financial consequences for the German budget outside of the control of the Bundestag. In a very broad outline, in this reasoning, the core constitutional concept of democratic self-determination requires that the Bundestag substantially retain control over significant budgetary expenditures, for which it is accountable to the citizenry. This stands in the way of the State assuming financial commitments or contingent liabilities under EU or international arrangements insofar as they may result in major expenditures for the German budget without *ex ante* approval in principle and continuous control by the Bundestag. Doing so would impair the Bundestag's budgetary autonomy as a constitutional matter.

630. The BVerfG has repeatedly stated these principles, including, *inter alia*, in its judgment of September 7, 2011 on various support measures for Greece,[875] its judgment of September 12, 2012 on the ratification of the ESM Treaty,[876] its order of April 15, 2021 dismissing an application for a preliminary injunction against Germany's approval of Council Decision (EU, Euratom) 2020/2053[877] and its judgment of December 6, 2022 on the merits in the same case. In this last judgment, those principles are summarized in the following terms:

> *"No permanent mechanisms may be created that would essentially entail an assumption of liability for decisions taken by other states, intergovernmental institutions or international organisations, especially if the commitments in question could have potentially unforeseeable consequences. When the Federation undertakes significant aid measures based on solidarity at the international or EU level that affect public spending, approval by the Bundestag is required in each individual case. Every single measure agreed upon at the supranational level which, by reason of its scale, may structurally affect Parliament's budgetary powers not only requires approval by the Bundestag, it must also be ensured that the Bundestag retains sufficient influence on how the means provided will be used [...]; this requirement applies, for instance, if guarantees were given that, in the event of default, could endanger budgetary autonomy, or if Germany participated in a financial guarantee system of such nature".*[878]

631. This is a sobering message for advocates of a greater measure of counter-cyclical fiscal capacity or other risk-shared financing at the European level. Yet, like a symphony of Wagner, it is not all as bad as it sounds. On what seems a fresh note, in the same judgment of December 6, 2022, the BVerfG applies those principles with a certain largesse and appears to set the door ajar for properly structured EU or intergovernmental financial support arrangements. It should be a helpful factor in the further debate on strengthening EU or euro area stability support in EMU's architecture. We will take a closer look at this judgment at the end of this chapter (*see* paragraphs 670-681 below).

875. BVerfG, September 7, 2011, ECLI:DE:BVerfG:2011:rs20110907.2bvr098710, §§121-132. An English translation of this judgment is reproduced on the BVerfG's website at http://www.bverfg.de/e/rs20110907_2bvr098710en.html.
876. BVerfG, September 12, 2012, ECLI:DE:BVerfG:2012:rs20120912.2bvr139012, §§106-111. For an English translation, *see* http://www.bverfg.de/e/rs20120912_2bvr139012en.html.
877. BVerfG, April 15, 2021, ECLI:DE:BVerfG:2021:rs20210415.2bvr054721, §85. The English translation may be found at http://www.bverfg.de/e/rs20210415_2bvr054721en.html.
878. BVerfG, December 6, 2022, ECLI:DE:BVerfG:2022:rs20221206.2bvc054721, §135, with English translation at http://www.bverfg.de/e/rs20221206_2bvr054721en.html.

2 THE EU BUDGET AND FINANCING MECHANISMS

a Budget and Off-Budget Financing

632. At present, the European Union's regular long-term (seven-year) budget under the 2021-2027 Multiannual Financial Framework ("MFF") is EUR 1,074.3 billion (in 2018 prices). Its annual budget, in a range of EUR 160 to 190 billion, represents between 1.1% and 1.2% of aggregate EU GDP and remains comparatively small. In absolute terms, it is in the same order of magnitude as the annual budget of Denmark. Macroeconomic stabilization has traditionally not been among the explicit objectives of the EU budget so far, although certain funds and spending programs undoubtedly have had and still have a limited stabilizing impact in cyclical downturns.[879]

633. Subsections b. through f. below summarily describe, in chronological order, certain special financing mechanisms within the EU legal framework which, although not reserved to euro area Member States, are of interest to the subject matter of this book. The Single Resolution Fund (*see* paragraphs 640-641 below) is an outlier among these mechanisms in that it is funded by contributions from the financial sector and will eventually be backstopped by a revolving credit line of the European Stability Mechanism ("ESM"), an intergovernmental financial institution outside the EU institutional framework.[880] The other financing mechanisms discussed here have in common that, somewhat at the periphery of the EU budgetary framework, they are funded by debt which the European Commission issues or contracts on behalf of the European Union in the financial markets, with the proceeds from these borrowings then being provided to Member States, for certain specified purposes, by way of onward loans (which I will refer to as the "loan-to-loan variant") or, as in the case of NextGenerationEU ("NGEU"), also in part by way of non-repayable grants (the "loan-to-grant variant").

634. The European Union can borrow at favorable rates on the strength of its high credit ratings, *i.e.*, currently a triple-A rating with Moody's, Fitch, DBRS and Scope and an AA+ rating with Standard & Poor's (all with stable outlook). Thus, even in the loan-to-loan variant, this should produce interest savings for Member States with lower ratings insofar as the Union's favorable interest terms are substantially passed on to the borrowing Member States.[881] In this sense, inasmuch as the European Union's superior

879. *Cf.* European Commission, *Spending review*, SWD(2018) 171 final, May 2, 2018, p. 32, https://eur-lex.europa.eu/legal-content/EN/TXT/PDF/?uri=CELEX:52018SC0171&from=EN, on the stabilizing impact of the European Regional Development Fund, the Cohesion Fund and the European Social Fund during the 2008-2012 financial crisis.

880. At the time of writing, the relevant amendments to the ESM Treaty had been ratified by all euro area Member States except Italy. On December 21, 2023, the Italian parliament voted down ratification but my working assumption still is that Italy's overdue ratification could only be a matter of time—and the right political *quid pro quo(s)*.

881. Under the mechanisms discussed here, the Union's onward loans to Member States are extended substantially on a back-to-back basis, except that loans under NGEU are not necessarily linked to specific EU borrowings (given the scale and timeframe of the program).

credit rating rests in part on the membership of the highest-rated Member States (as appears to be implicit in the reasoning of the credit rating agencies), such centralized financing at EU level operates a certain "transfer" to lower-rated Member States also in the loan-to-loan variant as these Member States "piggyback" on the stronger credit of the Union and, indirectly, on that of higher-rated Member States. But "transfer" may not be the apt word here so long as the interest gain derived by lower-rated Member States does not directly or indirectly give rise to a cost for higher-rated Member States (*i.e.*, broadly, so long as a loan default by the former does not in some way trigger contributory payments by the latter).

635. In the loan-to-loan variant, the financing mechanisms discussed below are essentially off-budget: the EU borrowings are not entered in the EU budget (except as *pro memoria* items to record the Union's contingent liability) and, so long as the beneficiary Member States timely meet their payment obligations on the onward loans received, the financing should have no impact on the EU budget. In the loan-to-grant variant of NGEU, the amount of EU borrowings allocated to non-repayable grants is recorded in the budget as external assigned revenue, *i.e.*, a form of "other revenue" within the meaning of Article 311, second paragraph, TFEU. In both variants, the European Union is liable for its borrowings vis-à-vis its creditors. In the event of a default of a beneficiary Member State in the loan-to-loan variant, the Union must cover any corresponding shortfall in interest or principal due on its own debt out of the EU budget's "headroom", *i.e.*, the difference ("margin") between (i) the own resources ceiling for annual payment appropriations (being the maximum amount that the Union may require Member States to contribute in a given year to finance expenditures), and (ii) the annual ceiling for payment appropriations under the long-term budget. In other words, in case of a shortfall due to a default by a beneficiary Member State on its onward loan, the Commission has to draw on the margin available under the own resources ceiling for payment appropriations in order to fully service the EU debt. In this sense, the EU borrowings are "guaranteed" by the EU budget headroom. In the loan-to-grant variant, payments due on the corresponding amount of EU borrowings are to be fully covered out of the EU budget headroom.

636. Obviously, EU budget headroom is limited and other expenditures (including expenditures resulting from contingent liabilities and unexpected expenditures like those on the war in Ukraine) compete for some part of it. And rising borrowing costs as a result of monetary tightening may squeeze available space under the margin. Accordingly, as financing mechanisms of this kind, especially those of the loan-to-grant variant, are put in place more frequently or at a larger scale (such as NGEU), careful planning of cash-flows on EU borrowings will be needed, and maturities and repayment schedules may have to be stretched, to ensure that available EU budget headroom can cope to cover debt service on EU borrowings in any given year. Back-up guarantee schemes may have to be established, as was done in the case of SURE (*see* paragraph 643 below). And to cover (re)payments under NGEU borrowings, a dedicated increase has been made in the own resources ceiling (*see* paragraph 646 below). In a longer-term perspective, new sources of own resources may have to be mined, as is a recurring and difficult subject of discussion (*see* paragraphs 666-669 below).

b Balance-of-Payments Assistance Facility for Non-Euro Area Member States

637. In 2002, an existing balance-of-payments assistance facility was recast as a medium-term loan facility reserved for non-euro area Member States experiencing, or seriously threatened with, balance-of-payments difficulties.[882] The loan envelope was initially capped at EUR 12 billion in principal amount outstanding, raised to EUR 25 billion at the end of 2008 and to EUR 50 billion in the spring of 2009, and the loans to Member States are conditioned on policy actions to address the underlying economic problems. During the financial crisis that began in 2008, loans under this facility were extended to Hungary, Latvia and Romania, each time as part of a package involving assistance from the IMF (and other sources).

c The European Financial Stabilisation Mechanism

638. In the spring of 2010, with the sovereign debt crisis then beginning to unfold, another EU loan facility, the European Financial Stabilisation Mechanism ("EFSM"), was established, on the basis of Article 122(2) TFEU, to provide loans to Member States experiencing, or seriously threatened with, *"a severe economic or financial disturbance caused by exceptional circumstances beyond its control"*.[883] This new loan facility broadly mirrors the earlier balance-of-payments facility for non-euro area Member States just described (which is maintained) but is available to all Member States, including those of the euro area. In parallel, as will be further discussed in Chapter 10, a (much larger) dedicated euro area facility, the European Financial Stability Facility ("EFSF"), was set up outside the EU legal framework, followed, in 2012, by the establishment of the ESM as its permanent successor. It was subsequently agreed that, save in exceptional circumstances, the ESM should be the first port of call for further financial assistance to euro area Member States, and that henceforth these Member States should hold the other Member States harmless for any liability they may incur as a result of a payment default by a euro area Member State under an EFSM loan.[884]

---

882. Council Regulation (EC) No 332/2002 of February 18, 2002 establishing a facility providing medium-term financial assistance for Member States' balances of payments, *OJ* L53, February 23, 2002, p. 1, amended by Council Regulation (EC) No 1360/2008 of December 2, 2008, *OJ* L352, December 31, 2008, p. 11, and Council Regulation (EC) No 431/2009 of May 18, 2009, *OJ* L128, May 27, 2009, p. 1. For a more detailed discussion of this facility, *see* A. Thiele, "Financial Assistance to Non-Euro Area Member States", in *The EU Law of Economic and Monetary Union* (F. Amtenbrink & Chr. Herrmann eds.), Oxford University Press, 2022, pp. 1039-1045, §§34.48-34.60.

883. Council Regulation (EC) No 407/2010 of May 11, 2010 establishing a European financial stabilisation mechanism, *OJ* L118, May 12, 2010, p. 1, amended by Council Regulation (EU) 2015/1360 of August 4, 2015, *OJ* L210, August 7, 2015, p. 1. For further discussion, *see* V. Borger, "EU Financial Assistance", in *The EU Law of Economic and Monetary Union* (F. Amtenbrink & Chr. Herrmann eds.), Oxford University Press, 2022, pp. 968-973, §§32.14-32.29.

884. *See* recital (4) to Council Regulation (EU) 2015/1360 and the new Article 3(2a) which this Regulation adds to Council Regulation (EC) No 407/2010. In fact, at its meeting of December

639. As with the balance-of-payments facility for non-euro area Member States, EFSM financial assistance is funded by borrowings of the European Commission on behalf of the European Union, with the proceeds being on-lent to the beneficiary Member States on a back-to-back basis. The loan envelope was limited in reference to the EU budget headroom margin, then estimated to accommodate a loan volume of up to EUR 60 billion.[885] EFSM financial support takes the form of loans or credit lines that are subject to economic policy conditionality. The facility has been used so far to extend loans to Ireland and Portugal between 2011 and 2014 (each time in tandem with the IMF and the EFSF) and to provide short-term bridge financing to Greece in July 2015 pending a further program of financial assistance by the ESM (*see* paragraph 719, Table 10.1, below). The EFSM was initially conceived as a temporary facility but it has remained in place until this day, available for further use if and when needed.

d The Single Resolution Fund

640. A targeted transfer mechanism outside the EU budget is the Single Resolution Fund ("SRF") of the Single Resolution Mechanism created in the framework of the Banking Union. The SRF was established in 2016 pursuant to Regulation (EU) No 806/2014 of July 15, 2014,[886] in order to avoid that the costs of resolving failing banks would (primarily) fall on public funds of individual Member States—as had happened in the 2008-2009 banking crisis, especially in Ireland and Spain, fuelling the so-called "bank-sovereign doom loop" (*see* paragraph 63 above).

641. The SRF is to provide the financial resources for the application of various resolution tools to failing banks. It is funded by annual levies (contributions) of some 2,777 banks and (certain) investment firms in the 21 Member States participating in the Banking Union (*i.e.*, all 20 euro area Member States and Bulgaria). It has been gradually built up, and mutualized, over an eight-year period from 2016 to 2023 to reach a target level of at least 1 % of the aggregate amount of covered deposits. It stood at EUR 66 billion by the end of 2022 and is estimated to reach about EUR 77.6 billion

---

16-17, 2010, the European Council had already agreed that, upon the establishment of the ESM as a permanent mechanism for dedicated euro area stability support, Article 122(2) TFEU should no longer be used for this purpose. *See* Conclusions of the European Council of December 16-17, 2010, §I.1, https://www.consilium.europa.eu/uedocs/cms_data/docs/pressdata/en/ec/118578.pdf.

885. *See Communication from the Commission to the Council and the Economic and Financial Committee on the European Financial Stabilisation Mechanism*, COM(2010) 713 final, November 30, 2010, p. 4, https://eur-lex.europa.eu/legal-content/EN/TXT/PDF/?uri=CELEX:52010DC0713.

886. *See*, in particular, Articles 67 to 78 of Regulation (EU) No 806/2014 of the European Parliament and of the Council of July 15, 2014 establishing uniform rules and a uniform procedure for the resolution of credit institutions and certain investment firms in the framework of a Single Resolution Mechanism and a Single Resolution Fund and amending Regulation (EU) No 1093/2010, *OJ* L225, July 30, 2014, p. 1, amended by Regulation (EU) 2019/877 of May 20, 2019, *OJ* L150, June 7, 2019, p. 226, Regulation (EU) 2019/2033 of November 27, 2019, *OJ* L314, December 5, 2019, p. 1, and Regulation (EU) 2021/23 of December 16, 2020, *OJ* L22, January 22, 2021, p. 1.

by the end of 2023. If the SRF is depleted and no additional funds can be mobilized from other sources on acceptable conditions, the plan is for the ESM to act as a backstop under a revolving credit line with a nominal cap of EUR 68 billion, to be repaid through *ex post* contributions from the industry (*see* paragraphs 721-722 below). But this still awaits the entry into effect of the 2021 amendments to the ESM Treaty which have meanwhile been ratified by all euro area Member States except, at the time of writing, Italy.

e The SURE Program

642. Several temporary "solidarity" mechanisms were put in place at the EU level to provide financial support to Member States in response to the COVID-19 crisis. An early initiative was a temporary EU loan facility, named "Support to mitigate Unemployment Risks in an Emergency" ("SURE"), for loans to Member States, up to a total program amount of EUR 100 billion, to assist them in addressing sudden increases in public expenditures to protect jobs and workers' income (through short-time work schemes and other measures) and, secondarily, for health-related measures at the workplace.[887]

643. These loans are funded by "social" bonds issued by the European Commission on behalf of the European Union. The bonds are "guaranteed" by the EU budget headroom but the risk borne by the European Union is counter-guaranteed by the 27 Member States, under a set of bilateral on-demand guarantees, for a total amount of 25% of the SURE envelope, *i.e.*, EUR 25 billion, with each Member State's share corresponding to its share in EU gross national income ("GNI").[888] Before calling on these guarantees, the Commission *"is expected"* to draw first on the EU budget headroom to the extent it considers this *"sustainable [...] having regard, inter alia, to the total contingent liabilities of the Union [...] and the sustainability of the general budget of the Union"*.[889]

644. Under SURE, loans for a total amount of EUR 98.36 billion have been granted to 19 Member States, with an average maturity of around 14.5 years,[890] mostly to Italy (EUR 27.44 billion), Spain (EUR 21.32 billion), Poland (EUR 11.24 billion), Belgium (EUR 8.20 billion), Portugal (EUR 6.23 billion) and Greece (EUR 6.17 billion).[891] The SURE window closed on December 31, 2022.

887. Council Regulation (EU) 2020/672 of May 19, 2020 on the establishment of a European instrument for temporary support to mitigate unemployment risks in an emergency (SURE) following the COVID-19 outbreak, *OJ* L159, May 20, 2020, p. 1.
888. Articles 11 and 12 of the same Regulation.
889. Recital (9) and Article 11(5) of the same Regulation.
890. *See* the European Commission's fifth and final bi-annual report on the implementation of SURE, COM(2023) 291 final, June 2, 2023, pp. 11 and 44, Table A1, https://eur-lex.europa.eu/legal-content/EN/TXT/PDF/?uri=CELEX:52023DC0291.
891. *Ibid.*, p. 9, Table 1.

f NextGenerationEU and the Recovery and Resilience Facility

645. At a special meeting of July 17-21, 2020, the European Council agreed on the key features of a much larger temporary support package, NextGenerationEU ("NGEU"), to address the economic fall-out of COVID-19 and stimulate post-COVID-19 recovery.[892] In this context, the European Commission is authorized to borrow up to EUR 750 billion, in 2018 prices,[893] in the capital markets, prior to 2027,[894] for the sole purpose of funding non-repayable grants (up to EUR 390 billion) and loans (up to EUR 360 billion) to Member States to support public investments and reforms aimed at ensuring sustainable recovery in the aftermath of COVID-19. It is a package of significant size in relation to the European Union's regular long-term budget, *i.e.*, EUR 1,074.3 billion, again in 2018 prices, under the 2021-2027 MFF. It has been estimated that, if all NGEU grants and loans are taken up for productive public investments, NGEU would lead to a persistent increase in output which for the euro area would peak at around 1.5% of GDP in 2025.[895]

646. The interest and principal (re)payments on the EU borrowings to fund NGEU (which stretch in time until the end of 2058) are "guaranteed" by the EU budget headroom, *i.e.*, the margin available under the own resources ceiling for payment appropriations (*see* paragraph 635 above). For the sole purpose of covering the financial obligations on those NGEU borrowings, Council Decision (EU, Euratom) 2020/2053 of December 14, 2020 has backed this up by a temporary *ad hoc* increase of the regular own resources ceilings in respect of annual payment and commitment appropriations (*i.e.*, 1.40% and 1.46%, respectively, of the European Union's GNI) by 0.6 percentage points to 2% and 2.06%, respectively.[896] This produces an additional

892. *See* the conclusions adopted by the European Council at its special meeting of July 17-21, 2020, pp. 2-7, https://www.consilium.europa.eu/media/media/45109/210720-euco-final-conclusions-en.pdf. The actual legal act setting up this instrument is Council Regulation (EU) 2020/2094 of December 14, 2020 establishing a European Union Recovery Instrument to support the recovery in the aftermath of the COVID-19 crisis, *OJ* L433 I, December 22, 2020, p. 23.

893. All budgetary amounts in this subsection f. are stated in 2018 prices, except as indicated otherwise. According to EU budgetary practice, these amounts are restated in current prices on the basis of a fixed deflator of 2% *per annum*, irrespective of actual inflation. *See* Article 4 of Council Regulation (EU, Euratom) 2020/93 of December 17, 2020 laying down the multiannual financial framework for the years 2021 to 2027, *OJ* L433 I, December 22, 2020, p. 11, amended by Council Regulation (EU, Euratom) 2022/2496 of December 15, 2022, *OJ* L325, December 20, 2022, p. 11. Thus, in current (2023) prices, the NGEU envelope of EUR 750 billion translates into EUR 806.9 billion, and the EU long-term budget of EUR 1,074.3 billion into EUR 1,210.9 billion.

894. Relevant provisions on the European Commission's borrowing authority, the use of proceeds and the repayment of the loans are set forth in Articles 4, 5, 6 and 9(4)-(9) of Council Decision (EU, Euratom) 2020/2053 of December 14, 2020 on the system of own resources of the European Union and repealing Decision 2014/335/EU, Euratom, *OJ* L424, December 15, 2020, p. 1.

895. *See* Kr. Bankowski, M. Ferdinandusse *et al.*, "The macroeconomic impact of the Next Generation EU instrument on the euro area", *ECB Occasional Paper Series No 255*, January 2021, pp. 10-11.

896. Article 6 of Council Decision 2020/2053.

layer of EU budget headroom as a dedicated guarantee for EU debt issued for NGEU. If at any time budgetary appropriations are not sufficient to meet those financial obligations and the Commission is unable to generate the necessary liquidity through active cash management or short-term financing, the Commission may, as a last resort, call on the Member States to provide the necessary resources, *pro rata* their estimated budget revenue and limited to their relative share in the *ad hoc* 0.6% increase in the own resources ceiling—with a further round of (provisional) true-up calls in case one or several Member States fail to fully pay up their share.[897]

647. As said, legal action was brought before the BVerfG challenging Germany's approval of Council Decision (EU, Euratom) 2020/2053 (as is required by Article 311, third paragraph, TFEU) on the ground, in particular, that it would violate the Bundestag's budgetary autonomy as a matter of German constitutional law insofar as it could give rise to budgetary costs for Germany outside of the Bundestag's control and, in addition, would breach the "no bail-out" rule of Article 125 TFEU. On April 15, 2021, the BVerfG rejected the application for a preliminary injunction, and on December 6, 2022, it dismissed the case on the merits. As will be discussed in the final section of this chapter (*see* paragraphs 670-681 below), the December 6, 2022 judgment is significant in that it appears to create an opening for EU or euro area NGEU-type financial support mechanisms. In that sense, it may reduce a legal obstacle to greater risk-shared financing at European level.

648. NGEU funds are allocated to several EU spending programs but as its centerpiece stands the temporary Recovery and Resilience Facility ("RRF").[898] RRF's resources come essentially from NGEU, *i.e.*, up to EUR 312.5 billion for non-repayable financial support and up to EUR 360 billion for loans (both in 2018 prices)[899]—a total of up to EUR 672.5 billion or almost 90% of NGEU. The RRF envelope has meanwhile been topped up by EUR 20 billion (in current prices), from allowances auctioned under the EU Emissions Trading System, earmarked for non-repayable grants to support projects in line with the REPowerEU Plan (*see* paragraph 448 above).[900]

649. The objectives and scope of RRF are broadly defined as providing financial support for public investments and reforms that contribute to post-COVID-19 recovery in *"policy areas of European relevance"* that are grouped into six general themes (*"pillars"*). RRF places significant emphasis on the green transition and digital transformation and, since its amendment in February 2023, also on strengthening the resilience, security and sustainability of the EU energy system in line with the

897. Article 9(4)-(9) of the same Decision.
898. *See* Regulation (EU) 2021/241 of the European Parliament and of the Council of February 12, 2021 establishing the Recovery and Resilience Facility, *OJ* L57, February 18, 2021, p. 17, amended by Regulation (EU) 2023/453 of February 27, 2023, *OJ* L63, February 28, 2023, p. 1.
899. Article 6(1) of Regulation 2021/241.
900. Article 21a(1) of the same Regulation and Article 10e of Directive 2003/87/EC of the European Parliament and of the Council of October 13, 2003 establishing a system for greenhouse gas emission allowance trading within the Union and amending Council Directive 96/61/EC, *OJ* L275, October 25, 2003, p. 32, amended multiple times and last by Directive (EU) 2023/959 of May 10, 2023, *OJ* L130, May 16, 2023, p. 134.

REPowerEU Plan.[901] Thus, when reviewing the Member States' recovery and resilience plans, the European Commission must specifically assess whether proposed measures contributing to the green transition (including biodiversity) and to the digital transformation account for at least 37% and 20%, respectively, of each plan's total allocation.[902] As a general matter, RRF's nexus with the repairment of economic damage caused by COVID-19 would seem fairly tenuous: COVID-19 appears more as a context for fiscal stimulus targeted at strategically desirable investments and reforms than as a causal condition.

650. RRF is not conceived as a stabilization instrument *pur sang* but primarily as a reform-delivery instrument. Yet, the following features of the instrument are of particular interest to the subject matter of this book:

(a) The distribution of RRF grants and loans among Member States has a clear "solidarity" dimension. Thus, the allocation keys for grants favor Member States with larger population, lower GDP *per capita*, higher average unemployment rate over the past five years compared to the 2015-2019 EU average, and a higher drop in real GDP in 2020 and 2021.[903] Loans for each Member State are capped at the lower of (i) the difference between the total cost of its recovery and resilience plan and its maximum grant allocation, and (ii) as a rule, 6.8% of its 2019 GNI in current prices.[904] One will note that these criteria present only an approximate nexus to the economic damage caused by COVID-19.

(b) RRF funds may not serve as a substitute for recurring national budgetary expenditures *"unless in duly justified cases"*.[905] This exception would seem to leave some margin for allowing (more heavily indebted) Member States to present ongoing projects, and use RRF grants to reduce corresponding government debt or RRF loans to refinance existing debt on more advantageous terms. It is unclear (at least to this author) whether this was intended or may have actually happened. It would obviously open the door for "creative accounting", but, in appropriate circumstances, it might arguably be the next-best use of RRF funds in the case of Member States with high debt and limited capacity to absorb RRF funds for additional public investments.[906]

(c) The Member States' recovery and resilience plans must be found to be consistent with country-specific challenges and priorities identified in the European Semester, as well as, in the case of euro area Member States, with

901. *Cf.* Articles 3 and 4 of Regulation 2021/241.
902. Articles 18(4)(e) and (f) and 19(3)(e) and (f) and Annexes V (points 2.5 and 2.6), VI and VII of the same Regulation.
903. Article 11 and Annexes I to IV of the same Regulation. A special allocation formula for additional grants in respect of REPowerEU projects looks to a Member State's population, GDP *per capita*, gross fixed capital formation price deflator and share of fossil fuels in gross domestic energy consumption (Article 21a(2) and Annex IVa of the same Regulation).
904. Article 14(4)-(6) of the same Regulation.
905. Article 5(1) of the same Regulation.
906. *Cf.* Kr. Bankowski, M. Ferdinandusse *et al.*, *supra*, pp. 14-15.

the most recent economic policy recommendations of the Council.[907] Also, financing commitments or disbursements may be put on hold in certain instances of a Member State's non-compliance with the EMU fiscal or macroeconomic surveillance frameworks.[908]

3 DISCUSSIONS ON A DEDICATED EURO AREA INSTRUMENT LINKED TO THE EU BUDGET

651. To this day, initiatives and proposals for some EU budget-linked stabilization mechanism reserved for the euro area, and tailored to its needs as a currency union, have not gone very far. In the context of the 2008-2012 financial crisis, a dedicated euro area stability support mechanism was eventually established outside the EU institutional framework, *i.e.*, the EFSF and its more permanent successor the ESM, as will be discussed in Chapter 10. But several ideas have been floated from time to time to create a euro area financing instrument of some kind within the EU legal framework—or to integrate the ESM in that framework. As of 2017, these discussions became intertwined with the preparation of the 2021-2027 MFF. In this process, proposals for a dedicated euro area instrument with stabilization properties were progressively watered down to a reform-delivery instrument, with the working title "Budgetary Instrument for Convergence and Competitiveness" ("BICC"), which in the end fell by the wayside to make way for the EU-wide NGEU and its RRF (*see* paragraphs 645-650 above). Still, it is a story well worth telling because it reveals the political dynamics and fault lines in the discussions on euro area stabilization capacity that continue to be relevant today—even if they episodically become more blurred by shifting alliances and economic fortunes.

a From the Five Presidents' Report to the Saint Nicholas Package

652. In 2015, the so-called "Five Presidents' Report" on the completion of EMU envisaged that, at some stage, "*as culmination of a process of convergence and further pooling of decision-making on national budgets*", "*a common macroeconomic stabilisation function*" should be put in place "*to better deal with shocks that cannot be managed at national level alone*".[909] This instrument, to be established within the EU framework, should prevent moral hazard and be tightly linked to compliance with the EMU fiscal and macroeconomic surveillance frameworks, but its exact design was left to further in-depth work. In his 2017 "State of the Union" address to the European

907. Article 17(3) of Regulation 2021/241. *See also* Articles 18(4)(b) and 19(3)(b) and Annex V (point 2.2) of the same Regulation.
908. Article 10 of the same Regulation.
909. *Completing Europe's Economic and Monetary Union*, Report by Jean-Claude Juncker, in close cooperation with Donald Tusk, Jeroen Dijselbloem, Mario Draghi and Martin Schulz, June 22, 2015, pp. 14-15, https://wayback.archive-it.org/12090/20191231140925/https://ec.europa.eu/commission/sites/beta-political/files/5-presidents-report_en.pdf.

Parliament, then Commission President Jean-Claude Juncker, in line with his general dislike for "*parallel structures*", tried to set the tone by clarifying that "*[w]e do not need a budget for the Euro area but a strong Euro area budget line within the EU budget*".[910]

653. In its "Saint Nicholas package" on EMU reforms of December 6, 2017, the European Commission outlined its ideas for (i) a stabilization function to maintain national investment levels in the event of large asymmetric shocks that eligible Member States would be unable to absorb by using their fiscal buffers and conducting SGP-compliant discretionary fiscal policies; (ii) a dedicated convergence facility for Member States on their way to joining the currency union; and (iii) a reform-delivery tool to provide extra grants and technical assistance to support national efforts to implement reforms identified as priorities under the European Semester.[911] As concerns the proposed stabilization function, the Commission's thinking at that time was that (i) while applicable to euro area Member States, it should be *"open to all who wish to participate"*;[912] (ii) support would consist of loans and a *"relatively limited"* grant component; (iii) such support would not be subject to *ad hoc* economic policy conditionality but to *ex ante* eligibility criteria, including pre-shock compliance with SGP; and (iv) the program's size should be *"economically meaningful"*, then estimated at a level allowing overall net disbursements of at least 1% of GDP.[913]

654. The Commission crystallized its thoughts in proposals for two regulations of the European Parliament and of the Council which it tabled in the context of its initial May 2, 2018 proposal for the 2021-2027 MFF:[914]

(a) A first draft regulation, based on Article 175, third paragraph, TFEU, would establish a European Investment Stabilization Function for the purpose of providing financial assistance to euro area Member States and Member States participating in ERM II (*see* paragraph 52 above) with a view to preserving eligible ("growth-friendly") public investments in case of large asymmetric shocks.[915] Access to financial assistance would be subject to *ex ante* eligibility

910. President Jean-Claude Juncker's State of the Union Address 2017, September 13, 2017, https://ec.europa.eu/commission/presscorner/detail/en/SPEECH_17_3165, at p. 8.

911. *See* Communication from the Commission to the European Parliament, the European Council, the Council and the European Central Bank, *Further steps towards completing Europe's Economic and Monetary Union: A roadmap*, COM(2017) 821 final, December 6, 2017, p. 8, https://ec.europa.eu/info/sites/default/files/economy-finance/com_2017_821.pdf, and, especially, *New budgetary instruments for a stable euro area within the Union framework*, COM(2017) 822 final, December 6, 2017, pp. 7-16, https://ec.europa.eu/info/sites/default/files/economy-finance/com_822_0.pdf.

912. COM(2017) 822 final, p. 13.

913. *Ibid.*, p. 14.

914. *See* Communication from the Commission to the European Parliament, the European Council, the Council, the European Economic and Social Committee and the Committee of the Regions, *A Modern Budget for a Union that Protects, Empowers and Defends: The Multiannual Financial Framework for 2021-2027*, COM(2018) 321 final, May 2, 2018, especially pp. 10-11, https://eur-lex.europa.eu/legal-content/EN/TXT/?uri=COM%3A2018%3A321%3AFIN.

915. Proposal for a regulation of the European Parliament and of the Council on the establishment of a European Investment Stabilisation Function, COM(2018) 387 final, May 31, 2018, https://eur-lex.europa.eu/legal-content/EN/TXT/?uri=COM:2018:387:FIN.

criteria looking to compliance with decisions and recommendations under the EMU fiscal and macroeconomic surveillance frameworks and would be triggered by a significant worsening in unemployment. Financial assistance would take the form of loans, subject to an overall cap of EUR 30 billion, and of related interest subsidies. The loans would be funded by Commission borrowings, while the interest subsidies would be financed out of a fund endowed with annual national contributions determined on the basis of the share of Eurosystem monetary income ("seigniorage") allocated to the national central banks. Interestingly, the Commission's May 2, 2018 communication added that the European Investment Stabilization Function could over time be scaled up by additional resources, outside the EU budget, such as *"an insurance mechanism financed from voluntary contributions by Member States as well as a possible role for the European Stability Mechanism and for the future European Monetary Fund"*.[916]

(b) A second draft regulation, based on Articles 175, third paragraph, and 197(2) TFEU, would set up a Reform Support Program providing grants and technical assistance in support of national reforms identified in the context of the European Semester.[917] Its overall financial envelope for the 2021-2027 period would be EUR 30 billion. It would be available for all Member States, except that a sub-envelope of some EUR 2.16 billion would be reserved for non-euro area Member States which have taken demonstrable steps toward adopting the euro within a given timeframe.

655. All in all, after the Five Presidents' 2015 vision of *"a common macroeconomic stabilisation function"* and Jean-Claude Juncker's 2017 call for *"a strong Euro area budget line within the EU budget"*, the European Commission had landed on programs of modest size, focused on supporting SGP-compliant public investments and reforms, with a limited grant component and subdued stabilization properties.

b Franco-German Proposals

656. In parallel, France, with measured support from Germany, had been advocating a genuine euro area stabilization function. In a speech of September 26, 2017 at the Sorbonne University, French President Emmanuel Macron called for *"un budget plus fort [...] au coeur de la zone euro"* with stabilization capacity to respond to economic shocks which a Member State alone cannot absorb when it can no longer conduct a

916. COM(2018) 321 final, May 2, 2018, p. 11.
917. Proposal for a regulation of the European Parliament and of the Council on the establishment of the Reform Support Programme, COM(2018) 391 final, May 31, 2018, https://eur-lex.europa.eu/legal-content/EN/ALL/?uri=COM%3A2018%3A391%AFIN.

monetary policy of its own.[918] Bilateral exchanges with Germany led to a joint Franco-German statement of June 19, 2018, the so-called "Meseberg Declaration", which, among other measures, proposed the establishment of a *"Eurozone budget [...] to promote competitiveness, convergence and stabilisation in the euro area"*. This budget would be defined on a pluriannual basis, within the EU framework, and be endowed with national contributions, allocation of tax revenues and European resources.[919] The size of the budget was not specified—quite probably because, in those days, France and Germany were still far apart on this issue.[920] Strategic decisions on the budget would be taken by the euro area Member States, while decisions on expenditures would be *"executed"* by the European Commission. Still in the context of a euro area budget, the Meseberg Declaration also proposed to jointly examine a European Unemployment Stabilization Fund for severe economic crises, but, as an obvious nod to Germany, *"without transfers"*.[921]

657. Notwithstanding push-back from other Member States (*see* paragraph 660 below), France and Germany pursued discussions on their concept of a euro area budget and, on November 16, 2018, submitted a two-pager with an outline of *"a possible structure"*.[922] The paper clarified that the euro area budget would serve in particular to co-finance growth-enhancing public investments and other expenditures, and *"could also play a stabilising function in the Euro-zone"* by avoiding harmful reductions in such investments and expenditures in times of pressure on national public finances. There was no explicit reference to unemployment stabilization. The euro area budget would be part of the EU budget and be financed *"primarily"* by external assigned revenue, consisting of regular national contributions pursuant to an intergovernmental agreement between the euro area Member States, and by European resources. Again, the paper did not give any indication of the possible size of the euro area budget but

918. *See* "Discours du Président de la République—Initiative pour l'Europe", Paris La Sorbonne, September 26, 2017, p. 10, https://www.diplomatie.gouv.fr/IMG/pdf/26.09_-_discours_du_president_de_la_republique_-_initiative_pour_l_europe_transcript_cle0cfdbe.pdf.

919. "Meseberg Declaration—Renewing Europe's promises of security and prosperity", June 19, 2018, https://diplomatie.gouv.fr/IMG/pdf/declarationconjointe_cle0c657a.pdf, at pp. 6-7.

920. In an August 30, 2017 interview with *Le Point*, Emmanuel Macron had hinted at a budget of several percentage points of euro area GDP (*"un budget qui représente plusieurs points du PIB de la zone euro"*), https://www.lepoint.fr/politique/exclusif-emmanuel-macron-le-grand-entretien-30-08-2017-2153393_20.php. In contrast, in a June 3, 2018 interview with *Frankfurter Allgemeine Sonntagszeitung*, then German Chancellor Angela Merkel spoke of a budget at the lower end of the double-digit billions range (*"im unteren zweistelligen Milliardenbereich"*), https://www.bundesregierung.de/breg-de/bundeskanzler/europa-muss-handlungsfaehig-sein-1141498.

921. Meseberg Declaration, at p. 7.

922. *Proposal on the architecture of a Eurozone Budget within the framework of the European Union*, November 16, 2018, https://www.consilium.europa.eu/media/37011/proposal-on-the-architecture-of-a-eurozone-budget.pdf. Following the Euro Summit of December 14, 2018, France and Germany submitted a further paper on February 21, 2019, *Eurozone Budgetary Instrument—possible ways forward after the December 2018 Summit*, https://www.euractiv.com/wp-content/uploads/sites/2/2019/02/French-German-Contribution-on-a-Eurozone-Budgetary-Instrument_2.pdf. But by then discussions had firmly moved in the direction of BICC, and away from any explicit stabilization finality. In fact, the February 21, 2019 paper ends by noting that *"[i]n parallel"*, separate technical discussions on a stabilization function continue. *Ibid.*, p. 4.

suggested that the proposed intergovernmental agreement set a multiannual cap, to be negotiated in the context of the MFF. Overall, one is left with the impression that, in an apparent concession to the dissenting Member States, the paper muted the stabilization function of the proposed budget somewhat and moved in the direction of what was to become the BICC proposal.

c The New Hanseatic League

658. In the process leading up to the 2021-2027 MFF, eight fiscally conservative Member States (including six euro area Member States) formed a more or less united front against a dedicated euro area budget with (significant) stabilization capacity. The coalition became occasionally referred to as the "New Hanseatic League" and included the three Scandinavian Member States (Denmark, Finland and Sweden) and three Baltic Member States (Estonia, Latvia and Lithuania), joined by Ireland and The Netherlands, which oftentimes was to take the *de facto* lead of the group.

659. On March 6, 2018, the Ministers of Finance of these eight Member States set the tone by publishing a joint statement on EMU reforms.[923] This statement defined, as guiding principles, that (i) EMU reforms are a matter for all Member States to decide, and new EMU initiatives should be open for participation, on equivalent terms, by non-euro area Member States on a voluntary basis; (ii) first and foremost, compliance with SGP and national structural reforms should allow the Member States to build up fiscal buffers so as to create fiscal policy space for smoothening economic downturns; (iii) rather than focusing on "nice-to-haves", priority should be given to finding consensus on "need-to-haves", notably the completion of the Banking Union and the transformation of the ESM into a European Monetary Fund; and (iv) the forthcoming 2021-2027 MMF should be better aligned with, and support, the implementation of structural reforms and could finance targeted investments to complement these reforms. It would be difficult to read this joint statement otherwise than as push-back against the Macronian vision of a common euro area budget with stabilization capacity (*see* paragraph 656 above) and some of the thoughts on a stabilization function outlined in the Commission's "Saint Nicholas package" of December 6, 2017 (*see* paragraph 653 above).

660. The New Hanseatic League was also quick to respond to the Meseberg Declaration (*see* paragraph 656 above). On June 23, 2018, Dutch Finance Minister Wopke Hoekstra sent a letter to Eurogroup President Mário Centeno, on behalf of the League members and three other smaller Member States (*i.e.*, Austria, Belgium and Luxembourg), in which he emphasized that there was a *"wide divergence"* on the need of any euro area budget with stabilization properties and *"clearly no consensus on starting to*

923. "Finance ministers from Denmark, Estonia, Finland, Ireland, Latvia, Lithuania, the Netherlands and Sweden underline their shared views and values in the discussion on the architecture of the EMU," March 6, 2018, https://www.government.se/statements/2018/03/finance-ministers-from-denmark-estonia-finland-ireland-latvia-lithuania-the-netherlands-and-sweden/.

explore options" at a forthcoming meeting.[924] In fact, from then onward, the League's reservations and red lines were to steer discussions more and more in the direction of an EU-wide financing instrument, of limited size, to support public investments and reforms, with minor stabilization features.[925]

d The Budgetary Instrument for Convergence and Competitiveness

661. On December 14, 2018, the Euro Summit mandated the Eurogroup to work on the design of a *"budgetary instrument for convergence and competitiveness"* for the euro area and, on a voluntary basis, ERM II Member States, that was to be part of the EU budget and coherent with other EU policies.[926] After months of discussions, on June 14, 2019, the Eurogroup agreed on an initial term sheet for what had now become BICC,[927] which was supplemented on October 10, 2019 with a further term sheet.[928]

662. In significant measure, BICC's design that emerged from this tortuous process reflected Hanseatic concerns. Noteworthy features included the following:

(a) While reserved for euro area Member States and for ERM II Member States choosing to participate, BICC would be part of the EU budgetary framework. Strategic priorities for BICC spending would be defined by the Euro Summit and the Eurogroup, but the program would otherwise be managed by the European Commission.

(b) BICC was to co-finance national public investments and structural reforms that promote the convergence and competitiveness of euro area economies. Financial support would be in the form of grants (not loans), without BICC-specific economic policy conditionality. But it would be subject to

924. *See* J. Brunsden & M. Khan, "Franco-German eurozone reform plan faces growing opposition", *Financial Times*, June 22, 2018, https://www.ft.com/content/19eba02a-75fd-11e8-b326-75a27d27ea5f.

925. *Cf.* M.G. Schoeller, "Preventing the eurozone budget: issue replacement and small state influence in EMU", *Journal of European Public Policy*, Vol. 28, 2021, pp. 1727-1747. https://doi.org/10.1080/13501763.2020.1795226.

926. Statement agreed by the Euro Summit on December 14, 2018, §4, https://www.consilium.europa.eu/media/37563/20181214-euro-summit-statement.pdf.

927. *Term sheet on the Budgetary Instrument for Convergence and Competitiveness*, https://www.consilium.europa.eu/de/press/press-releases/2019/06/14/term-sheet-on-the-budgetary-instrument-for-convergence-and-competitiveness/. The idea, in terms of legislative approach, was that BICC would be included as a distinct chapter in the draft regulation on the proposed Reform Support Program (*see* paragraph 654(b) above), complemented by a new proposed regulation on a specific governance framework for BICC, which the Commission submitted on July 24, 2019. *See* Proposal for a Regulation of the European Parliament and of the Council on a governance framework for the budgetary instrument for convergence and competitiveness for the euro area, COM(2019) 354 final, July 24, 2019, https://eur-lex.europa.eu/legal-content/EN/TXT/PDF/?uri = CELEX:52019PC0354&from = EN.

928. *Term sheet on the budgetary instrument for convergence and competitiveness (BICC)*, https://www.consilium.europa.eu/en/press/press-releases/2019/10/10/term-sheet-on-the-budgetary-instrument-for-convergence-and-competitiveness-bicc/pdf.

national co-financing of (as a rule) minimum 25% so as to ensure that beneficiary Member States would have skin in the game.

(c) BICC's size was left to be determined in the context of the 2021-2027 MFF. In its related "negotiating box", the then Finnish Presidency noted an indicative amount of—merely—EUR 12.90 billion for the seven-year period.[929] It was contemplated that BICC could be scaled up by voluntary national contributions (as external assigned revenue) under the terms of an intergovernmental agreement between euro area Member States. But a report of the Eurogroup on this subject, commissioned by the Euro Summit of December 13, 2019, did not go beyond general considerations.[930]

(d) BICC had no explicit stabilization features, except that the minimum national co-financing rate could be reduced from 25% to 12.5% for Member States experiencing severe economic circumstances (as defined in SGP). Redistributive effects were limited by guaranteed minimum allocations to Member States.

663. It was, all in all, a meager result of lengthy and difficult discussions. With the outbreak of COVID-19, attention shifted to what was to become the far more important EU-wide NGEU and RRF (*see* paragraphs 645-650 above) and, in the event, the BICC proposal was withdrawn.[931] Like a good many other things in European politics, it may bring to mind Evelyn Waugh's metaphor of soapsuds drifting off an old clay pipe, full of rainbow light for an instant and then phut!, vanished. But it was not all in vain.

4 THE ROAD AHEAD

a The Political Chessboard

664. The story of how the 2017 Macronian idea of a strong euro area budget with credible stabilization capacity ended up two years later in BICC is remarkable in several respects. It shows how an activist coalition of smaller fiscally conservative Member States effectively succeeded in blocking a separate euro area budget with genuine stabilization properties and in diluting a Franco-German compromise proposal that didn't even go very far in that direction. It is possible that, with the then imminent withdrawal of the United Kingdom from the European Union, those Member States felt

929. *Multiannual Financial Framework (MFF) 2021-2027: Negotiating Box with figures*, December 5, 2019, p. 28, https://www.consilium.europa.eu/media/41632/mff-negotiating-box_presidency.pdf.

930. *Eurogroup report on a possible inter-governmental agreement for the budgetary instrument for convergence and competitiveness*, February 17, 2020, https://www.consilium.europa.eu/en/press-releases/2020/02/17/eurogroup-report-on-a-possible-inter-governmental-agreement-for-the-budgetary-instrument-for-convergence-and-competitiveness/.

931. *See* Proposal for a Regulation of the European Parliament and of the Council establishing a Recovery and Resilience Facility, COM(2020) 408 final, May 28, 2020, p. 2, https://eur-lex.europa.eu/legal-content/EN/TXT/?uri=CELEX%3A52020PC0408.

even more pressed to form a counterweight to where Franco-German bilateralism might lead. Germany's position in the debate may seem curious. For many years, Germany had been known for taking a fiscally hawkish stance, epitomized by its former Finance Minister, the late Wolfgang Schäuble: fiscal discipline, no large budget deficits, no European fiscal transfers. In fact, Germany's traditional position was close to that of the New Hanseatic League and, substantively, it probably found itself in agreement with several of the positions expressed in the Hanseatic joint statement of March 6, 2018 (*see* paragraph 659 above). Yet, Germany kept its distance from the Hanseatic coalition and pursued its long-time pragmatic diplomacy of bilateral exchanges with France,[932] seeking to accommodate or at least assuage French concerns as a basis for brokering European consensus solutions that landed as closely as possible to its own objectives and constraints. It may have helped that, on March 14, 2018, Wolfgang Schäuble was succeeded as German Finance Minister by the more pragmatic Olaf Scholz, the later Chancellor.

665. In any event, BICC was not to be the last word. Olaf Scholz and his deputy Jörg Kukies, PhD of Chicago Business School and former Goldman Sachs banker, worked closely with French Finance Minister Bruno Le Maire in bringing about the EU-wide NGEU and RRF, semi-housed in the EU budget, with a sizable non-refundable grant component—a far more important EU budgetary instrument with risk-sharing properties than anything that had been discussed since Emmanuel Macron's 2017 Sorbonne speech. Undoubtedly, the sudden and largely common economic risks presented by COVID-19, possibly in combination with a certain political embarrassment over the May 5, 2020 judgment of the German Federal Constitutional Court in *Weiss* (*see* paragraphs 546-551 above), have been conducive to the German Government's active support for NGEU and RRF. But it would not be accurate to think of this as a sudden—or complete—Damascene conversion.

b A Question of Money

666. An obvious stumbling block for more budgetary or other risk-shared stabilization capacity at the EU level has to do with ... money. A sizable debt-funded financing mechanism with a significant grant component like NGEU may face budgetary constraints, especially when the margin under the MFF spending ceiling may also be needed for other pressing expenditures and when borrowing costs increase in times of monetary tightening.[933] It raises the question of the need to mine new sources for the European Union's "own resources".

932. *Cf.* D. Howarth & J. Schild, "Torn between Two Lovers: German Policy on Economic and Monetary Union, the New Hanseatic League and Franco-German Bilateralism", *German Politics*, Vol. 31, 2022, pp. 323-343, https://doi.org/10.1080/09644008.2021.2003331.

933. *Cf.* the concerns expressed in the report of the European Parliament's Committee on Budgets "on the impact on the 2024 EU budget of increasing European Union Recovery Instrument borrowing costs", A9-0163/2023, April 28, 2023, https://www.europarl.europa.eu/doceo/document/A-9-2023-0163_EN.pdf. Full coverage of NGEU interest payments may require some creative budgeting. *See* the cascade mechanism outlined in *Multiannual Financial Framework*

667. Thus, one new own resource was introduced by Council Decision (EU/Euratom) 2020/2053 of December 14, 2020, *i.e.*, national contributions of EUR 0.80 per kilogram of non-recycled plastic packaging waste.[934] In their Interinstitutional Agreement of December 16, 2020, the European Parliament, the Council and the European Commission agreed on a series of guiding principles and a timeline to *"work towards"* (a favorite diplomatic phrase) adding other kinds of own resources over the life of the 2021-2027 MFF.[935] The new own resources should be raised in an amount corresponding to the expected principal repayments on the EU borrowings used to fund non-repayable grants under NGEU (although without earmarking those resources for this specific purpose) so as to avoid that those expenditures would cut into other program expenditures or investment instruments under the MFF.

668. On December 22, 2021, the Commission tabled a proposal for a first basket of three new own resources, stating its expectation that it would propose a second basket by the end of 2023.[936] Then on June 20, 2023, the Commission submitted a revised and updated proposal to introduce four new species of own resources,[937] *i.e.*:

(a) 30% of (most) revenues from the auctioning of allowances under the EU Emissions Trading System;
(b) 75% of revenues from the sale of certificates of the Carbon Border Adjustment Mechanism;
(c) 15% of the share of residual profits of larger multinational companies that would be reallocated to Member States under future legislation giving effect to the OECD/G20 "Pillar One" agreement (once the relevant multilateral convention has been signed and ratified);[938] and

---

2021-2027: Negotiating Box, December 15, 2023, pp. 4-6, https://data.consilium.europa.eu/doc/document/ST-23-2023-INIT/en/pdf.

934. Articles 2(1)(c) and (2) of Council Decision 2020/2053.

935. Annex II of the Interinstitutional Agreement of December 16, 2020 between the European Parliament, the Council of the European Union and the European Commission on budgetary discipline, on cooperation in budgetary matters and on sound financial management, as well as on new own resources, including a roadmap toward the introduction of new own resources, *OJ* L433 I, December 22, 2020, p. 28, at pp. 44-46.

936. *See* Communication from the Commission to the European Parliament, the Council, the European Economic and Social Committee and the Committee of the Regions, *The next generation of own resources for the EU budget*, COM(2021) 566 final, December 22, 2021, 5 pp., https://commission.europa.eu/system/files/2021-12/com_2021_en_act_part1_v8.pdf, and Proposal for a Council Decision amending Decision (EU, Euratom) 2020/2053 on the system of own resources of the European Union, COM(2021) 570 final, December 22, 2021, https://eur-lex.europa.eu/legal-content/EN/TXT/PDF/?uri=CELEX:52021PC0570.

937. *See* Communication from the Commission to the European Parliament, the Council, the European Council, the European Economic and Social Committee and the Committee of the Regions, *An adjusted package for the next generation of own resources*, COM(2023) 330 final, June 20, 2023, 3 pp., https://commission.europa.eu/system/files/2023-06/COM_2023_330_1_EN_ACT_part1_v5.pdf, and Amended proposal for a Council Decision amending Decision (EU, Euratom) 2020/2053 on the system of own resources of the European Union, COM(2023) 331 final, https://commission.europa.eu/system/files/2023-06/COM_2023_331_1_EN_ACT_part1_v5.pdf.

938. *See* OECD/G20 Base Erosion and Profit Shifting Project, *Statement on a Two-Pillar Solution to Address the Tax Challenges Arising from the Digitalisation of the Economy*, October 8, 2021,

(d) a statistics-based (not tax-based) contribution of 0.5% of the sum of gross operating surplus reported under the European System of Accounts (ESA2010) for the sectors of non-financial and financial corporations (S.11 and S.12, respectively), pending the possible establishment of an own resource based on an underlying tax linked to the "Business in Europe: Framework for Income Taxation" ("BEFIT") initiative.[939]

669. Together, items (a), (b) and (d) above are estimated to deliver additional revenue of up to EUR 36 billion (in 2018 prices) *per annum* on average over the 2028-2030 period.[940] At the time of writing, the proposed amendments to Council Decision 2020/2053 were still pending before the Council, amidst reservations and disagreements of Member States on several aspects of the proposal.[941] Under Article 311, third paragraph, TFEU, the Council must act unanimously and its decision becomes effective only upon approval by the Member States in accordance with their constitutional requirements. It is a tough nut to crack.

c The BVerfG's Saint Nicholas Judgment

670. Another recurring stumbling block for more risk-shared financial support at the EU—or euro area—level has come from national constitutional concerns over budgetary autonomy, especially in Germany, as voiced prominently by the German Federal Constitutional Court ("BVerfG") (*see* paragraphs 629-630 above). These concerns have weighed on political discussions, and it is therefore of significant interest that, in a judgment of December 6, 2022, the BVerfG appears to have put forward a milder version of its budgetary autonomy doctrine that leaves the door ajar for NGEU-type financial support mechanisms. The judgment deserves a closer look because it shows a possible path for future similar initiatives, and it is important in this respect to understand the BVerfG's reasoning and its boundaries.

671. The feast of Saint Nicholas appears to be a propitious day for significant developments regarding EMU (*see also* paragraph 653 above). The case that gave rise to the BVerfG's judgment of December 6, 2022 involves constitutional challenges

https://www.oecd.org./tax/beps/statement-on-a-two-pillar-solution-to-address-the-tax-challenges-arising-from-the-digitalisation-of-the-economy-october-2021.pdf, and *Outcome Statement on the Two-Pillar Solution to Address the Tax Challenges Arising from the Digitalisation of the Economy*, July 11, 2023, https://www.oecd.org/beps/outcome-statement-on-the-two-pillar-solution-to-address-the-tax-challenges-arising-from-the-digitalisation-of-the-economy-july-2023.pdf.

939. BEFIT seeks to establish a set of common rules for determining and partially reallocating the taxable base for groups of companies having combined annual revenues in excess of EUR 750 million. *See* Proposal for a Council Directive on Business in Europe: Framework for Income Taxation (BEFIT), COM(2023) 532 final, September 12, 2023, https://eur-lex.europa.eu/legal-content/EN/TXT/?uri=CELEX%3A52023PC0532.

940. COM(2023) 330 final, June 20, 2023, p. 3.

941. *See* the November 24, 2023 status report of the Spanish Presidency at https://data.consilium.europa.eu/doc/document/ST-15858-2023-INIT/en/pdf.

brought against the German act ratifying Council Decision 2020/2053.[942] As indicated earlier (*see* paragraphs 645-646 above), this Council Decision authorizes the European Commission to borrow, on behalf of the European Union, up to EUR 750 billion (in 2018 prices) in the financial markets prior to 2027, in order to fund non-repayable grants and loans to Member States under NGEU (principally RRF). The interest and principal (re)payments on these EU borrowings (which may stretch until the end of 2058) are "guaranteed" by the EU budget's headroom, backed up by a temporary *ad hoc* increase of the own resources ceilings. Within these limits, the Commission may call on Member States to make the necessary resources available to cover any shortfall, with a further round of true-up calls if one or several Member States fail to pay in time.

672. By an order of April 15, 2021, the BVerfG turned down an application for a preliminary injunction against the German act ratifying Council Decision 2020/2053,[943] and by its judgment of December 6, 2022, the court rejected the constitutional complaints on the merits.[944] The BVerfG concluded that the act ratifying Council Decision 2020/2053 does not violate the constitutional right to democratic self-determination. It considered that this Council Decision (i) is not *ultra vires* insofar as it does not manifestly exceed the powers conferred by Article 311 *jo.* Article 122 TFEU and does not clearly violate the "no bail-out" clause of Article 125(1) TFEU, and (ii) does not unduly intrude upon the overall budgetary responsibility of the German Bundestag. As to point (i), the BVerfG did not believe it necessary to refer any questions to the CJEU for a preliminary ruling—in part, remarkably, because it saw no reason to assume that the CJEU would interpret the competences conferred by Articles 122 and 311 TFEU more narrowly than it does, and in part because it considered the interpretation of Article 125(1) TFEU an *acte éclairé*.[945]

673. On the ***ultra vires*** **question**, the BVerfG noted that, in the context of its constitutional review, an act of an EU institution can be held *ultra vires* only if it exceeds the competences conferred on that institution in a manner that is both obvious (*"offensichtlich"*) and of structural significance for the division of competences between the European Union and the Member States.[946] Applying this standard of review to Council Decision 2020/2053, the court then engaged in a lengthy analysis that is summarized in paragraphs 674 to 679 below.

674. ***First***, the Treaties do not specifically confer upon the European Union a power to borrow in the financial markets, and the prevailing view, reflected in Article 17(2) of

942. As said, under Article 311, third paragraph, TFEU, decisions of this kind become effective only upon approval by the Member States in accordance with their constitutional requirements.
943. BVerfG, April 15, 2021, ECLI:DE:BVerfG:2021:rs20210415.2bvr054721. An English translation of this order may be found at http://www.bverfg.de/e/rs20210415_2bvr054721en.html. This order lifted an earlier order of the BVerfG halting certification of the act by the Federal President pending the court's decision on the application for preliminary injunction (BVerfG, March 26, 2021, ECLI:DE:BVerfG:2021:rs20210326.2bvr054721).
944. BVerfG, December 6, 2022, ECLI:DE:BVerfG:2022:rs20221206.2bvr054721. For an English translation, *see* http://www.bverfg.de/e/rs20221206_2bvr054721en.html.
945. *Ibid.*, §236.
946. *Ibid.*, §129.

the EU Financial Regulation,[947] is that borrowing is not recognized as a permanent source of financing of the EU general budget.[948] Yet, so the BVerfG observed, the Treaties do not appear to expressly set out an absolute prohibition of borrowing either, and no such prohibition must be inferred from Article 310(1), third paragraph, TFEU.[949] It is not clearly implausible to consider that the authorization to borrow given by Council Decision 2020/2053 could validly be based on Article 311, second paragraph, TFEU, with the loan proceeds constituting a form of "other revenue" within the meaning of this provision.[950] But, according to the BVerfG, in order for this interpretation to be tenable (i) the loan proceeds could not serve for general financing of the EU budget but would need to be earmarked exclusively for some designated task within the competences conferred upon the European Union; (ii) the authorization to borrow must be limited in terms of volume and duration; and (iii) given that, under Article 311, second paragraph, TFEU, "other revenue" is to remain the exception in relation to own resources, the amount of other revenue may not exceed the total amount of own resources.

675. The BVerfG then concluded that *"[i]t cannot be clearly ruled out"* (*"[e]s ist jedoch nicht offensichtlich ausgeschlossen"*) that the borrowing authority given by Council Decision 2020/2053 satisfies these three conditions:

(a) As to condition (i), Article 4 of Council Decision 2020/2053 expressly excludes the use of the borrowed funds for the financing of operational expenditures, and Article 5(1) earmarks these funds exclusively for addressing the consequences of COVID-19 through the NGEU recovery instrument established by Council Regulation (EU) 2020/94. Since this Regulation is based on Article 122 TFEU, the BVerfG looked at whether the purpose of the financing could properly be anchored in the competence conferred by this Treaty provision. Given that Article 122 TFEU authorizes financial assistance only to Member States in difficulties or seriously threatened with severe difficulties, caused by natural disasters or exceptional occurrences beyond a Member State's control, it was not entirely clear to the BVerfG whether there exists a sufficiently close connection between NGEU recovery support and the

947. Regulation (EU, Euratom) 2018/1046 of the European Parliament and of the Council of July 18, 2018 on the financial rules applicable to the general budget of the Union, amending Regulations (EU) No 1296/2013, (EU) No 1301/2013, (EU) No 1303/2013, (EU) No 1304/2013, (EU) No 1309/2013, (EU) No 1316/2013, (EU) No 223/2014, (EU) No 283/2014, and Decision No 541/2014/EU and repealing Regulation (EU, Euratom) No 966/2012, *OJ* L193, July 30, 2018, p. 1, amended by Regulation (EU, Euratom) 2022/2434 of December 6, 2022, *OJ* L319, December 13, 2022, p. 1. According to Article 17(2) of this Regulation, the European Union *"shall not raise loans within the framework of the budget"*.

948. BVerfG, December 6, 2022, §§150-153.

949. *Ibid.*, §155. Article 310(1), third paragraph, TFEU requires revenue and expenditure shown in the budget to be in balance.

950. *Ibid.*, §149. Article 311, second paragraph, TFEU provides that *"[w]ithout prejudice to other revenue, the budget shall be financed wholly from own resources"*.

consequences of COVID-19.[951] Notwithstanding this concern, the court concluded that the financing scheme does not manifestly exceed the competence conferred by Article 122 TFEU, noting that the Council and the European Commission are afforded a wide measure of judgment in determining the prerequisites for the application of this provision, and that it is not untenable (*"nicht unvertretbar"*) to characterize the NGEU financing as a measure "appropriate to the economic situation" within the meaning of Article 122(1) TFEU.[952] The BVerfG further emphasized the exceptional nature of the COVID-19 crisis and referred to statements made in the oral hearing on behalf of the Federal Government and the Bundestag to the effect that NGEU is intended to be a one-time instrument in response to an unprecedented crisis and must not be viewed as a step toward a transfer union with institutionalized financial equalization.[953]

(b) As to condition (ii), the BVerfG noted that Council Decision 2020/2053 limits the Commission's borrowing authority by (i) volume, by setting a strict upper limit, albeit at the extraordinarily high level of EUR 750 billion (in 2018 prices), and (ii) duration, by barring new net borrowings after 2026 and requiring that all amounts due be fully repaid by December 31, 2058.[954]

(c) As to condition (iii), the BVerfG observed that, when comparing the amounts for each budget year separately, the borrowings significantly exceed own resources in budget years 2021 and 2022, which would seem incompatible with Article 311, second paragraph, TFEU.[955] However, *"it does not appear manifestly untenable"* (*"nicht offensichtlich unzutreffend"*) to take the 2021-2027 MFF as the relevant point of reference, in which case the borrowings exceed own resources only in two out of the seven budget years in question and remain well below own resources for the period as a whole, *i.e.*, EUR 750 billion against EUR 1,074.3 billion.[956] While this remains a significant amount in comparison, it does not manifestly violate Article 311, second paragraph, TFEU. Surely, a curious combination of law and mathematics.

676. *Second*, the BVerfG then considered whether the arrangement might involve either a direct violation or an unlawful circumvention of the "no bail-out" clause of Article 125(1) TFEU. The court saw no such direct violation since, under the scheme, neither the European Union nor the Member States assume liability for any Member

951. *Ibid.*, §§176-181. In this respect, the BVerfG noted that (i) some of the financial assistance appears to go beyond addressing the direct effects of COVID-19, including funds to support the green transition and digital transformation (*ibid.*, §178) and for ongoing EU programs unrelated to COVID-19 (*ibid.*, §180); (ii) the funds are to be distributed over the 2021-2026 period, which appears to be a longer time span than that needed to overcome the effects of COVID-19 (*ibid.*, §179); and (iii) the key for the allocation of the funds is only partially connected to the economic effects of COVID-19 (*ibid.*, §181).
952. *Ibid.*, §§182-184.
953. *Ibid.*, §187.
954. *Ibid.*, §§189-192.
955. *Ibid.*, §§197-198.
956. *Ibid.*, §§199-202.

State's debt.[957] As to a possible circumvention of the "no bail-out" clause, the court noted that the purpose of this clause is to ensure that Member States stand on their own feet in the conduct of their fiscal policies, without mutualization of responsibility for their respective obligations. EU law does not allow fiscal balancing (*"Finanzausgleich"*) among Member States.[958] In the case at hand, a circumvention of Article 125(1) TFEU cannot be ruled out altogether insofar as the debt-financed NGEU funds and particularly the non-repayable grants may serve to alleviate the pressure of market logic on Member States with excessive debt. But the BVerfG concluded that Article 125(1) TFEU ultimately does not stand in the way of the proposed financing mechanism on the basis of the competence conferred by Article 122 TFEU. Here, the court did not say that, as *lex specialis*, Article 122 constitutes an exception to Article 125(1),[959] but observed instead, somewhat cryptically, that the value judgments underlying Article 122 are not inconsistent with those of Article 125(1).[960]

677. Turning then to its fearsome **budgetary autonomy** doctrine, the BVerfG went on to examine whether Council Decision 2020/2053 did not compromise the Bundestag's budgetary prerogatives.

678. ***First***, the BVerfG found that Council Decision 2020/2053, viewed in isolation, does not substantially impair the budgetary powers of the Bundestag, notably for the following reasons:

(a) The Decision limits the European Union's borrowing authority as to the amount, duration and use of proceeds and is subject to the Bundestag's approval under Article 311, third paragraph, TFEU.[961]
(b) The financing scheme does not create any permanent mechanism that entails an assumption of liability by Germany for decisions taken by other Member States.[962]
(c) It does not appear that Germany's additional financial commitments under Council Decision 2020/2053 would affect the German federal budget or the Bundestag's overall budgetary responsibility to an extent that is structurally

957. *Ibid.*, §205.
958. *Ibid.*, §207.
959. In its 2012 *Pringle* judgment, the CJEU held that Article 125 TFEU is not intended, and must not be read, as an absolute prohibition of any form of EU or Member State financial assistance to another Member State, adding, curiously (and erroneously), that, if it had been intended that way, Article 122 TFEU would have had to specify that it derogated from Article 125. *See* CJEU, November 27, 2012, Case C-370/12, *Pringle*, ECLI:EU:C:2012:756, §§130-131. The CJEU concluded that Article 125 does not prohibit such financial assistance so long as the recipient Member State *"remains responsible for its commitments to its creditors"* and the financial assistance comes with conditions that *"prompt that Member State to implement a sound budgetary policy"*. *Ibid.*, §137.
960. BVerfG, December 6, 2022, §§208 and 210. The BVerfG also considered the consistency of the true-up arrangement under Council Decision 2020/2053 (*see* paragraph 646, *in fine*, above) with Article 125(1) TFEU. It noted that the true-up call in case one or more Member States fail to pay their additional contributions in the first-round call involves only a form of bridge financing and not an assumption of the defaulting Member States' liability. *Ibid.*, §209.
961. *Ibid.*, §§211 and 213-215.
962. *Ibid.*, §§217-218.

significant (*"von struktureller Bedeutung"*). This is true both for (i) the additional contribution pursuant to the *ad hoc* 0.6% increase of the own resources ceiling and (ii) the possible additional payments to be made under true-up calls if other Member States fail to pay up their share (*see* paragraph 646 above).

As to item (i), the court measured Germany's financial commitment by reference to the scheduled principal repayments on the portion of the EU borrowings used to fund non-repayable grants (up to EUR 390 billion in 2018 prices). According to estimates of the federal Government and the Bundestag as well as expert testimony, this could increase Germany's contribution by an annual amount in a range of (roughly) EUR 3.84 billion to EUR 7 billion. While these amounts are far from insignificant (*"zwar nicht unerheblich"*), they would not affect the German federal budget, or the Bundestag's overall budgetary responsibility, in a structurally significant manner.[963]

As to item (ii), the court acknowledged that, by ratifying Council Decision 2020/2053 and assuming this contingent liability, the current Bundestag would bind future parliaments and diminish their budgetary latitude significantly over many years, but considered that making long-term commitments is inherent in law-making. Given the budgetary principle of annuality, constitutional review must look at the financial burden *per annum* rather than the potential aggregate liability over time (until 2058). On the basis of government projections and expert testimony, Germany's potential maximum annual financial commitment would be between EUR 21 billion and EUR 28 billion if all other Member States were to default on calls for their additional contributions. Given the low probability of such a collective default, and considering the total size of the annual federal budget and total public debt, it was within the legislature's margin of judgment to consider that this contingent liability could tenably be assumed without excessively burdening the budget and vitiating its own budgetary powers.[964]

679. ***Second***, considering these financial commitments in combination with Germany's other payment obligations and contingent liabilities in relation to EMU, the BVerfG saw no apparent violation of the Bundestag's budgetary powers either. But it cautioned that the accumulation of such commitments may reach a point where these powers become in fact restricted to a degree that the Bundestag is no longer *"master of its own decisions"*.[965] While no reliable estimate of the aggregate exposure resulting from existing and new commitments (such as in relation to the EFSF, the ESM, SURE and NGEU) was at hand, it seemed clear to the BVerfG that they have significantly narrowed the Bundestag's financial margin going forward.[966] Consequently, so the court observed, the Bundestag has an ongoing duty to monitor the use of NGEU funds

963. *Ibid.*, §§221-222.
964. *Ibid.*, §§223-229.
965. *Ibid.*, §230.
966. *Ibid.*, §231.

and the evolution of liability risks for the federal budget under this mechanism and, when necessary, to immediately take suitable measures to protect the budget.[967]

680. But, all in all, the BVerfG's December 6, 2022 decision is a remarkably "dovish" judgment. In a scathing dissenting opinion, the lone voice of Justice Peter Müller severely criticized the majority view. He fustigated the majority for retreating from the substance of the BVerfG's standard *ultra vires* review, *i.e.*, that of *"a careful and meticulously reasoned interpretation of the law in accordance with general principles"*, in order to overcome its own hesitations and concerns as to the European Union's competence for adopting Council Decision 2020/2053.[968] While, under Article 311, second paragraph, TFEU, own resources are the primary source of financing of the European Union and "other revenue" remains the exception, the majority view accepts borrowing as such other revenue in an amount more than double the regular annual EU budget for the years 2021 and 2022. By the logic espoused by the majority, any EU borrowing could be justified to finance any matter within the EU competences so long as, when measured over the multiannual term of the MFF, its amount does not exceed that of own resources.[969] This, so Justice Müller pursued, opens the door to debt financing as a "second pillar" of EU financing on nearly equal footing with own resources—a fundamental change in the European Union's financial architecture that tilts it in the direction of a fiscal and transfer union and should require an amendment of the Treaties.[970]

681. I have spent some time on the BVerfG's Saint Nicholas judgment for good reason. In tone and demeanor, this judgment stands in marked contrast with the same court's May 5, 2020 judgment in *Weiss* (*see* paragraphs 546-551 above). Perhaps the controversy to which the *Weiss* judgment gave rise and the political importance of NGEU brought some *raison d'Etat* to bear on the BVerfG's analysis. The Saint Nicholas judgment is probably not among the court's best judgments in terms of logical rigor and consistency and, here and there, the reasoning takes awkward bends. But, importantly, the judgment proffers a more restrained *ultra vires* assessment of EU legal acts in the context of the BVerfG's constitutional review, and a milder version of its budgetary autonomy doctrine, that create more space for EU—or euro area—financial support mechanisms of the NGEU type. In a sense, it lays out a clearer roadmap for structuring such mechanisms. In any event, it should be broadly helpful in attenuating a legal concern (or excuse) in further political discussion on strengthening EU or euro area stability support in EMU's incomplete architecture.

967. *Ibid.*, §233.
968. Dissenting opinion of Justice Müller to the BVerfG's judgment of December 6, 2022, §6.
969. *Ibid.*, §25.
970. *Ibid.*, §§33-34.

CHAPTER 10

Stand-Alone Euro Area Financial Assistance

1 FROM THE EFSF TO THE ESM

a A Special Purpose Vehicle

682. When, in the early months of 2010, Greece found itself in dire need of financial assistance, an international financial support package of EUR 110 billion was put together—Greece's first financial assistance program (*see* paragraph 72 above). It consisted of the "Greek Loan Facility", a bundle of bilateral loans from euro area Member States in a total amount of EUR 80 billion, and an IMF stand-by arrangement of EUR 30 billion. As tensions were building up in the sovereign bond markets, it was soon recognized that a more robust financial support mechanism was needed, also to serve as a "firewall" against contagion spreading in the euro area. During high-level discussions in Brussels on the weekend of May 7 to 9, 2010,[971] it was eventually agreed to establish a new EU budgetary instrument on the basis of Article 122(2) TFEU, the European Financial Stabilisation Mechanism ("EFSM"), to provide loans or credit lines, subject to economic policy conditionality, to Member States experiencing, or seriously threatened with, *"a severe economic or financial disturbance caused by exceptional circumstances beyond its control"* (*see* paragraphs 638-639 above). But, insofar as constrained by the EU budget's headroom, the EFSM would have a loan envelope of only about EUR 60 billion, which was thought to fall way short of a "firewall" of sufficiently credible scale. A proposal of European Commissioner Olli Rehn to supplement the EFSM's resources, if and when needed, with Commission borrowings jointly and severally guaranteed by euro area Member States was opposed by Germany,

971. For an interesting narrative of these discussions, *see* European Stability Mechanism, *Safeguarding the euro in times of crisis: The inside story of the ESM*, Publications Office of the European Union, 2019, pp. 45-56.

apparently in part for reasons related to what was to become a recurring "turf war" over who was to control the mechanism.[972]

683. A compromise proposal eventually emerged under which a dedicated euro area financing mechanism would be put in place for a period of three years, in the form of a "special purpose vehicle" outside the EU institutional and budgetary framework. This vehicle would borrow funds in the financial markets with the backing of guarantees by the euro area Member States, in proportion to their respective shares in the ECB's paid-up capital. It would then on-lend the proceeds to euro area Member States in financial distress, subject to *ad hoc* macroeconomic policy conditionality aimed at restoring the debtor country's access to the financial markets on normal conditions.[973] The vehicle would have a lending capacity of up to EUR 440 billion—a number that does not appear to have been based on any rigorous estimate of potential needs but seems to have come about almost by coincidence at a late hour and had the appeal of producing both a solid and a round number of EUR 500 billion when added to the EFSM's envelope of EUR 60 billion.[974] It was announced that, in parallel, the IMF *"is expected to provide at least half as much as the EU contribution through its usual facilities"*.[975]

684. The "special purpose vehicle" was established on June 7, 2010, as a *société anonyme* of Luxembourg law, under the name "European Financial Stability Facility" ("EFSF"), by deed of notary Jacques Delvaux. The EFSF's governance, *modus operandi* and funding are set out in the "EFSF Framework Agreement" of June 10, 2010—a kind of shareholders' agreement between the euro area Member States (and the EFSF itself) governed by ... English law.[976] To mobilize the necessary funds for financial assistance to euro area Member States in distress, the EFSF was to borrow in the financial markets with the backing of (several but not joint) guarantees of its members, according to a contribution key based on their respective ECB capital subscriptions. In order to secure a top credit rating for the EFSF in circumstances where several of its guarantors fell

972. *Cf. ibid.*, p. 51.
973. *See* the press release issued after the extraordinary ECOFIN Council meeting of May 9-10, 2010, https://www.consilium.europa.eu/uedocs/cms_data/docs/pressdata/en/ecofin/114324.pdf.
974. On the somewhat haphazard origin of the EUR 440 billion number, *see* European Stability Mechanism, *supra*, p. 54.
975. *See* the press release referred to in fn. 973 above. In a May 11, 2010 news item on the IMF's website (https://www.imf.org./en/News/Articles/2015/09/28/04/53/sonew051110a), then IMF Managing Director Dominique Strauss-Kahn was quoted as saying that IMF assistance would be on a country-by-country basis and *"broadly in proportion"* to the IMF's recent European arrangements (in which IMF financing accounted on average for *"around one-third"* of total joint financing). John Lipsky, then First Deputy Managing Director, was reported emphasizing that the IMF *"had not earmarked a specific amount as financing for the IMF's European members"*. In the event, for the five euro area Member States that were to receive EFSF/ESM financial assistance, the IMF participated for a total amount of EUR 81.6 billion on a disbursement basis, representing about 16.88% of total financial assistance (*see* paragraph 719, Table 10.1, below).
976. Article 16(1). A consolidated text of the EFSF Framework Agreement (as amended effective October 18, 2011) can be found on the ESM's website, https://www.esm.europa.eu/sites/default/files/document/20111019_efsf_framework_agreement_en.pdf.

short of such a rating,[977] a "credit enhancement" package was put together that initially consisted of guarantee coverage of up to 120% (a form of over-collateralization to cover a possible default by some guarantors on their guarantee payments), loan-specific cash buffers and a cash reserve constituted by withholdings from the on-ward loans to Member States (prepaid margin and service fee). As of the fall of 2011, this was replaced by increased guarantee coverage of up to 165%, with no further retentions for the cash reserve.[978]

685. Until mid-2013, *i.e.*, during its three-year "active" life, the EFSF provided financial assistance to Ireland, Greece and Portugal in a total amount (on a disbursement basis) of EUR 187.58 billion (*see* paragraph 719, Table 10.1, below). Since July 1, 2013, the EFSF no longer engages in new lending activity, but it continues to exist, more or less as a run-off vehicle managing its existing loan portfolio and related borrowings. Article 40 of the ESM Treaty contemplates a possible transfer of the EFSF's rights and obligations to the ESM, but this had not yet happened by the time of writing.[979]

b A Euro Area Treaty Organization

686. Back in 2010, a political consensus soon emerged on the need to substitute a more permanent euro area crisis financing mechanism for the EFSF and the EFSM. At its meetings of October 28-29 and December 16-17, 2010, the European Council endorsed the idea of a euro area stability mechanism, as an intergovernmental arrangement, to provide policy-conditioned financial assistance to euro area Member States in financial distress where necessary to contain contagion risk within the euro area. Given concerns over a possible breach of the Treaty's "no bail-out" clause (Article 125(1) TFEU), the European Council also decided to put the arrangement on firmer legal ground by launching a simplified treaty revision procedure under Article 48(6) TEU in order to add a third paragraph to Article 136 TFEU. The new Article 136(3) now allows

977. The EFSF's initial credit ratings for long-term debt were AAA with Standard & Poor's and Fitch, and Aaa with Moody's, reduced in 2012 and 2013 to AA+ and Aa1, respectively. Standard & Poor's and Fitch further downgraded the EFSF to AA in 2013 and 2014. Moody's again upgraded the EFSF to Aaa in June 2022. In May 2023, Fitch downgraded the EFSF by one notch to AA– in view of its April 2023 downgrading of France from AA to AA–.

978. *See* Articles 2(3) and (8) and 5(1)(a) and (b) of the EFSF Framework Agreement. *See also* EFSF Financial Statements, Management Report and Independent Auditor's Report, December 31, 2022, pp. 25-26 and 38, https://www.esm.europa.eu/system/files/document/2023-06/EFSF_Financial%20Statements_31.12.2022.pdf. Euro area Member States in difficulties requesting financial assistance (notably Ireland, Greece and Portugal) have been allowed to suspend their guarantee commitments in respect of further EFSF borrowings. *See* Article 8(2) and Annex 1 of the EFSF Framework Agreement.

979. Under the new Article 40(4), added by the pending 2021 amendments to the ESM Treaty, the ESM's Board of Governors may facilitate this transfer by creating an additional tranche of authorized capital of the ESM, represented by non-voting shares and to be subscribed by some or all EFSF shareholders, up to a maximum amount of 165% of the aggregate principal amount outstanding under the EFSF loans transferred (to be reduced in line with the repayment of these loans).

euro area Member States to establish a stability mechanism *"to be activated if indispensable to safeguard the stability of the euro area as a whole"* and *"subject to strict conditionality"*.[980]

687. On January 27, 2011, Eurostat, the European Union's statistical office, ruled that, under applicable macro-sectoral accounting standards (then ESA95), the EFSF did not qualify as a separate institutional unit, with the consequence that its indebtedness should be directly attributed to the euro area Member States in proportion to their guarantee commitments.[981] This has likely been among the factors that prompted the ESM's architects to give more organizational substance to the ESM and to replace the guarantee arrangements with capital commitments by the euro area Member States. At its meeting of March 24-25, 2011, the European Council endorsed a detailed term sheet on the ESM in this sense.[982]

688. The new institution was finally put in place, outside the EU legal framework, by the Treaty Establishing the European Stability Mechanism of February 2, 2012 ("ESM Treaty"),[983] now as a treaty-based intergovernmental organization under public international law, backed not by guarantees but by capital subscriptions of the euro area Member States.

Significant amendments to the ESM Treaty were agreed in 2021 (*see* paragraphs 720-727 below) but, pending ratification by Italy, had not yet entered into effect at the time of writing.[984] On December 21, 2023, the center-right majority in the Italian Parliament even voted down ratification, but my working assumption boldly remains that Italy will eventually ratify before too long, probably in exchange for some suitable *quid pro quo*. Accordingly, in this book, article references to the ESM Treaty are to those of the amended ESM Treaty, except as indicated otherwise. Occasionally, references to a new or amended article or article subdivision will be followed by the mention "(new)" or "(as amended)" where relevant to the analysis.

980. *See* the conclusions of the European Council of October 28-29, 2010, §I.2, https://www.consilium.europa.eu/uedocs/cms_data/docs/pressdata/en/ec/117496.pdf, and those of the European Council of December 16-17, 2010, §§I.1-4 and Annexes I and II, https://www.consilium.europa.eu/uedocs/cms_data/docs/pressdata/en/ec/118578.pdf. The new Article 136(3) TFEU was eventually adopted by European Council Decision of March 25, 2011 amending Article 136 of the Treaty on the Functioning of the European Union with regard to a stability mechanism for Member States whose currency is the euro (2011/199/EU), *OJ* L91, April 6, 2011, p. 1.

981. *See* Eurostat News Release 13/2011 of January 27, 2011, https://ec.europa.eu/eurostat/documents/2995521/5034386/2-27012011-AP-EN.PDF, and the related background note of the same date, https://ec.europa.eu/eurostat/documents/1015035/2041337/Background-note-EFSF-27-January-2011.pdf.

982. *See* the conclusions of the European Council of March 24-25, 2011, §I.17 and Annex II, https://data.consilium.europa.eu/doc/document/ST-10-2011-INIT/en/pdf.

983. The consolidated text of the ESM Treaty prior to its 2021 amendment is to be found at https://www. esm.europa.eu/legal-documents/esm-treaty.

984. *See* Agreement Amending the Treaty Establishing the European Stability Mechanism, signed on January 27 and February 8, 2021, https://www.esm.europa.eu/about-esm/esm-reform-documents/esm-treaty-amending-agreement.

c Initial Legal Challenges

689. In the early days, legal action was brought in certain Member States to halt the ratification of the ESM Treaty. Few things have come easily in matters of the European currency union.

690. One such case was the *Pringle* case that we have encountered before (*see* paragraphs 514 and 577(c) above). Thomas Pringle, a member of the Irish Parliament, instituted legal proceedings before the Irish courts in which he questioned the lawfulness of the simplified treaty revision procedure adding Article 136(3) TFEU (*see* paragraph 686 above) and Ireland's ratification of the ESM Treaty. He did so on several grounds, arguing notably that these acts are inconsistent with the European Union's exclusive competence for monetary policy and with the "no bail-out" clause of Article 125(1) TFEU. In a preliminary ruling of November 27, 2012, on questions referred by the Irish Supreme Court,[985] the Court of Justice of the European Union ("CJEU"), in full setting, principally reached the following conclusions:

(a) The CJEU held, in essence, that ESM financial assistance does not encroach on the Union's exclusive competence for the monetary policy of the euro area. It considered that such financial assistance does not pursue a price stability objective but rather aims at securing access of euro area Member States to financing when needed to avoid destabilizing the currency union. This, so the CJEU concluded, places ESM financial assistance in the realm of economic policy, not monetary policy, even if it may have lateral effects on the stability of the euro or on inflation.[986]

(b) The CJEU also ruled that the "no bail-out" clause of Article 125(1) TFEU does not stand in the way of ESM financial assistance insofar as the euro area Member States, acting through the ESM, do not assume or guarantee existing indebtedness of the debtor Member State and, being subject to appropriate policy conditionality, such financial support does not take away that Member State's incentive to conduct sound fiscal policies.[987] Curiously, in its lengthy considerations on this question, the Court did not address the question of whether Article 136(3) TFEU could, as *lex specialis*, be viewed as (implicitly) derogating from Article 125(1) TFEU—as seems precisely to have been one of the reasons for adding Article 136(3) in the first place (*see* paragraph 686 above). The Court's silence on this point seems to imply that the Member States' actions through the ESM remain subject to review under Article 125(1).

985. CJEU, November 27, 2012, Case C-370/12, *Pringle*, ECLI:EU:C:2012:756.
986. *Ibid.*, §§93-98.
987. *Ibid.*, §§129-143.

691. In a German opinion poll conducted at the time, 54% of the respondents had expressed the hope that the German Federal Constitutional Court ("BVerfG") would block the ESM Treaty, and some 12,000 citizens signed on to applications seeking a temporary injunction to prevent ratification of this treaty. In a judgment of September 12, 2012,[988] the BVerfG held that the ESM Treaty would not infringe the Bundestag's budgetary autonomy as a matter of German constitutional law provided that it was clear that (i) Germany's financial commitments under the treaty could not go beyond its capital subscription without the Bundestag's consent,[989] and (ii) certain provisions of the treaty on the inviolability of documents and professional secrecy would not obstruct communication of such information as the Bundestag may need to exercise budgetary oversight.[990] On this basis, the BVerfG ruled that Germany must not ratify the ESM Treaty without making a reservation confirming these interpretations and clearly expressing that it cannot be bound by the treaty if this reservation is not effective.[991] Accordingly, on September 27, 2012, the euro area Member States all signed an interpretative declaration substantially to this effect.[992] The BVerfG then dismissed the case on the merits in its judgment of March 18, 2014.[993]

692. Unsuccessful challenges against the ratification of the ESM Treaty were also brought before the President of the District Court of The Hague,[994] before the Supreme Court of Estonia[995] and before the Constitutional Court of Austria.[996]

2 THE ESM'S KEY STRUCTURAL FEATURES

a Legal Status and Mandate

693. The ESM is not an EU institution, at least not yet. It is an intergovernmental organization outside the EU legal framework, governed by its own treaty and by public international law. Proposals have been made and ideas floated from time to time to integrate the ESM into the EU framework, as we will discuss later in this chapter (*see* paragraphs 735-737 below).

988. BVerfG, September 12, 2012, ECLI:DE:BVerfG:2012:rs20120912.2bvr139012. The avid reader will find an English translation of this judgment on the BVerfG's website at http://www.bverfg.de/e/rs20120912_2bvr139012en.html.
989. While Article 8(5) of the ESM Treaty appears clear on this point, the BVerfG considered that Article 25(2) gives rise to some ambiguity in respect of top-up payments that may be required if one or several ESM members fail to pay their share on capital calls. *Ibid.*, §§138-149.
990. On this point, the BVerfG's doubts concerned Articles 32(5), 34 and 35(1) of the ESM Treaty. *Ibid.*, §§150-155.
991. *Ibid.*, §§149 and 155.
992. The text of this declaration may be found at https://www.consilium.europa.eu/uedocs/cms_data/docs/pressdata/en/ecofin/132615.pdf.
993. BVerfG, March 18, 2014, ECLI:DE:BVerfG:2014:rs20140318.2bvr139012. For an English translation of this judgment, *see* http://www.bverfg.de/e/rs20140318_2bvr139012en.html.
994. Judgment of June 1, 2012, *Wilders et al.*, ECLI:NL:RBSGR:2012:BW7242.
995. Judgment of July 12, 2012, https://www.riigikohus.ee/en/constitutional-judgment-3-4-1-6-12.
996. Judgment of March 16, 2013, translated in relevant part in English and available at https://www.vfgh.gv.at/downloads/VfGH_SV_2-12_ESM_EN_4.4.2017_2.pdf.

694. The ESM's core mission is broadly the same as that of the EFSF, *i.e.*, to mobilize funds in the financial markets and, as a kind of lender of last resort, to provide financial assistance, *"under strict conditionality"*, to euro area Member States in financial distress, *i.e.*, which *"are experiencing, or are threatened by, severe financing problems"*, in circumstances where such assistance is *"indispensable to safeguard the financial stability of the euro area as a whole and of its Member States"*.[997] A separate mission, added by the 2021 amendments to the ESM Treaty, is to provide backstop financing to the Single Resolution Board ("SRB") as a kind of safety net in case of a shortfall of available resources in the Single Resolution Fund ("SRF") to cover expenses incurred in the application of the various bank resolution tools of the EU Single Resolution Mechanism.[998] We will briefly return to this second mission later in this chapter (*see* paragraphs 721-722 below) and focus for now on the ESM's core mission.

b Organizational Structure and Governance

695. The ESM started operations in October 2012. Its offices are located at Plateau Kirchberg in Luxembourg City—perhaps not exactly the city that never sleeps but one that exhales the soft airs of decennia of such venerable EU institutions as the Court of Justice, the European Investment Bank, the European Court of Auditors and Eurostat. The ESM has a fully developed organizational structure with significant expert professional staff.[999]

696. The ESM's core governance structure consists of a Board of Governors, a Board of Directors, a Managing Director, assisted by a Management Board, and a Board of Auditors. The Board of Governors is composed of the Ministers of Finance (or their alternates) of all 20 euro area Member States and, in character with the ESM's intergovernmental nature, must approve a fairly elaborate list of strategic (and indeed some less strategic) decisions *"by mutual agreement"*, *i.e.*, unanimously (not counting

997. Article 3(1) of the ESM Treaty. Article 136(3) TFEU refers only to the stability of *"the euro area as a whole"*. It is not clear what nuance the drafters of the ESM Treaty may have had in mind when adding the words *"**and** of its Member States"* in Article 3(1), which defines the ESM's core mission (and likewise in Article 12(1)), and the words *"**or** of its Member States"* in Article 13(1)(a), which concerns the prior assessment of risks to financial stability. This cannot be put to drafting inadvertence. Since successive drafts of the ESM Treaty were reviewed in various forums, the discrepancy with Article 136(3) TFEU must have been noted and discussed. Still, it is unclear, at least to this author, what the added wording was intended to achieve, especially since the use of the conjunctive *"and"* (rather than the disjunctive *"or"*) in Article 3(1) could be read to narrow the ESM's mission statement compared to its wording in Article 136(3) TFEU. So it remains a bit of a mystery and one that may well come up one day in a court case.

998. Article 3(2) (new) of the ESM Treaty.

999. On December 31, 2022, the ESM had a permanent staff of 228. *See* the ESM's 2022 Annual Report, p. 105, https://www.esm.europa.eu/system/files?file=document/2023-06/esm-annual-report-2022.pdf.

abstentions).[1000] This list[1001] notably includes the approval of financial assistance in each individual case, its policy conditionality and its financial terms and conditions.[1002] In other words, each euro Member State effectively retains veto power over whether, and on what terms, the ESM will grant financial assistance to another euro area Member State. In urgent cases, the European Commission and the ECB may jointly call for emergency voting on the granting or implementation of financial assistance, in which case the Board of Governors may act by a qualified majority of 85 % of the votes cast[1003]—but this still gives veto power to each of Germany, France and Italy.[1004]

c Capital Structure

697. In contrast to the EFSF's guarantee arrangements, the ESM borrows on the financial markets essentially on the strength of a robust capital structure. It currently has an "authorized" (yet fully subscribed) capital of EUR 708,493,700,000 of which, at the time of writing, EUR 80,970,690,000 had been paid in.[1005] Each ESM member has *"irrevocably and unconditionally"* committed to contribute its share,[1006] which, as a rule, is determined on the basis of the ECB capital subscription key.[1007] Capital calls can be made (i) by the Board of Governors, acting by mutual agreement, at any time; (ii) by the Board of Directors, acting by simple majority, to restore the minimum level of paid-in capital when it has been reduced by the absorption of losses; and, notably, (iii) by the Managing Director insofar as needed to avoid the ESM defaulting on any payment obligation to its creditors.[1008] To my knowledge, the latter feature is fairly unique for international organizations of this kind.

1000. Article 4(3) of the ESM Treaty. There is also a quorum requirement of two-thirds of the (voting) members representing no less than two-thirds of the voting rights (Article 4(2)). The voting rights correspond to the member countries' respective shares in the ESM's authorized capital (Article 4(7)).
1001. The (long) list of decisions requiring unanimity is set forth in Article 5(6) of the same treaty.
1002. Article 5(6)(f) of the same treaty.
1003. Article 4(4) of the same treaty.
1004. Outside of this emergency voting procedure, a series of less strategic decisions, listed in Article 5(7) of the ESM Treaty, require a qualified majority of 80 % of the votes cast, which still gives veto power to each of Germany and France.
1005. Article 8(1) and (2) and Annex II of the same treaty. Croatia became the 20th member of the ESM on March 22, 2023. Under the technical terms of Croatia's accession to the ESM, as approved by the ESM's Board of Governors on December 5, 2022, Croatia's regular share of authorized capital will be EUR 5,733,900,000 and its corresponding share of paid-in capital EUR 655,300,000. But since its 2022 GDP *per capita* is less than 75 % of the EU average, Croatia benefits from a 12-year reduction of these amounts under Article 42 of the ESM Treaty. Accordingly, prior to 2035, Croatia's share of authorized capital is reduced to EUR 3,695,000,000 on which EUR 422,290,000 is to be paid up in five annual instalments between 2023 and 2027. *See* the ESM's press release of December 5, 2022, https://www.esm.europa.eu/press-releases/esm-approves-croatias-application-membership.
1006. Article 8(4) of the same treaty.
1007. Article 11 and Annex I of the same treaty.
1008. Article 9 of the same treaty.

d Preferred Creditor Status

698. The ESM is at present triple-A rated with the major rating agencies[1009] which allows it to borrow at favorable rates that it then passes on in its own loans to euro area Member States (plus a margin, service fee and commitment fee, as the case may be). This top rating is primarily based on the ESM's robust capital structure and the credit strength of its highest-rated shareholders. The credit rating agencies also refer (albeit more obliquely) to the ESM's supposed "preferred creditor status" ("PCS") as an official lender of last resort to euro area Member States.[1010] This topic deserves a little digression.

699. PCS means, in essence, that the ESM would come ahead of other creditors (at least market creditors) in the repayment order in case of debtor distress or default and would be exempt from debt relief in a possible sovereign debt rescheduling. Under a looser formulation of PCS, debtor countries would have to prioritize debt service to official lenders like the ESM over debt service to market creditors. In recitals (13) and (14) to the ESM Treaty, it is said that (i) *"Heads of State or Government have stated"* that ESM loans will benefit from PCS in similar fashion to those of the IMF but second to them;[1011] (ii) the ESM's backstop loans to the SRB are to enjoy similar PCS; and (iii) *"[t]he euro area Member States will support"* equivalent creditor treatment of the ESM and other States lending bilaterally in coordination with the ESM, including in respect of backstop loans to the SRB. Thus, unlike the ECB which has expressly accepted *pari passu* treatment with other bondholders in respect of sovereign bonds acquired under its asset purchase programs (*see* paragraphs 222, 340(e), 360 and 535(b) above), the ESM claims PCS for its loans to euro area Member States and the SRB, junior only to the IMF and on the same footing as States having made loans in tandem with the ESM.

700. Said recitals (13) and (14) to the ESM Treaty can be retraced to earlier high-level political statements,[1012] but they have not been incorporated into the normative

1009. Moody's initially rated the ESM at Aaa but downgraded it to Aa1 in November 2012 (concomitantly with France's downgrade) and upgraded it back to Aaa in June 2022. Standard & Poor's first assigned an AAA rating to the ESM in August 2020. The ESM has had an AAA rating with Fitch from the beginning.

1010. For example, Fitch specifically mentions PCS among the factors supporting its assessment of the ESM's overall risk profile as "low". *See, e.g.*, its press release of July 8, 2022, https://fitchratings.com/research/sovereigns/fitch-affirms-european-stability-mechanism-at-aaa-outlook-stable-08-07-2022.

1011. An exception is made for ESM loans made under financial assistance programs pre-dating the ESM Treaty, for which the ESM will remain on equal footing with other creditors (and still junior to the IMF). By extension, a Euro Summit statement of June 29, 2012 *"reaffirms"* that the proposed financial assistance to Spain for the recapitalization of financial institutions will be transferred from the EFSF to the ESM, when it becomes operational, *"without gaining seniority status"*. *See* https:/www.consilium.europa.eu/media/21400/20120629-euro-area-summit-statement-en.pdf. *See also* European Stability Mechanism, *supra*, p. 223.

1012. *See*, in particular, the Statement by the Eurogroup of November 28, 2010, p. 2, https://www.consilium. europa.eu/media/25728/118050.pdf, and the Conclusions of the European Council of March 24-25, 2011, https://data.consilium.europa.eu/doc/document/ST-10-2011-INIT/en/pdf, which, in §1.17, endorsed a term sheet on the ESM that contained a statement on PCS substantially similar to the later recital (13) to the ESM Treaty (Annex II, p. 32).

provisions of the ESM Treaty. The rationale for a claim to PCS is clear enough and makes good sense. PCS protection is needed to justify that official lenders, ultimately backed by taxpayers' money, step in as lenders of last resort to provide financial assistance to countries in financial distress, on conditions to which these countries no longer have access in the financial markets. This is done to help these countries avoid default on their debt and regain financial market access on viable terms, which, in the end, serves the interests of existing market creditors as well. Such lender-of-last-resort financial assistance should not allow market creditors to reduce their loan exposure and then leave the official lender to incur loss in case of subsequent default or debt restructuring of the debtor country. The alternative would have been for the official lender to step in only after a prior rescheduling of the debtor country's market debt, and PCS in a sense (partly) replicates that outcome in case official lending could not avoid subsequent default or debt restructuring.

701. Yet, absent binding provisions in treaties, national laws or loan documentation, the legal status of the claim to PCS is doubtful. PCS is not clearly backed by customary international law or any general principle of EU law.[1013] One generally looks to the IMF for having set the precedent on PCS. PCS is not mentioned in the IMF's Articles of Agreement either, but the IMF laid (moral) claim to it in a statement issued by its Interim Committee following a meeting in Berlin on September 25-26, 1988.[1014] Later, the IMF observed that its PCS originated in the Paris Club where official bilateral creditors have been willing to exclude the IMF from debt restructuring.[1015] It attributed its PCS to *"the recognition by both the creditor community and sovereign debtors that it is in their interest and that of the international community at large to exclude the IMF from the debt restructuring process"*, as well as to legal limitations for the IMF to restructure its claims on its members. But it then candidly added that *"[t]he forbearance exercised by creditors is of a voluntary nature; unsecured creditors have not legally subordinated their claims to those of the IMF"*.[1016] Accordingly, PCS emerges more as a rule of civilized (and self-interested) conduct among creditors, a form of creditor etiquette, that is widely recognized—but not always observed, not even in Europe. Thus, on June 30, 2015, Greece (briefly) defaulted on a SDR 1.2 billion (about EUR 1.5

1013. Interestingly, in an old judgment rendered in a different context, the European Court of Justice denied PCS to the European Coal and Steel Community in respect of a debt owed by a company for steel production levies, in the absence of *"a clear and precise provision of Community law"*. *See* CJEU, May 17, 1983, Case C-168/82, *ECSC vs. Ferriere Sant'Anna*, ECLI:EU:C:1983:137, §18.

1014. IMF Press Release No 88/33 of September 26, 1988, §5, https//archivescatalog.imf.org/Details/archive/125087427. In the key sentence of this paragraph, the Interim Committee *"urged all members, within the limits of their laws, to treat the Fund as a preferred creditor and to lend their active and tangible support to this cooperative endeavor, so as to bring countries with overdue obligations back into the mainstream of international economic relations"*. The Committee did not invoke any existing rule or custom of international law or other legal authority.

1015. *See* International Monetary Fund, *IMF Financial Operations 2018*, April 18, 2018, p. 142, https://doi.org/10.5089/9781484330876.071.

1016. *Ibid.*

billion) repayment due to the IMF.[1017] One might also note that, in 2016 and 2018, the EFSF and the ESM consented to certain short-term and medium-term debt relief measures to Greece, involving maturity extensions, deferral of interest and amortization, and interest rate adjustments, while market creditors did not then participate in any debt relief, but it is true that those relief measures mostly concerned the EFSF loans and did not involve any nominal haircut.[1018]

3 THE ESM'S FINANCING TOOLKIT AND *MODUS OPERANDI*

a Toolkit

702. Leaving aside its backstop financing to the SRB for now (*see* paragraphs 721-722 below), the ESM's toolkit for financial assistance to euro area Member States consists of a variety of instruments. The regular tools are set forth in Articles 14 to 18 of the ESM Treaty but the list is open-ended insofar as, under Article 19, the ESM's Board of Governors may, acting unanimously, *"make changes to it"*. The Board of Directors has established detailed "guidelines" for the use of the various instruments and these are published on the ESM's website. The instruments that are or were at some point included in the ESM's toolkit are outlined in paragraphs 703 through 709 below.[1019]

703. *Macroeconomic adjustment loans*:[1020] The ESM may extend loans, under a macroeconomic adjustment program, to euro area Member States which no longer have access to the financial markets under viable conditions. The ESM has so far used this instrument twice, *i.e.*, for the 2013-2016 loan facility of up to EUR 10 billion[1021] to Cyprus (of which EUR 6.30 billion was disbursed) and for the 2015-2018 loan facility of EUR 86 billion to Greece (of which EUR 61.93 billion was disbursed) (*see* paragraph 719, Table 10.1, below).

704. *Loans for the recapitalization of financial institutions*:[1022] These are loans to euro area Member States to be used for the recapitalization of financial institutions that

1017. *See* IMF Pres Release No 15/310 of June 30, 2015, https://www.imf.org./en/News/Articles/2015/09/14/01/49/pr15310.

1018. *See* the EFSF/ESM press releases of December 4, 2017 and November 22, 2018, https://www.esm.europa.eu/press-releases/explainer-esm-short-term-debt-relief-measures-greece and https://www.esm.europa.eu/press-releases/explainer-efsf-medium-term-debt-relief-measures-greece, respectively. *See also* European Stability Mechanism, *supra*, pp. 341-343.

1019. For a more detailed discussion of these instruments, *see* U. Forsthoff & J. Aerts, "Financial Assistance to Euro Area Members (EFSF and ESM)", in *The EU Law of Economic and Monetary Union* (F. Amtenbrink & Chr. Herrmann eds.), Oxford University Press, 2020, pp. 984-996, §§33.20-33.87.

1020. Article 16 of the ESM Treaty.

1021. Following the IMF's decision to grant SDR 891 million in financial assistance to Cyprus, the amount of the ESM facility was reduced to EUR 8.96 billion by a notice of September 23, 2013 (https://www.esm.europa.eu/sites/default/files/migration_files/cyprusnoticerecital_epublication_version.pdf).

1022. Article 15 of the ESM Treaty.

are systemically relevant or otherwise present serious contagion risk for the euro area as a whole or the Member State in question. While part of a macroeconomic adjustment loan may also be earmarked for this purpose,[1023] this second instrument is specifically intended to address situations in which the financial stresses are primarily situated in the financial sector and not directly related to the relevant Member State's overall economic or fiscal policies. Accordingly, these loans are extended outside the framework of a macroeconomic adjustment program. The ESM has so far used this instrument on one occasion, *i.e.*, for the 2012-2013 loan facility of EUR 100 billion to Spain (of which EUR 41.33 billion was eventually disbursed) (*see* paragraph 719, Table 10.1, below).

705. ***Direct recapitalization of financial institutions***: This instrument, not included in the original treaty list, was adopted by the ESM's Board of Governors on December 8, 2014 pursuant to Article 19 of the ESM Treaty.[1024] It allowed the ESM itself, within an overall envelope of EUR 60 billion, to directly take equity participation (common stock or other capital instruments) in financial institutions of systemic relevance, as a last resort and on a temporary basis, to address capital shortfalls that could not otherwise be covered. In essence, this instrument offered a shortcut to the previous instrument (*see* paragraph 704 above) by bypassing the loan to the relevant Member State and, in this manner, avoiding a worsening of its government debt ratio. But the instrument lost a good part of its relevance when the bail-in mechanism of the Bank Recovery and Resolution Directive and the contribution of the SRF under the Single Resolution Mechanism came on stream. It has never been used thus far and will eventually be replaced by the ESM's backstop financing for the SRB (*see* paragraphs 721-722 below).

706. ***Primary market support facility***:[1025] As a complement to a macroeconomic adjustment loan (*see* paragraph 703 above) or to precautionary financial assistance (*see* paragraph 708 below), the ESM may acquire debt securities issued by a euro area Member State in the primary market (by participating in auctions or syndicated transactions). Under the related guideline, the ESM's purchases are ordinarily capped at 50% of the amount issued but they may go higher if needed to ensure that at least

1023. Thus, as part of the total financial assistance granted to Greece by the EFSF and the ESM, loans worth EUR 42.7 billion served specifically for the recapitalization or resolution of certain Greek banks. *See* U. Forsthoff & J. Aerts, *supra*, pp. 1009-1010, §§33.178-33.179. As concerns the ESM, an envelope of up to EUR 25 billion in the third (2015-2018) assistance program for Greece was earmarked for the recapitalization of Greek banks, and, in December 2015, the ESM disbursed EUR 5.43 billion to Greece for the recapitalization of Piraeus Bank and the National Bank of Greece. *See* the (original) Memorandum of Understanding of August 19, 2015 between the European Commission (acting on behalf of the European Stability Mechanism), the Hellenic Republic and the Bank of Greece, p. 18, https://ec.europa.eu/info/sites/default/files/01_mou_20150811_en1.pdf. In similar vein, as part of the ESM's financial assistance to Cyprus, an amount of EUR 1.5 billion was dedicated for the recapitalization of the Cooperative Central Bank. *See* U. Forsthoff & J. Aerts, *supra*, p. 1023, §33.248.

1024. This decision is published at https://www.esm.europa.eu/system/files?file=document/20141208_establishment_of_the_instrument_for_the_direct_recapitalisation_of_institutions.pdf.

1025. Article 17 of the ESM Treaty.

50 % of the originally targeted amount is placed.[1026] This instrument too has been lying idle so far.

707. ***Secondary market support facility***:[1027] Again as a complement to a macroeconomic adjustment loan but also on a stand-alone basis, the ESM may purchase a euro area Member State's government bonds in the secondary market. In the somewhat restrictive formulation of the current guideline, this instrument is intended for use in exceptional circumstances where a shortage of market liquidity in a Member State's government debt market creates financial instability risks by pushing up sovereign yields too high and causing refinancing problems for the Member State's banking system.[1028] Substantively, this tool bears resemblance to the ECB (Eurosystem)'s anti-fragmentation purchases of government bonds discussed in Chapter 5, except that the ESM's asset purchases would come with (additional) policy conditionality. But, insofar as they seek to contain an excessive rise in a Member State's sovereign bond yields and the consequent widening of sovereign bond spreads with those of other euro area Member States, they would seem to address similar fact patterns. In any event, the ESM has not so far used this instrument either.

708. Precautionary financial assistance:[1029] This is an earlier-stage instrument to provide financial assistance to euro area Member States *"with sound economic fundamentals, which could be affected by an adverse shock beyond their control"*. Precautionary financial assistance may be granted in the form of either a "Precautionary Conditioned Credit Line" ("PCCL") or an "Enhanced Conditions Credit Line" ("ECCL"). The key distinguishing factor between the two forms of credit line, once the 2021 amendments to the ESM Treaty will have entered into effect, is that the PCCL is subject to a series of *ex ante* eligibility criteria (and continuous compliance with these criteria) but not to additional *ad hoc* country-specific policy conditionality. These eligibility criteria, now set forth in Annex III to the amended ESM Treaty, essentially look to compliance with the numerical benchmarks and qualitative conditions of the EMU fiscal and macroeconomic surveillance frameworks. The ECCL, in contrast, is meant for Member States that fail to meet one or more of those eligibility criteria and remains subject instead to country-specific policy conditionality to be specified in a memorandum of understanding with the ESM. We will revisit the revised rules regarding precautionary financial assistance in a subsequent section on the ESM reforms (*see* paragraphs 723-725 below). Neither the PCCL nor the ECCL have so far been applied.

709. ***Pandemic Crisis Support***: This instrument became available in the spring of 2020 and offered longer-term credit lines of up to 2 % of a euro area Member State's GDP (as

1026. Article 4 of the Guideline on the Primary Market Facility, https://www.esm.europa.eu/sites/default/files/esm_guideline_on_the_primary_market_support_facility.pdf.
1027. Article 18 of the ESM Treaty.
1028. Article 1 of the Guideline on the Secondary Market Support Facility, https://www.esm.europa.eu/system/files?file=document/esm_guideline_on_the_secondary_market_support_facility.pdf.
1029. Article 14 of the ESM Treaty (as amended).

at the end of 2019) to support domestic financing of COVID-19-related healthcare and prevention costs.[1030] While being based on the ECCL, these credit lines would come without *ad hoc* policy conditionality other than the use of proceeds for eligible pandemic-related expenditures. No applications for support under this instrument were received before the December 31, 2022 deadline. This may seem somewhat surprising given that a number of euro area Member States could probably have borrowed more cheaply under the Pandemic Crisis Support than directly in the financial markets.[1031] The lack of interest may be explained in part by the availability of COVID-19 support from EU budget-linked instruments (*see* paragraphs 642 *et seq.* above). But certain euro area Member States may also have been hesitant to call on the ESM on account of the monitoring and surveillance that come as part of an ECCL as well as, perhaps, because of a certain stigma attached to ESM assistance. It seems a bit dysfunctional.

710. In partial summary, of those seven instruments, the ESM has effectively used only two so far, *i.e.*, macroeconomic adjustment loans (twice) and loans for the recapitalization of financial institutions (once). One instrument that has not been applied thus far, *i.e.*, the direct recapitalization of financial institutions, should be replaced by the ESM's backstop financing to the SRB upon entry into effect of the 2021 amendments to the ESM Treaty. And another instrument, *i.e.*, the Pandemic Crisis Support, has meanwhile expired unused.

b Prerequisites

711. A euro area Member State's request for financial assistance triggers, as a first step, a screening, to be conducted jointly by the ESM's Managing Director and the European Commission, acting *"in liaison with the ECB"*, of (i) the existence of a risk to the financial stability *"of the euro area as a whole or of its Member States"*; (ii) the sustainability of the relevant Member State's public debt and its capacity to repay the stability support; and (iii) the Member State's actual or potential financing needs.[1032] The assessment of debt sustainability and repayment capacity is to be made *"in a transparent and predictable manner"* while allowing for a *"sufficient margin of judgment"*, and is expected to be carried out *"[w]herever appropriate and possible"* together with the IMF.[1033]

1030. The ESM's Board of Governors approved this new instrument on May 15, 2020, https://www.esm.europa.eu/sites/default/files/migration_files/2020-05-15-bog-summary-of-decisions.pdf. A term sheet of May 8, 2020 is to be found at https//www.esm.europa.eu/sites/default/files/migration_files/20200508-pcs-term-sheet-final.pdf.

1031. *Cf.* K. Anev Janse & S. Ruhl, "Why the Covid-19 credit line still makes sense", *ESM blog*, July 29, 2020, https://www.esm.europa.eu/blog/why-covid-19-credit-line-still-makes-sense.

1032. Article 13(1) of the ESM Treaty (as amended).

1033. Article 13(1)(b) of the same treaty (as amended). For a high-level summary of the assessment criteria, *see* https://www.esm.europa.eu/content/how-will-esmec-perform-debt-sustainability-and-repayment-capacity-assessments. The expectation is that the institutions will reach a common view but, if this is not the case, the European Commission will have the *dernier mot* on debt sustainability and the ESM on repayment capacity. *See* the new recital

712. Recital (11b) (new) to the ESM Treaty states that the ESM should provide financial assistance only to Member States whose government debt is considered sustainable and whose repayment capacity is confirmed. Yet, this is not repeated as a prerequisite for financial assistance in the treaty's operative provisions, except, as to debt sustainability, for precautionary financial assistance.[1034] When addressing the Board of Governors' decision in principle to grant financial assistance, Article 13(2) (as amended) refers to a *"positive"* debt sustainability assessment only in respect of the precautionary instrument. This suggests that, for all other instruments, the Board of Governors would, at least as a theoretical matter, not be precluded by an inconclusive or even negative debt sustainability assessment from, unanimously, granting financial assistance nevertheless—just as it would not be bound to grant assistance in case of a positive assessment.[1035] This may be relevant in a crisis situation at the cliff's edge. It should be noted in this connection that, according to recital (12) to the ESM Treaty, where ESM stability support is granted under a macroeconomic adjustment program, *"an adequate and proportionate form of private sector involvement"* (a euphemism for debt relief in a sovereign debt restructuring) is to be considered *"[i]n exceptional cases"*.

713. Co-financing by the IMF is not a prerequisite to ESM financial assistance. Initially, during the euro area sovereign debt crisis in 2010-2012, the IMF became actively involved in providing financial assistance to certain Member States and in negotiating related policy conditionality as part of the notorious "Troika" (the European Commission, the IMF and the ECB). At that time, despite misgivings in certain European quarters, Germany appeared to favor IMF involvement because of the Commission's perceived lack of experience in dealing with sovereign crisis financing and its policy conditionality.[1036] But in later years, the IMF's role receded somewhat. It did not participate in the 2012-2013 financial assistance program for Spain, nor in the third (2015-2018) program for Greece.[1037] And while, in the original recital (8) to the ESM Treaty, euro area Member States requesting financial assistance were still expected to make a parallel request to the IMF *"wherever possible"*, this wording has been softened to *"whenever appropriate"* in the 2021 revision of the treaty.[1038]

(11b), *in fine*, to the ESM Treaty. Note that, under "Two Pack" Regulation 472/2013, the debt sustainability analysis is made by the Commission *"in liaison with the ECB and, where possible, with the IMF"*. *See* Article 6 of Regulation (EU) No 472/2013 of the European Parliament and of the Council of May 21, 2013 on the strengthening of economic and budgetary surveillance of Member States in the euro area experiencing or threatened with serious difficulties with respect to their financial stability, *OJ* L 140, May 27, 2013, p. 1.

1034. Article 14(1) of the ESM Treaty (as amended).

1035. *Cf.* J. Aerts & P. Bizarro, "The reform of the European Stability Mechanism", *Capital Markets Law Journal*, Vol. 15, 2020, pp. 169-170, https://doi.org/10.1093/cmlj/kmaa001.

1036. *Cf.* European Stability Mechanism, *supra*, pp. 78-79.

1037. In 2017, however, the IMF granted a further SDR 1.3 billion (about EUR 1.6 billion) precautionary Stand-By Arrangement to Greece.

1038. Also, language in the original recital (8) stating that the ESM will cooperate *"very closely"* with the IMF in providing stability support and seek the IMF's *"active participation"* at the technical and financial level, has been deleted in the 2021 amendments.

c Policy Conditionality

714. All ESM financial assistance under the existing instruments is granted subject to country-specific policy conditionality, except, under the 2021 amendments to the ESM Treaty, the PCCL which instead is made subject to a standard set of *ex ante* eligibility conditions and continued compliance with these conditions (*see* paragraph 724(c)-(f) below).[1039] Those policy conditions are specified in a memorandum of understanding ("MoU") which, under the amended treaty, is now to be negotiated with the euro area Member State in question jointly by the ESM's Managing Director and the European Commission, acting *"in liaison with the ECB"*, together *"wherever possible"* with the IMF.[1040] Once (unanimously) approved by the Board of Governors, the MoU is signed by the Managing Director and the Commission **on behalf of the ESM.**[1041] The same actors involved in the negotiation of the MoU are then tasked with monitoring the relevant Member State's compliance with the policy conditions.[1042]

715. As said, for the PCCL, conditionality consists of continued compliance with a standard set of eligibility conditions now set forth in Annex III of the amended ESM Treaty. For all other forms of ESM financial support, the ESM Treaty and "Two Pack" Regulation 472/2013 define the scope and content of the policy conditions only in broad terms:

(a) The ESM Treaty has little more to say on the subject than that (i) conditionality must be *"strict"*, echoing Article 136(3) TFEU;[1043] (ii) it must be *"appropriate to"*, *i.e.*, varies with, the type of financial assistance instrument[1044] and may *"range from a macro-economic adjustment programme to continuous respect of pre-established eligibility conditions"*;[1045] (iii) the content of the MoU must *"reflect the severity of the weaknesses to be addressed"*;[1046] and, significantly, (iv) the MoU must be *"fully consistent with the measures of economic policy coordination provided for in the TFEU, in particular with any European Union law, including any opinion, recommendation or decision addressed to the ESM Member concerned"*.[1047]

(b) Under "Two-Pack" Regulation 472/2013 (*see* paragraph 596 above), in the case of ESM financial assistance conditioned on a macroeconomic adjustment program, the Council must approve this program and the Commission must

1039. For a more detailed (and excellent) analysis of this subject, I happily refer the reader to U. Forsthoff & N. Lauer, "Policy Conditionality Attached to ESM Financial Assistance", in *The EU Law of Economic and Monetary Union* (F. Amtenbrink & Chr. Herrmann eds.), Oxford University Press, 2020, pp. 878-919, especially pp. 886 *et seq.*, §§30.41 *et seq.*
1040. Article 13(3) of the ESM Treaty (as amended).
1041. Article 13(4) of the same treaty (as amended).
1042. Article 13(7) of the same treaty (as amended).
1043. Article 3(1) of the same treaty.
1044. Articles 3(1), 12(1) and 13(3), first paragraph, of the same treaty.
1045. Article 12(1) of the same treaty.
1046. Article 13(3), first paragraph, of the same treaty.
1047. Article 13(3), second paragraph, of the same treaty.

ensure that the MoU is fully consistent with it.[1048] The macroeconomic adjustment program can be thought of as the backbone for the MoU, with the MoU defining the actual policy conditions and reforms in (considerably) greater detail.[1049] Regulation 472/2013 sets a limited number of general parameters for these programs, and thus indirectly for the MoUs, including that (i) such a program must address *"the specific risks emanating from the* [relevant] *Member State for the financial stability in the euro area"* and aim at *"rapidly re-establishing a sound and sustainable economic and financial situation and restoring the Member State's capacity to finance itself fully on the financial markets"*;[1050] (ii) the program must take due account of any recommendation addressed to the Member State concerned under Articles 121, 126, 136 or 148 TFEU;[1051] (iii) it must *"take into account"* the practice and institutions of wage formation in that Member State and *"fully observe"* the role of the social partners and the right of collective bargaining in accordance with EU and national laws and practices, as guaranteed by Article 28 of the Charter of Fundamental Rights of the European Union;[1052] and (iv) the fiscal consolidation efforts set out in the program must take into account *"the need to ensure sufficient means for fundamental policies, such as education and health care"*.[1053]

716. All in all, these parameters are fairly high-level and leave a wide perimeter for the negotiations on the MoU. Policy conditionality is not substantively limited to measures in the fiscal space but may cover a broad spectrum of economic, social and even legal reforms. In the ESM's macroeconomic adjustment loans to Cyprus and especially Greece, the policy conditions tended to be quite granular and intrusive. Thus, the MoU of August 19, 2015, in respect of the third (2015-2018) financial assistance program for Greece[1054] lists, over the length of some 30 pages, an elaborate series of relatively detailed measures, with target delivery dates, for raising tax revenue, improving

1048. Article 7(2) of Regulation 472/2013. The Council acts by qualified majority of the members representing euro area Member States, as such majority is determined in accordance with Article 238(3)(a) TFEU.

1049. By way of illustration, with respect to the third (2015-2018) financial assistance program for Greece, *compare* Council Implementing Decision (EU) 2015/1411 of August 19, 2015 approving the macroeconomic adjustment programme of Greece (*OJ* L219, August 20, 2015, p. 12), which in its Article 2 defines the key objectives and measures of the program in the space of about two pages, *with* the corresponding MoU dated August 19, 2015 (https://ec.europa.eu/info/sites/default/files/01_mou_20150811_en1.pdf) which is about 30 pages long (excluding annexes).

1050. Article 7(1), second paragraph, of Regulation 472/2013.

1051. Article 7(1), third paragraph, of the same Regulation.

1052. Article 7(1), fourth and fifth paragraphs, of the same Regulation. This slightly more specific parameter appears to be intended to push back on restrictions on collective bargaining included in policy conditionality attached to earlier EFSF financial assistance. *Cf.* A. Poulou, "Financial Assistance Conditionality and Human Rights Protection: What is the Role of the EU Charter of Fundamental Rights?", *Common Market Law Review*, Vol. 54, 2017, p. 993, https://doi.org/10.54648/cola2017087.

1053. Article 7(7), second paragraph, of Regulation 472/2013.

1054. This document is cited in fn. 1049 above.

collection of taxes, containing and controlling public expenditures, strengthening the budget process, further pension and healthcare reforms, recapitalizing certain banks and addressing non-performing loan ratios, additional labor and product market reforms (*"aimed at European best practices"*), pursuing an *"ambitious"* program of privatizations, and improving public administration, justice and action against corruption.

717. The policy conditionality attached to financial support from the ESM, as a non-EU intergovernmental organization of euro area Member States, has raised significant questions as to its interaction with EU rules on economic policy coordination, the role of the European Commission and the ECB as EU institutions in this process, and available judicial remedies under EU law. Several of these issues were addressed in the September 20, 2016 judgment of the European Court of Justice ("CJEU") in the *Ledra* case.[1055]

In *Ledra*, certain depositors who had suffered loss in the restructuring and resolution of the Cyprus Popular Bank and the Bank of Cyprus applied for the annulment of the relevant paragraphs of the ESM's MoU of April 26, 2013 with Cyprus[1056] and claimed damages from the European Union under Article 340 TFEU. On appeal from an earlier decision of the General Court, the CJEU reached the following conclusions:

(a) The CJEU first held that the involvement of the Commission and the ECB in the negotiation of the MoU does not allow to characterize the MoU (as such) as a legal act that can be attributed to these institutions. The manner of their involvement does not alter the nature of the MoU as an act of the ESM alone, which falls outside the EU legal order and which, accordingly, the CJEU has no jurisdiction to annul.[1057]

(b) However, the Court considered that, by the same token, the tasks conferred on the Commission and the ECB by the ESM Treaty do not detract from the essential character of their powers and duties under the TEU and TFEU which, in the case of the Commission, include its role as guardian of the

1055. CJEU, September 20, 2016, Joined Cases C-8/15 P to C-10/15 P, *Ledra Advertising and Others vs. Commission and ECB*, ECLI:EU:C:2016:701.

1056. This MoU pre-dated Regulation 472/2013, which entered into effect on May 30, 2013. Regulation 472/2013 in turn pre-dated the CJEU's judgment in *Ledra* but anticipated several of its findings.

1057. *Ledra*, §§52-54. This is in line with the Court's observations in the *Pringle* case, *see* CJEU, November 27, 2012, Case C-370/12, *Pringle*, ECLI:EU:C:2012:756, §161.

Under Article 7(2) of Regulation 472/2013, the Council now has to approve the macroeconomic adjustment program underlying the MoU (*see* paragraph 715(b) above) and this Council decision is an act that the CJEU could review and annul. Thus, since the Council is bound by the Charter of Fundamental Rights of the European Union, its decision could be annulled for violation of the Charter. Such a violation would likely be harder to establish given the higher-level content and lower degree of specificity of the Council's decision (as compared with the corresponding MoU). Also, private parties may have difficulty establishing standing under Article 263, fourth paragraph, TFEU, which requires that the decision either be addressed to them or be of direct and individual concern to them.

Treaties under Article 17(1) TEU. This means that the Commission should ensure that the MoUs concluded on behalf of the ESM are consistent with EU law, and that *"it should refrain from signing a memorandum of understanding whose consistency with EU law it doubts"* lest it engage the European Union's non-contractual liability under Article 340, second paragraph, TFEU.[1058]

(c) The Court then proceeded to examine the damages claim on the merits as it was based on an alleged violation of Article 17(1) (right to property) of the Charter of Fundamental Rights of the European Union. Significantly, the Court held that, while the Charter is not addressed to Member States when acting in the context of the ESM Treaty, it is addressed to EU institutions even when acting outside the EU legal framework, with the consequence that, when negotiating an MoU on behalf of the ESM, the Commission is bound to see to it that such an MoU is consistent with the fundamental rights guaranteed by the Charter.[1059]

(d) In the end, the Court found no breach of Article 17(1) of the Charter in the case at hand and dismissed the claim for damages.

718. Regulation 472/2013 already placed the European Commission in a key role in preparing the macroeconomic adjustment program with the Member State requesting financial assistance and in ensuring the consistency of the MoU with this program. The CJEU's *Ledra* judgment appears to further strengthen the Commission's hand in the determination of policy conditionality attached to ESM stability support, now that it clearly falls to the Commission to see to it that the policy conditions are consistent with *"EU law"* more broadly. This should include the rules of the EMU fiscal and macroeconomic surveillance frameworks, but a possible question is whether the *Ledra* consistency test should extend to the "soft law" elements of these frameworks (like policy guidelines and recommendations in the non-coercive phase). Yet, the Commission's Treaty guardianship role is broadly defined in Article 17(1) TEU to include *"ensur[ing] the application of the Treaties, and of measures adopted by the institutions pursuant to them"*. And the ESM Treaty itself does not seem to distinguish between "hard" and "soft" rules of the EMU frameworks. Its Article 13(3), second paragraph, provides that MoUs must be *"fully consistent with the measures of economic policy coordination provided for in the TFEU, in particular with any European Union law, including any opinion, recommendation or decision addressed to the ESM Member concerned"*.[1060]

It is also worth noting here that, echoing *Pringle* (*see* paragraph 577(c) above), the new recital (15a) to the ESM Treaty, added by the 2021 amendments, states that Member States are to coordinate their economic policies within the arrangements

1058. *Ledra*, §§55-59. This also echoes *Pringle*, §§162-164.

1059. *Ledra*, §§66-68. Here, the CJEU connects the dots between *Pringle*, §§179-180 and §§162-164.

1060. In a similar vein, Article 14(2), as replaced by the 2021 amendments, provides that the Commission will be tasked to review whether the policy intentions stated in the "letter of intent" to be submitted by a Member State applying for a PCCL (*see* paragraph 724(e) below) are *"fully consistent with the measures of economic policy coordination provided in the TFEU, in particular with any act of European Union law, including any opinion, warning, recommendation or decision addressed to the ESM Member concerned"*.

determined by the TFEU and that, accordingly, *"the ESM should not serve the purpose of economic policy coordination among ESM Members for which European Union law provides the necessary arrangements"*. To this effect, a final sentence added to Article 3(1) mandates the ESM's Managing Director to *"collaborate with the European Commission and the ECB to ensure full consistency with the framework for economic policy coordination provided for in the TFEU"*. The new Article 12(4) provides that, when exercising its tasks under the ESM Treaty, the Commission will ensure that the ESM's financial assistance operations are *"where relevant, consistent with European Union law, in particular with the measures of economic policy coordination provided for in the TFEU"*.

d Financial Assistance Granted

719. To wrap up this section, Table 10.1 provides an overview of the financial assistance granted so far by the EFSF and the ESM (on a disbursement basis)—all originating in the 2010-2012 euro area sovereign debt crisis.

Full particulars of the terms of these loans, the attached policy conditionality and related disbursements and repayments can be found on the ESM's website. Meanwhile, all beneficiary Member States have exited their respective financial assistance programs.

Table 10.1 EFSF/ESM Financial Assistance (Disbursements[a], Billions of Euro)

	EFSF	*ESM*	*Total*	*Weighted Average Maturity*	*EFSM*	*Bilateral Loans[b]*	*IMF*
Cyprus	–	6.30 (2013-2016)	6.30	14.9 years	–	–	1.0
Greece	141.84[c] (2012-2014)	61.93 (2015-2018)	203.77	42.45 years (EFSF) 32.35 years (ESM)	–[d]	52.9	32.1[e]
Ireland	18.41 (2011-2013)	–	18.41	20.8 years	22.5	4.8	22.5
Portugal	27.33 (2011-2014)	–	27.33	20.8 years	24.3	–	26
Spain	–	41.33 (2012-2013)	41.33	12.49 years	–	–	–
Total	187.58	109.56	297.14		46.8	57.7	81.6

Source: ESM data.

Notes: [(a)] These are amounts disbursed on a gross basis, *i.e.*, sums effectively disbursed plus certain amounts withheld upfront for various costs and fees, *i.e.*, any upfront portion of the service fee (where applicable) and prepaid margins on EFSF loans to Ireland and Portugal. [(b)] This includes the 2010 Greek Loan Facility of bilateral loans from euro area Member States and bilateral loans to Ireland from Denmark, Sweden and the United Kingdom. [(c)] This amount includes (i) the EFSF's contributions to the 2012 Greek sovereign debt rescheduling, *i.e.*, EUR 29.7 billion of one-year and two-year notes for bondholders as part of the debt exchange, and EUR 4.9 billion of six-month bills to cover accrued interest on Greek bonds, and (ii) EUR 10.9 billion of bonds issued by the EFSF for the recapitalization of Greek banks which were redelivered by the Hellenic Financial Stability Fund on February 27, 2015. [(d)] In July 2015, the EFSM extended a EUR 7 billion bridge loan to Greece pending adoption and disbursement of the third (2015-2018) financial assistance program to Greece. [(e)] This amount does not include a further SDR 1.3 billion (approximately EUR 1.6 billion) precautionary Stand-By Arrangement which the IMF Executive Board approved on July 20, 2017.

4 THE 2021 ESM REFORMS

720. After a drawn-out process, certain ESM reforms were agreed and reflected in the Agreement Amending the Treaty Establishing the European Stability Mechanism which was signed on January 27, 2021 (and by Estonia on February 8, 2021). This Agreement has meanwhile been ratified by all euro area Member States except, at the time of writing, Italy. The most significant amendments are reviewed below.

a Backstop to the Single Resolution Fund

721. In the context of the EU Single Resolution Mechanism for banks and certain investment firms, the ESM may provide "backstop" financing to the Single Resolution Board ("SRB")[1061] to cover a shortfall of its Single Resolution Fund ("SRF") in funding expenditures arising from the application of the bank resolution tools listed in Article 76 of Regulation (EU) No 806/2014 of July 15, 2014[1062] (*see* paragraphs 640-641 above). As said, the SRF pools annual risk-adjusted contributions paid by some 2,777 banks and certain investment firms across the 21 Banking Union Member States (*i.e.*, currently all euro area Member States and Bulgaria). It has been built up over the 2016-2023 period to reach at least 1 % of all covered deposits: it stood at EUR 66 billion at the end of 2022 and is estimated to reach about EUR 77.6 billion by the end of 2023.

1061. New Articles 3(2), 12(1a) and 18a and Annex IV of the ESM Treaty.
1062. Regulation (EU) No 806/2014 of the European Parliament and of the Council of July 15, 2014 establishing uniform rules and a uniform procedure for the resolution of credit institutions and certain investment firms in the framework of a Single Resolution Mechanism and a Single Resolution Fund and amending Regulation (EU) No 1093/2010, *OJ* L225, July 30, 2014, p. 1, amended by Regulation (EU) 2019/877 of May 20, 2019, *OJ* L150, June 7, 2019, p. 226, Regulation (EU) 2019/2033 of November 27, 2019, *OJ* L314, December 5, 2019, p. 1, and Regulation (EU) 2021/23 of December 16, 2020, *OJ* L22, January 22, 2021, p. 1.

722. The ESM's backstop facility would be available only as a last resort, *i.e.*, if and when the SRF's (non-committed) resources are depleted and the SRB is unable to borrow in the financial markets on acceptable conditions. It is supposed to be fiscally neutral over the medium term, in the sense that all of the SRF expenditures are eventually to be covered by contributions from the banking industry, and the support from "taxpayers' money" is to be fully reimbursed. The ESM backstop facility is capped at EUR 68 billion and takes the form of a revolving credit line, with parallel financing by non-euro area Member States participating in the Banking Union (currently only Bulgaria). It will replace the ESM's dormant instrument for the direct recapitalization of financial institutions upon entry into effect of the 2021 amendments to the ESM Treaty (*see* paragraph 705 above).

b Streamlining Precautionary Financial Assistance

723. Other amendments appear to be intended to streamline and facilitate access to the ESM's precautionary financial assistance or at least its PCCL variant (*see* paragraph 708 above). This is done essentially by conditioning access to a PCCL on a series of standard eligibility criteria and exempting it from (additional) *ad hoc* country-specific conditionality and the conclusion of a related MoU. Yet, these eligibility criteria are not particularly light. Also, several criteria and conditions for access to a PCCL and even an ECCL are now incorporated in the ESM Treaty that previously either did not exist (or at least were not expressly stated) or were included in the guideline for precautionary financial assistance that could be modified by the ESM's Board of Directors by a qualified majority of 80% of the votes cast.

724. Upon entry into effect of the 2021 amendments to the ESM Treaty, the revised conditionality matrix for precautionary financial assistance will look as follows:

(a) The amended treaty itself now restricts precautionary financial assistance, including both a PCCL and an ECCL, to euro area Member States *"with sound economic fundamentals which could be affected by an adverse shock beyond their control"*.[1063] These criteria are not expressly stated in the pre-2021 version of the treaty, and, while the current (pre-amendment) guideline limits precautionary financial assistance to euro area Member States whose economic and financial situation remains sound, it does not require the occurrence of some adverse shock beyond their control.[1064]

The added wording *"which could be affected ('pourraient être touchés', 'beeinträchtigt werden könnten') by an adverse shock beyond their control"* is a bit curious insofar as, in this uncertain world, any country *"could"* at any time be affected by an adverse shock which may turn out to be beyond its

1063. Article 14(1) of the ESM Treaty (as amended).

1064. Articles 1 and 2(2) of the current (pre-amendment) Guideline on Precautionary Financial Assistance, https://www.esm.europa.eu/sites/default/files/esm_guideline_on_precautionary_financial_assistance.pdf.

control. And what must be beyond a Member State's control: the occurrence of the shock itself, its magnitude and consequences, or both? And how bad must this "adverse shock" be? One would think that the purpose of precautionary assistance should be to allow timely support in a pre-crisis situation in order to prevent troublesome tensions from escalating into a serious crisis in which a Member State faces major difficulties in its access to market finance, with adverse spill-over effects elsewhere in the euro area. Legal wording often fails to properly characterize such an intrinsically fluid fact pattern—but some words more than others. It is not clear why precautionary assistance should now be conditioned on the possible occurrence of an adverse shock beyond a Member State's control.

(b) The amended treaty expressly conditions a Member State's access to precautionary financial assistance, again in either of its variants, on a prior **positive** assessment of the sustainability of its sovereign debt.[1065] The current (pre-amendment) guideline also includes sovereign debt sustainability among the criteria of eligibility for a PCCL but this did not necessarily apply to an ECCL.[1066]

(c) As said, the revised treaty subjects access to a PCCL to *ex ante* fulfillment of, and continuous compliance with, a series of standard eligibility criteria in lieu of *ad hoc* economic policy conditions.[1067] A Member State that fails *"some"* of these eligibility criteria may still qualify for an ECCL if its *"general economic and financial situation remains strong"* and its *"government debt is sustainable"*, but an ECCL remains subject to *ad hoc* economic policy conditionality to be specified in an MoU.[1068]

(d) The eligibility criteria for a PCCL are now set forth in section 2 of Annex III of the treaty (as amended). This section starts out by limiting access to a PCCL to euro area Member States whose *"economic and financial situation is fundamentally strong and whose government debt is sustainable"* and, *"as a rule"*, comply with the numerical benchmarks and qualitative conditions of the EMU fiscal and macroeconomic surveillance frameworks. This then is to be assessed *"on the basis"* of a list of more specific criteria. In particular, it is to be checked that the relevant Member State (i) is not under an excessive deficit procedure ("EDP") and has met the applicable numerical fiscal benchmarks as to government deficit, structural budget balance and government debt in the preceding two years;[1069] (ii) has not been identified as experiencing excessive imbalances; (iii) has a track record of access to international

1065. Articles 13(2) and 14(1) of the ESM Treaty (as amended).
1066. Article 2(2)(b) and (4) of the current (pre-amendment) Guideline on Precautionary Financial Assistance.
1067. Article 14(1) and (2) and section 2 of Annex III of the ESM Treaty (as amended).
1068. Articles 13(3) and 14(3) and section 3 of Annex III of the same treaty (as amended).
1069. As formulated in section 2(a) of Annex III, these benchmarks may need to be adapted to the outcome of the ongoing reforms of SGP. In particular, section 2(a)(iii) refers to the current debt reduction benchmark which is likely to be abandoned, at least in its current form (*see* paragraphs 613 and 621(a) above).

capital markets *"where relevant, on reasonable terms"*; (iv) has a sustainable external position; and (v) has no severe financial sector vulnerabilities that put its financial stability at risk. These criteria may well set the bar on the high side and diminish the relevance of the instrument as a prevention tool for euro area Member States most in need of it.

The above criteria essentially correspond to those stated in the current (pre-amendment) guideline, except that, under this guideline, a Member State would not be disqualified for being under an EDP or an excessive imbalance procedure so long as it takes the required corrective actions.[1070] And except that, under the pre-2021 treaty, the Board of Directors could change these criteria by amending the guideline by a qualified majority vote. Under the revised treaty, the eligibility criteria set forth in Annex III may be amended only by the Board of Governors, acting unanimously, in which case the changes become effective only after the completion of *"applicable national procedures"*.[1071] In other words, the 2021 amendments to the ESM Treaty appear to have tightened the eligibility criteria for a PCCL in some respects and made it more difficult to adapt them.

(e) In addition, when applying for a PCCL, a Member State must, in a letter of intent, commit to continuous respect of those eligibility criteria and *"highlight[...] its main policy intentions"*. The European Commission must then review whether those policy intentions are fully consistent with *"the measures of economic policy coordination provided for in the TFEU"* and *"any act of European Union law, including any opinion, warning, recommendation or decision addressed to the ESM Member concerned"*.[1072]

(f) Finally, in case of a subsequent finding of non-compliance with the eligibility conditions for a PCCL or the policy conditions attached to an ECCL, access to the credit line may be discontinued (unless maintained by the Board of Directors by unanimous vote) and, furthermore, an additional interest margin will be applied to any funds already drawn (unless the Board considers non-compliance to be due to events beyond the relevant Member State's control).[1073] Under a draft pricing guideline (now possibly somewhat outdated), this additional margin equals 50 basis points (115 basis points after six months), to be added to the regular margin of 35 basis points (85 basis points following a maturity extension).[1074]

725. In light of all of the above conditions, one may wonder whether ESM precautionary financial assistance would become that much more accessible and/or attractive

1070. Article 2(2)(a) and (c) of the (pre-amendment) Guideline on Precautionary Financial Assistance.
1071. Article 14(1), second paragraph *jo.* Article 5(6)(fa) of the ESM Treaty (as amended).
1072. Article 14(2) of the ESM Treaty (as amended).
1073. Article 14(7) of the same treaty (as amended).
1074. *See* the draft updated Pricing Guideline that was agreed in principle at the Eurogroup meeting of December 4, 2019, p. 10, https://www.esm.europa.eu/sites/default/files/migration_files/20191206_-_draft_pricing_guideline_-_publication_version.pdf.

than before, especially for euro area Member States that could most benefit from it when facing the risk of quickly worsening market dynamics:

(a) Why now confine the instrument in reference to the—possible—occurrence of some adverse shock beyond a Member State's control?
(b) Also, the affirmative requirement of a positive public debt sustainability assessment for both a PCCL and an ECCL may give pause, especially now that, in its latest (April 2023) Debt Sustainability Monitor, the European Commission found eight euro area Member States (Italy, France, Spain, Belgium, Greece, Portugal, Croatia and Slovakia) to be at high fiscal sustainability risk in the medium term, and six others (Austria, Slovakia, Malta and even Germany, The Netherlands and Finland) at medium risk.[1075]
(c) Why disqualify a Member State in EDP from access to a PCCL so long as it is taking the requisite corrective action?
(d) Furthermore, one may doubt the wisdom—in terms of reason, not politics—of making it more difficult to adapt the eligibility criteria for a PCCL to rapidly changing circumstances by subjecting changes to a unanimous vote of the ESM's Board of Governors and applicable national procedures.

c Other Amendments

726. In light of "Two Pack" Regulation 472/2013 and the CJEU's *Ledra* judgment (*see* paragraphs 596, 715(b) and 717-718 above), the amendments to the ESM Treaty seek to clarify the respective roles of, and interaction between, the institutions involved in the process notably with regard to the prior screening of public debt sustainability and repayment capacity, the negotiation of policy conditionality for the MoU, and subsequent compliance monitoring.[1076] The new Article 13(8) contemplates that these matters will be further articulated in a memorandum of cooperation between the ESM and the European Commission.[1077] At the end of the day, the fact remains that the Commission has the final say in the debt sustainability assessment and has a solid foot in the door in the negotiation of policy conditionality (*see* paragraphs 711, 714 and 718 above). In combination with its increasingly prominent role in the management of the EMU fiscal and macroeconomic surveillance frameworks, as discussed in Chapter 8,

1075. *See* European Commission, *Debt Sustainability Monitor 2022, European Economy Institutional Paper No 199*, April 2023, pp. 43-58.
1076. For further particulars, *see* J. Aerts & P. Bizarro, *supra*, pp. 166-168.
1077. On April 27, 2018, the Commission and the ESM had already signed a Memorandum of Understanding on the principles governing their "working relations" (https://www.esm.europa/system/files/document/20180427_esm_ec_mou.pdf). Building on these principles, they subsequently agreed on a joint position, set out in a note of November 14, 2018 (https://www.esm.europa.eu/press-releases/joint-position-future-cooperation-between-european-commission-and-esm). This joint position has been substantially incorporated in a Memorandum of Cooperation which will enter into effect at the same time as the 2021 amendments to the ESM Treaty.

the Commission has become a central actor in the domain of economic policy coordination and conditionality.

727. Significantly, another amendment requires that, as from January 1, 2022, the terms of all new euro area government bonds with a maturity in excess of one year include so-called "collective action clauses" ("CACs") that provide for "single-limb" aggregated voting (rather than the previous "double-limb" CACs requiring a majority vote per issuance and in the aggregate).[1078] Of course, that date has passed, but I understand that euro area Member States now include in government bond documentation a clause switching to single-limb CACs upon entry into effect of the ESM Treaty amendments.

d Nihil Obstat from Karlsruhe, Hesitations in Rome

728. In Germany, true to tradition, the act ratifying the 2021 amendments to the ESM Treaty was challenged before the Federal Constitutional Court ("BVerfG") on the ground that certain amendments transfer sovereign power to the ESM and the European Union and/or result in a *de facto* change of the EU legal framework. By an order of October 13, 2022, the BVerfG dismissed the complaint as inadmissible because it failed to sufficiently substantiate these claims.[1079] The court held, *inter alia*, that it cannot be ascertained that the revised PCCL fails to meet the requirement of "strict conditionality" of Article 136(3) TFEU.[1080] As conditionality must reflect the severity of the economic weaknesses to be addressed and may vary with the instrument chosen (as provided by Article 13(3) of the ESM Treaty), it may be sufficient for a PCCL to be conditioned on continued compliance with the eligibility criteria set forth in the new Annex III to the ESM Treaty, especially, as the court noted, since some of these criteria are stricter than before.[1081] The BVerfG also concluded that neither the revised PCCL nor the common backstop for the SRF implies *de facto* changes to the "no bail-out" rule of Article 125 TFEU.[1082]

729. The BVerfG's *nihil obstat* cleared the path for German ratification of the ESM Treaty amendments. But, at the time of writing, Italy's center-right governing coalition continued to hold off on ratification. Early in July 2023, the vote on ratification was deferred again, then until sometime in November. But November passed and still Italy had not ratified. On December 21, 2023, the Italian Parliament even voted down ratification. Italy's hesitations appear to derive in part from lingering distrust of the ESM as a mechanism associated with harsh policy conditionality favored by fiscally

---

1078. Recital (11) and Article 12(3) of the ESM Treaty (as amended).

1079. BVerfG, October 13, 2022, ECLI:DE:BVerfG:2022:rs20221013.2bvr111121. For an English translation of this decision, *see* https://www.bundesverfassungsgericht.de/SharedDocs/Entscheidungen/EN/2022/10/rs20221013_2bvr111121en.html.

1080. *Ibid.*, §§124-130.

1081. *Ibid.*, §129.

1082. *Ibid.*, §§131-133.

conservative (Northern) Member States. But there may be other more opportunistic considerations below the waterline.

5 POSSIBLE STEPS FORWARD

a Status Quaestionis

730. Let us first look back from this point in our narrative. A currency union among sovereign States remains a difficult proposition, even—and, in some sense, especially—if they are part of a free trade zone. A single monetary policy has to contend with country differences in the timing or amplitude of business cycles, inflation levels, yield curves and fiscal positions, and these differences are in part hardwired into long-standing differences in economic and social characteristics. Being deprived of exchange rate and monetary policy tools of their own, as well as from the possibility to impose restrictions on trade within the currency zone, member countries are left with economic and fiscal policy tools to smooth the business cycle or respond to external shocks in a manner that commands sufficiently broad domestic political acceptance. Yet, the cohesion of the currency union requires member countries to submit to a measure of discipline in the use of these tools in order to restrain public deficits, government debt and external imbalances. This further reduces their remaining policy space and may give rise to difficult issues of domestic political arbitrage. Domestic political constraints have a stubborn habit of challenging fiscal discipline. Effective and complementary coordination of economic and fiscal policies between surplus and deficit countries would help to alleviate tensions, but it has proven hard to force surplus countries into more expansionary policies for the common good. Situations may arise in which a concurrence of inflationary pressures and recessionary risks places conflicting demands on monetary policy and national fiscal policies. This may constrain monetary policy and require it to be less restrictive than would ordinarily be required for inflation control, so as to avoid that the most vulnerable economies run up excessive government deficits and debt and that widening bond spreads may eventually cause destabilizing market dynamics in the currency union. All of this points to the need for some robust centralized financial capacity to provide stability support to struggling economies and to largely unburden monetary policy from intra-union stabilization responsibilities that may interfere with inflation control. In an ideal world, this stabilization support would take the form of some central budget for (quasi-)automatic transfers triggered by the worsening of unemployment and other key economic performance indicators. A sufficiently robust stabilization capacity of this kind remains lacking in Europe's incomplete EMU.

731. At the **EU level**, the EU budget itself is comparatively small in size, has limited stabilization features and has no such instruments earmarked for the euro area. The EFSM is a loan facility of modest size and, while it has been used in the 2011-2013 financial assistance program for Ireland, in the 2011-2014 program for Portugal and for short-term bridge financing to Greece in July 2015, it is open to all EU Member States, and it has been agreed that the ESM should henceforth be the first port of call for euro area Member States (*see* paragraphs 638-639 above). Then, in a somewhat tortuous process from 2017 to 2019 in the run-up to the 2021-2027 MFF, discussions on some euro area stabilization budget ended up in a modest proposal for an EU budgetary instrument, BICC, of undetermined but likely small size, for grants to support public investments and structural reforms of euro area Member States (and ERM II Member States choosing to participate) (*see* paragraphs 651-663 above). In the event, this proposal fell by the wayside as political focus shifted to EU-wide measures in response to COVID-19, particularly NGEU and RRF. But the difficult discussions in the BICC trajectory suggest that a sizable EU budgetary stabilization instrument dedicated to the euro area remains an uphill battle for now—perhaps even a vertical uphill battle.

732. Yet, certain EU-wide funds and spending programs linked to the EU budget indirectly have a certain stabilization impact. Thus, certain (temporary) instruments created in response to COVID-19, including SURE and, especially, NGEU and its RRF with their significant grant component and allocation key favoring the more vulnerable economies (*see* paragraphs 642-650 above), should be helpful to convergence and cohesion within the euro area as well. After all, the 20 euro area Member States now represent approximately 85% of the EU economy's GDP. Prior to Brexit, it was only about 72% and, accordingly, Brexit has increased the overlap between the euro area and the European Union and the relevance of the EU budget and EU-wide financing schemes for the euro area.

733. Still, while NGEU is a most welcome development, it is a temporary instrument and it was not a particularly easy compromise politically—notwithstanding the fact that COVID-19 does not divide the Member States into good and bad students, ants and grasshoppers, which should make solidarity easier. Clearly, genuine risk-sharing fiscal capacity remains a difficult subject politically. The political bandwidth for transfers proper remains narrow, and progress is likely to be achieved only in slow and difficult steps, or when some external threat leaves little alternative. Money is limited and there is no shortage of competing expenditures. It may, however, be of some significance in this respect that the December 6, 2022 judgment of the BVerfG on Council Decision 2020/2053 seems to have opened the door somewhat for NGEU-type financial support instruments (*see* paragraphs 670-681 above). The BVerfG's greater leniency on the German constitutional requirement of budgetary autonomy may make it less persuasive for German (and other) politicians to take shelter behind national constitutional objections of that kind. This, and the clever political engineering that went into the design of NGEU/RRF, may make NGEU/RRF a convenient matrix for future EU-wide financial support initiatives. Still, large-scale programs of this kind, with a significant grant component, inevitably place the need for additional EU own resources on the political agenda—a difficult topic (*see* paragraphs 666-669 above).

734. It is likely that, for some time, the European currency union will have to continue to rely in significant measure on its own **dedicated stability support capacity** outside the EU budget. Here, one would look in the first instance to the ESM, which is a fully operational instrument and has significant firepower left in terms of uncommitted lending capacity, *i.e.*, up to EUR 422 billion at the time of writing.[1083] If one deducts the future EUR 68 billion credit line to the SRF (*see* paragraph 722 above) from this, the amount available for sovereign lending under the ESM's core mission remains EUR 354 billion.

This remaining firepower is perhaps not a "bazooka" but it is still considerable—EUR 354 billion represents about 2.63 % of total 2022 euro area GDP at market prices and 2.89 % of total euro area government consolidated gross debt at the end of 2022. Now that the financing instruments in the ESM's toolkit have either expired unused or been laying idle for over eight years (their last use dates back to August 19, 2015, when the ESM extended its loan facility to Greece under the third (2015-2018) financial assistance program for this country), one should think of sensible ways in which the ESM's firepower could be put to efficient use. This may require recalibrating existing tools or expanding the toolkit by adding one or several new tools, as we will discuss in subsections c. and d. below. But before doing so, we should briefly consider an unresolved question regarding the ESM's legal status.

b Toward a European Monetary Fund?

735. Conspicuously absent from the 2021 amendments to the ESM Treaty is the ESM's possible integration into the EU institutional fabric. Unlike the contemporaneous Treaty on Stability, Coordination and Governance in the Economic and Monetary Union of March 2, 2012,[1084] the original ESM Treaty did not contemplate such an integration, and its 2021 amendments do not provide for it either. From the outset, the ESM's existence in a parallel intergovernmental universe has been a source of discomfort for some, and from time to time proposals have been made, or ideas floated, to bring the ESM under the EU roof. Thus, the 2015 Five Presidents' Report noted that the ESM's intergovernmental structure rendered its governance and decision-making processes complex and called for full integration of the ESM's governance within the EU Treaties in the medium term.[1085] In December 2017, the European Commission submitted a proposal for a Council regulation under Article 352 TFEU to anchor the ESM, now renamed "European Monetary Fund" ("EMF"), in the EU legal framework.[1086]

1083. This amount corresponds to the difference between the ESM's maximum lending capacity of EUR 500 billion (*cf.* Article 39 of the ESM Treaty) and its outstanding loan commitments of EUR 78 billion at the time of writing.

1084. Article 16 (sometimes referred to as the "repatriation clause") of this treaty provides that the necessary steps will be taken by 2018 to incorporate the treaty's substance into the EU legal framework. This has happened only partially so far (*see* paragraph 575(a) above).

1085. *Completing Europe's Economic and Monetary Union*, Report by Jean-Claude Juncker, in close cooperation with Donald Tusk, Jeroen Dijsselbloem, Mario Draghi and Martin Schulz, June 22, 2015, p. 18, https://ec.europa.eu/info/publications/five-presidents-report-completing-europes-economic-and-monetary-union_en.

1086. Proposal for a Council Regulation on the establishment of the European Monetary Fund, COM(2017) 827 final, December 6, 2017, https://eur-lex.europa.eu/legal-content/EN/ALL/?uri=COM:2017:827:FIN.

736. Under the Commission's proposal, the EMF would succeed (and replace) the ESM as a separate legal entity under EU law, with a self-financed budget separate from the EU budget. It would substantially have the same missions (including the backstop financing for the SRF), institutional features, capital structure and lending tools as the ESM. One significant difference would have derived from the *Meroni* doctrine which, in broad outline, stands in the way of delegating powers involving the exercise of significant policy discretion to institutions not established by the Treaties themselves.[1087] In recognition of this limitation, the Commission's proposal provided that a series of decisions of the EMF's Board of Governors and Board of Directors would become effective only after approval by the Council, acting by qualified majority and with the votes of the members representing non-euro area Member States being suspended.[1088] The proposal drew significant criticism in euro area quarters, notably on this Council approval requirement. Yet, since the EMF's Board of Governors would consist of the finance ministers of the euro area Member States, it seems rational to expect that, when changing hats and sitting as members of the Council, they would generally approve their own decisions in the EMF's Board of Governors and those of their appointees in its Board of Directors.[1089] Still, *Meroni* and broader autonomy concerns prompted the alternative idea of recreating the ESM as a Treaty-anchored institution, possibly modeled on the European Investment Bank[1090]—but this would require a formal TFEU amendment which, even under the simplified procedure of Article 48(6) TEU, would involve a fairly lengthy and potentially difficult process.

737. In any event, the Commission's EMF proposal and alternative integration proposals have so far failed to get much traction. The theme of the ESM's integration into the EU legal order is bound to resurface from time to time. But, by and large, most euro area Member States, having made substantial capital commitments to the ESM and being accountable in the first instance to their national parliaments, seem broadly comfortable with the *status quo* and not in a particular hurry to change it. Discomfort over greater Commission influence undoubtedly plays a role in some European

1087. The *Meroni* doctrine is based on an early judgment of the European Court of Justice, *i.e.*, CJEU, June 13, 1958, Case C-10/56, *Meroni vs. High Authority*, ECLI:EU:C:1958:8. It has been clarified in the Court's later judgment in the short-selling case, CJEU, January 22, 2014, C-270/12, *United Kingdom vs. Parliament and Council*, ECLI:EU:C:2014:18, §§41-55.

1088. Article 3(1) and (4) of the proposed regulation. A possible legal issue is whether a Council regulation could validly extend the suspension of the voting rights of Council members representing non-euro area Member States to votes on the EMF's stability support, since this matter does not clearly fall within those referred to in Article 139(1) and (4) TFEU. This might conceivably be resolved by structuring the arrangement as a form of "enhanced cooperation" under Article 20 TEU and Articles 326 to 334 TFEU.

1089. Also, it would be highly unlikely if not impossible that, for EMF decisions subject to qualified majority voting, euro area Member States which failed to constitute a blocking minority under the EMF's weighted voting system could subsequently block approval of the decision at Council level under Article 238(3) TFEU.

1090. Klaus Regling, then Managing Director of the ESM, suggested this approach at the end of his speech "Strengthening the ESM and EMU" at the Inter-Parliamentary Conference on Stability, Economic Coordination and Governance in the European Union on September 30, 2019 in Helsinki. *See* https://www.esm.europa.eu/speeches-and-presentations/ "strengthening-esm -and-emu"-speech-Klaus-Regling.

capitals. The ESM, as an intergovernmental organization circling in the European Union's orbit, is a fully functioning structure and capable of interacting with EU institutions in the broader framework of EMU. Changing its legal status would not seem a compelling priority at this time. For now, I am not overly troubled, intellectually, by EMU's hybrid architecture of EU and intergovernmental components.

c Operational Improvements: Possible Hurdles

738. Putting the ESM's firepower to effective use in today's environment may require recalibrating some of its existing financing instruments and/or adding one or more new instruments to its toolbox. But there are hurdles to overcome for a broader and more proactive stability support role for the ESM, which we must consider first. Aside from political hesitations and bad memories of Troika policy conditionality, there are two legal hurdles (or what seem to be hurdles) under the ESM Treaty (as amended), at least under the working assumption that a further amendment of this treaty is likely not in the cards in the near future (for lack of political appetite or time).

739. ***First***, the ESM is essentially conceived as a **lending** mechanism: its stability support takes the form of loans (or purchases of sovereign bonds), not grants. ESM financing allows the beneficiary Member State to avoid additional borrowing in the financial markets at a higher cost or to refinance existing government debt on more favorable terms. But debt is still debt. Loans have less stabilization efficacy insofar as they produce interest-bearing debt for the beneficiary Member States and do not improve their government debt ratio. This first limitation should be nuanced in two respects:

(a) The ESM Treaty places no restrictions on the maturity or repayment schedule (including possible grace periods) of ESM loans to euro area Member States or on the ESM's ability to subsequently extend them. The ESM has a diversified funding strategy and need not simply relend the proceeds of its borrowings to Member States on a back-to-back basis. Thus, the loans disbursed by the ESM to Greece under the third (2015-2018) financial assistance program have a weighted average maturity of 32.35 years, with maturity dates between 2057 and 2060 and amortization schedules starting in 2034 or later. (And the EFSF loans made to Greece under the second (2012-2014) program have been "reprofiled" under short-term and medium-term debt relief measures, without nominal haircuts but with deferral of interest payments and principal repayments, resulting in amortization schedules now stretching to 2070.[1091]) The point is that ESM loans can offer beneficiary Member States a longer time horizon, and more favorable rates, than would be available to them in the market—producing, in effect, a significant subsidy equivalent in net present value terms.

1091. *See* European Stability Mechanism, *supra*, pp. 341-342 and 400-402.

(b) If one takes the reasoning one step further, it could make good sense too for ESM financial assistance in appropriate circumstances to include a form of grant component. In particular, in the case of a euro area Member State hit by some serious external shock that pushes some of its key economic indicators into the red, it could be stipulated that a certain portion of the financial assistance will become repayable only upon subsequent recovery to pre-crisis conditions or some other significant improvement in selected economic indicators.[1092] I realize that we are skating on thinner ice here. Yet, on a careful reading, the (amended) ESM Treaty does not expressly exclude that stability support may include terms of this kind. True, the treaty's implicit assumption is that stability support should eventually be repaid. This is reflected, in particular, in (i) Article 13(1)(b), which requires a prior repayment capacity assessment (although Article 13(2) does not condition the Board of Governors' decision to grant support on a **positive** assessment of repayment capacity); (ii) Article 13(6), which calls on the ESM to set up an appropriate warning system to ensure that it receives any payments ***"due"*** in a timely manner; and (iii) Article 20(1), which provides that the ESM should ***"aim"*** to fully cover its funding costs and a suitable margin.[1093] But, strictly speaking, none of these provisions excludes a contingent repayment feature of the kind described above. More broadly, if the ESM is allowed to effectively grant a subsidy equivalent in net present value terms by way of long maturities and repayment schedules and subsequent "reprofiling", why should such a feature be disallowed?

740. ***Second***, the other issue is that of **conditionality**. Article 136(3) TFEU requires financial assistance granted under a euro area stability mechanism to be made subject to *"strict conditionality"* but does not define this term. In *Pringle*, the Court of Justice observed that the purpose of this wording is to ensure that the ESM and the beneficiary Member States *"comply with measures adopted by the Union in particular in the area of the coordination of the Member States' economic policies, those measures being designed, inter alia, to ensure that the Member States pursue a sound budgetary*

1092. Such a contingent repayment feature would be a kind of *"retour à meilleure fortune"* clause, somewhat akin to value recovery instruments occasionally used as sweeteners for principal haircuts in sovereign debt restructurings, including the 2012 Greek debt rescheduling. *See* J. Zettelmeyer, Chr. Trebesh & M. Gulati, "The Greek Debt Restructuring: An Autopsy", *Peterson Institute for International Economics Working Paper Series No 13-8*, August 2013, p. 10.

1093. In the *Pringle* case, when addressing the compatibility of the ESM Treaty with the "no bail-out" clause of Article 125(1) TFEU, the Court of Justice seemed to attach some significance to the fact that the financial assistance pursuant to Articles 14 to 16 of the ESM Treaty takes the form of loans or credit lines that give rise to new debt to be repaid to the ESM. *See* CJEU, November 27, 2012, Case C-370/12, *Pringle*, ECLI:EU:C:2012:756, §139. But this appears to be no more than a dictum to support the Court's conclusion that the ESM does not assume or guarantee existing debt of the recipient Member State within the scope of Article 125(1) TFEU. In any event, I continue to believe that Article 136(3) TFEU must be viewed as a *lex specialis* (implicitly) derogating from Article 125(1) TFEU (*see* paragraph 690(b) above).

policy".[1094] The ESM Treaty explicitly incorporates the requirement of *"strict conditionality".*[1095] It further provides that the content of the MoU, which must *"detail"* such conditionality for all instruments (other than, under the 2021 amendments, the PCCL), must *"reflect the severity of the weaknesses to be addressed and the financial assistance instrument chosen"*, while being *"fully consistent with the measures of economic policy coordination provided for in the TFEU, in particular with any act of European Union law, including any opinion, warning, recommendation or decision addressed to the ESM Member concerned".*[1096] Little else is said about the nature and scope of the conditionality required other than that it may vary with the instrument chosen,[1097] ranging *"from a macro-economic adjustment programme to continuous respect of pre-established eligibility conditions".*[1098]

741. The amended ESM Treaty is more specific only for a PCCL for which conditionality consists of continued compliance with a series of standard eligibility conditions listed in an annex[1099] (*see* paragraph 724(c) and (d) above). As said, these conditions (in combination with the requirement of a prior positive debt sustainability assessment) may somewhat defeat the purpose of making a PCCL a more attractive and efficient earlier-stage instrument for crisis prevention, especially for the more vulnerable economies in the euro area. Those eligibility conditions (but not the requirement of a positive debt sustainability assessment) could be adapted by the ESM's Board of Governors, acting unanimously, and subject to completion of applicable national procedures.[1100] Interestingly, in its order of October 13, 2022, the BverfG held that it cannot be ascertained that the PCCL's form of conditionality falls short of the "strict conditionality" requirement of Article 136(3) TFEU (*see* paragraph 728 above).

742. But otherwise, the ESM Treaty's references to conditionality remain fairly abstract and should, by and large, leave a significant margin for judgment. Politics aside, neither Article 136(3) TFEU nor the ESM Treaty requires that policy conditionality attached to ESM financial assistance be as detailed and intrusive as that set forth, for example, in the MoU of August 19, 2015 in respect of the third (2015-2018) financial assistance program for Greece (*see* paragraph 716 above). Save for addressing new developments or difficulties, there is no compelling reason why such conditionality should substantively go much beyond applicable benchmarks and policy recommendations under the EMU fiscal and macroeconomic surveillance frameworks and encroach further on whatever autonomous economic and fiscal policy space may be left to the euro area Member State in question. In the very words of the new recital (15a) to the ESM Treaty, *"the ESM should not serve the purpose of economic policies coordination among ESM Members for which European Union law provides the necessary arrangements"*. And the European Commission, acting as the ESM's agent in

1094. *Pringle*, §143. In the same sense, *ibid.*, §69.
1095. Articles 3(1) and 12(1) of the ESM Treaty.
1096. Article 13(3) of the same treaty.
1097. Articles 3(1) and (4), 12(1) and 13(3) of the same treaty.
1098. Article 12(1) of the same treaty.
1099. Article 14(2) and Annex III of the same treaty (as amended).
1100. Article 14(1), second paragraph, of the same treaty (as amended).

negotiating and signing the MoU,[1101] should not derive greater powers from this delegation than those of its principal. *Nemo plus iuris ad alium transferre potest quam ipse habet*.

d Operational Improvements: Ideas for Further Exploration

743. Given the limited scope and prospects of genuine euro area stability support at the level of the EU budget, it makes eminent sense to have the ESM on stand-by for such additional euro area stability support as may become needed, and to make sure that its existing firepower and expertise can be deployed efficiently when necessary. The ESM Treaty does offer some scope for "tuning" existing instruments and, if needed, establishing suitable new ones pursuant to Article 19 so as to allow the ESM to assume a broader and more active stability support role within the European currency union and to respond in a targeted and timely fashion to potentially destabilizing developments for the currency union. It is, in the end, a question of political will and swift action to follow through.

744. Several ideas and proposals have been floated in this regard. There is little added value in critically reviewing them here. But I should single out a May 2022 paper by Florian Misch and Martin Ray not only for providing a bird's eye overview of earlier ideas but also, and mostly, for presenting a thoughtful proposal of their own. They propose to establish a EUR 250 billion loan facility, "stability fund", hosted by the ESM that would be activated in case of external shocks that put financial stability at risk, on the basis of numerical trigger conditions (in terms of the unemployment rate and other indicators of economic activity such as the Purchasing Managers' Index or PMI), complemented by expert assessment.[1102] The proposal is balanced and would be a step forward.

745. This author, for one, would like to see the following issues receive priority consideration:

(a) *Ad hoc* policy conditionality attached to ESM financial assistance should generally be tempered. Not only should it be fully consistent with applicable country benchmarks and recommendations under the EMU fiscal and macroeconomic surveillance frameworks, but it should also, as a rule, not go beyond them except to address intervening developments or for other compelling reasons.

(b) The design of precautionary financial assistance should be recalibrated so that it may serve as a genuine prevention tool that can be mobilized swiftly. Concern over euro area stability and cohesion should weigh more heavily than concern over moral hazard or rewarding the undeserving. Promptness of

1101. Article 13(3) and (4) of the same treaty.

1102. Fl. Misch & M. Rey, "The case for a loan-based euro area stability fund", *ESM Discussion Paper Series No 20*, May 2022, 32 pp.

decision-making and transparency could be aided by a pre-set matrix of trigger conditions that look to a sudden and serious worsening of selected high-frequency economic indicators.

(c) It should be explored whether and how the ESM could take over part or all of the current role of Eurosystem central banks in engaging in anti-fragmentation purchases of government bonds issued by euro area Member States at the high end of unduly widening government bond spreads. This calls for a further word of explanation.

746. As we discussed earlier, geographically targeted government bond purchases carried out by Eurosystem central banks with a view to containing financial fragmentation present various issues. Aside from being slightly unnatural acts for central banks, such purchases (i) may bring the ECB as monetary authority into conflict with its primary price stability objective, particularly in a higher-inflation environment calling for monetary tightening; (ii) notwithstanding the European Court of Justice's benevolent ruling in its 2015 *Gauweiler* judgment, raise legal doubts as to whether they are within the compass of the ECB's monetary policy mandate and are compatible with the monetary financing prohibition of Article 123 TFEU; and (iii) could hardly be made subject to economic policy conditionality without further calling into question their characterization as monetary policy (*see* paragraphs 382 *et seq.* above). These issues are more than pebbles in the ECB's shoe.

They would go away if the ESM were to step in in one of the following ways:

(a) Under Articles 17 and 18 of the ESM Treaty, the ESM could, in the secondary market and even in the primary market, engage in outright purchases of government bonds issued by euro area Member States experiencing serious difficulties in their access to market finance. Possible hurdles would include the requisite speed of execution and, more importantly, the fact that the ESM's uncommitted lending capacity (*see* paragraph 734 above) may be relatively modest for bond purchases on a larger scale and over a longer time span.

(b) Instead, I have long cherished the idea that the ESM could, pursuant to Articles 19 and 24 of the ESM Treaty, establish some interest stabilization fund of the kind proposed by Friedrich Heinemann in 2012, or, alternatively, that such a fund could be established by an intergovernmental agreement between euro area Member States, with the ESM managing the fund and providing backstop financing to it. I have described the idea in greater detail in Chapter 5 (*see* paragraphs 401-404 above). In broad outline, under such a scheme, a plausible yield corridor would be established (and adapted from time to time in light of market circumstances and the monetary policy stance of the moment) within which Member States' sovereign bond yields can be deemed to be broadly aligned with underlying macroeconomic fundamentals. Euro area Member States with government borrowing rates above the upper limit of their corridor would receive temporary interest subsidies from the fund on new debt, subject to appropriate conditionality linking the continuing flow of interest subsidies to ongoing fiscal and structural reforms in compliance with the applicable benchmarks and policy recommendations under the EMU fiscal and macroeconomic surveillance frameworks. On the other side of the equation, euro area Member States fortunate enough to see their government borrowing costs drop below their lower limit would contribute part of their interest savings to the fund. Thus, the scheme would be an interest stabilization mechanism, triggered by unwarranted deviations from underlying macroeconomic fundamentals, not an interest equalization mechanism. Properly structured, this scheme would unburden the ECB from having to conduct government bond purchases to contain financial fragmentation. Also, in a higher-inflation environment, an interest subsidy mechanism of this kind would minimize incremental liquidity injection into the system as compared to outright asset purchases and, accordingly, cause less interference with a more restrictive monetary policy stance.

Chapter 11
The End of All Things: Euro Exit

747. Spoiler alert: this final chapter will discuss a forbidden subject. In 2010, then ECB President Jean-Claude Trichet said that *"[o]ne cannot jump in and jump out of the euro area as one hops on and off from a bus"*.[1103] A partial, let alone total break-up of the European currency union has become somewhat of a taboo subject in official European circles, or at least one that is not regarded as a proper topic of civilized discussion among serious people. The mantra in official discourse remains that the euro is irreversible. But is it? And what happens if it isn't? How to deal with euro exit?

1 SLEEPLESS IN FRANKFURT

748. Keeping Greece on board in its crisis years in the first half of the previous decade required total financial assistance (on a disbursement basis) of approximately EUR 289 billion (including EUR 32.1 billion from the IMF) and about EUR 107 billion of debt relief in nominal terms (significantly more in net present value terms) (*see* paragraphs 70-74 above). The rescue effort was laboriously pieced together over a period of several years in a difficult and somewhat haphazard process, it came with stern policy conditionality that caused political and social tensions in Greece and, in the summer of 2015, Greece still came at the cliff's edge of exit from the European currency union. Greece stands for about 1.5% of aggregate euro area GDP, which begs the question of whether the currency union would have the resources, tools and decision-making processes to effectively deal with a serious crisis of a significantly larger economy.

749. Presently, the economic fallout of COVID-19, the armed conflicts in Ukraine and the Middle East, geopolitical tensions, climate change, the complex challenges of the green transition, and unfavorable demographics are significant disruptive events with asymmetric effects across the euro area. Rising social tensions, euroskepticism and

1103. Quoted in H. Hofmeister, "Goodbye Euro: Legal Aspects of Withdrawal from the Eurozone", *Columbia Journal of European Law*, Vol. 18, 2011, p. 134.

populist resentment in several euro area Member States threaten to narrow the political bandwidth for serious reforms. Against this backdrop, how can the cohesion of the European currency union be preserved in an extended period of elevated uncertainty with inflationary pressures, subdued GDP growth, increased public spending needs to contain recessionary risks, support the green transition and rebuild credible defense capability, and high levels and divergence of sovereign debt? Much political capital is invested in the currency union and its lines of defense may seem robust, but are they strong enough to hold up against a concurrence of serious challenges of this kind? These are the kind of questions that one would imagine keep at least some people awake at night at the ECB's offices in Frankfurt.

750. As we have seen in Chapter 5, since the 2010-2012 euro area sovereign debt crisis, the financial markets have become more sensitive, and the ECB more attentive, to episodic signs of excessive widening of sovereign bond spreads—which are viewed almost as the proverbial canary in the coalmine, warning of impending trouble. There has been some economic literature seeking to empirically determine to what extent different sovereign risk premiums are attributable to differences in macroeconomic fundamentals, and to what extent they are due to perceived "redenomination risk" (*see also* paragraph 376 above). Redenomination risk may broadly be defined as the risk that, following a partial or total break-up of the currency union, the public debt of an exiting Member State (as well as the private debt and contractual payment obligations of its residents) would be redenominated (and repaid) in a national currency that is worth less than the euro. Those studies have used various indicators to measure redenomination risk, and their results differ and, by and large, are somewhat inconclusive.

751. Sometimes, the residual, *i.e.*, the portion of the sovereign bond spread that cannot properly be explained by economic fundamentals, has been taken as a proxy for redenomination risk. This approach is quite approximative insofar as (i) the residual may (also) reflect other causes of market overreaction than the fear of redenomination; (ii) it is hard to identify all relevant fundamental variables; and (iii) there is bound to be significant auto-correlation between economic fundamentals and redenomination risk (since sovereign credit risk and redenomination risk should ordinarily in some measure depend on common fragilities affecting fiscal sustainability). An alternative approach would be to compare the spread on USD-denominated bonds issued by a euro area Member State (which should not be affected by redenomination risk) with that on its euro-denominated bonds of comparable maturity. Yet another method, used by Umberto Cherubini in a 2021 paper, looked at the difference between premiums on credit default swaps ("CDS") based on the 2003 ISDA Credit Derivatives Definitions and those on CDS based on the revised 2014 ISDA definitions, so long as CDS of both types are concurrently traded in the market. The point of this comparison is that redenomination constitutes a credit event ("Restructuring") under the 2014 ISDA definitions, but not under the 2003 ISDA definitions in the case of euro area Member States that are part of the G7 (Germany, France and Italy) or are OECD countries with AAA-rated debt (The Netherlands). That paper found that, measured in this manner, redenomination risk had risen since February 2017, when the UK Parliament approved the request to start the Brexit procedure. It even concluded that, since then, the CDS market has by and large priced redenomination as the most likely outcome of the next sovereign debt crisis in the euro area.[1104] Perhaps or perhaps not, but for present purposes, these academic attempts at detecting and measuring redenomination risk seem somewhat futile. Redenomination risk is in the eyes of the beholder. It exists when markets begin to perceive a significant risk of euro exit and to adapt their pricing and hedging conduct accordingly. It should usually be in plain sight, although perhaps, like the headlights of an incoming train in the fog, only at an uncomfortably close distance.

2 NO RULES OR PLAYBOOK FOR EURO EXIT

752. One would suspect that, especially after the 2010-2012 sovereign debt crisis and Greece's near-exit in 2015, playbooks must exist in official circles on how to deal with the exit of one or several Member States from the currency union. But if they do, they are veiled in secrecy—the financial equivalent of nuclear codes.

a The Silence of the Treaties

753. Neither the Treaty on European Union ("TEU") nor the Treaty on the Functioning of the European Union ("TFEU", together the "Treaties") contain any specific provisions on the termination or suspension of the currency union. They are also silent on the voluntary or forced withdrawal of a Member State from, or the suspension of its membership of, the currency union.[1105] Several commentators have inferred from certain provisions[1106] that the Treaties intend to exclude any exit from the currency union, and perhaps they do, in the way that marriage vows exclude divorce. Conversely, a lone voice has argued, entirely unpersuasively, that the Treaties should be understood to offer a possibility of (unilateral) euro exit when the admission conditions (convergence criteria) are no longer fulfilled.[1107]

754. Under the Treaties, the only certain path for withdrawal from the currency union would be for a Member State to leave the European Union altogether. Article 50 TEU, introduced by the Treaty of Lisbon of December 13, 2007, establishes the right of every

1104. U. Cherubini, "Estimating redenomination risk under Gumbel-Hougaard survival copulas", *Journal of Economic Dynamics and Control*, Vol. 133, 2021, Article No 104268, pp. 1-20, https://doi.org/10.1016/j.jedc.2021.104268.

1105. The procedure provided by Article 7 TEU for the suspension of certain of a Member State's rights under the Treaties would not be suitable for suspending a Member State's membership of the currency union.

1106. These authors would typically refer to such provisions as Article 123(4) of the pre-Lisbon Treaty establishing the European Community and Article 140(3) TFEU on the "irrevocable" fixing of a national currency's conversion rate in euro upon accession to the currency union, and to the old Protocol (No 24) on the transition to the third stage of economic and monetary union (1992) regarding the "irrevocable" character of this transition.

1107. J.S. Dammann, "The Right to Leave the Eurozone", *Texas International Law Journal*, Vol. 48, 2013, pp. 137 *et seq.*

Member State to unilaterally withdraw from the European Union. The Treaties then cease to apply to the departing Member State from the effective date of the withdrawal agreement or, absent such an agreement, two years after the Member State's withdrawal notification (or such longer period as may have been agreed).[1108] Perhaps somewhat surprisingly, this right of unilateral withdrawal is not subject to any substantive conditions. The general consensus view is that withdrawal from the European Union encompasses withdrawal from the currency union.[1109] Obviously, this "all-or-nothing" solution would further raise the costs of euro exit for a Member State whose continued currency union membership may have become economically harmful to it (as it may be harmful to the rest of the euro area). Also, under Article 50 TEU, withdrawal from the European Union involves a potentially lengthy process that may leave uncertainty for too long and give rise to destabilizing market speculation about the future terms of separation.[1110]

b Article 62 of the Vienna Convention

755. It has from time to time been suggested that Article 62 (fundamental change of circumstances) of the Vienna Convention of May 23, 1969 on the Law of Treaties, in combination with its Article 44 (separability of treaty provisions)—or the rules of customary international law codified by these provisions—[1111] would permit a Member

1108. Article 50(3) TEU.

1109. A paper by Phoebus Athanassiou, legal counsel at the ECB, considers Article 50 TEU ambiguous and flawed in this respect insofar as *"[a] potential right of withdrawal from EMU and the procedure for such withdrawal are too serious to be left to inference"*. *See* Ph. Athanassiou, "Withdrawal and expulsion from EU and EMU", *ECB Legal Working Paper Series No 10*, December 2009, pp. 27-30, at p. 29.

1110. Under the procedure set forth in Article 50 TEU, the exiting Member State must enter into negotiations with the remaining Member States on the conclusion of a withdrawal agreement setting out the arrangements for withdrawal and regulating the future relationship between the departing Member State and the European Union. The Treaties do not require that such negotiations be successfully completed: absent an earlier agreement on the terms of withdrawal, the Treaties would cease to apply to the Member State in question automatically two years after the Member State notified the European Council of its intention to withdraw (or such longer time interval as may have been agreed with the Member State concerned). Accordingly, the right to withdraw from the European Union could thus in effect be exercised unilaterally, although without a withdrawal agreement, it is bound to be an uncertain and potentially disorderly process.

1111. All euro area Member States are or have become parties to this 1969 Vienna Convention, except France. The European Union itself is not a party to the Convention. Nevertheless, many of its provisions, including Article 62, are generally considered as codifying rules of customary international law, as has been confirmed by the European Court of Justice. *See* CJEU, June 16, 1998, Case C-162/96, *Racke vs. Hauptzollamt Mainz*, ECLI:EU:C:1998:293, §24. In this judgment, the Court held that *"the rules of customary international law concerning the termination and the suspension of treaty relations by reason of a fundamental change of circumstances are binding upon the Community institutions and form part of the Community legal order"*. *Ibid.*, §46. Arguably, however, this dictum only concerns the Union's own treaty relations with third countries (as, in the case at hand, a cooperation agreement between the European Economic Community and the former Socialist Federal Republic of Yugoslavia)—and not the relations between the Union and its Member States, or among its Member States, under the Treaties.

State unilaterally to withdraw from the currency union **without** withdrawing from the European Union. Legally, this would be an uncertain path. Several conditions would need to be fulfilled for invoking Article 62, including that (i) there needs to be a change in the original circumstances of currency union adhesion that was not foreseen; (ii) said circumstances must have constituted an essential basis for the original consent; (iii) the effect of the change is *"radically to transform"* the extent of the obligations still to be performed; and (iv) the change does not result from a breach of Treaty obligations by the exiting Member State. When applied to withdrawal from the European currency union, these conditions leave plenty of room for discussion and doubt. Condition (iv), in particular, may be a tough nut to crack insofar as it would require that the adverse change of circumstances is not in some significant measure attributable to the exiting Member State's breach of its Treaty obligations including those under the EMU fiscal and macroeconomic surveillance frameworks.

756. Yet, this ground for unilateral selective withdrawal from the currency union only cannot be dismissed out of hand. Interestingly, in recital (18) to the Intergovernmental Agreement on the Transfer and Mutualisation of Contributions to the Single Resolution Fund of May 21, 2014,[1112] the signatory Member States (including all current euro area Member States) acknowledge that the provisions of the Vienna Convention and customary international law apply in case of any fundamental change of circumstances *"that has taken place against their will and that affects the essential basis"* of their consent to be bound. This *"essential basis"* is defined as consisting of the core elements of the Single Resolution Mechanism listed in recital (17) to the agreement. It is further specified that, if a Member State invokes such a fundamental change of circumstances, any other signatory Member State may refer the matter to the European Court of Justice for verification of the existence of such a change and the consequences deriving from it. Note, however, that similar wording is absent from the Treaty Establishing the European Stability Mechanism of February 2, 2012 and from the Treaty on Stability, Coordination and Governance in the Economic and Monetary Union of March 2, 2012.

c Treaty Amendment or Article 352 TFEU

757. Alternatively, to allow a Member State to exit the currency union without leaving the European Union altogether and to do so under conditions of legal certainty would require an amendment of the Treaties or, arguably, at least a Council decision under Article 352 TFEU.

758. The Treaties could be amended to suspend or terminate a Member State's currency union membership by adding a protocol that, in essence, would recognize this Member State's status as a Member State "with a derogation" or as an opt-out

1112. The text of this intergovernmental agreement may be found at https://data.consilium.europa.eu/doc/document/ST%208457%202014%20INIT/EN/pdf. It has been amended by an agreement of January 27, 2021, https://www.consilium.europa.eu/media/48068/agreement-amending-the-intergovernmental-agreement-on-the-transfer-and-mutualisation-of-contributions-to-the-single-resolution-fund-27-january-2021_en.pdf.

Member State. This could be accomplished through the simplified revision procedure of Article 48(6) TEU.[1113] But it would still effectively require the concurrence of all Member States (including those not part of the euro area) and ratification by Member States where constitutionally required. It would be a relatively lengthy process with lingering uncertainty, unsuitable for the instant clarity needed for the financial markets.

759. Article 352 TFEU may provide a faster track for officializing a Member State's (temporary) exit from the currency union. This so-called "flexibility clause" empowers the Council, acting unanimously on a proposal of the European Commission and after having obtained the consent of the European Parliament, to take appropriate action that is required to attain one of the objectives set out in the Treaties and for which the Treaties have not provided the necessary powers. Action under Article 352 TFEU could be justified on the ground that allowing a Member State to (temporarily) leave the currency union is necessary to safeguard the proper functioning and cohesion of the currency union which, as an integral part of EMU, is one of the stated objectives of the European Union.[1114]

d Article 2(1) TEU

760. An unconventional angle—mentioned here for intellectual pleasure more than as a well-considered possibility—is Article 2(1) TFEU. According to this provision, in areas of exclusive EU competence, only the European Union may legislate and adopt legally binding acts, *"the Member States being able to do so themselves only if so empowered by the Union"*. Monetary policy for the euro area is an exclusive EU competence[1115] and this must logically extend to the use of the euro as a single currency and to exchange rate policy for the euro.[1116] Therefore, is it conceivable that pursuant to Article 2(1) TFEU, the Union, presumably acting through the Council, would empower a Member State, probably only on a temporary basis, to adopt legislation reintroducing a currency of its own and organizing its monetary affairs? It would likely be too much of a stretch, and Article 352 TFEU would seem a safer albeit slower route.

1113. The simplified revision procedure should be available for the (temporary) withdrawal of one or several Member States from the currency union since the amendment should be limited to provisions of Part Three of TFEU and should not increase the competences conferred on the Union by the Treaties. It would likely be unavailable for a complete dissolution of the currency union since the establishment of EMU with the euro as its single currency is one of the core objectives of the European Union (Article 3(4) TEU).

The simplified procedure requires adoption of a decision by the European Council, by unanimous vote (and after having consulted the European Parliament, the Commission and, on monetary matters, the ECB), and the ratification of this decision by Member States when constitutionally required, but it does not require a formal convention or conference of government representatives.

1114. Article 3(4) TEU.

1115. Article 3(1)(c) TFEU.

1116. *Cf.* Articles 119(2), 127(2), 133 and 219 TFEU.

e Beyond Legal Fiction

761. The irreversibility of the euro is, in the end, a legal fiction. When politicians face unforgiving realities, legal fiction will yield to political and economic necessities. Unlikely and undesirable as it may seem, if and when euro membership of a particular Member State becomes unsustainable, a possible scenario might, in broad outline, unfold along the following lines. After secret high-level exchanges with the Eurogroup, the ECB and the European Commission, the exiting Member State, invoking a fundamental change of circumstances, would, over a weekend, prior to Monday trading hours, decide to terminate or temporarily suspend euro membership. It would pass a law introducing a new national currency as its lawful currency and redenominate payment obligations governed by its national laws from the euro into the new currency at some specified conversion rate. To bridge an inevitable period of transition, the exiting Member State would issue small-denomination treasury bills in its new national currency and impose certain restrictions on cross-border payments and capital flows, and the Council would adopt certain provisional measures. The matter would subsequently be officialized, by (simplified) Treaty amendment or pursuant to Article 352 TFEU, so as to reclassify the relevant Member State as a Member State with a derogation or an opt-out Member State.

762. One would assume that the authors of the Treaties believed it best not to provide for any organized exit from the currency union for fear that the very acknowledgment of a possibility of exit would increase its likelihood. They may also have thought that the prospect of an uncertain and potentially disorderly exit would dissuade Member States from pursuing it and would further cement their commitment to the currency union. It is a reasoning still widely shared today in European circles. But the flip side of this reasoning is that, when continued currency union membership becomes unsustainable and withdrawal desirable or inevitable, there is no pre-established process for orderly withdrawal (or at least none that is publicly known in advance). Which is worse? Should not rational financial markets, with limited belief in legal fiction, take greater comfort in the knowledge that the inevitable will not be chaotic but governed by thoughtful rules and procedures? And wouldn't such an *ex ante* framework, by making exit the *ultima ratio*, limit the possibility for rogue governments to make tactical threats of unilateral exit as a bargaining strategy? In fact, wouldn't the lack of binding exit rules reinforce the bargaining power of an exiting Member State?

3 COMPLEXITIES, COSTS AND UNCERTAINTIES

763. A Member State's withdrawal from the currency union would most likely be somewhat of a leap in the dark, with limited visibility on the probability, magnitude and duration of its economic and financial consequences. There are almost no relevant recent precedents of one or more countries breaking away from a currency union which otherwise continues to exist. And one would doubt that much relevant guidance is to be found in how former Soviet republics like Estonia, Latvia, Lithuania, Ukraine and Kyrgyzstan replaced the ruble with currencies of their own.

764. The drama and uncertainties surrounding a Member State's currency union exit could in some measure be mitigated if the exiting Member State did not let its new national currency float freely against the euro but was willing and able to commit to maintaining its currency within specified fluctuation margins around some specified central rate against the euro—whether or not as part of ERM II (*see* paragraph 46 above). But this may not always be feasible, at least not initially (unless within a wide fluctuation band).

a The First Hours

765. The redenomination process itself would involve countless large and small complexities, costs and uncertainties. This is especially so since such an exit would probably occur in crisis circumstances, with the exiting Member State having its back against the wall, and with little or no lead time for economic operators and financial markets to properly prepare for the event. Difficulties would be compounded if the exit were non-consensual, *i.e.*, if it were not from the outset recognized and minimally supported by EU legislative measures. In fact, this would not be the typical fact pattern of a disappearing national currency being replaced with a new one. With the euro continuing to exist, redenomination could cause serious controversy in respect of existing payment obligations expressed in euro, if not somehow validated by EU law as the euro's *lex monetae* (*see* paragraph 770 below).

766. For some transition period, the exiting Member State would most likely have to impose certain controls and restrictions on outbound payments and capital flows in foreign currencies, now including the euro. As a matter of EU law, such restrictions may be justifiable on public policy grounds,[1117] insofar as proportional, but always at the risk of giving rise to legal challenges. If they restrict or delay payments in euro or other foreign currency that fall due under existing contracts, they may give rise to contractual disputes. The exiting Member State's redenomination law may have to impose a temporary stay on attachments and other creditor enforcement action against residents for defaulting on euro or other foreign currency payment obligations, but measures of this kind could be legally challenged as well.

767. At a more mundane level, the replacement of the euro with a new national currency would present a fair number of practical challenges. In terms of logistics, it would require such measures as the production of new banknotes and coins, adjustments to payment and securities settlement systems, changes to bank programs and applications, the conversion and advertising of new prices, and the reprogramming of innumerable ATMs, point-of-sale terminals, cash registers, petrol pumps and vending machines. Imagine for a moment the undignified scramble for IT consultants and

1117. *Cf.* Article 65(1)(b) TFEU.

lawyers in those stressful first hours, and hold this thought. Additional bank holidays would likely be needed to allow banks and other businesses to carry out the practicalities of the transition. Still at the level of what I would classify as practicalities, a number of technical issues would have to be dealt with, and costs incurred, *inter alia*, in connection with the unwinding of transactions with Eurosystem central banks, the redenomination of outstanding debt and equity securities, and the tax treatment of gain or loss on restated values of assets and liabilities. Logistics and practicalities must never be underestimated, especially when needing to be handled at short notice and in a short time span. Such processes should be manageable, but not without difficulties and glitches. The authorities would need to have developed the necessary scripts to keep this process more or less orderly.

b Redenomination Issues

768. Redenomination would likely cause significant legal uncertainty and controversy in respect of payment obligations in euro under numerous commercial and financial contracts. During the Greek crisis in the first half of the previous decade, law firms were frequently called upon to advise clients on the possible implications of a Member State's currency union exit for a variety of contracts, securities and derivative instruments. This is obviously not the place for an in-depth review of the multiple legal issues that may arise in this broad subject area. Such a discussion would in large measure be hypothetical since the legal consequences in any given situation would be highly dependent on the terms of the relevant contract or financial instrument and its governing law, the precise content of the exiting Member State's currency redenomination law, and the provisions of EU supporting legislation (if any). Here, we must limit ourselves to a few general considerations.

769. To evoke a picture in the mind of the kind of contractual issues to which redenomination is likely to give rise, consider the straightforward example of an outstanding euro loan made by a financial institution in some Member State to a borrower residing in the exiting Member State. The loan agreement may be governed by the laws of the lender's Member State, either pursuant to an express choice-of-law clause or under the default rule of the Rome I Regulation.[1118] But one could also imagine the darker scenario of the loan being governed by the laws of the borrower's jurisdiction. And let us further assume, for the purpose of academic exposition, that we are dealing with an uncharacteristically plain-vanilla loan agreement with no special protective clauses addressing redenomination risk: redenomination is not listed among the events of default, there is no material adverse change clause (or at least none that

1118. Regulation (EC) No 593/2008 of the European Parliament and of the Council of June 17, 2008 on the law applicable to contractual obligations (Rome I), *OJ* L177, July 4, 2008, p. 6. Absent a choice of law by the parties, the default rule of Article 4(2) of this Regulation would look to the laws of the country of habitual residence of the party required to effect the characteristic performance of the contract, which, in the case of loan agreements, would generally be the act of lending. In the case of a consumer loan, however, the default rule of Article 6(1) would ordinarily point to the country of habitual residence of the consumer.

could plausibly be interpreted to cover redenomination), and there is also no clause requiring that, if payment needs to be made in another currency, the lender be made whole for any exchange loss at the time of payment. The exiting Member State now adopts a currency redenomination law that provides for mandatory redenomination of its residents' payment obligations in euro into the new national currency at some specified official conversion rate, without expressly "grandfathering" euro payment obligations under existing contracts from mandatory redenomination.

Since the exiting Member State likely faces serious economic difficulties (as one would ordinarily expect in the case of currency union exit), its new currency would tend to significantly depreciate against the euro, and its interest rate level to rise. As a result, the lender would now face a different and higher currency risk, with the prospect of suffering exchange loss on future interest payments and repayment of principal under the loan, while being locked into a lower interest rate set in reference to the euro yield curve. Could the lender enforce continued performance of the borrower's (re)payment obligations in euro against the terms of the exiting Member State's redenomination law and, if not, claim indemnification for any exchange loss suffered? Could the lender terminate (accelerate) the loan on general contract law grounds that may exist in the law governing the loan and that excuse performance or permit termination of a contract in the event of unforeseen developments that substantially change the economics of the contract (frustration, hardship, *imprévision*)? And, if the redenomination law were to "grandfather" payments in euro under pre-existing contracts but such payments were restricted by exchange controls, could the lender claim default in case payments are delayed by such controls, and could the borrower then invoke *force majeure* as a defense?

770. It seems broadly (but not universally) recognized that it is the law of the currency, the *lex monetae*, and not the law governing the contract, that determines what is legal tender for the purpose of validly discharging a debt expressed in the currency of that jurisdiction. That is clear in the standard situation in which a vanishing national currency is replaced by a new one. However, the peculiarity of the fact pattern here is that a new national currency is substituted for a supranational currency, the euro, that continues to exist and is governed by EU law as its *lex monetae*. This fudges the issue,[1119] at least in the absence of concomitant EU legislation that somehow validates the redenomination and determines its consequences as to existing payment obligations in euro. But what happens in case of a radically unilateral, non-consensual withdrawal from currency union membership with mandatory redenomination and no express "grandfathering" of euro payment obligations under existing contracts?

771. It is also widely recognized that the proper law of the contract or obligation, the *lex contractus* or *lex causae*, and not the *lex monetae*, determines questions regarding the possible effects of a change of currency on the continuation of the relevant contract and the effects of changes in value or purchasing power of a currency on the quantum of the relevant obligation. In particular, the question of whether redenomination or a

1119. *Cf.* H.S. Scott, "When the Euro Falls Apart", *International Finance*, 1998, pp. 223-224, https://doi.org/10.1111/1468-2362.00010.

consequent rise or fall in the value of the currency may be a ground for rescinding a contract or excusing performance of a contractual obligation, or may give rise to indemnification for the exchange loss suffered, are issues within the province of the *lex contractus*. But these governing laws may not always provide clear or convenient answers, in the absence of sufficiently specific contractual clauses. And what if, in its redenomination law, an exiting Member State were to include a provision to ensure continuity of contracts—*mutatis mutandis* as Article 3 of Council Regulation (EC) No 1103/97 did in respect of the introduction of the euro?[1120] Such a provision would say, in essence, that redenomination does not have the effect of altering any other term of an existing legal instrument or of discharging or excusing performance of any obligation under such an instrument, nor entitle a party unilaterally to alter or terminate such an instrument. But could such a mandatory provision of national law extend to contracts governed by other laws or override contractual clauses to the contrary? And, if it purported to do so, could it not be challenged as a deprivation of, or disproportionate interference with, existing contractual rights in violation of constitutional or treaty rules protecting property rights (in particular, Article 1 of the First Additional Protocol to the European Convention on Human Rights)? One could see a significant potential for litigation.

c Longer-Term Economics and Short-Term Politics of Euro Exit

772. These and other complexities, costs and uncertainties associated with the process of redenomination would come on top of unsettled and potentially disorderly market conditions in the short term and the uncertain economic fallout of currency union exit over a longer time span. And in an interconnected and "euro-ized" economy, the exiting Member State may find it difficult to re-establish control over its money supply. All of this combined should ordinarily constitute a serious deterrent against withdrawal from currency union membership for any Member State inclined to consider it. From the vantage point of the other euro area Member States, the departure of a member with an unsustainable fiscal position may reduce the heterogeneity of, and tensions within, the remaining euro area. But they too may suffer unsettled market conditions for a while, and a member's departure may increase the currency union's exposure to destabilizing market dynamics as future economic disturbances will more easily prompt "who is next?" market sentiment. Considerations of this kind create a strong incentive for seeking a cooperative solution that keeps the struggling member on board or at least makes the exit process as orderly as possible.

773. Still, one cannot be confident that it will always work out that way. Like in the Prisoner's Dilemma of game theory, national political calculations may lock parties

1120. Council Regulation (EC) No 1103/97 of June 17, 1997 on certain provisions relating to the introduction of the euro, *OJ* L162, June 19, 1997, p. 1, amended by Council Regulation (EC) No 2595/2000 of November 27, 2000, *OJ* L300, November 29, 2000, p. 1. *See* J. Meyers & D. Levie, "The Introduction of the Euro: Overview of the Legal Framework and Selected Legal Issues", *Columbia Journal of European Law*, Vol. 4, 1998, pp. 338-342.

into a process that eventually produces a suboptimal outcome for the group as a whole. In a difficult economic environment, social resistance to necessary fiscal restraint and reforms may at some point cause a Member State's governing coalition, especially one with euroskeptic and/or populist inclinations, to conclude that the political necessity of "taking back control" outweighs the (*ex ante* less visible) costs and uncertainties of currency union exit. Risks of this kind are inherent in the short-term horizon of political decision-making and electoral cycles. They have arisen in the history of the European currency union and there are no persuasive reasons for believing that they may not occur again.

774. It could have happened in Greece in 2015. After the radical left Syriza party led by Alexis Tsipras had won the parliamentary elections in January, negotiations on the terms of a third financial assistance program stalled for months. Greece imposed capital controls and a bank holiday on June 28 and missed an IMF payment around the same time. In a referendum of July 5, Greek citizens voted by a 61% majority against the Troika policy conditions for further financial assistance. That summer, Greece came within inches from currency union exit.[1121] A less dramatic but telling episode, a few years later, is the sharp widening of the spread of Italian government bonds in May 2018 during the formation of the new government between Movimento Cinque Stelle and Liga Nord. Paolo Savona, author of a plan (actually a plan B) for Italy's exit from the currency union,[1122] had initially been proposed as Minister of Finance in the new government but, following opposition by President Sergio Mattarella, was eventually moved to the post of ... Minister for EU Affairs (!). Notwithstanding assurances in Italian government circles to the effect that currency union exit was not part of the government's program, Cinque Stelle and Lega Nord representatives in the European Parliament voted for a (failed) amendment to a resolution on the EU 2021-2027 Multiannual Financial Framework[1123] that would have called for financial support for Member States planning to negotiate their exit from the currency union (!).[1124] *Stai scherzando?*

775. Nothing can ever be taken for granted in monetary affairs or, *a fortiori*, in contemporary European politics.

1121. *See* European Stability Mechanism, *Safeguarding the euro in times of crisis—The inside story of the ESM*, Publications Office of the European Union, Luxembourg, 2019, pp. 311-320.

1122. *Guida pratica per uscire dall' euro*, October 13, 2015, summarized by D. Gros, "How to exit the euro in a nutshell —'Il Piano Savona'", *CEPS Commentary*, June 1, 2018, https://www.ceps.eu/ceps-publications/how-exit-euro-nutshell-il-piano-savona/.

1123. European Parliament Resolution of May 30, 2018 on the 2021-2027 multiannual financial framework and own resources, *OJ* C76, March 9, 2020, p. 103.

1124. *See* https://www.reuters.com/article/uk-italy-politics-euro-idAFKCN1IX4ZL.

Conclusions

776. The euro saw the light of day a good 25 years ago in what now seems a different epoch. It was conceived in the late 1980s and early 1990s at a time of political and economic optimism—a *fin de siècle* looking to a brighter millennium. Following many years of mixed experience with snake-type semi-fixed exchange rate schemes, Europe boldly moved to a single currency under a single monetary policy. A common currency, shared by a number of fiscally sovereign Member States with relatively diverse economies, started out with only a bare set of common rules to ensure a measure of fiscal discipline and without a dedicated centralized financing mechanism for stability support within the currency area. It was once likened by Mario Draghi to a bumblebee in that, by all known laws of physics, it should not fly. Yet, it did fly and eventually weathered a 2008-2009 banking crisis, a 2010-2012 sovereign debt crisis, Greece's troubles and near exit in 2015 and, to this day, the 2020 outbreak of a pandemic and the political and economic fall-out of a large-scale military conflict on the borders of the European Union. In the process, the construction was reinforced, brick by brick and oftentimes in the haphazard ways of European politics, by successive reforms of the common fiscal framework in 2005, 2011, 2013 and 2023-2024 and by the two-step establishment in 2010 and 2012 of a dedicated euro area stability support mechanism.

777. The European currency union now faces, over an extended time span, the concurrent challenges of (i) increased geopolitical tensions and the consequent uncertainties for foreign trade and investment flows and for the supply and prices of fossil fuels and other commodities; (ii) climate change and the considerable complexities and uncertainties of the transition to a low-carbon economy; (iii) population aging and the task of integrating the influx of migrants; and, most probably, (iv) the need for Europe to significantly strengthen its defense and intelligence capabilities. It does not help that the currency union has to start addressing these challenges in years of higher inflation and monetary restraint in conjunction with an overall higher level of euro area sovereign debt with significant divergence among its Member States. These are also days of more polarized political discourse, increased national sentiment and broad societal resentment. By the look of things, Europe is in a difficult place.

778. Over its 25 years and intermittent periods of turbulence, the European currency union has most probably contributed to relative economic stability in the euro area. One need only imagine, counterfactually, the kind of tensions, conflicts and instability that the successive crises mentioned above would have caused if the Member States had been left with a snake-type semi-fixed exchange rate system or floating currencies. At the same time, however, economic performance and convergence within the euro area have shown a mixed picture, and some of the lesser results may even be due in part to restrictions flowing from the currency union (such as the insufficiently counter-cyclical fiscal policies or even pro-cyclical fiscal restraint applied by several Member States, under the common fiscal rules or policy conditionality attached to EFSF/ESM financial assistance, in the aftermath of the 2008-2012 financial crisis).

779. The developments that are the most concerning today include the following:

(a) At the end of 2022, the average euro area government debt ratio stood at a significantly higher level, with a higher degree of divergence among, broadly speaking, Northern and Southern euro area Member States, than in the early years of the currency union or even at the beginning of the euro area sovereign debt crisis in 2010. The increase in divergence has been particularly pronounced between the Big Five economies. In its latest (April 2023) Debt Sustainability Monitor, the European Commission found eight euro area Member States (Italy, France, Spain, Belgium, Greece, Portugal, Croatia and Slovakia) to be at high fiscal sustainability risk in the medium term, and six others (Austria, Slovakia, Malta and even Germany, The Netherlands and Finland) at medium risk.

(b) Public investment as a share of GDP has varied significantly among euro area Member States and was generally noticeably lower in the 2013-2019 period than in the 2000-2010 period, especially in higher-debt Member States. When fiscal policy space is limited, as it is in higher-debt countries, it is often politically more expedient to limit investment expenditures than it is to raise taxes and/or cut social transfers and other current expenditures of more immediate electoral consequence. *Ceteris paribus*, fiscal bias of this kind may be difficult to overcome in times of subdued growth and/or higher inflation, with monetary tightening raising government borrowing costs, as is presently the case. Given the need for considerable public investments notably in respect of climate change and the green transition as well as in defense capability, it is of critical importance to find a workable solution to reconcile public investment needs with government debt sustainability concerns. Such a solution will require both a proper calibration of common fiscal rules and shared financial support.

(c) Movements in inflation were directionally broadly synchronous but with significant variability of country rates in most years, especially since 2019. This is a complicating factor. A single monetary policy ordinarily produces similar nominal interest rate levels across the currency area. But the conjunction of similar nominal interest rates and significantly different country inflation rates would produce comparatively lower real interest rates in higher-inflation countries, which may unduly fuel domestic demand and credit and further add to inflationary pressures, and, conversely, comparatively higher real interest rates in lower-inflation countries, with opposite effects. For a single monetary policy to work effectively and evenly, a high degree of convergence of inflation rates across the currency area is of considerable importance.

(d) Over the 2007-2022 period, GDP generally grew at a lower rate in the euro area than in the OECD and in the United States, with again significant differences across the euro area. There has been no significant convergence of GDP *per capita* among euro area Member States and, if anything, the gap between the most and the least productive Member States appears to have stagnated or even widened over the past decade (with France, Spain and especially Italy lagging behind). This statistic is troublesome in that, in today's challenging and politically increasingly polarized environment, it should become more difficult to credibly lay claim to an "ever closer Union" without more visible progress toward "shared prosperity".

(e) Unemployment rates continued to diverge significantly among euro area Member States, with consistently high levels notably in Spain and Greece and very high youth unemployment rates in Italy, Spain and Greece. Addressing these issues will require increased public expenditures on education and vocational training, which again will be especially challenging for Member States with fiscal sustainability issues.

780. The Treaty confers the exclusive mandate of conducting a single monetary policy for the euro area upon the ECB/Eurosystem and says that its *"primary"* objective shall be to *"maintain price stability"* but without further defining what this all means. The ECB has taken it upon itself to define this core constituent of its mandate, in several iterations, as a symmetrical numerical benchmark of 2% for year-on-year increases in consumer prices over an otherwise unspecified (and seemingly elastic) medium-term horizon. The European Court of Justice has benevolently given its *nihil obstat* to this definition. More generally, the Court has used the (primary) inflation control objective as the decisive criterion for delineating the substantive compass of the monetary policy mandate in relation to (national) competences for economic and fiscal policies, thereby effectively tolerating significant incursions of monetary policy actions in these other competence spheres.

781. Yet, over the 16 years since 2008, euro area headline inflation (HICP) has never been close to the 2% target in any year, except in 2018 (1.8%), or over any rolling three-year period (if this can be taken as a proxy for the medium term). In recent years, the ECB/Eurosystem staff's quarterly projections of inflation over three-year periods have often been widely off the mark and, generally, have seriously underestimated inflation outcomes. It raises questions about the reliability of the models and simulations used in capturing inflation dynamics. They must be, and are being, continuously tested and improved to a lower level of imperfection. But there is simply no model of everything—no model that can accurately integrate and process the numerous relevant variables, interactions, non-linearities and trade-offs in a complex multi-country environment like the euro area. Monetary policy will inevitably be tentative and subject to a significant margin of error in such a multivariate setting.

782. One is left wondering about the scale and duration of monetary easing, including quantitative easing, from 2013 through 2021 and about the months that passed before the ECB eventually started a monetary tightening cycle in the summer of 2022. Was such a prolonged monetary easing partly needed to make up for insufficiently counter-cyclical fiscal policies and/or inspired by the obdurate and quite possibly outdated belief in a long-term trend decline in the natural (or neutral) rate of interest? Might it have allowed inflationary undercurrents to gain strength, especially in the later years of that period? Still in the sphere of the macroeconomic policy mix, could or should the ECB bend an uncompromising focus on inflation control, by tempering monetary tightening or intensifying monetary easing (as the case may be), in order to enlarge fiscal policy space notably for public investments required by the green transition? It is a significant trade-off that is now upon us.

783. A recurring message of the ECB since the spring of 2022 (with occasional variations in wording) is that going forward, it will take a "meeting-by-meeting approach" and maintain "optionality, data-dependence, gradualism and flexibility". Accordingly, the ECB has subdued explicit forward guidance on the future monetary policy path. This is tempting and appears to make good sense in a highly uncertain and fluid economic environment. But does it really? In circumstances of volatile and conflicting data, data dependence may be disorienting. When reading the published accounts (redacted minutes) of the monetary policy meetings of the ECB's Board of Governors over the past two years, one repeatedly has the impression of members decrypting the latest incoming data and focusing on a near-term horizon that in many instances does not seem to stretch much beyond the next monetary policy meeting. At times, it seems to involve a somewhat bizarre dialectic in which the financial markets are left speculating how the ticker tape of incoming data may affect the ECB's further course of action, and the Board of Governors then attempts to decipher and correct the markets' expectations of its own intentions. But it all comes with the risk that market expectations become volatile, unstable or simply wrong (as occurred on several occasions in recent times).

Elevated economic uncertainty should not inevitably command a higher degree of policy discretion and forward vagueness. One could invert this argument by saying that it is especially in times of economic fluidity that the markets need greater visibility on the future course of monetary policy. A good argument could be made in support of the proposition that effective inflation control would be better served by more articulate monetary policy guidance that exhibits a certain stability over a significant time interval so as to more firmly anchor market expectations as to inflation developments and the ECB's monetary policy reactivity. There are various ways of providing such guidance other than by way of Federal Reserve-type dotplotting or some Taylor-type or other formulaic policy rule. The ECB took a step in the direction of more guidance when, on March 16, 2023, it announced that, while remaining data-dependent, future policy rate discussions would be determined by its assessment of the inflation outlook in light of incoming economic and financial data, the dynamics of underlying inflation, and the strength of monetary policy transmission. But this is hardly more than stating the obvious and does not offer much substantive guidance. One could be thinking instead of a more substantive statement of the baseline monetary policy path for the near term and its critical underlying assumptions. In fact, following recent meetings, the ECB did provide some disjunct explicit or implicit clues on its forward thinking, and it should be a relatively modest step for the ECB to put indications of this kind together in a more articulate statement as to a baseline monetary policy path and its key conditionality. It would be one small step for the ECB and one giant step for the markets, more or less.

784. A fragility of the European currency union is that, with no intra-euro area exchange rates to target anymore, financial markets have from time to time directed their speculative inclinations toward government bonds of euro area Member States with weaker fiscal positions or persistent negative external imbalances. Widening sovereign bond spreads may then become detached from underlying fundamentals and get caught in destabilizing market dynamics. Under programs like OMT, PEPP (in part) and TPI, the ECB has stepped in by announcing or actually carrying out selective purchases of government bonds of Member States at the high end of the spreads. It has attached such asset purchases to its monetary policy mandate on the ground that excessive widening of sovereign bond spreads not warranted by underlying macroeconomic fundamentals causes financial fragmentation that impairs the proper functioning of the monetary policy transmission mechanism—a theory which the European Court of Justice accepted in its 2015 *Gauweiler* judgment. Excessive widening of sovereign bond spreads does interfere with proper monetary policy transmission, of course, but so may other things in the various channels and sub-channels of monetary policy transmission. It seems overreaching to broadly elevate the repair of the monetary policy transmission mechanism as a parallel criterion for defining the substantive scope of the exclusive competence of monetary policy, at least absent more precise criteria and boundaries.

In fact, geographically targeted government bond purchases carried out by the ECB/Eurosystem with a view to containing financial fragmentation present various issues. Aside from being slightly unnatural acts for central banks, such purchases (i) may bring the ECB as monetary authority into conflict with its primary price stability objective, particularly in a higher-inflation environment calling for monetary tightening; (ii) notwithstanding the Court's blessing in *Gauweiler*, raise legal doubts as to whether they are within the compass of the ECB's monetary policy mandate and are compatible with the monetary financing prohibition of Article 123 TFEU; and (iii) could hardly be made subject to any economic policy conditionality without further calling into question their characterization as monetary policy.

These problems would mostly be avoided if anti-fragmentation government bond purchases were taken outside the perimeter of monetary policy and carried out instead by a dedicated euro area mechanism like the ESM. As it is, the ESM may engage in selective government bond purchases, subject to economic policy conditionality, pursuant to Articles 17 and 18 of the ESM Treaty. A more cost-efficient alternative (or indeed parallel) scheme that is worth exploring would be an interest-stabilization facility that would be hosted by the ESM or, instead, established by an intergovernmental agreement among euro area Member States and managed and backstopped by the ESM.

785. When reviewing the ECB's monetary policy actions, the European Court of Justice has thus far adopted a fairly deferential approach in ruling on the scope of the monetary policy mandate, on its incursions ("indirect effects") in economic and fiscal policy spheres, on proportionality, and on the monetary financing prohibition of Article 123 TFEU. In view of the complexity and inherent uncertainties of monetary analysis, the Court has allowed the ECB a wide measure of discretion, liberally applying standards of marginal judicial review. Yet, marginal review must not become infra-marginal. Judicial review must remain effective, and suggestions have, respectfully, been offered in this book on how the Court could kick the tires of the ECB's stated reasoning some more.

786. A currency union among countries with different economic characteristics that retain a large measure of autonomy in the conduct of their economic and fiscal policies, needs common fiscal rules of the game to, at least, avoid imbalances that would put the currency union under stress and, better still, to mutually align those policies in a manner consistent with overall macroeconomic stability of the currency area. The European currency union started out with an optimistically simple set of common fiscal rules which, through successive reforms in 2015, 2011, 2013 and 2023-2024 and added codes of conduct, vade mecum's and compendiums, have been refined and expanded into a relatively complex and more intrusive corpus of rules, benchmarks and procedures. The ongoing 2023-2024 reforms mark a further stage on this continuing learning curve and, in several respects, should be a step in the right direction. But it remains to be seen how well the revised rules will address (i) the perennial issue of a more symmetrical allocation of the burden of adjustment between deficit and surplus Member States, and (ii) the now pressing challenge of reconciling government debt sustainability concerns with considerable public investment needs.

787. A viable multi-country currency union needs a workable mix of both risk containment and risk sharing. Risk containment, as just mentioned, requires credible rules of the game ensuring that member countries conduct responsible economic and fiscal policies, keep their government debt sustainable and carry out structural reforms and public investments needed to address weaknesses in productivity and competitiveness and to support the green transition. Risk sharing requires some centralized financial mechanism providing stability support to help member countries overcome asymmetric external shocks or bridge imbalances pending structural reforms.

Proposals and initiatives for some EU budget-linked stabilization mechanism reserved for the euro area have not gone very far. While being temporary and having limited explicit stabilization features, the EU-wide Recovery and Resilience Facility ("RRF") of NextGenerationEU ("NGEU") is still a most welcome step and, with the 20 euro area Member States now representing approximately 85% of EU GDP, should broadly be conducive to euro area cohesion as well. Interestingly, the December 6, 2022 judgment of the German Federal Constitutional Court has put the door ajar for financial support mechanisms of this kind. This, and the clever political engineering that went into NGEU/RRF, may make NGEU/RRF a convenient matrix for future initiatives. But larger-scale schemes of this kind, with a significant grant component, inevitably raise the question of additional EU own resources—not the easiest of subjects politically.

788. Still, the European currency union would need a financing mechanism of its own for genuine euro area stability support. The ESM should be the prime candidate for this role since it has the considerable advantage of existing as a fully-functioning organization with expert staff and capital backing that provides significant financial firepower, *i.e.*, at the time of writing, some EUR 422 billion (or EUR 354 billion after deducting the proposed EUR 68 billion credit line to backstop the Single Resolution Fund).

With few of its existing financing instruments having been used and its last stability loan dating back to the summer of 2015, it may be necessary to "revitalize" the ESM by recalibrating its existing instruments and/or adding one or more fresh instruments to its toolbox. In this respect, the following issues should receive priority consideration:

(a) *Ad hoc* policy conditionality attached to ESM financial assistance should generally be tempered. It should not, as a rule, go beyond applicable country benchmarks and recommendations under the EMU fiscal and macroeconomic surveillance frameworks except to address intervening developments or for other compelling reasons.
(b) The design of precautionary financial assistance should be recalibrated so that it may serve as a genuine prevention tool that can be mobilized swiftly. Promptness of decision-making and transparency could be aided by a pre-set matrix of trigger conditions that look to a sudden and serious worsening of selected high-frequency economic indicators.
(c) As mentioned in paragraph 784 above, it should be explored whether and how the ESM could take over part or all of the current role of Eurosystem central banks in engaging in anti-fragmentation purchases of government bonds issued by euro area Member States at the high end of unduly widening government bond spreads.

789. No human construct is irreversible. Neither is the European currency union. Yet, the political capital invested in it is considerable, and so would be the risks and uncertainties associated with its total or partial break-up. Under the circumstances, a common sense conclusion would be that it is worth serious efforts to preserve it and improve its resilience against the challenges of our days. In all this, deepening divisions along political fault lines are worrisome. In the end, political fragmentation is the greater enemy than financial fragmentation. It makes it more hazardous to rely on *ad hoc* compromises and increases the relevance of common rules that have a certain fixity.

INTERNATIONAL BANKING AND FINANCE LAW SERIES

1. Jan Job de Vries Robbe, *Innovations in Securitisation. Yearbook 2006*, 2006 (ISBN 90-11-2533-7).
2. Jim Bartos, *United States Securities Law: A Practical Guide*, Third edition, 2006 (ISBN 90-411-2362-8).
3. Hui Huang, *International Securities Markets: Insider Trading Law in China*, 2006 (ISBN 90-411-2557-4).
4. Barth et al., *Financial Restructuring and Reform in Post-WTO China*, 2007 (ISBN 90-411-2573-6).
5. Zhongfei Zhou, *Banking Laws in China*, 2007 (ISBN 978-90-411-2519-4).
6. Jan Job de Vries Robbe & Paul Ali, *Expansion and Diversification in Securitization Yearbook 2007*, 2007 (ISBN 978-90-411-2661-0).
7. Ross Buckley, *International Financial System. Policy and Regulation*, 2008 (ISBN 978-90-411-2746-4).
8. Jan Job de Vries Robbe, *Securitization Law and Practice: In the Face of the Credit Crunch*, 2008 (ISBN 978-90-411-2715-0).
9. Phoebus Athanassiou, *Hedge Fund Regulation in the European Union: Current Trends and Future Prospects*, 2009 (ISBN 978-90-411-2856-0).
10. Jan Job de Vries Robbe, *Structured Finance: On from the Credit Crunch: The Road to Recovery*, 2009 (ISBN 978-90-411-2787-7).
11. Gaetane Schaeken Willemaers, *The EU Issuer-Disclosure Regime: Objectives and Proposals for Reform*, 2011 (ISBN 978-90-411-3394-6).
12. Panagiotis Delimatsis & Nils Herger (eds), *Financial Regulation at the Crossroads: Implications for Supervision, Institutional Design and Trade*, 2011 (ISBN 978-90-411-3355-7).
13. Raffaele Scalcione, *The Derivatives Revolution: A Trapped Innovation and a Blueprint for Regulatory Reform*, 2011 (ISBN 978-90-411-3430-1).
14. Douglas Arner & Ross Buckley, *From Crisis to Crisis: The Global Financial System and Regulatory Failure*, 2011 (ISBN 978-90-411-3354-0).
15. Anton P. Trichardt, *Letters of Comfort: A Trans-Systemic Analysis*, 2012 (ISBN 978-90-411-3600-8).
16. Eddy Wymeersch, *Alternative Investment Fund Regulation*, 2012 (ISBN 978-90-411-3690-9).
17. Asif H. Qureshi & Xuan Gao (eds), *International Economic Organizations and Law: The Perspective and Role of the Legal Counsel*, 2012 (ISBN 97890-411-3427-1).
18. Rhys Bollen, *The Law and Regulation of Payment Services: A Comparative Study*, 2012 (ISBN 978-90-411-3818-7).
19. Ramandeep Kaur Chhina, *Standby Letters of Credit in International Trade*, 2012 (ISBN 978-90-411-4560-4).

20. Dirk Zetzsche (ed.), *The Alternative Investment Fund Managers Directive*, Third Edition, 2020 (ISBN 978-94-035-0910-5).
21. Lorenzo Sasso, *Capital Structure and Corporate Governance: The Role of Hybrid Financial Instruments*, 2013 (ISBN 978-90-411-4843-8).
22. Pablo Iglesias-Rodríguez, *The Accountability of Financial Regulators: A European and International Perspective*, 2013 (ISBN 978-90-411-3874-3).
23. Seraina Neva Grünewald, *The Resolution of Cross-Border Banking Crises in the European Union: A Legal Study from the Perspective of Burden Sharing*, 2014 (ISBN 978-90-411-4909-1).
24. Megan Bowman, *Banking on Climate Change: How Finance Actors and Transnational Regulatory Regimes are Responding*, 2015 (ISBN 978-90-411-5223-7).
25. Jin Sheng, *China's Listed Companies: Conflicts, Governance and Regulation*, 2015 (ISBN 978-90-411-5925-0).
26. Sven Schelo, *Bank Recovery and Resolution*, Second Edition, 2020 (ISBN 978-94-035-1881-7).
27. Luis M. Hinojosa–Martínez & José María Beneyto (eds), *European Banking Union: The New Regime*, 2015 (ISBN 978-90-411-5263-3).
28. Gill North, *Effective Company Disclosure in the Digital Age*, 2015 (ISBN 978-90-411-3815-6).
29. Hanneke Wegman, *Investor Protection: Towards Additional EU Regulation of Investment Funds?*, 2016 (ISBN 978-90-411-5252-7).
30. Ruth Plato-Shinar, *Banking Regulation in Israel: Prudential Regulation versus Consumer Protection*, 2016 (ISBN 978-90-411-6791-0).
31. Bader Alkhaldi, *Saudi Capital Market: Developments and Challenges*, 2017 (ISBN 978-90-411-8351-4).
32. Yves Mauchle, *Bail-In and Total Loss-Absorbing Capacity (TLAC): Legal and Economic Perspectives on Bank Resolution with Functional Comparisons of Swiss and EU Law*, 2017 (ISBN 978-90-411-8998-1).
33. Uzma Ashraf Barton, *Rethinking Regulation of International Finance: Law, Policy and Institutions*, 2018 (ISBN 978-90-411-8838-0).
34. Phoebus L. Athanassiou, *Digital Innovation in Financial Services: Legal Challenges and Regulatory Policy Issues*, 2018 (ISBN 978-90-411-8781-9).
35. Gu Bin, *The Law and Governance of the Asian Infrastructure Investment Bank*, 2019 (ISBN 978-94-035-0631-9).
36. Gerald Nels Olson, *Money, Morality and Law: A Case for Financial Crisis Accountability*, 2019 (ISBN 978-94-035-0941-9).
37. Scott Farrell, *Banking on Data: Evaluating Open Banking and Data Rights in Banking Law*, 2023 (ISBN 978-94-035-3116-8).
38. Jan Meyers, *A European Central Bank Standing Guard over a European Currency Union*, 2024 (ISBN 978-94-035-2148-0).